W9-BIF-449

New York Chapter,
American Institute of Architects

AIA GUIDE TO NEW YORK CITY

Norval White
Elliot Willensky
Editors

The Macmillan Company
New York

Collier-Macmillan Limited
London

ACKNOWLEDGMENTS:

The herculean task of researching, writing, photographing, and assembling this guide in six months could not have been possible without the concentrated efforts of a team of devoted individuals: our colleague, John M. Dixon, who has shared responsibility during this period, Roger Feinstein, Ann Douglass, and particularly, Hope Asrelsky who, as editors, coordinators, and expediters handled each of their many tasks with sensitivity, insight and dispatch, Jean Francis and Ghiday Belay, production assistants, and Lynn Davis.

Credit must go to the New York Chapter, American Institute of Architects for arranging the publication of this guide, and to its past president, Max O. Urbahn, to the Executive Committee, and to Dickson McKenna and Robert C. Weinberg. Special thanks is due the Chapter's public relations counsel, Andrew W. Weil, who developed and coordinated the sponsorship plan which made the initial publication of the book possible, and to the Arnold W. Brunner Scholarship Committee.

Needless to say, countless others have contributed to our work: the members of the New York Chapter of AIA and the many other individuals and organizations who supplied reference materials and photographs to assist us, particularly the Bronx County Historical Society, the City Planning Commission, the Landmarks Preservation Commission, the Long Island Historical Society, the N.Y.C. Housing Authority, the New York Society Library and the Staten Island Historical Society, to mention but a few.

Most of all, however, our thanks must go to our respective wives and families for bearing with us on those many days and nights and weekends and holidays when we were kept from them by the demands of this book.

Norval White/Elliot Willensky

CREDITS:

Manhattan: Lower, Astor Place/East Village, Four Squares, Upper East Side (Norval White); Midtown (remainder), Lincoln Square (John M Dixon); Greenwich Village (Ann Douglass); Upper West Side (remainder) Harlem (Roger Feinstein); Central Park (Sophia Duckworth & Henry Hope Reed); Upper Manhattan (Richard Dattner).

The Bronx: (Roger Feinstein).

Brooklyn: Brooklyn Heights, Fort Greene/Clinton Hill (Norval White); Grand Army Plaza/Prospect Park/Botanic Garden (John M. Dixon); West Central (remainder), Northern, Central, Southwestern, Southern, Southeastern, Eastern (Elliot Willensky).

Queens: (Elliot Willensky).　　**Design:** (Herb Lubalin, Fran Elfenbein).

Richmond: (Mina Hamilton).　　**Maps:** (Jerome Kuhl).

The City: (Elliot Willensky).　　**Photo & Literary Credits:** See page 416.

Production consultants to Publisher: Libra Studios, Inc.

Library of Congress Catalog Number 68-58489

FIRST PRINTING

The Macmillan Company, New York

Collier-Macmillan Canada Ltd., Toronto, Ontario

Printed in the United States of America

CONTENTS

MANHATTAN

MAPS

A Message from Mayor John V. Lindsay

Almost everybody visits New York at one time or another, but very few people actually see the tangible composition of the city —its old-country neighborhoods, its isolated parks, and its often scrambled street patterns. Even the casual visitor, obviously, sees the Empire State Building, Central Park and Times Square. They are uniquely New York's; but they comprise only part of the architectural aspect of the city.

One of my favorite buildings, for example, can be seen from the steps of City Hall. It is the Woolworth Building on lower Broadway, a grandly baroque skyscraper that stands as one of the finest achievements of the American Gothic school of architecture. The building is somewhat overdone to suit modern tastes, perhaps, but it maintains its stateliness even when contrasted with the puristically contemporary tower of glass and steel that flanks it on the North.

This Guide can direct the reader to similar architectural treasures in New York. It has all the credentials and expertise required to fulfill that objective for both residents and visitors, for it was researched and written under the auspices of the New York Chapter of the American Institute of Architects.

The Guide focuses on the continuing development of New York as a modern metropolis, a process that prompted someone to comment: "It will be a great city—if they ever finish it."

It describes the old and the new, but particularly the offbeat —those trees, lampposts, restaurants, manhole covers or cornices that give New York a visible relationship to its historical heritage. They are a thrill to discover amid the vastness of this city, for they represent permanence in an acutely transient place and time.

I hope you'll like and use the Guide; it's a good one.

John V. Lindsay
Mayor

A Message from the President, N. Y. Chapter AIA

This Guide to New York City was first published in 1967 under the auspices of the New York Chapter of the American Institute of Architects in commemoration of the one-hundredth anniversary of the Chapter.

The book, unprecedented in its scope and format was essentially available only to architects. It achieved, however, such an immediate popularity that it has now become necessary to issue a new and updated edition for both laymen and professionals.

The Guide's comprehensive, street-by-street, borough-by-borough, coverage of the significant buildings, neighborhoods and scenes of New York makes it an indispensable aid to all those who are interested in the world's most important city, be they visitors or residents, laymen or professionals, modernists or historians.

Such a thorough and complete work could not have been written were it not for the many months of untiring work and editorial guidance of two chapter members, Norval White and Elliott Willensky and their assistants; nor could it have been published without the able administration of Andrew Weil and the generous financial support of those manufacturers and trade associations of the building industry listed below.

The Guide is truly a major contribution toward an appreciation of the excitement and history of our city; and hopefully a means of putting into focus the serious urban problems that face us today.

We sincerely hope that the Guide will help you "discover" the City of New York.

LATHROP DOUGLASS, F.A.I.A.
President, New York Chapter
American Institute of Architects

Sponsors of the AIA Guide to New York City

Armstrong Cork Company, p. 25

Corning Glass Works, p. 51

Eaton, Yale & Towne, Inc. p. 69

Electric Heating Association, p. 91

Georgia Marble Company, p. 107

Indiana Limestone Company, Inc. p. 129

Johns-Manville Corporation, p. 147

Jones & Laughlin Steel Corporation, p. 169

Knoll Associates, p. 191

Koppers Company, p. 225

Libbey-Owens-Ford Glass Company, p. 271

Lupton Manufacturing Company, p. 283

Owens-Corning Fiberglas Corporation, p. 325

Pittsburgh Plate Glass Company, p. 359

United States Plywood Corporation, p. 373

United States Steel Corporation, p. 393

WHY WE DID IT

A city is a trading post and a beehive of industry. It is a seat of military command and governmental power. It is also a sanctuary for religious ceremony and meditation, a stage for parades, drama and communications in unending variety. It is the site of a vast array of schools, universities and scientific institutions. It is a history book where the treasures and archives of civilization are hoarded, and it is home for millions. It is the place where men gather to share their highest hopes, and it is a burying ground for the great and the forgotten.

All of these descriptive definitions fit any great city. The primary purpose of this book is to indicate, by way of thousands of examples, how the buildings, streets, tunnels, structures, monuments and public spaces, both open and enclosed, serve as backdrop, stage and roof for the myriad lively and life-giving activities whose totality make up the phenomenon we know as New York City.

Serious sight-seers will use this volume to locate landmarks in the history of education, business, science, religion, housing and popular culture. It will have immediate utility for architects and planners, demographers, businessmen and specialists in art and fashion. It will serve students and scholars as a framework on which they can launch future histories of the City and its people.

The use of this Guide will not, of course, be limited by this listing. The essential understanding shared by the authors is that the City—along with its importance as the primary focus for all sorts of productive activities of man—is also a place to be, a place for people to seek all types of adventures, or just to sit and watch the world go by. A place to see and to be seen. A place to gaze, to smell, to feel, to meet and to discover. A place to be a person.

The human activities of the metropolis are infinite and could be completely cataloged in no single book. This Guide limits itself to physical, largely permanent places and things, both man-made and natural, which have been preserved or built or restored in New York City, and which are recognized as points of enduring interest. But within the confines of the five boroughs of the City our nets have been cast widely, and the Guide locates, describes, and illustrates more human points of interest than any other such reference work ever prepared or published for New York or any other American city.

Each of the several thousand buildings, structures, monuments, places and spaces were qualified for inclusion on the basis of two standards. First, as an example of architectural, technical, social or historical significance. Second, in terms of its importance to the City in its function as a place to be; that is, as a place or thing that excites curiosity and gives interest, pleasure and identification to a wide variety of people regardless of their interests and occupations.

At the same time, we have included buildings that are important only in relation to the relative *lack* of architectural distinction of the sectors or precincts in which they are found. These buildings would not have the same role in such architecturally rich areas as Brooklyn Heights or lower Manhattan.

The ultimate purpose of the Guide is to enable New Yorkers—permanent or temporary—to enjoy themselves while at home and abroad in the City. It points out countless visual delights that tend to go unnoticed daily in this fast-paced metropolis. It attempts to tie landmarks, whether world-renowned or obscure, to their models and their architectural and historical relatives, whether far away on other continents or close-by in a neighboring precinct.

A serious attempt has been made to give credit to some important and often unique landmarks that have previously been neglected. These landmarks, located in the north of Manhattan and in the four outlying boroughs, have for too long been overshadowed by the more familiar treasures of "downtown" Manhattan.

Likewise, attention has been paid to non-architectural factors such as the park systems, transit and utility tunnels, and public markets and highways, all of which are essential to the life of a city of eating, breathing, mobile beings.

Important lessons of how the City can be made more habitable than it now is, are illustrated by the many references to existing housing projects that are truly human in scale; to boulevards carefully planned to serve a variety of forms of traffic; to industrial structures built with sensitivity and character; and to buildings both new and old whose exterior form and ornamentation announce their functions to those who enter and to those who merely pass by.

This Guide is meant to challenge you. It is, in a sense, your duty to make it more complete than it is by restoring, preserving and creating the neighborhood, the precinct, the borough, the City itself. It is your knowledge, concern, skills, and curiosity that make the physical City a City of life.

—THE AUTHORS

USING THE GUIDE

The Guide is designed to be a source of pleasure, knowledge, perhaps even amazement, both for New Yorkers who rarely venture west of the Hudson, and for visitors who want to see more than is usually revealed to tourists. You will be able to select and follow a wide variety of specific walking tours (and automobile tours for the outer fringes of the City), or you may use the book to design a "custom-tailored" tour or ramble that suits your own disposition.

Some of you will explore your own neighborhoods before venturing to unfamiliar places. Braver souls will immediately "go abroad" within the City, and taste some new or exotic precinct. Others may wish to start at the Battery, and systematically explore each neighborhood of the City in the chronological order of its development.

If you tend to be less peripatetic, you may leave the Guide on your coffee table, leaf through its pages at your leisure, and enjoy imaginary City excursions without ever stepping outside of your doors. You will also be able to use the Guide to conduct visitors from Paris, Venice, Los Angeles, or wherever, to New York's palaces, basilicas, and market places.

The stylistic purists among you will delight in the special Architectural Style Guide placed at the end of the text, before the Index, to enlarge your enjoyment of a favorite style or period, whether it be Georgian/Federal or Romanesque Revival.

Geographical Organization. Like the city whose face it attempts to reflect, the Guide is divided into the five boroughs. It begins with Manhattan, at whose lower tip the historic City began. The outlying boroughs, The Bronx, Brooklyn, Queens and Staten Island—Richmond to the cognoscenti—follow in the order in which they were incorporated into New York. A final section, titled *The City,* deals with the metropolis as a whole.

New York's complexity makes an entirely consistent format for the Guide impossible. Therefore, the various sections of the book are organized to illustrate the complexity and richness of the particular areas called sectors (e.g., Lower Manhattan, Northern Brooklyn and Northwestern Queens). The sectors, in turn, are often divided into neighborhood areas called precincts (e.g., The Financial District, Greenpoint and Long Island City).

Every borough, sector and precinct section is prefaced in the text by a short historical introduction and a capsule description of the area's topography and physical development.

Entries. Each item listed in the Guide is numbered within brackets and identified by name in bold type (sometimes also by former name or names), followed by street address and/or block location, as well as designer and date of completion. When no other title follows the name of the designer, it should be assumed that he is an architect. Throughout the Guide identification lines appear at the bottom of the page, indicating the borough, sector and precinct in which the entries fall. Lines at the bottom of left-hand pages indicate the borough. Right-hand pages show the sector and precinct of the entries. The latter also indicate, through the use of a letter code for each sector (e.g., N for Northern, SE for Southeastern), where the entries can be found on the guide maps. When several entries are located geographically close to one another, but are mentioned individually in the Guide, the same number is used for all the listings in the group but followed by a different letter for each entry (e.g., [3a.], [3b.], [3c.]). On the maps these geographical "clusters" are indicated only by the single number, itself. Bracketed notes at the end of some entries (e.g., [see . . .]) refer to entries of related interest.

In a number of cases, buildings considered worthy of mention in the Guide are no longer standing. In order to indicate the dynamic changes in the City—even if in a negative sense—these entries have been overprinted with the word "DEMOLISHED," in color. If buildings listed in the original edition have since been damaged by fire or abandoned before completion, the information has also been added to the entries.

Photographs that illustrate specific listings are identified with the same number as precedes the entry in the text. If there is no number next to the photograph, it does not illustrate a listed item. The photographs are not always immediately adjacent to the entry that they illustrate.

Maps. Each borough is illustrated with a specially designed map that delineates its sectors. In areas with heavy concentrations of entries, detailed maps for sectors and precincts also show the street systems, subway stations and major landmarks. The numbers on the maps correspond to the numbers of the text entries. As noted above, however, a *single* number on the map sometimes refers to a *group* of geographically adjacent entries mentioned in the text. Special symbols used in the maps throughout the Guide are shown below:

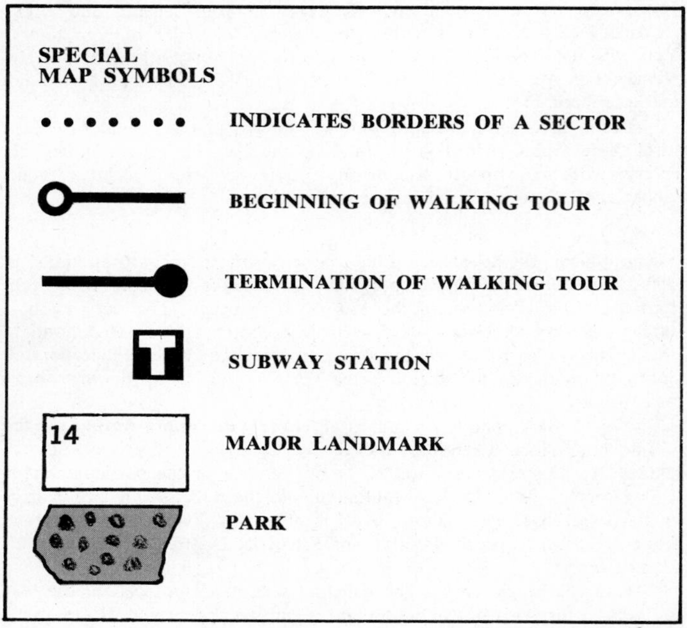

**SPECIAL
MAP SYMBOLS**

● ● ● ● ● ● ●   **INDICATES BORDERS OF A SECTOR**

○━━━━━   **BEGINNING OF WALKING TOUR**

━━━━●   **TERMINATION OF WALKING TOUR**

T   **SUBWAY STATION**

14   **MAJOR LANDMARK**

    PARK

Walking Tours. Routes for walking tours are specified in the text and are shown on the sector maps for the more complex areas. They are indicated by solid black lines, beginning with an open circle and terminating with a solid circle. Where tours are not specifically indicated, the entries are laid out so that by following the numerical sequence of the entries, the reader will naturally trace an easy-to-follow walking or motor tour. Almost all these tours begin at the point within the precinct closest to the Battery, so that the walker moves away from the City's historical "starting point" as he proceeds on his tour. Entries located away from the routes of walking tours are indicated at the end of some sections under the heading *Miscellany*. For outlying parts of the City we recommend an ordinary street map available at gasoline stations.

Restaurants, Bistros, and Emporia. These have not been numbered, except where they have been included primarily for their architectural distinction, but are listed in the index. Telephone numbers are provided for restaurants.

Official Landmarks. Items proposed for designation by the New York City Landmarks Preservation Commission are identified by an open star ☆; those officially designated are identified by a solid star ★. Since these designations are in a constant state of flux, we recommend that you check with the Landmarks Preservation Commission of the City of New York for the most up-to-date information.

Style Symbols. Special symbols in the margin indicate that an entry is a notable example of a building in one of nine significant architectural styles: Colonial, Georgian Federal, Greek Revival, Italianate, Gothic Revival, Classical Revival, Renaissance Revival, Romanesque Revival and Modern. The Architectural Style Guide lists, by style, all such buildings mentioned in the text.

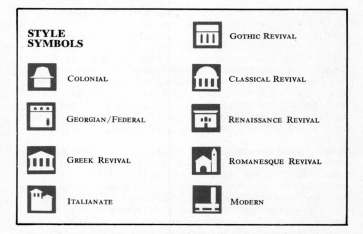

STYLE SYMBOLS

COLONIAL

GEORGIAN/FEDERAL

GREEK REVIVAL

ITALIANATE

GOTHIC REVIVAL

CLASSICAL REVIVAL

RENAISSANCE REVIVAL

ROMANESQUE REVIVAL

MODERN

Index. The large and very detailed Index has been designed to provide you with a number of useful and speedy "doors" to the City, as they reflect the information included in the Guide. Most basic of all, entries have been indexed to cover the three geographical levels utilized throughout the book: BOROUGH, SECTOR and precinct (neighborhood). In addition, the Index will help you to find places and things that you would like to locate but for which you don't have a precise name; every park, square, school, church, even cemetery, that is cited has been listed under a generic heading (in color), e.g., PARKS, etc. Many of these have also been cross-indexed alphabetically. All the names of ARCHITECTS and architectural firms and their works that are mentioned in the Guide are individually listed in the Index. The same has been done for sculptors, painters, landscape architects and artisans. And finally but, perhaps, most delightful, each walking tour suggested in the Guide may be quickly found by referring to the Index. They are indicated with map references under the heading of WALKING TOURS and also by area covered.

NEW YORK CITY IN A NUTSHELL

Name: The name New York dates from British conquest of Dutch Nieuw Amsterdam in 1664. The new colony was named for James, Duke of York, who received New World rights from Charles II of England. Name briefly became New Orange in 1673–1674 when recaptured by the Dutch. After Treaty of Westminster, the name New York was again bestowed by British.

Location: At the confluence of Hudson River, New York Harbor and Atlantic Ocean. Latitude at City Hall, 40°42′45″; longitude 74°0′23″.

Size and Makeup: Comprises five boroughs, each a county as well: Manhattan (New York County), The Bronx (Bronx), Brooklyn (Kings), Queens (Queens), and Richmond (Richmond), more commonly Staten Island. Including inland waters, NYC occupies 365.4 square miles; excluding inland waters except the area within U.S. Bulkhead Lines, total area is 319.8 square miles. From northern tip of the Bronx to southern tip of Richmond, NYC has extreme length of 36 miles. From western border of Richmond to eastern edge of Queens is 25 miles.

Geography: Permeated and bounded by water, navigable and not; New York is essentially an island city. Only the Bronx is on the mainland. Both Manhattan and Richmond occupy their own islands. Brooklyn and Queens share Long Island with two suburban counties. The waterways themselves are punctuated by numerous other islands, particularly in Queens' Jamaica Bay Wildlife Refuge. Highest natural point in NYC is 409.8 feet at Todt Hill, Richmond; average altitude: 55.0 feet.

Population: Leading the country as a city with a population in 1960 of 7,781,984, NYC has single boroughs that would form some of our most populous municipalities. The list would read: NYC (in toto), Chicago, Brooklyn, Los Angeles, Philadelphia, Queens, Manhattan, Detroit, Bronx, and Baltimore. Regional population in 1960 was 16,020,984. Estimate: 22,170,000 by 1985. Region includes 22 counties in 3 states.

Ethnically, 48% of NYC's population are either foreign-born or have at least one foreign-born parent. Estimates show 48.4% Catholic, 26.4% Jewish, 23% Protestant. Fourteen percent of all New Yorkers are Negro; 7.8% are Puerto Rican. There is a significant oriental population; also, 1960 Census listed 3262 American Indians.

History and Government: Sighted in 1524 by Verrazano; earliest European settlement delayed until 1624. Dutch settlers obtained charter in 1653, making New York the oldest incorporated large city in U.S.; English superseded Dutch in 1664. Following Revolution, some of whose battles were fought here, NYC briefly became first capital.

Year 1811 brought gridiron plan to Manhattan. 1816 saw Brooklyn incorporated as village, eventually becoming the independent City of Brooklyn. Census of 1820 first established NYC (only Manhattan Island) as country's largest. Annexation of parts of the Bronx in 1874 and 1895 paved way for unification; opening Brooklyn Bridge in 1883 provided added stimulus. Incorporation of the five boroughs occurred January 1, 1898.

Charter of 1898 and subsequent revisions gave Board of Estimate and Apportionment greater power than Board of Alderman. 1936 City Charter established Board of Estimate as its "board of directors;" City Council as its legislative body. 1963 Charter centralized great power in Mayor's office. New proposal would make formerly separate departments and agencies directly responsible to the Mayor as administrations.

Economy: Over 3.5 million persons are employed, 881,000 of them in manufacturing. NYC is financial capital of US, its largest port, most important management center, center of national advertising, heart of the publishing industry, the garment center, and nucleus of its cultural life in figurative arts, theater, ballet, music, and opera. More store clerks, warehouse workers, artists, musicians, bootblacks, publishers, brokers, bankers, telephone operators are in New York than in any other American city.

1

MANHATTAN

Borough of Manhattan/New York County

To most people, Manhattan **is** New York, a place to **"go to business,"** the **downtown of all downtowns.** This is **where the "action" is;** money is largely here earned, and here in large part spent.

To non-New Yorkers, Manhattan is known in **excerpts from the whole:** Fifth Avenue, Broadway, Greenwich Village, Wall Street, the caricatures of the chic, of **bright lights,** of **the off-beat,** of big business; excerpts symbolic of the public power and influence of Manhattan as the **capital of banking,** corporate headquartering, **the theater,** advertising, **publishing,** fashion; **of tourism,** of the United Nations. This passing parade of visitors mostly misses Manhattan's **myriad local neighborhoods** with handsome buildings and areas of visual delight. That there is **distinguished architecture** and **urban design** in **Harlem;** on the vast **Upper West Side** (of Central Park), or in the **loft districts** of the **Lower West Side,** will startle, and we hope, pleasantly surprise those visitors who have savored **only the well-publicized monuments, musicals and museums.**

L

LOWER MANHATTAN

THE FINANCIAL DISTRICT

The Battery

The "Battery" suggests to most New Yorkers the bottom of Manhattan Island, where **tourists** are borne by ferry to the **Statue of Liberty,** and **"provincial"** Staten Islanders start their trek to that distant island that turns out to be, surprisingly, part of New York. What was, in fact, the name for this namesake consisted of **a row of guns** along the old shorefront line, now approximated by **State Street** between **Bowling Green** and **Whitehall.** During the War of 1812, the status of the gunnery was elevated, and **Castle Clinton,** erected on a pile of rock some 300 feet off the shore, was known as West Battery; **Castle Williams,** built in 1811 on Governor's Island, became the "East Battery." Intervening years have seen land fill entirely envelop Castle Clinton (and its various **transmogrifications)** forming **Battery Park,** a flat and somewhat confused stretch of landscaping that provides **greenery and delight** to summer New Yorkers from nearby offices. A fresh, if sometimes pungent, breeze from the **Upper Bay** is an antidote for the doldrums or any bad mood aggravated by heat.

Walking Tour: From the Battery to Liberty Street and Broadway. (IRT Lexington Avenue or Seventh Avenue Subways to South Ferry station, or BMT local to Whitehall Street.)

 [1a.] Castle Clinton National Monument, Battery Park. 1807. John McComb, Jr. ★

Until recently, one of the most vitally involved structures in

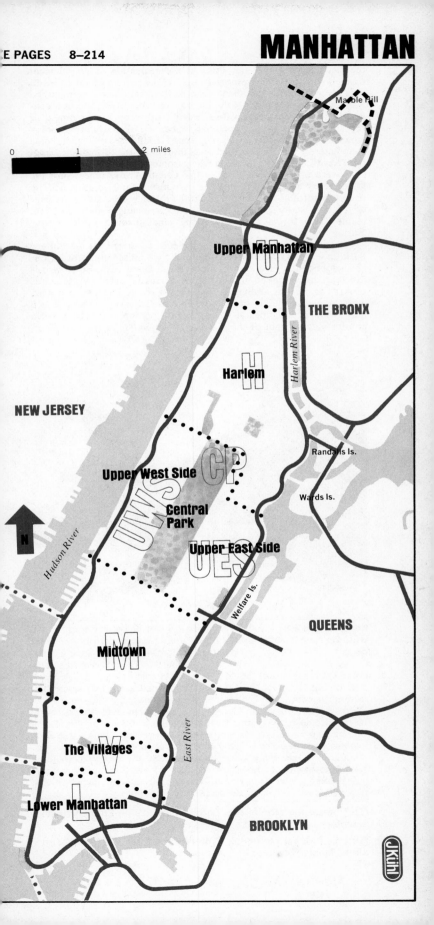

the city's history and life. Built as a **fortification** to complement
Castle Williams on Governors Island, it was 16 years later ceded to
the City. As a **civic monument** it served for reception of distinguished
visitors at the very edge of the nation. Remodeled in 1845 as a **concert hall,** and renamed **Castle Garden** (still at sea), its moment of
supreme glory was the much-ballyhooed P. T. Barnum-promoted
concert of the Swedish soprano, **Jenny Lind,** in 1850. Only nine
years later, it was transformed once more, into the **"Emigrant Landing Depot"** (pre-Ellis Island), where some 7.7 million new Americans were processed, some into the **Union Army;** others into the
Lower East Side. Scandal caused its closure, and replacement by
federal control at **Ellis Island** in 1890. Not one to be out of the center of the "action," it juggled its innards, changed its decor, and
reentered the fray as the **"Aquarium,"** much-beloved grotto of New
Yorkers until 1941.

   Then, apparently doomed by the cut and tunnel for the Battery
Park underpass, it was rescued by loud civic noises. Belatedly, Congress dubbed it a "National Historic Monument" in 1946. Now it is
just that: to be looked at, but not used. Having achieved the status
of **Art** (Architectural division), it is to be revered as a saintly relic,
not involved in the life of the city. The aquarium was removed to a
new group of buildings at Coney Island, perhaps to make the fish
comfortable in sight of the sea. [See S Brooklyn 7a.]

[1a.]   **[1c.]**

Staten Island Ferry, foot of Whitehall Street at Battery Park, ranks
with the Empire State Building as a tourist mecca not only of great
delight and exoticism, but one that explains the overall arrangement
of the city quickly, clearly, and pleasantly. For **five cents** (a ludi-
crous figure—it should be free, or self-supporting) you will experience one of the great short water voyages of the world, through the
teeming harbor, past Ellis and Liberty Islands, the Bayonne Navy
Yard, to the town of St. George at Staten Island's northeast shore.
If you decide to stay, turn to the Richmond section of this guide.
But for another nickel, travel the route in reverse. This is the **low-
income substitute** for a glamorous arrival in New York by trans-
atlantic liner, **receiving Liberty's salute,** and the romantic **wedding
cake silhouette** of the Lower Manhattan skyline. On a lucky day you
will diesel by and through the wakes of freighters, ferries, liners,
pleasure craft, and **even an occasional warship.**

[1b.] Verrazano Monument, Battery Park. 1909. Ettore Ximenes,
Sculptor.

[1c.] East Coast Memorial, Battery Park. 1960. William Gehron.
Albino Manca, Sculptor.

Statue of Liberty Ferry, in Battery Park. BO 9-5755.

Every hour on the hour, year-round, between 9 and 4. More frequently in summer [See 1e.]

[1e.] Statue of Liberty, Liberty Island/formerly **Bedloes Island,** across the Upper Bay. 1886, Frederic Auguste Bartholdi, Sculptor; Richard Morris Hunt, Architect of the base.

Perhaps three times the height of the Colossus of Rhodes, which was one of "Seven Wonders of the World." Liberty is considered **corny** these days, but corn is here a necessary ingredient. Like an old shoe to New Yorkers, she is always there, has worn and continues to wear well. Take the ferry out to her, ascend the spiral stairway through her innards to the crown, and you will look back on one of the romantic glories of the world: the New York skyline.

[3.] **[5.]**

[2.] Whitehall Building, 17 Battery Place, NE cor. West St. 1900–1910. Clinton and Russell.

[3.] Downtown Athletic Club (and adjacent office building), 18–21 West St. SE cor. Morris St. 1926. Starrett & Van Vleck.

A chromatic range of **salt-glazed** tile, from burnt oranges to brown. This is the material of which **silos** are frequently made, a natural glaze, resistant to urban "fallout" without the crassness of the popular white-glazed brick of post-World War II. The arcade with recessed ground floor is composed of corbeled arches, reminiscent of Moorish architecture. Corners are cantilevered, allowing corner windows naturally.

[4.] 90 West Street, bet. Albany and Cedar Sts. 1905. Cass Gilbert.

Limestone and cast terra cotta. Increasingly interesting and complex the higher you raise your eyes: designed for a view **from** the harbor, or the eyries of an adjacent skyscraper, rather than the ordinary West Street pedestrian. A similar, but less successful use of terra cotta than Gilbert's spectacular **Woolworth Building.**

[5.] Shrine of Blessed Mother Seton/originally **James Watson House,** 7 State St. bet. Pearl and Whitehall Sts. NE side. 1793–1806. Attributed to John McComb, Jr. ★

A single survivor of the **first great era of mansions,** this facade is original: Federal (both in the archeological and political senses, it was built in the fourth year of George Washington's presidency of the **Federal** Republic, in a style that is separately considered Federal: slender, elegant freestanding Ionic columns, and delicate late-Georgian detailing.)

[6.] Bowling Green (New York's first park), foot of Broadway. Formalized, 1732. Fence. ☆

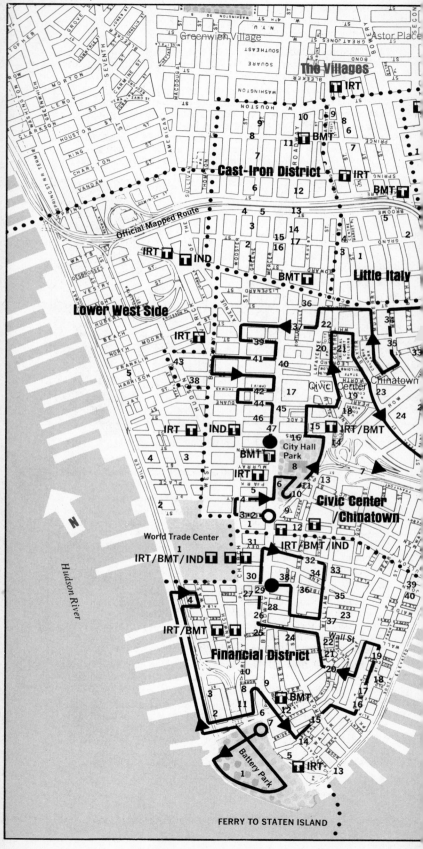

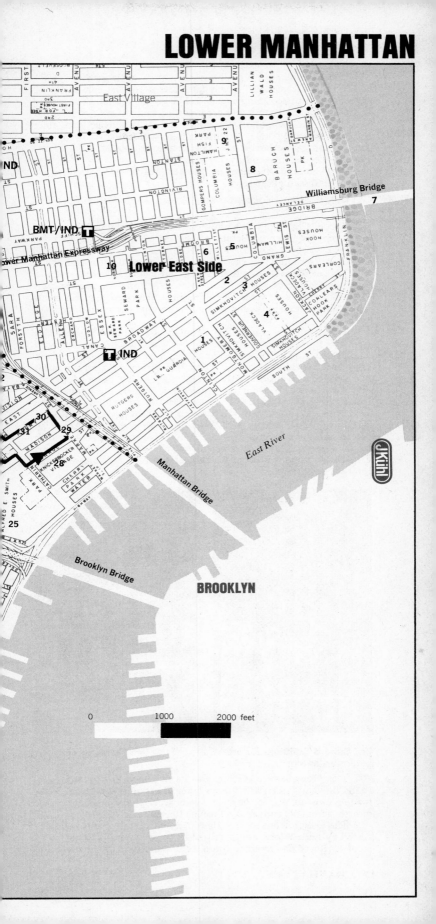

LOWER MANHATTAN

This spot as an extension of Battery Place (**Marcktveldt** or **Marketfield** originally) was part of the Dutch **cattle market** (1638–1647). Then a "parade," it was later leased for the annual fee of **one peppercorn**, becoming a quasi-public bowling ground (or green) in 1732, (for the beauty and ornament of said street as well as the recreation and delight of the inhabitants.) The fence remaining today was erected in 1771, although its decorative crowns were knocked off by **exuberant militia** after the reading of the Declaration of Independence on July 9, 1776.

The statue of **Abraham De Peyster** (Mayor, 1691–1695) is by George E. Bissell (1896).

[7.] U.S. Customs House, Bowling Green. S side. 1907. Cass Gilbert. ★

Daniel Chester French's four monumental sculptures are very much part of the architecture of the facade (left to right, **Asia, America, Europe, Africa**). Their whiteness (of limestone) against dark grey (granite) is a rich counterpoint of both form and color.

The **oval pavilion** within is a grand salon of bureaucracy—a flat domed space of public importance. When the Customs vacates in favor of the new **World Trade Center,** the challenge will be to make this building a viable participant in community and/or business affairs.

In the position a royal palace might assume in 17th and 18th Century European city planning, the Customs House replaced "Steamship Row", six town houses built as minor mansions and later used for shipping offices. These had earlier replaced the burnt and derelict **Government House,** first built (1790, John McComb, Jr.) for George Washington's presidency. When the capital was moved to Philadelphia, Government House served briefly as the Governor's Mansion until the State capital also moved, to Albany. A Dutch, then English, then Dutch, then English, then American fort occupied the same general premises under nine consecutive names, beginning as **Fort Amsterdam,** in 1625 and ending as **Fort George.** This was the fort of which East and West Batteries were the outward defenses.

[4.] [7.]

[8.] Cunard Building, 25 Broadway, SW cor. Morris St. 1921. Benjamin Wistar Morris.

This "Renaissance" facade and its neighbors handsomely surround Bowling Green with a high order of **group architecture.** What matters most at No. 25, however, is its great public interior spaces, directly accessible and on axis through the entrance lobby.

The elaborately decorated groined and domed vaults were designed by **Ezra Winter** and executed by imported **Italian** craftsmen; maps by **Barry Faulkner.** If you walk to either end of the vestibule, you can outflank the ticket office, and enter the main "freight distribution" hall. This and the domed **"Bill of Lading"** hall of the Customs House vie for honors as the most elegant places to work in New York.

[9.] 26 Broadway/formerly **Standard Oil Building,** NE cor. Beaver St. 1922. Carrère & Hastings; Shreve, Lamb & Blake.

The curve of this facade reinforces the street's group architecture, working well with its eclectic friend, No. 25. First THE Standard Oil Building, it served until that Trust was broken up by federal anti-trust action. Then the Trust's child, Socony (**S**tandard **O**il **Co**mpany **O**f **N**ew **Y**ork, later Socony Mobil, then Mobil) lived here until it built its own new building at 42nd Street in 1958.

The tower is squared to the grid of the city to the north, rather than to any geometry of the base or local streets. The architects were concerned with it as a **skyline** element, not a local form, and hence coordinated it with skyline neighbors.

[1a.]

[10.] U.S. Office Building, 45 Broadway bet. Morris and Exchange Alley, W side. 1886. Young and Cable.

[11.] 11 Broadway, Bowling Green. W side. 1898. W. G. Audsley.

"Eclectic" was really invented for confections like this. The battered **Egyptian pylons** framing the entrances are bizarre imports. Above the third floor, however, the spirit changes: strong glazed brick piers, with articulated spandrels have much of the bold verticality of buildings of the "Chicago School."

[12.] 2 Broadway, bet. Beaver and Stone Sts. 1959. Emery Roth & Sons.

"Whitehall", at 1 State Street, NW cor. Whitehall Street, (ca. 1657) was Peter Stuyvesant's mansion. Renamed Whitehall by the first **English** governor it occupied a tiny peninsula projecting from the east end of the Battery at this point. One hundred years later **Robert Fulton** was a resident in a different building on the same site.

[13.] Piers, 11 South St., foot of Whitehall. 1906. ★

The Late Victorian false front on these aging piers shows a raised porch with 40-foot columns to Whitehall. Green paint over sheet metal and steel structural members **simulates** verdigris copper. The Governors Island Ferry leaves from here. The only historical "style" which this inherits is the very idea of a colonnade: the columns, however, are original, and relate to the material, sheet metal.

[14.] U.S. Army Building, 39 Whitehall St. bet. Water and Pearl Sts. ca. 1886.

Broad Street, ca. 1695: Before it was so named, this was the **Heere Gracht,** a drainage and shipping canal reaching present day Exchange Place, where docked a ferry to Long Island. A short-lived function, ending with the filling of the canal 100 years before the Revolution, its effects remain in the **extraordinary width** of the street (for this part of town). The oldest streets of Manhattan cross Broad, most with matter-of-fact names as descriptive as Broad: Bridge Street, for example, was at the first bridge immediately adjacent to the waterfront at Pearl. Pearl should be Mother-of-Pearl, in fact, for the glistening **shells** that lined its shores. Stone Street was the first to be **cobbled.** The geometry of public space has not greatly changed, except that Broad's meeting with the shoreline is some 600 feet farther into the harbor than at the time of the canal's fill, making Water, Front, and South man-made land of later date.

[16b.]

[15a.] Fraunces Tavern, 54 Pearl St. SE cor. Broad St. 1907. William Mersereau. ★

The tavern of Samuel Fraunces occupied this plot and **achieved great historic note** in the Revolution: for ten days in 1783 it was the terminal residence of **General Washington.** On December 4th **he bade farewell** to his officers and withdrew to his estate at Mount Vernon, Virginia. He returned six years later **to take office as president** at old City Hall at the head of Wall and Broad five blocks away.

The present building is a **highly conjectural construction** (not restoration) based on typical buildings of "the period," part of the remaining outer walls, and guesswork. With enthusiasm more harmless when attached to geneology than **to wishful archeology,** the Tavern has been billed in the public's eyes as the "Real McCoy." Such charades have caused "George Washington slept here" architecture to strangle reality in much of suburban America.

[15b.] 62 Pearl Street, bet. Broad St. and Coenties Slip. 1827. ☆

Here is an architectural workhorse, used and still usable, a valid remnant of its period.

[15c.] 71 Pearl Street, bet. Broad St. and Coenties Alley. Foundations, 1641. Walls, 1700. Facade, 1826. ★

The Dutch **Stadt Huys,** seat of colonial government, stood here, and is invisibly memorialized in the foundations supporting the present visible structure. A plaque 12 feet up on No. 73 inaccurately records this. In fact, the Stadt Huys straddled both properties. Here the old shoreline was so close that **tides** at times **lapped against its steps.**

Coenties Slip, at South St.: As the fill crept seaward, this "slip" (a tiny artificial bay for wharfing ships) was created with a diagonal breakwater paralleling the present west boundary. Eventually the breakwater was absorbed as land projected even beyond its former tip.

[16a.] Seaman's Church Institute, 25 South St. at Coenties Slip. Additions, 1913, 1929, Warren and Wetmore.

An Episcopal Church-supported hostel for seamen docked in New York harbor, to be demolished when the Institute's new building is completed adjacent to Battery Park. Its **lighthouse tower** memorializes the sinking of the *Titanic*.

[16b.] 54, 55, 56, 57, 61 Front Street, bet. Coenties and Old Slips. 1837. ☆

[17.] 62, 64 Front Street, bet. Cuylers Alley and Old Slip. ca. 1837.

Remnants of handsome vernacular shipping warehouses. Even the most common structure had class when the Greeks were Revived.

[18a.] 1st Precinct Police Station, N.Y.C. Police Dept., at South St. Old Slip, 1909. Richard Howland Hunt and Joseph Howland Hunt.

[18b.] U.S. Assay Building, Old Slip, at South St. 1930. James A. Wetmore, Acting Supervising Architect, U.S. Treasury.

The "behind" is what impresses today. A massively sculptural granite monolith. Note the chimney. The front is fussy.

[19.] 96-110 Front Street, bet. Gouverneur Lane and Wall St. NE cor. De Peyster St. 142 Front St. ca. 1837.

[20a.] India House/originally **Hanover Bank,** 1 Hanover Square, bet. Pearl and Stone Sts. 1854. Richard J. Carman, Carpenter. ★

Florentine Palace, typical of many brownstone commercial buildings that once dotted this area, now replaced by newer and denser construction. The style is so associated with the New York brownstone row houses that we almost do a double-take on seeing it clothing a Wall Street building. Now a club, it harbors a **maritime museum.**

[18a.]

[18b.]

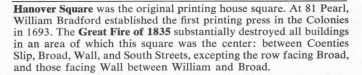

Hanover Square was the original printing house square. At 81 Pearl, William Bradford established the first printing press in the Colonies in 1693. The **Great Fire of 1835** substantially destroyed all buildings in an area of which this square was the center: between Coenties Slip, Broad, Wall, and South Streets, excepting the row facing Broad, and those facing Wall between William and Broad.

Stone Street, bet. Hanover Square and Broad St. ca. 1657: Paved with cobbles, the name changed from Brouwer to Stone Street in a society that was naively and happily literal. Its curve merely reflects the profile of the original shoreline.

[20b.] Delmonico's Restaurant/now **Oscar's Delmonico,** 56 Beaver St. at William St. 1891. James Brown Lord. ☆

Occupying, like 1 Liberty Street and the Flatiron Building, the valuable but awkward **triangular space** left between two converging streets. A distinguished restaurant for almost a century and a half. Lord designed this palatial headquarters at the height of their prestige and popularity. Try to remember another New York restaurant (without hotel) which is more than the outfitting of commercial "store space."

[21.] First National City Trust Company/originally **City Bank Farmers Trust Co.,** 22 William Street bet. Beaver St. and Exchange Pl. 1931. Cross and Cross.

A slender 57-story tower of limestone, from the awkward period of architectural history between buildings-as-columns and steel cage construction.

[22.]

[25a

[25

Wall Street: The Dutch Wall of 1653 was built as protection against attack from English colonies to the north. The English took it down, but the name remained.

[22.] First National City Bank/lower portion originally the **Merchants' Exchange,** 55 Wall St. bet. William and Hanover Sts. 1842. Isaiah Rogers. Remodeled and doubled in height, 1907. McKim, Mead & White. ★

After the destruction of the First Merchants' Exchange in the "Great Fire of 1835," Rogers erected a three-storied Ionic temple with a central domed trading hall on this same site. Later used as the Customs House, it was remodeled in 1907 after the Fed removal to Bowling Green as the head office of the then National City Bank: another tier of columns, this time **Corinthian,** was superimposed to double the cubic content.

[23.] 60 Wall Tower, 70 Pine St. bet. Pine, Pearl and Cedar Sts. 1932. Clinton and Russell.

Addressmanship at its most blatant: the tail on Wall wags the body on Pine. A slender tube (bridge) connects the two across Pine.

This is a skyline building, with a "Gothic" crown only to be appreciated as part of the skyline from a great distance or from a neighboring eyrie.

[24a.] 40 Wall Street/originally **Bank of the Manhattan Company,** bet. William and Nassau Sts. 1929. H. Craig Severance & Yasuo Matsui. Ground floor remodeled, 1963, Carson Lundin & Shaw.

Another skyline bank building, now best observed from the

composite bank to which it has removed its quarters: Chase Manhattan. The pyramidal crown was the strong and simple symbol of the original bank. Chartered originally (i.e., the Manhattan Company) as a water company and the first quasi-public utility, it became redundant in 1842 when the **Croton Reservoir** system began to feed Manhattan with water. Always permitted by clause in its charter to engage in banking, it continued, after 1842, solely as the Bank *of* the Manhattan Company, the latter parent organization becoming incidental to its former offshoot.

[24b.] Federal Hall National Memorial/formerly **Subtreasury Building,** 1862–1925/originally **Customs House,** 1842–1862, 28 Wall Street, NE cor. Nassau St. 1842. Town & Davis, with John Frazee. ★

A Doric-columned temple, this is the star of New York's Greek Revival. The Wall Street facade is a simplified Parthenon, without the sculptured frieze or pediment. Carved from marble quarried in **Westchester County,** it is raised on a high base to handle the change in grade from Pine to Wall. Inside is a very non-Greek rotunda, the principal, and startling, space (analagous to finding a cubical body in a conch shell).

[24b.]

The current name, Federal Hall National Memorial, commemorates the building on the same site in which Washington took the **oath of office** as president in 1789. It had been remodeled by Pierre L'Enfant from the shell of old City Hall to which local government had been removed from the old Dutch Stadt Huys on Pearl Street in 1701.

J(ohn) Q(uincy) A(dams) Ward's statue of **Washington** (1883) stands on the approximate spot where the man himself took the oath.

[24c.] J. P. Morgan & Co., 23 Wall St., SE cor. Broad St. 1913. Trowbridge and Livingston. ★

Interesting more for the contents than its architectural envelope. J. Pierpont Morgan epitomized Wall Street to capitalists, communists, radicals, and conservatives alike. And, of course, when Wall Street was to be bombed, this was considered its sensitive center of control: on September 16th, 1920, an anarchist ignited a wagonload of explosives next to the Wall Street flank; 33 persons were killed, four hundred injured. The scars are still visible in the stonework.

[24d.] New York Stock Exchange, 8 Broad St. bet. Wall St. and Exchange Pl. 1903. George B. Post. Addition, 1923. Trowbridge and Livingston. Pediment sculpture, J. Q. A. Ward and Paul Bartlett. ☆

One of the few great architectural spaces accessible to the public in this city. Guided tours are available to the galleries.

The original temple-facade by Post is a far cry from his Queen Anne Long Island Historical Society 27 years before. [See Brooklyn Heights 20h.] The Columbian Exposition of 1893 had swept such earth-colored picturesque architecture under the rug. The rage for neo-Renaissance architecture and cities was compelling even to those who had been the Goths of Architecture.

[25a.] Irving Trust Company, 1 Wall St., SE cor. Broadway. 1932. Voorhees, Gmelin & Walker. Addition, 1965. Smith, Smith, Haines, Waehler & Lundberg.

Ralph Walker's experiments with the plastic molding of skyscraper form, both in massing and detail, include this one example in limestone, and three in brick: two for the Telephone Company (140 West Street and 32 Sixth Avenue) and one for Western Union (60 Hudson Street).

[39.]

[25b.] Trinity Church, Broadway at the head of Wall St. 1846. Richard Upjohn. ★ **Chapel of All Saints,** 1913. Thomas Nash. **Bishop Manning Memorial Wing,** 1966. Adams and Woodbridge.

The attached chapels must not be confused with Trinity's Colonial chapels, which were, in fact, **separate and remotely located church buildings** serving this **immense Episcopal parish.** Typical of the latter is St. Paul's Chapel at Fulton and Broadway. The parish was and is an enormous landowner (Fulton to Christopher Streets, West of Broadway to the river, was **its original grant from Queen Anne,** 1705). Thus, the proselytizing of the faith through missionary activities could be financed comfortably (**St. Augustine's** and **St. Christopher's Chapels** on the Lower East Side are further examples). Nestled in the canyons of Broadway and Trinity Place, its tiny form is totally comprehensible to the pedestrian: on the axis of Wall Street the canyon walls read as **surfaces,** while Trinity sits importantly, an anthracite jewel, bedded in a green baize cemetery. The cemetery offers a green retreat for summer-tired office workers at noontime. **Bronze doors** designed by **Richard Morris Hunt** were executed by Charles Niehaus, Karl Bitter, and J. Massey Rhind. (Left entrance, main entrance and right entrance, respectively).

Cemetery monuments of particular note include those of Alexander Hamilton and Robert Fulton.

[26.] 100 Broadway, Bank of Tokyo/formerly **American Surety Company,** SE cor. Pine St. 1895. Bruce Price.

[27a.] Trinity and U.S. Realty Buildings, 111 and 115 Broadway at Thames St. 1906. Francis H. Kimball.

Rich buildings, from top to bottom, their narrow ends at Broadway are broken Gothic forms with strongly scaled detail. They have a great deal of personality vis-à-vis the passing pedestrian. Unlike the blank austerity of 1 Wall, the temple-entrance of 100 Broadway, or the modern open-ness of Chase Manhattan's vast transparent lobby for mass bureaucrats, these are buildings for **individual people.** One could feel possessive about them.

[27b.] Nichols Hall, N.Y.U. Graduate School of Business Administration, 100 Trinity Pl. bet. Thames and Cedar Sts. W side 1959. Skidmore, Owings & Merrill.

[28.] Equitable Building, 120 Broadway bet. Pine and Cedar Sts. 1915. Ernest R. Graham (Graham, Anderson, Probst and White, the Office of D. H. Burnham).

This was more famous for what it caused than what it is. An immense volume, it **exploited its site** as no building had before: 1,200,000 square feet on a plot of **just under an acre,** or a *floor* area of almost **30 times** the *site's* area—maximum permitted under the **1961 Zoning Resolution,** with special bonuses, 12.

The hue and cry after Equitable's completion led to the adoption of the **first Zoning Resolution** in **1916.**

[28.]

[29.] 140 Broadway, bet. Broadway, Liberty, Nassau and Cedar Sts. 1967. Skidmore, Owings & Merrill.

A taut skin stretched over bare bones. The sleek and visually flush facade is an almost melodramatic contrast to the ornamented environment. Matteness of the black spandrels breaks up the reflections of these neighbors into more random, mysterious parts. The plaza at Broadway is a perfect size to have a major impact on the feel of this neighborhood. (The same firm's Chase Manhattan Plaza next door on Pine suffers from an amorphous shape, and a separation (by elevation) from the street life around it except at the West or Nassau Street end.)

[30.] Singer Building, 149 Broadway, NW cor. Liberty St. 1908. Ernest Flagg.

Flagg had a dry run on the "little" Singer building at 561 Broadway a year earlier. This has some of the same original use of metal and glass, equally anticipating Mies van der Rohe and his lesser imitators, but in a frame of heavy and monumental eclectic palace architecture.

[31.] American Telephone and Telegraph Building, 195 Broadway bet. Dey and Fulton Sts. 1917. Welles Bosworth.

The **layer cake** of New York: eight Ionic colonnades (embracing three stories within each set) are stacked on a Doric order. All is surmounted by the famous telephone company symbol: **Spirit of Communication** by Evelyn Longman. Handsome parts are assembled into a bizarre whole: **more columns** than any building in the world!

[32.] John Street Methodist Church, 44 John St. bet. Nassau and William Sts. 1841. ★

More interesting because it is old and venerable in a hotbed of changing commercial uses than because of great architectural merit. Pink paint doesn't help, but rather demeans the architecture.

Nassau Street Shopping Area: From Maiden Lane to Beekman Street this serves as the most active local shopping strip: medium to modest-priced chain stores, discount houses, and small specialized shops. Nylons, radio equipment, dresses, shoes, all of the personal and portable items that a noontime **lunch-shopper** would be most inclined to inspect and purchase. The ground-floor activity and clutter of show windows and signs keep the eyes at street level. The form and detail of buildings above, no matter how tall, is rarely noticed, almost never observed.

[29.]

[30

[33.] Aetna Insurance Company, 100 William St. bet. John and Platt Sts. ca. 1890.

[34.] Home Insurance Company, 59 Maiden Lane, NW cor. William St. 1966. Office of Alfred Easton Poor.

A small plaza again shows that public space contained by buildings can benefit from being small; increasing the size would diminish rather than enhance its quality.

The **H. V. Smith Museum** occupies the 15th floor with the nation's most complete collection of equipment, art, and history of **fire fighting and fire insurance** (open Monday-Friday, 10 AM-4 PM; Saturday by appointment; 530–7051).

[35a.] 1 Liberty Street, at Maiden Lane. 1907. Hill and Stout.

Crane your neck to see one of the more spectacular cornices of New York: a giant **concave cantilever** of tan terra cotta tile, edged with ornamented copper, projects 12 feet. No question here of a firm architectural ending against the sky.

[35b.] 90 Liberty Street, bet. William and Pearl Sts. 1865.

[36a.] Chase Manhattan Bank and Plaza, 1 Chase Manhattan Plaza, bet. Nassau, William, Liberty and Pine Sts. 1960. Skidmore, Owings & Merrill.

David Rockefeller and his fellow board members, through their act of faith in building this behemoth, here cried "Excelsior," and the **flagging spirit** of the Financial District took courage. Architecturally less successful than the more sophisticated 140 Broadway by the same firm, it provides, however, the first gratuitous plaza to the Financial District. Two more have appeared since, the Home

Insurance Company, and 140 Broadway.

A sheer 800 feet of aluminum and glass rises from the paved Plaza surface, which is, in turn, accessible from both Nassau and Pine Streets. The topography unfortunately forces the Liberty and William Street sides down, detaching them from participation in the plaza's space.

The sunken circular courtyard is paved with undulating forms of granite blocks, crowned with sculpture, and caressed in summer by a fountain, pools, and rivulets: all by sculptor **Isamu Noguchi.** Goldfish were resident at first, but the **urban fallout** and sentimentalists' "coins in the fountain" destroyed even those resilient carp.

From the harbor, Chase is a jarring, box-like mass on the many-spired skyline.

[36b.] Federal Reserve Bank of New York, 33 Liberty St., Maiden Lane, William and Nassau Sts. 1924. York & Sawyer. ★

A "fortified" Florentine palace conserves within its dungeons more money than **Fort Knox.** This is a great neo-Renaissance building, with rusticated Indiana limestone, Ohio sandstone, and elegant ironwork. A **bank for banks,** this is the great stabilizer and equalizer of their separately erratic activities. Nations have rooms in **the five levels below the street,** where their **gold is stored** and moved, in the balance of trade, from nation to nation, without ever leaving the building. [Free tours available by appointment.]

The south wall, on Liberty Street, is **a magnificent foil** to the crystalline glass and aluminum of the Chase Manhattan Bank. We hope that the Federal Reserve Bank will long remain so.

[36a.]

[37.] Down Town Association, 60 Pine St. bet. William and Pearl Sts. 1887. Charles C. Haight.

This appropriately somber club building serves many distinguished financial executives, principally for **lunch.**

[38a.] Liberty Towers, 55 Liberty St., NW cor. Nassau St. 1909. Henry Ives Cobb.

[38b.] Chamber of Commerce of the State of New York, 65 Liberty St., NW cor. Liberty Pl. 1901. James B. Baker. ★

End of Tour. Nearest subway at either Wall Street or Fulton Street and Broadway (IRT Lexington Avenue Line) or at Fulton Street for IND Eighth Avenue Line.

MISCELLANY

[39.] Schermerhorn Row (or Block): 2–18 Fulton Street; ☆ 189–195 Front Street; ☆ 159–171 John Street; ☆ 91–92 South Street. ☆ 1811–1850.

As early as these buildings were built, (No. 2 at South Street is a vintage structure, 1811), the land had already been filled 600 feet out from its original shoreline to a wharf-frontage. Served by this block, among many others, South Street was lined with ships, parked, **bowsprit in,** oversailing the wheeled and pedestrian traffic

[36b.]

below. (The line of the bulkhead was approximately at the line of the supporting west or inner row of columns of the vehicular viaduct.)

Plans are being developed for a South Street Historical project with the objective of restoring the whole of "Fishmarket Square" to mid-19th century splendor, including shops and ships.

[40.] 170–176 John Street, bet. Front and South Sts. 1840. ☆

An austere granite facade, rare in that era, gives a dour face to the street.

Entertainments, Stimuli and a Full Stomach.

Sweet's Restaurant, 2 Fulton St. at South St. WH. 2-9628. A la carte. Closed weekends and holidays; first two weeks of July.

For those Latins and Russians who cannot bear to dine before 10 or later, this must be stricken from the list. They close promptly at 8 PM. At the foot of Schermerhorn Row [See 39], this venerable and fine seafood restaurant (est. 1845) occupies an even more venerable building of 1811.

Fraunces Tavern, 54 Pearl St., SE cor. Broad St. BO 9-0144. Closed Saturday evening, all of Sunday and holidays.

Not fascinating gastronomically, but the competition is limited. This is the cuisine of the American suburban roadhouse these days: steak, roast beef, scampi. [See 15a.]

Oscar's Delmonico, 56 Beaver St., at S. William St., BO 9-1180. Open until 10:30 PM. Closed Saturday evening, Sundays and holidays.

This, the downtown restaurant of the Delmonico family, has served in two guises and two buildings six generations of New Yorkers (since 1836). Oscar provides North Italian cuisine of high quality.

Chez Yvonne L'Escargot, 54 Stone St. bet. Broad St. and Hanover Sq. 944-9887. Open til 7 PM. Closed weekends and holidays.

Yvonne the Snail, not surprisingly, specializes in snails as an appetizer—they are notable. Rare lamb, another notable rarity in American-French cuisine is also available.

Whyte's Downtown, 145 Fulton St. bet. Nassau St. and Broadway, CO 7-2233. Closed weekends and holidays. A la carte.

An old shoe restaurant, fish is mandatory. Finnan Haddie is the most famous institution here.

While you're in New York, visit the Armstrong Product Center—a showcase for flooring, ceiling materials, and other interior finishes. It offers informative and imaginative displays—residential and commercial room settings. The Product Center is staffed by a resident interior designer and an Architect-Builder-Contractor Consultant. ☐ Hours: Monday through Friday, 9:30 a.m. to 5:00 p.m. Armstrong Product Center, 60 West 49th Street, Rockefeller Center, New York City, N Y.

Armstrong
CORK COMPANY

Hanover Square Restaurant, 1 Hanover Square, SW cor. Stone St. WH 4-9251. Closes 8:30 PM, weekends and holidays.

Within part of the west flank of India House, this public restaurant shares some of the volume of that private club. Schnitzel, hassenpfeffer, dumplings and other goodies devised to adjust the jowls to bankers' proportions. Good and inexpensive.

Zum Zum, 74 Broad St., SW cor. Marketfield St.

Another in the happily spreading empire of Restaurant Associates. Soup, salad, sausages and beer are standard.

Trefflich's (Bird and Animal Company) 144 Liberty St. bet. Washington and West Sts.

Rats and snails and puppy dogs with and without tails—that's what little boys are made for (also snakes, gerbils, tortoises, birds, lizards, monkeys, alligators). Larger and more exciting (some say vicious) animals can be had on order. Mr. Trefflich is a gracious and knowledgeable host, who will be delighted to advise you. Certainly one of the leading bird and animal stores in the country (to term it a "pet" store would demean it).

Kabuki Restaurant), 115 Wall St. 962-4677. Closed Sundays, holidays and for Saturday lunch.

A first-rate Japanese restaurant, where one may dine sitting on a chair, or if stoic, sit, Japanese-style, on the floor.

Ye Olde Chop House, 101 Cedar St. bet. Broadway and Trinity Pl. RE 2-6119. A la carte. Closes 7:30 PM, weekends and holidays.

Under normal circumstances a guide concerned with design would boggle at the thought of including anything termed "Ye Olde." But quality of food here shines through; the grilled meats are excellent. The specialty of the house is Smithfield Ham given such a grilling.

Lower Manhattan Plan, 1966, Wallace-McHarg Associates and Whittlesey, Conklin & Rossant. This thorough report commissioned by then City Planning chairman William F. R. Ballard gives prospect of a lively and handsome future for all the island south of Canal Street. It promises a pedestrian world, foot-eased by small and un-noxious electric buses. Cars are burrowed under the perimeter, feeding parking warehouses at key points, and land fill to the pierhead line will give opportunity for new residential communities surrounding riverside plazas, "windows on the waterfront."

LOWER WEST SIDE

Shipping shifted from the **East** to the **North** (Hudson) Rivers after the **Civil** War. The many-bowspritted streets on the east flank of Manhattan were abandoned for the many-berthed piers of **steam-powered** trans-Atlantic shipping, on the west flank. In much later years auto traffic needs caused the Miller Highway, that elevated portion of the West Side Drive to 72nd Street, to dominate West Street.

[1.] World Trade Center, West, Washington, Barclay, West Broadway, Vesey, Church and Liberty Sts. 1975. Minoru Yamasaki & Associates, and Emery Roth & Sons.

Twin 110-story towers will flank low buildings and a plaza larger than the Piazza San Marco in Venice. From the harbor, Brooklyn, or New Jersey this pair will dominate Lower Manhattan's skyline—stolid monoliths overshadowing the cluster of filigreed towers that still (except for Chase Manhattan) are the romantic symbols that once evoked the very thought of "skyline."

Ten million square feet of space will here be offered: seven times the Empire State Building, four times the Pan Am building.

[2.] New York Telephone Company, 140 West St. bet. Barclay and Vesey Sts. 1926. Voorhees, Gmelin and Walker.

This distinguished monolith borders the site of the new World Trade Center. An early experiment in massing large urban form within the zoning envelope permitted in the then-new law of 1916. The arcaded sidewalk along Vesey Street is handsome and pleasant: why not elsewhere in New York to protect the pedestrian from inclement weather and enrich the architectural form of the street? (Down the road a piece, at 21 West Street has a brief arcade as well).

[1.] **[2.]**

[3.] 75 Murray Street, bet. W. Broadway and Greenwich Sts., ca. 1865.

[4.] Cast-Iron Building, NW cor. Washington and Murray Sts., 1848. James Bogardus. ☆

[5.] 29-33 Harrison Street; 314, 315-317, 327-329, 331 Washington Street. 1797-1828. John McComb & friends. ☆

John McComb, Jr., designed 315-317, and lived there. Now market buildings, their original Federal spirit is still clearly apparent over the trucks and loading canopies.

CIVIC CENTER/CHINATOWN

The flavor of city life rests largely in sharp juxtapositions of differing activities: government, commerce, industry, housing, entertainment, and differing ethnic and economic groups. These precincts are a caricature of that idea.

Spreading out from City Hall, the neighborhood's center of gravity, are government offices at all levels (in the future to be coordinated with new construction to form a planned "Civic Center"), middle-income and public housing, commercial warehousing, the fringes of the financial district, Chinatown, and that ancient viaduct that made New York's consolidation with the City of Brooklyn possible: the Brooklyn Bridge.

These ancient streets are some of New York's most venerable, but only a smattering of the structures that originally lined them remain: slowly the blocks have been consolidated, and larger and larger single projects of all kinds built or planned: housing projects, government structures, and a college campus.

Civic Center

Walking Tour: From Fulton Street and Broadway to Chambers Street and Broadway via City Hall Park, Civic Center, and Chinatown. (IRT Lexington Avenue Subway to Fulton Street Station, or IND Eighth Avenue Subway to Broadway-Nassau Station.)

 [1.] St. Paul's Chapel and Churchyard, bounded by Broadway, Fulton, Church and Vesey Sts. 1766. Thomas McBean; Tower and steeple, 1796, James Crommelin Lawrence. ★

New York's only extant pre-Revolutionary building. Although the city's present territory contains a dozen other buildings that old or more, these were isolated farmhouses or country seats that bear no more relation to the city than do still-rural 18th Century houses in outlands surrounding the city proper. Unlike Fraunces Tavern, St. Paul's is as close to the original as any building requiring maintenance over 200 years could be.

McBean was a pupil of James Gibbs, whose St. Martin's-in-the-Fields (London) was undoubtedly a prototype for St. Paul's. Stone from the site (Manhattan schist) forms walls that are quoined, columned, parapeted, pedimented, porched, and towered in Manhattan's favorite 18th and 19th Century masonry: brownstone.

[5.]

[1.]

[2.] New York County Lawyer's Association, 14 Vesey St. bet. Church St. and Broadway. 1930. Cass Gilbert. ★

Law in America is based on English common law, and what better tie to the fount than to club together in a London club! Here a watery neo-Georgian.

[3.] Garrison Building/formerly **New York Evening Post Building,** 20 Vesey St. bet. Church St .and Broadway. 1906. Robert D. Kohn. ★

The interest here is at the top: sculptured limestone and cop-

28   **MANHATTAN**

per, art nouveau.

[4.] St. Peter's Church (Roman Catholic), 22 Barclay St. SE cor. Church St. 1840. John R. Haggerty and Thomas Thomas. ★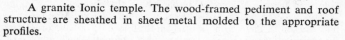

A granite Ionic temple. The wood-framed pediment and roof structure are sheathed in sheet metal molded to the appropriate profiles.

[5.] Woolworth Building, 233 Broadway bet. Park Pl. and Barclay St. 1913. Cass Gilbert. ☆

Much maligned for its eclectic Gothic detail, and charcoal "Gothic crown," this sheer shaft is one of the most imposingly sited skyscrapers of New York. Rising almost 800 feet from the street, it soars; only the Seagram's and CBS buildings have the combination of articulate architecture and massing to achieve similar drama.

[6.] City Hall Park/formerly **the City Common.** ca. 1700.

The bounds were determined by the two main "High" roads, from New York (the city barely went beyond Wall Street at this time): the westerly one to the north island town of Bloomingdale (near present Columbia University), and the easterly one to Boston.

The motto once seemed to be: "when in doubt, put it in City Hall Park." Happily, the motto is out of date: **Mullett's Post Office Building** (ca. 1865) which occupied the triangular south tip was demolished ca. 1938, and the **"Tweed" (N. Y. City) Courthouse** (1862) will be demolished in consonance with the new Civic Center plan. Assorted sculpture is placed seemingly at random, but each may have once related to a system of paths, of planting, of pavilions that no longer exist, although the sculpted figures remain unchanged: **Nathan Hale,** 1893, Frederick MacMonnies, Sculptor; base by Stanford White; **Horace Greeley,** 1890, J. Q. A. Ward, Sculptor.

[7.]

[7.] Brooklyn Bridge. City Hall Park, Manhattan, to Cadman Plaza, Brooklyn. 1860–1883. John A. and Washington Roebling. ★ [See Bridges and Tunnels.]

A walk across the raised central boardwalk to Brooklyn Heights is one of the great dramatic walks of New York. As a side tour from City Hall, it is a unique experience, viewing Brooklyn, Manhattan, their skylines and the harbor through a filigree of cables.

[8.] City Hall, City Hall Park bet. Broadway and Park Row. 1811. Mangin and McComb. ★

A mini-palace, crossing French Renaissance detail with Georgian form, perhaps inevitable where the competition-winning scheme was the product of a Frenchman and a Scot. Mangin (who had worked in Paris with Gabriel on the Place de la Concorde) was the principal preliminary designer and theorist; McComb supervised construction and determined much of the detailing.

Interiors were restored and refurbished between 1902 and 1920 under Grosvenor Atterbury, and the exterior peeled off, reproduced in new Alabama limestone (piece by piece), and re-

[8.]  [15.

stored under Shreve, Lamb and Harmon in 1959. The soft original Massachusetts marble had badly eroded by joint attacks of pollution and pigeons (the rear of the building had been built in brownstone to save money!).

The central domed space leads past the offices of mayor and city councilmen, up twin spiral, self-supporting marble stairs to the Corinthian-columned gallery serving both the City Council Chamber and Board of Estimate. The Governor's Room, originally for his use when in New York City, is now a portrait gallery replete with portraits by Sully, Inman, Jarvis, Trumbull, and others.

[9.] Park Row Building, 15 Park Row, bet. Ann and Beekman Sts. 1899. R. H. Robertson.

[10.] Potter Building, 38 Park Row, NE cor. Beekman St. 1883. N. Y. Starkweather.

An elaborately ornate confection in cast and pressed terra cotta, the first use in New York of a material that was to become the rage, producing repetitive elaboration economically.

The invisibly used structural steel of this building is the first (extant) in New York: also fireproofed by terra cotta.

Ye Old Herb Shoppe, 8 Beekman St. (in the Potter Building) bet. Park Row and Nassau Sts.

The cook and/or witch in your family can brew, savor, season with raw materials, rather than "blended seasonings" or totally prepared frozen food.

[11.] Pace College/formerly **The Times Building,** 41 Park Row bet. Beekman and Spruce Sts. 1889. George B. Post. Altered 1905, Robert Maynicke. ☆

[12.] Bennett Building, 99 Nassau St. bet. Fulton and Ann Sts. 1873. Arthur Gilman. ☆

A glassy building, with bold structural grid. The hectic shops of the ground floor distract the eye; few notice its quality.

Whyte's Restaurant, 145 Fulton St. bet. Park Row and Nassau St.
Instant half-timbering clads a fine fishery!

[13.] 150 Nassau Street Building/formerly **American Tract Society,** SE cor. Spruce St. 1896. R. H. Robertson.

The fascination here is at the roof, where giant "Romanesque" arches provide a geometry of architecture separate from the rusticated granite below.

[14.] Municipal Building, Chambers St. at Centre St. 1914. McKim, Mead & White (William M. Kendall and Burt Fenner). ★

This is urban architecture, irrevocably straddling a city street. In those days, the ways of traffic were entwined with architecture [See Warren & Wetmore's Grand Central Terminal of 1913]. The "Choragic Monument" topping the composition is, in turn, surmounted by "Civic Virtue" by Adolph A. Weinman.

[15.] Surrogates Court/Hall of Records, 31 Chambers St. bet. NW cor. Centre St. 1911. John R. Thomas and Horgan & Slattery. ★

Civic functions were designed to impress the citizen in those days (not merely humor as is most often the case today). Therefore his records were kept in a place of splendor.

[16.] Criminal Court of the City of New York, 52 Chambers St. bet. Broadway and Center Sts. 1872. John Kellum.

Maligned by all, conservatives and radicals alike, this suffers from the political burden of Boss Tweed's extortions. The building is not guilty, in spite of the fact it cost four times its real cost. A Palladian country house; the central well is one of the few great spaces our City government still maintains. The court house will go as part of the new Civic Center plan, for it occupies the bed of the proposed Mall between City Hall and the Municipal Building Annex.

[17.] U.S. Federal Building and Customs Courthouse, Broadway, Worth, to Duane St., on Foley Square. 1967. Alfred Easton Poor, Kahn & Jacobs, Eggers & Higgins, Associated Architects.

[18.] U.S. Court House, bet. Duane, Park and Pearl Sts., Cardinal Hayes Pl., on Foley Square. 1936. Cass Gilbert & Cass Gilbert, Jr.

[19.] New York County Courthouse, Foley Square. 1912. Guy Lowell. ★

The "Hexagon" anticipated the "Pentagon" by 30 years. Lowell's scheme won a competition, in the spirit of both City Hall and the Municipal Building. The imposing Corinthian portico is handsome Roman archeology, but doesn't measure up to the vigorous planning of the building.

[20.] Civil and Municipal Court, bet. Lafayette, White, Centre, and Franklin Sts. 1960. William Lescaze & Matthew Del Gaudio.

A sleek cube fills the site facing an open plaza, not for people, but for judges' parking. Bas-reliefs by William Zorach.

[21.] Criminal Courts Building and Prison, bet. Centre, White, Baxter, and Leonard Sts. 1939. Harvey Wiley Corbett.

A "ziggurated" construction overlaid with stylish detail of the thirties: limestone with cast aluminum spandrels.

[22.] Engine Company 31, N.Y.C. Fire Department, 87 Lafayette St. bet. White and Walker Sts. 1895. Napoleon LeBrun and Sons. ★

Country house for fire engines, disguised as French Renaissance chateau; still in use.

[23.] Chatham Towers, 170 Park Row bet. Park Row and Worth St. N side. 1965. Kelly & Gruzen.

Sculptured concrete, this joins the ranks of distinguished housing architecture; the Dakota, Butterfield House, 131 East 66, and Williamsburgh Houses are its peers from all eras. As with all strong architectural statements, it rouses great admiration and great opposition.

 [24.] Chatham Green, 185 Park Row bet. St. James Pl.; Park Row; Pearl and Madison Sts. 1961. Kelly & Gruzen.

A great undulating wall; open access galleries (architects term: "elevated streets") are served by vertical towers containing stairs and elevators. The stores at either end are an afterthought.

[23.]  **[24**

Castilla's Restaurant, 35 Madison St. bet. St. James Pl. and James St. BE 3-9492.

An adventure in Spanish food (cooked principally for local Spanish-speaking residents). A full bar available and reasonable prices.

[25.] Governor Alfred E. Smith Houses, bet. South, Madison, Catherine Sts., and St. James and Robert F. Wagner Sr. Pl. 1952. Eggers & Higgins.

Al Smith lived a short stone's throw away: his turf.

[26.] St. James Church (Roman Catholic), 33 James St. bet. St. James Pl. and Madison St. 1837. Attributed to Minard Lafever. ★

Brownstone Doric columned Greek Revival. Di-style (two columns) in antis (between flanking blank walls).

[27a.] First Shearith Israel Graveyard, 55–57 St. James Pl. bet. Oliver and James Sts. 1683. ★

The only man-made physical remnant in Manhattan from the 17th Century. One of three Manhattan graveyards of the Spanish-Portuguese Synagogue (Shearith Israel). They followed population movements from here to Greenwich Village to 21st Street west of Union Square; now Queens' Cypress Hills Cemetery serves their congregation. [See Greenwich Village 54a; Chelsea 18a.]

[27b.] St. Margaret's House (Lower East Side Mission), 2 Oliver St. bet. St. James Pl. and Henry St. 1822. ☆

[27c.] Mariner's Temple/Baptist Meeting House, 12 Oliver St. NW cor. Henry St. 1842. Minard Lafever. ★

A stone Greek Revival Ionic-columned temple. Servicios en espagnol (and Chinese). A wide cross-section of communicants worship in a sailor's church that might well be a temple to Athena.

[28.] Knickerbocker Village, Catherine to Market St., Monroe to Cherry St. 1934. Van Wart and Ackerman.

A blockbuster, with 1600 apartments on three acres (N.Y.

City public housing averages 80 to 100 units per acre). The central courtyards are reached through gated tunnels, and seem a welcome relief by contrast with their dense and massive surrounds. This was the very first major housing project even partially aided by public funds.

[29.] 51 Market Street/originally **William Clark House,** 1824. ★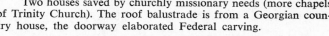

A rare four-story Federal house: they were almost always two or three (plus basement and/or dormered attic). Its parts are in superb condition.

[30.] Sea and Land Church and the First Chinese Presbyterian Church (dual use), NW cor. Market and Henry Sts. 1817. ★

Dressed Manhattan schist is close in scale to aged concrete block. Brownstone surrounds and trim.

[31.] St. Christopher's Chapel, 48–50 Henry St. bet. Market and Catherine Sts. 1830. ☆

Two houses saved by churchly missionary needs (more chapels of Trinity Church). The roof balustrade is from a Georgian country house, the doorway elaborated Federal carving.

[27c.]

[32.] Manhattan Bridge and Approaches, The Bowery, Canal, Forsyth and Bayard Sts. 1905. Gustav Lindenthal, Engineer; Carrère and Hastings, architects of the approaches. ☆ [See Bridges and Tunnels.]

Two regal and monumental sculptures ("Manhattan" and "Brooklyn" by Daniel Chester French) used to guard the adventurous traveler seeking Brooklyn. They now (owing to plastic surgery on the approach ramps by highway engineers) guard the Brooklyn Museum [See Park Slope/Prospect Park 45.]

[33.] 18 Bowery, SW cor. Pell St. 1795. ★

The oldest thing around here, it preserves its handsome Federal silhouette, in spite of ground-floor surgeries.

Olliffe's Pharmacy, 6 Bowery (1803, but remodeled).
The oldest drugstore in America.

Chinatown

In most major American cities Chinese have formed racial enclaves that are sought by tourists and relished by native city-dwellers with an interested palate. New York's Chinatown is centered in eight blocks bounded by Canal, Worth, and Mulberry Streets, the Bowery, and Chatham Square: its "main street" is Mott. Jammed with restaurants, some double-decked, largely great halls to accommodate tourist flocks, smallness becomes a virtue. Those most concerned with family ties, but equally concerned with an increased standard of living, have generated luxury apartment buildings, so that they might (justly) have their cake and eat it too.

[34.] Chinese Merchant's Association, 85 Mott St., SW cor. Canal St. 1958.

Grauman's Chinese Theatre Architecture.

[35.] Church of the Transfiguration, 25 Mott St. 1801. ★

Like "Sea and Land," [See 30] a Georgian church with Gothic windows inserted; although here with Gothic tracery, there with small-paned double-hung windows. Dressed Manhattan schist makes neat building blocks, with brownstone detail. The octagonal tower, copper-sheathed, is of a later date.

The Wing Woh Lung Co., 50 Mott St., SE cor. Bayard St.

Vegetables and dried goodies press against the glass, compartmentalized like an index to Chinese gastronomy.

Quong Yee Wo, 38 Mott St., SE cor. Pell St.

The tan and green-topped white roots that form the nucleus of Chinese vegetarianism; seeds and candy to complement.

Hong Fat Restaurant, 63 Mott St. WO 2-9588.

Gall and/or Chinese are needed here, but what they may command is exotic. Either intimidate the waiters or ply them with Cantonese.

Joy Luck Coffee Shop, 57 Mott St.

No telephone. No booze. No reservation. The food is excellent, and cheap.

King Wu Restaurant, 18 Doyers St. WO 2-8480.

Straightforward, excellent, inexpensive. Two for $5 at dinner. No liquor served.

Wo Ping, 24 Pell St. RE 2-0847.

Craig Claiborne of the *Times* describes it as "noisy as a gong, and earthy as a ginger root." Snails, crabs, fish: what the Chinese cannot grow underground, they catch underseas.

Cast-Iron District I (South of Canal Street): Cast iron gave possibility of reproducing (inexpensively) elaborate detail, previously only possible as carving in stone. More Corinthian, Ionic, Doric, Composite, Egyptian and Lord-knows-what-else-columns were cast for New York facades of the 1850's and 1860's than Greece and Rome turned out in a thousand years. The two great centers were those between Broadway and West Broadway, Canal to Duane (here cited); and Broadway to Wooster, Canal to Houston Streets.

These handsome loft spaces are used by assorted commercialdom, principally for warehousing, sometimes for light manufacturing, and by an occasional painter who has penetrated these precincts for a living-studio. Unfortunately, the buildings are not fireproof: steel and cast iron soften and buckle under heat, even before wood beams and columns collapse in a similar situation. Interior floors are of wood between wrought-iron beams and cast-iron columns.

[36.] 254–260 Canal Street, SW cor. Lafayette St. 1865. ☆

Cast iron over chaos, it gets few complimentary glances. **Nos. 60-66 White Street,** 1869, ground floors mutilated at 64-66. **Nos. 54-56 White Street,** Italianate brownstone over cast-iron ground floor. **Nos. 55-57 White Street,** ca. 1865, James Kellum and Son, mutilated ground floor. **No. 52 White Street,** note the appropriate sign.

 [37.] 46–50 White Street/formerly **Woods Mercantile Building.** 1865. ☆

A group organized by its pediment. **No. 10 White Street,** elaborated Tuscan columns. **No. 2 White Street,** ca. 1830, a genuine Federal barber shop, now propped up by a steel pipe column spiraled with the red and white banding, symbolic of barbering. A real building with a real (modern) use.

[38.] Western Union Building, 60 Hudson St. bet. Hudson,

Thomas and Worth Sts. and Broadway. 1930. Voorhees, Gmelin and Walker.

Nineteen shades of brick from brown to salmon form a subtle-shaded palette. Note the handsome graphics at the ground floor.

Teddy's Restaurant, 219 W. Broadway bet. Franklin and White Sts. Italian, busy, moderately expensive. A full bar, lunch and dinner, save Sundays.

[39a.] 112–114 Franklin Street.

Huge, cast-iron columns support Italianate facade above. **No. 71 Franklin Street,** attributed to Renwick & Co. **No. 70-72 Franklin Street,** Thomas and Sons. **No. 81-83 Franklin Street,** Italian brownstone over cast iron.

[39b.] 361–363 Broadway/formerly **Jas. S. White Building,** SW cor. Franklin St. 1882. W. Wheeler Smith. ☆

[40.] 346 Broadway/formerly **New York Life Insurance Company,** bet. Broadway, Leonard, Catherine and Lafayette Sts. 1870. Griffith Thomas. Remodeled by McKim, Mead and White.

Now offices for the Army, Navy and Air Force, this building served as New York Life's headquarters until the company was moved uptown in 1928. M, M & W lifted Mr. Thomas's Italianate face (at the Broadway end only), with some larger-scaled neo-Renaissance trappings.

[41a.] 87–89 Leonard Street, 1862. ☆ **85 Leonard Street,** 1862. James Bogardus. ☆

No. 85 was Bogardus' own warehouse: a larger scale than the usual cast-iron parts; the columns here embrace two stories.

37.]  [41e.]

[41b.] 80–82 Leonard Street, 1860. James H. Giles. ☆ **73 Leonard Street,** 1863. J. F. Duckworth. **71 Leonard Street,** 1860. S. A. Warner.

[41c.] 41 Worth Street, 1860. S. A. Warner.

[41d.] 43–45 Worth Street, 1860. S. A. Warner. **47 Worth Street,** ca. 1860.

No. 47 is a victim of "colonializing" by an innocent admirer of history, who, unfortunately, misunderstands architecture.

[41e.] 54 Worth Street/temporarily **N.Y.C. Police Dept. Hack Bureau,** ca. 1860. William Field and Sons.

[41f.] 65-85 Worth Street (commercial buildings).

[41g.] 58–60 Worth Street, 1869. Rebuilt 1879. Griffith Thomas (Morgan Slade). ☆ **66–68 Worth Street.**

[42a.] 341 Broadway, 1860. J. B. Snook. **319 and 317 Broadway,** 1865. ☆

Nos. 319 and 317 are a pair of handsome flanks to the entrance to Thomas Street, marred seriously, as usual, by grossly unsympathetic ground-floor (and mezzanine) alterations. Very elaborate in detail, these are gems of the first order.

[43.]

[44

[42b.] 10–12 Thomas Street, opposite end of 101–103 Duane St. 1870. Thomas Little. ☆ **8 Thomas Street,** ca. 1875.

No. 8, a local Ruskinian Gothic invader, is in superb condition.

[42c.] 62–66 Thomas Street, 1867.

A rare "Gothic" cast-iron building, suitably painted dark brown; polygonal columns.

[43.] New York Mercantile Exchange, 6 Harrison St. NW cor. Hudson St. 1884.

[44a.] Fire Department Museum (Engine 7, Hook and Ladder 1), 100 Duane St. bet. Broadway and Church St. 1905. Trowbridge and Livingston. Hours, 9 AM–3 PM weekdays, except by appointment.

English version of an Italian palace with double-hung windows.

[44b.] H. Boker and Company/101–103 Duane Street, bet. Broadway and Church St. 1870. Thomas Little. ☆

[44c.] National Council of the YMCA, 291 Broadway. 1910. Clinton and Russell.

A little bit of Renaissance trappings near street and cornice.

[45.] Fordham University, City Hall Division/Vincent (Astor) Building, 302 Broadway. 1899. George B. Post.

[46.] Ross Scientific Apparatus, 61 Reade St.

Binoculars, glass eyes, barometers, litmus, microscopes, novelties: new and used. For the mad scientist in your family (yourself), or merely the berserk gadgeteer (yourself again).

Suerken's Restaurant, 27 Park Place, NE cor. Church St.

Cast-iron Corinthian columns face the local home of dumplings, Lowenbrau, Sauerbraten; weight watchers, beware, the delights here offered are tempting, a caloric garden of Eden.

[47a.] 287 Broadway. 1872. John B. Snook. ☆ **Schraffts, 281 Broadway.** 1926. George B. Post and Sons.

[47b.] Old New York Sun Building/formerly **A. T. Stewart Store,** Chambers, Broadway, Reade Sts. 1846. Ottavio Groi, Stonemason.

Here Stewart founded the first great department store of America, later to occupy grand premises at Broadway, 8th-10th Streets (known to recent generations as Wanamaker's, who bought all of Stewart's enterprises). Henry James and Anthony Trollope both lavished words of wonder on these premises. Later the *Sun* was published here. Now a discount house.

End of Tour. Nearest subways are: IRT and BMT at Chambers and Centre Streets; BMT Local at City Hall; IND Eighth Avenue Line at Chambers and Church Streets.

CAST-IRON DISTRICT

The 20 blocks between Canal and Houston Streets, West Broadway and Broadway are a rich **architectural resource,** a highpoint in **commercial** architectural history. Cast-iron facades of great distinction and in quantity form a **total urban grouping.** These are not individual objects to be noticed as monuments, but parties to whole streets and blocks that together make one of the most glorious **commercial groupings** that New York has ever seen. Mostly Italianate, some might be called **Palladian.** They are surprising precursors of the exposed structural expression in **concrete** seen at Kips Bay Plaza or the American Bible Society. The heart of the area is threatened by the proposed **Broome Street Expressway.** [see map]. Starting at Canal and Greene Streets, the best pedestrian route is north on Greene to Houston, with side-steps down adjacent portions of Grand, Broome, Spring, and Prince Streets. Then Cross Houston to Broadway, and saunter down Broadway to Canal again.

[1.] Greene Street, bet. Canal and Grand Sts.

[1a.] 8 Greene St. 1884. John B. Snook. **[1b.] 10–12 Greene St.** 1869. John B. Snook. **[1c.] 16–18 Greene St.** 1880. Samuel A. Warner. He was the architect of the Marble Collegiate Church [see Four Squares 32.]. **[1d.] 15–17 Greene St.** 1895. Samuel A. Warner. **[1e.] 19–21 Greene St.** 1872. Henry Fernbach. The architect of Central Synagogue **[1f.] 20–26 Greene St.** 1880. Samuel A. Warner. **[1g.] 23–25 Greene St.** 1873. Duckworth. **[1h.] 27 Greene St.** 1871. W. Jose. **[1i.] 29 Greene St.** 1878. Webb & Son. **[1j.] 31 Greene St.** 1876 Da Cunha. Extraordinarily ornate. **[1k.] 32–34 Greene St.** 1873. C. Wright.

[17.]

[13.]

[2.] 83-87 Grand Street, SW cor. Greene St. 1872.

[3.] Greene Street, bet. Grand and Broome Sts.

[3a.] 37-43 Greene St. 1884. R. Berger. **[3b.] 45 Greene St.** 1882. J. M. Slade.

[4.] Broome Street, bet. Greene and Wooster Sts.

[4a.] 480 Broome St. 1885. Berger. **[4b.] 478–476 Broome St.**
1885. Griffith Thomas. Granite and brownstone over cast iron. **[4c.]**
479–477 Broome St. 1885. E. Shiffin. **[4d.] 475–469 Broome St.** 1873.
Griffith Thomas. Note the elegant curved and glazed corner.

[5.] Broome Street, bet. Greene and Mercer Sts.

[5a.] 467–465 Broome St. 1873. Duckworth. **[5b.] 463 Broome**
St. 1867. Henry Fernbach. **[5c.] 461–457 Broome St.** 1871. Griffith
Thomas. **[5d.] 455–453 Broome St.** 1873. Griffith Thomas.

[6.] Greene Street, bet. Broome and Spring Sts.

[6a.] 58–60 Greene St. 1871. Henry Fernbach. Bold Corinthian.

[6b.] 62–64 Greene St. 1873. Henry Fernbach. **[6c.] 66–68 Greene**
St. 1873. John B. Snook. **[6d.] 65 Greene St.** 1873. John B. Snook.
[6e.] 67–71 Greene St. 1873. Henry Fernbach. **[6f.] 72–76 Greene St.**
1873. Duckworth. The king of this block. Projecting pedimented
porch of magnificent Corinthian columns and pilasters. **[6g.] 78**
Greene St. 1873. Van Anken. **[6h.] 75–81 Greene St.** 1876–1878.
Henry Fernbach. **[6i.] 80–82 Greene St.** 1873. Griffith Thomas.

[7.] Greene Street, bet. Spring and Prince Sts.

[7a.] 93–99 Greene St. 1881. Henry Fernbach. Composite capitals support window heads like those of Kips Bay Plaza. **[7b.] 96**
Greene St. 1879. Henry Fernbach. **[7c.] 98–100 Greene St.** 1880.
Henry Fernbach. **[7d.] 103–105 Greene St.** 1879. Henry Fernbach.
[7e.] 112 Greene St. 1884. Henry Fernbach. **[7f.] 114–120 Greene St.**
1882. Henry Fernbach.

[8.] Prince Street, bet. Greene and Wooster Sts.

[8a.] 112–114 Prince St. 1889. **[8b.] 109–111 Prince St.** 1889.
J. M. Slade.

[9.] Greene Street, bet. Prince and Houston Sts.

[9a.] 121–123 Greene St. 1883. Henry Fernbach. Corinthian all
the way up. **[9b.] 132–140 Greene St.** 1885. A. Zucker. **[9c.] 142–144**
Greene St. 1871. Henry Fernbach. **[9d.] 135 Greene St.** 1883. Henry
Fernbach.

[10.] 600 Broadway. ca. 1886.

Corinthian columns of descending heights on each successive
floor. The ground-floor alteration is by those who don't understand
the value of what they have in hand.

[11.] Singer Building, 561 Broadway, facing both Broadway and
Prince St. 1907. Ernest Flagg. ☆

Steel, glass and terra cotta within a frame of masonry. This is
avant-garde for its time, the forerunner of the "curtain wall," that
light metal and glass skin cladding commercial New York, grossly,
compared to this 60-year-old charmer.

[12.] 502 Broadway, bet. Spring and Broome Sts. 1860. John
Kellum.

[13.] Haughwout Building, 488–492 Broadway, NE cor. Broome
St. 1857. J. P. Gaynor. Iron by Badger Iron Works. ☆

Palladio would have been proud of this progeny in cast iron, a
rich participant on the urban scene. A proud and handsome, but
not egocentric, building proves that quality does not demand originality for its own sake. It also houses the first practical passenger elevator installed by Elisha Graves Otis, founder of the famous elevator
company. There is a special door on the north side of Fifth Ave.
facade for it.

[14.] Roosevelt Building, 478–482 Broadway bet. Broome and
Grand Sts. 1874. Richard Morris Hunt.

[15.] Franklin National Bank, 461–467 Broadway, NW cor. Grand
St. 1967. Eggers and Higgins.

A neo-"Georgian" "suburban" bank building provides a tree-lined plaza. The intent is excellent, the result a strange and foreign one in this virile cast-iron environment.

[16.] A. J. Dittenhofer Building, 427–429 Broadway, SW cor. Grand St. 1871. Thomas R. Jackson.

[17.] 462–468 Broadway/originally **Lord and Taylor Store** NE cor. Grand St. ca. 1870. Griffith Thomas.

LITTLE ITALY

Canal to Houston Streets, Lafayette Street to the Bowery, is still the most important old **Italian center** of New York, but now with **old** Italians, as the newest generation has made the move to suburbia. (It returns, however, for festivals and family festivities; marriages, funerals, feast and holy days.)

[1.] Paolucci's Restaurant/originally **Stephen van Renssalaer House,** 149 Mulberry St. bet. Hester and Grand Sts. 1816. ☆

A Federal two-story and dormered brick house, a surprising remnant in these tenemented streets. The restaurant has been described as "Le Pavillon of **Little Italy.**"

[2.] Bowery Savings Bank, 130 Bowery, NW cor. Grand St. 1894. McKim, Mead and White. ☆

Roman pomp on the Bowery, and on the edge of Little Italy. It has served as an architectural and economic anchor through the Bowery's years of hard times. The interior is one of the great semi-public spaces of New York. Go in.

[3.] 165–171 Grand Street/originally **Odd Fellows' Hall,** SE cor. Centre St. 1849. John B. Snook. ☆

[4.] New York City Police Headquarters, 240 Centre St. bet. Grand and Broome Sts. and Centre Market Pl. 1909. Hoppin & Koen. ☆

In the manner of a French *hôtel de ville* (town hall), this is tightly arranged within the city's street system, not isolated palatially (as is City Hall or almost any state capitol). Ornate Renaissance Revival architecture is laced with bits of baroque. Even the shape of the building follows the wedge-shaped plot it occupies. It will soon be vacated for a new building east of the Municipal Building in the Civic Center.

[4.]  **[2.]**

The Feast of San Gennaro fills Mulberry Street from Canal to Spring Streets during the week of September 19th (autos are banned). Arcaded with a filigree of electric light bulbs, the street becomes a vast *al fresco* restaurant, interspersed with games of chance, for the benefit of the Church. Fried pastries and sausages steam the air, and for one evening you may be part of the gregarious Italian public life.

[5.] Engine Co. 55, N.Y.C. Fire Department, 363 Broome St. bet. Mott and Elizabeth Sts. 1895. R. H. Robertson.

Milan Laboratories, 57 Spring St., bet. Mulberry and Lafayette Sts.

The center of gastronomical chemistry, both for the ingredients and equipment: here you can outfit yourself to produce Chianti in your cellar. Apparatus and advice are available, as well as spices.

Grotta Azzurra, 387 Broome St., SW cor. Mulberry St.

The grandest spot in Little Italy. Those who have made the big time luxuriously return here to enjoy their **old** neighborhood.

[6.] Old St. Patrick's Cathedral, bet. Mott, Prince, and Mulberry Sts. 1815. Joseph Mangin. Restored after a fire in 1868. Henry Engelbert. ☆

The **original** Roman Catholic cathedral of New York; present St. Patrick's uptown replaced it after a disastrous fire. Restored, this building was demoted to parish church status. The interior is a grand, murky brown, "gothicized" space, with cast-iron columns supporting a timber roof. The original (pre-fire) shell is in the Gothic-decorated Georgian tradition of **Sea and Land** or the **Church of the Transfiguration,** both in the Civic Center/Chinatown area.

The Mott Street of Little Italy is as colorful as its Chinatown continuation below Canal Street. **Pushcart vendors** still tout their wares, mostly vegetables. Pick up (and pay for) an apple on your way through.

[7.] Old St. Patrick's Convent and Girl's School, 32 Prince St., SW cor. Mott St. 1826. ☆

A Georgian-Federal building with a handsome entry. Here the vocabulary of a Federal house was merely inflated to the program requirements of a parish school.

[8.] St. Michael's Chapel, 266 Mulberry St., bet. Prince and E. Houston Sts. ca. 1850. ☆

Built in a shape and location as if on a tenement lot: perhaps it once was, and the intervening buildings were since demolished.

[9.] Puck Building, 295–309 Lafayette St. bet. Lafayette, E. Houston, Mulberry, and Jersey Sts. 1885. Addition, 1892. Albert Wagner.

A gold leafed "Puck" holds forth from the third-story perch at the corner of Mulberry Street. Monolithic red brick Romanesque Revival. Note the handsome **gilt signs** of the Superior Printing Ink Company across the ground floor.

LOWER EAST SIDE

Far more significant **historically** than as individual structures—here are the legions of **tenement buildings** warehousing the **arriving immigrants of the 1880's, 1890's** and **teens.**

Six-story masonry blocks covered 90 percent of the lots in question, offering light and air (except for minuscule air shafts) only at the 90-foot distant ends of these railroad flats, (strung **end to end** like railroad cars).

On a 25 by 100-foot lot, ten families were the standard. Reaction against overcrowding has produced an unhappy over compensation: the density per acre remains the **same** or **greater,** but the Lower East Side is being dominated by high-rise, freestanding structures (it seems the taller and further spaced the better): **project dwellers** yearn for **light** and **air,** or at least the apparent virtues of light and air.

[1.] Congregation Beth Harnesses Synagogue/originally **Olive Branch Baptist Church,** 290 Madison St. SW cor. Montgomery St., 1856. ☆

The "pink synagogue" is an orphan amidst low- and mid-income housing.

[2.] Henry Street Settlement, 263-267 Henry Street, bet. Montgomery St. and Grand St. 1827-1834. ☆

Greek Revival townhouses now happily preserved by a distinguished private social agency, founded by Lillian Wald, who is personally memoralized in housing bearing her name between Houston and 6th Street on the River.

[3.] St. Augustine's Chapel, 290 Henry St., bet. Montgomery St. and Jackson St. 1828. Attributed to John Heath. ☆

Georgian body with Gothic-revival windows. Compare China-town's **Church of the Transfiguration** and the **Sea and Land Church.**

[4.] Vladeck Houses, Water, Madison, Gouverneur and Jackson Sts., 1940. William F. R. Ballard and Sylvan Bien.

Trees, and the patina of weathering brick have softened this large project of 1500 units.

[5.] Hillman Houses (including Amalgamated Dwellings, Inc.) bet. Grand, Broome, Willett, and Lewis Sts. 1926—1930. Spring-steen and Goldhammer.

Forty-one years ago Abraham Kazan (now President of the United Housing Foundation) explored the world of mass housing on behalf of the Amalgamated Clothing Workers (**male clothing,** not necessarily workers), providing, in concert with his architects, these pioneer projects. Times have changed, and his current 15,500-unit Co-op City in the Bronx (under construction) is not in the same class of avant-garde thinking as these, its antecedents.

The New York Chapter, AIA commended the Amalgamated Dwellings with a medal citing "the complete elimination of mean-ingless ornament and the sincerity with which they used the essential elements of the design to achieve esthetic results...."

[6.] Bialystoker Synagogue, 7-13 Willett St. bet. Grand and Broome Sts. 1826. ☆

Shifting ethnic populations cause changing religious uses of venerable buildings like this one. Originally a rural Protestant church, it now serves the dense urban Jewish population in this neighborhood.

[7.] Williamsburg Bridge, at Delancey St. 1903. L. L. Buck.

Note the unusual straight cables on land side of the towers (on most bridges cables in such positions hang in catenary curves). These merely anchor their center-supporting sections. The end portions of the bridge are supported from below.

[9.]

[8.] DeWitt Reformed Church, 280 Rivington St., NE cor. Columbia St. 1958. Edgar Tafel.

Used brick and a cross of tree trunks give this neighborhood church a rustic quality. A very human element amidst overpowering public housing.

[9.] Junior High School No. 22 Manhattan, and Branch Public Library, Stanton, and Columbia Sts. 1956. Kelly and Gruzen.

[10.] Beth Hamedrash Hagodol Synagogue/originally **Norfolk Street Baptist Church,** 60–64 Norfolk St., bet. Grand and Broome Sts. ca. 1852.

[11.] Mills Hotel No. 2, NW cor. Rivington and Chrystie Sts. 1897. Ernest Flagg.

~~DEMOLISHED~~

An abandoned hulk that once served as a low-income hostel. (See **Mills Hotel No. 1** in Greenwich Village.) Flagg is well known for his elegant Singer Buildings, but not so well for his avant-garde tenements for City and Suburban Homes (see Upper East Side), and the two Mills Hotels.

V

THE VILLAGES

GREENWICH VILLAGE

Settled over 300 years ago, slowly surrounded by a growing Manhattan, but still a community, lovingly referred to by its residents as **The Village.** At once the home of Madison Avenue art directors, young singles **eager to have their first liberal experience,** and entrenched Italian and Irish families, as well as a **community of zealous homeowners.** For part-timers, it has a fountain **to sing protest**

songs around and is a hangout for homosexuals; it's where Kew Gardens matrons come to **"tsk, tsk"** the degenerate youth. Formal entertainment embraces a number of famous **Off** and **Off-Off Broadway theaters,** some seedy striptease bistros, and **avant-garde events** in jazz and rock 'n roll.

A visitor is likely to arrive by subway, either the Eighth or Sixth Avenue IND Lines, at the center of things at **Village Square** (or at nearby Sheridan Square via the IRT Seventh Avenue local). At Village Square, Greenwich Avenue and West 8th Street abut Sixth Avenue (officially Avenue of the Americas, but not to most harried New Yorkers). The principal **shopping, voyeuristic,** and **tourist haunts** radiate from the square: up and down Sixth Avenue, 8th Street (which becomes Greenwich Avenue west of Sixth Avenue) and beyond.

West of it—**the West Village**—is Jane Jacobs territory, a quiet mixture of residential and commercial buildings. She has continually—and sucessfully—fought the Robert Moseses of officialdom against changing this area of **mixed land use** into a **coat of one cloth.** Within its labyrinth of narrow streets are Old Law tenements, the bulk of the city's early 19th Century dormered houses, newer ziggurated apartment blocks, loft buildings, and parking lots.

The north and east edges of Village Square are defined easily by Manhattan's street grid. Here are **proud town houses** and the "luxury" apartments and hotels. To the south is **Washington Square Park,** perhaps *the* urban park of the city. In it you find chess games between **WASP intellectuals** and **Italian papas; Grand Concourse beatniks** down for a day's worth of **individualism;** N.Y.U. students lounging illegally on its grass; and **working artists** as well as **the more numerous poseurs** taking in the scene. On Sunday afternoons cameras outnumber people.

South of the park is the **old Italian coffee house center** of the local artists and intellectuals, now overrun with expensive cabarets and **fly-by-night "art" galleries.** It is the **turf** of the black-leather-jacketed **dropout.** The surviving coffee houses are still there but are serving tourists; the artists either remain at home or move to the lower rents of the other—the East—Village, Chelsea, or downtown. Surprisingly though, the Italian colony flourishes. And below Houston is *Little,* Little Italy, best known for its joyous outdoor **Festival of San Antonio of Padua** in the middle of June.

Heritage: Always a village, the first one was an Indian community, Sapakanikan. The Dutch upon arrival quickly kicked out the natives, taking over their fertile, rolling farmland for their own profit and pleasure.

Growth came leisurely since the village was completely separated from the bustling community concentrated at the lower tip of the island; its stature, though, **took a sudden rise** in the 1730's with the land purchases of socially prominent naval captain **Peter Warren.** When Capt. Warren bought a large parcel in 1731, he was the first of **a long line of affluent individuals** to settle in the Village. His mansion was soon followed by **Richmond Hill** (owned by **Aaron Burr,** among others), **Alexander Hamilton's** estate, and the **Brevoort homestead.** Richmond Hill was the most well known of these homes which, for nearly 100 years, gave the Village an unsurpassed social status.

The city commissioners, already having contemplated the future growth of Manhattan, appointed **John Randel, Jr.,** who from 1808 to 1811 prepared maps and plans for the present gridiron of Manhattan's streets. The Village **escaped most of this layout,** however, since it was simply too difficult to impose it over **the well-established pattern.** The commissioners, though, had their way with the hills; leveling them all by 1811, and taking with them the grandeur of the old estates. These properties were then easily divisible into small city lots, and by 1822 the community was densely settled, many of the settlers being "refugees" from a series of "downtown" epidemics.

Sailors' Snug Harbor and Trinity Parish have both had leading roles in affecting the direction of growth within the Village. The Harbor was founded in 1801 when Capt. **Robert Richard Randall** deeded in perpetual lease 21 acres of land (around and north of Washington Square), together with a modest cash grant, for the support of **a home for aged seamen.** It was moved to Staten Island in 1833 [See Staten Island 3b.], and since then has received its income from its leased Village land.

Trinity Parish made great contributions to the development of the West Village in the 19th Century, encouraging **respectful care** and **beautification** of its leased land. In 1822 it developed a residential settlement around St. Luke's Church [See 20a] which to this day is a positive influence upon the neighborhood.

The Residents: Perhaps as important as the architectural heritage is the people the Village has attracted; the artists and writers, entertainers, intellectuals, and bohemians who have made their homes alongside of long-established but less-conspicuous Village families.

Walking Tour B

Walking Tour A

BMT/IND 🚇

IRT 🚇

🚇 IRT

Greenwich Ave.

Seventh Ave.

Ninth Ave.

Gansevoort St.

Jane St.

W. 12th St.

Bethune St.

Eighth Avenue

Bleecker St.

Bank St.

W. 11th St.

Perry St.

Charles St.

W. 10th St.

Christopher St.

Barrow St.

Morton St.

Leroy St.

West St.

Washington St.

Greenwich St.

Hudson St.

St. Luke's Pl.

Seventh Avenue South

Grove St.

Barrow St.

Commerce St.

Morton St.

W. 4th St.

Waverly Pl.

WEST SIDE (MILLER ELEVATED) HIGHWAY

Hudson River

N

W. Houston St.

King St.

Charlton St.

Vandam St.

Spring St.

0   500   1000 feet

23 45 43 44 42 41 40 39 38 37 36 35 34 33 32 31 30 29 28 27 26 25 21 20 19 18 17 16 15 14 13 12 9 67 68 65 87

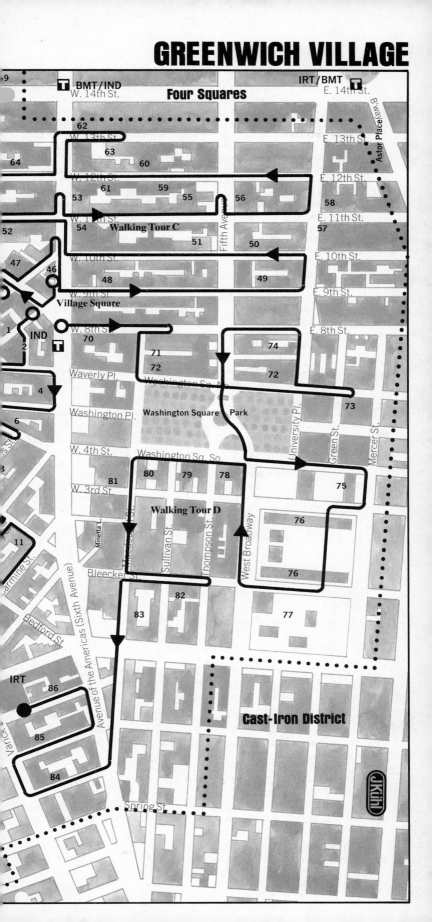

GREENWICH VILLAGE

Four Squares

T BMT/IND
W. 14th St.

IRT/BMT T
E. 14th St.

Astor Place

E. 13th St.

W. 13th St.
62
63
60
64

W. 12th St.
61
59
55
56
53
58

E. 12th St.

E. 11th St.
52
54
Walking Tour C
51
57
50

Fifth Avenue

W. 11th St.

47
46
48
49

E. 10th St.
W. 10th St.

E. 9th St.
W. 9th St.
Village Square

1
IND
2
T
70

W. 8th St.
71
72
74
72

E. 8th St.
73

Waverly Pl.

Washington Sq. No.
4
6

Washington Pl.
Washington Square Park

University Pl.
Green St.
Mercer St.

W. 4th St.
Washington Sq. So.
81
80
79
78
75

W. 3rd St.
Walking Tour D
76

Minetta L.
Sullivan St.
Thompson St.
West Broadway

11

Bleecker St.
82
76

83
77

Carmine St.
Bedford St.

Avenue of the Americas (Sixth Avenue)

IRT
86
Cast-Iron District

Varick
85
84

Spring St.

JKüh

The **artist-synonymous-with-Village** is today more legend than reality. The well-known performer has replaced the painter and writer; we find Lauren Bacall and Jason Robards, Jr., Theodore Bikel, Leontyne Price more typical residents. **Eugene O'Neill** and his group at The Provincetown Playhouse; **Maxwell Bodenheim; Edna St. Vincent Millay;** the delightul, "spirited" **Dylan Thomas** at the White Horse Tavern; and quiet **Joe Gould** accumulating material for his **"oral history" at the Minetta**—these are the ones who made the Village reputation **international.** Their forerunners were the local writers of the 19th Century who took up residence here, being attracted by modest rents, the leisurely pace, and delightful streets and houses. They included **Poe** and **Melville, Mark Twain,** and **Henry James.**

Though the future "writers-in-residence" of the Village will, more frequently than not, be well-paid copy writers, they will, more than likely, seek out the same **Georgian** and **Federal** houses and back-alleyed converted stables to live in that attracted the Mark Twains and E. St. V. Millays years ago.

To preserve the Village's overall physical quality, N.Y.C.'s **Landmarks Preservation Commission** has designated few individual buildings within the Village, in the hopes of establishing an Historic District which will encompass the entire fabric of the area. For this reason, few of the buildings in the entries that follow are shown as proposed for designation, although many are being considered, but in toto.

Walking Tour A—The Lower West Village: Village Square to Morton Street Pier: Begin at Village Square (IND Sixth and Eighth Avenue Subways to West 4th Street station).

 [1a.] 18 and 20 Christopher Street, bet. Gay St. and Waverly Pl. SE side. 1827. E. L. Kent, Builder. Alterations: store fronts.

There are so many early 19th Century houses in this section of the Village, one is tempted to say **"when you've seen one, you've seen 'em all."** Not so. They are always a surprise; sometimes they are squashed between six-story lofts, some bedecked with destructive but nostalgic wisteria vines, others are tucked away in back yards. It is this **rich texture** that makes them such a valuable contribution to the Village—take away the contrasts and the Village would be a dull place indeed.

[1b.] 14 Christopher Street, SE cor. at Gay St. 1895.

[2.] Gay Street, bet. Christopher St. and Waverly Pl.

My Sister Eileen territory. Once you get past the lofts with their scaly fire escapes you find a handful of little houses, delightful for being so close to the street and for the glimpses of rooftop gardens.

 [3.] Northern Dispensary, 165 Waverly Pl. on triangle with Waverly Pl. and Christopher St. 1831.

A fine example of the style, though most severe in its simple Georgian detailing. Remarkable both for lack of exterior alterations and for having continuously operated as a public clinic since its founding in 1827. Edgar Allan Poe was treated here for a head cold in 1837—without charge, as are all who can't afford the fee.

The triangular Northern Dispensary is the only building in New York with one side on two streets (Grove and Christopher) and two sides on one street (Waverly Place, forming a "Y," going off in two directions).

The Lion's Head (restaurant and bar), 57 Christopher St. bet. Waverly Pl. and Seventh Ave. WA 9-0670.

Originally a coffee house in West Village, now relocated. Not too tweedy, but not sandaled. Active dart board. Good food, reasonable prices.

[4.] Residence of the Graymoor Friars/formerly **St. Joseph's Church School,** 138 Waverly Pl. bet. Sixth Ave. and Grove St. S side. 1869. Renwick & Sands. **St. Joseph's Roman Catholic Church,** Sixth Ave. bet. Waverly and Washington Pls. 1833. **Cathedral High School, St. Joseph's branch,** 111 Washington Pl. bet. Sixth Ave. and Grove St. N side. ca. 1865. Renwick & Sands.

An unrelated though not displeasing group. The church is the oldest Roman Catholic sanctuary in Manhattan.

[5.] Sheridan Square, bounded by Washington, W. 4th, Barrow, and Grove Sts.

Now the most unused public space in the Village, marked out with a striped island stanchioned with "no parking" signs, surrounded by bland towers of housing. Parks Department hopes to extend a triangle from the base of No. 2 Barrow Street to create an outdoor café/park.

The Square is frequently confused with nearby Christopher Park—complete with grass, iron fence, benches, and bums, and where General Sheridan's statue happens, actually, to stand.

a.] [1b.]

2.] [4.]

[6.] 175–181 W. 4th Street (houses), at Jones St. N side. ca. 1830. **Le Bijou** (restaurant and bar), 168 W. 4th St. bet. Cornelia and Jones St. S side. CH 2-9338. Dinner only. Daily to 11 PM.

A good, quiet bar. Top notch French cuisine and service; the following are recommended: vichysoisse, paté, Dover sole. Backroom has unusual intimate character. Medium-priced.

[7a.] 15 Barrow Street, bet. W. 4th and Bleecker Sts. E side. 1896.

Originally a four-story stable—note the horse's head protruding from just below the cornice (and also the tenement "sculpture" on both sides of block).

[7b.] 19–19½–21, 25 Barrow Street (houses), bet. W. 4th and Bleecker Sts. E side. 1834. No. 25, prior to 1808.

[7c.] Greenwich House, 29 Barrow St., bet. W. 4th and Bleecker Sts. SE side. 1917. Delano & Aldrich.

The building, a finely kept Georgian Revival, is most significant for what it stands for: social reform. At the turn of the century, Jones Street kept 1400 people—975 to the acre—then the **highest density** on the lower west side. These were second-generation Irish, first-generation Italian, some Negro, some French. From Greenwich House, founded in 1901 on Jones Street by **Mary K. Simkhovitch,** came the **Greenwich Village Improvement Society,** the first neighborhood association in the city—and today a leading organization in the Village.

[8.] 26–30 Jones Street (houses), bet. W. 4th and Bleecker Sts. S side. 1843–1844. ★

[9.] 262–268 Bleecker Street (houses), bet. Leroy and Morton Sts. S side. ca. 1828.

[10.] 7, 12–20 Leroy Street (houses), bet. Bleecker and Bedford Sts. NW and SE sides. No. 7, 1830. Nos. 12–20, 1835. ☆

Faicco's Sausages, 260 Bleecker St. at Cornelia St.

Tipico Italiano.

Caesar's Pastry Shop, 243 Bleecker St. bet. Carmine and Cornelia Sts.

Great Italian ices for a summer stroll. The Italian rum cake (these with luscious frosting!) is not to be believed.

[13.]

[11a.] 27 Carmine Street (house), bet. Bedford and Bleecker Sts. N side. 1833.

The jewel of the block: with original wood-carved frieze and other Late Federal details.

Chez Vous Restaurant, 78 Carmine St. bet. Bedford St. and Seventh Ave. CH 2-2576. Reservations only.

Good French cooking, but fairly expensive.

Mary's Restaurant, 42 Bedford St. bet. Carmine and Leroy Sts. CH 2-9588. Lunch and dinner until 10:30 (closed Mondays).

One of the original Italian kitchen restaurants, dating from Prohibition and still expanding; now on two floors with the kitchen half-way between. A hangout for politicians. Recommend the "specials." Very moderate prices.

[12.] Seventh Avenue South, bet. Carmine St. and Greenwich Ave. 1914–1917.

The building of the Seventh Avenue IRT Subway left huge scars in its wake, as it cut a diagonal path through these West Village blocks leaving the backs and sides of buildings crudely exposed. Isolated triangles of land are now filled with dingy gas stations and parking lots.

[13.] 6–13 St. Luke's Place, bet. Seventh Ave. South and Hudson St. N side.

One of the most splendid blocks in Manhattan. (This one-block stretch of Leroy St., from Hudson St. and east to the elbow, changes its name here to St. Luke's Pl.) Consistent overall proportions and lavish Federal detailing; home-owners' pride rarely exceeds the care lavished on the small front-yard gardens, private lamp posts, and the like. Ginkgo trees flourish on both sides of street, spaced at lot-width intervals. These houses overlook the sunken **James J. Walker Park** (the Mayor's home was No. 6), which was, from 1812 to 1895, part of Trinity Parish Cemetery until it was moved up to 155th Street.

[14a.] Engine Co. 25, N.Y.C. Fire Dept., 78 Morton St. bet. Hudson and Greenwich Sts. S side. 1864.

With few exceptions, fire house architecture is fun. So it is here.

5.]   [16a.]

[14b.] 449½–451 Hudson Street (houses), bet. Morton and Barrow Sts. W side. 1827, 1828, respectively. George Sutton, Builder. ☆

[15.] Morton Street, from Hudson to Bedford Sts.

If there is a typical Village block, this is it. It bends; it has a private court with its own, out-of-whack numbers (Nos. 44A, 44B). It is full of **surprising changes** of scale, setbacks, facade treatments. No. 66 has an awkwardly bowed front; No. 59 has possibly the finest Georgian doorway in the Village. The Old Law tenements interrupt the street, greedily consuming their property right out to the building line; in them live Italians and Irish—groups that remind their more affluent neighbors of an earlier, less moneyed Village.

[16a.] "Narrowest house in the Village," 75½ Bedford St. bet. Barrow and Grove Sts. W side. 1873.

It's 9½ feet wide, originally built to span an alley to the rear court (where its main entrance is). Though narrow by any standards it was wide enough for the carriages that used to pass through. This is one of the several residences of Edna St. Vincent Millay which remain in the Village.

[16b.] Isaacs-Hendricks House, 77 Bedford St., SW cor. Grove St. 1799. Alterations, 1836, 1928.

[16c.] 39 and 41 Commerce Street, at Bedford St. E side. 1831 and 1832, respectively. ☆ Additions: common garden wall.

This extraordinary one-of-a-kind pair proclaims the elegance once surrounding this and neighboring St. Luke's Place. They were reputedly built by a sea captain for his two daughters; one for each because they could not live together.

[16d.] 64–66 Barrow Street, bet. Commerce and Bedford Sts. N side.

What ten-year-old Batman could resist cat-walking from one section to the other of this curiously spliced tenement?

[16c.]

[16

Chumley's Restaurant, 86 Bedford St. bet. Barrow and Grove Sts. N side. CH 2-9512. Open daily until 3 or 4 AM.

Famed ex-speakeasy whose reputation still lingers; there is still no sign nor any other outside indication that this is a pub. Medium prices. Excellent hamburgers at any hour.

[17.] 41–51 Barrow Street, bet. Bleecker and Bedford Sts. SE side. 1826–1828.

A terrific little street: Nos. 47–49 have original store fronts (tobacconist and mason, respectively); both built in 1826. No. 51 has no record of alterations.

The Deli Gallery, Christopher St. bet. Bleecker and Bedford Sts. N side.

The corned beef and pastrami combi is one of the best in the Village. If it's a nice day, get a couple of sandwiches here and save them for the Morton Street Pier. [See 23.]

Carpenter-Musicians: Zuckerman Harpsichords, at 115 Christopher Street, sells a kit for *do-it-yourself* harpsichordists. It includes fixin's like strings, hardware, keyboard ivories and blacks. A list of necessary lumber and complete instructions are included. The rest is up to you!

[18a.] 17 Grove Street, NE cor. Bedford St. 1822. Alterations: cornices.

William Hyde built this as his house. He was a sash-maker and later put up a small building around the corner [See 18b] for his workshop. His home is the most whole of the few remaining wood-frame houses in the Village.

[18b.] 100 Bedford Street, bet. Grove and Christopher Sts. E side. 1833. Second story, 1852.

Built as a workshop for sash-maker William Hyde. [See 18a.]

[18c.] "Twin Peaks," 102 Bedford St., bet. Grove and Christopher Sts. E side. ca. 1835. Renovation, 1923.

The renovation was the work of a local resident, Clifford Reed Daily; it was financed by the wealthy Otto Kahn whose daughter lived here for some time. Daily considered the surrounding buildings "unfit for inspiring the minds of creative Villagers," and set out to give them this "island growing in a desert of mediocrity." Great fun for the kids—pure Hansel and Gretel.

[19a.] 14 Grove Street, bet. Bedford and Hudson Sts. 1839. First recorded alterations, 1966–1967.

[19b.] Grove Court, viewed bet. 10 and 12 Grove St., bet. Bedford and Hudson Sts. S side. 1853–1854. Alterations.

With its irregular site, this private plot with its story-book frame houses gives a good hint of what early 19th Century property lines were. Evidence of similar holdings are glimpsed throughout the West Village; only a study of old maps and tax books can give a thorough, and thoroughly confusing picture.

[19c.] 4–10 Grove Street, bet. Bedford and Hudson Sts. S side. 1824–1836.

An excellent row of wood-frame houses with brick side walls; No. 4 was the first of this dormered group.

Honest and humble. The Georgian houses at 4–10 Grove Street [See 19c.] represent the prevailing style of the 1820's. Americans then had few architects; instead, the builders—carpenters and masons—copied and adapted plans and details from the English builder's books. In translation, the detailing is less pretentious, adapting to the needs of speculative housing; nonetheless, there is a faint, pleasant echo of Sir Christopher Wren.

[20c.]

[21

[20a.] St. Luke's Episcopal Chapel of Trinity Parish/formerly **St. Luke's Church,** 485 Hudson St. bet. Barrow and Christopher Sts. at Grove St. W side. 1822. James N. Wells. Interior remodeling, 1875, 1886. Open daily.

The land to the south of the chunky tower remains much as it was in the early 19th Century with some of the row houses. The handsome interior—essentially as it was in 1875 (rebuilt in that style after a fire of 1886)—comes as a welcome surprise.

The original church was founded independently by local residents, with some financial help from the wealthy, downtown Trinity

Parish; **Clement C. Moore** ("The Night Before Christmas") was its first vestryman. With the influx of immigrants in 1892, the carriage-trade congregation moved uptown to Convent Avenue. [See Hamilton Heights 3a.] St. Luke's reopened the next year, now under the auspices of downtown Trinity Parish which had bought the property in the interim.

[20b.] 473–477, 487–491 Hudson Street, flanking St. Luke's Chapel, bet. Barrow and Christopher Sts. W side. 1825. **90–96 Barrow Street,** bet. Hudson and Greenwich Sts. N side. 1827. James N. Wells.

Unifying cornices and simplicity make an appropriate and well-planned frame for the austere chapel, also the work of Wells [See 20a] but a complete row to the ends of the block would even better set it off.

[20c.] 95 and 97 Barrow Street, bet. Hudson and Greenwich Sts. S side. 1847. ☆

[21.] U.S. Federal Building, 641 Washington St. Washington to Greenwich St., Barrow to Christopher St. 1892–1899. Willoughby J. Edbrooke. ★

This ten-story government building was originally a U.S. appraiser's warehouse—**sited to face the local docks,** naively expected to become center of the city's port facilities. The building remains an isolated and splendid example of the robust tradition of **early Chicago School architecture.** It is not surprising that Edbrooke's practice was in Chicago. He went to Washington in 1891–1893 to take the federal post of Supervising Architect of the Treasury, during which time he designed this building. It now houses a post office and is **the record center of the National Archives for the eastern area.**

This "interloper" has a scale that is entirely different from the nearby 19th Century Federal houses. It is probably for this reason that it is scorned by some Villagers, many of whom have been acclimatized to equate a livable environment with nothing higher than a four-story residence.

[22.] 6 Weehawken Street, bet. Christopher and West 10th Sts.

Like 77 Bedford Street [See 16b] this little house reveals skeletal remains of the 18th Century—their appearances shouldn't be taken seriously as Early Federal architecture but valued more for the wonder that anything remains of them at all.

[23.]

[23.] Morton Street Pier, at West St. beyond the Miller Elevated Highway (better known as the West Side Highway).

"Renovated" only a few years ago (and only because of local demand), the flat pier is graced with the black hull of a Board of

Education and Maritime High School ship and neat and humorously painted stanchions warning smokers to puff elsewhere. Nonetheless, it's crowded year-round with West Villagers **desperate for any open space,** water, and a smoke-stacked view of New Jersey.

End of Tour. Walk up to West 10th Street, where the crosstown bus will take you back to Greenwich Avenue and Village Square.

Walking Tour B—The West Village: Village Square to the Gansevoort Market area. (IND Sixth and Eighth Avenue Subways to West 4th St. Station.) Begin at Village Square.

[24.] Engine Co. No. 18, N.Y.C. Fire Dept., 132 W. 10th St., bet. Greenwich Ave. and Waverly Pl. S side. 1891. N. LeBrun & Sons.

Casey's (bar & restaurant), 142 W. 10th St. bet. Greenwich Ave. and Waverly Pl. S side. 989-8925. Lunch except Sunday; dinner daily to 10:30, weekends 11 PM.

Owned by **K. C.** (Casey) Li (Cornell graduate son of a Chinese millionaire) as a sideline; serves French food. We do know that the food is consistently good. High-priced.

[25a.] 176–184 Waverly Place, bet. Christopher and W. 10th Sts. W side. 1834–1839. ☆

[25b.] 156 and 158 West 10th Street, bet. Waverly Pl. and Seventh Ave. South. 1855. ☆

Two sets of representative Federal row houses.

[26.] Sayat Nova (restaurant), 91 Charles St., NW cor. Bleecker St. 1957. Haroutiun Derderian. Extensive remodeling 1958, 1962, 1965–1966: Robert H. Gans, Industrial Designer. OR 5-7364. Daily 5–10 PM.

One of the first and best "designed" restaurants in area. Very popular, excellent Armenian kitchen; garden. Complete dinners around $5–$6.

[27.] 248 West 4th Street, bet. Bleecker and Hudson Sts.

A private courtyard rumored to contain a stable from Alexander Hamilton's estate.

[28.] 510–518 Hudson Street (houses), bet. Christopher and W. 10th Sts. E side. ca. 1840.

The Other Side of the Tracks: The deserted N.Y. Central elevated tracks west of Washington Street (south to Leroy Street) for all appearances form the western boundary of The Village. But scattered beyond these tracks are quite a few 19th Century houses—some restored, others decaying—originally built for speculation or in the rush to house those fleeing the epidemics of lower Manhattan. An area to investigate if you have lots of time.

[29.] 271 West 10th Street/originally **Primary School 33–34,** bet. Greenwich and Washington Sts. N side. 1846.

[30.] 727 Greenwich Street (house), bet. Charles and Perry Sts. E side. 1826. ☆

[31a.] 131 Charles Street, bet. Greenwich and Washington Sts. N side. 1834. ★

[31b.] Sixth Precinct, N.Y.C. Police Dept., 135 Charles St. bet. Greenwich and Washington Sts. N side. 1895. John Fais.

When this building was dedicated, the Commissioner of **New York's Finest** was Teddy Roosevelt, prior to his Rough Rider days.

[32.] 335 West 11th Street (house), bet. Washington and Greenwich Sts. N side. ca. 1830.

[33a.] 276–282 West 11th Street, bet. W. 4th and Bleecker Sts. S side. 1817–1820.

No. 282 is one of the rare houses with few alterations and in excellent condition.

[33b.] 265 and 267, 282 West 11th Street (houses), bet. Bleecker and W. 4th Sts. ca. 1845.

[34a.] 282 West 11th Street (house), bet. Bleecker and W. 4th Sts. S side. ca. 1845.

[34b.] St. John's in the Village (Episcopal), SW cor. W. 11th St. and Waverly Pl. 1846.

All churches of the era resembled Greek temples: here is another variation of the Classical Revival Style. This one cost only $15,000 when built, was wood, but it was stuccoed to resemble "the more expensive spread." Interior has been unfortunately changed to a dark, uninspiring hall.

[a.]

[31b.]

[34c.] 223 Waverly Place, bet. Perry and W. 11th Sts. NE side. 1966–1967. Robert Bruce Cousins.

Low-budget, well-designed facade was the happy solution for Cousins' ex-storefront architectural office. After dark, one can often find a local crowd enjoying rear-projected slides and movies or listening to the **live rock 'n roll** group (willfully gathered from among his students).

[35.] 2–10 Perry Street, bet. Greenwich Ave. and Seventh Ave. South SE side. ca. 1845.

Papier Maché Ltd., 55 Greenwich Ave. SW cor. Perry St. CH 3-2017. Hours: Noon–8 PM (closed Sundays).

Everything paper: replicas of Tiffany lampshades and French castles to be cut out and ingeniously interlocked.

1, 2 Kangaroo (toys), 201 W. 11th St. SW cor. Greenwich Ave. 255-8697. Hours: 10 AM–10 PM. Daily.

Over 50 architectural toys—many not sold elsewhere—are to be found in this tiny "adult" toyland (or toy adultland). Here is the work of Bruno Munari, the Kurt Naef line of modular building sets, Eames' *House of Cards,* and *Cubi,* the *Super Egg,* among others. Take the kids; there are "children's" toys too.

[36.] 243–247 Waverly Place, bet. W. 11th St. and Bank St. N side. ca. 1880.

Triplicate Romanesque Revival curiosities reduced here to a mid-19th Century Village scale. Their **leafy neighbor,** at 241, is doing the best it can to hide its Georgian simplicity behind a beard of greenery.

Ye Waverly Inn, 16 Bank St. SW cor. Waverly Pl. CH 3-9396. Lunch except weekends; dinners till 8, weekends 8:30.

Quaint, New England-style restaurant, tucked away in the basement nooks and crannies of an early 19th Century house. Year-round garden; free wine with Sunday dinner. Moderate prices.

[37a.] 37 Bank Street (house), bet. Waverly Pl. and W. 4th St. N side. ca. 1850.

One of the best of the style in the Village. The block is a striking one—despite the curious lintel details (Nos. 16–34) and some ghastly refacing across the street.

[37b.] 55 and 57 Bank Street (houses), bet. W. 4th and Bleecker Sts. N side. 1842. ☆

[37c.] 61 Bank Street (house), bet. W. 4th and Bleecker Sts. N side. 1840.☆ 1841, rear building. ☆

The private back yard structure should be seen, but is guarded from the curious with a new twist on an old sign: "Keep gate securely closed—dog within." (There may also be a dog!)

[37d.] 68, 74 and 76 Bank Street, bet. W. 4th and Bleecker Sts. S side. ca 1840–1845.

[38.] New Abingdon Square Park, at Hudson, Bank, and Bleecker Sts. 1966. Arnold Vollmer, landscape architects and engineers, with a committee of community architects.

Here we see evidence of one of the first chinks in the armor of the Park Department—a sprightly, imaginative non-institutional playground. It *can* be fun to play.

[39.] 767 Greenwich Street, bet. W. 11th and Bank Sts. E side. 1965. Leonard Feldman, Architect; Helmut Jacoby, Designer.

One of the most recent—and rare—of the city's town houses. This one successfully copes with its drab neighbor to the north; complements the Federal house to the south.

[40a.] 41 Bethune Street, bet. Greenwich and Washington Sts. S side. ca. 1835.

A gem: the short stoop is unusual for this sized house, but is entirely in keeping with the delicate proportions and detailing. (Unfortunately, so many others of its size and scale have pompous and clunky stoops.)

[40b.] 19–29, 24–36 Bethune Street (house), bet. Greenwich and Washington Sts. ca. 1835–1840. 1836. No. 25.

[41a.] 9 Jane Street (house), 9½ Jane Street (rear house), bet. Greenwich Ave. and W. 4th St. N side. 1844, 1854 respectively. ☆

[41b.] 39 Jane Street/formerly **Con Edison DC Substation,** bet. Eighth Ave. and Hudson St. NE side. ca. 1923. Remodeled, 1967.

The imaginative builder, in remodeling to apartments, has fitted several duplex apartments with inner balconies between the original floors, making the most of their high ceilings. Every interior wall is *solid* masonry.

[42.] 65 Jane Street, bet. Hudson and Greenwich Sts. W side. ca. 1865.

Here, open space is all we get: no inviting entry, blood clot-colored brick. Relief is the contrast with the chummy backs of Nos. 58–62 Horatio with their pleasantly cluttered and sagging wooden balconies.

[43.] 83 Horatio Street, bet. Washington and Greenwich Sts. N side. ca. 1835.

This typical Federal house built for speculation has the horse walk that led to the stable in the rear.

[44a.] 345–351 West 4th St. (houses), bet. Horatio and Jane Sts. E side. 1867. ☆

[44b.] 1–5 Horatio Street (houses), bet. W. 4th St. and Eighth Ave. N side. 1848. ☆

[44c.] 51 and 53 Eighth Avenue (houses), bet. Horatio and W. 13th Sts. W side. 1848. ☆

[45.] Gansevoort Market area, W. 14th St. to Gansevoort St., and

Ninth Ave. to Hudson River.

Hiding behind the 19th Century two-story Federal facades are thoroughly modern meat-packing and refrigeration systems. From these, as well as the newer buildings, comes the meat for most of Manhattan's restaurants and institutions. Herman Melville worked here on what was then the Gansevoort Dock as an outdoor custom's inspector for 19 years. He came to this job, discouraged and unable to earn a living as a writer. It was sometime during these years that he completed *Moby Dick*.

Old Homestead Restaurant, 57 Ninth Ave., bet. W. 14th and 15th Sts. E side. CH 2-9040. Lunch and dinner daily.

A good stopping place for the end of this tour. This is New York's oldest steak house: 1868. Yes, the fine meats come direct from the local market.

End of Tour. A 14th Street bus can take you to subways: the IND (at Eighth and Sixth Avenues), the IRT (at Seventh Avenue and Union Square), or the BMT (at Union Square).

[45.]

[46.]

[34c.]

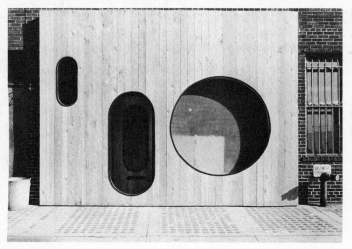

Walking Tour C—Pre-Civil War Elegance: From Village Square to 14th Street. Begin at Village Square (IND Sixth and Eighth Avenue Subways to West 4th Street Station).

[46.] Jefferson Market Library/formerly **Jefferson Market Courthouse,** SW cor. Sixth Ave. and W. 10th Sts. 1876. Vaux & Withers. Exterior restoration, interior remodeling, 1967. Giorgio Cavaglieri.

The original courthouse complex, including a jail, replaced **an active shopping and marketing area** and **a fire lookout tower** (photo, p. 57) that dated from 1830. (The new tower was separate from the courthouse functions.) In 1885 it was voted **America's fifth most beautiful building.**

In 1927, an adjoining jail was replaced by the **Women's House of Detention** (where any time you are likely to hear one of the badly overcrowded residents shouting down to a friend? below). Since 1945, the courthouse had remained vacant. Then, with threats to demolish this **Neuschwansteinian assemblage** of stained glass, Venetian-style embellishments, and **its watchtower and clock,** Village associations formed to revive the building—the first success being the lighting and reactivation of the clock. This good fortune encouraged residents to press for reopening the building, and they helped achieve its present use—a new regional branch of the New York Public Library.

The exterior has been cleaned and repaired and a metal covering of Terne Follansbee has been placed over the roof. The interiors retain much of the **lusty spirit** of the original, **a welcome change for a library.**

[46.]

[47

La Crêpe (restaurant), 15 Greenwich Ave., bet. Christopher and W. 10th Sts. CH 3-2555. Hours: 11:30–1 AM (closed Mondays). Wine only.

Over 100 varieties of *crêpes* (French pancakes)—from *beurre d'escargot* to those filled with caviar. All served in the neat decor of Brittany. Very reasonable prices.

[47a.] Paraphernalia (boutique), 28 Greenwich Ave. bet. W. 10th and Charles Sts. 1966. Ulrich Franzen & Associates.

The walk past the spot-lit pedestal displays—all stark and uptown gallery-like—leads to a back room crammed with kicky boutique fashions, swinging chicks with boy friends, as well as curious grandmother types.

Sutter's French Café, 18 Greenwich Ave. bet. W. 10th and Charles Sts. 255-0666. Hours: 7:30 AM–10 PM (counter), 11 PM (café).

For all self-respecting self-indulgent snackers, any wait is worth the while. The original bakery still sells its real butter-and-eggs goodies to an evergrowing clientele. Outstanding is lemon meringue pie; the croissants are about the closest to those in Paris in the city. (If buying at the counter, be sure to take a number.)

[47b.] Patchin Place, off W. 10th St. bet. Greenwich and Sixth Aves. NW side. 1849. **Milligan Place,** Sixth Ave. bet. W. 10th and 11th Sts. W side. 1848.

The earliest records of these two **private courts** date from 1799 when Samuel Milligan purchased the surrounding farmland. His daughter Isabella married Aaron D. Patchin, who reputedly fell in love with her when employed by her father to survey his property.

In 1848 and 1849, respectively, Milligan and Patchin Places were built as second-class boarding houses for the Basque waiters and workers at the old Brevoort Hotel on Fifth Avenue (and it is rumored they also housed some **French feather workers** who made a living **curling ostrich and egret plumes**).

It was not until the 1920's that Patchin Place became famous for its writer residents; though **Theodore Dreiser** lived there in 1895. Its most renowned tenant was **e. e. cummings.**

[48.] 14–18 West 9th Street (house), bet. Sixth and Fifth Aves. S side. 1859–1860. E. Kelley.

The Brevoorts: an early Village family. The first records were of John Hendricks Brevoort with a 41-acre farm there in 1701. One of the Brevoort houses, on the east side of Fifth Avenue and 8th Street, was opened as a hotel in the mid-19th Century, becoming a New York institution — with such guests as **Queen Emma of the Sandwich Islands** and later the Duke of Argyll and his daughters a few years later. The hotel is gone; only its name is preserved on its monolithic replacements.

.]   **[50.]**

[49.] 3 East 9th Street, bet. Fifth Ave. and University Pl. N side. ca. 1845.

The best of what once was an elegant row of houses, looks out upon the Hotel Brevoort block complex (lying mostly on Sailors' Snug Harbor property).

[50.] 7 and 9 East 10th Street (town houses), bet. University Pl. and Fifth Ave. N side.

Owner Ardsley Van Arsdale was justly proud of his architect's work and had him put his (AVA's) initials on the teakwood parlor-floor tablet of No. 9. The carving was commissioned in India by a well-known connoisseur of the art, also a painter of the day, Lockwood de Forest.

[51a.] The Church of the Ascension (Episcopal), NW cor. Fifth Ave. at 10th St. 1840–1841. Richard Upjohn. Remodeling of interior, 1885–1889. McKim, Mead & White: John La Farge, altar mural, and stained glass. St. Gaudens, marble altar relief. Open daily.

One of the few churches that lights up the stained glass at night, allowing evening strollers on lower Fifth Avenue to enjoy the colors. If you are wondering about the inconsistent quality of the stained glass, you're correct: not all the windows are La Farge's.

[51b.] 12 West 10th Street, bet. Fifth and Sixth Aves. S side. ca.

1820. Extensive renovations.

Breaking from the more popular Italianate town house style, this one is unique. There have been several renovations; one of them was the subdivision into four apartments, one for each daughter, by one owner, architect Bruce Price. One of those daughters, **Emily Post,** tells of having President Wilson to Thanksgiving dinner (and it is rumored he proposed to his second wife here).

[51c.] 15 West 10th Street (house), bet. Fifth and Sixth Aves. N side. 1847.

[51d.] "The English Terrace" Row, 20–40 W. 10th St., bet. Fifth and Sixth Aves. S side. 1855–1856.

These were the first group of row houses in the city to abandon the high, Dutch "stoop" (which is Dutch for step), making the entry floor only two or three steps up from the street. Being the first builders in *Nieuw Amsterdam,* they followed the home style: high stoops way off the canal or street to protect the basement from periodic flooding—despite no threat from the local waters.

"Terrace," does not refer to the handsome balcony that runs the length of these houses, but is an English term for a *row of houses,* such as found in the Kensington and Paddington districts of London of the 1840's, 1850's, and 1860's. **New Yorkers** visiting England **were impressed** with this style, and saw good reason to bring it to New York. [See Astor Place/East Village 17b.]

[51f.] 56 West 10th Street, bet. Fifth and Sixth Aves. S side. 1832. Modifications: window lintels, braided cornice.

Among the oldest houses in this part of the Village, it has much of its original detail (including the pineapple posts that have all but disappeared, ironwork in mint condition, door with fluted colonnettes and leaded lights).

Charles French Restaurant, 452 Sixth Ave. bet. W. 10th and 11th Sts. E side. GR 7-3300. Reservations preferred. Lunch weekdays, dinner daily til 10 (weekdays), 11:30 weekends.

Parisian Grand Hotel atmosphere; excellent cuisine, rather expensive.

Rhinelander Gardens: In 1955, P.S. 41, on the south side of West 11th Street, just off Sixth, replaced the Rhinelander Gardens designed by James Renwick, Jr. These were a one-of-a-kind group of wrought-ironed balconied row houses, in the manner of Bourbon Street, New Orleans. For nostalgia's sake a bit of the wrought iron was applied to the school's rear facade.

[52.] 130–158 West 11th Street, bet. Sixth and Seventh Aves. S side.

If you like to play architectural guessing games here is a row to practice on.

[53.] 462–470 Sixth Avenue, bet. W. 11th and W. 12th Sts. E side. ca. 1840. ☆

The remains of Federal buildings on this predominantly commercial street are scanty. Their shabbiness recalls the days of the noisy and filthy Sixth Avenue "el."

[54a.] The Second Cemetery of the Spanish and Portuguese Synagogue, Shearith Israel, in the City of New York, 72–76 W. 11th St. bet. Sixth and Fifth Aves. 1805–1829.

The **original cemetery is at Chatham Square.** It expanded here in 1805, onto what then was a much larger, **square plot** covering what now is the street. The commissioners' grid was drawn up by 1811; but not until 1830 was West 11th Street cut through, at that time slicing the cemetery into **its present triangle.** The remaining plots were moved farther uptown to 119 West 21st Street, west of Sixth Avenue. In 1852, City law **forbade burial within Manhattan,** and subsequent interments have been made in Cypress Hills, Long Island. [See Civic Center 27a; Chelsea 18a.]

[54b.] West 11th Street, bet. Sixth and Fifth Aves.

This is a fine street, and a number of houses should be pointed out: Nos. 54 and 35 as **beautifully preserved examples** of the Greek Revival; No. 30 is Italianate. No. 16 was built by **Henry Brevoort,** a very wealthy landowner (but not for his home) in 1844–1845. Its neighbors (built at the same time) have added Grecian graces, **fanlights and wreathed plaques,** at a much later date. No. 11 was built in 1831.

These one-family houses are **highly prized** and **seldom change hands.** The few that have been sold in recent years have brought prices of between $100,000 to $150,000 each.

[55.] First Presbyterian Church, Fifth Ave. bet. W. 11th and 12th Sts. W side. 1845. Joseph C. Wells. South parish house, 1893, McKim, Mead & White. Church house, 1960. Edgar Tafel.

The church tower by Wells is an adaption of Magdalen Church tower at Oxford. The south parish house is a curious addition to the impressive list of McKim, Mead & White buildings; in any case, it is an early work of a firm significant for the originality and great range soon to appear from their drawing boards. Tafel's five-story church house blends with the older buildings by repeating the quatrefoil motif of the original church in his treatment of the cornices and balcony.

The cast iron fence on the Fifth Avenue side was brought from the church's original location on Wall Street.

[56a.] 43 Fifth Avenue, NE cor. 11th St. 1904. Henry Anderson.

One can still rent a half-floor apartment in this florid baroque building, completely intact with separate entrances for the servants' quarters.

[56b.] Salmagundi Club/formerly **home of William G. Park/**originally **home of Irad Hawley,** 47 Fifth Ave., bet. E. 11th and 12th Sts. E side. 1852–1853. Open daily 1 to 5 PM. ☆

The Salmagundi Club is America's oldest artist's club (founded in 1870). This private, **all-male club** moved to Fifth Avenue in 1917; members included **John La Farge, Louis C. Tiffany,** and **Stanford White.** The basement billiard room is a handsome relic of a bygone era. The parlor floor, which is the only one open to the public, gives a good picture of the interiors of the period.

[57.] Hotel Albert, SE cor. University Pl. and E. 11th St. 1883. Henry J. Hardenbergh. Additions by others.

Lawners Auction Galleries, 81 University Pl., NE cor. E. 11th St.

One of several large and popular auction houses in this neighborhood. Times of preview and sale vary; consult newspapers.

[58a.] Police Athletic League Headquarters/originally **a public school,** 34½ E. 12th St., bet. University Pl. and Broadway. S side. 1856. ☆

[58b.] East 12th Street, bet. University Pl. and Broadway. N side.

Il Bambino Restaurant, 94 University Pl. SW cor. E. 12th St. OR 5-9844. Lunch and dinner (closed Sundays).

A reasonably priced Italian restaurant with exceptionally good kitchen. Try one of the "specials"; they're each from a different region of Italy.

Sixty-Eight Restaurant, 59 Fifth Ave.

Italian, with a well-stocked bar and cellar. $4-7 *table d'hote.* The perils of naming yourself after your address are obvious; restaurant was across Fifth Avenue for many years. Considered one of the Village's best.

[59a.] 31-33 West 12th Street, bet. Fifth and Sixth Aves. N side. 1890. J. B. Snook & Son.

Buildings on the north sides of Manhattan streets have an advantage working for them: **the sun.** Here, the delicate iron balconies take on additional character when their shadows augment the crusty rhythm. Both work to make this studio building a fine contrast with its next two neighbors.

[59b.] 35 West 12th Street, bet. Fifth and Sixth Aves. N side. 1840. Altered 1868; right half removed in 1893.

[59a.]
[59b.]

[59e

[59c.] Butterfield House, 37 W. 12th St. bet. Fifth and Sixth Aves. N side. 1962. Mayer, Whittlesey & Glass, William J. Conklin, associate partner in charge of design and James S. Rossant.

Superb use of irregular site. On residential 12th Street, this cooperative apartment goes to only seven stories on a 50-foot-wide plot; variation in fenestration, bays, and balconies combine not only to break up the size of the facade but to relate it in a thoroughly successful and contemporary way to the prevailing 19th Century residential scale of the street. Glazed courtyard passage to rear building on 13th Street captures the backyard charm of the West Village. On 13th Street, though, with numerous lofts and 20th Century apartment towers, the building rises agreeably (and economically) to 13 stories.

[60.] 45 West 12th Street, bet. Fifth and Sixth Aves. N side. 1846.

Look carefully at the east side of this building for the acute angle. The side wall slants back because it originally faced the once-above-ground Minetta Brook. Frank Lloyd Wright's sister, Mrs. William Pope Barney, owned and lived in the house at one time.

[61.] The New School for Social Research, 66 W. 12th St. bet. Fifth and Sixth Aves. S side. 1930. Joseph Urban. **11th and 12th Street additions, Interior court,** 1958, Mayer, Whittlesey & Glass, William J. Conklin, associate partner in charge of design. Isamu Noguchi, Sculptor.

It became the "university in exile" in 1933, a home for the intelligentsia fleeing Nazi Germany. In the original (east) building, note the progressive narrowing of the horizontal band between strip windows and the slight setting back of the street wall as it rises— these subtleties render it a shorter, less imposing structure, more in scale with the adjacent residences. The new sculpture court is a welcome and popular addition.

[62.] Noma Building, 55 W. 13th St., bet. Sixth and Fifth Aves. S side.

[63.] Rambusch Building, 40 W. 13th St., bet. Sixth and Fifth Sts. S side.

This narrow, and out-of-square building (the east side follows the underground route of Minetta Brook) has kept its "flapping" iron shutters; they are a marvelous up beat to the loft tempo of the street.

[64.] 117 W. 12th Street, bet. Sixth and Seventh Aves. N side. ca. 1825.

[65.] National Maritime Union of America, AFL-CIO, 36 Seventh Ave. bet. W. 12th and 13th Sts. W side. 1964. Albert C. Ledner.

In the wake of Frank Lloyd Wright, this huge double-dentured monument is without precedent. The on-the-hour tours (9 AM to 4 PM) show a more human side of the building: part hiring halls and training room for working seamen, and part executive offices, the latter approached around a "parrot jungle" in the stairwell. Compare with its sibling on 346 West 17th Street. [See Chelsea 23.]

[62.]

[66.] Village Presbyterian Church and The Brotherhood Synagogue, 143 W. 13th St. bet. Sixth and Seventh Aves. N side. 1846. Samuel Thompson (?).

One of the best of the Greek Revival temple-type churches.

[67.] Jackson Square, bound by Greenwich Ave., Horatio St., and Eighth Ave.

All is unimaginatively squared up, but paved with those nice hexagonal bricks and graced with 28 trees. Toward Village Square to the east is the Van Gogh apartments; **the artist's touch in name only** (ditto for the Cezanne, on Greenwich Avenue between Bethune and Bank).

Piemonte Restaurant, 240 W. 14th St. bet. Eighth and Seventh Aves. S side. CH 2-4010. Hours: from Noon weekdays and 4 PM

Saturdays to 10:30 PM. (closed Sundays).

Cozy neighborhood restaurant and bar owned by the waiter. Piano player some evenings. Italian food consistently well-cooked and served. Recommend special dinner menu; also shrimp *Provinciale,* sweetbreads *Bordelaise. Camerieri* are very nice to well-behaved children. Moderate, but wide, price range.

14th Street: West as well as East 14th Street has seen better days, when **Wanamakers' magnetism** radiated throughout the area. The remaining vitality is a small Spanish neighborhood, west of Seventh Avenue, recognizable by a handful of good, inexpensive restaurants and an occasional shop.

[66.]

[72

Oviedo Restaurant (and bar), 202 W. 14th St. bet. Eighth and Seventh Aves. S side. 929-9454. Lunch and dinner until 1 AM, daily.

Spanish cooking: we recommend the *paella* and the seafood. A la carte from $2.25.

Casa Moneo (Spanish and South American imports), 218 W. 14th St. bet. Eighth and Seventh Aves. WA 9-1644.

This is **the** Spanish *bodega,* crammed with all the makings for *paella* or *tacos;* books, records, cooking pots two feet wide, wine carafes (both the portable *botas* and the glass *parrones*) are just a sampling.

[68.] 56 West 14th Street, bet. Sixth and Fifth Aves. S side.

This thin building, pompously laden with Beaux Arts eclectic detail, now sports the sign of the Bunnie Baby Wear Shops, Inc.—typical of the odd juxtapositions of a once elegant past and today's aging honky-tonk.

 [69.] Painting Industry Welfare Building, 45 W. 14th St. bet. Sixth and Fifth Aves. N side. 1960. Mayer, Whittlesey & Glass, William J. Conklin, associate partner in charge.

Hopefully, this witty and elegant refacing of a tired facade will inspire its neighbors to follow.

End of Tour. The IND Subway is at Sixth Avenue, and the BMT and Lexington Avenue IRT east at Union Square. The Sixth Avenue bus goes uptown, the Fifth, down to Eighth Street.

Walking Tour D—Washington Square, N.Y.U., and the South Village: From West Eighth Street at Sixth Avenue to King Street. Begin at Village Square (IND Sixth and Eighth Avenue Subways to West 4th Street Station).

[70a.] The Eighth Street Playhouse (movie theater), 52 W. Eighth

St. bet. Sixth Ave. and Macdougal St. S side. 1929. Frederick J. Kiesler. Extensive alterations.

Kiesler's original design is barely recognizable today, as apparently the successive theater owners did not value his visionary designs, which have been applauded and applied by several theater architects throughout the world. In this movie theater he made provisions for simultaneous slide projections on the side walls and created a main screen where the projection surface area could be altered in size; film projection concepts that today—nearly 40 years later— are still considered avant garde.

[70b.] Tenth Church of Christ Scientist, 171 Macdougal Street bet. W. 8th St. and Washington Square North. W side. 1967. Victor Christ-Janer.

[71.] Macdougal Alley, at Macdougal Street bet. W. 8th St. and Washington Square North. E side.

This private street is jointly owned by property holders on Washington Square North and on the south side of 8th Street that back up on the alley. The two gas lamps are *not* the last remaining ones in New York—there are none. These were privately installed.

[72a.]

[72a.] Washington Square Park, at the foot of Fifth Ave.

Originally marshland with **Minetta Brook** meandering through, then a potters field, and later the site of the **hanging gallows;** in the 1820's a less sadistic citizenry converted it to a **public park and parade ground** for the military. With this change, building quickly came to all sides of the Park; for instance, the north side with its "Row" [See 72b.], and the east, in 1837, with the **first N.Y.U. building.** The present park design dates from the 1880's. **The Memorial Arch** (1889–1892) was first erected in wood in 1876 for the centenary celebration by McKim, Mead & White. It was so well liked that pianist **Jan Paderewski** gave a benefit concert to help finance the permanent arch. (The **Washington statue** on the west face was sculpted by **Alexander Calder's** father, **Alexander Stirling Calder.**)

Since 1964, when local as well as city-wide civic-oriented groups pressured for complete removal of vehicular traffic, the Park has been the exclusive domain of the pedestrian.

[72b.] "The Row," 1–13, 21–26 (originally Nos. 1–28), Washington Square North. ca. 1831. Nos. 21–26, Martin Thompson or Town and Davis.

When built, these homes housed the most socially prominent New Yorkers, such as the **Delano family.** Later, **Edith Wharton, William Dean Howells,** and **Henry James,** all lived and worked at No. 1. In this century **John Dos Passos** wrote "Manhattan Transfer" in No. 3; others living there have been **Edward Hopper** and **Rockwell Kent.** No. 8 was once the **official residence of the Mayor.**

The first six (Nos. 21–26) established the overall style, leaving the details for the others which followed to other architects or builders. Over the years community pressure and **artful illusion** have maintained The Row in a fairly whole condition. Those from 7–13, to the east of Fifth Avenue, retain the shell of their front and side facades only: **Sailor's Snug Harbor** gutted them for multiple-dwelling housing; and entrance to these now N.Y.U.-owned apartments is via a **curious pergola** facing Fifth Avenue. On the west side of Fifth, when the huge No. 2 Fifth Avenue apartment tower was being planned, citizens put up an outcry, and a neo-neo-Georgian wing was designed for the Washington Square frontage, conspicuously *lower* than the adjacent buildings. (Nos. 14 and 15 were the original **Rhinelander mansions** converted in 1922 into a 6-story apartment, in turn demolished with 16, 17, and 18 for No. 2 Fifth Ave.)

[73.] Harout's Restaurant, 14 Waverly Pl. bet. Green and Mercer Sts. 1961. Haroutiun Derderian. 254-4190. Hours: 10 AM to Midnight and 4 AM on weekends (closed Sundays).

Pleasant, low-budget job, capitalizing on the original brick walls and cast iron columns (note the original, encircling radiator).

[74a.] Washington Mews, at University Pl. and Fifth Ave. bet. E. 8th St. and Washington Square North.

Merrill Ames (gift and housewares shop), 41 E. 8th St. bet. University Pl. and Broadway. N side.

The finest contemporary design sold in the Village. Many imitators.

[74b.] 4–26 East 8th Street, bet. University Pl. and Fifth Ave. S side. ca. 1870. Remodeled, 1916. Harvey Wiley Corbett.

Sailors' Snug Harbor directed the 1916 renovation which turned a failing commercial group into very attractive and spacious quarters for artists. This faked Tudor is acceptable, whereas the faked Colonial (the supermarket over at West 8th Street on the south side) is offensive.

[74c.] Brentano's Book Shop, 20 University Pl. NW cor. E. 8th St. 1966. Warner, Burns, Toan & Lunde.

New York University. Over the years, N.Y.U.'s expansion has left records of quiet—and not so quiet—feuds with the local residents. The latter are fearful the University will wall in the square. It has only partially succeeded, although much property in the immediate area—though now used residentially—is owned by or on long-term lease to N.Y.U. The south end of the park, excepting Judson Memorial Church [See 79.] is lined with the School's buildings. [See 78a, 78b; 80.] East of the Loeb Student Center [See 78a.] is the site of the proposed Elmer Holmes Bobst General Library and Study Center.

[75.] Warren Weaver Hall, 251 Mercer St. bet. W. 4th and 3rd Sts. W side. 1966. Warner, Burns, Toan & Lunde.

This vigorous, classroom tower may try a shade too hard to attract attention. But it is the first that N.Y.U. has built in recent years to make a decisive architectural statement. A bold and not cosmetic addition to the expanding campus.

[76.] Washington Square Village, Nos. 1 and 2, W. 3rd to Bleecker Sts., W. Broadway to Mercer St. 1956–1958. S.J. Kessler; Paul Lester Weiner, consultant for design and site planning.

The first and only slab housing in the Village, now owned by N.Y.U. The apartments themselves are well-planned, yet the multi-color facade treatment doesn't succeed in making these block-long, 16-story buildings into town houses. Corridors are endless; planting not well maintained.

[77.] University Village, bet. Bleecker and Houston Sts., W. Broadway and Mercer Sts. 1966. I. M. Pei & Partners.

Of these three, nearly identical towers, the one closest to West Broadway is Mitchell-Lama middle income housing—undoubtedly the finest in the city, and much better than Pei's Kips Bay Plaza. [See Four Squares 37.] All three are owned by N.Y.U. With each, the exterior expresses the pinwheel plan; the result is exceptional for high-rise housing, where one can, for a change, grasp the size of the individual apartments. Inside, corridors are very short—not the usual labyrinth—and handsomely lit and carpeted. Viewed from Houston Street their bases disappear behind the mound ending in a wall at the sidewalk, isolated from the scrubbiness of Houston Street; and from the north they appear as *the* logical and elegant termination of the progression of recently built, structures.

[77.]

[79.]

[78a.] Loeb Student Center, SE cor. Washington Square South and W. Broadway. 1959. Harrison & Abramovitz; sculpture by Reuben Nakian.

A center for many Village activities.

[78b.] Holy Trinity Chapel of the Generoso Pope Catholic Center of N.Y.U., SW cor. Washington Square South and Thompson St. 1964. Eggers & Higgins.

Walking down Fifth Avenue one is delighted with Washington Square Park, announced by the Memorial Arch—and then the eye looks through the arch and framed in the middle is this incongrous chapel.

[79.] Judson Memorial Baptist Church, 55 Washington Square South, **Judson Hall and Tower,** 51–54 Washington Square South, bet. Thompson and Sullivan Sts. 1892. McKim, Mead & White. John LaFarge, stained glass. Herbert Addams, marble relief south wall of chancel (after plans of St. Gaudens). ☆

One of the earliest and best of many eclectic styles to be built by the firm in the next two decades. The Tower (attributed to McKim, Mead & White), now used by N.Y.U. as a women's dorm, is reminiscent of the simpler yellow brick campaniles of Renaissance Rome. The interior of the church is, at first, a bit of a shock; pews are removed, lighting equipment hangs hapazardly about, the glass windows are partly hidden by large screens. The sanctuary has been converted into a flexible rehearsal hall-theater; yet none of the interior architecture has been remodeled, only obscured by the temporary baffles.

[80a.] Vanderbilt Law School, N.Y.U., Washington Square South to W. 3rd St., Macdougal to Sullivan Sts. 1951. Eggers & Higgins.

One can sympathize with the desire to place this building in context with its neighbors on the square, but the solution chosen seems a bland and unnecessarily derivative approach.

[80b.] 132 and 134 West Fourth Street (houses), bet. Washington Square West and Sixth Ave. S side. 1839. Alexander Masterton and Robert Smith, Builders. ☆

[80c.] 141 Macdougal Street (apartments), SW cor. W. 4th St. 1889–1890. Thom & Wilson. ☆

The Peacock Cafe (coffee house), 149 W. 4th St., bet. Macdougal and Sixth Ave. Hours: 4 PM to Midnight (later on weekends).

One of the oldest—and most authentic—coffee houses in the Village. (Here, 18 years of continuous business is ancient.) Also offers Shish Kebab, pastries, and a limited, moderate-priced dinner menu.

[81a.] 127–131 Macdougal Street, bet. W. 4th and 3rd Sts. W side. 1829. ☆

These houses were built for Aaron Burr. The **pineapple newel posts** on the ironwork at No. 129 are a rare remaining pair. **The Piñata Party** which imports the unusual from Mexico and South America is typical of the unique shops in the Village vicinity.

[81a.]

[81b.] 125 Macdougal Street, NW cor. W. 3rd St. 1829. Mansard roof, ca. 1860.

The street floor houses the gracious **Granados Restaurant.** Dining is amidst Goya prints; Flamenco and classical guitar is heard after 10 PM. *Sangria*, a wine punch, is delightful. Moderate prices; dinners only. OR 3-5576. Open til 2 AM and later.

O'Henry's Steak House, 345 Sixth Ave., NW cor. W. 4th St. CH 2-2000. Hours: daily til 1:30 AM, til Midnight on Sundays (charge cards honored).

Butcher-block tables (some probably from when it was a meat market), sawdust, straw-hatted waiters in large, white aprons—the whole bit, including sidewalk service and gas lamps. Can be relied upon for good steaks. Reservations recommended Wednesdays and Saturdays.

Folklore Center, 321 Sixth Ave. (below the Waverly Theatre). W side.

Founded in 1957 and run by **Israel Young,** one of folk music's most knowledgeable and loving supporters. If female and attractive, Izzy is likely to persuade you to accompany him on his own excellent tour of Greenwich Village.

[81c.] 130–132 Macdougal Street, bet. W. 3rd and Bleecker Sts. E side. 1852. ☆

Twin entrances and ironwork portico are uncommon. Louisa

On the finest buildings

YALE®

Looks as good as it locks

**Yale Lock & Hardware Division
Rye, New York 10580**

EAT⊕N
YALE &
TOWNE
INC.

May Alcott once lived here.

Minetta Tavern, 113 Macdougal St. SW cor. Minetta Lane. 473-9119.

A drinking man's museum of Greenwich Village. The walls are crammed with photographs and other proof of the famed characters who claimed Minetta's a second home. Note especially the **Joe Gould memorabilia.** Italian cooking, moderate prices.

The psychedelic emporium in the Village is *The Head Shop,* at 124 Macdougal Street at Minetta Lane. You can buy imported water pipes, tarot cards, temple bells, diffraction discs. The record collection has the latest "acid" rock. Many Hicksville hipsters as well as local *heads.*

[82a.]

[88

Caffé Reggio (coffee house), 119 Macdougal St. bet. Minetta Lane and Bleecker St. GR 5-9557. Hours: daily 1 PM to 1:30 AM (later on weekends).

The real brass *machina,* marble-topped (not formica) tables, dim-lit chandeliers—*tutti gentile.* Most seats are close to the large windows, so the whole Street can be considered.

Grand Ticino (restaurant), 228 Thompson St. bet. Bleecker and W. 3rd Sts. GR 3-8876. Hours: 12–3 PM; 5:30–10:30 PM. (closed Sundays).

A quiet, Italian, Italian restaurant; moderate prices, decent food.

[82a.] Hotel Greenwich/originally **Mills Hotel No. 1,** 160 Bleecker St. bet. Thompson and Sullivan Sts. S side. 1896. Ernest Flagg. ☆

Built to house poor "gentlemen" on a short-term basis (originally 20¢ a night; the profit was made on the 10 and 25¢ meals) this brick and Indiana limestone building was a milestone in concept and plan. Though tiny, every bedroom (there are 1500) has a window: either on the outside or overlooking one of two interior courts. (These courts are now paved and protected from weather with skylights; they once were grass.) Overlooking the near-derelict clientele, they are still marvelous spaces. A smaller version of the Hotel exists on the Lower East Side.

[82b.] Village Hotel, 154 Bleecker St. SW cor. Thompson St. 1832. ☆

[83.] The Macdougal-Sullivan Gardens, bet. Macdougal and Sullivan Sts., Bleecker and W. Houston Sts. ca. 1923. ☆ **170–188 Sullivan Street,** bet. Bleecker and W. Houston Sts. E side. ☆ **74–96 Macdougal Street,** bet. Bleecker and W. Houston Sts. W side. ca. 1840. 1920–1921. Arthur C. Holden. ★

The whole-block renovation started with the idea of Mr.

William Sloane Coffin (then president of W. & J. Sloane & Co.) to develop from a slum neighborhood a pleasing residence for middle-income professionals. He formed the **Hearth and Home Corporation** which bought the block, renovated it, and, by 1921, the following year, had rented nearly all the houses. Coffin's dream of a private community garden was realized around 1923; each house has its own low-walled garden that opens onto a central mall with grouped seating for adults and, at one end, a small playground.

Joe's Restaurant, 79 Macdougal St. bet. Bleecker and W. Houston Sts. CA 8-2710. Hours: noon to midnight (closed Tuesdays).

An excellent home cooked Italian meal. Specialties are hot antipasto, shrimp in wine sauce, *zabaglione* à la Joe. Wide price range.

The Half Note (jazz), 296 Spring St., SW cor. Hudson St. AL 5-9752. Hours: 9:30 PM to 3:30 AM (closed Mondays). $3.50 minimum; $4.50, weekends.

The place for authentic and avant garde jazz in the Village.

[84.] 9–29 Vandam Street (houses), bet. Sixth Ave. and Varick St. N side. ★

[85.] 15–43 Charlton Street (houses), bet. Varick St. and Sixth Ave. N side. 1824 on. ★

[86.] 15–21, 43–45 King Street (houses), bet. Sixth Ave. and Varick St. N side. 1830–1840. ★

The buildings between these fine old houses are in some ways more endearing: No. 29, Public School No. 8, New York, has a robust quality rare for school architecture, matching in spirit its neighboring tenements and those opposite it.

Richmond Hill once stood at the corner of Charlton and Varick Streets. This country mansion was built in 1767 by an English paymaster, Major Abraham Mortier. (Yes, at one time General George Washington slept here.) It was most famous, though, for the hospitality of its later owner, Vice President and Mrs. John Adams. It was bought by Aaron Burr, who, in 1797, broke up the 26 acres (leased from Trinity Parish) into lots.

At that time, Richmond Hill still stood on a 100-foot rise and had a magnificent view. But by 1811 the city's commissioners leveled this and other Village hills to their present flatness, literally taking the mansions down off their pedestals. After 1811 Richmond Hill lost its status, becoming a tavern, and finally an unsuccessful theater.

The present growth on Charlton Street didn't start until the property changed hands—from Burr to John Jacob Astor. (It later changed back to Burr.) Building began in the 1820's on this and the surrounding two blocks (King and Vandam Streets).

[87.] James Brown House, 326 Spring, bet. Greenwich and Washington Sts. 1817. ☆

[88.] 284 and 288 Hudson Street (houses), bet. Spring and Dominick Sts. E side ca. 1815.

Incredible that these remain!

End of Tour. The nearest subway is the Seventh Avenue IRT Local one block up at Varick Street and West Houston. To the east any Sixth Avenue bus goes straight uptown to 59th Street. At Houston Street (and Sixth Avenue) the number 5 bus, one of the city's nicest bus rides, goes north to Fort Tryon Park via Riverside Drive.

ASTOR PLACE/EAST VILLAGE

For one brief generation in the changing fashions of New York, **Lafayette Street** (then Lafayette **Place**) was its most wealthy and elegant residential precinct. Then running only from **Great Jones Street** to **Astor Place,** it was a short, tree-lined boulevard, flanked by town houses of **Vanderbilts, Astors** and **Delanos.** Now the trees are

gone, and only **Colonnade Row (LaGrange Terrace)** remains, albeit
in shoddy condition. Its character and quality were, however, so
strong, that they still suggest the urban and urbane qualities present
up to the Civil War. Mostly developed circa **1831,** the Street's construction replaced **Sperry's Botanic Gardens,** later **Vauxhall Gardens,** a summer entertainment enclave, where music and theatrical
performances were held in the open air. **John Lambert,** an English
traveler of **1808,** noted it as a "neat plantation...the theatrical corps
of New York City is chiefly engaged at **Vauxhall** during the summer." Only twenty years after this residential development the
Street's principal families moved away to Fifth Avenue in the thirties. At this same point in time, the **Astor Library** (later to become a
major part of New York's Public Library) and the **Cooper Union
Foundation Building** were built (started in **1854** and **1853,** respectively), seeding the precinct with different uses: now Lafayette is
primarily a light manufacturing and warehousing street, with erratic
or isolated physical remnants of past moments in its variegated history. Conversion of the Astor Library from its former use by **HIAS**
(Hebrew Immigrant Aid Society) into an indoor theater for the
Shakespeare Festival (via the good offices of the **NYC Landmarks
Commission)** offers hope for the future.

[1.] Saint Barnabas House, 304 Mulberry St. SE cor. Bleecker
St. 1949. Ketchum, Gina and Sharp.

A **modern pioneer** (though badly maintained) in these precincts,
it is a temporary "shelter" for homeless women and children.

[2.] 153 Crosby Street, bet. Houston and Bleecker Sts. ca. 1840.

A **Greek Revival** warehouse from the days when one's wares
had a house equal to the house of their owner: defaced by crude
concrete block infill, and a modern "front" on Lafayette Street.

[3.]   [5

[3.] Bayard Building/formerly **Condict Building,** 65 Bleecker St.
at Bond St. 1898. Louis H. Sullivan. ☆

This was a **radical** building in its time, a direct confrontation
with the architectural establishment that had embraced **"American
Renaissance"** architecture after the **Columbian Exposition** of **1893.**
Sullivan, the principal philosopher and leading designer of the
"Chicago School," was the employer and teacher of **Frank Lloyd
Wright.** (The sextet of angels supporting the cornice were added,
over Sullivan's objections, but still by his hand, at the request of his
client, **Silas Alden Condict**). It had little influence in New York, for,
as **Carl Condit** has stated: "Who would expect an aesthetic experience on Bleecker Street?"

[4a.] Cable Building, 621 Broadway, NW cor. Houston St. 1894.
McKim, Mead and White.

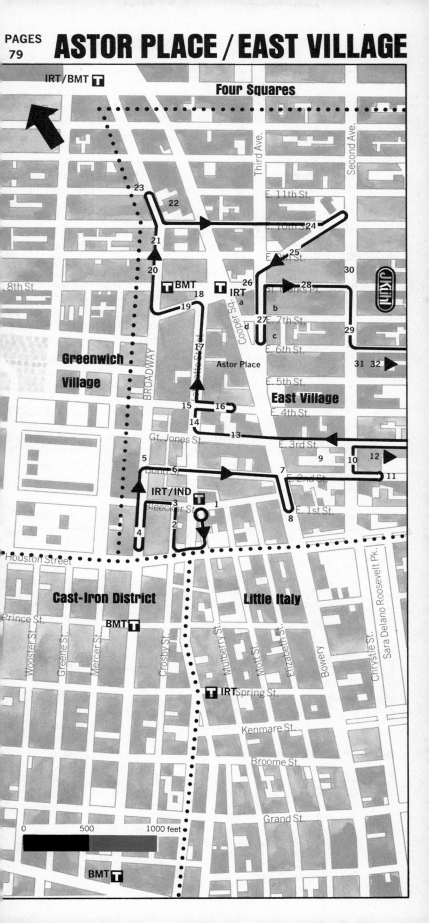

IRT/BMT 🚇

Four Squares

Third Ave.

Second Ave.

E. 11th St.

23

22

E. 10th St. 24

21

E. 9th St. 25

20

🚇 BMT   🚇 IRT

18   St. Marks Pl.   28   30

19   26   b

a

27   E. 7th St.   29

c

d

17   E. 6th St.   31   32

Greenwich

Village

BROADWAY

Astor Place

E. 5th St.

East Village

15   16   E. 4th St.

14

Gt. Jones St.   13   E. 3rd St.

5   9   10   12

Bond St.   6   7   E. 2nd St.

IRT/IND   11

3   1

Bleecker St.

4   2   8   E. 1st St.

Houston Street

Cast-Iron District   **Little Italy**

Prince St.   BMT 🚇

Wooster St.   Greene St.   Mercer St.   Crosby St.   Mulberry St.   Mott St.   Elizabeth St.   Bowery   Chrystie St.   Sara Delano Roosevelt Pk.

🚇 IRT Spring St.

Kenmare St.

Broome St.

0   500   1000 feet

Grand St.

BMT 🚇

[4b.] New York Mercantile Exchange, 626 Broadway bet. Houston St. and Bleecker St. 1860.

[5a.] Broadway Central Hotel/formerly **Grand Central Hotel** (1871–1892)/formerly **La Farge House** (1854–1869), 673 Broadway bet. Bleecker and West 3rd Sts. Rebuilt, 1871. Henry Engelbert. ☆

New York's **oldest** hotel of any size. Jim Fisk, spectacular financial speculator of the post-Civil War, was shot on the back stair by a rival in a love triangle.

[5b.] 670 Broadway/formerly **Brooks Brothers Store,** NE cor. Bond St. 1874. George E. Harney.

A romantic commercial structure (at the **third of five sequential locations** of Brooks Brothers).

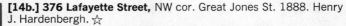

[6.] 1–5 Bond Street/formerly **Robbins and Appleton Building,** SE cor. Jones Alley. 1871. S. D. Hatch. ☆

Five white-painted stories of elegant **Corinthian** cast-iron, occupying the site of the house of **Albert Gallatin,** Jefferson's secretary of the treasury, and later Minister to France.

[7.] Bouwerie Lane Theatre/formerly **Bond Street Savings Bank,** 330 Bowery, NW cor. Bond St. 1874. Henry Engelbert. ☆

[8.] 305 Bowery, NE cor. First St. ca. 1808. ☆

The oldest extant building in these parts. Its end wall, stepped and gabled, is strong form.

[9.] New York Marble Cemetery, interior of the block bet. 2nd and 3rd Sts., Second Ave. and the Bowery. 1830. ☆

One of the earliest sophistications of burial practices, anticipating, and therefore preventing, a **"marble orchard"**; the interred are noted by tablets inlaid in the perimeter brick wall.

[10.] Church of The Nativity, 46 Second Ave. bet. 2nd and 3rd Sts. 1832. Town and Davis (A. J. Davis, J. H. Dakin and James Gallier). ☆   Now a seedy and uncared-for remnant.

[11.] New York City Marble Cemetery, 52–74 East 2nd St bet. First and Second Aves. 1832. ☆

President James Monroe was originally interred in this one of two remaining cemeteries in a part of town that contained many in the 1830–1850 period. The latest burial there took place as late as 1964.

[12.] First Houses, 2nd to 3rd Sts. and Avenue A. 1935.

The first houses built, or rather rebuilt in this instance, by the N.Y.C. Housing Authority. In a block of tenements every third was demolished, allowing the remaining pairs light and air on three exposures. This, as a remodeling, and **Williamsburgh Houses** as new construction, are still the brightest lights in the history of this city's public housing.

[13.] Engine Co. No. 33, 44 Great Jones St. (Third St.), bet. Lafayette St. and the Bowery. 1898. Ernest Flagg and W. B. Chambers. ☆

[14b.] 376 Lafayette Street, NW cor. Great Jones St. 1888. Henry J. Hardenbergh. ☆

Free-swinging **Romanesque Revival** by the architect who has graced New York with more romantic symbolism than any other.

[15.] 399 Lafayette Street/formerly **DeVinne Press Building,** NE cor. 4th St. 1885. Babb, Cook & Willard. ★

A powerful brick building in the utilitarian manner of late 19th Century industrial buildings. The waterfront of Brooklyn is graced with the poor country cousins of this magnificent pile. Certainly, here is a sample of "less is more," when juxtaposed with 376 down the block.

[16a.] Old Merchant's House/formerly **Seabury Treadwell House,** 29 E. 4th St. bet. Lafayette St. and the Bowery. 1832. Attributed to Minard Lafever. ★

Relic from New York's past when blocks surrounding this spot had houses of equal quality. A foundation now keeps it. Open to the public.

[16b.] 37 East 4th Street, bet. Lafayette St. and the Bowery. ca. 1830.

[17a.] New York Shakespeare Festival/formerly **Hebrew Immigrant Aid Society/**originally **the Astor Library,** 425 Lafayette St. bet. 4th St. and Astor Pl. 1849–1881. Center Section, Griffith Thomas; South Section, Thomas Thomas; North Section, Thomas Stent. Remodeled, 1967. Giorgio Cavaglieri. ★

John Jacob Astor here contributed New York's first free library, later combined with its peers (**Lenox Library,** which was sited where the **Frick Collection** is today, and the **Tilden Foundation**) to form the central branch of the New York Public Library at 42nd Street. A central skylit space formed the main reading room, off which supporting library spaces were strung. Now this grand core contains

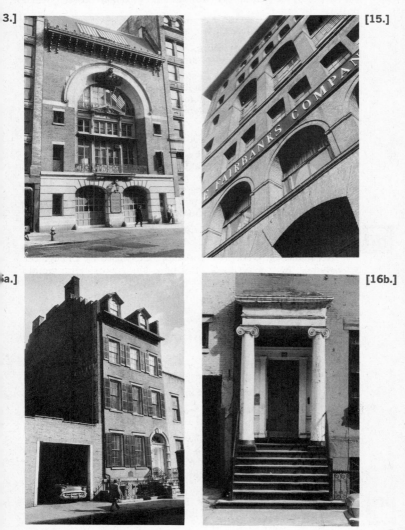

a 300-seat theater for **Joseph Papp's** Shakespearean repertory.

[17b.] Colonnade Row/also known as **LaGrange Terrace,** 428–434 Lafayette St. bet. 4th St. and Astor Pl. 1833. Alexander Jackson

Davis. ★

Four of nine houses built speculatively by **Seth Geer** in **1831.** Five at the south end were demolished for the still existing **Wanamaker warehouse.** An elegant urban arrangement of private structures subordinated to an imposing **Corinthian** colonnade (compare the **Rue de Rivoli** in Paris). **Delanos, Astors** and **Vanderbilts** lived here, until their game of "social" musical chairs sent them uptown.

[18.] District 65 Building/formerly **Mercantile Library Building,** 13 Astor Pl. bet. Astor Pl. and 8th St. at Fourth Ave. 1890. George E. Harney.

Harney's ode to **Ruskin** at 670 Broadway 16 years earlier is here replaced by an "establishment" Harney.

District 65 rests on the site of the **Astor Place Opera House,** where, in **May, 1849,** rioting between the competing claques of the American actor, **Forrest,** and the English actor, **Macready,** caused the death of 34 stalwarts. The **Seventh Regiment** quartered in an armory on the site of the present **Hewitt Building** of **Cooper Union,** quelled the passions forcibly.

[19.] 442 Lafayette Street, SW cor. Astor Pl. ca. 1885.

[20.] "New" Wanamaker Store, Broadway to Fourth Ave. 9th to 10th St. 1903. Daniel H. Burnham and Co.

This squat and stolid 15-story monolith contains approximately as much space as the **Empire State Building!** No courtyards subtract space, as in normal structures, for this was built as a selling store, although used by the **Federal Government** today for its own mysterious purposes.

[21.] Stewart House, 60 East 10th St. 1961.

This site was once graced by one of the finest cast-iron, post-Civil War buildings of New York: the **"old" Wanamaker store.** Built around a central court rising through the building to a huge skylight, it was the most gracious shopping space in New York, in European tradition of a **galleria** (the concept of the bazaar comprehensible as a whole, yet subdivided into articulated specialty shops).

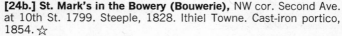 **[22.] Grace Church (Protestant Episcopal),** 800 Broadway, Broadway to Fourth Ave. at 10th St. 1846. James Renwick, Jr. ★

A magnificent **Gothic Revival** church, designed by an engineer who studied the copybooks of the **Pugins,** the great English Gothic theorists and detailers. At the bend of Broadway, its tower dominates the vista from the south.

[23a.] 806 Broadway, opposite 11th St. 1888. Renwick, Aspinwall and Russell.

A **Gothic Revival** wall provides a visual backdrop for **Grace Church,** by Renwick's later firm.

[23b.] 801–807 Broadway/formerly **James McCreery Store,** NW cor. 11th St. 1868. John Kellum. ☆

Cast-iron, neatly maintained in battleship gray.

[24a.] "Renwick" Triangle, 114–128 10th St. 23–35 Stuyvesant St. embraced by Stuyvesant and 10th St. ca. 1880.

Building with differing plans, but uniform facades (actual buildings vary in depth from 16 to 48 feet, in width from 16 to 32 feet) make a handsome urban grouping, being carefully restored by new owners as one- and two-family houses. **Stanford White** was born at **118 East 10th Street.**

[24b.] St. Mark's in the Bowery (Bouwerie), NW cor. Second Ave. at 10th St. 1799. Steeple, 1828. Ithiel Towne. Cast-iron portico, 1854. ☆

Only **St. Paul's Chapel** is older than this handsome church, built on the site of a garden chapel of **Peter Stuyvesant's** estate.

The interior is typical of many handsome churches of the pre- and post-Revolutionary War period (cf., **St. Paul's Chapel, Mariner's Temple**). The graveyard is interesting in that it contains the Stuyvesant vault and was the scene of the A. T. Stewart body-snatching episode in 1878.

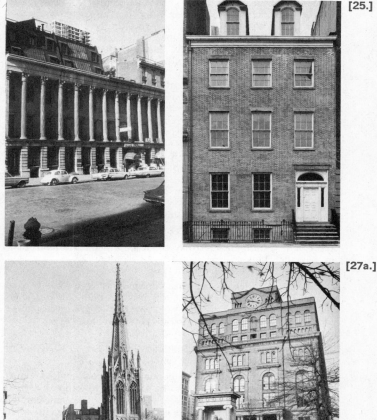

Peter Stuyvesant's mansion sat roughly at the intersection of **Tenth** and **Stuyvesant Streets,** and Second Avenue. The Bowery was then the Bouwerie (Dutch, for "farm") Road, bounding the southwest flank of the Stuyvesant estate (which extended north to 23rd Street, east to Avenue C, and south to 3rd Street). **Stuyvesant Street** was the driveway from the **Bouwerie Road** to the ex-governor's mansion.

[25.] Stuyvesant-Fish House, 21 Stuyvesant St. bet. Third and Second Ave. 1804. ★

A fat Federal house, of width unusual for its time: only five years newer than the body of **St. Mark's** down the block. **Nicholas Stuyvesant** lived here, **Hamilton Fish** was born here.

[26.] Cooper Union Engineering Building, 8th to 9th St. Fourth to Third Ave. 1961. Vorhees, Walker, Smith, Smith, and Haines.

This neither conforms to the street pattern, nor establishes an alternative. The building could equally well be on a freestanding rural site.

[27a.] Cooper Union Foundation Building, 7th St. to Astor Pl. Fourth Ave. to the Bowery, on Cooper Square. 1859. Frederick A. Peterson. ★

A high-rise brownstone, **Cooper Union** is the **oldest extant building** framed with steel beams in America. **Peter Cooper,** its founder and benefactor, in the great Victorian paternalistic tradition (he gave presents to Cooper Union on his birthday), was a partner of **Samuel F. B. Morse** in laying the first Atlantic cable; builder of the **Tom Thumb** steam locomotive, and, as an iron-maker, rolled the first steel railroad rails. Such rails were used as Cooper Union's beams, spanning between brick bearing walls. In turn, brick floor arches jump from rail to rail. The facade is in the same **Italian-ate** brownstone tradition popular at the time with cast-iron designers (see 6.), but heavier, as it is in masonry except at the ground floor. In the 1860's the first and second floors were shops rented to the public; the reestablishment of such uses would lend much life and activity to what is now a dead urban area.

The Bowery, popularly known for its "bums", is much more complex than that. South from **Cooper Square to Canal Street,** the vista includes the center of commercial kitchen equipment distribution and manufacturing of New York, and one of the principal wholesale lighting fixture precincts of the city. Interspersed are the hotels **(flophouses to some),** resting places of the unwanted, the alcoholic, the derelict.

[27b.] First Ukrainian Assembly of God/formerly the **Metropolitan Savings Bank,** 59–61 Third Ave. NE cor. Cooper Sq. and Seventh St. 1868. Attributed to Carl Pfeiffer. ☆

Marble parallel to the then-current **Cast-Iron** world: such **material** denoted class (cast iron was used to gain elaboration **inexpensively).** The church use is a happy fate to preserve a grand old neighborhood friend...not too old, however; McSorley's Saloon down the block is 14 years its senior.

[27c.] Cooper Union Hewitt Building, Cooper Sq. to Hall Pl. 6th to 7th St. 1905. Clinton and Russell.

In the effort to honor the donor, a pompous and unrelated architecture is introduced; built, by the way, to support several more floors on the existing steel and foundations. The **Ionic** column in the main entryway is the **white elephant gift** of the Hewitt sisters (Cooper's granddaughters), who gave the building.

[27d.] Peter Cooper's Statue, in Cooper Sq., off 7th St. 1897. Augustus St. Gaudens, Sculptor; Stanford White, Architect of the base.

[28a.] Deutsch-Amerikanische Schuetzen Gesellschaft, 12 St. Mark's Pl. bet. Third and Second Ave. 1885.

A German shooting club reveled here, and shot elsewhere.

[28b.] 20 St. Mark's Place/formerly **Daniel LeRoy House,** 1832.

Greek Revival swings again as an expresso cafe. ☆
Bowl & Board, 7 St. Mark's Pl.

This small basement shop vends laminated chopping blocks.

St. Mark's Place, although the standard width **(60 feet)** in theory, is actually wider, as most of the buildings are built (unusual for Manhattan) ten feet back of their respective property lines. The cast-iron stairs jumping from street to parlor floors modulate it: matter-of-fact, pop-sculpture. Basement shops of considerable design elegance now line both sides, including those for **dresses, jewelry, beads, buttons** & **posters.** A somewhat seedy **Turkish bath** rounds out this block, the swinging area of what is now called Village East. (Artists from Greenwich Village have largely fled increasingly soaring rents. They who made it famous and desirable now must go elsewhere.)

[29.] Isaac T. Hopper Home, 110 Second Ave. 1839. ☆

A very grand (for its surrounds) late **Federal** building. "Wayward" girls, to use the **Horatio Alger** term, are here given a chance to rehabilitate themselves.

[30.] New York Public Library, Ottendorfer Branch, 135 Second Ave. bet. St. Mark's Pl. and 9th St. ca. 1890.

Originally a free German public library in the period of heavy German immigration to these surrounding streets. Note the equally ornate and unfortunately painted (white) **Stuyvesant Polyclinic** adjacent.

[31.] Community Synagogue Center/formerly **United German Lutheran Church,** 323 East 6th St. bet. Second and First Ave. 1848. ☆

[32a.] Tompkins Square Park, 7th to 10th St. Avenues A to B.
Sixteen blessed acres, in these tight and dense streets.

[32b.] Riis Plaza, in Jacob Riis Houses, 6th to 10th Sts. Avenue D to the East River Dr. 1966. Pomerance and Breines, Architects; M. Paul Friedberg, Landscape Architect.

This is well worth the trip. Public space (between buildings) is usually either filled with traffic or parked cars, or grassed and fenced off from the pedestrian. Here is space made available, in a construction to delight all ages: pyramids to climb on for the small, an amphitheater that spans all age groups, places to **sit, stand, walk, talk, hop, skip, scoot** and **tag.** Given an asphalt street down the block from a local park, kids will most frequently pick the street to play; Riis is planned to be the alternate to streets; and is where the action is in these parts, these days.

Entertainment, Stimuli and a Full Stomach

To appreciate the buildings and urban design of the area, the **"native"** cuisine adds greatly:

Ratner's Restaurant, 111 Second Ave. bet. 6th and 7th Sts.

A famous **Kosher** (dairy) restaurant, featuring **Blintzes,** lox and cream cheese on a bagel, matzoh brei (a matzoh omelet), and scrambled eggs with a variety of ingredients: peppers, lox, et cetera. One can make a meal largely on the rolls (soft, glazed and seeded) at every table.

Rapoport's Restaurant, 93 Second Ave. bet. 5th and 6th St.

The "peoples" Ratner's: try the barley soup.

McSorley's Old Ale House/formerly **McSorley's Saloon,** 15 East 7th St. bet. Cooper Sq. and Second Ave.

Opened in **1854,** the year construction on Cooper Union started, it was made famous by painter **Reginald Marsh** and the **New Yorker** stories by **Joseph Mitchell.** Ale, brewed to their own formula, is sold in pairs of steins, two for a quarter; lunch is cheap and good.

The Surma Book and Record Company, 11 East 7th St. bet. Cooper Sq. and Second Ave.

A fascinating **Ukrainian** store (books, records, Ukrainian decorated **Easter Eggs)** retains the old flavor of this neighborhood's Eastern European society.

Booksellers' Row, up Fourth Ave. and Broadway from Cooper Sq. to Union Sq.

Lined with bookshops with old, frequently fascinating, and sometimes rare books. The **Strand,** at Fourth Avenue and 12th Street, sells quantities of reviewer's copies at half price; and all have books sorted by topic. The least expensive are displayed on racks along the street, a browser's delight, particularly in balmy weather.

Il Faro East Italian and French Restaurant, 325 East 14th St. bet. First and Second Aves. GR 7-9999.

A garden is available. Open every day including **Sunday.**

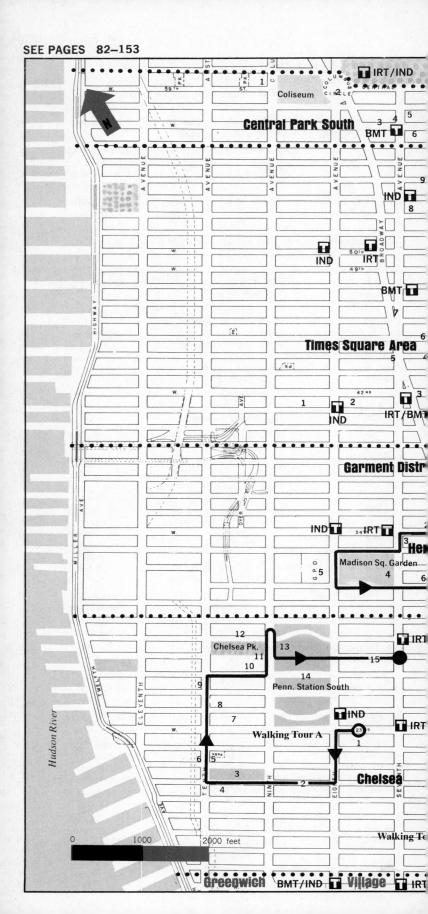

W. 59TH ST.

PK. ST.

1

Coliseum

COLUMBUS CIRCLE

T IRT/IND

CENTRAL PARK

2

Central Park South

3 4 5

BMT T 6

AVENUE

AVENUE

AVENUE

AVENUE

AVENUE

9

IND T

8

W.

BROADWAY

50TH

IND T IRT T

49TH

W.

BMT T

7

PL.

Times Square Area

5

6

42ND

3

T

1 2

IND IRT/BMT

Garment District

AVE.

MILLER AVE.

DYER AVE.

IND T 34TH IRT T

3 Herald

G.P.O.

Madison Sq. Garden

5 4 6

HIGHWAY

T IRT

12

Chelsea Pk. 13

11 15

10

TWELFTH

ELEVENTH

14

Penn. Station South

9

8

T IND

7

23 T IRT

Walking Tour A

1

Hudson River

6

5

3

2

Chelsea

4

NINTH

EIGHTH

SEVENTH

TENTH

0 1000 2000 feet

Walking Tour

T BMT/IND T **Village** T IRT

Greenwich

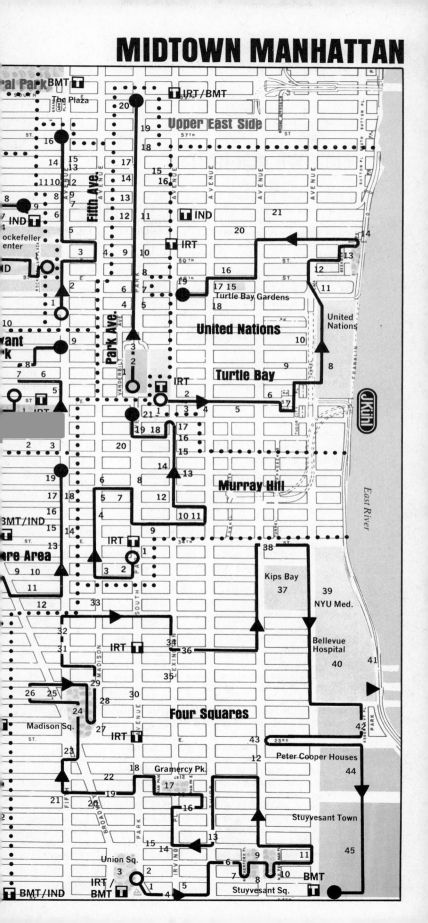

MIDTOWN MANHATTAN

M

MIDTOWN MANHATTAN

If Manhattan is the center of the city, Midtown is **the center of the center.** Here are most of the elements one expects to find in a city core: the major **railroad** and **airline terminals,** the vast majority of **hotel rooms,** the **biggest stores,** the **main public library** and **post office.** Of the four major activities that sustain New York, two—the **garment industry** and the **offices of nationwide corporations**—are concentrated in Midtown. Another of the four—**shipping**—is seen here at its most glamorous, in the **docks of the great liners.** Only one—the **financial center**—is concentrated in **another part of the island.**

Social status in Midtown once followed a **clearcut pattern:** all the fashionable shops and living quarters ran up a central spine along **Fifth and Park Avenues.** But **Central Park,** by driving a cleft between this spine and the Upper West Side, **diverted fashionable Manhattan a bit to the east,** and the purposeful development of **Park Avenue** in the 1920's shifted the weight a bit further, encouraging some colonies of high society to move far to the east. With the construction of the **United Nations Headquarters** on the East River, a **whole new profile** took shape.

CHELSEA

Almost a century and a half of ups and downs have left Chelsea **a patchwork** of town houses, tenements, factories, and housing projects. The name was originally given by **Captain Thomas Clarke** to his estate, **staked out in 1750,** which extended roughly from the present 14th to 27th Streets, from Seventh Avenue west to the Hudson, boundaries which still apply except that the northern one is now at about 30th Street.

Captain Clarke's grandson, **Clement Clarke Moore,** who grew up in the family mansion just southwest of the present corner of 23rd Street and Eighth Avenue, was the one who **divided the estate up** into lots about 1830. Moore, noted as a biblical scholar in his time, is remembered now mainly for his poem *A Visit from Saint Nicholas,* which sealed the unscholarly but imperishable connection between Saint Nick and Christmas. Moore donated one choice block for the **General Theological Seminary,** which is still there, and the surrounding blocks prospered as a desirable suburb. Then the **Hudson River Railroad** opened along Eleventh Avenue in 1851, began to fill nearby blocks with slaughterhouses, breweries, and so on, followed quickly by the shanties and tenements of workers.

In 1871, the **dignity of town house blocks,** unaffected by the railroad, was **shattered by the steam locomotives** of New York's first elevated railroad, which ran up Ninth Avenue. In the 1870's, a **declining Chelsea** was brightened by the blossoming of the city's **theater district** along West 23rd Street. For a decade or so, these blocks were ideally convenient to both the **high society** of Madison Square and the **flourishing vice district** along Sixth Avenue in the upper 20's and 30's. When the theater world moved uptown, artists and literati stayed on to make Chelsea **New York's Bohemia;** early in this century Bohemia moved south to Greenwich Village, but the writers never quite deserted 23rd Street.

Around 1905–1915, **a new art form,** the motion picture, was centered in Chelsea, whose old lofts and theaters made economical studios, but the **sunshine of Hollywood** soon lured the industry away. In the 1920's and 1930's, Chelsea got a lift from some impressive new **industrial buildings** near the piers and some **luxury apartments** inland. But the greatest improvements were on the grade-level freight line, long since part of the New York Central, which ran along Eleventh Avenue (a **"Death Avenue Cowboy"** riding on horseback and carrying a red flag of warning ahead of each train); it was replaced by an inconspicuous through-the-block elevated line just west of Tenth Avenue. During World War II, the rattling **Ninth Avenue "el"** was finally torn down.

In the 1950's and 1960's public housing and urban renewal uprooted some large chunks of slum housing, and rehabilitation of Chelsea's many fine town houses followed **a slow upward trend.**

Walking Tour A: From West 23rd Street between Seventh and Eighth Avenues (23rd St. stations of IRT Seventh Avenue or IND Eighth Avenue Subways) to Seventh Avenue and 27th Street (one block south of IRT Seventh Avenue 28th Street station).

Best time for tour is Sunday morning, when churches are open.

[1a.] Chelsea Hotel, 222 W. 23rd St. bet. Seventh and Eighth Aves. 1884. Hubert, Pirsson & Co. ★

Built as one of the city's first cooperative apartment houses, the Chelsea became a hotel in 1905, but has a high ratio of permanent tenants even today. The 12-story **brick bearing-wall structure** has been called Victorian Gothic, but its style is hard to pin down. The most prominent exterior features are the **delicate iron balconies,** made by **J. B. and J. M. Cornell,** that screen the hefty brickwork. Of four bronze plaques around the entrance, one concerns the building; the other three honor **writers who have lived here:** Thomas Wolfe, Dylan Thomas, and Brendan Behan, three of **a long list that runs from Mark Twain and O. Henry** to **Tennessee Williams and Jessica Mitford.** Guests from other arts have included Sarah Bernhardt, Virgil Thomson, John Sloan, and Larry Rivers. Edgar Lee Masters wrote a poem about the Chelsea and **Andy Warhol** made it the scene of his movie **"Chelsea Girls."** The lobby is a bit of a letdown, but the rooms are reported to be well kept and full of **Edwardian atmosphere** — and quite reasonable by midtown standards.

[1b.] 240, 244, and 248 West 23rd Street, bet. Seventh and Eighth Aves.

Just to the west of the Chelsea, a row of commercial buildings with fanciful facades of brick, stone, and cast iron.

Cavanaugh's Restaurant, 256 W. 23rd St. AL 5-1100.

Serving up Irish and American fare here since 1876. The front is tricked out in Gay Nineties style, but the interior still looks much as it did when Diamond Jim Brady escorted Lillian Russell here.

Grand Opera House stood on the northwest corner of 23rd Street and Eighth Avenue until 1960, when land was cleared for the surrounding Penn Station South. [See Chelsea 14.] Bought by the notorious financier, impresario, and bon vivant, "Jubilee" Jim Fisk, in the late 1860's, it did double service as head office of his Erie Railroad. It withstood repeated assaults by irate Erie stockholders (with steel doors reputed to be 12 inches thick) and was the scene of Fisk's funeral in 1872, after he was shot by Edward S. Stokes, hot-blooded third corner of a triangle whose apex was the Josie Mansfield, Fisk's one-time mistress.

[2a.] St. Peter's Church (Episcopal), 344 W. 20th St. bet. Eighth and Ninth Aves. 1836–1838. James W. Smith, Builder, after designs by Clement Clarke Moore. ☆

[2b.] St. Peter's Rectory, 346 W. 20th St. bet. Eighth and Ninth Aves. 1831–1832. ☆

These two buildings form a remarkable study in the popular adaptation of styles. **The rectory,** which apparently served first as the church, is in a very **stripped-down Greek Revival style,** but its **fine proportions** give it **dignity.** By the time the much larger church was built, the congregation was ready to make one of New York's earliest ventures into the **Gothic Revival.** Its fieldstone walls, massively buttressed, with spare trim of cut granite, give it **a military look.**

The third building in the group, **the hall east of the church,** is an example of later common-brick Gothic, started in 1854 and given its **strangely church-like front** in 1871. The wrought-iron fence along the street is older than *any* of the buildings. It dates from about 1790 and was a **hand-me-down** from **venerable Trinity Church,** which was putting up its third edifice in the 1830's.

Around the church are many **interesting town houses.**

Oldest Building in Chelsea: Clearly visible from the corner of 20th Street and Ninth Avenue. A house dating from 1785, it stands at the northwest corner of 21st Street and Ninth Avenue (183 Ninth Avenue), its ground floor occupied by a store, but its original gabled roof and dormers intact.

[3a.] General Theological Seminary, W. 20th St. bet. Ninth and Tenth Aves. Main buildings, 1883–1900. Charles C. Haight.

[3b.] West Building, General Theological Seminary, "5 and 6 Chelsea Square," W. 20th St. bet. Ninth and Tenth Aves. N side. 1836.

The stoutly fenced full city block of the seminary is accessible, if at all, through the recent (1960) building on the Ninth Avenue front, but the major buildings can be seen from 20th Street. The **West Building,** one of the oldest examples of Gothic Revival in the city, was modeled after an even earlier, matching **East Building** (built, 1827; razed, 1892). Haight's surrounding red brick and brownstone buildings are, for their period, **quite simple in massing and ornament.**

[4a.] 404–418 West 20th Street, bet. Ninth and Tenth Aves. 1830's or 1840's.

Built by **Don Alonzo Cushman** (Don was his *first* name), a friend of Clement Moore, who became a millionaire developing Chelsea. Their fine Greek Revival detail, except for losses here and there, is intact: tiny, **wreath-encircled attic windows;** deeply recessed doorways with brownstone frames; **handsome iron balustrades,** newels, and fences.

[4b.] 446, 448, 450 West 20th Street, bet. Ninth and Tenth Aves.

[5.] 465–473 West 21st Street, NE cor. Tenth Ave.

Five exceptional Italianate brick houses facing the austere rear walls of the seminary.

[6.] Church of the Guardian Angel (Roman Catholic), Tenth Ave. NW cor. 21st St. 1930. John Van Pelt.

Also known as the "Shrine Church of the Sea," it serves a parish with many sailors' lodgings.

[4a.]

[4b.]

[3b.]

[7.] London Terrace, W. 23rd to W. 24th Sts., Tenth to Ninth Aves. 1930. Farrar & Watmaugh.

This vast buff brick pile, in **protomodern planar style** with faintly Gothic verticality, is actually two rows of connected apartment buildings flanking **a block-long private garden.** All in all, it contains 1670 units, with swimming pool, solarium, and shops and banks on the avenue fronts. The name comes from **a row of four-story houses** that once stretched along the same 23rd Street frontages, facing the 18th Century Clarke mansion. When the present complex was new, doormen were **dressed as London "bobbies,"** as a play on the name.

Two Scavenging Spots occupy shabby buildings across the avenue from London Terrace. "Stuff and Nonsense" (227 Tenth Avenue) is a typical modern off-beat fashion, houseware, and poster emporium with a used furniture basement. "The Pottery Barn" (231 Tenth Avenue) is a very busy four-floor bargain loft for pottery, glass, housewares, and furniture.

[8a.]

[1

[8a.] 437–461 West 24th Street, bet. Tenth and Ninth Aves.

Just east of Tenth Avenue is a small, two-story Greek Revival house (Celia Beauty Shoppe) dating from the 1830's. To the east of it is a row of later Italianate brick houses (Nos. 437-459), unusual in being set well back from the street.

[8b.] 242–258 Tenth Avenue, bet. 24th and 25th Sts. E side.

[9.] H. Wolff Book Manufacturing Co./formerly **Williams Company Warehouse,** 259–273 Tenth Ave. bet. W. 25th and W. 26th Sts. W side.

Ten-story block of bare reinforced concrete, with conventional influence in massing and modeling of facade, but no nonessentials.

[10.] The Hudson Guild, 441 W. 26th St. S side of Chelsea Park bet. Tenth and Ninth Aves. 1967. Edelbaum & Webster.

[11a.] Public School 33, Manhattan, Ninth Ave. NW cor. 26th St. 1952. Eric Kebbon.

In a 1952 *New Yorker* "Sky Line" piece, Lewis Mumford praised this school for its genial scale and dynamic massing, comparing it with the "funereally decorated" health center to the north. Fifteen years later, the difference in quality is hard to distinguish.

[11b.] District Health Center, 303 Ninth Ave. SW cor. 28th St. 1936.

Monumental buff brick and polished black granite. Modernistic.

[12a.] Model Tenement, 441 W. 28th St. bet. Tenth and Ninth Aves. 1916. ~~DEMOLISHED~~

Built as a demonstration by the Hudson Guild, it is now distinguished from its neighbors mainly by its less ornate facade.

[12b.] 403–405 West 28th Street, near Ninth Ave.

Two isolated houses, set back, with rare vine-covered verandas.

[13.] Church of the Holy Apostles (Episcopal), 300 Ninth Ave. SE cor. 28th St. 1846–1848. Minard Lafever. Transepts, 1858, Richard Upjohn & Sons. ☆

This remarkably independent work, now threatened with visible deterioration, fits into no stylistic slot. It has been called an early effort at Romanesque Revival, but its brick details, **bracketed eaves,** and its **unique bronze and slate spire**—completely dominating the low nave—mark it as an equally early appearance of Italianate style, rarely seen in churches. The interior has the simple **barrel-vaulted geometry** of early Italian Renaissance, without the classical details. The windows, by **William Jay Bolton,** are as unusual as the building, if less vigorous; each is composed of square panels of colorful abstract design, with central medallions painted in delicate, monochrome, realistic style.

[14.] Penn Station South, 23rd to 29th Sts., Ninth to Eighth Aves. 1962. Herman Jessor.

This 2820-unit urban-renewal development is a cooperative sponsored by the International Ladies' Garment Workers Union ("ladies'" refers to the *garments*), conveniently located at the southwest corner of the **Garment District** (which extends north to 40th Street and east to Fifth Avenue).

[13.]

Belly-Dancing Center of the Western World: Around Eighth Avenue between 28th and 29th Streets. Exotic night clubs, remnant of a 19th Century Greek colony that later spread north up Eighth Avenue, are housed in a rich variety of Victorian buildings. Their names—Grecian Cave, Ali Baba, Britannia, Arabian Nights, Egyptian Gardens, Port Said, and Istanbul—show some geographical confusion, which extends to the dancers themselves, many reported to be just plain American although quite accomplished.

[15a.] Fashion Institute of Technology, W. 27th St. bet. Eighth and Seventh Aves. **Main Building,** N side, 1958; **[15b.] Nagler Hall** (dormitory), S side, 1962. Both by DeYoung & Moscowitz.

End of tour. IRT Seventh Avenue Subway's 28th Street station is the closest.

Walking Tour B: From 23rd Street and Avenue of the Americas (Sixth Avenue) south to 14th Street. IND Sixth Avenue Subway to 23rd Street station.

Sixth Avenue Magazines: The block-long ghosts lining Sixth Avenue (officially Avenue of the Americas) recall the latter part of the 19th Century when this was fashion row. Though now all used for loft and office space, their splendor is still quite evident. "Meet you at the fountain!" [See Chelsea 22.]

[16.] Stern Brothers Department Store, 695–711 Sixth Ave. bet. 23rd and 22nd Sts. W side.

A high quality cast iron facade; where Sterns (now on 42nd Street overlooking Bryant Park) got its start.

[17.] Adams Dry Goods Store, 675–691 Sixth Ave. bet. 22nd and 21st Sts. W side.

[18a.] Third Cemetery of the Spanish-Portuguese Synagogue, Shearith Israel, 98–110 W. 21st St. bet. Sixth and Seventh Aves. 1829–1851. ☆

Contained by painted brick loft buildings on three sides, this is a handsome, though private, oasis graced with a venerable ailanthus tree. This cemetery is one of three on Manhattan Island (the youngest of the trio). [See Civic Center 27a; Greenwich Village 54a.]

[18b.]

[18b.] Hugh O'Neill Department Store, 655–671 Sixth Ave. bet. 21st and 20th Sts. ca. 1875.

Cast iron Corinthian columned and pilastered facade, with almost full circle towers interlocked at its two corners. The name remains clearly visible in relief at the pediment.

Bazar Francais, 666 Sixth Ave. bet. 21st and 20th Sts. CH 3-6660.

Tous les articles pour la cuisine, comme les moulins, plus les poteries.

[19.] Church of the Holy Communion, 47 W. 20th St. NE cor. Sixth Ave. 1846. Richard Upjohn. ☆

More notable because Upjohn did it, than because of its intrinsic architectural quality.

[20.] Simpson–Crawford Department Store, 641 Sixth Ave. bet. 20th and 19th Sts. W side.

Seven stories of limestone, a sober work of architecture.

[21.] B. Altman Department Store/now **Warner Hudnut Building,** 621 Sixth Ave. bet. 19th and 18th Sts. W side. 1876–1880. D. & J. Jardine.

B. Altmans (or Baltmans to some) forsook this cast iron emporium for its imposing stone edifice at Fifth Avenue and 34th.

[22.] Siegel–Cooper Department Store/now **television scenic studio,** 616–632 Sixth Ave. bet. 19th and 18th Sts. E side. 1896. De Lemos & Cordes.

Fifteen-and-a-half acres of space are contained in this latecomer to the area. **Elaborately embellished** in glazed terra cotta, it clearly bears the stamp of the **Chicago World's Fair Style** of 1893. At one time it was a favored meeting place; "Meet you at the fountain!" referring to the jet of water graced by the figure of the Republic by **Daniel Chester French** (now reposing at California's Forest Lawn Cemetery). After a brief but turbulent history it was converted to a military hospital during World War I.

End of tour: The Sixth Avenue IND 14th Street station is the nearest although a short walk along the street will get you to a wide range of rapid transit.

MISCELLANY

[23.] National Maritime Union, Joseph Curran Annex, 346 W. 17th St. bet. Eighth and Ninth Aves. 1966. Albert C. Ledner.

A startling white tile-faced, **porthole-pierced** front wall sloping **8½ degrees from vertical** was the architect's way of meeting the setback requirement of the *old* Zoning Law. **As novel as the union's main building** [See Greenwich Village 65] on the exterior, the building is efficiently laid out inside to accommodate "retraining and upgrading programs" for about **2000 seamen a year** as well as medical and recreational facilities for union members.

[23.]

[24.] Starrett–Lehigh Building, W. 26th to W. 27th St., Eleventh to Twelfth Aves. 1931. Russel G. and Walter M. Cory; Yatsuo Matsui, associated architect.

Literally miles of strip windows and bands of brick, streaking and swerving around this block-square, 19-story factory-warehouse structure have made it a landmark of modern architecture ever since it rose over the air rights Lehigh Valley Railroad Freight terminal.

Famous Players in Famous Plays: Adolph Zukor, who originated this title, produced a number of old films in Chelsea. Nor was his the only studio, others being Kalem, Charles O. Bauman & Adam Kessel Films, Reliance, Majestic, etc. Famous Players Studios was at 221 West 26th Street; its roster of stars contained such names as Mary Pickford and John Barrymore.

THE FOUR SQUARES

More than a hundred years ago, the laying out of Gramercy, Union, Stuyvesant, and Madison Squares gave promise of urbane residential precincts for wealthy New Yorkers.

Union Square. First Union Place, it joined the Bloomingdale Road (Broadway) from the north, to the Bowery Road (Fourth Avenue) from the south. Before the Civil War, it was a grand **residential** square, with a **private park,** locked and gated for the residents surrounding it (as Gramercy Park still is today). In 1854, the first glimmer of its future as a new **theatrical district** appeared with the opening of the **Academy of Music** (opposite its movie palace namesake of today and where now are the Consolidated Edison offices). When it later became the center of "radicalism," thousands of **protesters** here waited news of the execution of **Sacco** and **Vanzetti.** May Day celebrations were centered here, the precinct of the *Daily Worker,* and many other more or less **radical publications** and organizations were in the neighborhood.

Walking Tour: From Union Square to First Avenue at East 14th Street via Gramercy Park, Madison Square Park, Stuyvesant Square. (Arrive via Lexington Avenue IRT, 14th Street station; or BMT Subway, Union Square station.)

[1.] S. Klein's, 6 Union Square bet. 14th and 15th Sts. E side.

A clutch of small buildings serves the most modest woman's budget, occasionally with high style for those who search the racks frequently and with keen eyes. Some day you will find that $5 Dior or $1 Chanel skirt here. Chic and tawdry intermixed place the burden on customer talent! (Annex is between 15th and 16th Streets.)

[2.] Union Square Savings Bank, 20 Union Square, NE cor. 15th St. 1907. Henry Bacon.

A classy Corinthian colonnade is somewhat forlorn in these precincts.

[3.] Union Square, 14th to 17th St., Union Square West to Park Ave. South.

Small crowds still assemble here around their favorite debater to heckle, support, or berate him; New York's "Hyde Park" was made a sacred precinct for orators and agitators after police excesses in repressing the Depression unemployment rallies of 1930.

Washington, (H. K. Brown, Sculptor). A copy of a Houdon original, erected in 1856, it is the oldest statue in New York in its original location. Brown also contributed **Lincoln** in 1866; and in 1876, Bartholdi, sculptor of the Statue of Liberty, left **Lafayette** as token of Franco-American relations (early in his indefatigable campaign to raise funds for "Liberty").

[4.] Lüchow's, 110 E. 14th St., at Irving Pl.

One of the great gastronomic landmarks of New York. This is North German, not Chinese! There are few places where schmaltz is dished out in **both** quality and quantity; this wins crossed forks for both. With an ancient band playing "Tales from the Vienna Woods," aged and mellowed mahogany, and mirrors, sauerbraten, dumplings, and draft German beer.

[5.] Consolidated Edison Company, 4 Irving Pl., NE cor. 14th St. 1915–1929. Henry J. Hardenbergh. Tower, 1926, Warren and Wetmore.

A landmark clock tops Con Ed's GHQ. This is the site of the old "Academy of Music"; its namesake, a movie theater, is opposite.

[6.] St. George's Church, Rutherford Pl., NW cor. 16th St. facing Stuyvesant Square. 1856. Restored, 1897. Blesch and Eidlitz. ★

Parish House, 207 E. 16th St. 1887. Cyrus L. W. Eidletz. **Chapel,** 4 Rutherford Pl. 1911. M. L. and H. G. Emory. ☆

J. P. Morgan's church. Stolid brownstone, cut and dressed.

The Electric Heating Association,
on behalf of its electric utility company
and its manufacturing company members, is pleased to
play a part in making possible this
publication on one of the world's great cities.

The chapel is not in the same bold class as its parent: it is over-decorated in a Byzantine-Romanesque fashion.

[7.] Friend's Meeting House and Seminary, 221 E. 15th St. facing Stuyvesant Square (Rutherford Pl) bet. 15th and 16th Sts. 1860. Charles T. Bunting.

Appropriately plain Quaker architecture. Spartan designs of the Civil War era speak well to modern architects.

[8.] St. Mary's Catholic Church of the Byzantine Rite, 246 E. 15th St. 1964. Brother Cajetan and J. B. Baumann.

Essentially a stained-glass box, ornamented with sculpture and mosaics.

[9.] Stuyvesant Square, Rutherford and Perlman Pls., 15th to 17th St. 1837. Rutherford Stuyvesant, Donor.

Given this handsome urban "square," not only the city, but the owners of the surrounding lands, benefited: the one in urban graces, the others in future profit(s). Statuary: **Washington Irving,** 1885 by Frederick Beer; **Peter Stuyvesant** by Gertrude Vanderbilt Whitney (founder of the Whitney Museum).

[10.] New York Infirmary, Nathan D. Perlman Pl. 15th to 16th St. 1950. Skidmore, Owings & Merrill.

[11.] Beth Israel Hospital/Belle and Jack Linsky Pavilion, First Ave., 16th to 17th St. 1967. DeYoung, Moscowitz & Rosenberg.

[6.]

[7.

[13a.]

[17

[12.] Church of the Epiphany, Second Ave., SW cor. 22nd St. 1967. Belfatto and Pavarini.

Plastically contoured of dark brown brick, this is the phoenix of a former church on this site that was gutted by fire. It is undoubtedly the most sophisticated modern church on Manhattan Island save Victor Lundy's for the East Harlem Protestant Parish. [See E. Harlem 1b.]

[13a.] Joe King's Rathskeller. (The German-American)/formerly **Scheffel Hall,** 190 Third Ave. bet. 17th and 18th Sts. 1894. Weber & Drosser. ☆

Four generations of collegians have used this place to drink beer, sing, and make out. An ornate Victorian import from Germany, built to express the nationalism of this precinct's formerly large German population.

[13b.] Wilburt's, 194 Third Ave. bet. 17th and 18th Sts. 1964. Space Design Group.

Housewares, glass, china, pottery, candles, and endless details of good design are sold here. The Bonniers of the Bowery. The shop itself is as handsome as its contents: unpretentious, elegant, except, perhaps, for the wooden lily pods on a gravel sea.

[12.]

Paul and Jimmy's Place, 54 Irving Pl. bet. 17th and 18th Sts. OR 4-9463.

Superb Southern Italian cooking in a small, popular restaurant. Cocktails and wine; complete dinner can be had from $3 to $5.

[14.] Washington Irving House, 122 E. 17th St., SW cor. Irving Pl. 1845.☆

Though the house has no known connection with Washington Irving, the most significant fact about it is that Elsie de Wolfe and Elizabeth Marbury lived there from 1894 to 1911. They maintained a salon where notables from all walks of life could meet and the "white" decor was the beginning of Elsie's career as Lady Mendl, the founder of American interior decorating as a paying business.

[15.] Guardian Life Insurance Company, 105 E. 17th St. bet. Park Ave. South and Irving Pl. 1961. Skidmore, Owings & Merrill.

Pete's Tavern, 129 E. 18th St., NE cor. Irving Pl. GR 3-7676.

A social landmark in a corner bar that is not garish, has a patina of age, and a sophisticated clientele. In summer a shallow sidewalk café bounds two sides. Cocktails and wines.

[16.] "The Block Beautiful," 19th St. bet. Irving Pl. and Third Ave.

A handsome architectural unit, more notable for the sum of

the parts than the parts themselves was redesigned mostly by Frederick Sterner, who initiated the effort to rehabilitate the block. No single building is of great note; in spite of this, it is one of the best "places" of New York. Tree-lined, with limited traffic, it is quiet, serene, urbane.

[17.] Gramercy Park, Gramercy Park West and East, Gramercy Park North and South (21st and 20th Sts.), on axis of Lexington Ave. (Irving Pl. S of the Park). 1831. Samuel Ruggles.

Enlightened self-interest here graces this neighborhood with a park; although private and restricted to the tenants now occupying the original plots that defined it, it is a handsome space for all to enjoy. This was the same attitude the Dukes of Bedford employed in London, where Bloomsbury and Covent Garden, speculative housing precincts, were made not only more delightful, but more profitable, by the addition of varied parks and squares and a consistent architectural quality control.

Edwin Booth (who lived at No. 16) stands as placed by sculptor Edmond T. Quinn in 1916.

[17a.] Friends' Meeting House, 144 E. 20th St. bet. Gramercy Park and Third Ave. 1859. King and Kellum. ★

[17b.] 34 and 36 Gramercy Park East, ca. 1883 and 1905, respectively.

Two dowagers, whose uptown brethren have been mostly demolished to build apartments with more floors and lowered ceilings.

No. 34 Gramercy Park East has the additional distinction of having one of New York's few remaining bird cage elevators.

[17c.] The Players (private club), 16 Gramercy Park South bet. Irving Pl. and Park Ave. South. 1845. Remodeled, 1888. Stanford White. ★

Edwin Booth's house later became a club for those in the theater (loosely defined). He was a star in a sense not easily conceivable today, when stars are neither so rare nor so influential.

[17d.] National Arts Club, 15 Gramercy Park South bet. Irving Pl. and Park Ave. South. 1874. Calvert Vaux. ★

Here the Vaux of Olmsted & Vaux reverted to a single architectural commission for Samuel J. Tilden, elected governor of New York the year this mansion was completed. Two years later Tilden ran for President against Rutherford B. Hayes; he won the popular vote by 250,000, but lost in the electoral college. Fearful of his personal security, Tilden had rolling steel doors built into the Gramercy Park facade (behind the windows) and a tunnel to 19th Street for speedy exit. Gothic Revival in the manner of John Ruskin.

[17e.] 3 and 4 Gramercy Park West, 1846. Alexander Jackson Davis.

[18a.] Calvary Church, 273–277 Park Ave. South, NE cor. 21st St. 1846. James Renwick, Jr.

[18b.] Church Missions' House, 218 Park Ave. South, SE cor. 22nd St. 1894. R. W. Gibson and E. J. N. Stent. ☆

[19.] Theodore Roosevelt Association/formerly **Theodore Roosevelt House,** 28 E. 20th St. bet. Broadway and Park Ave. South. 1848. Remodeled, 1923. Theodate Pope Riddle. ★ Hours: 9 AM–4:30 PM daily, children under six free.

For 50¢ you can absorb, over the period of an hour's tour, the flavor of New York in the time of Teddy Roosevelt. Built by his father, this house saw Teddy's birth in 1858.

[20a.] 881 Broadway/formerly **Arnold Constable Store,** SW cor. 19th St. 1873. Griffith Thomas.

Constable probably felt limestone and brick to be more imposing architecturally than the then currently popular cast iron.

Note the steep two-storied mansarded roof.

[20b.] 889–891 Broadway, NW cor. 19th St. 1883. Edward H. Kendall.

The skyline is desperately labored to achieve a varying picturesque profile: bits and pieces of roof interlock at random with the brick facade.

[20c.] 900 Broadway, SE cor. 20th St. 1887. McKim, Mead & White.

[20d.] 901 Broadway/formerly **Lord & Taylor Store,** SW cor. 20th St. 1870. James M. Giles.

Exuberant cast-iron facade, unusually capped with a single-storied, dormered, mansarded roof. The corner pavilion is reminiscent of the Renaissance castle architecture of Prague. The ground floor has been altered with no respect for its uppers.

[21.] 150 Fifth Avenue, SW cor. 20th St. ca. 1895.

[22.] 21 East 21st Street, bet. Broadway and Park Ave. South. 1878. Bruce Price.

[23.] Flatiron Building/formerly **Fuller Building,** 22nd to 23rd St., Fifth Ave. to Broadway. 1902. D. H. Burnham and Co. ★

The diagonal line of Broadway formed triangular buildings here and at Times Square. Burnham was the "master of architectural ceremonies" of the Columbian Exposition (Chicago World's Fair), an architectural event that changed the course of civic architecture for a generation.

Rusticated limestone uniformly detailed from ground to sky in the manner of an Italian Palace. The acute-angled corners give it a dramatic perspective.

3.]   [27.]

[24.] Madison Square/formerly planned as **The Parade/**formerly **a potter's field,** Fifth to Madison Ave., 23rd to 26th St. 1847.

The city crept to and past this point just prior to the Civil War. Madison Avenue springs from the east flank of the square at 23rd Street. The **Commissioners' Plan of 1811,** establishing a surveyor's grid for the city, showed a "Parade" from Third to Seventh Avenue, 23rd to 34th Street. The present square is all that remains of it—being replaced in scale by **Central Park,** which was not planned by or part of the Commissioners' scheme.

Chester A. Arthur statue, 1898, George Bissell, Sculptor. **Admiral David G. Farragut** statue, 1880, Augustus St. Gaudens, Sculptor. Stanford White, Architect of the base. A great and melancholy memorial. **Roscoe Conkling** statue, 1893, J.Q.A. Ward, Sculptor. Republican political leader. **William H. Seward** statue, 1876,

Randolph Rogers, Sculptor. Seward was Lincoln's secretary of state: here, owing to unsuccessful fund-raising, the body is one that Rogers modeled of Lincoln. With Seward's head attached, it holds the *Emancipation Proclamation!*

[25.] Worth Monument, 24th to 25th St., Fifth Ave. to Broadway. 1857.

General William J. Worth, hero of the Seminole and Mexican Wars, is literally buried here, marked by 51 feet of granite.

[26.] Serbian Eastern Orthodox Church of St. Saba/formerly **Trinity Chapel,** 15 W. 25th St. bet. Fifth and Sixth Aves. 1855. Richard Upjohn. ★

A boldly detailed, simple brownstone block; the stone blocks are dressed and tooled. Originally built as the uptown Trinity (Parish) Chapel, it was bought by the Serbian Orthodox Church in 1943. The clergy and parish house to the east (1860, Upjohn) forms an alley in common with the church proper, which is a handsome pedestrian route between 25th and 26th Streets.

[27.] Metropolitan Life Insurance Company, 1 Madison Ave., 23rd to 25th St., Madison Ave. to Park Ave. South. 1893–1961. Tower, 1909. Napoleon LeBrun and Sons.

[27a.] North Bldg. (annex), 1932, Harvey Wiley Corbett and D. Everett Waid.

Retained as a symbol after its adjacent base was rebuilt, the tower is now used as storage for company records. On the North Building, two marks to note are the polygonal modeling of the upper bulk to make it less ponderous—an early search for form in the history of modern architecture. The second is the vaulted entrance space at each of its four corners.

[28.] Appellate Division, N. Y. State Supreme Court, NE cor. 25th St. and Madison Ave. 1900. James Brown Lord. ★

This small marble palace is a reincarnation of an English 18th Century country house. The sculpture is extravagant: **Wisdom** and **Force,** by Frederick Ruckstuhl, flank the portal; **Peace,** by Karl Bitter, is the central figure on the balustrade facing the Square; **Justice** (fourth from the left on 25th Street) is by Daniel Chester French.

[29a.] 32 East 26th Street/formerly **Manhattan Club/**formerly **Leonard Jerome House.** 1859, T. R. Jackson. ★   DEMOLISHED

[29b.] New York Life Insurance Company, 51 Madison Ave., 26th to 27th St., Madison Ave. to Park Ave. South. 1928. Cass Gilbert.

Limestone Renaissance at the bottom, Birthday Cake at top. Gilbert was obsessed with pyramidal caps to his buildings: compare the Woolworth Tower and the Federal Courthouse at Foley Square (1913 and 1936, respectively) [See Civic Center 5; 18]

This site has a rich urban history. Originally it was the New York terminal of the New York and Harlem Railroad, Union Depot. After 1871, the old Union Depot's shell was converted into Barnum's Hippodrome; then to the first Madison Square Garden. Stanford White (McKim, Mead & White) designed a lavish replacement complete with a tower copied from the **Giralda** in Seville. White was murdered in the roof garden restaurant in 1906 by Harry Thaw, whose wife, the former Evelyn Nesbitt, was reputedly (before Thaw's marriage to her) White's mistress. One added irony is the fact that the Madison Square Garden's new quarters, two buildings later, is on the former site of Pennsylvania Station, McKim, Mead and White's greatest New York work.

[29c.] Wel-Met Camps, 50 Madison Ave., NW cor. 26th St. 1896. Renwick, Aspinwall & Sands.

A proper London club in delicately tooled limestone.

[30.] 165th Regiment Armory/formerly **69th Regiment Armory,** Lexington Ave. to Park Ave. South, 25th to 26th St.

A brick, mansarded palace with gun bays surveying Lexington. This is the Armory of the "Armory Show" of 1913, the bombshell entry of Cubist painting.

[31.] 250 Fifth Avenue, NW cor. 28th St. 1907. McKim, Mead & White.

One of few McKim, Mead & White office buildings.

[32.] Marble Collegiate Reformed Church, 272 Fifth Ave., NW cor. 29th St. 1854. Samuel A. Warner. ☆

Most noted for its pastor, Norman Vincent Peale.

[32a.] Church of the Transfiguration (Little Church Around The Corner), 1 E. 29th St. bet. Fifth and Madison Aves. 1849–1856. ★

Its notorious nickname has stuck since 1870, when a local, fashionable pastor declined to perform the funeral of George Holland, an actor, and suggested "the little church around the corner." It has been a church for those in the theater ever since. Pleasant small scale with a garden.

[33.] American Academy of Dramatic Arts/formerly **The Colony Club,** 120 Madison Ave. bet. 30th and 31st Sts. 1905. McKim, Mead & White. ★

Georgian-Federal revival seemed appropriate for venerably connected and socially prominent ladies. Unusual brickwork, with the short ends (headers) of brick facing outward. The false balcony is an irritating mannerism from a firm of talent.

[29.]

[34.] 123 Lexington Avenue, bet. 28th and 29th Sts. 1855. ☆

This was President Chester A. Arthur's house: Garfield's vice president was sworn in here as president when the former was assassinated. On the ground floor: no architecture, but rich color in Mr. Kalustyan's **Oriental Trading Company** seeds, nuts, honey, hookahs.

[35.] Associated Hospital Service of New York, 80 Lexington Ave. SW cor. 27th St. 1958. Carson, Lundin & Shaw.

A crisp, limestone and stainless steel office building for Blue Cross. Neatness without making a spectacle can be a virtue.

[36.] St. Stephen's Church (Roman Catholic), 149 E. 28th St. 1854. James Renwick, Jr. Restored, 1949. ☆

Brownstone Romanesque: an airy hall, slender cast-iron (plaster-encased) columns with elaborate foliated capitals supporting multi-ribbed vaulting. The transepts have unusual galleries overseeing the nave. Interior mural by Constantino Brumidi, "decorator" of the Capitol in Washington.

Caliban's (bar), 360 Third Ave. bet. 26th and 27th Sts.

Elegant modern bar: exposed brick with oak Victorian bar counter.

Trinacria Importing Co., 415 Third Ave. NE cor. 29th St.

Don't let the name fool you. Their imports are largely food-stuffs (though Turkish coffee makers, etc. are among their wares). The foods are wide ranging, Greek, Armenian, Near Eastern and magnificent hero sandwiches—have your lunch *al fresco*. The atmosphere (visual and olefactory) is Old World.

Hye Oriental Food Shop, 539 Second Ave. bet. 29th and 30th Sts.

Lahmajin, a pizza-like Lebanese pastry spread with ground lamb and beef, tomatoes, and varied seasoning. Eat it here or take it out.

El Parador (restaurant), 561 Second Ave., SW cor. 31st St. MU 4-8819.

A necessary seasoning to local Kips Bay environment. Here, excellent Mexican dinners cost from $5 to $7. Cocktails, wine; try Cresta Blanca beer from Monterrey. And a Margarita.

[42.]   [41

Marchi (restaurant), 251 E. 31st St. bet. Second and Third Ave. OR 9-2494.

Italian cuisine, the quality and quantity of which has made it famous for years.

[37.] Kips Bay Plaza, 30th to 33rd St., First to Second Ave. **South Building,** 1960. **North Building,** 1965. I. M. Pei & Assoc.; S. J. Kessler, Associate Architects.

New York's first exposed-concrete apartment house, joined soon after by **Chatham Towers,** 1965 (Kelly & Gruzen), and Pei's **University Plaza (1966).** Surprisingly, the resident density is similar to that in Greenwich Village or Brooklyn Heights (122 units/acre gross).

The vast open space compensates for the huge 21-story building slabs. These are stepchildren of Le Corbusier's Marseilles Block: the giant and beautifully detailed building in a park. Here, the city planning decision is more important than architectural detail (although the latter is handsome). Do buildings define urban pedestrian spaces—streets, boulevards, and plazas—or shall they be freestanding objects in a park?

[38.] Cathedral of the Armenian Church in America, Second Ave., 34th to 35th St. E side. 1967. Steinmann & Cain.

A huge (to accommodate cathedral-size congregations) version of Armenian churches of Asia Minor.

[39.] New York University-Bellevue Medical Center, 30th to 34th St., First Ave. to the East River Dr. 1950. Skidmore, Owings & Merrill.

A teaching hospital can attract staff and faculty of the highest stature. Here they are housed in complementary facility to Bellevue Hospital, designed in a single master plan by SOM, and constructed over a number of years.

[40a.] Bellevue Hospital, 25th to 30th St., First Ave. to East

River Drive. McKim, Mead & White.

Its old brick hulk is now squeezed between the parking garage addition on First Avenue and a giant 22-story "wing" facing the river. The top floors and roof contain the only serious architectural embellishments: roman brick Corinthian columns, pitched tile roofs. "Belle Vue" was the name of a farm that originally occupied this site.

[40b.] New Building, Bellevue Hospital, 27th to 28th Sts., East River Dr. ca. 1968. Katz Waisman Weber Strauss; Joseph Blumenkranz; Pomerance & Breines, Feld & Timoney. **Parking Garage,** 1965.

A behemoth: each floor will be an acre and a half of loft space served by 20 elevators.

[41.] Waterside Apartments, 23rd to 30th St., E of East River Dr., ca. 1970. Davis, Brody & Assocs.

A notch in the edge of Manhattan will give opportunity to project construction into the river without interfering with river traffic or water flow. Sixteen hundred apartment units, shopping, restaurants, boat-docking facilities, and pedestrian plazas will give a share of Manhattan's glorious waterfront back to its residents. The nonresident public will be able to walk through the whole complex, enjoying its river aspect, café restaurant, and boating facilities.

[43.]

[42.] Public Baths of New York City, 23rd St. and Asser Levy Pl. at East River Dr. 1906. Arnold Brunner and Martin Aiken.

[43.] American Musical and Dramatic Academy/originally **DeMilt Dispensary,** 245 E. 23rd St., NW cor. Second Ave. 1851.

[44.] Peter Cooper Village, 20th to 23rd St., First Ave. to East River Dr. 1947. Irwin Clavan and Gilmore Clarke.

More space and more rent make this the richer stepbrother of Stuyvesant Town.

[45.] Stuyvesant Town, 14th to 20th Sts., First Ave. to East River Dr. 1947. Irwin Clavan and Gilmore Clarke.

Tax abatement allowed this Metropolitan Life Insurance Company project to supply middle-income housing to the returning servicemen from World War II. Huge and dense (8755 families), the 20-year-old trees now soften its early brutality.

End of Tour: The 14th Street Canarsie Line BMT Subway connecting at Union Square with other BMT Lines; at Sixth and Eighth Avenues with IND Lines. Crosstown bus is number 14; use First Avenue buses for uptown.

HERALD SQUARE AREA

In the 1870's and 1880's the whole area between the respectability of Fifth Avenue and the slums of **Hell's Kitchen** (West of Seventh Avenue), from the 20's through the 30's, was New York's Tenderloin. The present **Herald Square** was right in the middle of it. Dance halls and cafes were lined up under the "el" along Sixth Avenue, with bordellos on the shady side streets, all flourishing under the **Tammany Hall** political machine. A brief period of **reform** in the 1890's dimmed the gaiety of Tenderloin, and it slowly faded away. Both the theater and the press made brief stops at Herald Square in the Nineties on their way to Times Square—leaving the square with a newspaper's name.

In 1904 the Pennsylvania Railroad opened its tunnel under the

Hudson and cut a broad swath to its monumental two-square-block station (opened 1910), erasing some of Hell's Kitchen tenements. (In the 1930's, Lincoln Tunnel approaches cut down more of the slums.) The new station quickly attracted the equally monumental General Post Office, some major hotels, and a cluster of **middle-class** department stores, which found the square an ideally convenient goal for their march up Sixth Avenue from 14th Street. By the 1920's, **garment manufacturing** had moved from the **Lower East Side** into the streets surrounding these pivot points. Today's **garment industry** is concentrated in the 30's between Sixth and Eighth Avenues, with suppliers of fabrics, trimmings, and such located to the east as far as Madison Avenue.

Walking Tour: Broadway and 34th Street (BMT and IND Sixth Avenue Lines, 34th Street Station) to Fifth Avenue and 38th Street.

[1a.] Herald Square, 34th–35th St., Sixth Ave. and Broadway. Present design, 1940. Aymar Embury II.

The small triangular park is dominated by the clock that stood from 1895 to 1921 on top of the New York Herald's two-story palazzo (by McKim, Mead & White) just to the north. Every hour **Stuff** and **Guff,** the two bronze mannequins, pretend to strike the big bell as Minerva supervises from above. At noon they make an especially joyful sound.

[1b.] Greenwich Savings Bank, NE cor. Broadway and 36th St. 1924. York & Sawyer.

Giant-order Corinthian columns march around three sides of this temple-like bank, interrupted only by columnar signs on two facades that almost undo the effect. Inside, columns define an **oval** rotunda with central skylight.

Keen's English Chop House, 72 West 36th Street, just east of Sixth Avenue. Founded 1878, known for fine mutton chops and thousands of **clay pipes,** signed by satisfied customers, on the ceiling. WI 7-3636.

[1c.] Gate of Cleve, in Sheraton-Atlantic Hotel (formerly McAlpin Hotel) SE cor. Broadway and 34th St. PE 6-5700.

[2.] Macy's, 34th to 35th St. and, Broadway to Seventh Ave. original (Broadway) building 1901. DeLemos & Cordes.

"The world's largest store" is sheathed in a dignified Palladian facade. In the south corner there appears to be the **world's busiest hot-dog** stand with a "Macy's" sign on top, it's actually a five-story 19th Century house bought at the outrageous price of $375,000 (ca. 1900) by Robert S. Smith, Macy's next door neighbor and bitter rival at their old 14th Street location. Smith's store has long since folded, but his heirs annually collect a fortune from Macy's for the sign.

The Broadway entrance and show-windows have been remodeled, but the 34th Street side shows the handsome original details; note the canopy, clock, and the **hefty** turn-of-the-century lettering.

Old-time-eating. Between Macy's and Penn Station are several hearty, old, unpretentious places: **Paddy's Clam House,** 215 W. 34th St. (CH 4-9123), big and inexpensive, with the atmosphere of a tramp freighter, but the seafood is good (no liquor); **Shine's** 426 Seventh Ave. bet. 33rd and 34th Sts. (LO 5-3900), is not so inexpensive, known for steaks and sandwiches; across the street **Solowey's,** 431 Seventh Ave. (LA 4-2077), has real garment-center fare, elaborate sandwiches, and rich desserts; **P. J. Moriarty's,** 213 W. 33rd St. (MU 8-6060), offers an Irish-American menu, moderately high prices (closed weekends).

[3.] Statler-Hilton Hotel/formerly **Hotel Pennsylvania,** Seventh Ave., SE cor. 33rd St. George B. Post & Sons.

Like its neighbor to the south [See 6.], this Classical block is set back about 15 feet from the building line to leave extra public space. It was a center for the big bands of the 1930's, and Glenn Miller wrote a tune called *PE 6-5000,* still the hotel's number.

[2.]

[13

[4.] Madison Square Garden Center, 31st to 33rd St., Seventh to Eighth Ave. 1968. Charles Luckman Associates.

Anybody who remembers the vast Classical waiting room and even vaster iron and glass train shed of **McKim, Mead & White's** 1910 station will feel bereaved here.

The new entertainment and office complex covering 2 blocks, includes a 20,000-seat "garden," a 1000-seat "forum," a 500-seat cinema, a 48-lane bowling center, a 29-story office building, an exposition "rotunda," an art gallery, and the usual dining, drinking, and shopping areas—all above the railroad station, which was underground to begin with, but **used** to have a ceiling 150 feet high. The new "garden," the third one, and closer to Madison Square than the second—is housed in a precast-concrete-clad cylinder, and roofed by a 425-foot-diameter cable structure which only **physically** replaces the grand and beautiful spaces of its noble predecessor.

[5.] General Post Office, Eighth Ave. bet. 31st and 33rd Sts. W Side. 1910–1913. McKim, Mead & White. ☆

The two block row of tall Corinthian columns, and what is probably **the world's longest inscription,** once faced the equally long, stubbier, row of Doric columns of Penn Station.

[6.] Montgomery Ward Building/formerly **Equitable Building,** NE cor. Seventh Ave. and 31st St.

Another of the Classical blocks built to **complement** the former Penn Station, this office building is notable mainly for its tall vaulted lobby with **polished marble,** gilding on the vault—a rich, well-preserved period piece. Notice the display of Singer **knitting machines** working away in a showroom on the 31st Street side.

[7.] Church of St. Francis of Assisi, W. 31st St. bet. Seventh and Sixth Aves.

A confection of yellow brick and rosy sandstone, complete with polychrome mosaics and **trompe l'oeil niches,** that looks like a set for *Cavalleria Rusticana.*

[8.] Greeley Square. 32nd to 33rd St., and Broadway to Sixth Ave.

[9a.] Hotel Martinique, NE cor. Broadway and 32nd St. 1897. Henry J. Hardenbergh. Alterations.

An opulent **French Renaissance pile,** topped with several stories of Mansards; the south facade is the real front. The hotel houses a theater (47 W. 32nd) now popular for "Off-Broadway" productions (although it is closer to Broadway itself than most "Broadway" theaters).

[9b.] Stanford Hotel, 43 W. 32nd St. bet. Broadway and Fifth Ave.

[10.] Hotel Aberdeen, 17 W. 32nd St. bet. Broadway and Fifth Ave.

[11.] Hotel Clinton/formerly **Life Building,** 19–21 W. 31st St. bet. Broadway and Fifth Ave. 1894. Carrère & Hastings.

This opulent Classical facade once enclosed the offices of a very literate humor magazine *Life* (from which the present Time-Life organization bought the name in 1936). Visible **mementoes** include the inscriptions **"wit"** and **"humor"** and a pattern of **L's** back-to-back on handsome iron balconies.

[12.] Wolcott Hotel, 4–10 W. 31st St. bet. Broadway and Fifth Ave.

One of the many variations on the Classical hotel.

[13.] Empire State Building, 350 Fifth Ave. bet. 33rd and 34th Sts. 1931. Shreve, Lamb & Harmon.

The world's tallest building was originally 1250 feet high to the top of its dirigible mooring mast (never used as such). That height remains unequalled, although it may soon be challenged by the projected World Trade Center towers. The 222-foot television antenna is used by all New York stations. Planned during the **booming Twenties,** it went up during the Depression. Largely vacant in its early years, the building relied on the stream of **sightseers** to the observation decks to pay its taxes.

The monumental Fifth Avenue entrance is not as interesting as the modernistic stainless steel canopies of the two street entrances. All of them lead to two-story-high corridors around the elevator core (with 67 elevators in it), which is crossed here and there by stainless steel and glass-enclosed bridges. **The Observation Deck** (ticket office on 34th St.) is open daily 9:30 AM–Midnight.

Empire State site: This pivotal spot has been occupied by two previous sets of landmarks. From 1857 to 1893 it was the site of two mansions belonging to the **Astor** family. Mrs. William Astor's place, on the corner of 34th Street, was for years undisputed center of New York social life, and the capacity of her ballroom gave the name "The 400" to the city's elite. But in the early 1890's a feud developed between Mrs. Astor and her nephew, William Waldorf Astor, who had the house across the garden at 33rd Street. He and his wife moved to Europe and had a 13-story hotel built on his property, naming it the **Waldorf** (the name of the first John Jacob Astor's native village in Germany). Within a year after it opened in 1893, Mrs. Astor wisely decided to move out of its ominous shadow (up to 65th Street and Fifth Avenue) and put a connecting hotel, the **Astoria,** on her property. When the 17-story structure was completed in 1897, the hyphenated hotel immediately became a social mecca. The requirement of full formal dress (tails) in the Palm Room created a sensation, even then, but made it the place to be seen. Successful as it was, the old Waldorf-Astoria operated under a curious agreement that the elder Mrs. Astor could have all connections between the buildings walled up at any time on demand.

[14.] B. Altman and Company, Fifth Ave. bet. 34th and 35th Sts. 1906, extended 1914. Trowbridge & Livingston.

Even after the Waldorf-Astoria opened in the Nineties, Fifth Avenue from the 30's north remained solidly residential. Benjamin Altman made a prophetic breach by moving his department store from Sixth Avenue and 18th Street to this corner. To make the change less painful, it was designed as a dignified eight-story Classical block. The Fifth Avenue entrance shows the atmosphere Altman was trying for. Altman's set off a rush of fashionable stores to Fifth Avenue above 34th Street. Many of them made a second jump from the upper 30's to the 50's, leaving Altman's ironically isolated.

[15.] 366 Fifth Avenue/formerly **Best & Company,** SW cor. 35th St. 1910.

[16.] 390 Fifth Avenue/formerly **Russek's/**formerly **Gorham Building,** SW cor. 36th St. 1905. McKim, Mead & White. Alterations.

When Altman's opened at 34th Street, the famous jewelers had just completed their Italian Renaissance palace. Russek's kept the fine architecture largely intact. Since then, the lower floors have now been inappropriately altered, but the original columns and arches are visible on the 36th Street side.

[17.] Stewart & Co., SW cor. 37th St.

[18.] 409 Fifth Avenue/formerly **Tiffany's,** SE cor. 37th St. 1906. McKim, Mead & White.

Finished only a year after Gorham [16] by the same architects, this more massive structure was modeled after the **Palazzo Vendramini** in Venice. The 37th Street side retains the original motif of three ranks of giant-order columns shouldering up a broad cornice.

[19a.] W. & J. Sloane/formerly **Franklin Simon & Co.,** SW cor. Fifth Ave. and 38th St. 1922.

[19b.] Lord & Taylor, NW cor. Fifth Ave. and 38th St. 1914. Starrett & Van Vleck.

[12.]

[16

A Few Notions: The side streets between Fifth and Sixth Avenues in the upper 30's are full of suppliers of trimmings for garments and millinery, and their windows are a great show. Beads, rhinestones, spangles, and laces predominate on 37th Street, milliners' flowers and feathers on 38th.

End of Tour. Fifth Avenue buses downtown, Sixth and Madison Avenue buses uptown.

MURRAY HILL

The country home of **Robert Murray** once stood approximately where 37th Street now crosses Park Avenue; it was here that Murray's wife is said to have **served tea to General Howe and his staff** while the **Revolutionary troops escaped to the northwest.** In the late 19th Century, social status on **the fashionable hill** was highest near the great mansions of Fifth Avenue, dropping off toward the east, where carriage houses gave way to tenements at **el-shaded Third Avenue.** When commerce moved up Fifth Avenue in the early 1900's, Murray Hill beccame an isolated but **vigorous patch of elegance,** centered about Park Avenue, where through traffic (first horse-cars, then trolleys, now cars) was diverted into an old railroad tunnel from 33rd to 40th Streets. Fashionable Murray Hill has gradually shifted to the east, where **carriage houses** have become residences, and commerce has made slow but steady inroads on the other three sides.

Walking Tour: Park Ave. and E. 33rd St. (IRT Lexington Ave. line, 33rd St. station) to Park Ave. and 42nd Street.

[1.] 71st Regiment Armory, Park Ave. bet. 33rd and 34th Sts. E side. 1904. Clinton & Russell.

A burly brick mass topped by a medieval Italian tower decorated bizarrely with American flags back to back on each face.

[2a.] 4 Park Avenue/formerly **Vanderbilt Hotel.** 1912. Warren & Wetmore. Remodeled, 1967, Schuman, Lichtenstein & Claman.

The change from transient hotel to "elegant apartment suites" is understandable; but why did the widely admired Adam detail of the lower stories have to be sacrificed?

[2b.] 2 Park Avenue, bet. 32nd and 33rd Sts. W side. 1927. Ely Jacques Kahn.

A very neat pier-and-spandrel pattern on the walls of this office block bursts into angular terra cotta decoration in primary colors at the top.

[3.] 29 East 32nd St./formerly **Grolier Club,** bet. Madison and Fifth Aves. 1889. Charles W. Romeyn & Co. ☆

Superb Richardsonian, with brownstone—smooth, rough, and carved.

[4a.] Church of the Incarnation, 205 Madison Ave. NE cor. 35th St. 1865. Emlen T. Littel. ☆

[3.]

[4b.]

[4b.] Percy Silver House, 209 Madison Ave. bet. 35th and 36th Sts. E side. 1868. Robert Mook. ☆

[4c.] 211 Madison Avenue, bet. 35th and 36th Sts. E side.

A former J. P. Morgan carriage house, occupied by the Anthroposophical Society in America, which holds classes in cosmology.

[5a.] Morgan Library, 33 E. 36th St. bet. Madison and Park Aves. 1903–1906. McKim, Mead & White. Addition at 29 E. 36th St. NE cor. Madison Ave. 1928. Benjamin W. Morris. ★

Through unostentatious on the exterior, the original library is lavishly built of perfectly fitted marble, which does not depend on mortar for its strength. The addition, built on the site of the J. Pierpont Morgan, Sr., mansion after his death modestly defers to the older part. The interior is notable not only for its exhibits of rare prints and manuscripts, but for Morgan's opulent private library, maintained just as he left it.

[5b.] Lutheran Church in America/formerly **J. P. Morgan, Jr. Residence,** 231 Madison Ave. SE cor. 37th St. ★

A Classical block that has suffered from additions and restoration of its brownstone. The iron balustrades on the first-floor windows are outstanding.

[6a.] National Democratic Club/originally **DeLamar Mansion,** 233 Madison Ave. NE cor. 37th St. 1905. C. P. H. Gilbert. ☆

The interiors of this Dutch sea captain's mansion are as opulent as the exterior, and largely intact. The club has added some paintings of its own since 1925.

[6b.] 19 and 21 E. 37th Street, bet. Madison and Park Aves.

Exceptionally fine town houses. Note the Corinthian porch of No. 19, the doorway and iron balustrades of No. 21.

[7.] Union League Club, 38 E. 37th St. SW cor. Park Ave. 1931. Morris & O'Connor.

Correctly Georgian red brick home of a club founded by Republicans who left the Union Club [See UES 39] in 1863, incensed by its failure to expel Confederate sympathizers.

[8a.] Olympic House/originally **Adelaide L. Douglas Residence,** 57 Park Ave. bet. 37th and 38th Sts. E. side. 1911. Horace Trumbauer. ☆

[8b.] Church of Our Savior (Roman Catholic), 59 Park Ave. SE cor. 38th St. 1959. Paul C. Reilly.

Remarkably correct Romanesque for its date, but modern appurtenances like auxiliary rooms *above* the nave give it away.

[9.] The New Church (Swedenborgian), 112 E. 35th St. bet. Park and Lexington Aves. 1859.

A small-scaled whitewashed Italianate structure that adds a bit of open space to a block of good townhouses.

[10.] 157 and 159 East 35th Street, bet. Lexington and Third Aves

[11.] Sniffen Court, 152 E. 36th St. bet. Third and Lexington Aves. ca. 1850–1860. ★

A group of early Romanesque Revival brick carriage houses on a mews, tastefully enhanced with black paint on the gateway houses, light colors on those in the mews. Well chosen accessories, too.

[12.] 130 East 37th Street, SW cor. Lexington Ave.

Colorful example of 1920's-style house remodeled, Latin variety.

[13a.] 150 and 152 East 38th Street, bet. Lexington and Third Aves. 1862, 1858, respectively. Remodeled, 1935, Robertson Ward. ★

The Regency treatment for some old houses. A delicate loggia leads from the street into a garden at No. 152.

[13b.] 149 East 38th Street, bet. Lexington and Third Aves. 1902.

A Dutch Renaissance carriage house with carved heads of animals.

[14.] 125 East 38th Street. NW cor. Lexington Ave.

A large house redone in Old Charleston style.

[15.] Syska & Hennessy, Inc., 144 E. 39th St. bet. Lexington and Third Aves.

Very fine brick and brownstone carriage house well restored. Carriage houses at Nos. 134 and 142 also have interesting details.

[16.] 143, 148, and 152 East 40th Street, bet. Lexington and Third Aves.

Three carriage houses in various styles. The Second Empire detail of 148 is outstanding, but a bit obscured by exuberant painting.

[17.] 140 East 41st Street/formerly **Tiffany & Co. stables,** bet. Lexington and Third Aves. 1904. McKim, Mead & White.

[18a.] 113 and 115 East 40th Street/formerly **the Architectural League of New York,** bet. Lexington and Park Aves.

Connected houses that have for decades sheltered the New York Chapter of the AIA, the League, and other art and architectural organizations.

[18b.] Armenian General Benevolent Union of America, 109 E. 40th St. bet. Lexington and Park Aves. ca. 1900. Ernest Flagg.

The house Flagg built for himself has an intriguing entrance leading to a complex, multilevel interior.

[19.] Architects Building, 101 Park Ave. NE cor. E. 40th St.

Scores of architects' offices fill the office floors above the Architectural Materials Center on the first floor.

[9.]

[11.]

[20.] 90 Park Avenue, SW cor. 40th St. 1964. Emery Roth & Sons.

A clear dinstinction between 41-story tower and symmetrical wings flanking a court gives dignity to this brown aluminum and glass office building. Note the straightforward SCM showroom in the south wing and the Colonial style bank in the north wing.

End of Tour: Grand Central offers a variety of rapid transit and commuter connections.

BRYANT PARK AREA

The land where Bryant Park now is was set aside by the city as **a potter's field** in 1822. The Egyptian style **Croton Reservoir,** with walls 50-feet high and 25-feet thick around a four-acre lake, was completed on the Fifth Avenue side (site of the New York Public Library) in 1842. The locale was still at **the northern fringe of the city** in 1853 when New York's **imitation of London's Crystal Palace** was put up on the park site in 1853; it **burned down** in 1858. In 1884 the park was named for **William Cullen Bryant,** well-known poet and journalist; in 1900 **the reservoir was razed** to make way for **the library.**

Walking Tour: West 42nd Street between Fifth and Sixth Avenues (IRT Flushing Line, Fifth Ave. Station; IND Sixth Ave. Line, 42nd St. Station) to Fifth Avenue and 46th Street. Tour passes through two buildings open during week-day business hours: the Bar Building (37 W. 43rd St.; 36 W. 44th St.) and the Berkeley Building (19 W. 44th St.; 20 W. 45th St.).

[1.] Bryant Park, Sixth Ave. bet. 40th and 42nd Sts. E side.

After decades of evolution, the park reached its present formal layout in the early 1930's. As a void at the heart of Midtown, it offers excellent views of surrounding towers.

[1a.] Bush Terminal Building, 132 W. 42nd St., bet. Sixth and Seventh Aves. 1918. Helmle & Corbett.

Visible only from the park, this building rises 480 feet from a base only 50 by 200 feet. The sheer verticality of the east face is now interrupted by a vast sign board.

[2.] American Radiator Building, 40 W. 40th St. bet. Fifth and Sixth Aves. 1924. Raymond M. Hood.

Centerpiece in a row of Renaissance club facades is Hood's black brick and gold terra cotta Gothic-inspired tower. The first floor facade, of bronze and polished black granite, and the black marble and mirror-clad lobby are worth a close look. The plumbing fixture showroom is a later addition.

[3.] Republic National Bank/formerly **Knox Building,** 452 Fifth Ave. SW cor. 40th St. 1902. John H. Duncan.

This exuberant Classical showcase, built for Col. Edward Knox, hatter to presidents, was sympathetically renovated in 1965.

[1.]

[4.]

[4.] New York Public Library, Fifth Ave. bet. 40th and 42nd Sts., W. side. 1898–1911. Carrère & Hastings. ☆

It has been criticized for "overabundant detail" and its designer Hastings, reportedly wanted it altered, but the library facade, according to Alan Burnham, "probably comes closer than any other in America to the complete realization of Beaux-Arts design at its best." Contributing to its success are the handsome terraces, with the well-known lions (E. C. Potter) and figures over the fountains (Frederick MacMonnies). The white marble foyer is one of the city's great interiors, embellished with busts of the architects in the two stairways (Hastings by MacMonnies and Carrère by Jo Davidson). A tiny shop selling cards, books, gifts, etc. related to literature and reading is located under one of the stairs.

[5a.] 500 Fifth Avenue, NW cor. 42nd St. 1931. Shreve, Lamb & Harmon.

A fine example of zoning-ordinance massing, with vertical brick piers and bronze spandrels, a 699-foot-high contemporary of the Empire State Building. [See Herald Square 13.]

[5b.] Manufacturers Hanover Trust Co./formerly **Manufacturers Trust Co**. 510 Fifth Ave., SW cor. 43rd St. 1954. Skidmore, Owings & Merrill.

The elegant glass cage with the exposed vault door remains as handsome as ever. Interior details, however, became much more refined in the firm's later banks, especially at 410 Park Ave. [See Park Avenue 14.]

[5c.] Israel Discount Bank/formerly **Manufacturers Trust Company,** 511 Fifth Ave. SE cor. 43rd St. Remodeled 1962. Luss, Kaplan & Assocs. Ltd.

Superb renovation of a Renaissance bank interior. All old fittings that could be kept have been; everything added is clearly *new*.

[6.] Century Association, 7 W. 43rd St. bet. Fifth and Sixth Aves. 1889–1891. McKim, Mead & White. ☆

A delicate Palladian facade for an intellectuals' club. The large window above the entrance was originally an open loggia.

[7.] The Association of the Bar of the City of New York, 42 W. 44th St. bet. Fifth and Sixth Aves. 1895. Cyrus L. W. Eidlitz. ★

A Classical limestone structure with the massive sobriety of the law.

The Algonquin: The hotel and restaurant at 59 West 44th Street has a 1902 Renaissance facade like many others, but it has been a rendezvous for theater and literary figures for over 50 years. In the 1920's, its Rose Room housed America's most famous luncheon club, the *Round Table*, at which F. P. Adams, Robert Benchley, Harold Ross, Dorothy Parker and others sat. Stop for refreshment in the closet-sized Blue Bar or on one of the easy chairs in the lobby. (MU 7-4400).

[5b.]

[8a.] New York Yacht Club, 37 W. 44th St. bet. Fifth and Sixth Aves. 1899. Warren & Wetmore. ☆

A fanciful example of Beaux-Arts work, with windows that look like the sterns of old ships worked in among the columns.

[8b.] Mechanics' Institute/originally **Berkeley Preparatory School,** 20 W. 44th St. bet. Fifth and Sixth Aves. 1891. Lamb & Rich.

A free, evening technical school founded in 1820 is housed in this grim Classical structure. The interior is the surprise: a three-story gallery ringed drill hall housing a library and exhibits of old locks.

[8c.] Harvard Club, 27 W. 44th St. bet. Fifth and Sixth Aves.

1894 (major additions 1902, 1915). McKim, Mead & White. ☆

A modest Georgian exterior housing some imposing spaces; their large scale can be seen in the 45th Street facade.

Train Treasurehouse: The Model Railroad Equipment Corp. at 23 W. 45th St. claims to be the world's largest train store, and well worth a visit.

[8a.]  [8b.]

[9.] Fred F. French Building, 551 Fifth Ave. NE cor. 45th St. 1927. Fred F. French Company.

The headquarters of the prosperous designer-builder company has strange multicolored faience at the upper-floor setbacks, a well-preserved ornate lobby.

End of Tour: Most convenient subways are at Grand Central.

Schrafft's: The most imposing quarters (Carrère & Hastings' Knoedler Gallery, 1911) of the omnipresent candy-confections-restaurant chain, at 558 Fifth Ave. (bet. 45th and 46th Sts.), has great arches of vermiculated stone framing a lavish interior only slightly altered since the 1920's. "Frank G. Shattuck & Company," engraved on the facade (see photo p. 111), means the same as "Schrafft's."

TIMES SQUARE AREA

Up to the 1890's, all of the 40's and 50's west of Seventh Avenue was written off as **Hell's Kitchen,** a seething mixture of factories and tenements where **even the cops moved in pairs.** The rich ventured in only as far as Broadway in the upper 40's, an area of **carriage shops** called **Long Acre** after a similar district in London.

Then big things happened quickly. Charles Frohman ventured **to open a theater** at 40th Street and Broadway, just north of the then-new Metropolitan Opera, in 1893; **Oscar Hammerstein I** did him one better in 1895 by opening the Olympia, **a block-long palace** on Broadway between 44th and 45th Streets (then a muddy stretch) with a concert hall, a music hall, and a theater in it. Soon **lavish restaurants** like **Rector's** and **Café de l'Opera** were dispensing lobster and champagne to **Diamond Jim Brady, George M. Cohan,** and the rest of the turn-of-the-century theater and sporting world. When the city decided to route its first subway west from Grand Central along 42nd Street, then north on Broadway, New York Times publisher Adolph Ochs saw a chance to outdo his competitors by **erecting an imposing tower** at Broadway and 42nd. He got the station there officially named **"Times Square"** on April 19, 1904.

By then the area was established as **the theater district,** and the evening crowds and broad vistas attracted the early electric sign makers; **the 1916 Zoning Ordinance** made specific allowances for vast signs in the area. In the 1920's **neon and movies** took over. In Hollywood's heyday, movie-and-variety palaces pre-empted the valuable Broadway frontage and legitimate theater retreated to the side

streets. The signs got bigger as the crowds got bigger, and began to feature moving things like **waterfalls** and **smoke rings.** As big-time movies waned in the 1950's and 1960's, most of **the palatial theaters were razed,** and Times Square was on the verge of an office building boom.

Another old-time **festive activity** of the district is the **sailing of ocean liners.** Most of the big ones dock between 42nd and 52nd Street, and can be boarded before their noisy, streamer-happy departures.

Egg Cremes: To some New Yorkers simply a chocolate soda with a bit of milk, but to many others, ambrosia, nectar of the gods. Like Manhattans, though definitely non-alcoholic, it comes sweet and dry. The former is topped by a head of creamy foam; the latter by none, achieved by premixing syrup and milk and storing both chilled. Best resource for the latter at Kass & Goldstein Soda Fountain, Seventh Avenue NW corner 41st Street. Incidentally, whether eggs or "creme" actually find their way into this concoction is highly conjectural.

 [1.] McGraw-Hill Building, 330 W. 42nd St. 1931. Raymond M. Hood, with Godley & Fouilhoux.

Hood designed this tower with continuous horizontal bands of blue-green terra cotta at the time his vertically-striped Daily News Building [See Turtle Bay-U.N. 5] was going up at the other end of 42nd Street. The lobby carries out the visual theme. This was the only New York building shown in Johnson and Hitchcock's epoch-making book "The International Style" in 1932.

Paddy's Market: A stretch of Ninth Avenue, between 36th and 42nd Streets, was once full of push-cart food venders, which were banished in the 1930's. The market soon revived, however, as shops with big outdoor displays featuring fresh fruit and vegetables, Italian, Greek, Polish, and Spanish products.

[2.] Franklin Savings Bank, Eighth Ave. SE cor. 42nd St. 1899. York & Sawyer.

One of the earliest of several banks by this firm, in massive Classical style.

[3a.] Allied Chemical Tower/formerly **Times Tower,** Broadway, NW cor. 42nd St. 1904. Eidlitz & MacKenzie. Remodeled, 1966, Smith, Smith, Haines, Lundberg & Waehler.

The New York Times moved into its 25-story tower with dramatic timing on December 31, 1904, marking the occasion with a fireworks display at midnight that made Times Square the place to see the New Year in ever since. The paper moved out in a couple of decades to larger quarters on West 43rd St. but the name remained until the original Italian Renaissance terra cotta skin was stripped off to be replaced with something less ornate.

Home-town news: A long-established news-stand at the north end of the Allied Chemical Tower sells newspapers from scores of cities. Hotaling's, on the first floor of the building sells foreign periodicals and books, 8 a.m. to 11 p.m. except Sunday, when their shop at 142 W. 42nd is open, Noon–8 PM.

-b.]

[6.]

[3b.] 142 West 42nd Street/formerly **Knickerbocker Hotel.** E cor. Broadway. 1901–1902. Marvin & Vavis (Bruce-Price, consultant).

An office building now fills the Classical, mansard topped shell of a hotel—originally commissioned by Col. John Jacob Astor—where Enrico Caruso and George M. Cohan once lived. It had a $10,000 gold service for 60 and a bar so fashionable in the 1890's that it was known as the "42nd Street Country Club." A mural from this bar now sets the theme for the King Cole Bar at the St. Regis-Sheraton Hotel [See Fifth Avenue 12b.]

[4a.] The Lambs Club, 128 W. 44th St. bet. Broadway and Sixth Ave. 1904. McKim, Mead & White. ☆

A tidy Federal-style clubhouse for a still lively actors' group.

[4b.] 1-2-3 Hotel, 123 W. 44th St. bet. Broadway and Sixth Ave.

A tan brick and limestone pile, extravagantly decked out with German Renaissance gables and dormers.

[5a.] 1515 Broadway, bet. 44th and 45th Sts. W side. 1969. Kahn & Jacobs.

A 50-story office building that replaces one of Times Square's best-known landmarks, the Astor Hotel. It will have a 125-foot-deep court facing Broadway.

[5b.] Shubert Alley, from W. 44th St. to W. 45th St. bet. Seventh and Eighth Aves.

Now a convenience for theater-goers, this private alley was once where aspiring actors gathered in front of the offices of J. J. and Lee Shubert when plays were being cast. It will be more spacious after the adjoining office tower [5a.] is completed.

Sardi's: The restaurant at 234 West 44th Street, strategically located among theaters and at the back door to *The New York Times,* has for decades been the place for actors to be seen—except during performance hours. Fine Italian food. Closed Sundays. LA 4-0707.

[6.] Lyceum Theater, 149 W. 45th St. 1903. Herts & Tallant. ☆

[7.] Duffy Square, W. 46th St. to W. 47th St. bet. Broadway and Seventh Ave.

The northern triangle of the crossroads is dedicated to Father Duffy (a national hero in World War I as "Fighting Chaplain" of New York's 69th Regiment, later a friend of actors, writers, and mayors as pastor of Holy Cross Church on West 42nd St.). His statue faces the back of one representing George M. Cohan, another Times Square hero—both of them facing south toward the square.

[8.] Americana Hotel, Seventh Ave. bet. 52nd and 53rd Sts. E. side. 1962. Morris Lapidus.

Dining and Dancing, Times Square style: Jewish-American delicatessen style food, long favored by entertainers, reaches its peak at venerable *Lindy's,* 1655 Broadway, NW cor. 51st St. (CO 5-0288) which set the style back in 1921, and the *Stage Delicatessen,* a small, crowded place at 834 Seventh Ave. (CI 5-7334). Big dance halls, once common around the square, survive in the sedate *Roseland,* in a former ice-skating palace at 239 W. 52nd (bet. Broadway and Eighth Ave.) and, in a new form, at the *Cheetah* a vast teen-age discotheque-boutique-amusement arcade at 1680 Broadway, SE cor. 53rd St.

[9.] Al and Dick's Steak House, 151 W. 54th St., bet. Sixth and Seventh Aves. 1948. George Nemeny and Abraham Geller.

Sound architecture—rare in popular restaurants. A plain wood front leads to a masculine interior of stone, brick, brass, and wood.

PARK AVENUE

This one-mile stretch from Grand Central Terminal to 59th Street— **the busiest and best known portion of Park Avenue**—is a uniquely successful **integration of railroad and city.** The avenue itself is built over the main New York Central lines (also used by the New Haven), and, up to 50th Street, the buildings along it are **built over the fan-shaped yards.**

The railroad's **right of way,** down what was originally Fourth

Avenue, **dates back to 1832** when the New York and Harlem Railroad terminated at Chambers Street. The **smoke and noise of locomotives** was later banned below 23rd Street, then 42nd Street, as the **socially prominent residential** areas moved north from Astor Place through Gramercy Park to Murray Hill. At 42nd Street the original Grand Central Depot, **a cupolaed confection** with a vast **iron and glass train shed,** was opened in 1871.

In the early 1900's, when electric locomotives were introduced, the railroad took audacious steps that increased the value of its property many times over and gave the city **a three-dimensional urban composition** that was one of the major achievements of the **City Beautiful** era. The terminal itself was made more efficient—and compact—by dividing its 67 tracks between **two subterranean levels.** The portions of Park Avenue north and south of the terminal were **joined together for the first time,** with a **system of viaducts** wrapping around the station.

New engineering techniques for isolating tall buildings from railroad vibrations made possible a complex of offices and hotels around the station and extending north above the yards and tracks. By the late 1920's the avenue north through the 50's **was lined with remarkably uniform rows** of office buildings, apartments, and hotels,

[3.]

[2-9.]

all solid blocks about 12 to 16 stories high, punctuated here and there by the divergent form of a church or club. Although some of the buildings had **handsome central courtyards,** their **dense ground coverage** must have made summer living unbearable in pre-air-conditioning times—but then people who lived here **never summered in the city.**

Firm as these palaces appeared, most of them lasted only a few decades. Their convenience to Grand Central and **the air of elegance** they had created made them **prized targets** in the building boom of the 1950's and 1960's. Today **less than half a dozen** buildings of their type **survive** below 59th Street.

Walking Tour: Park Avenue and 42nd Street (IRT Lexington Avenue, the shuttle, and Flushing Line, Grand Central station) to Park Avenue and 59th Street.

[1.] Grand Central Terminal, 42nd St. at Park Ave. N side. 1903–1913 (viaducts completed 1920). C. A. Reed and Warren & Wetmore. ★

The remarkably functional scheme of the terminal and its approaches is housed in **an imposing Beaux Arts Classical structure.** The main facade, facing down Park Avenue, is a fine symmetrical composition of **triumphal arches,** filled in with steel and glass, surmounted by a **clock and sculpture group** (by Jules Coutan) in which **Roman deities fraternize** with an American eagle—confusing symbolism perhaps, but very effective scale and composition.

The main room inside is unexpectedly spare in detail, a virtue now obscured by advertising displays. The simple ceiling vault, 125 feet in span and 116 feet high, is actually hung from steel trusses. Smaller spaces are spanned by **Guastavino hollow tile vaulting,** left exposed, with handsome effect, in parts of the Lower Level.

Grand Central Oyster Bar: This restaurant is world-renowned for its shellfish stews and pan roasts. The oyster bar and its equipment are worth seeing, and extending around it is dining space for hundreds, under exposed tile vaulting low enough to touch.

[2a.] Pan Am Building, 200 Park Ave. 1963. Emery Roth & Sons, Pietro Belluschi, and Walter Gropius.

This latter-day addition to the Grand Central complex can be entered directly from the main room of the terminal. A purely **speculative venture,** Pan Am aroused protest both for its **enormous volume of office space**—2,400,000 square feet, the most in any commercial office building, by a slight margin over even the RCA Building—and for **blocking the vista** up and down Park Avenue, previously punctuated, but not stopped, by the New York General Building tower [See 3.]. The precast concrete curtain wall was one of the first in New York.

The busy **Pan Am lobby** is accessible from the terminal, street level, and viaduct level, and is "enriched" by art works, including a vast **Josef Albers mural,** a **Richard Lippold space sculpture,** and screen-like **metal works by Gyorgy Kepes** in the north lobby.

Note the staid Classical buildings across Vanderbilt Avenue from Pan Am at 44th Street: the **Yale Club** (NW corner) **[2b.],** identified in letters only one inch high, and the **Hotel Biltmore** (SW corner) **[2c.],** noted for the clock in its elegant lobby where college students traditionally meet, and for its traditionally clubby Men's Bar.

Pan Am restaurants: The east side of the Pan Am lobby, at street level, has a row of three eateries, with lively decoration representing three nations: Charley Brown's (Edwardian English Club), Zum Zum (wursthaus German), and the Trattoria (jet-age Italian).

[2d.] Pan American World Airways Ticket Office, Vanderbilt Ave. SE cor. 45th St. 1963. Edward Larrabee Barnes and Charles Forberg.

The major tenants gave the Pan Am Building its most noteworthy public space. The arrangement of freestanding curvilinear elements against a brightly lighted undulating white wall is especially effective seen from outside.

[3.] New York General Building/formerly **New York Central Building,** 230 Park Ave. 45th to 46th St. W side. 1929. Warren & Wetmore.

This office tower, symbol of the then-prosperous railroad, was once visible for miles north and south along Park Avenue. Its fanciful cupola and opulent but impeccably detailed lobby departed from the sobriety of the terminal and the surrounding buildings. The lobby remains much as designed—even **the ornate elevator cabs** are meticulously preserved.

The north facade, once a **remarkably successful molding of urban space,** maintained the cornice line of buildings flanking the avenue to the north, carrying it around in small curves to create **an apse-like space** of grand proportions, crowned by the tower. Only a fragment of the original composition now remains, in the relation of the building to 240 Park Avenue. Carved into this north facade are **two tall portals** for automobile traffic, clearly differentiated from the central lobby entrance and the **open pedestrian passages** to the east and west.

[4.] Union Carbide Building, 270 Park Ave. bet. 47th and 48th Sts. W side. 1960. Skidmore, Owings & Merrill.

The 53-story sheer tower is articulated with bright stainless steel mullions against a background of gray glass and black matte-finished steel panels. The 13-story wing to the rear (well related in scale to Madison Avenue) is linked to the tower by a narrow transparent bridge, dramatically placed at the north end of Vanderbilt Avenue. Site of the building over railroad yards made it necessary to start elevators at the second floor, reached by escalator.

[5.] Chemical Bank New York Trust Company Building, 277 Park Ave. bet. 47th and 48th Sts. E side. 1964. Emery Roth & Sons.

Notable for both the kinship of its metal curtain wall with that of Union Carbide and its hospitable plaza sitting area.

[6.] Banker's Trust Building, 280 Park Ave. bet. 48th and 49th Sts. W side. 1963. Emery Roth & Sons; Henry Dreyfuss, Designer.

A rare example of an industrial designer (Dreyfuss) playing a major role in the design of a large building, most obvious in the very neat concrete curtain wall. The effort to fit into the old Zoning Law envelope without a wedding-cake silhouette has produced two rectangular masses that simply coexist.

[7.] Westvaco Building, 299 Park Ave. bet. 48th and 49th Sts. E side. 1967. Emery Roth & Sons.

[8.] Waldorf-Astoria Hotel, 301 Park Ave. bet. 49th and 50th Sts. E side. 1931. Schultze & Weaver.

When this world-famous institution moved from its original site, where the Empire State Building now rises, it chose to build in a sedate version of the modernistic style. The facades and lobbies once were a picture of 1930's chic, but in the early 1960's the management tried to turn back the clock to the Edwardian period; whatever couldn't be replaced was gilded. The 625-foot towers, which have a separate entrance on 50th Street, have been home to such notables as President Hoover, General MacArthur, and the Duke of Windsor.

a.]   [12.]

[9a.] Colgate-Palmolive Building, 300 Park Ave. bet. 49th and 50th Sts. W side. 1955. Emery Roth & Sons.

[9b.] I.T.T. Building, 320 Park Ave. bet. 50th and 51st Sts. W side. 1960. Emery Roth & Sons.

[9c.] Manufacturers Hanover Trust Building, 350 Park Ave. bet. 51st and 52nd Sts. W side. 1960. Emery Roth & Sons.

These three in a row show what happened when the old Zoning Law envelope was filled to capacity. The newer two—the gray ones—were built simultaneously and are almost twins.

Knoll Showrooms: High in 320 Park Avenue are handsome exhibits of Knoll Associates' furniture, which somehow got isolated from most of New York's interior design world (open only to architects, interior designers, and clients with proper credentials).

[10a.] St. Bartholomew's Church (Episcopal), Park Ave. bet. 50th and 51st Sts. E side. 1919. Bertram G. Goodhue. Entrances, 1902. McKim, Mead & White. ☆ **Community house,** 1927. B. G. Goodhue Assocs. ☆

[10b.] General Electric Building, 570 Lexington Ave. SW cor. 51st St. 1931. Schultze & Weaver.

St. Bartholomew's and the buildings behind it gave the old Park Avenue what it desperately needed: open space, color, variety of form and detail. Around its open terrace at the 50th Street corner are arrayed picturesque, polychrome forms that rise to the ample dome of the church, dip, then soar to the 570-foot pinnacles of the General Electric tower. Supporting roles in the related composition are played by Cathedral High School, just south of G.E., and the turrets of the Beverly Hotel, on the far side of Lexington Avenue.

[11a.] Seagram Building, 375 Park Ave. bet. 52nd and 53rd Sts. E side. 1958. Mies van der Rohe and Philip Johnson; Kahn & Jacobs.

Many consider Seagram Distillers' headquarters the most refined metal-curtain-wall structure yet built. Almost half of the multimillion dollar site has been set aside as a formal setting for the tower —with granite paving, green marble benches, gingko trees, and fountain pools. The building walls are entirely of bronze, with brown-tinted glass (made especially for the building; now commonly available). Even lavatory fixtures for this building were custom designed (some later becoming standard items). To show off the tower at night, a strip of lights around its perimeter is kept on all evening.

[11b.] The Four Seasons (restaurant), 99 E. 52nd St. bet. Park and Lexington Aves. 1959. Philip Johnson Assocs. Closed Sundays. PL 1-4300.

An entrance dominated by a Picasso stage backdrop for "Le Tricorne" (1929) leads from the Seagram lobby into the restaurant to the north, and the bar to the south. The walnut-paneled dining room is laid out around a square pool, the other room around the square bar, over which is a quivering brass rod sculpture by Richard Lippold. Both rooms are impeccably designed to the last napkin. A stair connects the bar with the 52nd Street lobby, one floor below, adorned with modern paintings. At this entrance, planting boxes and doormen's uniforms are changed quarterly to mark the seasons.

Dining at the Four Seasons is elegant and expensive. Sightseers are not generally welcome, but during the afternoon lull (around 4 PM) the management may be more permissive.

Brasserie: The Seagram Building's second restaurant, less lavish but well designed, is entered at 100 East 53rd Street. Its menu is basically Alsatian (quiche, choucroute), but you can have anything from a beer or a sundae to a full-course dinner (from about $5 up—but beware of lunch-hour crowds). The Brasserie also makes up picnic baskets, with wine if you wish. PL 1-4840.

[12.] Racquet and Tennis Club, 370 Park Ave. bet. 52nd and 53rd Sts. W side. 1918. McKim, Mead & White. ☆

The urban significance of this Italian Renaissance building exceeds its excellence as a work of architecture; it forms an ideal west wall for the space opened up by the Seagram plaza. Its rusticated granite and bronze trim no doubt influenced the choice of materials for Seagram. Despite modernization of shops on the first floor, most of it very sensitive, the building is well preserved on the exterior.

[13.] Lever House, 390 Park Ave. bet. 53rd and 54th Sts. W side. 1952. Skidmore, Owings & Merrill.

This glass-walled building caused a sensation when built and remains a major architectural landmark today. Its use of only a fraction of the allowable building volume was unprecedented among New York office buildings and had a strong effect on later "prestige" buildings—ultimately on the city's zoning laws (which now would prohibit its construction!). The tinted glass curtain wall, laced with a thin stainless steel grid, created an unprecedented effect of weightless volume. The vertical slab of 18 office floors (plus mechanical rooms) seems to hover above a horizontal slab floating one floor above the street. Recessed, metal-clad columns contribute to the floating effect.

The lower element, with an employees' garden on its roof, wraps around a street-level public court that is sunny and pleasantly removed from the street, but with rudimentary seating arrangement and landscaping. The deep colonnades around it, especially on the north side of the building, can be gloomy.

[14.] Chase Manhattan Bank Branch, 410 Park Ave. SW cor. 55th St. 1959. Skidmore, Owings & Merrill (bank), Emery Roth & Sons (building).

A building of the common wedding-cake form of its time, with a better than usual metal and glass curtain wall, designed to meet the needs of the bank on the lower two floors. The bank interior has unusually refined details, even compared to SOM's other banks. The high second-floor banking room is an impressive setting for an excellent Calder mobile.

[15.] East 55th Street, bet. Park and Lexington Aves.

Just off Park Avenue is a remnant of what many streets in the East 50's once were like. For most of the block it is tree-shaded and not shaded by high buildings. The fine old houses along it house many enterprises, including fashionable wig-makers. The tall, polished granite facade of the new Central Synagogue community building (121 E. 55th St., 1967, Kahn & Jacobs) has destroyed the scale of the street. **[15a.]**

[16.] Central Synagogue (Congregation Ahawath Chesed Shaar Hashomayim), 652 Lexington Ave. SW cor. 55th St. 1872. Henry Fernbach. ★

The oldest building in continuous use as a synagogue in New York, this one represents the rough-hewn Moorish style considered appropriate in the late 1800's. Although solemn on the exterior, except for the star-studded bronze cupolas, the synagogue has an interior almost gaily stenciled with rich blues, earthy reds, ochre, and gilt—presumably Moorish but distinctly American 19th-Century.

P. J.'s: One block further east (915 Third Ave., NE cor. 55th St.) is another characteristic 19th-Century relic, this bar with a dining room in the rear has always been known officially as Clarke's Bar, but to generations of collegians it has been "P. J.'s," and it is partly responsible for the rash of other places called P. J. "Something." Seen by millions as the set for movie "Lost Weekend," it has lots of real cut glass and mahogany, and one of the most lavish old-fashioned men's rooms in the city. Open till 4 AM. PL 9-1650.

[17a.] 430 Park Avenue, bet. 55th and 56th Sts. W side. 1954. Emery Roth & Sons.

Converted to office use by remodeling an existing apartment building, built before the 1916 Zoning Law took effect—thus the tall, unbroken form.

[17b.] Mercedes-Benz Showroom, 430 Park Ave. SW cor. 56th St. 1955. Frank Lloyd Wright.

In the master's first New York City work, his creativity seems to have been smothered by the cramped space. The ramp scheme is almost lost among the cars (attractive enough in themselves) and the wax plants.

[18.] Universal Pictures Building, 445 Park Ave. bet. 56th and 57th Sts. E side. 1947. Kahn & Jacobs.

This was the first office building built on a once-residential portion of Park Avenue and achieved distinction while adhering to the wedding-cake form prescribed by the zoning law.

[19.] Ritz Tower, Park Ave. NE cor. 57th St. 1925. Emery Roth and Carrère & Hastings.

This 42-story tower in the form of a stepped obelisk stood out conspicuously on the skyline when it was built. Rich details around the street-level walls are matched only by the opulent enterprises behind them such as Charles of the Ritz. Le Pavillon in the building, at 111 East 57th Street, was almost undisputed as the pinnacle of *haute cuisine* in the United States from its founding by Henri Soulé in 1939 until his death in 1966. It has been at this location since 1955 and remains, for many gastronomes, at the top. It is, of course, expensive and formal. PL 3-8388.

[13.]
[2●

[20.] Pepsi-Cola Building, 500 Park Ave. SW cor. 59th St. 1960. Skidmore, Owings & Merrill.

The apparently simple design of this corporate headquarters (to be moved to the suburbs) overcomes the limitations of a constricted site and maintains the scale of neighboring older buildings. Undivided bays of clear glass—made feasible by the almost sunless exposures—are enlivened by the random adjustments of vertical blinds. The joining of the building to its neighbor to the south, with a windowless link (and its exit doors) clad in polished black granite, is especially successful. The lobby (used for lively exhibits) and the plaza are both finely detailed, but pinched for space.

End of Tour: BMT at Fifth Avenue and 60th or IRT/BMT at Lexington.

TURTLE BAY-UNITED NATIONS

The tract known by the Mid-18th Century as **Turtle Bay Farm** extended roughly from 40th to 49th Street, from Third Avenue to the East River. The little cove that gave it its name is now covered by the gardens on the northern half of the **United Nations grounds.** Bucolic in the early 19th Century, the area was invaded around 1850 by **riverfront industry,** with **shanty towns** inland that were replaced by **tenements.** By 1880, "el" trains were rumbling along both Second and Third Avenues. Town houses on **the Beekman tract** along the river around 50th Street remained respectable (due to deed restrictions against industry) until about 1900, and were among the first in the area **to be rehabilitated.** There was **much ambitious building** and renovation in the 1920's, but it was not until six city blocks of **slaughterhouses** along the river were razed in 1946 for the United Nations and the Third Avenue El (the last one to operate in Manhattan) closed down in 1955, that Turtle Bay was ready for thorough rehabilitation.

Walking Tour: E. 42nd St. bet. Park and Lexington Aves. (IRT Grand Central station) to Lexington Ave. and E. 49th St. The entire tour is about two miles long.

[1a.] Bowery Savings Bank, 110 E. 42nd St. bet. Park and Lexington Aves. 1923. York & Sawyer. ☆

A tall arch leads to a vast banking room rich in colorful mosaics and marble, elegant and imaginative in its details.

[1b.] Chanin Building, 122 E. 42nd St. SE cor. Lexington Ave. 1929. Sloan and Robertson.

Surprising combinations of angular, floral decoration—even Gothic buttresses—sprout on this exuberant office tower. See the lobby, especially the extraordinary convector grilles.

1b.]   [2.]

[2.] Chrysler Building, 405 Lexington Ave. NE cor. 42nd St. 1930. William Van Alen.

Tallest building in the world for a few months, before the completion of the Empire State Building [See Herald Square 13], Chrysler remains the second tallest. It reaches a height of 1048 feet to the top of its spire. One of the first uses of stainless steel over a large exposed building surface. The decorative treatment of the masonry walls below changes with every set-back and includes story-high basket-weave designs, radiator-cap gargoyles, and a band of abstract automobiles. The lobby is a modernistic composition of African marble and chrome steel.

[3.] Socony Mobil Building, 150 E. 42nd St. bet. Lexington and Third Aves. 1955. Harrison & Abramovitz.

A 1,600,000-square-foot building covered almost all over with embossed stainless steel panels.

[4.] Third Avenue, bet. 39th and 45th Sts.

The stretch near Grand Central Station began attracting big office buildings as soon as the "el" was torn down in 1955. Most of them are visible from East 42nd Street: **[4a.] Lorillard Building,** 200 E. 42nd St., (SE cor. Third Ave.) 1958, Emery Roth & Sons; **[4b.] Continental Can Building,** 633 Third Ave., (SE cor. 41st St.) 1962, Harrison & Abramovitz—Distinguished by its dark green brick and glass walls; **[4c.] Burroughs Building,** 605 Third Ave., (SE cor. 40th St.) 1963, Emery Roth & Sons—Black aluminum and gray glass, striped with bright aluminum; **[4d.] 201 East 42nd Street,** (NE cor. Third Ave.) 1965, Emery Roth & Sons; **[4e.] 711 Third Avenue,** (NE cor. 44th St.) 1956, William Lescaze—A low ivory brick block topped by a blue brick block.

[5.] Daily News Building, 220 E. 42nd St. bet. Third and Second Aves. 1930. John Mead Howells and Raymond M. Hood. Addition, SW cor. Second Ave., 1958, Harrison & Abramovitz. ☆

Here Hood abandoned the Gothic sources of his verticality, using stripes of windows and brown brick spandrels alternating with white brick, with abstract decoration at the street floor. The 1958 addition wisely repeated the same stripes, in different proportions to yield wider windows. See the globe, weather instruments, and other exhibits in the modernistic old lobby.

Old Third Avenue Flavor: It survives in the beer at places like Meenan's, Blarney Stone, and Old Seidelberg (all between 40th and 41st Streets) in old brownstone buildings.

 [6.] Ford Foundation Building, E. 42nd St. bet. Second and First Aves. N side. 1967. Kevin Roche, John Dinkeloo Assocs.

Offices arranged in an L around a 130-foot-high glassed-in garden, an indoor continuation of parks to the east. The scheme is less extravagant than it seems when the value of the garden as a waste air chamber and thermal buffer is considered.

[7.] Tudor City, E. 40th St. to E. 43rd St. bet. Second and First Aves. 1925–1928. Fred F. French Co.

An ambitious private renewal effort that included 12 buildings, with 3000 apartments and 600 hotel rooms along its own street (Tudor City Place). Restaurants, private parks, shops, and a post office round out the little city, all in Tudor style. Everything faced in toward the private open space, away from the surrounding tenements, slaughterhouses, and generating plants. As a result, almost windowless walls now face the United Nations.

[8.] United Nations Headquarters, United Nations Plaza (First Ave.) bet. 42nd and 48th Sts. E side. 1947–1953. International Committee of Architects, Wallace K. Harrison, chairman. Library addition, NE cor. 42nd St. 1963. Harrison, Abramovitz & Harris.

John D. Rockefeller's donation of the $8,500,000 site, already assembled by William Zeckendorf for a private development, decided the location of the headquarters. The team of architects included **LeCorbusier** of France, **Oscar Niemeyer** of Brazil, and **Sven Markelius** of Sweden, and **representatives from ten other countries.** The whole scheme is **clearly a LeCorbusier concept** (seconded by Niemeyer), but the **details are largely Harrison's.**
The 544-foot-high slab of the Secretariat (only 72 feet thick) dominates the group, with the library to the south, the General Assembly to the north—its striking form played against the Secretariat's size—and the Conference Building extending to the east over Franklin D. Roosevelt Drive, out of sight from U. N. Plaza. Every major nation has donated some work of art to the headquarters. Immediately noticeable is England's gift, a Barbara Hepworth stone sculpture standing in the pool (a gift from U. S. school children) in front of the Secretariat. Probably the most interesting are the Council Chambers donated by three Scandinavian countries.
The city, under Robert Moses' direction, made way for the U. N. by diverting First Avenue through traffic into a tunnel under United Nations Plaza and opening up a half-block-wide landscaped park along East 47th Street—a meager space in the shadow of tall buildings, with no view at all of the U. N. Headquarters.

Guided tours of the U. N. Headquarters 9–4:45 daily except for Jan. 1 and Dec. 25. U. N. Delegates Dining Room, weekday lunch only; pass required. PL 4-1234. Coffee shop, lower level.

[9.] Beaux Arts Apartment Hotel, 307 and 310 E. 44th St. 1930. Kenneth Murchison and Hood, Godley & Fouilhoux.

A pair of cubistic compositions in light and dark tan brick facing each other across the street.

[10.] United Nations Plaza, bet. 45th and 48th Streets. W side.

A row of institutional offices not quite equal to their setting: **[10a.] United States Mission to the United Nations,** 799 United Nations Plaza, 1961, Kelly & Gruzen and Kahn & Jacobs; **[10b.]**

Institute of International Education, 809 United Nations Plaza. 1964. Harrison, Abramovitz & Harris—The penthouse Edgar J. Kaufmann Conference Rooms suite is one of the two U.S. works of Alvar Aalto; [**10c.**] **Carnegie Endowment International Center,** 345 E. 46th St., 1953, Harrison & Abramovitz; [**10d.**] **United Engineering Center,** 345 E. 47th St., 1961, Shreve, Lamb & Harmon.

[8.]

[6.]

[7.]

[**11.**] **860/870 United Nations Plaza,** bet. 48th and 49th Sts. E side. 1966. Harrison, Abramovitz & Harris.

Twin 32-story apartment towers rising from a six-story office block. A street-level garden court between the towers gives an outlook for the apartment lobby (N side), some street-floor shops and lower-floor offices. Note the change in scale of the bronze-colored aluminum and gray glass walls between office and apartment portion. Projections on the north and south faces of the towers are the ends of shear (bracing) walls.

[**12.**] **Beekman Tower Apartments**/originally **Panhellenic Hotel,** First Ave. NE cor. 49th St. 1928. John Mead Howells.

The almost undecorated brick tower is given vertical emphasis by the deep vertical window recesses and the chamfered corners.

[**13.**] **Beekman Place Neighborhood,** E. 50th St. bet. First Ave. and Beekman Place; Beekman Place bet. 50th and 51st Sts.

These two blocks have the best survivors of the town houses rehabilitated in the 1920's along Beekman Place and adjoining streets. Worth special note are: [**13a.**] **416-420 East 50th Street**—

Interesting detail on mansards; **[13b.] 417 and 419 East 50th Street** —Remodeled with steel windows in perfectly flat limestone facades; **[13c.] 17 Beekman Place** (SE cor. E. 50th St.) Remodeled 1929, Harold Sterner; **[13d.] 25 and 27 Beekman Place**—Two houses sharing an iron balcony and a windowless pediment, remodeled 1927, Pleasance Pennington; **[13e.] 33 Beekman Place**, 1927, H. T. Lindeberg—Note picturesque attic, twisted bronze downspout.

[14.] Unnamed Park, east end of E. 51st St.

Steps lead down to a small park and a footbridge over the Franklin D. Roosevelt Drive. Cross the bridge for a back view of Beekman Place and a view of the drive disappearing at East 52nd Street under a Sutton Place South apartment house. A few rocks in the river off 52nd Street mark what was Cannon Point before the drive was built. From the walk along the river there is a good view of: **[14a.] River House,** 447 E. 52nd St., 1931. Bottomley, Wagner & White. A palatial 26-story co-operative apartment house. The River Club, on its lower floors includes squash and tennis courts, a swimming pool, a ballroom, and it once had a private dock on the river where the best yachts tied up.

[13d.]   **[14**

[15.] Turtle Bay Gardens, 226-246 E. 49th St. bet. Second and Third Aves. (also 227–247 E. 48th St.) Remodeled 1920. Clarence Dean. ☆

Two rows of ten houses each, back to back, assembled by Mrs. Walton Martin. A six-foot strip was taken from the backyard of each house to form a common path and garden. Near a very old willow tree at the center of the group is a fountain copied from the Villa Medici. Low walls and planting mark off the private yards. House interiors were remodeled with living rooms opening to the yard, lowered front doors in pastel-painted stucco fronts. Such notables as Katharine Hepburn, Leopold Stokowski, E. B. White, and Tyrone Power have lived here.

Everything for the Home: Second Avenue in the 40's and 50's has a wild variety of shops selling new and old furniture and things to go with it. The Greenhouse (254 E. 51st St. SW cor. Second Ave.) is jammed with exotic plants that spill onto the sidewalk. Nearby are Furniture Et Cetera (250 E. 52nd St.) and the Workbench (241 E. 51st St.). For do-it-yourselfers, there's the Door Store (210 E. 51st St.). Back on the avenue are Pier 16 (SW cor. E. 51st St.), Be Seated (950 Second Ave.), a Salvation Army shop (947 Second Ave.) and an Unclaimed Railroad Furniture shop (937 Second Ave.). Once it's furnished, stock it up at the Nyborg & Nelson Swedish delicatessen.

[16a.] 219 East 49th Street, bet. Second and Third Aves. 1935. Morris Sanders.

A ground-floor office and two duplexes, all clearly expressed on the facade. Dark glazed brick was used to fend off soot, balconies to control sunlight.

[16b.] Amster Yard, 211–215 E. 49th St. bet. Second and Third Aves. 1870. Remodeled, 1945, Harold Sterner. ★

A passage with a slate floor and iron settees leads into the garden, from which office of James Amster Associates, other interior designers, and a few shops can be reached. Look carefully for the mirror at the end of the garden vista. Sculptor Isamu Noguchi once did his work in this yard.

[17a.] U. S. Plywood Building, 777 Third Ave bet. 48th and 49th St. E side. 1964. William Lescaze.

Handsome dark gray glass and aluminum walls rising from an arcade of dark gray granite columns, the massing and open space following the new zoning law. Automated plywood exhibit in the street-floor showroom.

[17b.] William Lescaze Residence, 211 E. 48th St. bet. Third and Second Ave. 1934. William Lescaze.

A pioneering modern townhouse, protected from city atmosphere by glass block and air conditioning. The office is at the bottom, house above, with a living room occupying the whole top floor.

c.]  [21.]

[18.] Harcourt Brace & World Building, 757 Third Ave. NE cor. 47th St. 1964. Emery Roth & Sons. **Book store** by Cloethiel W. Smith.

The recessed loggia (with benches) behind the red granite columns leads to the unusual store by America's best-known lady architect.

[19.] Shelton Towers Hotel, Lexington Ave. bet. 48th and 49th Sts. 1924. Arthur Loomis Harmon.

One of the first tall buildings (34 stories) to use the setback requirements of the 1916 Zoning Law creatively, it made a great impression on architects and artists of the 1920's. Brick masses accented with sparse, vaguely Romanesque, details.

[20.] Barclay Hotel, 111 E. 48th St. NW cor. Lexington Ave.

An elegant survivor of the Park Avenue development of the 1920's. Cocktails are served on the terrace overlooking the lobby, the centerpiece of which is a large gilded bird-cage.

MISCELLANY:

[21.] 242 East 52nd Street/formerly **the Museum of Modern Art Guest House,** bet. Second and Third Aves. 1950. Philip Johnson.

An understated front of brick and translucent glass that hides a two-part house around a central pool.

[22.] 312 and 314 East 53rd Street, bet. First and Second Aves. 1866. ★

A pair of wood town houses of Second Empire inspiration, with interesting corbeled entrance hoods and round-topped dormers.

FIFTH AVENUE—47th-57th STREETS

This stretch of the Avenue, where fashionable shops have been concentrated since the 1920's, was **a solid line** of **mansions, churches,** and **clubs** at the turn of the century. Two factors maintained the elegance of Fifth Avenue as the **stores moved north along it:** the Fifth Avenue Association (whose members have fought off billboards, bootblacks, parking lots, projecting signs—even funeral

parlors) and the lack of "els" or subways. To provide a genteel alternative for rapid transit, the **Fifth Avenue Transportation Company** was established in 1885, using horse-cars until 1907, followed by the fondly remembered open-top (until 1936) double-deck buses, until 1953. Despite a fight by the Association, the ordinary buses, as all traffic, on today's avenue run only southward.

[1a.] Olivetti Underwood Corp. Showroom, 584 Fifth Ave. bet 47th and 48th Sts. W side. 1954. Belgiojoso, Peressutti & Rogers.

With its typewriters on green marble pedestals growing out of the floor and its Constantino Nivola sand mural it is perennially avant-garde.

[1b.] Brentano's, 586 Fifth Ave. bet. 47th and 48th Sts. W side. Alterations, 1965, Warner, Burns, Toan & Lunde.

Three narrow passages lead from the avenue and two streets into a multi-level central space full of books, jewelry, ceramics, etc.

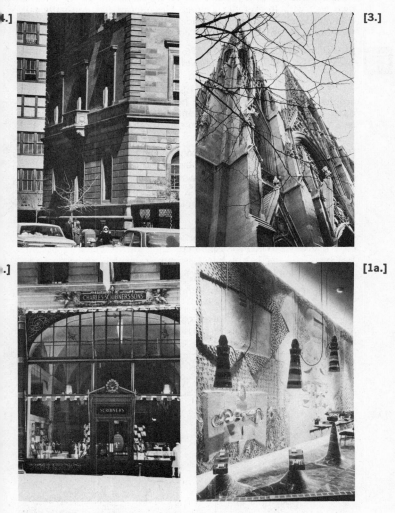

[4.]

[3.]

[.]

[1a.]

[1c.] Spanish National Tourist Office, 587 Fifth Ave. bet. 47th and 48th Sts. E side. 1964. Javier Carvajal.

An austere plaster and oak cave (by the designer of the Spanish Pavilion at the 1964-1965 World's Fair) sometimes obscured by displays.

[2a.] Chas. Scribner's Sons. 597 Fifth Ave. bet. 48th and 49th St. E side. 1913. Ernest Flagg. ☆

Flagg used a big handsome glass front to show his superb two-story book store interior.

[2b.] KLM-Royal Dutch Airlines Ticket Office, 609 Fifth Ave. SE cor. 49th St. 1959. Raymond & Rado.

The tall space, with, mural of moving lights by Gyorgy Kepes covering a whole wall, is all but smothered in displays.

[3.] St. Patrick's Cathedral (Roman Catholic), Fifth to Madison Aves. bet. 50th and 51st Sts. E side. 1858—1879. Archbishop's residence (452 Madison Ave. NW cor. 50th St.) and Rectory (460 Madison Ave. SW cor. 51th St.) 1880–1884. James Renwick. Lady Chapel, 1906, Charles T. Mathews. ★

Renwick's adaptation of French Gothic was weakened by his use of unyielding granite and his deletion of the flying buttresses (without deleting their pinnacle counterweights). But the cathedral, with its twin 330-foot towers, has an imposing mass that holds its own well with Rockefeller Center. The interior has unusually tall, thin columns screening off tall side aisles. The Lady Chapel behind the altar is in more academically correct French Gothic style.

[4.] Villard Houses, Madison Ave. bet. 50th and 51st Sts. E side 1882-1886, 1909. McKim, Mead & White. Also Babb, Cook & Willard. ☆

Mansions in chaste early Italian Renaissance style grouped around a formal court, now the headquarters of several organizations including Random House and the Roman Catholic Archdiocese of New York. Note the ironwork, both in the great gates and in ground floor window grilles.

[5.] Cartier, Inc./formerly **Morton F. Plant Residence,** 651 Fifth Ave. SE cor. 52nd St. 1905. Robert W. Gibson. ☆ Remodeled as shop, 1917, William Welles Bosworth. **Extension at 4 E. 52nd St.**/ formerly **private residence,** 1905, C. P. H. Gilbert.

Two fine mansions well adapted to the needs of a fine jewelry shop.

Twenty-one Club: Jack and Charlie's place, at 21 W. 52nd St. was only one of several Prohibition-era clubs on its block to become fashionable in the 1930's, but it alone remains, having become successor to Delmonico's and Sherry's as society's dining room.

[6.] 666 Fifth Avenue, bet. 52nd and 53rd Sts. W side. 1957. Carson & Lundin.

A million square feet of office space wrapped in embossed aluminum. Note the sculpture-waterfall and ceiling by Isamu Noguchi in the arcade.

Scandinavian Elegance: Georg Jensen has been selling Jensen-designed silver, Lunning furniture, and other fine Scandinavian crafts at 667 Fifth Ave. (SE cor. 53rd St.) for decades.

[11.]  [1

[7.] Samuel Paley Plaza, 3 E. 53rd St. bet. Fifth and Madison Aves. 1967. Zion & Breen Landscape architect, Albert Preston Moore, Consulting Architect.

A parklet contributed by William S. Paley, head of CBS.

[8a.] St. Thomas' Church and Parish House (Episcopal), 1 W. 53rd St. NW cor. Fifth Ave. 1909–1914. Cram, Goodhue & Ferguson. ★

The addition to the Irving Trust Company Building in New York City was completed in 1966. This building is located about 1 block south of Wall Street. Contractor: Turner Construction Company; Architects: Smith, Smith, Haines, Lundberg & Waehler.

Indiana Limestone... nature's best ...man's finest building material

Above all others, Indiana Limestone stands out as the best building material you can use. Whatever your requirements are . . . strength, durability, low upkeep, quiet colors, pleasant textures . . . Indiana Limestone offers them all. But most important, it gives buildings that unique appearance which makes them outstanding, impressive, memorable . . . a credit to their owners, a major contribution to beautifying our cities, and a joy to the eyes of all beholders. Irving Trust Company of New York selected Indiana Limestone for their stately new addition to the city's beautiful skyline. Across the country, thousands of architects are using Indiana Limestone for buildings, houses, stores, schools, factories, churches, in hundreds of new and exciting ways. Indiana Limestone is a perfect building material for most of the existing architectural styles. So if your specifications call for a good building material, check nature's best . . . Indiana Limestone.

INDIANA ▌▌ LIMESTONE COMPANY, INC.
Bedford, Indiana

One of Goodhue's finest essays in picturesque massing and detail, built on a constricted corner. Note the play of dense detail against big plain surfaces. The interior is like a small, rich cathedral.

[8b.] INTRA Bank Building/formerly **Canada House,** 680 Fifth Ave. SW cor. 54th St. 1958. Eggers & Higgins.

Its massing and neutral Alabama limestone walls were meant to complement St. Thomas' Church—and succeed very well.

[9.] America-Israel Cultural Foundation/formerly **William H. Moore Residence,** 4 E. 54th St. bet. Fifth and Madison Aves. 1900. McKim, Mead & White. ☆

[10a.] University Club, 1 W. 54th St., NW cor. Fifth Ave. 1899. McKim, Mead & White. ☆

An imposing Italian Renaissance palazzo. Three extra-tall stories—for the first-floor salon (visible from the street in the evening), the library, and the main dining room—alternate with normal stories for auxiliary rooms. If you can get in, be sure to see the vast library, with its wood colonnades and hide-and-seek mezzanines.

[10b.] Philip Lehman Residence, 7 W. 54th St. bet. Fifth and Sixth Aves. 1900. John H. Duncan. ☆

[10c.] Rhodes School, 9—11 W. 54th St. bet. Fifth and Sixth Aves. 1898. McKim, Mead & White. ☆

Masks and Spears: The Museum of Primitive Art is in another interesting old house at 15 W. 54th St. (bet. Fifth and Sixth Aves.)

[13b.]

[11.] Rockefeller Apartments, 17 W. 54th St. bet. Fifth and Sixth Aves. 1936. Harrison & Fouilhoux.

Two buildings (on 54th and 55th Sts.) back-to-back around a central garden. Note the fine details of the cylindrical dining bays. The Italian Pavilion restaurant, in the building at 24 W. 55th St. has tables in the garden (JU 6-5950).

[12a.] T. Jones, 697 Fifth Ave. bet. 54th and 55th Sts. E side. 1965. Morris Ketchum, Jr., & Associates.

Colorful shoe boxes used as decoration, played against earthy, textured surfaces.

[12b.] St. Regis-Sheraton Hotel, 2 E. 55th St. SE cor. Fifth Ave. 1901—1904. Trowbridge & Livingston. ☆

A richly decorated Beaux-Arts mass that gets better toward the top. Second only to the Plaza in number of prominent guests, the hotel is especially popular with foreign diplomats. The Maisonette in winter and the St. Regis roof in summer have long attracted High Society for dining and dancing. The King Cole Bar is designed around a Maxfield Parrish mural that once graced the Knickerbocker Hotel bar. [See Times Sq. 3b.]

[12c.] Mario Buccellati (shop), 701 Fifth Ave. SE cor. 55th St. Remodeling, 1964, Fleishman & Sedlis.

One of a row of elegant well designed shops where the St. Regis dining room used to be. Each shows a strong effort to relate to the building, but unfortunately no two do it the same way.

[12d.] Gotham Hotel, 2 W. 55th St., SW cor. Fifth Ave. 1902–1905. Hiss & Weeks. ☆

The mate of the St. Regis across the street, a little more angular, but just as ornate—and almost as fashionable, mainly with movie stars. All control over Fifth Avenue shop fronts was lost here.

[13a.] Sona the Golden One, 7 E. 55th St. bet. Fifth and Madison Aves. 1965. Richard Meier and Elaine Lustig Cohen Associates.

An oriental bazaar.

[13b.] Lederer de Paris, 711 Fifth Ave. bet. 55th and 56th Sts. E side. 1939. Morris Ketchum, Jr. and Victor Gruen.

Pace-setting shop perfectly preserved, frameless showcases and all.

[14a.] Rizzoli International Book Store/formerly **Cartier Building,** 712 Fifth Ave. bet. 55th and 56th Sts. W side. 1907. A. S. Gottlieb. ☆

A street-floor front of Neapolitan opulence leads into a treasury of fine books, open to browsers until midnight, except Sunday.

[16.]

[14b.] Former Coty Building, 714 Fifth Ave. bet. 55th and 56th Sts. W side. 1908. W. Leeming. ☆

[14c.] Harry Winston, Inc. 718 Fifth Ave. SW cor. 56th St. 1959. Charles Luckman Assocs.

The once modernistic Corning Glass Building transformed into a travertine-coated setting for extravagant jewels.

Eat Street: That's what columnist Earl Wilson calls W. 56th St. between Fifth and Sixth Aves. It holds a record for a single block, with about two dozen restaurants—from French and Italian to Japanese and Korean. Above the close ranks of canopies are some interesting house fronts.

[14d]. Hallmark Gallery, 720 Fifth Ave. NW cor. 56th St. 1965. Edward Durell Stone.

Another travertine remodeling, classical only in spirit. The intriguing exhibits (mementoes, photographs, etc.) can be seen by looking down from the street but reached only via the greeting card showroom.

[15.] Corning Glass Building, 717 Fifth Ave. SE cor. 56th St. 1959. Harrison & Abramovitz & Abbe.

Mirror-smooth walls of green glass rise out of a plaza pool. The lobby (entered from both 55th and 56th Sts.) has a mirrored ceiling and huge Albers reliefs on its white marble walls.

Fiberglas Showroom: Products of the Owens-Corning Fiberglas Corp. are on display in their street level showroom in the Corning Glass Building (56th St. side).

[16.] I. Miller Shoe Salon, SW cor. Fifth Ave. and 57th St. 1961. Victor Lundy. (in Genesco Building/formerly Heckscher Building. 1921. Warren & Wetmore.)

Tree-like wood-clad columns in the two-story space spread at the ceiling with cathedral-like effect. The original muted colors have been livened up by the owners.

Tiffany's: One of the oldest and most famous jewelers in the world came to the corner of Fifth Ave. and 57th St. in 1940. The show windows in its massive polished granite facade (727 Fifth Ave.) are famous for their miniature stage-setting displays.

ROCKEFELLER CENTER AREA

The waves of elegant construction that rolled up Fifth Avenue never reached as far west as Sixth Avenue. Rockefeller Center was expected to **trigger renewal in the 1930's,** but the Sixth Avenue "El," running up to 53rd Street until 1940, was too grim an obstacle. It was not until the **Time and Life Building** went up in 1960 that a Sixth Avenue building boom started.

[1.] Rockefeller Center, W. 48th to W. 51st Sts., Fifth to Sixth Aves. 1931–1940. Reinhard & Hofmeister; Corbett, Harrison & MacMurray; Hood & Fouilhoux. Esso Building, 15 W. 51st St. at Rockefeller Plaza. 1947. Carson & Lundin. Guided tours 9:30 AM–5:30 PM (including RCA observation deck). Deck open 9 AM–7 PM, Midnight April to October.

This 17-acre cluster, with almost 10,000,000 square feet of rentable space, is the most successful effort at high-density urban design in the nation. The 13 buildings constructed up through 1947 have a uniform vertical wall treatment of gray Indiana limestone that identifies them as a group. Three later buildings included in the statistics are not visually part of the center.

The best introduction to the massing and spatial sequence of the center is the promenade that leads into the middle of it from Fifth Avenue between 49th and 50th Streets. Passing between low buildings, with a series of planting beds and fountains stepping down the center, it descends a whole floor from the avenue to the edge of the skating rink that is the focus of the whole complex. One's attention is held by the gradually revealed complex of terraces around the rink, heralded by flags and the well-known gilded figure of Prometheus by Paul Manship, until the whole terraced composition is visible; only then does one look up the 850-foot prow of the RCA Building, its height emphasized both by the sunken rink and by the vertically striped gray walls. A slight difference in level is remarkably effective in isolating the space around the rink from the busy streets all around. (The developers actually *added* space for automobile circulation.) Another device that makes the center seem tranquil is the underground truck delivery system, serving all buildings, entered on the north side of 50th Street

Restaurants include Rainbow Room (and Grill) at RCA 65th floor (dining, dancing, expensive, PL 7-9090); Cafe Français and English Grill, flanking skating rink.

[1a.] Singer Showroom, La Maison Française at Rockefeller Plaza. 1965. Victor Lundy.

[1b.] EL-AL Israel Airlines, La Maison Francais at Channel Gardens. 1964. Samton Assocs. Wall relief, Glen Michaels.

[1c.] Japan Airlines Ticket Office, British Building at Channel Gardens. 1956. Raymond & Rado; Junzo Yoshimura, Associate architect.

Armstrong Product Center: 60 W. 49 St. showcase for flooring, ceilings, and other interior finishes.

[1.]

[2.] Time and Life Building, 1271 Avenue of the Americas (Sixth Ave.) NW cor. 50th St. 1960. Harrison, Abramovitz & Harris.

When Time and Life outgrew its building in the original Rockefeller Center (now General Dynamics Building), the Center management made its first venture west of Sixth Avenue and started a trend. Time and Life relates to the Center's original buildings in its massing, vertical lines, and in the pleasant sitting space at its southeast corner, but it is clearly a separate event.

[2a.] La Fonda del Sol (restaurant), 123 W. 50th St. bet. Sixth and Seventh Aves. (in the Time and Life Building). 1960. Alexander Girard.

The toy displays may be too extensive, but otherwise the forms spaces, and materials are impeccably controlled, though exuberant.

Note especially the bar and the ladies' room, the "exterior" of which is visible to all. The menu selects wisely from all over Latin America. Prices are moderate at lunch, jump up at dinner. PL 7-8800.

Wax Museum: New York's only example of this subtle art form is the Museum of Famous People at 135 W. 50th St.

[3.] Equitable Building, 1285 Avenue of the Americas (Sixth Ave.) bet. 51st and 52nd Sts. W side. 1961. Skidmore, Owings & Merrill.

An SOM effort to get maximum working space for the price.

[4.] Sperry Rand Building, 1290 Avenue of the Americas (Sixth Ave.) bet. 51st and 52nd St. E side. 1962. Emery Roth & Sons.

Like Time and Life, this is officially part of Rockefeller Center; but the resemblance is weak—and the exterior open space minuscule.

[4a.] Xerox Showroom, 1290 Avenue of the Americas (Sixth Ave.) SE cor. 52nd St. 1963. Eliot Noyes & Assocs.

A lively showroom that shows both architect and industrial designer at work; the client, typically, has tried to liven it up even more.

[5.] J. C. Penney Building, 1301 Avenue of the Americas (Sixth Ave.) bet. 52nd and 53rd Sts. W side. 1965. Shreve, Lamb & Harmon Assocs.

The interest here is in making the level below the street rentable by opening up a sunken plaza—fairly agreeable as a concept.

[2a.]  [7.

[6.] New York Hilton, 1335 Avenue of the Americas (Sixth Ave.) bet. 53rd and 54th Sts. 1963. William B. Tabler.

Clearly designed for conventions, this 2200 room hotel has a low, horizontal box of public spaces hovering above deeply recessed entrances; rising from it is a thin vertical slab of guest rooms. The rick-rack blue glass walls of the slab give each room a bay window and have a pleasing crystalline look when seen at an angle. The clarity of the exterior volumes is not reflected in the interior.

[7.] CBS Building, 51 W. 52nd St. NE cor. Sixth Ave. 1965. Eero Saarinen & Assocs. (Interior architects, office floors: Carson, Lundin & Shaw, Interior designers, office floors: Knoll Planning Unit.)

Saarinen's only high-rise building is a sheer, freestanding 38-story, concrete-framed tower clad in dark gray honed granite; a somber and striking understatement.

One of several buildings of its time to depart from established post-and-beam framing, CBS supports its floors instead on its central core and a dense grid—in effect a bearing wall—at the exterior. But it is the only one to carry the closely-spaced members down to the ground, rather than transferring structural loads to widely spaced piers at the lobby. (CBS' service requirements are handled through a low freestanding rear element connected underground.)

The Ground Floor, an elegant restaurant whose name gently spoofs the many top-floor restaurants, was designed down to table settings by the Saarinen office.

Early American Folk Arts: A small museum on this very pleasant subject can be found upstairs in an old house at 49 W. 53rd St.

[8a.] Museum of Contemporary Crafts, 29 W. 53rd St., bet. Sixth and Fifth Aves. 1956. David Campbell.

Some very nice spaces on many levels carved out of an old row house. The exhibits are often staged with great sophistication.

[8b.] America House, 44 W. 53rd St., bet. Sixth and Fifth Aves. 1961. David Campbell.

[9.] Museum of Modern Art, 11 W. 53rd St. bet. Sixth and Fifth Aves. 1939. Philip L. Goodwin and Edward Durell Stone. Additions and alterations, 1951 and 1964, Philip Johnson Assocs.

The museum has been a trail-blazer for modern design, not only in its exhibits, but in its buildings and gardens. Besides its vast collection of fine arts, photography, and motion pictures (selections shown daily), it has small permanent exhibits of modern architecture and industrial design (and frequent large temporary ones). The 1939 building survives now in the upper floor facades of the central building, the basement lounge and auditorium, and the main stairwell. The greatly enlarged lobby and most of the exhibition spaces are by Johnson. His 1951 west wing and 1964 east wing depart progressively farther from the original flat International Style surfaces, ending with deeply three-dimensional grids of painted steel standing free of the wall.

His finest contribution is the garden, an expansion and remodeling of his own earlier one. Here elegant stone, plantings, pools, and fountains have been composed into one of the handsomest gardens of its size to be seen anywhere. From its upper level, there are excellent views of the garden and museum, some surrounding towers, and a remarkable row of buildings on the north side of 54th Street. [See Fifth Avenue 10 and 11.]

MISCELLANY:

[10.] Phoenix Building, 1180 Sixth Ave. NE cor. 46th St. 1963. Emery Roth & Sons.

Perhaps the finest handling of an office tower within the maximum envelope of the old Zoning Law. The syncopated setbacks and the carefully studied detailing of the strip windows and tiers of continuous brick spandrels make this a fine work. The attempt to be "pretty" at street level is the building's major failing.

CENTRAL PARK SOUTH

The neighborhood stretching between the south side of the park and parallel 57th Street has a sense of unity generated by these strong lines and the cultural institutions at **Columbus Circle** and nearby in the **Carnegie Hall area.** It is a transition, a zone between Times Square **honky-tonk** and Central Park **gentility,** with Fifth Avenue's elegance percolating west through it into the general shabbiness of the far West Side.

[1.] Church of St. Paul the Apostle (Roman Catholic), 415 W. 59th St., NE cor. Columbus Ave. 1876-1885. Jeremiah O'Rourke.

An unadorned fort on the outside, except for one inexplicable mural, it turns into a Roman basilica inside, embellished with the works of such as St. Gaudens, MacMonnies, and John LaFarge, with the advice of Stanford White and Bertram Goodhue. All of their efforts are lost in the thick atmosphere.

[2.] Columbus Circle, Broadway at 59th St.

This focal point, where Broadway glances the corner of Central Park, was the obvious place for monumental treatment, but it turned out to be a few sculptures in a tangle of traffic. Gaetano Russo's statue of **Columbus** (1892) is at the hub; Architect H. Van Buren Magonigle's **Maine Memorial** (1913) wallows in from the park corner, with a boatload of figures by sculptor Attilio Piccirilli.

[2.]

[2a.] Gallery of Modern Art, 2 Columbus Circle. bet. Eighth Ave. and Broadway. S side. 1965. Edward Durell Stone.

A compact white marble confection, shaped to the constricted site. It shows off well when seen from the north on Broadway, gleaming among larger, darker structures.

Automobile Row: The main midtown showrooms of U.S. car makers are lined up on Broadway from 53rd St. to Columbus Circle, as they have been since the days of the Hupmobile.

[2b.] 240 Central Park South, SE cor. Broadway. 1941. Mayer & Whittlesey.

Two apartment towers rising from a one-story, **garden-topped podium** give all the big windows and balconies a good view. There are some problems of form in the **ziggurat top,** but the detailing is fine. Note the zigzag store fronts on Broadway.

Central Park South east of 240 is an impressive cliff, including luxury hotels and apartments, but there is little, except for the care-free decoration on the old **Gainsborough Studios,** No. 222, that calls for a close look.

[3.] Art Students League/formerly **American Fine Arts Society,** 215 W. 57th St. 1892. Henry J. Hardenbergh. ☆

A stately French Renaissance structure, originally built for an organization that included the Architectural League, is now an art school.

[4.] The Osborne Apartments, 205 W. 57th St. NW cor. Seventh Ave. 1885. James E. Ware.

The crazy-quilt exterior of Classical and Chicago School stone-work and glassy store-fronts hides elegant interiors, hinted at in the marble vestibule and lobby.

[5.] Alwyn Court Apartments, 180 W. 58th St. SE cor. Seventh Ave. 1909. Harde & Short. ★

A French Renaissance exterior literally encrusted with decoration.

[6.] Carnegie Hall, SE cor. 57th St. and Seventh Ave. 1891. William B. Tuthill; William Morris Hunt, Dankmar Adler, consultants. ★

The chaste Classical block of the hall itself is engulfed in the bristling offices and studios above and around it. The hall, noted more for its sound than its appearance, was almost lost in the early 1960's when Philharmonic Hall went up, but is now constantly booked. The building also houses a fine recital hall and a cinema.

3.]

[4.]

[7.] Manhattan Life Insurance Building/formerly **Steinway Hall,** 111 W. 57th St. bet. Seventh and Sixth Aves. 1925. Warren & Wetmore.

A sober Classical tower built by one of the many music concerns clustered around Carnegie Hall. The change of ownership has not changed the colorful street-floor piano showroom.

Fun Furs and Fun Food: Among West 57th Street's motley wares are off-beat furs—**second-hand** in shops between Sixth and Seventh Aves., brand-new between Fifth and Sixth. **Pick-it-yourself food** is available at the Horn & Hardart Automat at 104 W. 57th St., one of the more palatial of their 40 coin-in-the-slot restaurants. For a more elegant (and expensive) selection, try the smorgasbord at the **Copenhagen,** 68 W. 58th St. (MU 8-3690). The **St. Moritz Hotel** at Sixth Avenue and 59th St. offers a real sidewalk **Cafe de la Paix** and **Rumpelmayer's** lavish ice cream and confections (PL 5-5800).

UPPER WEST SIDE

A great deal of whatever it is that is New York, is concentrated in the **Upper West Side.** Between Central Park and the Hudson River, from Lincoln Square north to Morningside Heights, this area has been defamed as both an **air-tight cage** and a **gilded ghetto.** But, it is neither. Despite **massive problems,** it is an area of **liveliness** and hope and contains a **diversity of people,** buildings, stores, and institutions rubbing shoulders with one another. With the completion of the **West Side Urban Renewal Development,** the blossoming of Lincoln Square, the projected growth of Columbia University, and **a revival of interest** in the City's parks, this strategically located precinct will survive and even prosper as **an alive and attractive residential area.**

LINCOLN SQUARE

Developed quickly in the 1880's along the Ninth Avenue "el," which ran right through the Lincoln Square crossroads, **the area was never fashionable** except right along Central Park. By the late 1940's, the portion west of Broadway was **a slum,** now almost obliterated by a 12-block **renewal project** that includes Lincoln Center, Lincoln Towers apartments, and Fordham University's in-town campus. Before they crumbled, some of the tenements had their day in the limelight as **the location for filming** Leonard Bernstein's musical saga **"West Side Story."**

 [1.] American Bible Society Building, 1865 Broadway, NW cor. 61st St. 1966. Skidmore, Owings & Merrill.

The precast structural skeleton of this burly building is exposed, with bridge-sized beams making a giant ladder of the Broadway end.

[2.] Century Apartments, 25 Central Park West bet. 62nd and 63rd Sts. 1931. Office of Irwin S. Chanin.

Like the Majestic Apartments [see 10b.] by the same architects, it makes some pleasant gestures toward modern style. The name recalls the lavish and unprofitable Century Theater, designed by Carrère & Hastings, which stood on the site from 1909 until razed for the apartments.

[3a.] Society for Ethical Culture, 2 W. 64th St. SW cor. Central Park West, 1910. Robert D. Kohn.

Tavern-on-the-Green: The entrance to this bucolic eating-drinking-dancing spot, built around an 1870 sheepfold, is at 67th St. and Central Park West. Fairly expensive. TR 3-3200.

[3b.] Congregation Shearith Israel, 8 W. 70th St. SW cor. Central Park West. 1897. Brunner & Tryon.

The newest home of New York's oldest Jewish congregation, founded downtown by Spanish and Portuguese immigrants in 1655.

A connected "Little Synagogue," reproduces the Georgian style of the congregation's first real synagogue, built in 1730; it contains many furnishings used in that building.

[4.] Hotel des Artistes, 1 W. 67th St. bet. Central Park West and Columbus Ave. 1915–1918.

The fanciful facade clearly shows the balconied studios behind it. An early tenant, Howard Chandler Christy, painted a pin-up girl (his specialty) to decorate the cozy *Cafe des Artistes* on the first floor.

[5.] Lincoln Center for the Performing Arts, W. 62nd to W. 66th Sts. Columbus to Amsterdam Aves. 1962–1968. Wallace K. Harrison, Director of Board of Architects (composed of architects of individual buildings).

This **acropolis of music and theater** represents an investment of more than $165 million, most of it **private contributions**—along with **Federal aid** in acquiring the site and a **state contribution** to the New York State Theater.

The project **has aroused dissent** on both **urbanistic and architectural grounds.** The congestion caused by the location of so many large theaters **in one cluster** (with only meager public transportation) has been an obvious problem, left unsolved by the vast underground garage beneath the project. Making **a single impressive group** out of structures with such **demanding interior requirements** has imposed inhibitions on the individual buildings. As a result, *New York Times* critic Ada Louise Huxtable, has said, "Philharmonic Hall, the State Theater, and the Metropolitan Opera are lushly decorated, conservative structures that the public finds pleasing and most professionals consider a failure of nerve, imagination and talent."

"Fortunately," she continued, "the scale and relationship of the plazas is good, and they can be enjoyed as pedestrian open spaces." And the project **has spurred new development** of this once shabby neighborhood, at least in the immediate vicinity.

[5a.] New York State Theater, SE cor. Lincoln Center, Columbus Ave. bet. 62nd and 63rd Sts. 1964. Philip Johnson and Richard Foster.

This 2800-seat theater, designed mainly for ballet and musical theater, also includes a vast four-story foyer suitable for receptions and balls. It is the most frankly Classical building in the group. The plaza-level lobby is **a Baroque space** that seems to have been carved from the enveloping travertine. The grand foyer above it, by contrast, is bounded by **tiers of busy metal balconies,** glass with gold-colored chain drapery, and gold-leafed ceiling. It is dominated by two white marble sculptures, enlargements of earlier **Elie Nadelman** works. The "Delancey Street rhinestone" lights and chandeliers inside and out are a false note.

[5b.] Philharmonic Hall, NE cor. Lincoln Center, Columbus Ave. bet. 64th and 65th Sts. 1962. Max Abramovitz.

The many-tiered lobby of this concert hall has a completely transparent enclosure of clear glass between tapered columns. Richard Lippold's gleaming metal construction in two symmetrical clusters hangs in the tall narrow space at the front. The interior of the hall had widely-publicized acoustical problems at first, which have led to a series of changes in its design and materials.

[5b.]

[5c.] Metropolitan Opera House, W side of Lincoln Center, bet. 63rd and 64th Sts. 1966. Wallace K. Harrison.

The focal building of the complex and its largest hall, the new "Met" shows its dominance with a high, vaulted portico facing the central plaza. Inside, the lobby is a **sensuous composition** of red-carpeted stairs winding around themselves and two freestanding columns. Brilliant **Austrian crystal chandeliers** hang in the middle of the tall space, as they do inside the hall itself until performance time, when they silently rise to the **goldleafed ceiling.** The café at the top of the lobby offers a dizzying view down into the lobby and out across the plaza.

[5d.] Vivian Beaumont Theater, NW cor. Lincoln Center, Amsterdam Ave. and 65th St. 1965. Eero Saarinen & Associates. **[5e.] Library-Museum of the Performing Arts,** 1965, Skidmore, Owings & Merrill.

An unusual collaboration, with the library filling the massive attic story over the 1100-seat repertory drama theater. The building is a **handsome backdrop** for the **formal pool** with its **Henry Moore** sculpture, especially when the glass-enclosed, split-level lobby is lighted and populated. In the theater, neutral, dark interior surfaces do not compete with the colorful tiered seating or the action of the **highly flexible stage.**

The library-museum, entered from the link leading from the Opera House, has typically meticulous SOM details and some lively audio-visual exhibits.

[5f.] Juilliard School of Music, Broadway bet. W. 65th and 66th Sts. 1968. Pietro Belluschi, with Eduardo Catalano and Westermann & Miller.

Statue of Liberty: The roof top lady at 43 W. 64th Street is 55 feet high, or about one-third full size. Built in 1902, she had a spiral stair to her head, now closed; and her torch has blown away.

[6.] American Red Cross Building, 150 Amsterdam Ave. bet. 66th and 67th Sts. W side. 1964. Skidmore, Owings & Merrill.

A simple, low-rise structure with an external concrete frame.

[7.] Litho City, W. 59th St. to W. 72nd St.; West End Ave. to the Hudson River. Proposal, 1963. Kelly & Gruzen.

This riverfront project, originally sponsored by the Amalgamated Lithographers of America, would have placed housing for 15,000 people—along with shopping, park, piers, an international student center, and a new headquarters for the New York Times—over exposed freight yards and on sites of existing piers. Opposed by local interests, this project would have stimulated the Upper West Side, but has now been abandoned.

[5d.]

[8.] Public School 199, Manhattan, 70th St. SE cor. West End Ave. 1963. Edward Durell Stone.

The beginning of a modest trend to give city school commissions to prominent architects, it was built in connection with the awe inspiring mega-slabs of the 4000-odd-unit Lincoln Towers urban renewal project around it.

SHERMAN SQUARE

[9a.] Christ Church, 211 W. 71st bet. Broadway and West End Ave. 1890. Charles C. Haight. ☆

A Romanesque Revival church in orange brick with terra cotta trim built in the form of a Greek cross; this church is unusual in that it runs parallel with the street.

[9b.] The Dorilton, 171 W 71st St. NE cor. Broadway. 1900. Janes & Leo.

Luxury apartments in the Second Empire style.

[9c.] Sherman Square IRT Subway Entrance, Broadway at 72nd St. 1904. C. Grant LaFarge.

[9d.] Sherman Square Studios, 160 W. 73rd St. bet. Broadway and Columbus Ave. ca. 1925.

Behind a banal facade are soundproof studio apartments, specially constructed to house professional musicians.

[9e.] Verdi Square and Giuseppe Verdi Statue, Broadway at W. 73rd St. 1906. Pasquale Civiletti, Sculptor.

This small green, on the site of the ancient village of Harsenville honors the great Italian composer. At the base of the marble statue are life-size figures of four characters from Verdi's operas, *Aida, Falstaff, Otello,* and *Forza del Destino.*

[9f.] Central Savings Bank, 2100 Broadway NE cor. 73rd St.

1928. York & Sawyer. ☆

Offices above a Palladian Palace. Wrought-iron lanterns and window grilles by Samuel Yellin are the finest features of this richly embellished limestone bank building.

[9g.] Ansonia Hotel, 2107 Broadway, 73rd to 74th Sts. 1902. Graves and Duboy. W. E. D. Stokes, Designer. ☆

This richly ornamented apartment hotel, in the style of the resort hotels of the French Riviera, is the product of Stokes' (cousin of architect I. N. Phelps Stokes) studies at the Ecole des Beaux-Arts.

[9h.] Astor Apartments, W Side of Broadway, 74th to 75th Sts. ca. 1905.

[10a.] Majestic Apartments, 115 Central Park West, W. 71st to W. 72nd Sts. 1930. Office of Irwin S. Chanin.

One of four twin-towered apartment buildings which make the skyline along Central Park West a unique visual treat. This stream-lined building has wide banks of windows that extend around its sides. The much-copied brickwork patterns and futurist forms were designed by sculptor Rene Chanbellan.

[10b.] Dakota Apartments, 1 W. 72nd St. NW cor. Central Park West. 1884. Henry J. Hardenbergh. ☆

The city's first luxury apartment house dominated Central Park before the park drives were paved. It has been a prestige ad-dress, particularly for those in the arts, since the days when this part of the city was thought to be out in the Dakota Territory.

[10b.]

[10c.] The Langham, 135 Central Park West, W 73rd to W. 74th Sts. 1907. Clinton & Russell.

[10d.] Georgian Row Houses, 18–52 W. 74th St. bet. Central Park West and Columbus Ave. 1904. Percy Griffith.

[10e.] San Remo Apartments, 145 Central Park West, 74th to 75th Sts. 1930. Emery Roth.

[11a.] Church of the Divine Paternity, 4 W. 76th St. SE cor. Central Park West, 1898. R. H. Robertson & W. A. Potter.

A well-proportioned interior dominated by a huge mosaic.

[11b.] New-York Historical Society, 170 Central Park West, W. 76th to W. 77th Sts. Central portion, 1908, York & Sawyer; North and South Wings, 1938, Walker and Gillette. ☆

A restrained Classical palace is both an important museum and a research library for American history. Included in its vast holdings are the McKim, Mead, & White files and 432 original drawings of Audubon's Birds of America. [See U Manhattan 1a; 2.]

[12a.] American Museum of Natural History, Manhattan Sq. Central Park West, 77th to 81st Sts. 77th Street Building, 1877. J. C. Cady and Co.; Hayden Planetarium, 1935. Trowbridge and Livingston; Roosevelt Memorial Building, 1936. John Russell Pope. ★

One of the great scientific collections of the world. Cady's original building, gains its strength through the use of rough-hewn red granite in the Romanesque Revival style. Pope's pink granite Classical front facing Central Park is saved by the handsome equestrian statue of Theodore Roosevelt.

[14a.]

[9c.]

[9g.]

[12b.] Beresford Apartments, 1 W. 81st St., NE cor. Central Park West. 1928. Emery Roth.

[13.] West 78th Street, bet. Columbus and Amsterdam Aves.

A polyglot block of row houses undergoing sensitive if varied renovations. While facades, cornices, lintels, and stoops from the late 19th Century are being carefully retained and restored, tasteful yet jazzy exterior painting anchors this block firmly in the present.

[14a.] Apthorp Apartments, Broadway to West End Ave. W. 78th to W. 79th Sts. 1908. Clinton & Russell. ☆

This unusually handsome, richly ornamented limestone building occupies an entire block. The individual entrances are reached through high vaulted tunnels and a large interior court with a fountain in its center. Probably the best of the surviving Astor properties in New York. [See 18 and 21a; Harlem 11a; and W Bronx 4c.]

[14b.] First Baptist Church, Broadway, NW cor. W. 79th St. 1891.

[15.] West End Collegiate Church, West End Ave., NE cor. W. 77th St.·1892. Robert W. Gibson. ☆

Flemish gables and rich orange brickwork, provide a handsome home for this ancient congregation and cement its ties to the Netherlands.

[16.] Riverside Park, Riverside Drive, W. 72nd to W. 124th Sts. 1872–1910. F. L. Olmsted. Reconstruction, 1937, Clinton F. Lloyd.

To the endless relief of stifled West Siders this green ribbon of hills and hollows, monuments, playgrounds, and sports facilities fringes some 50 blocks of winding Riverside Drive, all the while covering the N. Y. Central freight-line tunnel. One of its most complex parts is the three-level structure at 79th Street: traffic circle at the top, masonry arcade and pedestrain paths surrounding a splendid, circular, single-jet fountain **[16a.]** at the middle level, and, at the bottom, parking space for the 79th Street boat basin yachtsmen.

Zabar's Gourmet Foods, 2245 Broadway bet. W. 80th and W. 81st Sts. 8 AM-midnight; till 2 AM Sunday morning.

A fantastic array of good things to take home and feast on.

Steinberg's Dairy Restaurant, 2270 Broadway bet. W. 81st and W. 82nd Sts. EN 2-2030.

Enjoy the carefully preserved streamlined decor from the 1930's, while ordering the classic blintzes and the like.

[18.]  **[**

[17.] Louis D. Brandeis High School, 151 W. 84th St. bet. Amsterdam and Columbus Aves. 1965. Charles Luckman Assocs., Charles W. Stanton, partner in charge.

BLOOMINGDALE

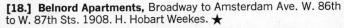 **[18.] Belnord Apartments,** Broadway to Amsterdam Ave. W. 86th to W. 87th Sts. 1908. H. Hobart Weekes. ★

Like its cousin the Apthorp [See 14a.] this massive structure is built around a garden court.

[19a.] Church of St. Paul & St. Andrew, West End Ave., NE cor. W. 86th St. 1895. R. H. Robertson & W. A. Potter.

[19b.] St. Ignatius Church, 552 West End Ave. SE. cor. W. 87th St. 1902. Charles C. Haight.

These churches and other groups of churches, schools, and row houses along West End Avenue provide relief from what would otherwise be an oppressive canyon walled by high apartment houses.

[19c.] Congregation B'nai Jeshurun, 257 W. 88th St. bet. West End Ave. and Broadway. 1918. Henry B. Herts and Walter Schneider.

A richly carved limestone portal set in a Moorish facade of orange granite conceal an ornate polychromed interior.

[20a.] Yeshiva Chofetz Chaim/formerly **Residence of Bishop Henry Codman Potter,** W. 89th St. SE cor. Riverside Dr. ca. 1901.

One of the last surviving free standing mansions which once lined Riverside Drive.

[20b.] Soldiers' and Sailors' Monument, Riverside Dr. at W. 89th St. 1902. Stoughton and Stoughton. Paul Duboy, Sculptor.

A marble memorial to the Civil War dead modeled on the choragic Monument of Lysicrates in Athens; a landmark along Riverside Drive.

[21a.] Astor Court Apartments, E. Side of Broadway, W. 89th to W. 90th Sts. 1916. Charles A. Platt.

The central garden court, ornamental balconies, and a rich cornice distinguish this excellent apartment building.

[21b.]

[21b.] Stephen Wise Towers, 90th to 91st Sts. bet. Amsterdam and Columbus Aves. 1964. Knappe & Johnson. Play area by Richard G. Stein & Associates; Constantino Nivola, Sculptor.

A modern horse fair for West Side cowboys is a permanent feature of the handsome play area of this public housing development.

[21c.] Trinity School, 139 W. 91 St. bet. Amsterdam and Columbus Aves.

Founded in 1709. An Anglo-Italianate brownstone main building; the Romanesque Revival pink granite eastern building (by William A. Potter) was once the parish house of the demolished St. Agnes Chapel. A tall apartment house will rise on the air rights over the new gymnasium building to be constructed on Columbus Avenue.

[22.] Eldorado Towers, 330 Central Park West, 90th to 91st Sts. 1930.

[23.] First Church of Christ, Scientist, 1 W. 96th St. NW cor. Central Park West. 1903. Carrère & Hastings.

White New Hampshire granite, handsome proportions, and an excellent steeple distinguish this church.

[24a.] RNA House, 150 W. 96th St. bet. Columbus and Amsterdam Aves. 1967. Edelbaum & Webster.

[24b.] East River Savings Bank, 743 Amsterdam Ave. NE cor. 96th St. 1927. Walker & Gillette. ☆

A Classical temple inscribed with exhortations to the thrifty.

[24c.] Holy Name of Jesus Church, 207 W. 96th St. NW cor. Amsterdam Ave. 1892-1900.

An intricate beamed ceiling is the most handsome feature of this large rough-hewn granite church.

[25.] Pomander Walk, W. 94th to W. 95th Sts. bet. Broadway and West End Ave. 1921. King and Campbell.

Pomander Walk is a tiny street in the London suburb of Chiswick. It came to New York in 1911 as the name of a stage play. This double row of small town houses is modeled after the stage sets used for the New York production.

[26.] Joan of Arc Statue, Riverside Dr. at W. 93rd St. 1915. John V. Van Pelt, Architect; Anna Vaughn Hyatt, Sculptor.

[27a.] Cliff Dweller's Apartments, Riverside Dr. NE cor. W. 96th St.

A mediocre building notable only for the mountain lions, rattlesnakes, and buffalo skulls on the frieze. They symbolize the life of the Arizona cliff dwellers and serve to tie these prehistoric people to the modern cliff dwellers of Manhattan.

[27b.] Carrère Memorial, Riverside Park at W. 99th St. 1916. Thomas Hastings.

A small granite terrace at the park entrance contains a barely noticeable memorial to one of New York's great architects, John Merven Carrère, who was killed in an automobile accident in 1911.

[27c.] Firemen's Memorial, Riverside Dr. at W. 100th St. 1913. H. Van Buren Magonigle, Architect; Attilio Piccirilli, Sculptor.

Courage and *Duty* guard this large pink marble monument to "soldiers in a war that never ends."

[28a.] St. Michael's Church, 225 W. 99th St. NW cor. Amsterdam Ave. 1891. Robert W. Gibson.

The interiors of this large limestone church complex are enhanced by Tiffany glass and mosaics.

[28b.] Park West Village, Amsterdam Ave. to Central Park West, W. 97th to W. 100th Sts.

This large and banal housing development was the site of the Manhattantown urban renewal scandal. Developers acquired six blocks of tenements at a reduced price from the City under the urban renewal program. Instead of redeveloping the site they sat tight, collected rents, neglected repairs, and invented ingenious schemes to exploit their unhappy tenants.

[29a.] Master Institute and Riverside Museum/formerly **Roerich Museum,** 310 Riverside Dr. NE cor. W. 103rd St. 1929. Helmle, Corbett & Harrison, and Sugarman & Berger.

A school and museum housed in a residential hotel. Nicholas Roerich, whose art museum was once housed here, is responsible for the shading of this building's exterior brickwork, from black and dark red at the base to light yellow at the top. [See 29f.]

[29b.] West 105th Street, bet. Riverside Dr. and West End Ave.

Both sides of this block are lined with handsome town houses with classical fronts in the Beaux-Arts style.

[29c.] New York Buddhist Church/formerly **Marion Davies Residence,** 331 Riverside Dr. bet. W. 105th and W. 106th Sts.

Johns-Manville, producer of new
and improved building materials, and
The American Institute of Architects,
creators of better buildings
and finer environments,
have a record of more than . . .

A Century of Association

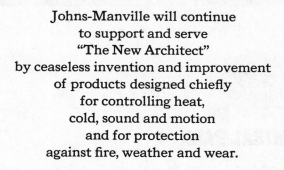

Johns-Manville will continue
to support and serve
"The New Architect"
by ceaseless invention and improvement
of products designed chiefly
for controlling heat,
cold, sound and motion
and for protection
against fire, weather and wear.

Johns-Manville

22 East 40th Street · New York, N.Y. 10016

A mansion serving as a church and social center. The heroic-size statue of a Buddhist saint has become a local landmark.

[29d.] Equestrian Statue of Franz Sigel, Riverside Dr. at W. 106th St. 1907. Karl F. Bitter, Sculptor.

[29e.] Former Schinasi Residence, Riverside Dr. NE cor. W. 107th St.

The last freestanding French chateau along Riverside Drive.

[29f.] Nicholas Roerich Museum, 319 W. 107th St. bet. Riverside Dr. and Broadway.

Permanent collection of the work of Nicholas Roerich, prolific artist, designer, explorer, and philosopher. Architectural landmarks of his native Russia were the subjects of many of Roerich's early paintings, and he contributed to the design of 310 Riverside Drive. [See 29a.]

[29g.] Straus Park and Fountain/formerly **Bloomingdale Square,** Broadway at W. 106th St. 1914. H. Augustus Lukeman, Sculptor.

[30.] Towers Nursing Home/formerly **New York Cancer Hospital,** 2 W. 106th St. SW cor. Central Park West. 1887. Charles C. Haight.

A castellated palace with squat circular towers, a high chapel and a handsome arcaded porch facing the park.

[24b.]

CENTRAL PARK

This great work of art, the grand-daddy of American landscaped parks, was named a **National Historic Landmark** in 1965.

Who made possible this **840-acre masterpiece** in the center of New York City? One of the first was poet **William Cullen Bryant** who in 1844 called out for a large, public pleasure ground **(at the time, Washington Square was considered uptown).** After landscape architect **Andrew Jackson Downing** appealed for a park the idea caught on and both mayorality contestants made it a promise in the 1850 campaign. The winner kept his word and the Common Council took action.

UPPER WEST SIDE

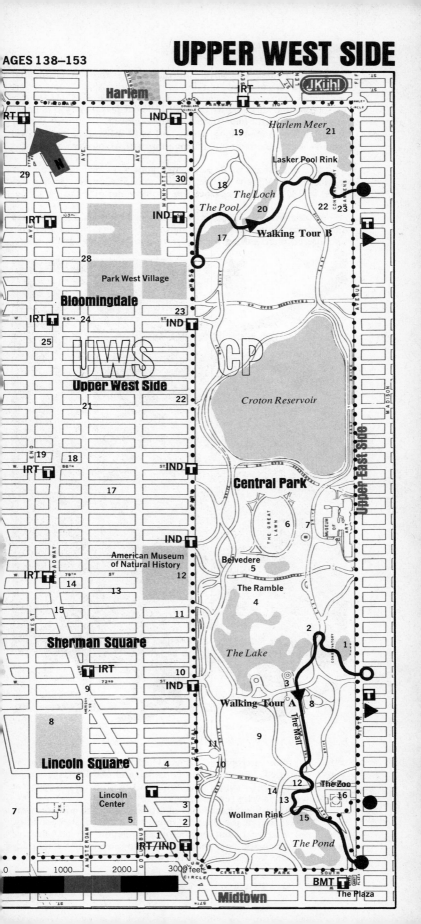

Harlem

IRT

IND

N

29

30

18 *The Loch*

19 *Harlem Meer* 21

Lasker Pool Rink

The Pool

20

Walking Tour B

22 23

17

28

Park West Village

Bloomingdale

IRT 96TH 24

IND

23

25

UWS

Upper West Side

21 22

CP

19 18

IRT 86TH

IND

17

Croton Reservoir

IND

Central Park

American Museum
of Natural History

12

THE GREAT LAWN 6 7

MUSEUM OF ART

13

14 79TH IRT

15

Belvedere 5

The Ramble

4

11

2

1

Sherman Square

IRT 72ND

The Lake

9

IND

3

8

Walking Tour A

The Mall

8

9

11

10

12 *The Zoo*

4

14 16

6

Lincoln Square

13

3

Wollman Rink 15

Lincoln
Center

2

The Pond

7

5

1

IRT/IND

0   1000   2000   3000 feet

BMT The Plaza

Midtown

Upper East Side

The site then was **physically unprepossessing:** "A pestilential spot where misamic odors taint every breath of air," one report concluded. But it was available. **Land was acquired** (1856) for $5,500,000 and surveyed by Egbert L. Vielé. Clearing began the next year: **squatters** and **hogs** were **forcibly removed,** often with the aid of the police; **bone-boiling works** and **swill mills** were **torn down, swamps** were **drained,** and the omnipresent **Manhattan schist was blasted.**

The first **Board of Park Commissioners,** helped by a committee including William Cullen **Bryant** and Washington **Irving,** decided in 1857 an **open competition** should determine the park's design.

"Greensward," so named by winners **Frederick Law Olmsted** and **Calvert Vaux,** won out among the 33 designs. It was a simple, uncluttered plan, **calling for a picturesque landscape:** glade, copse,

water, and rock outcropping. Bridges (each individually designed by Vaux) separated footpaths, bridle-paths, and the carriage drives (curved to prevent racing). The four sunken transverse roads for cross-town traffic were revolutionary.

Ten million **horse cart-loads** of stone, earth, and top soil were moved into or out of the site as "Greensward" became an actuality. It took nearly 20 years, but long before completion, the park became *the place* for **rich and poor to promenade,** to see and be seen. Today it is even more the playground for New Yorkers; for some a place to enjoy nature, for many the only "country" they have ever seen, and for everyone, a magnificent, designed Garden of Eden to ease the strains of city living.

Walking Tour A: Conservatory Water to Grand Army Plaza or the Zoo. (Arrive via 68th Street Station of Lexington Avenue IRT Subway; Madison or Fifth Avenue buses).

Enter at **Inventor's Gate,** Fifth Avenue and 72nd Street (N side of road), one of Vaux's eighteen named gates piercing the park wall. Descend **Pilgrim Hill** dotted with particularly nice evergreens. **Conservatory Water [1a.],** the formal pond, was named for the conservatory planned but never built on its eastern shore. Model boats, for rent at the **Kerbs Model Boat House [1b.],** are usually sailing here. Two statues overlook the water: **Alice-in-Wonderland** (José de Creeft) and **Hans Christian Andersen** (George Lober). Not of great artistic merit, the figures are, nevertheless, swarmed over by young children.

Continue around the western shore to the path leading west to **Trefoil Arch,** and pass under the East Drive to reach the shore of the **Lake [2.]** where a gondola and circuiting public launch once accompanied the flotilla of rowboats. The **72nd Street Boat House** (1954) **[2a.]** is in the "brick Colonial" style favored for almost all park buildings of the last thirty years.

The Boat House has a snack bar and a pleasant terrace overlooking the Lake. The **bicycle concession,** to the right, is jammed on Sundays, when the drives, closed to traffic, become the cyclist's province.

The path along the southern shore reaches the **Terrace [3.]** the only formal architectural element of the "Greensward" Plan. Jacob Wrey Mould designed the detailed stone work, Calvert Vaux, the general outline. **Bethesda Fountain [3a.];** beneath the Angel of the Waters, huddle, for some reason, Purity, Health, Peace, and Temperance. Since 1966, the **Fountain Cafe** has been open for lunch and dinner during the warmer months and is highly recommended for its country club atmosphere without high prices and pedigree admission.

Side Trip: The bosky **Ramble [4.]** where even vigilant bird-watchers have been known to lose their way on the maze-like paths. The meandering stream, exotic trees and shrubs, and small, hidden lawns are among the surprises. At the north the ramble ascends to Vista Rock, topped by **Belvedere Castle [5.]** home of the city's Weather Bureau Station. Below, further north, is **Belvedere Lake [5a.],** the last vestige of the old reservoir which was drained in 1929. The reservoir's dry bed was used by squatters during the Depression, then filled in, becoming the **Great Lawn [6.],** today's favored spot for touch-football, soccer, and softball matches (the latter, with "professional" teams of architects, theater people, etc.). The **Delacorte Theatre [6a.]** with summer Shakespeare hovers over the New Lake's western shore. **22nd Precinct, N.Y.C. Police Dept. [6b.]** ☆, on Transverse Rd. No. 3, is another Calvert Vaux building (1871). East, before the **Metropolitan Museum of Art** [See UES 76a.] rises the **Obelisk [7.]** built by King Thutmose III in 1600, B.C. A gift to the city from the Khedive of Egypt, it was erected in the park in 1881. Resume Tour.

The **Mall [8]**, the park's grand promenade, lies south of the Terrace Arcade. Pass through, noting the Minton tile ceiling. The Mall's axis points to Belvedere Castle, deliberately kept small by architect Vaux to lengthen the perspective. On the hillock behind the bandshell is the **Pergola [8a.],** one of the few remaining wisteria-covered arbors.

Side Trip: West of The Mall, past the closed Center Drive, stretches the **Sheep Meadow [9.],** a sweeping lawn where sheep grazed until banished in 1934, now the last open meadow in the park. From the north end is a splendid view of the skyscrapers. To the southwest, along Central Park West, stands the **Tavern-on-the-Green [10.],** a restaurant converted from the old Sheepfold. Nearby is Central Park's first **"Adventure Playground,"** (Richard Dattner). Resume Tour.

At the southern end of The Mall, bear left and cross the drive, and don't blame the designers for not providing an underground passage as part of the separation of traffic scheme; **Marble Arch,** the park's most famous bridge, was found here until the 1930's. Take the southeast path along the drive and while crossing over the 65th Street Transverse Road notice how little the sunken road intrudes on the park. To the right, a path leads past the **Dairy [12.]** a sturdy Gothic Revival building (now shorn of a handsome canopy) designed by Vaux; it is now used for storage.

Side Trip: Head west, to the north of the hill-site of the Kinderberg, once a large arbor. It's now replaced by the squat Chess and Checkers House, **[13.]** the gift of Bernard Baruch. Continue west, under Playmates Arch beneath the drive to the **Carousel [14.]** Resume Tour.

From the Dairy, after dropping down to the left, the path passes east of the Chess and Checkers site. Skirt southeast around **Wollman Memorial Rink [15a.]** and go up the hill along the fence enclosing the **Bird Sanctuary [15b.]** Gapstow Bridge, crossing the **Pond [15.],** is a good place to admire the reflection of the city's towers in the water below. A few swans and many ducks are usually swimming around. Swanboats, the same as those still in the Boston Common, sailed here until 1924. The café that Huntington Hartford tried so hard to donate was intended for the east corner. Leave the park by the gate across from the Sherman statue, or, if you want to feed the animals, go, via **Inscope Arch [15c.]** under the East Drive, northeast of the Pond.

End of tour: Nearest transit is BMT Line at the Plaza; Fifth Avenue Buses.

Side Trip: The **Zoo [16.],** off Fifth Avenue at 64th Street, is a favorite haunt of New Yorkers. A cafeteria and terrace overlooking the Seal Pond is a good place to rest and have a beer and a hot dog. **The Arsenal, [16a.]** N.Y.C. Dept. of Parks Administration Building, ★ facing 64th Street (1841), was designed by Martin Thompson. It housed troops during the Civil War and has had numerous and diverse tenants since. The original "Greensward" Plan is displayed on the third floor.

Walking Tour B: The Pool to Conservatory Garden. (Arrive via IND 8th Avenue Subway to 96th Street Station). Begin at Central

Park West and 100th Street.

The **Boy's Gate** gives access to a path descending to the Pool. **[17.]** It is the start of the waterway which flows east to Harlem Meer, and once the course of Montayne's Rivulet that led to the East River.

Side Trip: North of the Pool is the **Great Hill [18.]** where picnickers once enjoyed an unobstructed view of the Hudson and East Rivers. Perched on a cliff to the northeast is a lonely **Blockhouse [19.]**, a remnant of the fortifications built during the War of 1812 when the British threatened the city. Resume Tour.

At the eastern end of the **Pool**, the **Glen Span** carries the West Drive over the Ravine. On the other side flows **the Loch,** formerly a healthy sized body of water, now a trickle. This is very picturesque and completely **cut off from the city.**

Side Trip: To the south, behind the slope, is the **North Meadow [20a.]**, scene of hotly contested baseball games: to get there, take **Springbanks Arch [20b.]** Resume Tour.

In wet weather the Loch cascades down before disappearing under the East Drive at **Huddlestone Bridge.** Through the arch in front of **Harlem Meer [21.]** you can see the park's most disastrous "improvement," the **Loula D. Lasker Pool-Rink [21a.]**. New Yorkers have always tried to give things—especially buildings—to their park. Few succeeded until recent years when park administrators misguidedly encouraged philanthropic bequests.

To the right of the Loch find **Lamppost No. 0554.** (All the older lampposts were designed by Henry Bacon in 1907 and all bear a street-designating plaque; here, the first two digits indicate that this one stands at 105th Street.) A path goes sharply uphill and then turns east, crossing the East Drive below **McGown's Pass,** which was fortified by the British during the Revolutionary War. **The Mount [22.]**, to the right, was for many years the site of a tavern; its chief ornament today is the park's mulch pile.

The path descends to **Conservatory Garden [23.]** designed by Thomas D. Price in 1936. The "Greensward" Plan called for a large arboretum of native trees and shrubs to be planted here. Instead, a conservatory was built at the turn of the century but torn down in 1934. On the east side the **Vanderbilt Gate** opens on Fifth Avenue. Nearby is the **Museum of the City of New York,** where historical material of the park is on display. [See UES 96b.]

Special events: All sorts take place in the park, with each Park Commissioner choosing his own brand. Daily information on what's doing may be had by calling the special recorded announcement: 755-4100.

End of Tour. Transportation: IRT Lexington Avenue Subway stations at 96th or 103rd Streets, and via Fifth or Madison Avenue buses.

UES

UPPER EAST SIDE

"**Brownstones**" first filled the blocks from **Turtle Bay** to and through **Yorkville,** east of **Park Avenue. Yorkville,** a rural town early populated by **Germans,** was gathered up in the boom, leaving, however, its German identity in the same general location but with a different physical form. Here were the single-family row houses of the middle class, a smaller and more select group in the 1880's than those bearing the same stamp today. Quantity housing, it was built by the Levitts of that era for a market that was relatively similar —the product of a booming postwar (**Civil,** in this case) population, producing large new families; that is, wherever the newly and more widely distributed industrial wealth gave possibility of "moving up" the social and economic ladder.

The noxious smoke and noise of the railroads on **Fourth Avenue** (later to be renamed **Park Avenue)** were diminished when the tracks were placed in a cut, coincidental with the construction of **Commodore Vanderbilt's** new **(1871) Grand Central** train-shed, an enormous glass and cast-iron structure, which was itself to survive for only 39 years: demolished in 1910. Still a strong barrier, the new cut and tracks isolated the bulk middle-class housing to the east from the town palaces lining **Fifth Avenue** (so-called **Millionaire's Row)** and related side streets as far north as 96th. Marble chateaux marched up Fifth Avenue from **The Plaza,** while outposts of splendor, like **Andrew Carnegie's** garden palace of **1901,** skipped ahead of the march's regular cadence. A sudden halt at 96th Street, although not rational at Fifth Avenue, reflected the emergence of the railroad tracks over the **Harlem** "flats" from **Carnegie Hill,** on Park Avenue. This was the last great precinct of one of the most mobile social elements of New York; the *town palace.* It first appeared barely 100 years before at the Battery (where the former **Watson** house amazingly remains as the single remnant), passed up lower Broadway, rested at **Lafayette Place** (later Street), moved into the 30's on Fifth Avenue and then relentlessly northward, paced by the pressures of other moving centers of land use.

The third and last great wave of construction followed the First World War and the complete covering of the New York Central and New Haven Railroads' Fourth Avenue tracks and yards, coeval with the completion of the new Grand Central Station. Park Avenue became a social **mecca** rather than a social wall. Not only the well-to-do, but the very **rich,** were party (by supplying the demand) to the construction of uniformly organized high-rise mansions that still, today, define the form of this formal boulevard. Flats were and are, of course, common, but duplex and triplex units filled the need of mansion-like space for the rich, when land cost had driven private mansion land even out of their grasp. Social grace no longer required a competitive palace for social posture.

The fringe benefits of this surge filled the side streets toward Fifth as far east as Third Avenue (further in special cases) with similar, but **less expensive** or less pretentious structures. Now, slowly but surely, the remaining ex-brownstones and town houses are being consumed by inexorable apartment construction, and the beleaguered brownstone, once a bore, has become a venerable friend in its increasingly sparse groupings or complete isolation (particularly because it lends itself to conversion to duplex or smaller apartments).

Residents in Residence: Still the principal in-town concentration. of the rich, as well as the merely well-to-do, the Upper East Side

UPPER EAST SIDE

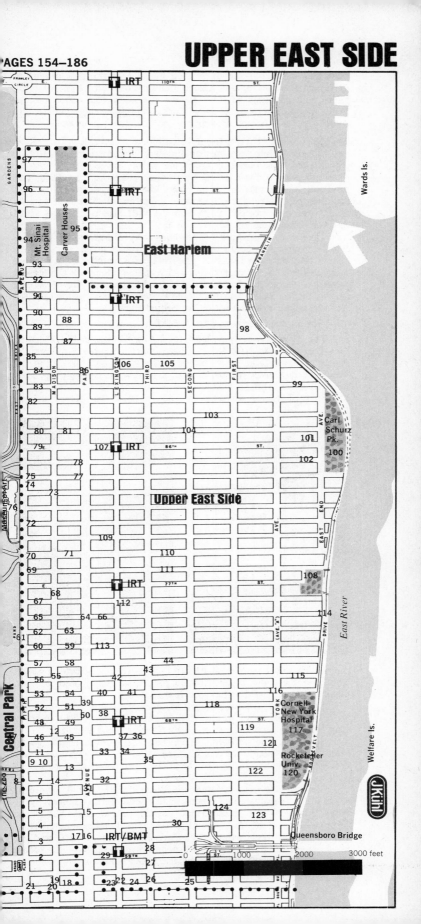

Wards Is.

IRT

110TH ST.

T IRT

ST.

Carver Houses

East Harlem

Mt. Sinai Hospital

GARDENS

AVENUE

Franklin

T IRT

ST.

T IRT

ST.

98

88
87
89
90
91
92
93
94
95
96
97

106 105
86 MADISON PARK LEXINGTON THIRD SECOND FIRST

99

Carl Schurz Pk.
100
101
102
103
104

80 81
79E
78
77
107 T IRT 86TH ST.
75
74
73
76 Metropolitan Mus of Art

Upper East Side

72
109
110
111
108
114

70
71
69
68
67 E
65 64 66
62 63
60 59 113
57 58
56 55
53 54
52 51
48 49
46 45
11
9 10
8
7
6
5
4
3
2

East River

AVE. END EAST

112
T IRT 77TH ST.

44
43
42
40 41
39
50 38
37 36
33 34
35
13
32
31
15
17 16
IRT/BMT
29 59TH
27
23 22 24 26 25
19 18
21 20

Central Park
THE ZOO

118
119
121
122
123
124
30

115
116
Cornell New York Hospital
117
Rockefeller Univ.
120

York Roosevelt Drive (Ave. "A")

Welfare Is.

Queensboro Bridge

0 1000 2000 3000 feet

FLIP

continues to harbor the decreasing number of the old immigrant German, Hungarian, and Czech middle class that had been the solid underpinnings of The **Brown Decades.** Ambitious college graduates, first moving to New York, use this as their habitat and mating ground before moving to child-oriented suburbs.

The 1811 Grid: A Plan for Speculation: Surveyor Randel's (Randall) original map, drawn for the city commissioners of 1811, shows very little variation from the reality of today. The major differences lie at the edge of the island along the East River (remodeled in the process of inserting the F.D.R. Drive), the construction of Central Park, and the elimination of Hamilton Square, which was first mapped from 66th to 68th Street, Fifth to Third Avenue, then extended north to 69th.

Under the imaginary (in 1811) overlay of streets and avenues lies the random geometry of hills, rocks, forests, farms, and country estates that were the reality of the area, now erased almost without a trace, the "almost" supported by such sparse remains as the present headquarters of the Society of Colonial Dames at 421 East 61st Street (Smith's Folly) and Archibald Gracie's country estate of 1799, now the **mayor's residence,** in Carl Schurz Park.

[1a.] The Plaza, Fifth Ave. 58th to 60th St.

The Plaza, properly called **Grand Army Plaza,** is **The** Plaza to New Yorkers, and New York's only public urban plaza for people. Plazas at **Rockefeller** and **Lincoln Centers** are, and the one at the **World Trade Center** will be, parts of private building complexes; but here, in the European tradition, is an outdoor room contained by buildings of varied architecture and function, an isle of urbane

[1b.]

repose. The more significant half (it is in two parts, bisected by 59th Street) to the south is centered on the Plaza (Hotel) and the new **General Motors** building now under construction.

The Plaza is ornamented by varied paving and trees enclosing the Pulitzer fountain, surmounted by **Abundance,** a lithe lady by Karl Bitter on a cascade of pools by Carrère and Hastings.

South are the buildings of Bergdorf Goodman (1928, Buchman & Kahn) and the Paris Theatre (1948, Emery Roth & Sons, theater interiors, 1948, by Warner-Leeds, architects of Bonniers, a long block away).

General Sherman occupies the Plaza's northern half: more of a traffic turn-around than a pedestrian enclave. The General (William Tecumseh) is here marching, not through Georgia but rather through the plot of allegory; Augustus Saint Gaudens (saynt gawdens) presented this casting at the Paris Exposition of 1900, and the good general mounted his present pedestal in 1903. Now the **oldest resident** of this place, he antedates the Plaza Hotel by four years.

[1b.] The Plaza Hotel, 58th to 59th St. facing The Plaza. 1907. Henry J. Hardenbergh. ☆

A gracious vestige of Edwardian elegance. Hardenbergh, its designer, graced New York with another, and equal, social and architectural monument: the **Dakota** (apartment house). The white glazed brick and green copper-and-slate roof have been returned to their pristine splendor in a recent cleaning. One of the most exciting views of New York (Eloise-style) is from any room on the north side, between the third and fifth floors. Eyes just skim the trees in a dramatic perspective of Central Park and Fifth Avenue. **Frank Lloyd Wright** was a devoté of the Plaza; he used it as his New York headquarters.

[1c.] General Motors Building, 58th to 59th St., Fifth to Madison Ave. 1968. Edward Durell Stone; Emery Roth and Sons, Associated Architects.

Here lay the **Savoy Plaza** (Hotel) and a miscellany of others, none particularly distinguished. The hue and cry over the new behemoth was based, not on architecture but, rather, first on the loss of the hotel's elegant shopping amenities in favor of automobile salesmanship (an **auto showroom** is particularly galling at the spot in New York most likely to honor the pedestrian); and second, the potential loss of definition to the space of The Plaza.

The 50-story tower will be clad in glistening white Georgia marble.

F.A.O. Schwarz, 745 Fifth Ave., SE cor. 58th St.

Toy store to the world. The second floor contains every gadget a father would care to buy for himself (in the name of his son).

[1d.] Sherry-Netherland Hotel, Fifth Ave. NE cor. 59th St. 1927. Schulze and Weaver.

[2a.] L'Etoile restaurant, 3 E. 59th St. 1966. Alexander Girard (Lee Schoen, Associated Architect).

Elegant, moderately expensive (complete dinner $6.25–$7.95), and reminiscent of the salons of a first-class French liner. Austere, polished, and bright, as only "French" modern can be, it has first-class graphics, first-class food. No English translations on the menus, which are lengthy, encyclopedic: try an omelette.

[2b.] The Playboy Club, 5 E. 59th St. bet. Fifth and Madison Aves. Remodeled, 1962. Oppenheimer, Brady & Lehrecke.

Formerly the Savoy Art Galleries, this structure is the key link in an international bacchanal. The matter-of-fact facade belies the multileveled stack of balconies, mezzanines, and intertwining spaces behind. The canopy is a later addition.

[2c.] C.I.T. Building, 650 Madison Ave. bet. 59th and 60th Sts. 1957. Harrison & Abramovitz.

A wrap-around, from the Playboy Club to the Copacabana, it nestles between the new and the old high life. Black granite and stainless steel; victimized by its tenancy at the ground floor; life insurance, banking, brokerage, do little to enliven the active pedestrian street. Oh for a bar or elegant shop!

Copacabana, 14 E. 60th St. (in the Hotel Fourteen).

A huge night club by contemporary standards, of the era of big bands and big shows, à la Ziegfeld. Have a drink at the bar and see (no cover), or sit at a table, see and dance.

[3a.] The Harmonie Club, 4 E. 60th St. bet. Madison and Fifth Aves. 1905. McKim, Mead & White.

[3b.] The Metropolitan Club, 1 E. 60th St., NE cor. Fifth Ave. 1893. McKim, Mead & White. ☆

J. P. Morgan organized this club, primarily for friends who were not accepted in others. An Italian Palazzo is crossed with a proper English carriage entrance and courtyard. The interior is an extravaganza of space, marble, coffers and gilt; Corinthian columns, velvet ropes, and scarlet carpeting. Wing to the east, 1912, Ogden Codman, Jr.

[4a.] Hotel Pierre, 2 E. 61st St., SE cor. Fifth Ave. 1928. Schultze & Weaver.

[4b.] Getty Building, 660 Madison Ave., SW cor. 61st St. 1958. Emery Roth & Sons.

Interesting because it contains in its bowels additional ball-rooms for the adjacent Pierre: a clever use of normally inefficient or unusable space.

[4c.] Mrs. M. Hartley Dodge House, 800 Fifth Ave., NE cor. 61st St.

A lone, undistinguished red brick and limestone row house without a row, owned but unused by a Rockefeller kin. A kind of wistful elegance still exudes from its meticulous maintenance.

[5b.]

[2

[5a.] Knickerbocker Club, 2 E. 62nd St., SE cor. Fifth Ave. 1914. Delano & Aldrich.

[5b.] The Fifth Avenue Synagogue, 5 E. 62nd St. 1959. Percival Goodman.

An urban temple, occupying a typical mansion site of the 60's. Limestone, with sharply incised, oval-pointed windows, filled with stained glass; as with all buildings where stained glass is a major design element, these read as black voids from without, until the interior is illuminated (just after sunset on a winter evening).

Le Provençal, 21 E. 62nd St. TE 8-4248.

Popular, crowded, a good solid French kitchen. Dinners from $5 to $8. A neighborhood restaurant that has crept into place on the edge of "haute cuisine," but still retains neighborhood scale and flavor.

[6a.] 817 and 820 Fifth Avenue, SE and NE cor. of 63rd St. 1916. Starrett & Van Vleck.

A pair of high-rise palazzos of limestone, copper-corniced, these are two of the great eclectic apartment houses of New York: magnificent relics of the irrational Twenties.

[6b.] The New York Academy of Sciences/formerly **Frank (F. W.) Woolworth House,** 2 E. 63rd St. 1918. Attributed to L. Steiner.

[6c.] 14, 16, and 18 East 63rd St. ca. 1885.

The **"brownstone"** is here elevated to mansion status, unlike the endless rows to the east of Park Avenue. Note particularly the original brownstone stoop and railings at **No. 18.**

[7a.] Wildenstein & Co., 19 E. 64th St. bet. Fifth and Madison Aves. 1932. Horace Trumbauer.

Marble in and marble out: an art palace (never a house) that marked the end of **Trumbauer's** rich, eclectic career with a bow.

[7b.] New India House/formerly **Mrs. Marshall Orme Wilson House,** 3 E. 64th St. 1903. Warren & Wetmore.

Powerful, molded limestone; slate and copper roofed; **W & W's** only "modest" remnant (they were the architects of **Grand Central Station**). It is now owned by the **Indian Government**, a happy fate which preserves this ex-private palace, like others in similar straits, for a little while if not forever.

[7c.] The Institute of Aeronautical Sciences/formerly **Edward Berwind House,** 2 E. 64th St., SE cor. Fifth Ave. 1896. N. C. Mellon.

Edward Berwind built this house for "town" and **"The Elms"** in **Newport** for "country." Berwind, then the largest owner of coal mines in the world, fueled the U.S. Navy through the First World War. Note the rich verdigris (brass or copper oxidation) on the ornamental railings that surround the **"moat."**

[8.] The Arsenal, in Central Park facing Fifth Ave. at 64th St. 1848. Martin E. Thompson. ★

The **fortified retreat** of New York's Parks Commissioners and their staffs. Originally the central cache of military explosives in the state, it became city property only nine years after completion. The zoo was at first in its basement. Now the **Arsenal** participates in the design of the zoo **"plaza"** as an object, but has nothing to do with its zoo workings.

[9.] Temple Emanu-El, 1 E. 65th St. 1929. Robert D. Kohn, Charles Butler & Clarence S. Stein; with Mayers, Murray & Philip, Consultants.

Occupying the site of **Mrs.** (Caroline Schermerhorn) **Astor's** mansion, this is one of the largest bearing-wall halls extant: that is, the east-west walls are solid masonry, supporting transverse steel beams for the roof. A huge hall (for 2500) seats more worshippers than **St. Patrick's Cathedral.**

[10.] Sherman M. Fairchild House, 17 E. 65th St. 1941. George Nelson and William Hamby.

A totally new (even now) concept of the relation of building and urban lot, continued by **Philip Johnson** in his **Museum of Modern Art guest house of 1951.** Two separate functional elements, one at the street (living rooms) and one at the rear lot line (bedrooms), are joined by a court, within which ramps of glass form flying bridges over the garden below. The facade belies what it shields. Above, the overhanging second and third floors are screened by continuous, power-driven wood louvers.

 [11a.] Lotos Club/formerly **William J. Schieffelin Residence**/originally **Margaret Shepard Residence,** 5 E. 66th St. 1900. Richard Howland Hunt.

An elaborate **Second Empire** limestone and brick extravaganza.

[11b.] Polish Delegation to the UN/originally **Charles Scribner Residence,** 9 E. 66th St. 1912. Ernest Flagg.

[11c.] Philippine Mission to the UN/originally **Harris Fahnestock Residence,** 15 E. 66th St. 1918. Hoppin & Koen.

[12a.] Paraphernalia, 795 Madison Ave. bet. 67th and 68th Sts. 1966. Ulrich Franzen.

A local center of **jet-set** fashion. A wood shell (barrel vault) recalls and continues, in friendly fashion, the brick-arched facade. Tractor seats for the weary, or those being adorned. The venerable ladies and gentlemen dining at **"Kirby Allen"** next door must get quite a start (or kick) out of it!

[12b.] Vidal Sassoon/Charles of the Ritz, 803 Madison Ave. bet. 67th and 68th Sts. 1965. Gordon and Ursula Bowyer.

For the **Ondine** in your family. When dressed at Paraphernalia, down the block, it is essential to patronize one of these two piggyback parlors. **Frank Lloyd Wright** noted that the decoration and "grooming" of the human body was most important at its extremities: feet, hands and head. Here the head is deified—but not for those seeking boarding-school bobs or molded extravaganzas of the "Miami Beach school." The very architectural interiors are rich, sleek, and grand, all in the space of a venerable brownstone.

[13a.] The American Federation of the Arts, 41 E. 65th St. 1910. Trowbridge & Livingston.

Galleries **open** to the public. Home of the Architectural League.

[13b.] 47–49 East 65th Street, 1907. Charles A. Platt.

Twin brick and limestone houses commissioned by **Mrs. James Roosevelt**. No. 47 was occupied by her; No. 49 by her son, **Franklin Delano Roosevelt**. It was here, in the fourth-floor front bedroom, that he began his recovery from polio.

[13c.] 55 East 65th Street, 1893. Thomas & Wilson.

An early **apartment** house of brick and brownstone.

Le Voisin, 30 E. 65th St. SE cor. Madison Ave. LE 5-3800.

French, elegant, expensive; $10.25 for a complete dinner, plus drinks, wine and/or tips.

[14.] The Verona, 32 E. 64th St. SE cor. Madison Ave. ca. 1900.

Names were once as important as numbers, the entrance of this **Edwardian** apartment house (it rates **"block of flats"**) is elegantly flanked by bronze lamp standards.

[15.] The Colony Club, 560 Park Ave. NW cor. 62nd St. 1924. Delano & Aldrich.

Female social leadership is split between the **Colony** and the **Cosmopolitan Clubs,** the former more oriented to grandes dames, the latter to the activists. The **Colony** was founded in **1903** by the wives of those who mattered.

A neo-Georgian red brick and limestone town palace.

Charles & Company, 681 Madison Ave. bet. 61st and 62nd Sts.

Goodies as far as the eye can see. If you want pomegranates or persimmons, dates as large as golf balls, marmalade made from oranges grown in Peking, this is your store. Excellent sandwiches from the highly sophisticated delicatessen. Buy a kit for a picnic in **Central Park** (beer, soft drinks, soups and salads available for accompaniment, too).

The Colony Restaurant, 30 E. 61st St. TE 8-6745.

Not the **jet set** exclusively, but the old guard and heads of state are frequenters as well. All you need is money: about **$10** for à la carte lunch items. There is a convenient parking garage across the street in the **Regency Hotel** for your **Rolls**.

Mme. Romaine de Lyon, 32 E. 61st St. 758-2422.

A superb idea for lunch, and you don't need much money. Extraordinary, formidable—its menu offers **538** varieties of **omelettes**. Bring your own wine, if necessary, for no such beverages are available here. Depending on ingredients, omelette prices vary from **$2.25** to **$7.75**.

[16.] Christ Church (Methodist), 520 Park Ave. NW cor. 60th St. 1932. Ralph Adams Cram.

A self-consciously aged church, the random limestone and brick is intended to look like a sophisticated patch job, centuries old. Similarly, the marble and granite columns appear to be, in the **Romanesque** and **Byzantine** manner, pillage from **Roman** temples. Handsome and of impeccable taste, it is an archeological and eclectic stage set for well-to-do parishioners.

[17.] The Grolier Club, 47 E. 60th St. 1917. Bertram G. Goodhue. ☆

Named for the French bibliophile (16th Century), **Jean Grolier,** this club is nominally devoted to the bookmaking crafts.

[18.] D/R (Design Research), 53 E. 57th St. 1965. Altered by Benjamin Thompson.

A modern architect's dream. Collected in one four-storied store are furniture, kitchen equipment, cutlery, dresses—in fact, everything that has been touched by the wand of good design. It could well be an exhibition from the Museum of Modern Art; but in this case the exhibits are for sale. **Benjamin Thompson,** an architect from Boston, started **D/R** in Cambridge on Brattle Street.

c.]

[12a.]

Paraphernalia

[19.] Bonnier's, 605 Madison Ave. bet. 57th and 58th Sts. 1949. Warner-Leeds Associates.

Originally commissioned as a **bookstore** for the Swedish publishing house, it always sold furnishings and gifts. Now the books are gone.

It is elegant, understated, and without stylistic mannerisms: Bulky, built-up wood mullions (dividing posts), taut orange canopy (awning). The two-story stairwell with a gangplank stair has become one of the **source materials of modern design.**

[20.] IBM Showroom, 590 Madison Ave., SW cor. 57th St. Altered, 1959. Eliot Noyes.

[21.] Manufacturers Hanover Trust Company, 1 E. 57th St., NE cor. Fifth Ave. 1966. Skidmore, Owings & Merrill.

[22.] 137 East 57th Street, 1930. Thompson & Churchill; Herbert Lippman.

A pioneering piece of **structural virtuosity:** the columns are recessed 9 feet from the skin. Steel tensile straps hang the perimeter wall and floor from the roof girders.

[23.] Acquavella Building, 119 E. 57th St. bet. Park and Lexington Aves.

Even **Hollywood** could not match this magnificent **Tudor** house. Somebody cared to simulate reality, rather than the unfortunate practice of tacking on boards and calling them half-timbering.

[24.] The Colombian Center, 138 E. 57th St. 1966. Paul Lester Weiner, Richard Bender, Associate.

The ground floor and mezzanine have been transformed into a showcase for **Colombia,** its culture, and its coffee (freely dispensed from 10 to 6, except Sundays). A statuary (oiled dark) bronze facade screens a simple brace of spaces whose most delightful aspect is the glazed yellow tile floor.

Café Nicholson, 323 E. 58th St. 355-6769.

Bizarre bazaar? Victorian nightmare or daydream? A delightfully off-beat package deal in delightfully off-beat surroundings: described by **Craig Claiborne** of the **New York Times** as **"Lewis Carroll."** Dinner (seven courses) with wine and cognac is $14. Cocktails are available, and a handsome parrot presides.

[25.] High School of Art and Design, Second Ave., 56th to 57th St. 1956. William Lescaze; Kahn & Jacobs, associated architects.

[32a.]

[2

[26.] RKO 58th Street Theatre, 964 Third Ave. bet. 57th and 58th Sts.

One of the few remaining movie palace interiors of the Twenties in central Manhattan. Many others, including most of the **Loew's** chain have become sites for hotels and apartment buildings. (Don't let the streamlined marquee fool you; the interior is exultant **Valentino**).

[27a.] Alexander's, Lexington to Third Ave., most of 58th to 59th St. 1965. Emery Roth & Sons.

[27b.] Decoration and Design Building, 979 Third Ave. NE cor.

58th St. 1965. David & Earl Levy.

The **ziggurratted** New York zoning envelope is here capitalized into a positive architectural statement (if you look skyward).

[28a.] Bloomingdale's, 59th to 60th St., Lexington to Third Ave.

An aggregation of Victorian and modern structures completely interlocking on the interior. One of the most comprehensive and sophisticated medium-priced stores in the country. **Good taste** is prevalent but not infallible; the modern furnishings on the fifth floor are surprisingly fresh, if not avant-garde: very different from the modernistic schmaltz of most department stores. The bargain basement is what it claims to be. On your way home, we suggest a stop at the first-floor gourmet shop for perhaps a **Boursault, white grapes in brandy**, or one of the many other irresistibles shelved here.

Baronet and Coronet, 995 Third Ave. bet. 59th and 60th Sts.

A **piggyback** pair of movie theaters.

Bookmasters, 999 Third Ave. bet. 59th and 60th Sts.

A spacious, eclectic store, displaying mostly paperbacks. The current, off-beat, controversial, are always available. Subjects (including **planning** and **architecture**) are arranged by general headings.

[28b.] Cinema I and II, 1001 Third Ave. bet. 59th and 60th Sts. 1962. Abraham W. Geller & Assocs.

Another **piggyback pair,** of great architectural quality. **Abe Geller** and his wife (who did the interiors) have produced a simple elegance, with counterpoints of rich paintings and graphics, the antithesis of the **RKO** down the street. Instead of escapist entertainment in escapist environments, movies here are serious business.

Yellowfingers, 1009 Third Ave. SE cor. 60th St.

New in the summer of **1966,** this aims to be a place for swingers. Short-order food, beer, and wine may be carried to outdoor tables along the 60th Street side.

[29a.] Argosy Book and Print Store, 115 E. 59th St. 1966. Kramer & Kramer.

A new location for an old neighborhood activity: the sale of used books, maps, and prints next to the sidewalk. Twenty years ago this whole block, from **Park** to **Lexington**, was a thriving sequence of similar stores (less elegant than this new **Argosy** location, to be sure). Upstairs (by elevator) are floors devoted to old prints, paintings, and specialized books. Perhaps too elegant, too stylish, too neat, for such a bookstore, **Argosy** is the current uptown outpost of a trade that still flourishes on the flanks of Fourth Avenue, in dusty storefronts **between Astor Place and 14th Street**.

[29b.] The Lighthouse: N. Y. Assn. for the Blind, 111 E. 59th St. 1964. Kahn & Jacobs.

A back-to-back addition to an existing building facing 60th Street, this institution puts the blind to work and play. A **ground-floor shop** sells their craftmanship, particularly delightful in straw, wicker, soft children's toys, and fine house wares. Note **sound** in architecture in the constant rhythmic tone signalling the entrance to the sightless.

The simple limestone facade with tall, color-anodized, aluminum-framed windows, is unassuming background architecture. It leaves the realm of background, however, by its placement, forming a tiny plaza with the wall of the corner **Aramco Building.** The four stacks release air conditioning exhaust, without subjecting pedestrian passersby to the usual blasts of warm, stale "air."

Le Veau d'Or (restaurant), 129 E. 60th St. TE 8-8133.

Excellent. Certainly the best food (basically French) for its price in Manhattan: **$6-$10** for dinner, drink, and tips. Crowded in two ways: the tables are small and close together, and deserved popularity brings customers in droves. **Phone first.**

Gino's (restaurant), 780 Lexington Ave. bet. 60th and 61st Sts. TE 8-9827.

A good Italian restaurant of the **pasta-is-only-one-aspect-of-Italy variety.** Moderate in price: dinner including a drink and tips will be **$6-$8.**

Au Canari d'Or, 134 E. 61st St. TE 8-7987.

Back to back with **Le Veau d'Or.** Prices **$4.50-$6.**

Joe's (restaurant), 1017 Third Ave. bet. 60th and 61st Sts. 838-9693.

One of three **Joe's,** landmarks of this area for two generations. They grew up under the **"El,"** before the new wave of chic activities that has invaded this precinct since the demise of the **"El."** Identity was a serious problem with three, and so is (or was) **seniority.** Each was, in turn, the **Original Joe's;** one is gone now, one removed to a new site on 59th Street off Third Avenue.

Serendipity 3, 225 E. 60th St.

Pop, Op, chic, in, old, off beat: a store for all the senses in terms of what is old and new; odd objects, whimsically collected: **Tiffany** glass, hats—all within the realm of availability. Food and beverages can be an excuse for a visit and a tour of the **exotica** currently in stock.

[30.] Trinity Baptist Church, 250 E. 61st St. 1930. Martin Hedmark.

An early modern building with **Art Nouveau** moments: total architecture from concept to the smallest detail, this is perhaps the last example in New York of **creative craftsmanship** complementing architecture.

Weyhe's Bookstore and Gallery, 794 Lexington Ave. bet. 61st and 62nd Sts. ca. 1920. Henry Churchill.

A **non**-American experience of great charm is in store here. One of four basic sources of new and old art and architecture books (**Wittenborn, Hacker** and **Architectural Book Publishing Co.** are the others), this delightful shop is packed with books of all vintages. Upstairs (by a flight immediately inside the shop door) is a small **gallery** of etchings, engravings, silk screens, and lithographs.

Phoenix Pan American Shop, 793 Lexington Ave. bet. 61st and 62nd Sts.

Latin American fabrics, and handicrafts in their most esoteric sense: **Mexican** tinware, pottery, papier maché, beads, bracelets: all rich in design and craftsmanship.

[31a.] Third Church of Christ, Scientist, 585 Park Ave., NE cor. 63rd St. 1923. Delano & Aldrich.

[31b.] Central Presybterian Church, 593 Park Ave., SE cor. 64th St. 1922. Pelton, Allen & Collems.

Rock-faced (stone-tooled to exaggerate its rough rockiness), granite **neo**-Gothic.

[32a.] Asia House, 112 E. 64th St. 1959. Philip Johnson. Open weekdays, 10AM–5PM; Saturday, 11AM–5PM; Sunday, 1–5PM.

The **Asia Society** maintains a small gallery here in the space of a double-width brownstone; tinted glass and white-painted steel are composed into a delicate street-wall. The opacity of the glass is sometimes disturbing, causing the building to appear solid, a mirror of the opposite side of the street. Only at night is the volume of interior space apparent.

[32b.] Edward Durell Stone House, 130 E. 64th St. 1959. Edward Durell Stone.

The body remodeled into its present form was similar to the three "brownstones" adjacent. The facade, and hence space, of the structure was extended to the permissible building line and clad with the same grillage **Stone** used so elegantly at the **American Embassy** at **New Delhi, India.**

[33a.] Seventh Regiment Armory, Park Ave. bet. 66th and 67th Sts. 1880. Charles W. Clinton. ☆

A friendly fort. New York armories were composed of two distinct elements: a three- or four-story collection of office, meeting, and social spaces, and a vast drill hall. The latter is, in this instance, **187** by **290** feet of clear space, sufficient for maneuvering large, modern military vehicles.

[34b.]

[33a.]

The **Armory** was in large part furnished and detailed on the interior by **Louis Comfort Tiffany,** son of Charles, founder and owner of Fifth Avenue's **Tiffany & Co.** Louis rejected the business world for that of the applied arts. His studios eventually specialized in decorative crafts ranging from the stained glass for which he is best remembered today to stonecarving, metalworking, casting of bronze: all the crafts complementing the ornate Late Victorian architecture of his architect-clients. In this case some tables were turned: **Stanford White** worked under Tiffany's direction on this interior work, rather than the later, and more obvious, reversed relationship.

[33b.] John Hay Whitney Garage, 126 E. 66th St. 1895. W. J. Wallace & S. E. Sage.

A handsome brick arch is portal for nine **Whitney** cars: rarely does even consciously monumental architecture achieve such power.

[34a.] Church of St. Vincent Ferrer, 66th St. and Lexington Ave. 1923. Bertram Goodhue. ☆

A **fashionable** parish church built during the post-World War I boom: rock-face granite with limestone trim, detailing and sculpture. Academically correct and precise. The uniformity of materials and details give a somewhat manufactured quality: the **"rock-face"** is self-conscious.

[34b.] 131–135 East 66th Street and 130–134 East 67th Street. 1905. Charles Platt. ☆

Twin residential palaces, ranking with the **Dakota** in architectural distinction.

[35a.] Manhattan House, 200 E. 66th St., 65th to 66th St. Second to Third Ave. 1950. Skidmore, Owings & Merrill and Mayer & Whittlesey.

This is the closest New York offers, philosophically, to the blocks of **Le Corbusier,** as machines for living (misinterpreted by many as implying a mechanistic way of life).

The subtle esthetic decision to choose pale gray glazed brick and white-painted steel windows by itself raised this block substantially above its **coarse new neighbors** (white-glazed brick and pasty aluminum sash). The balconies become the principal ornament, but unfortunately are small and precarious for those with any trace of vertigo.

[35b.] Sign of the Dove (restaurant), 1110 Third Ave. NW cor. 65th St.

Two hundred years ago there was a **Dove Tavern** near this spot. The present **Dove** is an elegant neo-Victorian bar-cum-hothouse, the product and property of a talented amateur (dentist).

[36a.] Park East Synagogue (Congregation Zichron Ephraim), 161 E. 67th St. 1890. Schneider & Herter.

Inside, a **Victorian** preaching space, nominally made Jewish through **Saracenic** detail. Stripped to its essentials it could be Civil-War-period Catholic or Congregational! Outside, it is a confection that might have been conceived in a Middle Easterners **LSD** trip: a wild, vigorous extravaganza.

[37.] 19th Precinct Police Station, N. Y. City Police Dept., 153 E. 67th St. ca. 1890.

Limestone **"Florentine Palace"** architecture. Rusticated (stone blocks cut with deep reveals) base.

Oscar's Salt of the Sea. (restaurant), 1155 Third Ave. bet. 68th and 69th Sts.

Bright, clean, packed with people, this restaurant caters mostly to local trade. A simple, natural, unself-conscious interior, serving well-prepared sea food in like manner. If you are alone, sit at the counter.

[38a.] Hunter High School/formerly **Hunter College,** 930 Lexington Avenue, bet. 68th and 69th Sts. 1913. O. B. J. Snyder.

The last gasp of **John Ruskin** here caused quality education to be housed in an "English Gothic" shell. The first building of Hunter College (then a "Normal" school), it now houses the prestige Hunter High, part of the City Public School system, enrolling talented girls from throughout the city, through a competitive examination program.

[38b.] Hunter College, Park Ave. bet. 68th and 69th Sts. 1940. Shreve, Lamb & Harmon and Harrison & Fouilhoux.

An interruption in the pace of Park Avenue: **Hunter** is not

[36a.]

only modern and (relatively) glistening with glass, it is set back ten feet from the regular lot line.

This is on a portion of what was, originally, **Hamilton Square** (66th to 69th, Fifth to Third Avenue; first stopping at 68th, in accordance with the Commissioner's Plan of 1811, it was later extended to 69th Street). It had a short life as a park and parade ground, becoming, in the opinion of the city, redundant when **Central Park** was built.

[39.] Union Club, 101 E. 69th St., NE cor. Park Ave. 1932. Delano & Aldrich.

An 18th Century English club building houses the oldest club in New York. Limestone and granite English Renaissance with a slate mansarded roof.

[40a.] 723 Park Avenue/formerly **Milliken House,** NE cor. 70th St. and Park Ave.

The spiral fire stair at the rear (off 70th Street) is an unconscious architectural highlight of this somber, conservative, brownstone town house.

[40b.] The Visiting Nurse Service of New York/formerly **Thomas W. Lamont Residence.** 107 E. 70th St. 1921. Walker & Gillette.

"**English Gothic**" for the taste of the country parson's son who became head of J. P. Morgan & Son. Ashlar with cut limestone; gabled shingle roofs: unexpected in the continuous facade architecture of these blocks—a **welcome break** in rhythm.

[40c.] 111 East 70th Street. 1911. William Adams.

[40d.] 117 East 70th Street. 1932. Frederick Rhinelander Kind.

[40e.] 120 East 70th Street. 1903. Gay & Nash.

[40f.] 121 East 70th Street. 1910. Delano & Aldrich.

[40g.] 124 East 70th Street. 1941. William Lescaze.

See his **own** house at **211 East 48th Street.**

[40h.] Paul Mellon House, 125 E. 70th St. 1965. H. Page Cross.

One of only six town houses built in **Manhattan** since the Second World War. Anachronistic, a charming confection.

[41.] 157, 163 and 165 East 70th Street. 1919, 1901, 1901, respectively. Mainzer, Gilbert & Gilbert.

[42a.] Elihu Root House. SE cor. 71st St. and Park Ave. 1903. Carrère & Hastings. ☆

A freestanding Georgian manor.

[42b.] 131 East 71st Street/formerly **Elsie De Wolfe House,** remodeled, 1910. Ogden Codman, Jr.

 [43.] Tower East, 200 E. 72nd St. 1962. Emery Roth & Sons.

A sheer, freestanding tower; four apartments per floor, with magnificent views. If economics had not forced a ground floor of shops in whole or in part, a local plaza could have been gained for the neighborhood. A pleasant neighborhood **"art"** movie occupies the 71st Street corner: **the Tower East Cinema.**

[40h.]

[4

[44a.] 205 East 72nd Street, remodeled 1947. Lewis J. Ordwein.

[44b.] St. Mary's Home for Working Girls, 225 E. 72nd St. 1966. Rogers, Butler and Burgun.

[45a.] 660 Park Avenue, NW cor. 67th St. 1927. York & Sawyer.

[45b.] 51-53 East 67th Street, ca. 1880.

Long before the rise of Park and Fifth Avenues, these were town houses of the well-to-do.

[45c.] Dresden Madison Nursing Home, 36 E. 67th St. 1906. Henry Bacon.

Bacon did the **Lincoln Memorial.**

[45d.] 33 East 67th Street. 1903, Robertson & Potter.

[46a.] 16 East 67th Street/formerly **Jeremiah Milbank House.** 1906. John H. Duncan.

Some finishes start things.

A new bank building in California; Shigenori Iyama, A.I.A., architect;
F. P. Lathrop Construction Company, general contractor.

...ings like new possibilities in design.

The richly glowing finish of this J&L stainless steel was just one considera-
...n in the choice of these handsome doors for a new bank. Stainless offers so
...any other benefits. But because finish is so important, J&L offers a special
...e, in addition to the standard grades. GRAIN LINE (from .018″ to .078″)
...aits the architect or designer who starts things with new finishes.

...Maximum light floods through these doors because stainless steel is strong
...ough to permit narrow-stile design, while it provides vital security. (Not
...ery architectural metal can.) Perfect alignment and close tolerance are
...ssible because stainless is warp-resistant. Stainless entrances are now avail-
...le, from stock, at prices sure to interest architects and builders. Other
...nefits are gleaming beauty . . . easy care . . . and long life. Wherever metal
... a possibility, stainless is the probability. Its finish gets a lot of exciting
...ings started!

Jones & Laughlin Steel Corporation
STAINLESS and STRIP DIVISION · Detroit 48234

STAINLESS

[46b.] Regency Whist Club, 15 E. 67th St. 1904. Ernest Flagg.

A turn-of-the-century Paris town house by the architect of **Scribners'** store and the two **Singer** buildings. Note the railings for security (mostly psychological) at the casement windows.

[46c.] 13 East 67th Street/formerly **Martin Beck House,** 1921. Henry Allan Jacobs.

[46d.] 9 East 67th Street. 1913. Hiss & Weeks.

Their great contribution to New York is the **Gotham Hotel.**

[46e.] 7 East 67th Street, 1900. Clinton & Russell.

[46f.] 4 East 67th Street. 1909. Carrère & Hastings.

[47.] Seventh Regiment Monument, Fifth Ave., on axis with 67th St. at Central Park. 1927. Karl Illava, Sculptor. ★

[48a.]

[4

[49f.]

A memorial to those of the **107**th infantry who died in **World War I.**

[47a.] Yugoslav Mission to the U.N./formerly **R. Livingston Beekman House,** 854 Fifth Avenue, bet. 67th and 68th Sts. 1905. Warren and Wetmore. ☆

[48a.] Indonesian Delegation to the U.N./originally **J. J. Emery House,** 5 East 68th Street. 1894. Peabody and Stearns.

[48b.] 8 East 68th Street/formerly **Otto Kahn House,** 1900.

Facade by John H. Duncan.

Part of a **trio** formed with number **6** and **10**.

[48c.] 9 East 68th Street/formerly **George T. Bliss House**, 1906. Heins and LaFarge.

Sir John Soane, 100 years too late.

[49a.] 35 East 68th Street, 1900. Carrère and Hastings.

[49b.] Dominican Academy/formerly **Michael Friedsam House**, 44 East 68th St., 1921. Frederick G. Frost.

[49c.] National Municipal League, 47 East 68th St. 1906. Adams and Warren.

[49d.] 420 Madison Ave./formerly **Clarence S. Day House**, 1903. Tracy & Swarthout.

The native habitat of Clarence Day, Jr. described on Broadway in **"Life with Father."**

[49e.] 49 East 68th Street, 1914. Trowbridge & Livingston.

[46b.]- [46e.]

[49f.] Council on Foreign Relations/formerly **Harold I. Pratt House,** 58 E. 68th St. 1920. Delano & Aldrich.

The last of the sons of Brooklyn's leading 19th Century citizen, **Charles Pratt,** kerosene magnate and later a large shareholder with **John D. Rockefeller** in the Standard Oil Company. Each son received a minor palace as a wedding present, the first three along **Clinton Avenue** in Brooklyn, opposite their father's mansion. When Harold's turn came, due to the *changing fashions* of New York (Manhattan) vis à vis Brooklyn, he chose **Park Avenue** for this English Renaissance limestone "palace."

[50a.] 680 Park Avenue/formerly **Percy Pyne House,** 1911. McKim, Mead & White.

Most recently the Russian Delegation to the U.N.

[50b.] Institute of Public Administration, 684 Park Ave. 1926. McKim, Mead & White.

[50c.] Istituto Italiano di Cultura/formerly **William Sloane House,** 686 Park Ave. 1918. Delano & Aldrich.

Sloane gave his name to **W. & J. Sloane,** the great New York furniture store.

[50d.] Italian Consulate/formerly **Henry P. Davison House,** 690 Park Ave. 1917. Walker & Gillette.

Built for the founder of the **Bankers Trust Company.** *Crisp* Georgian; delicately detailed.

[50a.]-
[50d.]

The parts (of the above facade, 50a.–50d.) are far less important than the **whole:** Georgian architecture's greatest contribution to remember today was **not the style** of individual buildings, but an **attitude toward urban design.** Buildings of character, quality and refinement were subordinated to a larger system of designing cities.

[51.] 69th Street, Park to Madison Avenue.

[51a.] 52 East 69th Street, 1917. Walker & Gillette.

[51b.] 50 East 69th Street, 1918. Henry C. Pelton.

[51c.] 46 East 69th Street, 1926. Mott Schmidt.

[51d.] 42 East 69th Street, 1930. Edward S. Hewitt.

[51e.] 36 East 69th Street, 1923. Carrère & Hastings and Shreve, Lamb & Blake.

[51f.] 35 East 69th Street, 1910. Walker & Gillette.

[51g.] 34 East 69th Street, 1930.

[51h.] 33 East 69th Street, 1910. Howells & Stokes.

[51i.] 31 East 69th Street, 1917. C. P. H. Gilbert.

[51j.] 27 East 69th Street, 1922. York & Sawyer.

[51k.] 25 East 69th Street, 1930. Noel & Miller.

[52.] 69th Street, Madison to Fifth Avenue.

[52a.] 16 East 69th Street, 1929.

[52b.] 13 East 69th Street, 1928. William A. Hewlett.

[52c.] 12 East 69th Street, 1914. Welles Bosworth.

[52d.] 11 East 69th Street, 1924. Delano & Aldrich.

[52e.] 9 East 69th Street, 1915. Grosvenor Atterbury.

[52f.] 6 East 69th Street, 1937.

[52g.] **Richard Morris Hunt Memorial,** 70th St. at Fifth Ave. 1898. Bruce Price; Sculptor, Daniel Chester French.

[53.] 70th Street, Fifth to Madison Avenue.

[53a.] **Frick Collection**/formerly **Henry Clay Frick Residence,** 1 E. 70th St. 1914. Carrère & Hastings. Renovated as a public museum in 1935 by John Russell Pope. Open to the public (Tuesday–Saturday, 10 AM–6 PM; Sunday, 1–6 PM.)

The garden is a pleasant break in the almost continuous east wall of Fifth Avenue.

Bland, sometimes fussy, frequently indecisive, the exterior

belies a rich interior, both in architecture and contents. The glass-roofed courtyard, entered almost directly, is a **delightful transition** from the noisy, bustling street: damp, still, except for what seems, in contrast, to be the *rich noise of water* from a central fountain, this is a place for pause, utterly relaxing: not surprising in the work of the same architect who created similar islands of light, sound, and repose at the **Mellon Gallery** in **Washington.**

[53b.] 5 East 70th Street, 1911. Warren & Wetmore. Remodeled, 1927. Horace Trumbauer.

[53c.] 11 East 70th Street, 1909. C. P. H. Gilbert.

[53d.] 13 East 70th Street, 1909. John H. Duncan.

[53e.] 15 East 70th Street, 1907. Charles I. Berg.

[53f.] 17 East 70th Street, 1919. Heins & LaFarge and A. L. Jackson.

[53g.] 19 East 70th Street, 1909. Thornton Chard.

[53h.] 21 East 70th Street, 1918. William J. Rogers.

[54.] 70th Street, Madison to Park Avenue.

[54a.] 30 East 70th Street, 1886. Charles W. Clinton.

[54b.] 32 East 70th Street, 1910. Taylor & Levi.

[54c.] 36 East 70th Street, 1884. Remodeled 1919. Louis S. Weeks.

[54d.] 43 East 70th Street, 1929. Mott B. Schmidt.

[54e.] 45 East 70th Street, 1929. Aymar Embury, 2nd.

[54f.] Explorer's Club/formerly Stephen C. Clark House, 46-48 East 70th St. 1912. Frederick J. Sterner.

[55.] St. James (Protestant Episcopal) Church, NE cor. 71st St. and Madison Ave. 1881. Robert H. Robertson; Altered, 1922, 1927. Ralph Adams Cram. Restoration of collapsed tower, 1950, Richard Kimball (tower replaced by spire).

Crisp brownstone and crisp steel produce a most **un-Gothic** appearance.

[56.] 71st Street, Madison to Fifth Avenue.

[56a.] 22 East 71st Street, 1923. C. P. H. Gilbert.

[56b.] 18 East 71st Street, 1911. John H. Duncan.

[56c.] 14 East 71st Street, 1913. York & Sawyer.

[56d.] 10 East 71st Street, 1935. John Russell Pope.

[56e.] Herbert N. Straus House, 9 E. 71st St. 1932. Horace Trumbauer.

[57a.] 7 East 72nd Street, 1899. Flagg & Chambers.

Rich opulence of the Paris of **Napoleon III.**

[57b.] Lycée Français/formerly **James Stillman House,** 9 E. 72nd St. 1896. Carrère & Hastings.

The French have occupied their own image: an architectural home away from home.

[57c.] 19 East 72nd Street, 1936. Rosario Candela & Mott B. Schmidt.

Styled in the "modern" manner. The site was that of **Charles Tiffany's** Romanesque mansion (an early **McKim, Mead and White** masterpiece), later decorated and occupied by his son, **Louis Comfort** (Tiffany).

[58a.] 867 Madison Avenue/formerly **Olivotti Building/**originally **Gertrude Rhinelander Waldo House,** 1898. Kimball & Thompson.

Every part of this exudes personality. Now used principally as a commercial structure, housing galleries and interior decorators (the most celebrated being **Christie's** of **London** who use the original salon and conservatory for exhibition galleries), each space has a strong external character, the antithesis of the flexible, universal office building.

[58b.] Manufacturers' Hanover Trust Company, 35 E. 72nd St. 1931. Cross & Cross. ☆

A bank, of all things, in the manner of the **Brothers Adam** (who worked in **18th Century London** and **Edinburgh**).

[58c.] 54 East 72nd Street. ca. 1950.

Glass is here used for **natural light, not sight,** except for a random glimpse through the louvered slots.

[58d.] 750 Park Avenue, SW cor. 72nd St. 1951. Horace Ginsbern and Associates.

A strong statement in the relatively bland wall of **Park Avenue.**

[59a.] Presbyterian Home, 49 E. 73rd St. 1870.

[59b.] Madison Avenue Presbyterian Church, NE cor. 73rd St. and Madison Ave. 1899. James Gamble Rogers. Altered, 1960. Adams & Woodbridge.

Sheer walls contrast sharply with ornate detail, to the end that what is normal **neo-Gothic** sculpture seems more ornate and complex by contrast.

[60.] 73rd Street, Madison to Fifth Avenue.,

[60a.] 38 East 73rd Street, 1897. Charles Buck and Co.

[60b.] 36 East 73rd Street, 1897. Charles Buck and Co.

[60c.] 26 East 73rd Street, 1896. Alexander M. Welch.

[60d.] 20 East 73rd Street, 1896. Alexander M. Welch.

[60e.] 16 East 73rd Street, 1907. Beatty & Stone.

[60f.] 12 East 73rd Street, 1921. Harry Allan Jacobs.

[60g.] 11 East 73rd Street/formerly Joseph Pulitzer Residence. 1903. McKim, Mead & White. ☆

[60h.] 5 East 73rd Street, 1902. Buchman & Fox.

[60i.] 4 East 73rd Street, 1913. Donn Barber.

[60j.] 920 Fifth Avenue, SE cor. 73rd St. 1922. J. E. R. Carpenter.

[61a.] 925 and 926 Fifth Avenue bet. 73rd and 74th Sts. 1899 and 1891. C. P. H. Gilbert.

[61b.] 927 Fifth Avenue, SE cor. 74th St. 1917. Warren & Wetmore.

[61c.] French Consulate, 934 Fifth Ave. bet. 74th and 75th Sts. 1926. Walker & Gillette.

[62.] 74th Street, Fifth to Madison Avenue.

[62a.] 5 East 74th Street, 1917. Edward Necarsulmer.

[62b.] 7 East 74th Street, 1891. James E. Ware.

[62c.] 9 East 74th Street, 1919. George & Edward Blum.

[62d.] 11 East 74th Street, 1919. George & Edward Blum.

[62e.] 15 East 74th Street, 1913. Hewitt & Bottomley.

[62f.] 18 East 74th Street, 1923. A. Wallace McRea.

[63.] 32 East 74th Street, 1935. William Lescaze.

A handcrafted vision of the machine esthetic (common to most **Bauhaus-inspired** design and architecture; the IDEA of the machine, or machine-made product, preceded reality).

[64.] Whitney Museum, Madison Ave. SE cor. 75th St. 1966. Marcel Breuer and Hamilton Smith.

Almost as startling on the city street as the **Guggenheim,** it vends its wares with a vengeance. Reinforced concrete, moated, bridged, cantilevered in progressive steps overshadowing the mere patron, it is a forceful place and series of spaces. The cantilevered floors recall the machicollations (stepped, overhanging battlements) of **Carcassonne.** Beware of boiling oil! The Whitney joins the list of **must-be-seen modern** "objects" in New York, along with **Seagram's,** the **Guggenheim,** and **Lever House.**

[64.]

[65a.] The Commonwealth Fund/formerly Edward S. Harkness House, 1 E. 75th St. 1905. Hale & Rogers. ☆

[65b.] Harkness House for Ballet Arts/formerly Thomas J. Watson House, 4 E. 75th St. 1896. Carrère & Hastings; Renovated, 1965. Rogers, Butler and Burgun.

[65c.] 5 and 7 East 75th Street, 1902. Welch, Smith & Provot.

[65d.] 13 East 75th Street, 1911. Walter Chambers.

[66.] The Hewitt School (Miss Hewitt's Classes)/formerly Dr. Ernest Stillman House, 45 East 75th St. 1925. Cross & Cross.

A late neo-Georgian town house.

[67.] 8 East 76th Street, 1896. Parish & Schroeder.

[68a.] Parke-Bernet Galleries, 980 Madison Ave. bet. 75th and 76th St. 1950. Walker and Poor; Sculpture, Wheeler Williams.

Parke-Bernet has understood and catered to America's culture starvation: buy history or at least live vicariously with the remnants of history.

[68b.] Hotel Carlyle, 35 E. 76th St. 1929. Bien & Prince.

One of the last gasps of the Great Boom, this became New York headquarters for both the Truman and Kennedy Administrations. Both presidents usually stayed here when visiting the City. **Ludwig Bemelmans** was unleashed with delightful success in the bar **(Bemelmans Bar);** even the ceiling was not spared his whimsical brush: airplanes and birds float overhead.

[69.] Institute of Fine Arts (New York University)/formerly

James B. Duke House, 1 E. 78th St. 1912. Horace Trumbauer. Interior remodeled, 1958. Robert Venturi, Cope & Lippincott.

Reputedly a push here and a pull there made a Bordeaux house into this town house, originally built for the **Dukes,** whose resources were those of the **American Tobacco Company.** Now it serves **New York University** graciously.

[70.] 2 East 79th Street/formerly **Augustus van Horn Stuyvesant House,** SE cor. Fifth Avenue.

[71a.] New York Society Library, 53 East 79th St. 1917. Trowbridge and Livingston. ☆

A great collection of and about New York's history lies here, **open to the public** for research and browsing, available to the public for loan on a yearly membership fee: **150,000 volumes.**

[71b.] Greek Consulate/originally **George L. Rives House,** 69 East 79th St. 1908. Carrère and Hastings. ☆

[71c.] 900 Park Avenue/originally **James Stillman House,** NW cor. 79th St.

The Stanhope Hotel Outdoor Cafe. 997 Fifth Avenue, SE cor. 81st St. 1965.

A new and pleasurable addition to an old and elegant hotel. The sights are equal to those offered café-sitters worldwide: girls, the **Metropolitan Museum,** tottering dowagers, **Rolls-Royces** and the jet set.

[72.] 998 Fifth Ave., at 81st St. 1910. McKim, Mead & White. ☆

[73.] 25 East 83rd Street. 1938. Frederick L. Ackerman, Ramsey & Sleeper.

Not to be confused with those buildings which superficially appear "modernistic"; centrally air-conditioned **(the first in the city);** note that there are **no grilles** penetrating the walls. Air is drawn in at the roof and distributed by interior ductwork.

[76a.]

[74.] 1025 Fifth Avenue, bet. 83rd and 84th Sts. 1955. Entrance spaces designed by Raymond Loewy-William Snaith, Inc.

This circuitous entrance allowed a Fifth Avenue address to buildings that would have been **70 East 84th Street** or **51 East 83rd Street.**

[75.] Marymount School/formerly **Burden House/**originally **Mrs. Harriet V. S. Thorne House,** 1028 Fifth Ave., at 84th St. 1902. Charles P. H. Gilbert.

[76a.] Metropolitan Museum of Art, Central Park, facing Fifth

Ave. bet. 80th and 84th Sts. Rear facade, 1880. Calvert Vaux & J. Wrey Mould; SW wing and facade, 1888. Theodore Weston. Central part, 1895. Richard Morris Hunt and (1902) Richard Howland Hunt. Side wings, 1906. McKim, Mead & White. Thomas J. Watson Library, 1965. Brown, Lawford & Forbes. ★

The **Columbian Exposition** (Chicago World's Fair) of **1893** was the **neo-Renaissance** design example for this elegant warehouse of art. (The opposing **Romanesque Revival** lost the battle at the "Fair," now the grounds of Chicago's **Jackson Park.**)

Instead of **Queen Anne Front** and **Mary Anne Behind,** this is the **City Beautiful Front** and a **Ruskinian Gothic Behind.** Confronting the city across an edge (a street) in the manner of **Versailles,** the building participates in both the urban order of Fifth Avenue and the rural order of **Olmsted and Vaux's Central Park.**

Architectural remnants were incorporated into the structure: one, the old **Assay Office** facade became the facade of the American Wing (**Grosvenor Atterbury,** architect of the alteration, **1924;** it had been built as the **Bank of the United States** in **1823,** and became the **U.S. Assay Office** from **1854** to **1912.**) The main hall is one of the great spaces of New York: our only New York suggestion of the great visionary **neo-Roman** spaces of the 17th Century Italian draughtsman, **Piranesi.** *Free, Monday through Saturday, 10 AM– 5 PM; Sundays and legal holidays, 1–5 PM.*

[76b.] Cleopatra's Needle, behind the Metropolitan Museum, ca. 1600 B.C. (reign of Thutmose III).

A gift of the **Khedive of Egypt** in **1880,** it was rolled over tortuous topography from the Hudson River on cannonballs to the **"worst place within the city for getting an obelisk to".**

[77a.] St. Ignatius Loyola (Roman Catholic) Church, SW cor. Park Ave. and 84th St. 1899. Schickel & Ditmars. ☆

Vignola in the American manner, with a German accent.

[77b.] Regis High School, 55 E. 84th St. 1917. Maginnis & Walsh.

[78.] Park Avenue Christian Church, SW cor. Park Ave. and 85th St. 1911. Cram, Goodhue & Ferguson.

Native materials, here Manhattan schist, were assembled with inspiration from the **Sainte Chapelle** in Paris. Such were the words of **Cram,** but the inspiration seems to have been effective largely in the fleche.

[79a.] The Town Club/formerly **William Woodward House,** 9 East 86th St. 1918. Delano & Aldrich. ☆

[79b.] 5 East 86th Street, ca. 1880.

An early **outpost** in this then undeveloped area.

[79c.] Yivo Institute/formerly **Mrs. Cornelius Vanderbilt House/** originally **William Starr Miller House,** SE cor. Fifth Ave. and 86th St. 1914. Carrère & Hastings. ☆

An emigré—from the **Place des Vosges** without the **Place:** a town palace of limestone and brick.

[80.] Buttinger House, 10 E. 87th St. 1958. Felix Augenfeld and Jan Pokorny.

Residence built around a private library which occupies a handsome, two-story glass-walled space.

[81.] Milton Steinberg House (Park Avenue Synagogue), 50 E. 87th St. 1955. Kelly & Gruzen.

A sleek stained-glass facade (**Adolf Gottlieb**) which at night visually floats (Friday night is the best time to see it) in front of this activities- and office-building.

[82a.] The Guggenheim (Solomon R. Guggenheim Museum) on Fifth Avenue, 88th to 89th St. 1959. Frank Lloyd Wright.

The **central space** is one of the greatest modern interiors in the world: more important as architecture than the contents it serves. To appreciate it, take the elevator (half-round) to the top and meander (literally between the structural baffles) down the ramp.

[82b.] **12, 14, and 16 East 89th Street**/formerly the **Cutting Houses.** 1919. Delano & Aldrich.

[82c.] **National Academy of Design,** 3 and 5 East 89th St. and 1083 Fifth Ave. No. 3 designed and 1083 remodeled in 1914 by Ogden Codman, Jr.; 5 added by William & Geoffrey Platt, 1958.

A center of conservatism in the arts. Founded in **1825,** it includes architects, painters, sculptors, graphic designers.

[82a.]

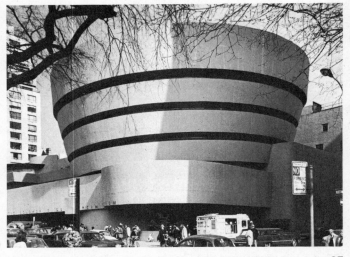

[83a.] **Church of the Heavenly Rest (Protestant Episcopal),** SE cor. Fifth Ave. and 90th St. 1928. Mayers, Murray & Philip; Malvina Hoffman, sculptor of pulpit Madonna; Ulrich Ellerhusen, exterior sculptor.

Stripped Gothic, this has some of the strong, but austere, massing that prefigures modern as a style if not a fact.

[83b.] **17 East 90th Street,** 1917. F. Burrall Hoffman, Jr.

[83c.] **15 East 90th Street,** 1927. Mott B. Schmidt.

[84a.] **Columbia School of Social Work**/formerly **Andrew Carnegie Mansion,** 2 E. 91st St. 1901. Babb, Cook & Willard.

When Carnegie built this chateau, squatters occupied the whole area.

[84b.] **Convent of the Sacred Heart**/formerly **Otto Kahn House,** 1 E. 91st St. 1918. C. P. H. Gilbert & J. Armstrong Stenhouse.

A huge house: an American version of an English version of an Italian Renaissance palazzo (cf. **Papal Chancellory** in Rome). It is rich but subdued, as expected in **Boston** or **Florence.**

[84c.] **Duchesne Residence School**/formerly **James A. Burden Residence,** 7 E. 91st St. 1902. Warren & Wetmore.

Built by the industrialized ironmonger from Troy whose commercial legacy is the **American Machine and Foundry Company** (AMF).

[84d.] **9 East 91st Street**/formerly **John H. Hammond House,** 1902. Carrère & Hastings.

Hammond was the father-in-law of **Benny Goodman.**

[84e.] **11 East 91st Street.** Trowbridge & Livingston.

[84f.] **The Spence School,** 22 E. 91st St. 1929. John Russell Pope.

[85a.] **1107 Fifth Ave.,** SE cor. 92nd St. 1925. Rouse & Goldstone.

Mrs. Marjorie Meriwether Post (Toasties), commissioned this vertically stacked town palace to allow herself a superb 54-room triplex **vantage point in space.**

[85b.] The Jewish Museum/formerly **Felix M. Warburg House,** 1109 Fifth Avenue. NE cor. 92nd St. 1908. C. P. H. Gilbert. New building, 1963. Samuel Glazer.

[86.] Brick Presbyterian Church, NW cor. Park Ave. and 91st St. 1938. York & Sawyer; Louis Ayres, designer. Chapel of the Reformed Faith, 1952. Adams & Woodbridge.

The safe, brick and limestone lanterned neo-Georgian of the Thirties.

[87a.] Russian Orthodox Church Headquarters/formerly **Francis Palmer House**/originally **George F. Baker, Jr. Residence,** 1180 Park Ave. NW cor. 93rd St. 1917 and 1928. Delano & Aldrich. ☆

A **lesson in town design** in itself, and how to respect and reinforce the form of street and avenue, while creating both private garden space and a richness and variety of architectural form.

[a.]
[77a.]

[.]
[84c.]

[87b.] 69 East 93rd Street, Delano & Aldrich. ☆

[87c.] Rumanian Delegation to the UN/formerly **Mrs. William K. Vanderbilt II House,** 60 East 93rd St. 1930. John Russell Pope. ★

[87d.] 56 East 93rd Street/formerly **Billy Rose House**/originally

William G. Loew House, 1931. Walker & Gillette. ☆

The last great mansion, it has the manners of **John Soane,** the avant-garde **Regency** architect who used classic parts with a fresh attitude to form and space.

[88a.] Squadron "A" (Eighth Regiment) Armory (Western portion), Madison Avenue, 94th and 95th St. 1895. John Rochester Thomas. ☆

Saved by the bell (and from the ball), this contained the offices and meeting rooms serving the great drill hall (used also as a polo arena) to the east, now demolished: to be used as a community building in conjunction with **I.S. 29** described below. A fantasy of brick-masons' virtuosity: arches, corbels, machicollations, crenellations; plastic, neo-medieval modelling.

[88b.] I.S. 29, Manhattan, Park to Madison Ave. 94th to 95th St. 1969. Morris Ketchum, Jr. and Associates.

The preliminary scheme is of castellated brick, complementary to its old machicollated neighbor.

[89a.] 5 through 25 East 94th Street, ca. 1880.

A speculators' row of brownstone and rock-faced ashlar **Romanesque revival** houses with a variety of detail for "individuality."

[99a.]

[88

[89b.] National Audubon Society/formerly **Williard Straight House,** 1130 Fifth Ave. NE cor. 94th St. 1914. Delano & Aldrich. ★

Elegant, distilled, refined, a sharp, precise, intellectually studied, American **neo-Georgian** house, with a homely residential scale.

[90.] Lycée Française de New York/formerly **Mrs. Amory S. Carhart House,** 3 E. 95th St. 1913. Horace Trumbauer. ☆

[91.] 7 and 15 East 96th Street, ca. 1915. Ogden Codman, Jr. ★

[92.] Russian Orthodox Cathedral of St. Nicholas, 15 E. 97th St.

An **exotic form** amongst the dour surroundings made by (predominantly) rich northern European Protestants. One of two onion domes in Manhattan; the other is at **St. George's** on 7th Street.

[93.] St. Bernard's School, 4 E. 98th St. 1918. Delano & Aldrich.

For boys, not the dogs of monks.

[94.] Mt. Sinai Hospital, 98th to 101st St. Fifth to Madison Ave., original buildings, 1904. Arnold W. Brunner; Klingenstein Pavilion, 1952. Kahn & Jacobs.

Like Topsy, it tried to grow within the grid (absorbing two cross streets). Similar to **Roosevelt** and **Lenox Hill Hospitals,** it rebuilt itself, in the same manner that the body remains and gradually changes its appearance.

[95.] Carver Houses (Plaza), 99th to 101st St. Madison to Park Ave. 1965. Pomerance & Breines; M. Paul Friedberg, Landscape Architect.

Messrs. **Breines** and **Friedberg,** by manipulating levels, giving surfaces of various textures for different active individual and group uses, have given us a practical and handsome plaza.

[96a.] New York Academy of Medicine, 2 E. 103rd St. 1926. York & Sawyer. Library open to the public.

Literal eclecticism: a little bit of **Byzantine** detail and mannerism; a pinch of **Lombardian** (northern Italian) **Romanesque:** monolithic and massive, windows and doors are tiny apertures.

What may be the world's largest collection of cookbooks is, surprisingly, housed here, the gift of **Dr. Margaret Barclay Wilson.** She (if not all physicians) believed that the enlightened, disciplined and/or enriched palate led to well being of the mind and/or body.

[96b.] Museum of the City of New York, 1220 Fifth Ave. bet. 103rd & 104th St. 1932. Joseph H. Freedlander. ☆

The product of a **competition** between five invited firms, this is a bland neo-Georgian building. The contents make up for any architectural deficiencies: "dioramas" demonstrate the physical form and history of the city to children (both old and young).

(**Adolf A. Weinman** statues of **Alexander Hamilton** and **DeWitt Clinton** in niches facing the entrance courtyard.)

[97a.] Flower & Fifth Avenue Hospitals/New York Medical College, 105th to 106th Sts. on Fifth Ave. 1921. York & Sawyer.

A **"homeopathic"** medical school (see your doctor for an explanation).

[98.] Stanley Isaacs Houses, First Ave. 93rd to 95th Sts. 1966. Frederick G. Frost, Jr. and Associates.

The poor have the best views, and breezes in New York. Open access corridors modulate the standard brick and aluminum windows of this small (**coat-, not vest-**pocket) housing project. The barrel-vaulted community center is another architectural and social step to give a place for **participation in the community** to project residents.

[99a.] Municipal Asphalt Plant, First Ave. to the East River Dr. 90th to 91st St. 1944. Kahn & Jacobs.

Exposed concrete over a steel (arched) frame, this **bold work of "industrial architecture"** has not been matched in New York for bald functional and esthetic logic.

[100a.]

[99b.] Gracie Square Gardens, through the center of the block 89th to 90th St. bet. York & East End Aves. (Nos. 520 and 530 East 90th; 515 and 525 East 89th).

An unpretentious group of six-story (non-fireproof) brick apartment buildings whose principal charm is their **common central garden.**

[100a.] Gracie Mansion (Residence of New York's Mayors), in Carl Schurz Park opposite 88th St. 1799. ☆ Public ballrooms added in 1966. Mott B. Schmidt.

A remote country residence in its day, **Archibald Gracie's** house has been through the mill of reconstruction and restoration. The addition permits the mayor to use the house while others think they are using it.

[100b.] Carl Schurz Park and John Finley Walk, East End Ave. to the River, 84th to 90th St.

Carl Schurz, general, minister, senator, Secretary of the Interior, editor: the most prominent German immigrant of the 19th century, he lived in Yorkville near this park.

The construction of the **F.D.R. Drive (Harvey Stevenson** and **Cameron Clark)** brought it its greatest glory: the edge of the city is enjoyed, in common, by the motorists below, at the water's edge, and pedestrians above.

From the edge are views of the **Triborough Bridge, Hellgate Bridge, Ward's Island, Welfare Island, Queensboro Bridge** and the **Astoria and Long Island City sections of Queens.** River traffic is the most fascinating sight, largely because the channel formed between the park and **Welfare Island** keeps boats and ships very close to the shore.

[101.] Henderson Place, North side of 86th St. bet. York & East End Aves.

A **charming cul-de-sac** lined with tiny, three-story houses.

[102.] 525 East 85th Street, 1958. Paul Mitarachi.

Two stories of glass-sheathed space; the garden is in front so that a raised living room overlooks it to the south.

[103.]

[103.] Church Of The Holy Trinity, 316 E. 88th St. bet. First and Second Aves. 1897. Barney & Chapman. ☆

A little bit of the **Loire Valley** (laced with bits of French Gothic), plus a great deal of imagination, produced this urban complex that respects its neighbors and creates, within its own embrace, a **garden oasis** for this parkless and plazaless precinct. **Modern** glass in the cloister chapel is by **Robert Sowers.**

[104.] 245 East 87th Street, 1966. Paul and Jarmul.

The same economics, the same materials, the same zoning and building laws, here in the hands of **someone who cares:** the bold massing of the balconies reads with great richness on the avenue.

[105a.] Ruppert Brewery, Second to Third Aves. 90th to 93rd Sts.

Thirty-four buildings gradually accrued on this one set of blocks, for the glory of the **German beer-hall** (this is **Yorkville**).

.]   **[108b.]**

[105b.] Renewal Project/formerly **Ruppert Brewery,** Second to Third Ave. 90th to 93rd St. in design 1967. Whittlesey, Conklin & Rossant.

[106.] YMHA (Young Men's Hebrew Association), SE cor. Lexington Ave. and 92nd St. ca. 1928. Gehron and Ross.

A city-wide center for cultural affairs, the **Kaufmann** auditorium holds readings from the resident **Poetry Center** and presents concerts and lectures of general interest.

[107.] RKO 86th Street, Lexington Ave. NW cor. 86th St.

Another of the now-rare movie palaces of the Twenties (see RKO 58th Street). Just to sit in the lobby and eat popcorn is a classy experience. Soon to be replaced by Gimbel's!

Cheese Unlimited, 1263 Lexington Ave. NE cor. 85th St.

Sol Chackam is the **cheese-god.** Pay obeisance at his shrine and you will be enriched by **Wensleydale** (old and decrepit as possible), **Israeli Blue,** any of assorted **Bries** or **Camemberts,** for sensual, immoral bliss: **Triple Crème or Boursault.**

Fox's Nut Shoppe, 1267 Lexington Ave. bet. 85th & 86th St.

Nuts (and candy) in bulk, for those who care to escape universally packaged America.

Martell's, 1469 Third Ave. SE cor. 83rd St.

More drinking than eating takes place here in this pleasant, handsome bit of nostalgia for something that never was.

[108a.] John Jay Park, Cherokee Place (E. of York Ave.) to the East River Dr. 76th to 78th St.

A small, neighborhood park with swimming pools and playgrounds; intensively used.

[108b.] Cherokee Apartments, 77th to 78th St. on Cherokee Place, ca. 1900. Ernest Flagg.

A second glance is here well-deserved. These simple buildings are rich in new architectural thoughts for their time: the triple-hung windows allow a tenant to step onto a narrow French Balcony and **view the river;** and even if he doesn't make the step, he has a dramatic sense of space and view (open almost to the floor), psychologically and physically protected by the railings. The units are entered through brick, **barrel-vaulted tunnels,** into central courtyards from which, at each corner, stairs rise five flights!

[108c.] City and Suburban homes, York Ave. to the East River Dr. 78th to 79th St. 1900. Ernest Flagg.

More Flagg.

[109.] Junior League of the City of New York/formerly **Vincent Astor House,** 130 E. 80th St., bet. Lexington and Park Aves. 1928. Mott Schmidt. ★

[110.] Yorkville Branch, New York Public Library, 222 East 79th St. bet. Second and Third Aves. 1915. James Brown Lord. ☆

Another **Palladian** (neo-Renaissance) **London Club;** but here for the masses, not the classes!

[111a.] 180 East 78th Street. ca. 1940.

A bland exterior hides one of the cleverest urban ideas in Manhattan: **row houses piggybacked over shopping.** When the "El" was still up, the small windows facing the avenue provided minimum vision and air required by the City Building Code.

[113.]

[1

[111b.] 78th Street, Lexington to Second Ave. (157–165 ★).

A variety of architecture: **Georgian rows, Victorian terraces,** and even **a sleek modern alteration.** The quality of this pair of blocks is first-rate urban architecture; note particularly nos. **153 to 165; 208 to 218; 233 to 241; and 255–261.**

[111c.] 235 East 78th Street, 1964. Bruce Campbell Graham.

A fourteen-foot town house, handsomely remodeled for separate use of upper and lower duplexes. The brick walls and black wrought-iron fences are strong, simple, and **appropriate** to the Victorian facade behind.

Circa 1890, 265 East 78th Street.

Mrs. Gassner professes to hate Victoriana and, therefore, sells it with gusto. **Bentwood furniture, Tiffany-style lamps and objects** are the most popular and hence most expensive things present.

[112.] St. Jean Baptiste (Roman Catholic Church), Lexington Ave. SE cor. 76th St. 1913. Nicholas Serracino. ☆

Pomp, but not pompous. Various Roman parts are clustered about a nave and transepts, unfortunately with a pasty result. It seems more **stage architecture** than the real stuff of which cities are made, but has a picturesque silhouette.

[113.] The Buckley School (Addition), 113 E. 73rd St. 1962.
Brown, Lawford & Forbes.

A simple, **well-scaled facade,** extension through the block from
74th Street for a venerable private (boys') grammar school.

[111b.]

[114.] New York City Transit Authority Coal Loading Facility, East
River Dr. (river side) at 75th St. 1952. J. G. White Engineering Co.,
C. Herbert Wheeler, designer.

A **common industrial facility** achieves elegance of detail and
bold sculptural form: almost an architectural **"happening."**

[115.] Institute for Muscle Disease, 515 E. 71st St. 1961. Skidmore, Owings & Merrill.

[116.] Payson House, 435 E. 70th St. on York Ave. bet. 70th and
71st Sts. 1966. Frederick G. Frost, Jr. and Associates.

Three staggered slabs straddle two service corridors: a **dramatic**
freestanding form.

[117.] New York Hospital/Cornell University Medical College,
York Ave. 68th to 70th St. 1933. Coolidge, Shepley, Bulfinch and
Abbott.

The word **massing** could have been invented to describe this
great medical complex.

[118.] The Premier, 333 E. 69th St. bet. First and Second Aves.
1963. Mayer, Whittlesey & Glass; William J. Conklin, Designer.

A simple **crisp** but forceful, facade of exposed concrete and
brick. The contained balconies are far more useable and weather
proof than the cantilevered leaves seen toothily projecting from
innumerable lesser buildings.

[119a.] Memorial Sloan-Kettering Cancer Center, 444 E. 68th St.
bet. First and York Aves. ca. 1935. James Gamble Rogers, Inc.

**[119b.] James Ewing Memorial Building, Memorial Sloan-Ketter-
ing Cancer Center,** First Ave. 67th to 68th Sts. 1950. Skidmore,
Owings and Merrill.

**[120a.] The Rockefeller University (Rockefeller Institute for Med-
ical Research),** E. of York Ave. 64th to 68th Sts.

A campus for research and advanced education occupies a high
bluff overlooking the East River, once the summer estate of the
Schermerhorn family of **Lafayette Street.** The first building (**Central Laboratory**) opened in **1906.**

[120b.] Caspary Auditorium, 1957. Harrison & Abramovitz.

The **dome** adjacent to York Avenue.

[120c.] Detlev W. Bronk House, 1958. Harrison & Abramovitz.

A **country house** in the city, this modern limestone building cannot be seen from the street.

 [121.] Nurses Residence (Cornell University Hospital, School of Nursing), 1320 York Ave. bet. 66th and 67th St. 1965. Harrison & Abramovitz.

A **tower** of glass, rare in New York, faces the **Caspary Auditorium.**

[122.] City and Suburban Homes, York to First Ave. 64th to 65th St. 1915. Ernest Flagg.

Fifteen super-tenements from the same experimental group **Flagg** did for City & Suburban at Cherokee Place, between adjacent 78th and 79th Streets.

[123.] Colonial Dames of America/ originally **Abigail Adams Smith House,** 421 E. 61st St. 1799. ☆

A modest but real **Georgian** ashlar stone building. Built as a stable by the son-in-law of President John Adams, it served a never-completed manor house that burned to the ground in **1826.** Subsequently the stable was promoted in status and served as a hotel, until in turn converted to use as a private house in **1833.**

[124.] Wall in front of Chermayeff House, 347 E. 62nd St. Ivan Chermayeff.

A simple remodeling is enhanced by the playful **graffiti** of a bicycle.

H

HARLEM

"...there is so much to see in Harlem." Langston Hughes.

To those who haven't been above 110th Street, Harlem means the **Negro ghetto,** wherever it may be. But New York is different from all other cities, and its Harlem is different from all other ghettoes. This Harlem consists of a **variety of contrasting little Harlems,** some distinct, some overlapping. Saturday night Harlem is one place. It is a very different place on Sunday morning. Then you have **literary** Harlem, **political** Harlem, **religious** Harlem, **West-Indian** Harlem, **Black Nationalist** Harlem, and **philanthropic** Harlem. To the east and south of Negro Harlem are Spanish Harlem and Italian Harlem, distinct districts with their own turfs and institutions.

In other cities the ghettoes either radiate from the oldest and most **dilapidated neighborhoods** or are relegated to the wrong side of town, where they sorely lack transportation and social facilities. But Harlem became New York's Negro ghetto when its housing was relatively new. Here we find churches and institutions set on **wide boulevards** or facing **well-designed parks** and plazas. Three major subway lines give Harlem access to other parts of the City. The stores, restaurants, and hotels of 125th Street maintained their largely white clientele long after the departure of the area's white population.

The old village of **Nieuw Haarlem** was established by Peter Stuyvesant in 1658 in what is now East Harlem and connected with New Amsterdam, ten miles to the south, by a road built by the **Dutch West India Company's** Negro slaves. Eight years later the British Governor drew a diagonal across Manhattan, from the East River at 74th Street to the Hudson River at 129th Street, to separate New

York from Harlem. Early in the 19th Century **James Roosevelt** cultivated a large estate along the East River before moving to **Hyde Park.** A country village existed at 125th Street and First Avenue.

The opening of the Harlem River Railroad in 1837 marks the beginning of Harlem's development as a **suburb for the well-to-do.** Many of the handsome brick and brownstone rows of this era still survive. The extension of the elevated to Harlem in 1879 was followed by the construction of tenement houses along the routes of the "els" and apartment houses—some on a **lavish scale**—along the better avenues. These were augmented by schools, clubs, theaters, and commercial buildings.

The building of the IRT Lenox Avenue Subway in 1901 encouraged a **real estate boom** in Harlem; many more apartments were built than could be rented. Entire buildings adjacent to Lenox Avenue near 135th Street were unoccupied. Just at this time the **Tenderloin,** west of Herald Square, where a large part of the city's Negroes were living, was being redeveloped. The construction of Pennsylvania Station, Macy's department store, large hotels, office and loft buildings was forcing the Negro population to seek living space elsewhere. But in no other part of the city were Negroes welcome.

The Negro settlement in the high-prestige neighborhood of Harlem was made possible by **Philip A. Payton,** a remarkable Negro realtor. Alert to both the opportunity in Harlem and the desperate housing situation in the Tenderloin, he was able to open Harlem's many **vacant apartment buildings** to Negroes by assuming the man-

[5c.]

agement of individual buildings and guaranteeing premium rents to their landlords. The availability of **good housing for Negroes** was unprecedented; the hard-pressed Negro community flocked to Payton's buildings, often paying exorbitant rents but, for a short while at least, enjoying good housing.

Since Payton's day, **Harlem's troubles** have been due not to the area's physical shortcomings, but to the abuse and exploitation which our society visits upon its Negro members. The great **Negro immigration** of the Twenties, instead of being allowed to spread, was bottled up in this one area. The privations of the **Great Depression,** the inadequacy of public and private measures to deal with poverty, and the failures of urban renewal have further burdened Harlem and its people.

In spite of exploitation, neglect, and the passing of time, **Harlem has survived** as one of New York's real places of interest and opportunity. Handsome parks, fine patrician rows of private houses, excellent churches, handsome theaters, communal buildings, and commercial blocks, which progress has erased from more fashionable neighborhoods, survive in Harlem.

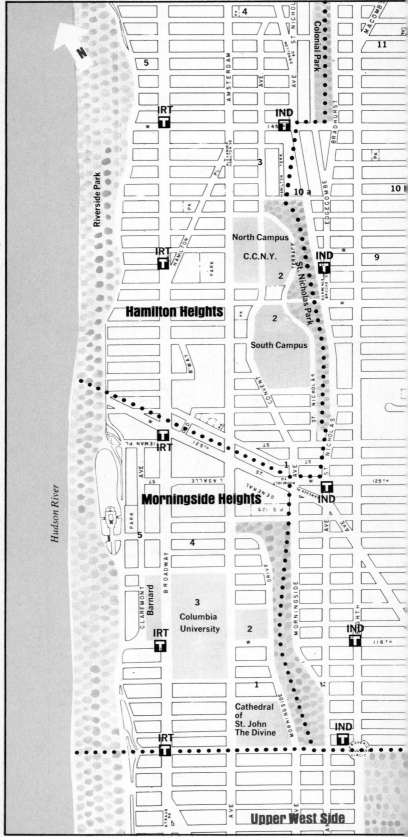

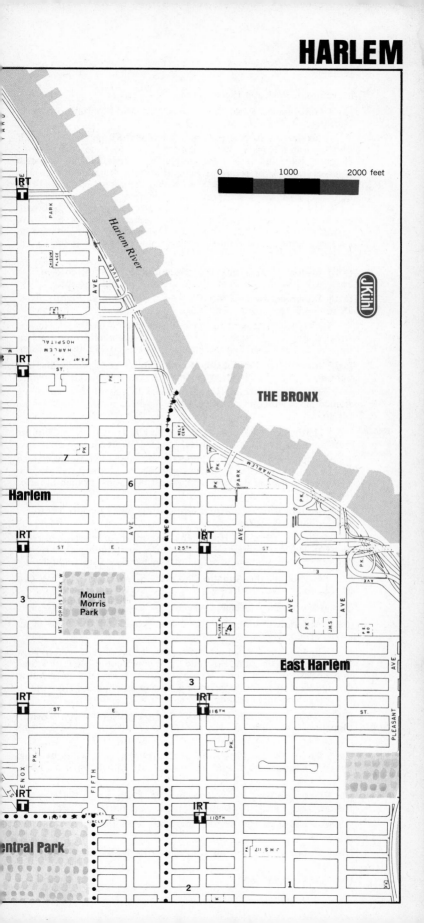

HARLEM

THE BRONX

Harlem

Mount
Morris
Park

East Harlem

Central Park

Harlem River

0   1000   2000 feet

JKtfi|

Morningside Park and Dewey Square

[1a.] Morningside Park, Cathedral Pkwy. and Manhattan Ave. to Morningside Ave. and W. 123rd St.

This narrow strip of parkland contains the high and rocky cliff that separates Harlem, below and to the east, from Morningside Heights, above and to the west. Designed by **Frederick Law Olmsted,** it preserves a bit of **primeval Manhattan** in a dramatic foreground to the Cathedral of St. John the Divine. Proposals of the mid-60's aimed to solve the social problems of Harlem and the space problems of the institutions on the Heights by cluttering the park with buildings. A public school has already eaten away the northwest corner of the park, and a proposed Columbia University gymnasium usurping two acres of public park, will block the view of the Cathedral.

[1b.] Statue of Lafayette and Washington, Manhattan Ave. SW cor. 114th St. 1900. Frederic Auguste Bartholdi, Scuptor.

[1c.] Rehabilitation, 114th St. bet. Seventh and Eighth Aves. 1966–1967. Horowitz and Chun.

Thirty-seven tenements on both sides of this typical Harlem street renovated through the auspices of two philanthropic foundations, with the aid and cooperation of various government agencies.

[1d.] Junior High School 88, Manhattan/formerly **Wadleigh High School,** 215 W. 114th St. W of Seventh Ave. 1905. C.B.J. Snyder.

This red brick school is embellished with a number of handsome stained-glass windows installed when it was a prestige high school for girls.

[1e.] 115th Street Branch, N. Y. Public Library, 203 W. 115th St. W of Seventh Ave. 1908. McKim, Mead & White. ★

Rusticated limestone, arched windows, and a handsome, carved seal of the city, guarded by a pair of angels, recall the Pitti Palace in Florence, and make this one of the most handsome branch libraries in the city.

[1f.] Graham Court Apartments, Seventh Ave. NE cor. 116th St. 1901. Clinton & Russell. ☆

Built for the Astor Estate, this, the most luxurious apartment house in Harlem, contains eight elevators. Surrounding a court, it is entered through a splendid arched passageway, two stories high.

[2.] St. Thomas the Apostle Church, 262 W. 119th St. SW cor. St. Nicholas Ave. 1907.

Mount Morris Park to Lenox Avenue

[3a.] Watchtower, Mount Morris Park, Madison Ave. SW of E. 121st St. ca. 1857. James Bogardus. ★

The lone survivor of many fire towers that once existed in New York. Employs the same post-and-lintel construction Bogardus used in his cast-iron warehouses. The watchtower is set on a steep hill in the middle of the Harlem plain and is an excellent place from which to survey the neighborhood.

[3b.] Commandment Keepers' Congregation/former **Dwight Mansion,** 1 W. 123rd St. NW cor. Mt. Morris Park W. 1890. Frank H. Smith.

[3c.] Mount Morris Presbyterian Church/formerly **Harlem Presbyterian Church,** W. 122nd St. SW cor. Mt. Morris Park W. 1905. T. H. Poole.

[3d.] Victorian row, Lenox Ave. bet. W. 120th and W. 121st Sts. E side. 1888. F. A. De Meuron and J. T. Smith.

A handsome row of ten mansions with distinctive Mansard roofs.

[3e.] Mount Olivet Baptist Church/formerly **Temple Israel,** 201

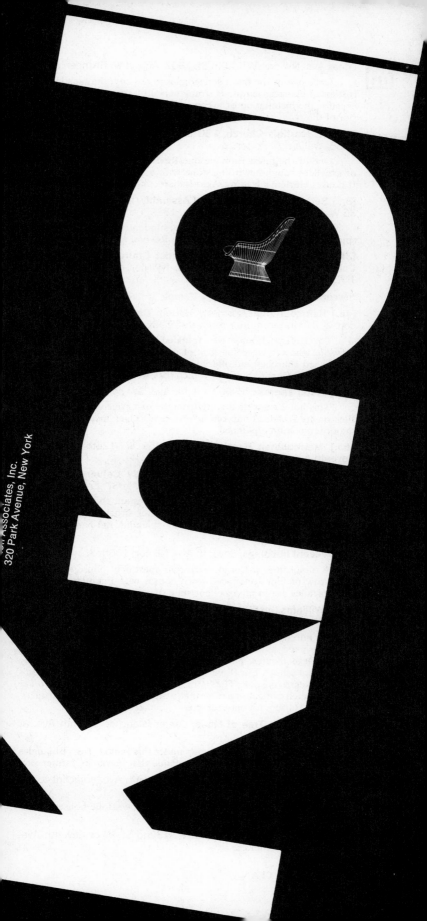

Knoll

Associates, Inc.
320 Park Avenue, New York

Lenox Ave. NW cor. W. 120th St. 1907. Arnold W. Brunner. ☆

Once one of the finest synagogues in the city; the facade of this rusticated classical temple is strengthened by four tall columns. Except for the installation of a baptismal pool, the lavish marble interior of the synagogue is intact.

[3f.] St. Martin's Church, 230 Lenox Ave. SE cor. W. 122nd St. 1888. William A. Potter. ★

One of the finest Romanesque Revival buildings in New York, of excellent rough-hewn limestone with a fine carillon in its tower. It houses Harlem's leading West Indian congregation.

[3g.] Bethel Gospel Pentecostal Assembly/formerly **Harlem Club,** 36 W. 123rd St. SE cor. Lenox Ave. 1889. Lamb & Rich. ☆

This clubhouse which once accommodated Harlem's elite is a splendid example of the Romanesque Revival expressed in brick.

[3h.] Ephesus Seventh Day Adventist Church/formerly **Second Collegiate Church,** 267 Lenox Ave. NW cor. W. 123rd St. 1887. J. R. Thomas.

Seventh Avenue: From Refuge Temple to the Tree of Hope.

[4a.] Refuge Temple/formerly **Harlem Casino,** Seventh Ave. NE cor. W. 124th St. Interior renovated 1966, Costas Machlouzarides.

The Refuge Temple was founded in 1919 by the Rev. R. C. Lawson, who criticized the lack of emotionalism in Harlem's more established churches and offered recent migrants the fire, brimstone, and personal Christianity with which they were familiar down South.

[4b.] Hotel Theresa, 2090 Seventh Ave. SW cor. W. 125th St.

This hotel gains its dignity from the extensive use of terra cotta tiles on its facade. Long one of Harlem's chief meeting places. A major renovation is planned.

[5a.] Metropolitan Baptist Church, 151 W. 128th St. NE cor. Seventh Ave. 1884.

[5b.] Salem Methodist Church/formerly **Calvary Methodist Church,** Seventh Ave. NW cor. W. 129th St. 1887. Enlarged, 1890.

This church once had the largest Protestant church auditorium and membership in the city. The simple brick structure is embellished by a carefully detailed bell tower and splendid, red-paneled arched doors.

[5c.] Vacant buildings, Seventh Ave. NE cor. 130th St.

A handsome, red brick Victorian apartment house and an unusual row of limestone-faced town houses with Egyptian motifs on their facades are in an excellent state of exterior preservation.

[5d.] Williams Institutional Church/formerly **Lafayette Theatre,** 2225 Seventh Ave. bet. W. 131st St. and W. 132nd St. E side.

A church now occupies this complex of three buildings, originally designed as a complete neighborhood entertainment center, with a large theater, ballroom, restaurant, tavern, public meeting rooms, and offices. For three decades the Lafayette was the nation's leading Negro theater. The 1913 production of *Darktown Follies* drew so much critical applause that it started the vogue of outsiders' coming to Harlem for entertainment.

[5e.] Site of the Tree of Hope, center island of Seventh Ave. at W. 131st St.

Negro actors exchanged news under this famous tree; **Bojangles Bill Robinson** presented the brass plaque that marks its former site.

[5f.] Residences, W. 132nd St. near Seventh Ave. adjacent to the Lafayette Theater building.

A row of unusually fine, high-stoop, brownstone houses, in excellent preservation.

[5g.] St. Aloysius' Church, 209 W. 132nd St. W of Seventh Ave. 1904. W. W. Renwick. ☆

An ornate and intricate facade of brick, cast stone, and terra cotta graces this charming eclectic church. Its most unusual detail is a wrought-iron Greek cross placed on the high rose window.

[1a.]   [1c.]

[3d.]

[5h.] St. Philip's Church, 214 W. 134th St. W of Seventh Ave. 1911. Vertner W. Tandy and George W. Foster.

This spare, Gothic-style, brick church has probably the wealthiest Negro congregation in the nation. It was founded in the notorious **"Five Points"** section of the Lower East Side in 1809. A century later it was able to sell its properties in the **Tenderloin** for almost $600,000. With this windfall the church purchased its present site, as well as a row of ten apartment houses on West 135th Street previously **restricted to whites.** When the congregation began its move to Harlem, white tenants living in the apartment houses were evicted, and their places were made available to Negroes.

MISCELLANY

[6a.] Intermediate School 201, Manhattan, Madison Ave. NE cor. 127th St. 1966. Curtis and Davis.

A handsome and successful attempt at sculptural ornamentation. A building which attempts to solve the social problems of Harlem with mechanical gadgets. The absence of windows prevents rock throwing, but the hostility that causes rock throwing will find other outlets in this vulnerable building.

[6b.] St. Andrew's Church, 2067 Fifth Ave. NE cor. 127th St. 1890. Henry Congdon. ★

This large church was built in 1873 at Park Avenue and East 128th Street. Sixteen years later it was dismantled and reerected on its present site and has stood firm ever since.

[6c.] All Saints' Church, Madison Ave. NE cor. E. 129th St. 1889–1894. Renwick, Aspinwall & Russell. ☆

[6d.] All Saints' Rectory, 47 E. 129th St. near Madison Ave. 1886–1889. Renwick, Aspinwall & Russell. ☆

[6e.] All Saints' School, Madison Ave. SE cor. E. 130th St. 1904. W. W. Renwick. ☆

Gothic structures built in materials of the day: orange brick, cast stone, and terra cotta. Exceptionally fine details.

[7a.] St. Ambrose' Church/formerly **Church of the Puritans,** 15 W. 130th St. near Fifth Ave. 1875.

[7b.] The Astor Block, W. 130th St. bet. Fifth and Lenox Aves.

Three-story brick, single-family row houses with wooden porches and large front and side yards.

[7c.] Riverbend Apartments, Fifth Ave., W. 138th St., Harlem River Dr. 1968. Davis, Brody & Assocs.

Respectful of street lines, dense, compact, of vernacular materials, mammoth red bricks and concrete, duplex apartments in the sky for moderate income residents; in short, a superb example of urban housing. Particularly impressive from the Bronx side of Harlem River.

From the Schomburg Library to Macomb's Place.

[8a.] Schomburg Collection/formerly **135th Street Branch, N. Y. Public Library,** 103 W. 135th St. NW cor. Lenox Ave. 1905. McKim, Mead & White.

This reference library was the unofficial headquarters of the Negro literary renaissance of the Twenties. **Arthur A. Schomburg** was a Puerto Rican Negro who privately undertook the task of collecting the raw materials of American Negro history, which were then in danger of loss through neglect by the academic community. In 1926 the **Carnegie Corporation of New York** purchased the collection and had it deposited here with Schomburg as its curator.

[3e.]

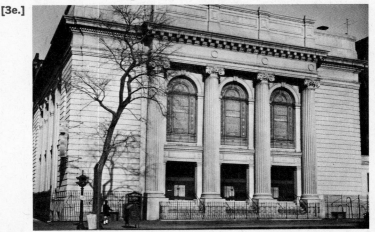

[8b.] Countee Cullen Branch, N. Y. Public Library, 104 W. 136th St. SW cor. Lenox Ave. 1942. Louis Allen Abramson.

This simple contemporary building is an extension of the former 135th Street Branch. It serves as a circulating library and contains an auditorium, art gallery, and the **James Weldon Johnson Collection** of children's books. Its name honors a **poet of the Harlem**

renaissance, and it is on the site of the home of Madame C. J. Walker, one of N. Y.'s first Negro millionaires, who made her fortune selling beauty aids.

[9a.] Abyssinian Baptist Church, 132 W. 138th St. bet. Lenox Ave. and Seventh Ave. 1923. Charles W. Bolton.

Congressman Adam Clayton Powell preaches from this pulpit on his infrequent visits to his constituency. An especially strong building, New York bluestone, with a large Tudor Gothic window in its facade. Founded in 1808, this is the largest Protestant congregation in the nation.

[9b.] Casino Renaissance, 2351 Seventh Ave. SE cor. W. 138th St.

The casino and adjacent theater constitute a commercial community center, which combines a variety of places for entertainment and accommodation, and which seems to survive only in Harlem.

[9c.]

[9c.] The King Model Houses (Striver's Row), W. 138th St. and W. 139th St. bet. Seventh Ave. and Eighth Ave. 1903. McKim, Mead & White.

Built as a demonstration by a wealthy private investor, these 158 individual buildings, are probably the best large row-house development in New York. Three-story yellow brick houses with limestone and terra cotta trim are on 138th Street. The houses on 139th Street have subdued classical ornamentation on orange-brown brickfronts rising above rusticated brownstone first stories. Small front yards and rear driveways with wrought-iron gates add to the distinction and urbanity of this street.

[9d.] St. Mark's Methodist Church, 55 Edgecombe Ave. SW cor. 138th St. 1924.

[10a.] St. James Presbyterian Church/formerly **St. Nicholas Avenue Church,** St. Nicholas Ave. NW cor. W. 141st St. 1905.

[10b.] St. Charles Borromeo Church, 211 W. 141st St. bet. Seventh Ave. and Eighth Ave. N side.

[11a.] Paul Lawrence Dunbar Apartments, W. 149th St. to W. 150th St. Seventh Ave. to Eighth Ave. 1928. Andrew J. Thomas.

Six well-designed apartment houses, each with several entrances are grouped around a landscaped inner court. The development was originally a cooperative **financed by John D. Rockefeller, Jr.,** who hoped it would be a model to solve Harlem's housing problem. When the Great Depression struck, Rockefeller foreclosed his mortgage and sold the property. But it remains one of the most desirable living places in Harlem. [See W Bronx 2a.]

[11b.] Harlem River Houses, W. 151st to W. 153rd Sts. Seventh

Ave. to Macombs Pl. 1937. Archibald M. Brown, Horace Ginsbern, Charles F. Fuller, Richard W. Buckley, John L. Wilson, Frank J. Forster, Will R. Amon.

One of the earliest and most successful attempts at public housing. Four-story houses built around open courts, malls, and terraces.

EAST HARLEM

East Harlem, which includes Spanish Harlem and Italian Harlem, was never the prestigious area that Negro Harlem once was. For a century it has been the home of **working-class** immigrants, and in the past it was the home of sizable Irish, Jewish, German, and Scandinavian populations. The Italian community was established here before 1890. Large numbers of Puerto Ricans have been in East Harlem for five decades.

[1a.] Metro North Community Plan, E. 99th St. to E. 106th St. E. of Third Ave. 1967. Whittlesey, Conklin & Rossant.

Developed in cooperation with local residents, this plan calls for the renewal of 11 blighted blocks, through the rehabilitation of existing buildings, selective clearance and redevelopment, and by the strengthening of community institutions.

[1b.] Church of the Resurrection, East Harlem Protestant Parish, 325 E. 101st St. bet. First and Second Aves. 1965. Victor A. Lundy.

A windowless red brick pillbox, falling somewhere between a fallout shelter and a Maginot Line fortress. Designed for a setting among grimy tenements; its starkness was meant as a bold and powerful contrast. Economy dictated substitution of a built-up roof for the original brick pavers. The interior is more inviting.

[1c.] Rehabilitated housing, 303–327 E. 102nd St. bet. First and Second Aves. 1967.

A gypsum company's attempt to renovate and modernize a row of tenement buildings. High hopes and a bright step forward.

[1d.]

[4

[1d.] Franklin Plaza Cooperative, E. 106th St. to E. 108th St. First to Third Aves. 1959. Holden Egan Wilson & Corser.

One of the most graceful groups of residential towers in Manhattan. First intended for public housing, this development became a cooperative under the auspices of community groups. The gardens and play areas were designed later by Mayer and Whittlesey.

[2a.] Public School 107, Manhattan, 1680 Lexington Ave. bet. E. 105th and E. 106th Sts.

Patterned brickwork and a handsome tower give solidity and authority to this venerable schoolhouse, while ivory paint hides its age.

[2b.] St. Cecilia's Church, 120 E. 106th St. bet. Park and Lexington Aves. 1883–1887. Napoleon Le Brun.

Romanesque Revival church with terra cotta decoration resembling richly carved stone. The handsome facade is dominated by a huge bas-relief of St. Cecilia as a youthful organist.

[2c.] Pathe Laboratories, Park Ave. SE cor. E. 107th St. 1946. Mayer & Whittlesey; M. Milton Glass, partner-in-charge.

One of Manhattan's few contemporary industrial buildings.

[3a.] Park Avenue Enclosed Market, Park Ave. bet. 111th and 115th Sts. under railroad viaduct.

A hothouse of small business. Sheltered by the elevated viaduct of the New York Central and New Haven Railroads is one of the most colorful, fast moving, fragrant, and boisterous of New York's commercial pageants. A mecca for both bargain hunters and those who love to bargain. Open courts timidly outfitted with bland, self-conscious street furniture exist at 113th and 114th Streets for those who want to sit down and take a breath of air.

[3b.] James Weldon Johnson Houses, E. 112th St. to E. 115th Sts. Park to Third Aves. 1947. Julian Whittlesey, Harry M. Prince, and Robert J. Reilly.

Handsomely proportioned buildings of varying heights and a sensitive site plan distinguish this development from the other low-rent developments here extending in a row from First to Lenox Avenues. A large plaza, small courts, and well-placed sculpture further enhance this development.

[3c.] Public School 57, Manhattan, 176 E. 115th St. SW cor. Third Ave. 1964. Ballard, Todd, and Snibbe; Richard W. Snibbe, partner-in-charge.

A large protective cornice, small paned windows and molded bricks make this school a warm, safe, and friendly place. The scale of this building would enhance and respect a block of row houses; in its setting amidst large housing projects, its attention to scale is lost.

[2a.]

[3d.] St. Paul's Church, 121 E. 117 St. bet. Park and Lexington Aves. 1908. Neville and Bagge. ☆

[3e.] St. Paul's Rectory, 113 E. 117th St. bet. Park and Lexington Aves. 1908. Neville and Bagge. ☆

A magnificent limestone church with handsome towers; late Romanesque Revival.

[4a.] Public School 7, Manhattan, 160 E. 120th St. SE cor. Lexington Ave. 1958. Perkins & Will.

Three glass and paneled pavilions connected by glass-enclosed ramps house the classrooms of this bright contemporary school. The building is now covered with steel mesh screening to curtail rock-throwing vandalism. The nearby I. S. 201 [See Harlem 6a.] built without windows is another answer to this problem.

[4b.] Harlem Courthouse, 170 E. 121st St. SE cor. Sylvan Place. 1893. Thom & Wilson. ★

This handsome brick and stone courthouse is a model turn-of-the-century governmental palace. It is adjacent to a small sitting park.

[4c.] Sylvan Court, E. 121st St. N of Sylvan Place.

Seven ivory-colored brick town houses grouped around a pedestrian walkway.

[4d.] Elmendorf Reformed Church, 171 E. 121st St. bet. Sylvan Pl. and Third Ave.

A small church with an unusual, but undistinguished, limestone facade is the oldest congregation in Harlem and the successor to the Dutch church founded here in 1660.

MORNINGSIDE HEIGHTS

Many of Manhattan's most impressive visual, architectural, and cultural delights are found on Morningside Heights. The site of a Revolutionary skirmish, in the 19th Century the **Bloomingdale Insane Asylum** and the **Leake and Watts Children's Home** were located here. The opening of Morningside Park in 1887, Riverside Drive four years later and the simultaneous settlement here of major cul-

tural institutions permitted the development of several magnificent groups of buildings, each in a well-designed setting. High-density housing along Riverside and Morningside Drives provided **people-power** for the institutions and for an active community life.

[1a.] Cathedral Church of St. John the Divine, Amsterdam Ave. W of W. 112th St. Begun 1892. 1891–1911, Heins and LaFarge; 1911–1942, Cram & Ferguson; 1966, Adams & Woodbridge. ☆

The largest church of modern times. The apse, choir, and crossing follow Heins and LaFarge's combined Romanesque Byzantine plan. Ralph Adams Cram redesigned the Cathedral along French Gothic lines, and from 1924 until 1941 his great nave and west front were built.

In spite of its incompleteness and mixing of styles, this is one of the nation's **magnificent** interiors. Its vastness is due both to its great height and length and to the side aisles' being built as high as the nave. Sculpture, glass, tapestry, metalwork, and woodwork are found here in quality and quantity. The seven ambulatory chapels illustrate the expansion of Christianity and display a variety of European church architecture and decoration.

Present plans call for completion of the church with modern materials. The **crossing** will be covered with a drum of concrete louvers, interspersed with stained glass and covered with a low dome. The Greek Revival building that remains from the Leake and Watts Children's Home and serves as the Cathedral exhibit hall, will be preserved.

[1b.] St. Luke's Hospital, Morningside Dr. bet. W. 113th St. and W. 114th St. 1896. Ernest Flagg.

The western pavilions have been replaced, and the handsome baroque drum and dome are in danger of being lost; but the high Mansard roofs and the profusion of classical detail give these buildings their dignity and charm.

[1c.] Église de Notre Dame, 405 W. 114th St. NW cor. Morningside Dr. 1915. Cross & Cross. ☆

Like the nearby Cathedral, this church is unfinished, but it should not be overlooked. It is our nearest approximation to the Church of the Invalides in Paris. The well-proportioned details, from the Corinthian portico to the rectory arcade, are carefully executed. A replica of the **grotto of Lourdes** is behind the altar. The interior is lighted artificially because the oversized drum and dome, designed to bring light into the church, were never built. The low dome built in its place is roofed with a tar paper structure.

[2a.] Statue of Carl Schurz, Morningside Dr. at W. 116th St. 1913. Karl Bitter, Sculptor; Henry Bacon, Architect.

This is an excellent place from which to view Harlem from afar. The steps into Morningside Park lead to 114th Street, where Bartholdi's statue of Washington and Lafayette may be seen.

Columbia University. Columbia University is one of the nation's oldest, largest, and wealthiest institutions. The renown of its undergraduate college is complemented by the influence of its professional and graduate programs. The Morningside Heights campus has few peers.

Designed by McKim, Mead, and White, this is one of the great urban spaces in New York. North of 116th Street, the original campus buildings are situated on a **high terrace,** two flights of stairs above the surrounding streets, and separated from the streets by high granite basements. The south campus, terraced below the level of 116th Street, further enhances these buildings.

Arranged on classical lines, the campus is dominated by the great, domed, limestone **library.** The instructional buildings, of red brick, limestone trim, and copper-green roofs, are arranged around the **periphery** of the campus and are augmented by excellent planting, tasteful paving, statues, plaques, fountains, a pavilion, and a variety of classical ornament and detail.

Yet, in spite of the success of this campus, its development violates the original concept; the architects planned a **densely built-up** campus, with a narrow central quadrangle and six intimate and sheltered side courts. The court between Avery and Fayerweather Halls is the only such court to have been completed. The alternative to this plan is the present open campus and the resulting spread of university buildings on to the neighboring blocks.

[2b.] President's House, Columbia University, Morningside Dr. NW cor. W. 116th St. 1912. McKim, Mead & White.

[2c.] Law School, Columbia University, Amsterdam Ave. NE cor. W. 116th St. 1963. Harrison & Abramovitz.

The Penthouse Restaurant, Butler Hall, 400 119th St. SE cor. Morningside Dr. MO 6-9490.

Excellent food and views can be enjoyed at this highest public restaurant in upper Manhattan.

[3a.] Low Memorial Library. 1893–1897. McKim, Mead & White; Charles Follen McKim, Partner-in-charge. ★

Three flights of stairs above street level, this magnificent building dominates the campus and sets a dignified, serious, and high-minded tone for the University. Lacking sufficient stack space and difficult to light, it was less successful as a **library** and now houses **administrative offices.**

[3b.] Butler Library. 1934. James Gamble Rogers.

One of the first buildings to depart from the original plan, this building is successful both as a library and as a focal point to the now-open south campus.

[3c.] St. Paul's Chapel. 1904. Howells and Stokes. ★

Classical and Byzantine elements are combined here to form the most beautiful building on the Heights. The porched facade and brick-vaulted interior are especially successful.

[3a.]

[3.]

[3c

The **last surviving building** of the Bloomingdale Insane Asylum is just south of the Chapel.

[3d.] Avery Hall. 1912. McKim, Mead & White.

One of nine similar instructional buildings, Avery Hall houses the School of Architecture and the **largest architectural library** in the nation.

[3e.] Barnard College, W of Broadway, from W. 116th St. to W. 120th St.

This college is named for **Frederick A. P. Barnard,** president of Columbia from 1864 to 1889, foremost advocate of the admission of women to Columbia University.

a. Barnard Hall. 1917. Arnold W. Brunner.
b. Helen Reid Dormitory. 1959. O'Connor & Kilham.
c. Lehman Library. 1959. O'Connor & Kilham.

The Battle of Harlem Heights: The first battlefield victory of the American army took place on September 16th, 1776, in a buckwheat field, now the site of Barnard College.

[4b.]

[4a.] Teachers College, Broadway to Amsterdam Ave. W. 120th St. to W. 121st St.

The names of great educators are carved along the pediment of Horace Mann Hall.

[4b.] Public School 36, Manhattan, Amsterdam Ave. NE cor. Morningside Dr. 1967. A. Corwin Frost & Fredrick G. Frost, Jr.

This school is actually a group of separate buildings situated on top of outcroppings at the northern end of Morningside Park. Simple brick stair towers, cast concrete construction, and large rectangular windows mark the first arrival of the new **brutalism** in upper Manhattan.

[4c.] Jewish Theological Seminary, 3080 Broadway. NE cor. W. 122nd St. 1930. William Gehron & Sidney F. Ross.

An uninspired and oversized Georgian building houses the central institutions of the **Conservative** movement in American Judaism. The tower, used as library stacks, was the scene of a tragic fire in 1966.

[5a.] Union Theological Seminary, Broadway to Claremont Ave. W. 120th St. to W. 122nd St. 1910. Allen & Collens, Charles Collens, partner-in-charge; 1952. Collens, Willis & Beckonert. ★

A stronghold of theological **modernism** and **social consciousness** is housed in a Collegiate Gothic quadrangle of rock-faced granite with limestone trim. Two handsome perpendicular towers, an exquisite chapel, library, refectory, and dormitories recall medieval Oxbridge.

[5b.] Juilliard School of Music/formerly **Institute of Musical Art,** 120 Claremont Ave. NE cor. W. 122nd St. 1910, Donn Barber; 1931, Shreve, Lamb, Harmon.

[5c.] Riverside Church, Riverside Dr. and W. 122nd St. 1927–1930. Charles Collens & Henry C. Pelton. South Wing, 1960. Collens, Willis & Beckonert.

A great church, built of Indiana limestone and distinguished for its fine glass, sculpture, and religious art, has many unusual features and has been described as a "late example of bewildered eclecticism." The oversized tower contains offices, classrooms, and is the home of a **Quaker meeting.** The width of the nave conceals its great height. The main entrance is at the side and contains a leaded-glass revolving door. Curiosity caused Albert Einstein to visit the church which had placed his statue in the recess above the west porch.

[5d.] Statue of General Daniel Butterfield, Sakura Park, Riverside Dr. NE cor. W. 122nd St. Gutzon Borglum, Sculptor.

[5e.] International House, 500 Riverside Dr. N. of Sakura Park, 1924. Lindsay & Warren, Louis Jallade, partner-in-charge.

[5f.] Grant's Tomb, Riverside Drive at W. 122nd St. 1897. John H. Duncan.

A granite and marble tomb, a great ornament of the city; its north lawn is a good place to watch the Hudson River and a favorite **kite-flying** area.

HAMILTON HEIGHTS

This precinct, west of St. Nicholas and Colonial Parks from West 125th Street north to Trinity Cemetery, includes the old village of Manhattanville and the once famous gilded ghetto known as "Sugar Hill." It takes its name from the country estate of Alexander Hamilton. Hamilton's home and other 19th Century houses, churches, and institutional buildings survive, but most of the existing buildings here date from the construction of the Broadway Subway, which opened in 1904.

[1.] St. Joseph's Church, 401 W. 125th St. NW cor. Morningside Ave. 1889. Herter Brothers. ☆

[2a.] City College-South Campus/formerly **Manhattanville College,** W. 133rd St. E of Convent Ave.

Manhattanville College and the convent for which Convent Avenue is named were established here in 1841. This property was sold to the City in 1952 and has since been used by City College.

[2a.]

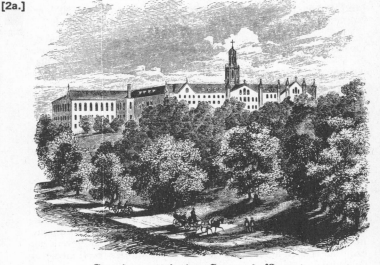

𝔄𝔠𝔞𝔡𝔢𝔪𝔶 𝔬𝔣 𝔱𝔥𝔢 𝔖𝔞𝔠𝔯𝔢𝔡 𝔥𝔢𝔞𝔯𝔱,
Manhattanville, New York.

[2b.] Lewisohn Stadium, City College, Convent Ave. bet. W. 136th and W. 137th Sts. W. side. 1915. Arnold W. Brunner.

Graced by a handsome colonnade, this stadium was designed for athletics, but it is most famous as the site of a popular summer concert series. The Stadium is scheduled for demolition and replacement by classroom buildings and new athletic facilities.

[2c.] City College-North Campus, W. 138th St. to W. 140th St. Amsterdam Ave. to St. Nicholas Terrace. 1903–1907. George B. Post.

This magnificent campus is a by-product of the city's transit system. It is built of Manhattan schist, which was excavated during the construction of the Broadway Subway.

[3a.] St. Luke's Church, Convent Ave. NE cor. W. 141st St. 1892. R. H. Robertson.

[3b.] Hamilton Grange, 287 Convent Ave. adjacent to St. Luke's Church. 1802. John McComb. ★

This historic shrine has been temporarily stored here for 68 years, and a suitable permanent site for it has not yet been found. A Federal country house with a large front porch and handsome interior woodwork, it remains in precarious condition despite a generous Congressional appropriation for its restoration. It is now closed to the public. A statue of Hamilton stands on the front lawn.

[3c.]

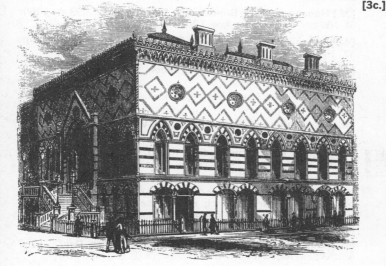

National Academy of Design

[3c.] Our Lady of Lourdes Church, 467 W. 142nd St. bet. Convent and Amsterdam Aves. 1904. O'Reilly Bros.

This unusual church consists of parts of two other important buildings. The grey-and-white marble and bluestone facade, recalling a Venetian Gothic palace, once adorned the National Academy of Design which stood on the northwest corner of 23rd Street and Fourth Avenue (Park Ave. South).

When the Academy was demolished, its building stones were marked and stored until they were incorporated into this structure. The rear wall of the church is the former rear wall of St. Patrick's Cathedral, which once faced Madison Avenue, removed to make way for the present Lady chapel. The lower church contains a stone grotto modeled after that in Lourdes. The upper church is embellished with an unusual set of support brackets for a balcony that was never built. A handsome bronze bust of Father Joseph McMahon is in the lobby. An outstanding and outspoken priest, he, more than any other person, was responsible for this church.

[3d.] Convent Avenue, from W. 141st to W. 145th St.

A street of extremely fine private residences and institutional buildings, graced by well-trimmed front gardens and an unusually wide pair of curbside grass strips. The row houses are an eclectic array of Richardsonian, English, and Dutch town house styles; brick with a variety of stone trimmings.

[4d.]

[3e.] Convent Avenue Baptist Church, 420 W. 145th St. SE cor. Convent Ave. 1897. Lamb & Rich.

This handsome Gothic Revival church has a checkerboard-patterned marble facade usually associated with Romanesque Revival buildings.

[3f.] Hamilton Grange Branch, N.Y. Public Library, 503 W. 145th St. NW cor. Amsterdam Ave. 1906. McKim, Mead & White. ☆

[4a.] Church of the Crucifixion, Convent Ave. NW cor. W. 149th St. 1967. Costas Machlouzarides.

[4b.] M. Marshall Blake Funeral Home, 10 St. Nicholas Pl. NE cor. W. 150th St. 1887.

Eclectic Victorian limestone residence once belonging to the Gimbel family.

[4c.] Milestone and aqueduct right-of-way, W. 152nd St. bet. St. Nicholas and Amsterdam Aves.

[4d.] Upper Manhattan Medical Group, 1865 Amsterdam Ave. NE cor. W. 152nd St. 1953. Nemeny, Geller & Yurchenco.

Functional, textured, balanced, this building retains its freshness after more than a decade of use. A layman's lesson in architecture, the exterior design clearly informs the patients what this building, a series of examining rooms and laboratories, is all about. An interior garden court brings light into every room.

[4e.] 30th Precinct Police Station, N.Y.C. Police Dept., 1854 Amsterdam Ave. SW cor. W. 152nd St. 1872. N. D. Bush. ☆

A simple brick police station with brownstone quoining and a dignified Mansard roof.

[5.] Temple B'nai Israel, 610 W. 149th St. bet. Broadway and Riverside Dr. 1920.

Limestone facade, battered walls, and a handsome high dome.

U

UPPER MANHATTAN

A history of habitation could be written in Upper Manhattan, the area of the island northward from Trinity Cemetery.

Indian **cave dwellers** once lived in Inwood Hill Park; the father of our country not only gave part of this area its name, **Washington Heights,** but he slept here; his headquarters having been preserved, and the **sites of the forts** he established remaining easy to find. This district was once a **country preserve of the wealthy,** and some of their estates have remained intact in a variety of forms, even though very rich people no longer live here. Museums, parks, a medical center, bus terminal, and a university, occupy sites here; an assortment of **other sacred and secular institutions** are ornaments to this urban district. But mainly it is **an apartment house area;** these houses make it one of the most densely populated parts of the city, while its parks, institutions, and **dramatic river views** make it **one of the most livable.** The Broadway subway reached Dyckman Street and St. Nicholas Avenue in the spring of 1906, and was the **major impetus** for the development of the eastern section. The Eighth Avenue Subway opened in the fall of 1932, encouraging still more apartment house construction.

Within Upper Manhattan and particularly in the subdivision called Washington Heights is **a maze of ethnic sub-communities.** The once predominant **Irish** now share this district with **more recent newcomers** to the city, **Negroes, Puerto Ricans,** and many other **Latin Americans.** The **Greek** and **Armenian** colonies here are large. After the rise of Hitler, so many **German** refugees settled here that the area became known as the "Fourth Reich."

[1a.]

[1a.] Trinity Cemetery, Riverside Dr. to Amsterdam Ave. 153rd to 155th Sts.

The cemetery climbs the hill from a spot near the river to the crest at Amsterdam Avenue and affords some idea of the topography of Upper Manhattan before all the brick and asphalt arrived. This was once part of the farm of J. J. Audubon, the great artist-naturalist, whose home was near the river at 155th Street and who is buried here. Every Christmas Eve carolers visit the grave of Clement Clarke Moore, author of *The Night Before Christmas.*

[1b.] Chapel of the Intercession and Rectory, Trinity Parish, Broadway SE cor. W. 155th St. 1914. Cram, Goodhue & Ferguson. ★

Set in Trinity Cemetery, this is the largest chapel in Trinity Parish. Here is the dream of the Gothic Revivalist come true: a large country church with a ceiling as high as a cathedral's, with a tower, cloister, parish house, and vicarage, all set on a bucolic hillside overlooking the romantic Hudson.

[2b.]

[2.] Audubon Terrace, Broadway, NW cor. W. 155th St. 1908. Charles Pratt Huntington.

Five small museums are reached through a well-proportioned Classical court.

[2a.] Museum of the American Indian (Heye Foundation), Audubon Terrace. 1916. Charles Pratt Huntington. Hours: 1–5 PM. Closed Mondays, holidays, and month of August. Free.

Originally the private collection of George G. Heye, this is now a comprehensive museum concerned with the prehistoric Western Hemisphere and the contemporary American (North, Central and South) Indian.

[2b.] American Geographical Society, Audubon Terrace. 1916. Charles Pratt Huntington. Mondays–Fridays, 9 AM–5 PM.

The largest geographical library and map collection in the Western Hemisphere is housed in this building.

[2c.] Hispanic Society of America, Audubon Terrace. South Building, 1908. Charles Pratt Huntington. North Building and additions to South Building, 1910–1926. Charles P. Huntington, Erik Strindberg, H. Brooks Price. Hours: Tuesdays–Saturdays, 10 AM–4:30 PM; Sundays, 2–5 PM.

This is a richly appointed storehouse of Hispanic painting, sculpture, and the decorative arts.

[2d.] American Numismatic Society, Audubon Terrace. 1908. Charles Pratt Huntington. Hours: Tuesdays–Saturdays, 9 AM– 5 PM.

A museum devoted entirely to coins, medals, decorations, and paper money; also the most comprehensive numismatic library in the country.

[2e.] National Institute of Arts and Letters/American Academy of Arts and Letters, Audubon Terrace. **Administration Building,** 633 W. 155th St., 1923. William Mitchell Kendall. **Auditorium and Gallery,** 632 W. 156th St., 1930. Cass Gilbert. Hours: Exhibitions open 1–4 PM. Closed Mondays and holidays.

The Institute and Academy were founded to honor distinguished persons in literature and the fine arts. The administration building contains a permanent exhibition of the works of Childe Hassam, the American painter, a library and a museum of manuscripts by past and present members.

[2f.] Church of Our Lady of Esperanza (Roman Catholic), 624 W. 156th St. bet. Bway and Riverside Dr. 1912. Charles Pratt Huntington. 1925, Lawrence G. White.

The green and gold interior of this church adjoining Audubon Terrace contains stained-glass windows and a lamp given by the King of Spain in 1912.

IRT's Hoosick: After the Hoosick Tunnel (northeast of Troy, N. Y.) which holds the record, the longest two-track tunnel in the U.S. cut through solid rock is on the IRT Broadway Line. The tunnel lies below Broadway and St. Nicholas Avenues and runs between West 157th Street and Fort George.

[3.] Morris–Jumel Mansion, Edgecombe Ave. NW cor. W. 160th St. ca. 1765. ★

Built by Roger Morris as a summer residence for his family. During the Revolution it served for a time as Washington's headquarters. But for most of that war the house was in British hands. It then served as a roadside tavern until 1810 when Stephen Jumel purchased it and completely renovated the house in the Federal style.

At one time this location commanded the finest view in Manhattan; even the hills of Staten Island being visible.

[3.]

[4.] Columbia-Presbyterian Medical Center, 622–630 W. 168th St. to below W. 165th St., Broadway to Riverside Dr. 1928–present. 1928–1947, James Gamble Rogers, Inc. 1947–1964, Rogers & Butler. 1964–date, Rogers, Butler, & Burgun.

Carcassonne on the Hudson; as the years pass more and more additions of varying heights and shapes (but all in related materials) populate the site. Present plans call for expansion east across Broadway.

Freud's Library: In the Freud Memorial Room of the Neurological and Psychiatric Institutes is shelved part of Freud's personal library.

[5.] Highbridge Park, W. 155th St. to Dyckman St. Amsterdam Ave. to Harlem River Dr.

Once the site of an amusement park, marina, and promenade, this park gains its beauty from a steep slope, and rugged topography, and as an excellent vantage point to survey the Harlem River valley.

[6a.] High Bridge/formerly **Aqueduct Bridge,** Highbridge Park at W. 174th St. 1839–1848, 1895.

This is the oldest remaining bridge connecting Manhattan to the mainland. It was built to carry Croton water to Manhattan. Originally the bridge consisted of closely spaced masonry arches, the central group of which were replaced by the present steel arch at the time of the building of the Harlem River Ship Canal. The pedestrian walkway has been closed for several years, but a recent proposal calls for its reopening. [See Bronx 8a.]

[7b.]

[6b.] Highbridge Tower, Highbridge Park at W. 173rd St. ca. 1842. Attributed to John B. Jervis. ★

A local landmark, this tower, originally used to equalize pressure ·in the Croton Aqueduct, now simply marks the Manhattan end of High Bridge. Adjacent is the site of a large (and well-used) public outdoor swimming pool.

[7.] Henry Hudson Parkway.

Driving southward into Manhattan on this parkway hugging the Hudson is one of New York's great gateway experiences. Leaving Riverdale in the Bronx there is the passage across the high-level Henry Hudson Bridge (more dramatic seen from the distance than driven across) and then the descent to the banks of the Hudson: past the Cloisters romantically surmounting a hill top, lonely and beautiful; through a wooded area; then under the majestic George Washington Bridge. And all of a sudden the skyline of Manhattan materializes and the transition is complete.

[7a.] Fort Washington Presbyterian Church, 21 Wadsworth Ave. NE cor. W. 174th St. 1914. Carrère and Hastings.

This handsome church is reminiscent in its details and in its feeling of Wren's London. The columns and pediment of the facade are particularly fine.

[7b.] Loew's 175th Street Theatre, Broadway, NE cor. W. 175th St. 1930. Thomas Lamb.

A thrilling and fantastic example of "Movie Palace Moorish," a reminder of those days when Hollywood ruled the world and everyone went to the movies on Saturday night. The lobby is cavernous and ornate, the theater is vast, and the popcorn still tastes the same! The lion roars: "MGM PRESENTS. . . ."

[8.] George Washington Bridge, Hudson River at W. 178 St. 1931. [See Bridges and Tunnels.]

"The George Washington Bridge over the Hudson is the most

beautiful bridge in the world. Made of cables and steel beams, it gleams in the sky like a reversed arch. It is blessed. It is the only seat of grace in the disordered city. It is painted an aluminum color and, between water and sky, you see nothing but the bent cord supported by two steel towers. When your car moves up the ramp the two towers rise so high that it brings you happiness; their structure is so pure, so resolute, so regular that here, finally, steel architecture seems to laugh. The car reaches an unexpectedly wide apron; the second tower is very far away; innumerable vertical cables, gleaming against the sky, are suspended from the magisterial curve which swings down and then up. The rose-colored towers of New York appear, a vision whose harshness is mitigated by distance."

Charles Eduard Jeanneret (Le Corbusier) from *When the Cathedrals Were White* Reynal and Hitchcock, 1947.

The lower level, added in 1962, has markedly changed the proportions of this bridge.

[8.]

[8a.] **"The Little Red Lighthouse,"** U.S. Coast Guard, Ft. Washington Park below the George Washington Bridge. 1921.

Directly under the east tower of the George Washington Bridge, the lighthouse was built to steer grain barges away from the shoals of Jeffrey's Hook. When navigational lights were mounted on the bridge, it was no longer used, and was put up for auction in 1951. A barrage of letters from children, who had read *The Little Red*

Lighthouse and The Great Gray Bridge by Hildegarde Hoyt Swift, saved the lighthouse, which is presently owned by the Department of Parks.

[9a.] George Washington Bridge Bus Station, E of Washington Bridge bet. Ft. Washington and Wadsworth Aves. 1963. Port of N.Y. Authority and Dr. Pier Luigi Nervi, Architects and Engineers.

The terminal provides direct access to the George Washington Bridge for short and long distance buses, and access for pedestrians to the IND Eighth Avenue subway. The concrete roof structure was designed to provide natural ventilation to the loading platforms with a minimum of columns inside the station.

[9a.]

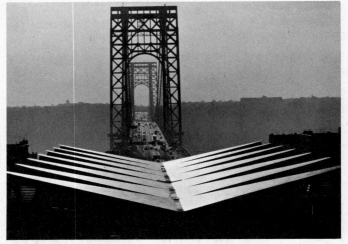

[9b.] Bridge Apartments, bet. W. 178th and W. 179th Sts., Wadsworth to Audubon Ave. 1964. Brown & Guenther.

These four apartment towers dominate Washington Heights visually, and, together with the George Washington Bridge and Bus Station, form a distinctly 20th Century architectural complex — potentially a great example of overlapping uses of land in an urban core. Housing 960 families, they are the first middle-income facility to be built using air rights over a highway. Unfortunately, large openings were left between the buildings in the platform that spans the roadway, resulting in a loss of precious ground-level area, and vast amounts of fumes, dirt and noise. These buildings are most dramatic at a distance.

[10.] Washington Bridge, 181st St. and Amsterdam Ave. to the Bronx. 1888. [See Bridges and Tunnels.]

[11.] Alexander Hamilton Bridge, 178th to 179 Sts. to the Bronx. 1964. [See Bridges and Tunnels.]

The Washington Bridge, with its flanking abutments of tall granite arches and its roadway carried on rectilinear space frames resting on its two central arches of steel, is one of New York's finest bridges. The best view, from below, enmeshes the eye with the constantly changing perspective of the frame—a sightseeing tour around Manhattan Island provides the finest vantage point.

The newer Alexander Hamilton Bridge, a few hundred feet downstream, diminishes the drama of its neighbor; adds redundancy, not delight.

[12.] Yeshiva University Campus, W. 184th to W. 187th St. along Amsterdam Ave.

[12a.] Main Building, Yeshiva University, Amsterdam Ave. SW cor. W. 186th St. 1928. Charles B. Meyers Assocs.

This is one of the great romantic structures of its decade. Its domes, tower, and turrets can be seen miles away, and the architect's lavish use of orange colored stone, copper and brass, ceramic tile, and Moorish architectural detail, makes for a visual treat.

[12b.] Central University Library, Yeshiva University, Amsterdam Ave. bet. W. 185th and W. 186th Sts. W side. 1967. Armand Bartos & Assocs., Martin Price, associate.

A rich composition of brick and concrete highly articulated to make the best of sun and shadow.

[12c.] Science Center, Belfer Graduate School of Science, Yeshiva University, Amsterdam Ave. and W. 184th St. E side. 1968. Armand Bartos & Assocs., Martin Price, associate.

[20a.]

[12b.]

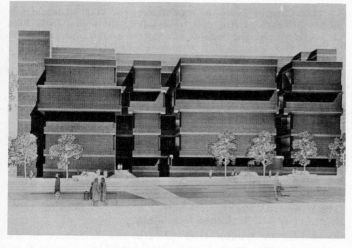

[13.] Isabella Neimath Home, 501 W. 190th St. 1875. Addition, 1965, Joseph D. Weiss.

The old building is a fine example of the institutional architecture of its day. The home serves elderly women, the new addition providing small private apartments designed to meet the special needs of the aged. Note the unusual roof line designed in deference to its older neighbor.

[14.] Fort Washington Collegiate Church, Ft. Washington Ave. NE cor. W. 181st St. 1907.

This small country church situated in a large churchyard

harkens back to the days when suburbia occupied Washington Heights.

The highest point: In Bennett Park, along the west side of Fort Washington Avenue between West 183rd and West 185th Streets is a rock outcropping which is the highest point in Manhattan, 267.75 feet above sea level. An added bonus is the outline of Revolutionary Fort Washington marked by stone pavers.

[15a.] Hudson View Gardens, 116 Pinehurst Ave. bet. W. 183rd and W. 185th Sts. 1925. George F. Pelham II.

Carefully located away from traffic and noise, on a quiet, sheltered street, this is a "country village" of Tudor Gothic six story elevator apartment houses.

[15b.] Castle Village Apartments, 120–200 Cabrini Blvd. bet. W. 181st to W. 186th Sts. 1938. George F. Pelham II.

Each floor of the cross-shaped buildings contains nine apartments, eight of which have river views. The site was formerly occupied by the Paterno estate—its massive retaining walls are used by the present buildings, and are visible from Henry Hudson Parkway.

[17.] Fort Tryon Park, W. 192nd St. to Dyckman St., Broadway to Riverside Dr. Frederick Law Olmsted Jr.

A gift of the Rockefeller family to New York City, this site was formerly the C. K. G. Billings estate (the triple arched driveway on Riverside Drive was the entrance to the estate). This is one of the best maintained city parks and famous for its flower gardens.

[17a.] The Cloisters, Metropolitan Museum of Art, Fort Tryon Park. 1934–1938. Charles Collens of Allen, Collens and Willis. Alterations to receive Fuentaduena Chapel, 1961, Brown, Lawford & Forbes. Hours: Weekdays except Mondays, 10 AM–5 PM. Sundays and holidays, 1 PM–5 PM (1 PM–6 PM May–September). Free.

The Cloisters house the medieval art collection of the Metropolitan Museum of Art, and are a gift to the public from John D. Rockefeller Jr. The building incorporates sections from medieval buildings such as a Twelfth Century chapter house, parts of five cloisters from medieval monasteries (from which the name is derived), a Romanesque chapel and a Twelfth Century Spanish apse, the Fuentaduena Chapel. It also contains the beautiful Unicorn tapestries. More a place with a character of its own than a museum, the Cloisters is more than the sum of its parts. Check with them for concerts of early music held in one of the cloisters.

Into the depths: The two deepest subway stations in the city are both in this vicinity. The IRT Broadway Line at 191st Street and St. Nicholas Avenue (180 feet below the street) and the IND station at 190th Street and Fort Tryon Park (165 feet down). In both cases elevators whisk passengers to the street.

[18a.] Dyckman House, Broadway, NW cor. W. 204th St. 1783. Hours: 11 AM–5 PM. Closed Mondays. ★

Rebuilt by William Dyckman after the destruction of the previous buildings by the British, this the only 18th Century farmhouse remaining in Manhattan. With its gambrel roof and fieldstone lower walls, the house shows a strong Dutch influence. The interior, with its random width chestnut floors and the original family objects and furnishings is well worth a visit.

Nash Pastry Shop, 182 Dyckman St.

Delectable French pastries and a tea room in the back for a leisurely repast. This is the neighborhood gathering place for local pastry lovers.

[18b.] Church of the Good Shepherd, 4967 Broadway, cor. Isham St. 1937. Paul Monahan.

The large barrel-vaulted interior is worth seeing for both its stained glass and the marble altar.

[19a.] 207th Street Yards, N.Y.C. Transit Authority, 3961 Tenth Ave. bet. W. 207th and W. 215th Sts. E side. 1928. F. Gardner.

[19b.]

[19b.] Metropolitan Street Railway Co., Ninth Ave. NE cor. 216th St.

[19c.] Kingsbridge Division, Third Avenue Railway System/now **MaBSTOA (Manhattan and Bronx Surface Operating Authority),** Broadway SE cor. W. 218th St. ca. 1895.

Three relics from the days when trolley cars and elevated trains were revered. Their bold and sometimes exuberant architecture seems to have departed with their occupants.

[20.] Baker Field, Columbia University, W. 218th St. at Seaman Ave. N side. Stadium, 1905–1930. **Field House and Lounge,** 1944–1954, Eggers & Higgins. **Boat House [20a.],** 1930, Polyhemus & Coffin.

Marble Hill: A tiny part of Manhattan lies on the mainland of North America though it has not always. When the Harlem River was deepened in 1895 to provide for shipping access, its name changing at the time to the Harlem River Ship Canal, its old course at the north end of Manhattan was altered and a new channel blasted through the rock. The meandering, shallow stream was filled in leaving a high rock outcropping which is still visible and known as the community of Marble Hill. The sheer rock face on the south side, over the river, is decorated by numerous signs and greek-letter fraternity emblems clandestinely applied at great risk to the painters.

THE OUTER ISLANDS

Ellis Island

[1.] United States Immigration Station, Ellis Island. 1898. Boring and Tilton.

Fanciful **bulbous turrets** proclaim the now unused buildings of Ellis Island where the **majority of European immigrants** landed on these shores following the turn of the century (1,285,349 entered the U.S. in 1907, the peak year). Now designated a **National Park,** Philip Johnson has been commissioned to design a **monument to immigration** to be built there.

Outer Islands: Ellis, Governors, Randalls, Wards, Welfare   213

Governor's Island

[2a.] Castle Williams/formerly **East Battery,** Governor's Island. 1811. Lt. Col. Jonathan Williams. ★

The twin of Castle Clinton [See L Manhattan 1a], both built to **fortify New York harbor** for the War of 1812. The architect, **Benjamin Franklin's nephew,** was the individual after whom Williamsburg, Brooklyn was named.

[2b.] Fort Jay, Governor's Island. 1798. ★

[2c.] The Block House, Governor's Island. 1843. Martin E. Thompson. ★

[2d.] Governor's House, Governor's Island. Late 18th Century. ★

[2e.] Commanding General's Quarters. Governor's Island. 1840. ★

Liberty Island: The site of the statue so symbolic of America's freedoms. Formerly known as Bedloe's Island.

 [3.] Statue of Liberty, Liberty Island. 1886. Frederic Bartholdi, Sculptor; Gustave Eiffel, Engineer; Richard Morris Hunt, Architect of the base.

Randall's and Ward's islands: located in the vicinity of **the turbulent Hell Gate** at the junction of the East and Harlem Rivers; at one time separate islands but today joined as a result of **landfill operations.** Randalls, the northernmost of the two, is the home of the Triborough Bridge interchange as well as the administrative headquarters of the **Triborough Bridge and Tunnel Authority.** In Downing Stadium are held a variety of entertainment and sporting events as well as the **Festival of San Juan,** the patron saint of Puerto Rico.

Welfare Island: Formerly Blackwell's Island, named after the land-owning family, it has long served to house a variety of municipal hospitals and other activities.

Wards Island is a recreation area **(joined to Manhattan** by a **pedestrian bridge** at East 103rd Street) and is the site of Manhattan State Hospital and a Department of Sanitation facility.

Hoffman and Swinburne Islands: Two slivers of land off Richmond in Lower Bay one day to be joined in a massive land-fill project. Today the "burial grounds" of the harbor's bird life.

[4a.] Blackwell Mansion, Welfare Island. ca. 1800. ☆

[4b.] Chapel of the Good Shepherd, Welfare Island. ca. 1875. Frederick C. Withers. ☆

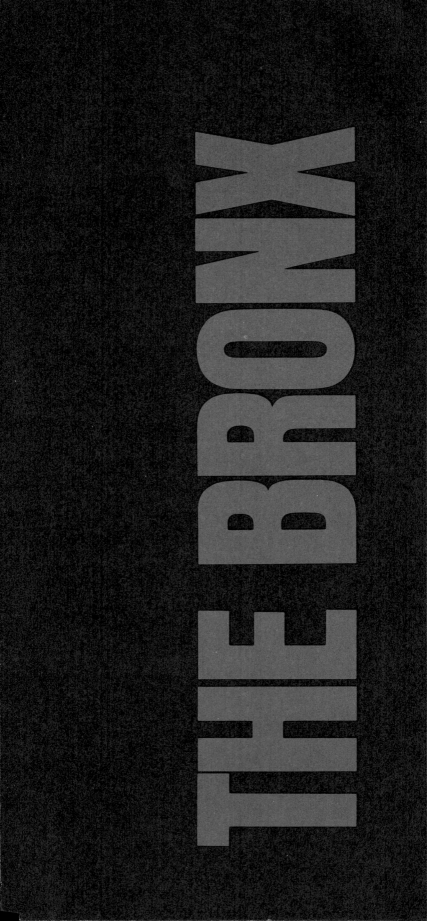

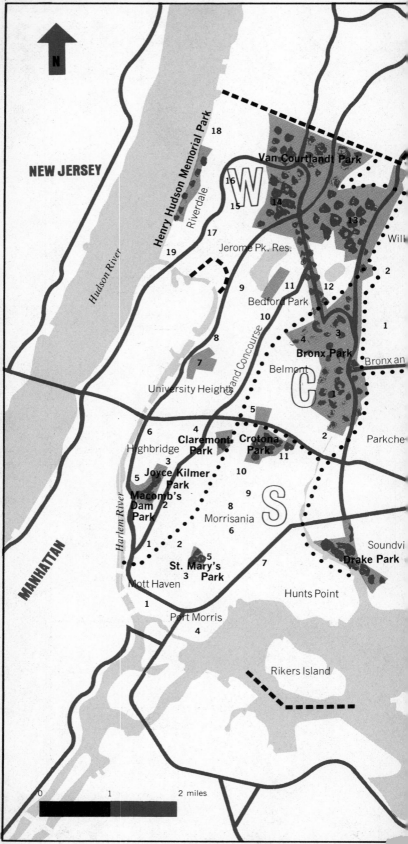

N

NEW JERSEY

Henry Hudson Memorial Park

18

Van Courtlandt Park

16
W
15
14
13

Riverdale

Will

17

Jerome Pk. Res.

2

Hudson River

9

11

12

1

Bedford Park

10

Bronx an

8

4

3

7

Bronx Park

Belmont

C

University Heights

5

6

4

Parkche

Claremont Park

Crotona Park

Highbridge

3

11

Joyce Kilmer Park

10

5

9

Macomb's Dam Park

8

S

2

Morrisania

6

Soundvi

Harlem River

1

2

5

7

Drake Park

St. Mary's Park

3

Hunts Point

Mott Haven

1

Port Morris

4

MANHATTAN

Rikers Island

0   1   2 miles

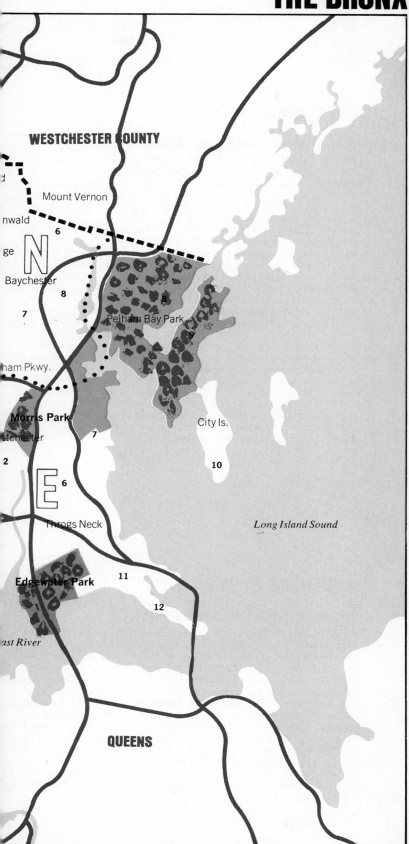

WESTCHESTER COUNTY

Mount Vernon

nwald

d

ge

6

N

Baychester

8

7

8

8

Pelham Bay Park

9

ham Pkwy.

Morris Park

stchester

7

2

E

6

Throgs Neck

City Is.

10

Long Island Sound

Edgewater Park

11

12

ast River

QUEENS

THE BRONX

Borough of The Bronx/Bronx County

The only one of New York's five boroughs that is on the mainland. For more than 200 years the Bronx was part of Westchester County, and the borough's topography is similar to that of its sylvan neighbor. To the west are steep hills, rocky outcroppings, and valleys running north and south. To the east is a marshy plain with peninsulas extending into Long Island Sound.

In the 19th Century the Bronx was covered with farms, market villages, embryo commuter towns, country estates, and a number of institutions. It was then a place of **rural delights.** In 1874 the western portion of the Bronx (designated **Western** and **Central Bronx** in this guide) was annexed to the City. Bridge-building and the extension of elevated lines, and then a growth of population, industry, and institutions followed political union. The eastern Bronx (designated as **Eastern** and **Northern Bronx** in this guide) became part of New York City in 1895. With a few exceptions, the development of the borough in the 20th Century has submerged the old villages and neighborhoods, and the Bronx became home to **hundreds of thousands** of families of average means. The South Bronx originally contained the **bulk** of the borough's commercial, civic, and cultural **institutions;** they are now **diffused** throughout many of its precincts.

An extensive system of parks and parkways was planned here in 1883 and largely executed in the following two decades. The plan provided for continuous chains of **uninterrupted greenery,** with paths and speedways for walkers, cyclists, and horse-drawn vehicles. It remains the most generous park system in the city.

SOUTHERN BRONX

MOTT HAVEN, HUNTS POINT, AND MORRISANIA

Village names persist into the present, but the country villages that once existed in the South Bronx have long disappeared. Soon after the **Civil War** the farms that existed here from colonial days began to give way to private homes and tenement rows. In more recent days these in turn have given way to **arterial highways** and **public housing** developments. The rapid growth of other parts of the Bronx in the 20th Century eclipsed the South Bronx and shifted the focus of commerce, entertainment, and government to other parts of the borough. Successive waves of immigrants and industries have passed in and out of the South Bronx, but their **footprints** are hard to find. Without money, power, or prestige, the South Bronx has been unable to cultivate its ornaments. **Landmarks** venerated in other places are overlooked in this area. Some have completely disappeared; others are marked for demolition, but many survive and are waiting to be rediscovered.

[1a.] Site of Jordan Mott Iron Works, 1828–1906.

Mott, inventor of a coal-burning stove, purchased 200 acres from Gouverneur Morris II, and established a factory west of Third Avenue, between East 134th Street and the Harlem River in 1828. The venture prospered and grew. The buildings of the iron works can still be seen from the western walkway of the Third Avenue Bridge. Mott founded the village of Mott Haven, whose monogram "MH" persists in the mosaics of the 138th and 149th Street stations of the IRT Lexington Avenue Line. [See S Bronx 2a and W Bronx 1a.]

Bronck's: The site of the Jonas Bronck farmhouse of 1639 is believed to have been located within the present New Haven railroad yards east of the Third Avenue Bridge. The name "The Bronx" derives from this early settler's family name.

[1b.] The Bertine Block, 414–432 E. 136th St. E of Willis Ave.

A handsome row of private houses. Low stoops, limestone foundations, a variety of ornament, some stained glass, yellow-face brick. Slum clearance has not yet reached this street.

[1b.]

[1c.] St. Jerome's Church, Alexander Ave. & SE cor. E. 138th St.

Spanish Renaissance brick and limestone church with an unusual cupola.

[1d.] Alexander Avenue from E. 138th St. to E. 142nd St.

This is the old Bronx at its best. Seven blockfronts encapsule an elegant and urbane world of the 19th Century.

[1e.] Mott Haven Branch, New York Public Library, 321 E. 140th St. NE cor. Alexander Ave. 1905. Babb, Cook & Willard.

One of the earliest and most handsome products of Carnegie's gift, with high ceilings, tall windows, red brick, and rusticated limestone trim; we are reminded of McKim, Mead & White's early buildings on Morningside Heights.

[2a.] Mott Haven Reformed Church, 350 E. 146th St. W. of Third Ave. 1852.

[2b.] "The Hub", intersection of E. 149th St. Westchester, Third, Melrose, and Willis Aves.

At least five important business streets come together at the junction point of the Third Avenue "El" and the Seventh Avenue and Lexington Avenue Subways. This is one of the focal points of Bronx business. The original of the Alexander's department store chain is at 2952 Third Avenue.

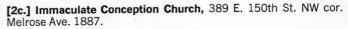

[2c.] Immaculate Conception Church, 389 E. 150th St. NW cor. Melrose Ave. 1887.

This austere yet handsome brick Gothic church boasts the highest steeple in the borough and recalls the days when the Germans were the most populous ethnic group in the Bronx and their prominence in the building trades, brewing, and in the manufacture of musical instruments were of central importance to the borough's prosperity.

[2d.] Brook Avenue Wholesale Meat Market, Brook and Westchester Aves.

Oversized refrigerator trucks contribute to the traffic jams that further detract from an already unsightly and congested area. The market has been proposed for urban renewal. To the south of the railroad yard, on Westchester Avenue between Brook and St. Ann's Avenues, was the site of the Janes and Kirkland Iron Works where the Capitol dome was cast.

[3.]

[3.] St. Ann's Church, W side of St. Ann's Ave. at E. 140th St. 1841. ★

A pleasant Greek Revival church whose interior walls contain plaques honoring members of the Morris family, whose remains lie in the crypt and in the **churchyard tombs.** With a limestone parish house built in 1917, this church and its shaded churchyard form an **oasis of tranquility** in a tense and dreary neighborhood. The break in the gridiron street pattern here is an unexpected bonus.

[4.] Port Morris, E of Bruckner Blvd. N & S of E. 138th St.

This industrial area was developed as a deep-water port by the Morris family during the mid-19th Century, in the hope of rivaling New York. The Hell Gate Plant of the Consolidated Edison Company and Richard Hoe and Company, manufacturers of printing press machinery are located here.

Schlitz Inn, 767 E. 137th St. NW cor. Willis Ave. 669-8770.

The last remaining German restaurant in the South Bronx now caters almost exclusively to executives from neighboring industrial buildings.

[5.] St. Mary's Park, E of St. Ann's Ave. from E. 143rd to E. 149th St.

This park is named for **St. Mary's Church,** a wooden country church that stood on Alexander Avenue and East 142nd Street until its demolition in 1959. The crest of the hill at the north end of the park is a good place from which to **survey this neighborhood.** It was once known as **Janes' Hill** and belonged to Henry E. Janes, whose iron works was only a few blocks away. [See S Bronx 2d.]

[6a.] St. Anselm's Church, 673 Tinton Ave. NW cor. 152nd St. 1917. Gustave Steinbach.

[6a.]

El Radiante Restaurant, 640 Prospect Ave. cor. Kelly St. 669-8163.

One of the finest Puerto Rican restaurants.

[7a.] American Bank Note Company, Lafayette Ave. NE cor. Tiffany St.

Paper money and stamps for many nations and stock certificates for domestic and foreign corporations are all produced in this large and spare Gothic fortress that guards the entrance to Hunts Point as it guards the valuable paper printed within its walls.

[7b.] Corpus Christi Monastery, 1230 Lafayette Ave. at Barretto St. 1899.

A cloistered community of Dominican nuns. The limestone church was the gift of the Crimmins family, whose vault is in the crypt. The best time to visit the monastery is on Sunday afternoon, when the nuns sing their office. The church, with its beautiful polished mosaic floor, bare walls, and scores of candles, is then fully lighted.

[7c.] Bright Temple AME Church/formerly **Temple Beth Elohim/** formerly **Brightside,** Faile St. NE cor. Lafayette Ave. 1860.

Handsome Gothic revival stone mansion was originally the residence of Col. Richard M. Hoe, inventor of the rotary printing press.

[7d.] New York City Terminal Market, Halleck St. S of Lafayette Ave. 1965. Skidmore, Owings & Merrill.

Spacious facilities for trailer trucks and railroad cars are provided in this new fruit and vegetable wholesale market. A model of SOM efficiency, enhanced by black-painted steel, blue-tinted glass, and occasional walls of carmine red brick.

[7e.] Drake Park, Hunts Point and Oakpoint Aves.

This small park contains the graves of poet Joseph Rodman Drake (1795–1820), members of the Hunt family, and other early settlers.

[8a.] Former Ebling Brewery, St. Ann's Ave. and E. 156th St.

These old brick buildings are now a hothouse of small industries, including several garment factories, machine shops, a *paella*-pot factory, and a pizza oven manufacturer who uses the beer-cooling caves as a warehouse.

[8b.] Former Hupfel Brewery, St. Ann's Ave. and E. 161st St.

Now used as a warehouse, the handsome wooden cooling tower has seen better days.

[8c.] Commercial building, Third and Brook Aves. SE cor.

The smallest building in the City on a tiny triangular lot.

[8d.] Old Bronx County Court House, E. 161st St. Third and Brook Aves. 1906. Michael J. Garvin. ☆

[8d.]   **[9d**

Strong vertical lines make this handsome classical structure a monument as well as a building. In spite of six decades of smoke, grime, neglect, and the rattling of the Third Avenue "El," it remains grand, even though its walls are tarnished and its windows are covered with soot. A leaf-crowned statue of **Justice** by G. E. Roine sits on the south facade and peers into every passing train.

[9a.] Morris High School, E 166th St. E of Boston Road. 1901. C. B. J. Snyder.

A powerful, turreted central tower, gabled green copper roof, buff brick and terra cotta trim make this a model of Public School Gothic.

[9b.] 105th Artillery Armory, 1122 Franklin Ave. cor. E. 166th St. 1910.

A dark red brick fortress with slit-like windows looks down on a steep street of stairs. Together with Hines Park and the facade of St. Augustine's Church, the Armory provides the backdrop for one of the city's exciting urban spaces. It is the perfect stage for a medieval melodrama or a childhood game of knights-in-armor.

[9c.] St. Augustine's Church, 1183 Franklin Ave. NW cor. E. 167th St. 1894.

[9d.] St. Augustine's School, 1176 Franklin Ave. bet. E. 167th St. and E. 168th St. 1904.

Romanesque and classical elements are combined in the handsome facade of this church. The parish school is decorated with a large classical pediment containing a sculptured frieze.

[10a.] Former Eichler Mansion, Fulton Ave. SW cor. E. 169th St.

Now a part of the Bronx-Lebanon Hospital, this handsome rococo building was once the home of a brewery magnate.

[10b.] St. John's Lutheran Church, 1343 Fulton Ave. bet. E. 169th St. and E. 170th St. 1896.

A German Gothic church with high windows, a tall, spired steeple, and a quaint brass historical plaque. Situated on a tree-lined street of private homes, adjacent to a spacious playground, it gives an idea of how the Bronx must have looked before the turn of the century.

[11a.] Crotona Park, Claremont Pkwy. E of Fulton Ave.

Formerly the Bathgate estate, this is one of the six parks purchased by the City after its selection by a citizens' committee in 1883. The park contains a wide array of sports facilities, and it takes its name from Croton, an ancient Greek city renowned as the home of many Olympic champions. The bathhouse at Fulton Avenue and East 173rd Street was built by the WPA. Red-face brick and green glass blocks create a festive but durable park pavilion.

[11b.] Junior High School 98, Bronx, Boston Rd. SW cor. E. 173rd St.

Named for Herman Ridder, a philanthropist who was publisher of the *New York Staats-Zeitung.* The entire building is faced with limestone. On a difficult irregular site the architect has employed a handsome round tower as a point of focus.

CENTRAL BRONX

The Central Bronx includes the Bronx Zoo, Botanical Garden, Fordham University, and the district north of East Tremont Avenue and east of Webster Avenue. Within this area, can be found a great variety of flora, fauna, land uses, housing types, and building conditions. Institutions of world prominence are within sight of humble and exotic neighborhood establishments, and long-forgotten landmarks are close to excellent contemporary structures that may become landmarks for future generations.

BRONX PARK AND FORDHAM UNIVERSITY

The Bronx Zoo to West Farms: From Pelham Parkway Gate of the Bronx Zoo to Boston Road and E. Tremont Ave. (177th St. Station IRT White Plains Rd. Line.)

The Bronx Zoo is the only one of the four zoos in the city maintained by the New York Zoological Society. (The others are maintained by the Parks Department.) The Society, a private membership organization, founded in 1895, also maintains the Aquarium in Coney Island. [See S Brooklyn 7b.]

This is the largest zoo in the United States, and it is a leader in the care, feeding, and exhibition of animals, birds, and other living creatures. The original buildings and grounds, designed by Heins and LaFarge and begun in 1899, comprise one of the most pleasing urban landscapes in the City. Exciting and significant exhibits and structures have been added in recent decades.

[1a.] Paul Rainey Memorial Gate, Pelham Parkway Entrance. 1934. Paul Manship, Sculptor; Charles A. Platt, Architect. ☆

This large and lavish bronze gate is probably the most handsome gate in the city. It portrays the animal kingdom and suggests a jungle setting.

[1b.] Rockefeller Fountain, S of Concourse Entrance, Pelham Pkwy. 1910. ★

[1c.] Baird Court Promenade, Lion House, 1903. **Primate House,** 1901. **Administration Building,** 1910. **Main Bird House,** 1905. All, Heins and LaFarge. **Head and Horns Building,** 1922. ☆

This quadrangle contains the administration building, major exhibition buildings, and the ever-popular sea lion pool. The classical pavilions of orange brick with limestone trim are decorated with bas-reliefs of the animals that live inside. The large medallions on the walls of the Lion House are especially good. The excellent maintenance of the grounds and the vigor of the elms add to the delights of the court.

[1d.] Aquatic Bird House, W of Bird House. 1964. Goldstone & Dearborn.

[1e.] Elephant House, S of Baird Court. 1908. Heins and LaFarge. ☆

This grand limestone palace with a high dome and colored terra cotta decoration could serve as the capitol of a banana republic. It is the home of the elephants, hippos, and rhinos, who enjoy the double treat of a classical palace with a Byzantine interior.

[1f.] The World of Darkness. 1966. Morris Ketchum, Jr. & Assocs.

A windowless building that reverses day and night in order to display nocturnal animals and cave dwellers. Built in the shape of a horseshoe around the zoo's famous **Rocking Stone,** a reminder of ancient glaciers, the battered, precast concrete panels of black granite aggregate indicate the dark world inside.

[1f.]

[1g.] The African Plains, S of World of Darkness. 1941. Harrison & Fouilhoux.

Moats rather than bars protect the public from the lions, while other moats protect the animals of the Savannah from both lions and visitors. Full-size replicas of indigenous buildings add to the realistic recreation of African landscape.

[2a.] Former Peabody Home, Boston Rd. NE cor. E. 179th St. 1901.

A red brick building in the Tudor Gothic style boasts an extremely fine central tower decorated with gargoyles. It is now occupied by followers of the late Father Divine.

[2b.] Beck Memorial Presbyterian Church, 980 East 180th St. W of Bryant Ave. S. side. 1903.

The tower of this limestone-faced Gothic church is richly decorated with buff colored terra cotta and has long been a neighborhood landmark. Across the street from the church is the old churchyard that contains the graves of four wars and a statue of a Union soldier in the familiar mourning pose. ☆

The Botanical Garden

The Botanical Garden, incorporated in 1891 and patterned after the Royal Botanical Gardens at Kew, England is one of the leading institutions of its kind in the world. Its scientific facilities include a conservatory, museum, library, herbarium (a collection of dried plants), research laboratory, and a variety of groves and gar-

unrequired reading

Tangents I

Tangents II

ANATOMY
OF A
COLOSSUS

HOW TO BUILD AN
IGLOO

*Certain pitfalls
to avoid
in building
a ten million
dollar house*

Neolithic Notes
on Urban Planning

Tangents III

Tangents IV

Rush? Must? For immediate attention? Not these. These are Tangents. Read them if and when you feel like it. They don't deal with the most important developments in the history of architecture, although they do get into some of the most intriguing.

Koppers started the Tangents series about a year ago. Four booklets have been published, and others are in preparation. In case we have missed you, or if you would like to have extra copies of any of them, write Koppers Company, Inc., 1331 Koppers Building, Pittsburgh, Pa. 15219.

KOPPERS

dens. By the accident of its location the Garden performs a second valuable function, it preserves and maintains the beautiful gorge of the Bronx River and the historic buildings which were here before the Park was created.

[3a.] Lorillard Snuff Mill, ca. 1840. ★

This mill, at a bend in the Bronx River, is now a public restaurant during the summer months. It was built by Peter and George Lorillard to manufacture snuff. The rose garden here was used to provide rose petals to perfume the snuff.

[3b.] Lorillard Gatehouse, N of rose garden. 1856. ☆

The Lorillard mansion was destroyed by fire, but its Victorian gatehouse has survived.

[3c.] Lorillard Stables, N of Gatehouse. ☆

[3d.] High Footbridge N of the Snuff Mill.

Provides a view of the gorge and waterfall of the Bronx River. To the north of the waterfall is the Hemlock Forest, the last remaining part of the forest that once covered most of New York City.

[3e.] Museum Building, W of Hemlock Forest, near main entrance to the Garden. 1902. Robert W. Gibson.

An archetypical turn-of-the-century museum building contains the herbarium, library, auditorium, in addition to its exhibition halls.

[3f.] Laboratory Building, 1957. Brown, Lawford, & Forbes.

[3g.] Conservatory Range, 1900. Lord & Burnham Company. ☆

The Conservatory consists of 11 ornate glass houses whose climates range from a tropical rain forest to the desert, and which display a fantastic array of plant life.

[3g.]

Fordham University: One of the major universities in the nation under Roman Catholic auspices, Fordham has been controlled by the Jesuits since 1846, five years after it was founded by Bishop John Hughes. Originally known as St. John's College, it took its present name in 1905. In 1964 St. Thomas More College, an undergraduate college for women, was established here.

[4a.] Keating Hall, at East Entrance, Southern Blvd. N of Fordham Rd. 1936.

The very model of collegiate Gothic.

[4b.] William L. Spain Seismograph Building, SW of Keating Hall. 1924.

[4c.] Administration Building/formerly **Rose Hill Manor House.** 1838. ☆

The charm of this old building has survived several additions and renovations.

[4d.] University Church. 1845. William Rodrigue. ☆

A handsome Gothic Revival church, on a cruciform plan, with a lantern over the crossing.

[4e.] St. John's Residence Hall, Queen's Court, S of University Church. 1845. William Rodrigue. ☆

[5a.] Old Borough Hall, Tremont Ave. SE cor. Third Ave. 1895–1897. George B. Post. ☆

Situated on a high bluff, this abandoned seat of local government is really two buildings, built at different times, one behind the other, connected by a ramp. It has recently been damaged by fire.

[5b.] 48th Precinct Police Station, 1925 Bathgate Ave. N of Tremont Ave. 1901. Horgan & Slattery.

A miniature of the Farnese Palace in orange-gold colored brick.

[5c.] St. Joseph's Church, 1949 Bathgate Ave. 1899.

A fortress exterior of rough hewn dark granite blocks protects an interior which is one of the most handsome spaces in the borough.

Dominick's Oyster & Chop House, 539 E. 180th St. E of Third Ave. LU 4-3723.

Italian Market: Arthur Avenue north of East 184th Street is the market place for the large Italian community of Belmont. On sunny days many good things are displayed on the sidewalks and curbs. Excellent restaurants and bakeries cluster on and near this street.

W

WESTERN BRONX

WEST BRONX

The West Bronx is known as a place of wholesome blandness. The pairs of diminutive **cast-stone lions** that guard the entrances to so many of the area's apartment houses are an attempt at elegance but result in a **dreary sameness.** But a closer look at this area will yield **some surprises.** An array of housing, schools, parks, hospitals, industries, and public works of social and architectural interest are all located here. This, too, though you may not believe it, is a place of urban diversity.

The Grand Concourse: From East 149th Street (IRT Lenox Ave. and Lexington Ave. Lines) to Cross-Bronx Expressway (175th St. Station, IND Concourse Line).

The Grand Concourse, one of the **grand boulevards** of New York, was designed in 1892 by Louis Risse as the **"Speedway Concourse,"** to provide access from Manhattan to the large parks of the Bronx. The original design provided **separate paths** for horse-drawn vehicles, cyclists, and pedestrians, and for grade separation through bridges at all major intersections.

[1a.] IRT Subway Junction, E. 149th St. and Grand Concourse 1904, 1917.

Here two subway stations have been built one above the other, separated by a mezzanine. (The trains on the upper level are marked "Woodlawn Road," a nonexistent destination.) The lower station, **in the Parisian manner,** is one large barrel vault. Despite uninspired decoration, poor lighting, and minimal maintenance, this station is one of the exciting spaces of the subway system.

 [1b.] Security Mutual Insurance Company, 500 Grand Concourse. SE cor. E. 149th St. 1965. Horace Ginsbern & Associates.

The first office building in the Bronx in 25 years. Precast concrete panels give a sculptured texture to this handsome structure.

[1c.] Bronx Post Office, 558 Grand Concourse. NE cor. 149th St. 1935. Louis Simon.

An excellent palace of government set on a classical terrace. Chaste gray brick walls and windows set in tall arches lined with marble add to its dignity. The lobby murals by Ben Shahn were a project of the WPA.

[2a.] Thomas Garden Apartments, 840 Grand Concourse bet. E. 158th and E. 159th Sts. 1928. Andrew J. Thomas.

A development of five-story walkup buildings grouped around a sunken court. All the houses are reached through the court, and the short flights of stairs leading into the court effectively separate the building entrances from the busy highway outside. This project, named for its architect, is one of two [See Harlem 11a.] designed by him for John D. Rockefeller, Jr., who hoped to solve the problem of the slum by investing in middle-income housing.

[2b.] Concourse Village, one block east of the Concourse, E. 156th to E. 158th St. Harry M. Prince.

This high-rise development, sponsored by the Amalgamated Meat Cutters and Butcher Workmen's Union, is built on air rights above the New York Central Railroad yards.

[2c.] Bronx County Building, 851 Grand Concourse. SW cor. E. 161st St. 1934. Joseph H. Freedlander and Max Hausle.

[2d.] Yankee Stadium, E. 161st St. and River Ave. 1922.

Best seen from the 161st Street Station of the Jerome Avenue IRT line. The plan of the stadium is asymmetrical in order to insure a short right field, which made it easier for Babe Ruth to hit home runs.

[3a.] The Lorelei Fountain, Joyce Kilmer Park, Grand Concourse. SW cor. E. 164th St.

The fountain honors the author of *Die Lorelei,* Heinrich Heine, whose bas-relief portrait is on the south side of the base. The statue was presented to New York in 1893 after it had been rejected by Dusseldorf, Heine's birthplace. The donors wanted it placed at the Plaza, where the Sherman statue now stands. But Heine's being both a German and a Jew, together with the statue's questionable artistic merits, made this site unavailable. After six years of debate the statue was placed in its present location, but even here its troubles continued. After its unveiling the fountain was vandalized, restored, and then put under constant police protection.

[3b.] Andrew Freedman Home, 1025 Grand Concourse. SW cor. McClellan St. 1924. Wings, 1928. Joseph H. Freedlander and Harry Allan Jacobs.

This subdued gray-and-yellow limestone palace is French-inspired, but its setting in a garden gives it the air of a large English country house. It is a home for the aged endowed by a leading contractor known as the "Father of the New York subway." The panic of 1907 made him fearful of losing the comforts to which he had become accustomed, and he established this home for aged indigents who could show that they once enjoyed affluence. (A retired czarist general was a guest here for a time.)

[3c.] Home and Hospital of the Daughters of Jacob, 321 E. 167th St. SW cor. Teller Ave. 1920. Louis Allan Abramson.

[4a.] Dollar Savings Bank, 101 East 170th St. E of Grand Concourse. 1957. Skidmore, Owings & Merrill.

A cool, clean glass box with a black metal frame. Strength and serenity comes to a hustle-bustle Bronx shopping street through this bank's understatement.

[4b.] Buildings and parking lot, E. 172nd St. W of Grand Concourse at head of Wythe Pl. 1908–1955.

Harold Swain, an attorney, built a tennis court, an indoor swimming pool, and four other structures just for the fun of doing it. Even after he abandoned his Bronx home for **Park Avenue,** he worked on his buildings each morning before going to his office. Swain mixed concrete, set brick and stone, built a window out of **bottles** and **jars.** Using bottle **caps, pebbles,** pieces of **wire** and **glass,** he made countless funny faces in the wet cement. The property is now used as a commercial parking lot, but three of Swain's buildings have survived. Could these be the **Watts Towers** of the Bronx?

[4c.] Astor Concourse, 1420 Grand Concourse. SE cor. E. 172nd St.

Like other Astor properties, this building is in the form of a hollow rectangle. The houses are entered from the well-shaded inner court, reached through a tunnel.

[4d.] Bronx-Lebanon Hospital, Grand Concourse. NE cor. Mount Eden Pkwy. 1940. Charles B. Meyers.

A tower rising in a garden, with its facade toward the south rather than facing the Concourse, steel balconies, and a plate glass solarium. This was the first really modern building to be built on the Grand Concourse. It stands in contrast to the many apartment houses built in this area during the 1930's, which were decorated in the modern style—in light-colored brick, with polychrome terra cotta, glass block, and steel casement windows—but which in terms of structure and layout exhibited no innovation over their older neighbors.

[4e.] The Cross-Bronx Expressway, at Grand Concourse.

Four levels of traffic pass this point. At the lowest level is the Expressway. Above and south of the expressway is a tunnel for the local streets. The next level going up is the IND Subway, and the top level is the Grand Concourse itself.

[4f.] The Lewis Morris Apartments, 1749 Grand Concourse. NW cor. E. 175th St.

This grand apartment house was an attempt to extend the fashion of Park Avenue and Riverside Drive to the Bronx. Built over the side of a cliff, the back of this house reaches down five stories to Walton Avenue. The house is named after a colonial judge whose controversy with the British governor led to the famous libel suit against Peter Zenger. [See N Bronx 6b.]

[5a.] Macomb's Dam Park, Jerome Ave. and W. 161st St.

[5a.]

This is the site of a dam erected in 1813 by Robert Macomb, who used the tidal flow of the Harlem River to operate a mill until his neighbors demolished it in 1838, in order to open the river to shipping.

[5b.] Unused subway tunnel, Anderson and Jerome Aves. at W. 162nd St.

Once an extension of the Ninth Avenue "el," this five-block subway tunnel was opened in 1918 and closed in 1955. Now vacant, it has been proposed as the site of a trolley museum.

[6.] Carmelite Monastery, 1381 University Ave. at W. 170th St.

The house of this cloistered community is best seen from the walkway of Highbridge. Built on a steep river bank, the elements of this medieval-style building—its tower, cells, chapel, cloister, and gardens—all become visible without revealing the life of contemplation within its walls.

UNIVERSITY HEIGHTS, KINGSBRIDGE HEIGHTS, FORDHAM HEIGHTS, BEDFORD PARK, AND GUN HILL

These neighborhoods follow the University Avenue and Grand Concourse ridges northward to **Van Cortlandt Park** and **Woodlawn Cemetery.** They contain hundreds of the familiar Bronx apartment houses, older one-family wooden homes, and a variety of institutions, public works, and landmarks, many of national fame and importance.

[7a.] New York University, University Heights Campus.

[7b.] The Hall of Fame, 1896–1900. McKim, Mead & White. ★

A semicircular colonnade frames three university buildings with which it forms a unit. At the crest of a steep ridge the colonnade offers one of the fine vantage points of the city and, because of its site, is a highly visible landmark itself.

[7c.] Gould Library. 1900. McKim, Mead & White. ★

One of Stanford White's finest buildings, a Palladian palace with flat green dome and an extended portico in the form of a classical temple. It houses both the library and chapel.

[7d.] Cornelius Baker Hall of Philosophy, N of Gould Library. 1912. McKim, Mead & White. ★

[7e.] Hall of Languages, S of Gould Library. 1894. McKim, Mead & White. ★

[7f.] Memorial Monument, N of Memorial Flagpole.

A spire from the original building of New York University, which was erected on Washington Square East in 1831. Another spire from this old building is used as the base for the sundial in front of the Library, and limestone pinnacles are scattered around the campus in the form of road blocks and fence posts.

[7g.] Memorial Flagpole. E of Technology Building. Presented in 1926.

The mast of the America Cup challenger *Shamrock IV* marks the site of Revolutionary Fort Number Eight, now armed with artillery of World War I vintage.

[7h.] South Hall/formerly **Justus H. Schwab Mansion,** S of Flagpole. 1857.

Red brick Anglo-Italian villa is also on the the site of the old Revolutionary fort. At the time of its building, cannon balls, grape shot, British coins and uniform buttons, and other remains were excavated.

[7i.] Technology Building and Begrisch Lecture Hall, W of Memorial Flagpole. 1964. Marcel Breuer; Hamilton Smith, Associate.

[7i.]

This handsome contemporary building uses yellow brick and reinforced concrete to match the brick and limestone trim of the Hall of Fame group. A second Technology Building, also by Breuer, is now under construction.

[7j.] Julius Silver Residence Center, W of Technology Building. 1964. Marcel Breuer; Robert F. Gatje, Associate.

In order to take good advantage of a difficult site, access to the dormitories from the dining hall and social rooms is through a pair of ramps that enter the building at its fourth story.

[8a.] The Croton Aqueduct, parallel to and 30 yards E of University Ave.

The Aqueduct is used as a sitting park and walkway. It is proposed to rebuild the aqueduct's viaducts and develop a 32-mile trailway from the Highbridge to the Croton Reservoir in Westchester.

[8b.] St. Nicholas of Tolentine Church, University Ave. SW cor. Fordham Rd. 1928. O'Connor & Delaney.

[8c.] Fordham Hill Apartments, Webb Ave. NE cor. Sedgwick Ave.

One of the first large apartment developments to use colored brick. Set on a commanding hill, these buildings offer excellent views of Upper Manhattan and the Harlem River valley.

[8d.] U.S. Veterans' Hospital, Kingsbridge Rd. SE cor. Sedgwick Ave. 1922.

The site of Revolutionary Fort Number Six, later the estate of circus magnate William H. Bailey. The Catholic Orphan Asylum was established here in 1901, and its buildings have been incorporated into the present hospital.

[9a.] 2744 Kingsbridge Terrace, N of Kingsbridge Rd.

A stucco castle with a handsome tile roof, numerous gables, balconies, crenelated turrets, a weather vane, a TV antenna, and a tunnel leading from the dungeon to the street.

[9a.]

[9

[9b.] Junior High School 143, Bronx, 231st St. SW cor. Sedgwick Ave. 1958. Ketchum, Gina, & Sharp; J. Stanley Sharp, Partner-in-Charge.

A large school on a compact and steeply sloping site, this is a model exercise in good manners in architecture. Skillful handling enables the Sedgwick Avenue wing to avoid clashing with either the rooflines of the commercial buildings to its south or with those of the row houses to its north.

[9c.] Jerome Park Reservoir, Sedgwick and Goulden Aves. 1895–1905.

The existing **reservoir** has a capacity of 773,000,000 gallons. A **second basin,** with a capacity almost twice as large as the first, was planned and excavated to the east of the present reservoir, from Mosholu Parkway along Jerome Avenue to Kingsbridge Road, but **abandoned** before its completion. This second basin is now the site of a college, a park, an armory, two subway yards, three high schools and a publicly aided housing development!

The reservoir takes its name from the **Jerome Park Race Track** that occupied this site from 1876 until 1890. The track was sponsored by the American Jockey Club, which attempted to elevate horse racing in this country to the status of an **aristocratic sport.**

[9d.] Bronx High School of Science, W. 205th St. NE cor. Goulden Ave. 1959. Emery Roth & Sons.

[9e.] Hunter College, Bedford Park Blvd. and Paul Ave. 1932. Thompson, Holmes, and Converse.

A branch of the college whose main building is on Park Avenue [See UES Manhattan 47b], which in turn is a part of the City University. Unlike the main center, men are admitted to classes here and in point of numbers predominate. The first four buildings are part of a never-completed Gothic quadrangle and are connected by subterranean tunnels.

[9f.] Hunter College, Library and Classroom Buildings, 1959. Marcel Breuer; Robert F. Gatje, Associate.

The south and east facades of these buildings are shielded by tile screens: vertical bands for the library and horizontal bands for the classroom building. The undulating roof of the library consists of six reinforced-concrete inverted umbrellas. Exciting structures.

[9g.] Kingsbridge Armory, W. Kingsbridge Rd. NW cor. Jerome Ave. 1912. Pilcher & Tachau.

[10a.] The Fordham Road-Grand Concourse Intersection.

Far beneath this busy commercial crossroads, the Fordham Station on the IND Concourse Subway is built around the tunnel that carries the Grand Concourse under Fordham Road. For more than three decades Alexander's Department Store has dominated this intersection from an unadorned brick building with horizontal bands of glass blocks and a huge neon sign on the roof. Two blocks to the south is the Loew's Paradise, one of the largest and most ornate motion picture palaces in the city, and one of the few without a marquee.

[10b.] Saint James' Church, Jerome Ave. and E. 190th St. NE cor. 1864. ☆

A granite Gothic Revival church whose large and quiet churchyard is enhanced by its proximity to St. James Park.

[10c.] St. James Park, Jerome Ave. to Creston Ave. E. 191st to E. 193rd Sts. 1901.

Once a wet and marshy tract, now one of the best neighborhood parks in the city.

[10d.] Poe Cottage, Poe Park, Grand Concourse. SE cor. Kingsbridge Rd. 1816. ★

The cottage was moved into Poe Park from an adjacent site in 1913. Edgar Allan Poe lived here from 1846 until a few months before his death in 1849. He came here in the hope that the clear country air would aid his ailing young wife. (She died during their first winter in the small house.) The raven silhouette on the cottage is misleading since *The Raven* was written before Poe came here.

[11a.] St. Philip Neri Church, 3025 Grand Concourse. N of Bedford Park Blvd. 1899.

[11b.] Bedford Park Presbyterian Church, Bedford Park Blvd. NW cor. Bainbridge Ave. 1900. R. H. Robertson.

[11c.] Academy of Mount St. Ursula, Bedford Park Blvd. and Bainbridge Ave.

[11d.] The Bedford Park Casino, 390 Bedford Park Blvd. bet. Webster and Decatur Aves. S side.

Now occupied by a manufacturer of violin bows.

[11e.] Mosholu Parkway, connecting Bronx and Van Cortlandt Parks.

One of the few completed links in the network of parkways that was proposed to connect the major parks of the Bronx. At the entrance to the parkway a sculptural group serves to divide traffic.

[11f.] 52nd Precinct Police Station, 3016 Webster Ave. at Mosholu Pkwy. North. 1905. Stoughton & Stoughton.

A high point of our provincial civic architecture. This solid red brick building gains authority from a large terra cotta municipal seal and grace from its handsome clock tower and its bright terra cotta face.

[12a.] St. Brendan's Church, Perry Ave., E. 206th to E. 207th St. 1966. Belfatto & Pavarini.

There are two churches in this building, and the slope of the site permits us to enter both at ground level. The lower church is entered from West 206th Street. The upper church, entered from East 207th Street, is under a steeply sloped ceiling. Near the entrance the ceiling is low, and the church dark, but as we move toward the altar the space and light around us grow. The steeple is part of the roof. This exciting new church is probably one of the best buildings in the Bronx.

[12b.] Isaac Varian Homestead, Bainbridge Ave. bet. Van Cortlandt Ave. East and E. 208th St. 1775. ★

This fieldstone farmhouse has recently been moved on to City-
owned land from its original site. It is now headquarters of the
Bronx County Historical Society. Varian was the 63rd mayor of
New York.

[12b.]

[12c.] Williamsbridge Oval, Bainbridge Ave. and Van Cortlandt
Ave. East. 1888.

Playground situated in the bowl of the former Williamsbridge
Reservoir, which once served a large part of the Bronx. The granite
house on Reservoir Oval between Putnam Place and Reservoir Place
was built for the reservoir keeper.

[12d.] Montefiore Hospital, E. 210th St. Bainbridge Ave., E.
Gun Hill Rd. 1913. Arnold W. Brunner.

Numerous additions, alterations, and entirely new buildings that
now crowd this medical campus make it difficult to pick out Brunner's handsome set of hospital buildings.

[12e.] Henry L. Moses Institute, Montefiore Hospital, Bainbridge
Ave. SE cor. Gun Hill Road. 1966. Philip Johnson & Assocs.

A crisp, angular tower. Unusual squared bay windows, set in
vertical panels, emphasize the height of this handsome brown brick
research laboratory which now dominates this area.

[13.] Woodlawn Cemetery, entrances at Jerome Ave. N of Bainbridge Ave. and at E. 233rd St. and Webster Ave.

A lavish array of tombstones, mausoleums, and memorials in a
richly planted setting. Many wealthy and distinguished people are
buried here. Tombs and mausoleums are replicas and small-size
reproductions of several famous European chapels and monuments.

RIVERDALE AND SPUYTEN DUYVIL

[14.] Van Cortlandt Manor, Van Cortlandt Park, E. Side of Broadway at W. 246th St. 1748. ★

A carefully preserved fieldstone country house for a wealthy
landed family. A simple exterior hides a richly decorated interior.
This large park was held by the Van Cortlandts for over 200 years
until it was sold to the City in 1899. The large meadow north of the
manor house was the site of the Van Cortlandt's farm. A great
number and variety of athletic fields are laid out here, including
cricket fields for New York's large West Indian population.

Vault Hill overlooking the Van Cortlandt Manor to the East contains the Van Cortlandt family vault. When the British occupied New York in 1776, Augustus Van Cortlandt, the city clerk, hid the municipal records in the vault. In 1781, General Washington had campfires lit here to deceive the British, while he marched to Yorktown for the battle against Cornwallis.

[15a.] Horace Mann School, 231 W. 246th St. NW cor. Post Ave.

A prestige school once associated with Teachers College. Its most handsome building is Pforzheimer Hall, a neat yellow brick structure by Victor Christ-Janer, built in 1956.

[15b.] Manhattan College, Manhattan College Pkway. and W. 242nd St. 1921. O'Connor & Delany.

[15c.] Fieldston School, Manhattan College Pkway. at Delafield Ave. 1926. Clarence S. Stein & Robert D. Kohn.

[16a.] Conservative Synagogue, Henry Hudson Pkway. NE cor. W. 250th St. 1961. Percival Goodman.

[16b.] Christ Church, Henry Hudson Pkway. SE cor. W. 252nd St. 1866. Richard M. Upjohn. ★

A small, picturesque church, of brick and local stone, with a simple pierced wall belfry. Minimal alterations and careful maintenance have preserved this delightful church.

[16c.] Henry Ittleson Center for Child Research, 5050 Iselin Ave. SE cor. Grosvenor Ave. 1967. Abraham W. Geller, Michael A. Rubenstein, design associate.

[16c.]

An architect's attempt to contribute to the baffling battle against schizophrenia. A careful complex of simple buildings in which the structural elements employed explain their functions, as well as provide a protective shelter for disturbed children.

[16d.] Riverdale Presbyterian Church, 4765 Henry Hudson Parkway, NW cor. W. 249th Street. 1863. James Renwick, Jr. ★

A fieldstone country church, with a steep roof and a fine steeple. Its former manse, the Duff House, combines a Gothic Revival rectory with a Mansard roof.

[17a.] Fieldston Hill, Residence of Edward C. Delafield, 680 W. 246th St. SE cor. Douglas Ave.

A large fieldstone house with a stately portico. The Delafields have been one of Riverdale's leading families since 1829. A part of the extensive gardens are used by Columbia University for horticultural research.

[17b.] Greystone/formerly **Cleveland E. Dodge Residence,** 690 W. 247th St. SW cor. Independence Ave. 1863. James Renwick, Jr.

The Dodge family has long been associated with Teachers College, which now operates a conference center in this large, granite Gothic Revival mansion.

[17c.] Riverdale Country School for Girls, W. 248th St. NE cor. Palisade Ave. 1967. R. Marshall Christensen.

This new study center has an unusual set of roofs, both handsome and practical, with skylights along the ridges.

[17d.] Anthony Campagna Estate, Independence Ave. SE cor. W. 249th St. ca. 1922. Dwight James Baum.

Long considered one of the nation's finest country palaces, this stucco and tile mansion is adorned with classical ornamentation.

[17e.] Wave Hill, 675 W. 253rd St. at Sycamore Ave. ca. 1830. ★

This largest of Riverdale's mansions is now the home of Wave Hill Inc., a foundation devoted to science and the arts and situated on the 28-acre Perkins-Freeman Estate. The handsome Federal-style house has had several additions including a large Gothic hall once used as an armory. Mark Twain, Theodore Roosevelt, George W. Perkins, and Arturo Toscanini have lived here.

[18a.] Ladd Road E. of Palisade Ave.

A group of handsome contemporary houses built around a swimming pool.

[18b.] Addition to Hebrew Home for the Aged, 5901 Palisade Ave. SW cor. W. 261 St. 1967. Kelly and Gruzen.

The new brutalism has come to Riverdale with this concrete and brick building. A handsome terrace takes advantage of the sloping riverbank.

[18c.] Library/formerly **Fonthill Castle,** College of Mt. St. Vincent, W. 261st St. at Palisade Ave. 1852. ★

[18c.]

This handsome stone castle—six octagonal towers, joined together, but rising to different heights—was built as the home of a Shakespearean actor. The unusual tile floors, woodwork, and fireplaces of the interior match the castle's romantic exterior.

MISCELLANY

[19.] Henry Hudson Memorial, Henry Hudson Memorial Park, Independence Ave. at W. 227th St.

A statue of the explorer, twice life size, surveys the river from a column on a high bluff.

EASTERN BRONX

At the center of this area lies the old village of Westchester, whose village green is now known as Westchester Square. The neighborhood that surrounds and takes its name from the Square is a conglomeration of single-family homes, stray apartment buildings, and all types of minor commercial, industrial, and institutional establishments. To the north is a new and large concentration of **medical facilities.** Pelham Bay Park is to the east. To the south are Throgs Neck and Ferry Point, the sites of two of the region's **major bridges;** and Clason Point, once a resort and amusement center, but now the site of the variety of housing developments. **Parkchester,** almost a city within the city lies west of Westchester Square.

PARKCHESTER, WESTCHESTER SQUARE AND MORRIS PARK

[1a.] Parkchester, E. Tremont Ave. Purdy St., McGraw Ave. White Plains Rd. 1938—1942. Board of Design: Richmond H. Shreve, Chairman; Andrew J. Eken, George Gove, Gilmore D. Clarke, Robert W. Dowling, Irwin Clavan, and Henry C. Meyer, Jr.

[1a.]

One of the largest housing developments in the nation and, in terms of urban design, almost a model of what good high-density housing might be. It was built for the Metropolitan Life Insurance Company on a site previously occupied by the Roman Catholic Protectory. The development includes more than 12,000 apartments, garage space for more than 3000 automobiles, a large theater, a variety of stores, offices, and places of public accommodation. **More than half** the site is landscaped or used for playgrounds.

The avoidance of the gridiron street pattern, the extensive separation of automobile and pedestrian traffic, generous planting and sensitive landscaping, the use of sculpture and terra cotta ornamentation, all add to the benefits that come from a carefully planned development. Criticism of Parkchester has centered around its **high density**—almost 250,000 people per square mile—and the scarcity of apartments designed for large families.

[1b.] St. Raymond's Church, Tremont Ave. SW cor. Castle Hill Ave. 1897—1898.

Founded in 1843, this is the oldest Roman Catholic parish in what is now the Bronx, and it is housed in one of the grandest church buildings of the borough.

Dominick's Restaurant, 2356 Westchester Ave. cor. Parker St. 822-8810. A good place to eat for over a century. Down a few steps from the street.

[2a.] Westchester-Bronx Branch, YMCA, 2244 Westchester Ave. Bet. Castle Hill Ave. and Havemeyer Ave. 1850. ☆

Red brick Victorian country residence is one of the last examples of its type in New York. Once the rectory of St. Peter's Church, it is now in poor repair, and is slated for replacement by its present owners.

[2b.] St. Peter's Church, 2500 Westchester Ave. at St. Peter's Ave. 1853. Leopold Eidlitz. ☆

A strong and handsome Gothic Revival granite church is the third building to house this congregation, founded in 1693. An altar and baptismal font were gifts of **Queen Anne** in 1706.

[2c.] Huntington Free Library and Reading Room, 9 Westchester Square. 1893.

A gingerbread survivor of the 19th Century and the gift of Collis P. Huntington, railroad magnate, whose portrait hangs in the reading room. The collection is scanty, and books may not be taken out of the building.

[2d.] Westchester Square.

The remains of the village green of the ancient town of Westchester, founded in 1653 and known as **Oostorp** under the Dutch. Under British rule it was the seat of Westchester County from 1683 until 1759. It is now a focus of local shopping and service activities and the terminus of several bus routes.

Morris Park: From Westchester Square (Westchester Sq. station, IRT Pelham Bay Line) to Pelham Parkway. (Pelham Parkway station, IRT Dyre Ave. Line).

[3b.]

[3a.] Bronx State Hospital, 1500 Waters Pl. 1959. The Office of Max O. Urbahn.

This large hospital is part of a still larger complex of State, Municipal, and private facilities for medical research and treatment which have been built here in the past decade. One of the weaknesses of current city planning is highlighted by the fact that these institutions, built at the same time, serving similar functions, and situated so close to each other, bear no relationship to one another and share no common facilities. A children's psychiatric hospital (by the same architects) in a distinct architectural style **[3b.]** will bring a rich collection of forms and a pleasant domestic scale to this otherwise institutional campus.

[4a.] Yeshiva University, Albert Einstein College of Medicine, 1300 Morris Park Ave. SW cor. Eastchester Rd.

> **Forcheimer Medical Science Building,** 1955, Kelly & Gruzen.
> **Robbins Auditorium, Friedman Lounge & Gottesmann Library,** 1958. Kelly & Gruzen.
> **Ullmann Research Center,** 1963, Kiesler & Bartos.

[4b.] Bronx Municipal Hospital Center, Morris Park Ave. to Pelham Pkwy. W. of Eastchester Rd. **Van Etten Hospital,** 1955. Pomerance & Breines. **Jacobi Hospital,** 1955. Pomerance & Breines.

[5a.] Bronx and Pelham Parkway.

A wide and handsome parkway connecting the two parks for which it is named and leading to the Bronx Zoo, Botanical Gardens, and Fordham University. The parkway is richly planted and well used by motorists, walkers, and equestrians. Prior to World War II the center lanes were closed off on **Sunday mornings** and were used for bicycle racing.

[5b.] Pelham Parkway Station, Dyre Avenue IRT Subway Line. Williamsbridge Rd. N of Pelham Pkwy.

This one-story concrete pillbox contains two small stores and the subway entrances. Formerly part of the New York, Boston, and Westchester Railroad, a commuter line that went bankrupt during the Depression. A 4-mile stretch of the right-of-way was acquired by the city, refurbished, and appended to the transit system in 1941.

[5c.] New York Institute for the Education of the Blind, 999 Pelham Pkwy. NW Cor Williamsbridge Rd. 1924. McKim, Mead, & White.

This pleasant and spacious campus contains 21 buildings and is an elementary and college preparatory school for the blind and visually handicapped.

PELHAM BAY PARK AND CITY ISLAND

Pelham Bay Park: The largest of the six parks purchased as a result of the new Bronx parks program of 1883. At that time this one was a distance outside the city limits. It contains two golf courses, an archery range, bridle paths, a firing range, and ample facilities for hiking, cycling, and motoring. Shell racing is held in the North Lagoon. During the 1911 season, a **monorail** traversed the park from the New Haven Railroad line to City Island.

[6.]

[6.] Museum of the American Indian, Heye Foundation Annex, Bruckner Expwy. SW cor. Middletown Rd.

This is a warehouse and research center for the Museum whose public galleries are on **Audubon Terrace** in Manhattan. [See U

Manhattan 2.] Totem poles, Indian houses, and wigwam replicas are displayed on the lawns, but you can't go inside.

[7a.] Rice Stadium, Pelham Bay Park. E of Bruckner Expwy. and N of Middletown Rd. Hertz & Robertson.

The concrete stadium is unusual because of the small temple containing Louis St. Lannes' heroic statue "American Boy" at the top of the bleachers. The stadium and athletic facilities around it were given to the City by Isaac L. Rice, who was president of the Electric Battery Corp. A grateful City Council honored the donor by assigning such electronic names as **Watt, Ampere, Ohm,** and **Radio** to the city streets south and east of the stadium.

[7b.] Pelham Bay Park World War Memorial, Shore Rd. E of Bruckner Expwy. John J. Sheridan, Architect; Belle Kinney, Sculptor.

[8.] Bartow-Pell Mansion Museum, Shore Road. 1675. ★
Hours: Tuesday, Friday, and Sunday afternoons; 25¢ admission.

Lords of the **Manor of Pelham** once owned this house which was enlarged, renovated, and remodeled in Federal style, probably by Minard Lafever, from 1836 to 1845. The mansion became the home of the International Garden Club in 1914 when it was restored by Delano and Aldrich. The Pell family plot, a magnificent formal garden, a view of Long Island Sound, and rare and tasteful furnishings combine to make a visit to this house worthwhile.

[8.]

[9.] Orchard Beach, East Shore of Pelham Bay Park on Long Island Sound. 1936.

A large sandy beach reopened in 1936 after extensive remodeling by the WPA and the Department of Parks. The bathhouses are enhanced by a strong set of concrete colonnades, chastely decorated with blue terra cotta tiles. The beach restaurant is under the spacious entry terrace. This is a good public place, monumental without being overpowering, and efficient without being crowded.

[10.] City Island. Off City Island Rd., in Long Island Sound.

This tight little island is part of New York City according to law, but otherwise it is a piece of the 19th Century surviving into the present. It is a community of small homes and stores that bears little resemblance to any other part of the city. For many generations a large **yachting** industry was located here.

Throgs Neck: At the eastern end of East Tremont Avenue, East 177th Street, and the Cross Bronx Expressway. Its name is derived from John Throckmorton who settled here in 1643, when New York was still under **Dutch rule.** Until the early part of the 20th Century this area was covered with estates. Today its inhabitants are modest, homeowning families.

[11a.] Edgewater Park, N of Cross-Bronx Expwy. at end of E. 177th St.

One of three communities in the Bronx where only the building is owned by the occupant, and ground rent is paid to the owner of the land. These buildings were originally summer cottages, but they are now winterized.

[11b.] Silver Beach, S of Cross-Bronx Expwy. at end of Hollywood Ave.

Another community of cottages on rented land. The Indian Trail affords excellent view of both the Whitestone and Throgs Neck bridges. The former Hammond-Havermeyer Mansion (1810) here was once known as the **Gibraltar of Long Island Sound** and serves as the community center.

[11c.] Preston High School/formerly **Collis P. Huntington Residence,** 2780 Schurz Ave. SE cor. Brinsmade Ave.

[12.] Fort Schuyler, New York State Maritime College, E end of Pennyfield Ave. 1834—1838. Capt. I. L. Smith. ★

Dormitory and Mess Hall, 1962; **Health and Physical Education Building,** 1964; **Science and Engineering Building,** 1966; Ballard, Todd, Assocs. Interior alterations to Fort, 1966—1967, William A. Hall.

NORTHERN BRONX

The Northern Bronx has been settled since the 17th Century, and for two months in the 18th Century the nation's executive mansion was here, but most of this area's modest homes and scattered groups of apartment houses have been built in the 20th Century. Here we find the neighborhoods known as Williamsbridge, Wakefield, Eastchester, and Baychester.

[1.] Lourdes of America, Bronxwood Ave. NW cor. Mace Ave. 1939.

A replica of the famous French shrine on the grounds of a modest parish church, it boasts of many cures and claims to have been constructed without architectural supervision. The *Santa Scala,* adjacent to the shrine consists of a Nativity crêche, Calvary, miniature chapels, catacombs, and countless saints and angels.

[2.] Williamsbridge Square, Gun Hill Rd. and White Plains Rd.

This is the green of the village that grew up around the bridge built over the Bronx River in 1673 by John Williams. The Square is occupied by a two-decked elevated subway station, completed in 1920 when the Third Avenue "El" was extended here from Fordham Road, to join the White Plains Road Elevated Line.

Louis Restaurant, 3531 White Plains Rd. at E. 211th St.
Excellent Italian-American food. 655-9369.

[3.] Hillside Homes, five city blocks, W of Boston Rd. bet. Wilson Ave. and Eastchester Rd. 1935. Clarence S. Stein.

High land costs make it impossible to duplicate this highly successful moderate-rental housing development. Most of the buildings here are only four stories high, and they occupy one-third of the land. A large central playground and community center is provided for school-aged children, while sand boxes and tot lots are placed away from street traffic inside seven large sunken interior courts that are reached through tunnel passageways. Basement apartments are in greatest demand here. They come with private, terraced gardens facing on the quiet and verdant courts.

 [4.] Our Lady of Grace Church, Bronxwood Ave. SW cor. E. 226 St. 1967. Belfatto & Pavarini.

Well done! A new upper church over an existing lower church, a successful attempt to introduce the Mansard roof into contemporary architecture.

[5a.] Misericordia Hospital, Bronx Blvd. SE cor. E. 233rd St. 1960. Kiff, Colean, Voss & Souder.

[6a.] Vincent-Halsey House, 3701 Provost Ave. NW cor. Conner St. Mid-18th Century. ☆

A nondescript old building that once was a handsome colonial farmhouse. John Adams moved the executive mansion here in 1797 to escape a yellow fever epidemic raging in Philadelphia, at that time the national capital. Adams governed the nation from this place for two months, but tragedy did not escape him. A son drowned while swimming in Eastchester Creek, and he was buried in St. Paul's Churchyard.

[6b.] St. Paul's Church, Columbus Ave. and Third St. Mount Vernon. 1765.

Situated just outside the city limits, this historic church occupies part of the village green of the old village of Eastchester. A handsome Georgian building with a 19th Century tower, fieldstone walls, brick detailing around the doors and windows. The mortar used was a mixture of sand and crushed seashells. The interior is restored to its original condition.

The Village Green of Eastchester was the site of the trial (1736) of Peter Zenger, the New York printer who was charged with libel for his criticism of the British Governor. His acquittal is regarded as the cornerstone of our traditions of a free press. [See W Bronx 4f.]

[7.] Junior High School 144, Bronx, Allerton Ave. SE cor. Lodovick Ave. 1968. The Office of Max O. Urbahn.

[7.]

[8.] Co-op City, E of New England Thruway, W of Hutchinson River Pkwy. to the Hutchinson River. 1968–1970. Herman Jessor.

A gargantuan middle-income housing community grouping 35 high-rise towers and 236 two-family houses in large-scale clusters on a marshy tract (once an amusement park, Freedomland). Its population of 60,000 persons is the equivalent of adding Atlantic City, New Jersey to this sparsely populated section of the Bronx (but without its boardwalk or salt water taffy.)

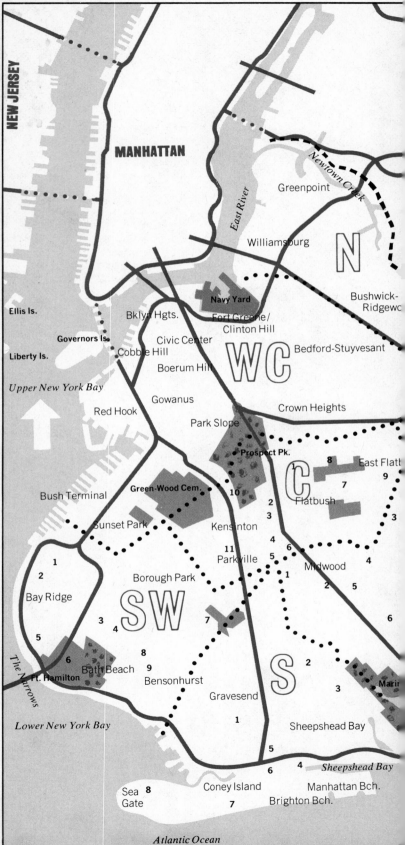

NEW JERSEY

MANHATTAN

East River

Greenpoint

Newtown Creek

Williamsburg

N

Bushwick-
Ridgewo

Ellis Is.

Navy Yard

Bklyn Hgts.

Fort Greene/
Clinton Hill

Governors Is.

Civic Center

Liberty Is.

Cobble Hill

Boerum Hill

WC

Bedford-Stuyvesant

Upper New York Bay

Gowanus

Crown Heights

Red Hook

Park Slope

Prospect Pk.

8

East Flatb

Bush Terminal

Green-Wood Cem.

10

1

7

9

Sunset Park

Kensinton

2

C

Flatbush

3

3

1

11

Parkville

4

6

4

2

Midwood

Bay Ridge

Borough Park

5

1

2

5

3

SW

7

1

6

5

4

8

6

Bath Beach

9

S

2

Marir

Ft. Hamilton

Bensonhurst

3

The Narrows

Gravesend

Sheepshead Bay

Lower New York Bay

1

5

6

4

Sheepshead Bay

Sea
Gate

8

Coney Island

Manhattan Bch.

7

Brighton Bch.

Atlantic Ocean

BROOKLYN

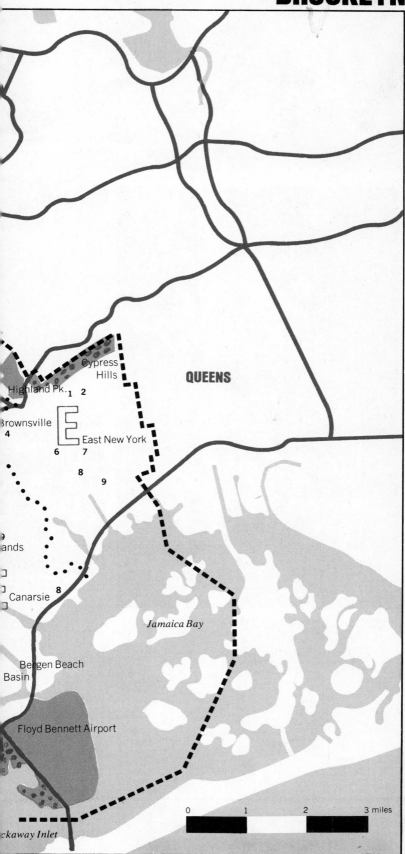

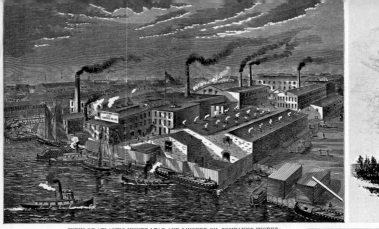

VIEW OF ATLANTIC WHITE LEAD AND LINSEED OIL COMPANY'S WORKS;

VIEW OF THOS. F. ROWLAND'S CONTINENTAL IRON WORKS AND SHIPYARD, GREENPOINT, NEW YORK.

BROOKLYN CL

E. KETCHAM & CO

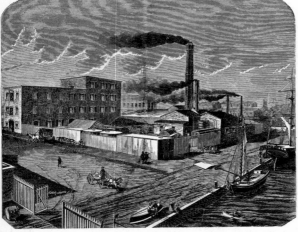

Valvoline Works of Leonard & Ellis, foot of Sullivan Street, South Brooklyn, New York.

O GREENWOOD (FROM WITHIN.)

EAST RIVER BRIDGE, NEW YORK.

WORKS, BROOKLYN, NEW YORK.

VIEW OF HAVEMEYERS & ELDERS SUGAR REFINERY, WILLIAMSBURGH, NEW YORK.

MANUFACTORY, BROOKLYN.

A. W. FABER.
LEAD PENCIL & PENHOLDER FACTORY.

E. FABER.
DEPOT 133 WILLIAM ST. NEW YORK.

A. W. Faber's Branch Lead Pencil and Penholder Manufactory, Brooklyn, N. Y.

BROOKLYN

Borough of Brooklyn/Kings County

Endless rows of buildings, many tree-lined streets, rubbish on the pavement, kids playing **stick-ball,** a glance upward at a steeple silhouetted in the smoggy sky, and the drama of the borrowed skyline across the bay—these are only some of the visual ingredients of Brooklyn's scene. How this scene changes from generation to generation!

The physical objects themselves do not really undergo the transformation. With certain notable exceptions they seem only to age and get **grimier.** It is, rather, the way in which we *see* them

that changes. Brooklyn today, even to many of its residents, is very often the image of Brooklyn absorbed from driving the limited-access highway: the industry of north end, the products of American industry awaiting shipment on the docks below Brooklyn Heights, the spin along the Narrows with the Verrazano Bridge punctuating the contrast between man and nature. Motorists remember the intricate spider web of Coney Island's **Wonder Wheel,** the endless stretches of **swampland** at Jamaica Bay, or the 25-mile-an-hour curves in a 50-mile-an-hour car in verdant Interboro Parkway. The placement of our highways and the speed of our cars tends to deemphasize the residential aspects of Brooklyn and to play up its other attributes.

What a different image Brooklyn must have provided in other periods.

It is an amazing thing that the footprints of civilization have not only been left on Brooklyn's 80 square miles, but have in many instances been preserved virtually intact to mark the path of people and culture. They are subtle footprints—after all, time both erodes and covers artifacts of the past. But the sense of Brooklyn as an **organism** which has grown from a settlement barely 300 years old is concealed to us, not by any lack of evidence, but by the changes in the manner of our observation. The rediscovery of parts of Brooklyn by a **young and sophisticated** middle class in the past decade may mark yet another change in the way we see. Viable residential communities of the past, backwaters in the mainstream of physical change, Brooklyn Heights, Park Slope, and the Hills: **Clinton, Cobble,** and **Boerum,** are once again becoming desirable neighborhoods. Perhaps the renaissance of these communities will provide the motivation to explore the rest of the borough. Perhaps that process will provide new opportunities for the renewal and reinterpretation of the lessons and landmarks of history.

WC

WEST CENTRAL BROOKLYN

Town of Brooklyn/Breukelen

Established as a town in 1657; as a city in 1834. Annexed City of Williamsburgh and Town of Bushwick in 1855, Town of New Lots in 1886, Towns of Flatbush, Gravesend, and New Utrecht in 1894, and Town of Flatlands in 1896. Consolidated into Greater New York City in 1898.

The original Town of Brooklyn, later City, encompassed all the brownstone neighborhoods once again becoming fashionable today, the **civic** and **financial nerve centers** of Brooklyn, and its **central business district.** Brooklyn Heights, Fort Greene-Clinton Hill, Park Slope, Bedford-Stuyvesant, Crown Heights, and what is now Cobble Hill and Boerum Hill are all within the boundaries of the original town; so is the Brooklyn Civic Center and "department store row" along Fulton Street. In addition, the teeming **waterfront facilities** from the Manhattan Bridge south to the deactivated Brooklyn Army Terminal lie within the area, as do the backup **residential communities** of Red Hook, Gowanus, and Sunset Park. And within the old boundaries are half of both Prospect Park and Green-Wood Cemetery, as well.

Although the extent of the old town can still be accurately charted, it is of little significance today as a locality when compared to the **individual communities** that comprise it. For many of the individual precincts to be described, we have included a short introduction outlining their characteristics.

BROOKLYN HEIGHTS/DOWNTOWN BROOKLYN

Colonized by well-to-do merchants and bankers from New York across the River, Brooklyn Heights as we know it today is the suburban product of a combined **land** and **"transit"** speculation (in this case the "transit" was the new **steam-powered ferry**). **Robert Fulton's** invention, with financial backing from **Hezekiah Pierrepont,**

first connected the two newly renamed **Fulton** Streets of New York (Manhattan) and Brooklyn by fast boats, giving occasion to Pierrepont and others **(Middagh, Hicks,** et al.) for profitable division and sale of their Heights "farm land." With the new ferry it was quicker and easier to go from **Fulton** to **Fulton** than to cross northward on Manhattan (beyond **Canal** Street). This status continued until the **New York and Harlem Railroad** was opened. A surveyors' grid marked the Heights into 25 by 100-foot lots as the system for parcel sales; although other subdivisions were made by speculators, the 25-foot dimension is today the basic module of the Heights.

That the oldest building still existing was built in 1820 (24 Middagh Street) is not surprising; **Pierrepont's** lots came on the market in 1819. Prior to this, as late as 1807, there had been but **seven** houses on the Heights, with perhaps 20 more at or near the ferry landing at the river's edge below. By **1890** the infill was substantially complete, and the architectural history of the Heights primarily spans those dates. Occasional buildings were built in random locations much later, but the principal pre-**1890** urban fabric remained intact when the district was designated an **Historic District** by the **City,** under its **Landmarks Preservation Law,** in 1966. Vacant lots on **Willow Place** afforded architects **Joseph and Mary Merz** the one chance, to date, to add buildings in serious modern architectural terms, but within the scale of the surrounding environment; four houses, Nos. **38, 40, 44** and **48 Willow Place** extend a previously truncated architectural history to the present moment.

North Heights Walking Tour: From Borough Hall to St. George Hotel. Borough Hall station of IRT Lexington and Seventh Avenue lines or Court Street station of BMT local.

[1a.]

[1a.] Borough Hall/formerly **Brooklyn City Hall,** 209 Joralemon Street at Fulton and Court Sts. 1846–1851. Gamaliel King. Cupola, 1898. C. W. & A. A. Houghton. ★

A **Greek Revival** palace, later crowned with a **Victorian** cupola, it presents a bold face to **Cadman Plaza,** made particularly monumental by the long, steep mass of steps to its entrance colonnade. First intended to be a lesser copy of New York's **City Hall** across the river, **Borough Hall** went through four designs. In the elapsed time, aesthetic moods changed, and the Federal world of 1812 (City Hall's completion date) became the **Greek Revival** world of 1830–1860. According to Brooklyn's City Directory, **King** was a grocer until **1830,** then a carpenter, not unusual in an era when **Thomas Jefferson** designed the **University of Virginia** and the capitol of the United States was the competition-winning design of a doctor, **William Thornton.**

[1b.] Municipal Building, SE cor. Court and Joralemon Sts. opposite Borough Hall. 1924. McKenzie, Voorhees, Gmelin and Walker. ☆

[2a.] Cadman Plaza (officially S. Parkes Cadman Plaza), bounded by Fulton, Court, Joralemon, and Adams Sts. and the Brooklyn Bridge approaches. 1950–1960. Designed by various City and Borough agencies; John Cashmore, Borough President.

Scarcely a plaza, this is an amorphous park created by demolition of several blocks east of **Brooklyn Heights.** A principal goal was the creation of a new setting for **Civic Center** buildings, to complement **Borough Hall.** Almost equally important fringe benefits were the elimination of the elevated (rapid transit) tracks that crossed the **Brooklyn Bridge** and crowded Fulton Street, and the easing of automobile traffic through street-widening.

[2b.] New York State Supreme Court, 360 Adams St. S part. Cadman Plaza opposite Montague St. 1957. Shreve, Lamb & Harmon.

The architects are best known for the **Empire State Building** (1933). Note the lamp standards at the south end, from the old **Hall of Records,** 1905, **by R. L. Daus.**

[2c.] Statue of Henry Ward Beecher, near Johnson St. S part Cadman Plaza. 1891. John Quincy Adams Ward, Sculptor; Richard Morris Hunt, Architect of the base.

[3a.]

[3a.] Brooklyn Central Post Office (U.S. Post Office), 271 Washington St. NE cor. Johnson St. at Cadman Plaza. 1885–1891. Mifflin E. Bell (first designs); William A. Freret, successor (successive supervising architects for the Treasury Dept.) North half, 1933. James Wetmore. ★

Exuberant granite **Romanesque Revival.** Deep reveals and strong modeling provide a rich play of light.

[3b.] Federal Building and Court House, 275 Washington St. NE cor. Tillary St. on Cadman Plaza. 1961. Carson, Lundin & Shaw.

The embassy to Brooklyn from Washington.

[4a.] Brooklyn War Memorial, Cadman Plaza, opposite Orange St. N portion. 1951. Eggers & Higgins; Charles Keck, Sculptor.

[5.] St. James' Pro Cathedral, Jay St. bet. Chapel St. and Cathedral Pl. E side. 1822.

Georgian, with a handsome verdigris copper-clad steeple.

"Pro" in this instance means "in place of," for the Bishop of Brooklyn (Roman Catholic) lacks a true cathedral of his own. **Cathedral** means, literally, that church which contains the *cathedra,* or chair, of the bishop. Each diocese can, therefore, have only one. Many tourists, particularly in France, are in the habit of elevating important-looking churches to cathedral status in their own minds; it bears no relation to size, merely to function.

[6a.] Institute of Design and Construction/formerly **Old Bridge Street Methodist Church,** 311 Bridge St. bet. Johnson St. and Myrtle Ave. E side. 1844. ☆

A Greek Revival temple in brick with wood columns and entablature; chaste, excepting the later Victorian stained glass, which is **exuberant** even from the outside.

[6b.] Gilbert School, 341 Bridge St. bet. Myrtle Ave. and Willoughby St. E side. ca. 1845.

Drastically altered Greek Revival.

[6c.] New York Telephone Co., Long Island Headquarters, 101 Willoughby St. NE cor. Bridge St. 1931. Voorhees, Gmelin & Walker.

Brick with a **graded** palette; a delicate aesthetic. Note the equally delicate grillages over the ground floor show windows.

[7a.] Engine Co. 207, Hook and Ladder Co. 110 N.Y.C. Fire Department/formerly **Brooklyn Fire Headquarters,** 365 Jay St. bet. Willoughby St. and Myrtle Ave. E side. 1892. Frank Freeman. ★

This is a building to **write home about.** A powerful **Romanesque Revival,** brick, granite, and tile structure, it is the New York branch (with Louis Sullivan's Condict Building) of the "Chicago School." **Freeman** learned much from afar, viewing **H. H. Richardson's** work, as did Sullivan.

[7b.] Transportation Building, 370 Jay St. NW cor. Willoughby St. 1948. William E. Haugaard & Andrew J. Thomas.

Headquarters of the **New York City Transit Authority.** The two gracious lobbies to the subway, at north and south ends, are pleasant fringe benefits gained from a building contiguous with subway lines (four). Windows here read as "skin" rather than punctured holes in masonry, by the device of detailing the glass to be flush. Nightly **money-trains** bring the till from all boroughs directly to a spur line in the building's bowels.

Gage & Tollner's (restaurant), 374 Fulton St. bet. Boerum Pl. and Smith St. TR 5-5181. ca. 1890.

Building and restaurant are much as they were the day they opened: plush, dark woodwork, mirrors and crystal glitter give a real, rather than **decorator's** version of the Nineties. The seafood is excellent, cooked to order.

[8a.] Abraham & Straus, 420 Fulton St. bet. Gallatin Pl. and Hoyt St. E side.

Eight assorted buildings are interconnected to form **the** great department store of Brooklyn. Its closest Manhattan counterpart is Bloomingdale's. The section at the northeast corner of Livingston Street and Gallatin Place (1895) has the only particular architectural interest: granite, brownstone, and Roman brick combined with superb Victorian craftsmanship.

[8b.] Martin's Department Store/formerly **Offerman Building,** Fulton St. bet. Bridge and Duffield Sts. N side. 1891. Lauritzen & Voss.

[8c.] RKO Albee, 1 DeKalb Ave. at Albee Square. ca. 1924.

The last of the Twenties' movie palaces in downtown **Brooklyn. Albee** was an impresario whose legacies to our present day include this extravagant theater and a foster son who is one of the leading avant-garde playwrights: **Edward Albee.**

[8d.] The Dime Savings Bank, 9 DeKalb Ave. at Albee Square. N side. 1907, 1932. Halsey, McCormick & Helmer. ☆

A movie version of **Rome,** appropriately next to a great movie palace. Money must be well-managed by those who could afford such splendor.

[9a.] Central Court Building, 120 Schermerhorn St. SW cor. Smith St. 1930. Collins & Collins.

[9b.] Brooklyn House of Detention (for men), 275 Atlantic Ave. bet. Smith St. and Boerum Pl. N side. 1955. LaPierre, Litchfield and Partners.

Cheerfully described as the "Brooklyn Hilton."

[10a.] Brooklyn Friends Meeting House and School, 110 Schermerhorn St. SE cor. Boerum Pl. ca. 1854. Enoch Straton, Builder.

[10b.] Board of Education, 110 Livingston St. SE cor. Boerum Pl. 1926. McKim, Mead & White.

[10c.] Society For The Prevention of Cruelty To Children, 67 Schermerhorn St. bet. Court and Smith Sts. N side. ca. 1890.

Sam's (hardware store), 117 Court St. NE cor. Schermerhorn St.

There is no screw, nut, saw, tool, paint, plastic, device or thingamajig that Sam's does not have. Spilling richly onto the Court Street sidewalk, it is a **museum** of American hardware and gadgetries.

[11a.] Packer Collegiate Institute, 170 Joralemon St. bet. Court and Clinton Sts. S side. 1854. Minard Lafever. Addition (Katherine Sloan Pratt House), 1957.

A brick and brownstone Victorian "Gothic" castle. Collegiate only in the sense that it prepares students for college, not a college itself.

[11b.] St. Ann's Church (Protestant Episcopal), Clinton St. NE cor. Livingston St. 1869. James Renwick, Jr.

Brown- and lime-stone of different colors and textures make an exuberant and unrestrained extravaganza. **Renwick** produced more academically correct Gothic Revival churches at **Grace** and **St. Patrick's** (**1846** and **1858–1877,** respectively). Perhaps by the time of St. Ann's his self-confidence had mushroomed. The copybooks of the **Pugins,** used at **Grace,** were discarded in favor of the current events of the architectural scene, particularly the "new" museum at Oxford, by **Deane & Woodward,** designed and built with the eager assistance of **John Ruskin,** hence "Ruskinian Gothic."

[12a.] Title Guarantee Company, 186 Remsen St. bet. Court and Clinton Sts. ca. 1890.

[12b.] Brooklyn Club/formerly **James H. Post Residence,** 131 Remsen St. bet. Clinton and Henry Sts. N side. ca. 1858.

The paired Corinthian columns and pilasters are strong and elegant.

[12c.] Brooklyn Bar Association/formerly **Charles Condon Residence,** 123 Remsen St. bet. Clinton and Henry Sts. N side. ca. 1875.

Relatively jazzy chromatics of limestone and brick make this an exuberant note on Remsen Street.

[12d.] Our Lady of Lebanon Roman Catholic Church (Maronite Rite)/formerly **Congregational Church of the Pilgrims,** NE cor. Remsen and Henry Sts. 1846. Richard Upjohn.

Certainly **Upjohn** was avant-garde for his time. This is a bold massing of ashlar stonework, a solid, carven image. The spire was removed due to deterioration and the cost of its replacement. The doors at both the west and south portals are salvage from the ill-fated liner, *Normandie,* that burned and sank at its Hudson River berth in 1942.

[12e.] 87 Remsen Street, bet. Henry and Hicks Sts. N side. ca. 1895.

[13.] 82 Remsen Street/formerly **William Saterlee Packer House,** bet. Henry and Hicks Sts. S side. 1843.

Spartan, painted gray and white exterior with a curious "Gothicized" doorway.

[12e.]  [1

[14.] Hotel Bossert, 98 Montague St. SE cor. Hicks St. 1909–1912. Helmle and Huberty.

This "modern" hotel was, only **40** years ago, one of the fashionable centers of Brooklyn social life: the **Marine Roof** (decorated like a yacht) for dining and dancing offered an unequaled view of the Manhattan skyline and harbor. The home of its founder, Louis Bossert, a millwork manufacturer, still stands. [See N Brooklyn, Bushwick-Ridgewood 8c.]

[15.] 1–13 Montague Terrace, bet. Remsen and Montague Sts. ca. 1886.

A complete "terrace" (in the English sense of "set" of row houses) in almost perfect condition.

[16.] The Esplanade, W of Columbia Hts., Montague Terrace and Pierrepont Pl. 1950–1951. Andrews & Clark, Engineers; Clarke & Rapuano, Landscape Architects.

The **Esplanade** is a fringe benefit from the construction of this section of the Brooklyn-Queens Expressway, earlier proposed by Robert Moses to bisect the Heights. Fred Tuemmler of the City

Planning Commission created one of the few brilliant solutions for the relationship of automobile, pedestrian, and city. A cantilevered esplanade was extended out from the level of the **Heights** to overlook the harbor on a fourth level over two levels of traffic and the feeder road for piers below: Furman Street. It is simple and successful: mostly hexagonal asphalt paving block, painted steel railings, hardy shrubbery and mimosa trees.

[17.] 2 and 3 Pierrepont Place/originally **Alexander M. White and Abiel Abbot Low Houses,** bet. Pierrepont and Montague Sts. W side. 1857. Richard Upjohn.

The most elegant brownstones left in New York. Two of an original row of three, all by **Upjohn:** No. 1, the **Henry E. Pierrepont** House, was demolished in **1946** in favor of a playground at the time of the esplanade-expressway construction.

Seth Low, father of **Abiel,** was a New Englander who made a "killing" in the China trade. Seth Low, **son** of Abiel, was president of Columbia College **(Low Library),** mayor of Brooklyn, then mayor of consolidated New York.

[)c.] [21b.]

[18a.] 6 Pierrepont Street, ca. 1890.

Romanesque Revival with strong, rock-faced stair, elaborate foliate carved reliefs, and a bay window (overlooking the bay!).

[18b.] 8–14 Pierrepont Street.

Another "terrace" where the whole is greater than the sum of its parts.

[18c.] 35 Pierrepont Street.

The roofscape and silhouette have every stop pulled out. A pleasantly synthetic "renaissance" bag of tricks.

[18d.] 36 Pierrepont Street/originally **George Hastings House.** ca. 1844.

[18e.] 43 Pierrepont Street. ca. 1865.

[19a.] Hotel Pierrepont, 55 Pierrepont St. 1928. Herman I. Feldman.

From the days when even speculative hotels had lion finials and griffin gargoyles!

[19b.] The Woodhull, 62 Pierrepont St. 1911.

The grundy ground floor belies the extravagant Edwardian French architecture above: neither Edward's England nor his contemporary France had this. A local Heights entrepreneur filled in the sad gap!

[19c.] Franciscan House of Studies/formerly **Palm Hotel**/originally **Herman Behr House,** Pierrepont St. SW cor. Hicks St. 1890. Frank Freeman. Addition, 1919.

Behr's house now serves as a residence for many of the students (brothers) of **St. Francis College.** After Behr, it was, with a six-story addition to the south, the **Hotel Palm,** which in its declining years was credited by legend to have housed the local **Polly Adler.**

[20a.] 161 Henry Street, NE cor. Pierrepont St. 1905.

Compare to **62 Pierrepont.** In the last 30 years, has the external architecture of an apartment building meant anything to an apartment dweller? This strong character shows that it used to, giving identity to its residents as does Manhattan's **Dakota.**

[20b.] 104 Pierrepont Street. ca. 1857.

A brownstone row-mansion. Note the ornate console brackets and verdigris bronze "stoop" railing.

[20c.] 106 Pierrepont Street. ca. 1890.

Here style definitions break down. This beautifully maintained, well-crafted house has many sorts of detail, in quantity. The oak, iron, and bronze entrance doors and intricate stained glass are of particular note.

[20d.] 108 Pierrepont Street/formerly **Campbell House**/originally **P. C. Cornell House.** 1840.

Harried remnants of a great **Greek Revival** double house; the only actual original part is the anthemion-ornamented pediment over the front door. Once two stories and basement, it was made three when No. 114, its adjacent twin, was converted from mirror-image into a Romanesque Revival town castle. The cornice is, therefore, late Victorian, and the false shutters and crass entrance light fixtures strictly **schmaltz.**

[20e.] The Brooklyn Women's Club/formerly **George Cornell House.** 114 Pierrepont St. 1840.

Originally the mirror image of 108: altered (drastically would be a mild adjective here) in 1887 for **Alfred C. Barnes.**

A tower for **Rapunzel** is available here. Note the single granite column, Romanesque-capped, supporting the "bay."

Monroe Place: a 700-foot-long (70-foot-wide) space, a quiet backwater on axis of the famous Cornell houses (108 and 114 Pierrepont Street) described above. The proportion of the street and its blocking at both ends are far more important than the buildings it contains, for this, as at **Sidney, Garden** and **Willow Places,** is a product of the staggered grid that fortuitously made this area so much richer than most of grid-planned Manhattan or Brooklyn.

[20f.] Appellate Division, New York State Supreme Court, Monroe Pl. NW cor. Pierrepont St. 1938. Slee & Bryson.

A prim and proper **Classic Revival** monument of the Thirties. Not an ugly building, but a boring one.

[20g.] First Unitarian Church/properly **Church of the Saviour,** NE cor. Pierrepont St. and Monroe Pl. 1844. Minard Lafever.

[20h.] Long Island Historical Society, 128 Pierrepont St. SW cor. Clinton St. 1878. George B. Post.

Post used a bright but narrow range of "Italian reds" in a time when earth colors were popular, from the polychromy of Ruskin—see St. Ann's Church—to the near monochromy of Richardsonian Romanesque, such as the Jay Street Fire House.

High-pitched slate roofs are visible only from abnormal points of view such as cater-corner across the temporary parking lot, from **Cadman Plaza.** However, the tower over the entrance stair, hall and elevator, bears a very visible slate-sheathed pyramid. The monochromatic palette tempers an exuberant range of detail: pilasters, arches, medallions, cornices, sculpture. At the entrance,

Viking and Indian flank the doors over Corinthian pilasters.

[20i.] St. Ann's Building and Episcopal School/formerly **Crescent Athletic Club,** 129 Pierrepont St. NW cor. Clinton St. 1906. Frank Freeman.

Montague Street: In Civil War days and later, this was the road to the Wall Street ferry, dipping down (until 1946, the time of the Esplanade) to a water edge terminal, where Pier 4 is now located. A stone bridge (1855, Minard Lafever) just west of Pierrepont Place carried the line of the Heights over cable cars and carriages descending the street.

[21a.] Brooklyn Savings Bank, 205–215 Montague St. 1962. Carson, Lundin & Shaw.

[21b.] Chase Manhattan Bank, 185 Montague St. 1929. Corbett, Harrison & MacMurray.

Original brick and limestone Cubistic massing and decoration gave this an **avant-garde** expression in its time.

[21c.] First National City Bank/formerly **People's Trust Company,** 183 Montague St. 1903. Mowbray & Uffinger. Pierrepont Street addition, 1929. Shreve, Lamb & Harmon.

This is a **D. W. Griffith's** version of a Roman temple. The bank, unfortunately, is neither staffed nor patronized by bacchanalian revelers, so that the total effect is a little wistful, like last year's disused movie set. In marble, not just wire-lath and plaster, it states: "more is better." The sculpture in the pediment is **"Pop,"** particularly when overlaid with anti-pigeon spikes.

[21d.] Manufacturer's Hanover Trust Company/formerly **Brooklyn Trust Company,** 177 Montague St. 1915. York & Sawyer.

The bottom is an Italian palace; the top, some Englishmen's version of an Italian palace: Corinthian engaged columns rest on rusticated tooled limestone.

[22a.] Franklin Trust Company, 164 Montague St. SW cor. Clinton St. 1888. George L. Morse.

A granite, rock-faced base sunk within a **moat** bears limestone arches and, in turn, brick and terra cotta piers, columns and arches; capped with a dormered red tile roof.

[22b.] Holy Trinity Protestant Episcopal Church, 157 Montague St. NW cor. Clinton St. 1847. Minard Lafever.

Brownstone, unfortunately, weathers poorly. The interior is cast and painted terra cotta, rather than carved stone. Reredos by **Frank Freeman.** A bust of **John Howard Melish,** by **William Zorach,** is bracketed from the north side of the entrance vestibule.

Meunier's, 140 Montague St. (up the outside stair).

The **Bonniers** of Brooklyn. High style and quality in glassware, china, toys, and household objects. The innocent can here trust to the **Meuniers'** judgment, and the knowledgeable can find that well-designed, well-made "whatever it is." Unusual items include paper (cut-out and paste-together) architectural models.

[22b.]

[21

[23a.] The Berkeley-The Grosvenor, 111–115 Montague St. 1885.

Twin "Queen Anne" brownstone, terra cotta, and brick apartment houses. Look **up!**

[24.] The Heights Casino, 75 Montague St. bet. Hicks St. and Montague Terrace. 1905. W. A. Boring, Jr.

Its founders described this indoor squash and tennis club as a "country club in the city." Handsome brickwork.

[25a.] 132–138 Henry Street. ca. 1843.

A row of four brick **Greek Revivals.** The volute railings are stylish.

[25b.] 137–143 Henry Street. ca. 1828.

Doric-columned porches. These were all **wood** [See 24 Middagh and 135 Joralemon]; No. 141's clapboard is painted, as all should still be.

[25c.] First Presbyterian Church, 124 Henry St. 1846. W. B. Olmsted. Memorial doorway, 1921. James Gamble Rogers.

A solid and stolid rock-faced brownstone, free standing and set back within a row of town houses. It looks bourgeois, compared to Lafever's **Church of the Saviour,** or **Trinity,** but it isn't: it houses the Heights Montessori School. Single-slab brownstone crenellations; bronze lanterns.

[26.] St. George Hotel, 57 Clark St. bet. Henry, Hicks, Clark, and

Pineapple Sts. 1899–1929.

Surprisingly, the largest hotel in New York, with a veritable ocean for a swimming pool **(Hippolyte Kamenka, Architect).** In it, while floating on your back at sea, you can navigate by watching your own and your neighbors' reflections in the mirrored ceiling (a little fogged at this writing).

The Cadman Plaza (urban renewal area)

[27a.] Whitman Close, Pineapple to Middagh Sts., Henry to Fulton Sts. 1967 (in construction). Morris Lapidus.

The "upper-middle"-income section of the renewal area. Row houses give a change of pace between the **35**-story tower and its complementary **25**-story middle–middle–income slab to the north.

[27b.] Cadman Plaza North, Middagh, Henry and Fulton Sts. 1967. Morris Lapidus.

Both projects attempt to match the scale of Brooklyn Heights by means of token row houses in one case **(Whitman Close),** and a grilled garage matching the heights, if not scale, of nearby buildings, in the other **(Cadman Plaza North).** However, the street as an urban space (rather than a **surface** on which **autos** navigate) has no definition, a principal essence of the Heights. One might as well put a Greek Revival townhouse from Sidney Place on an acre in Scarsdale.

[30.]

[28.] Cranlyn Apartments, 80 Cranberry St. SW cor. Henry St. 1931.

[29.] Cadman Plaza Artists' Housing/formerly **Mason Au & Magenheimer Candy Co.,** 22 Henry St. NW cor. Middagh St. 1885. Theobald Engelhardt. Scheduled renovation, 1968. Lee Harris Pomeroy.

[30.] Brooklyn Children's Aid Society, 57 Poplar St. bet. Henry and Hicks Sts. 1883.

This was a home for **indigent newsboys,** abandoned because of the urban renewal designation that included all blocks facing Cadman Plaza, from Montague Street to the Expressway. Brick and limestone arches form a Ruskinian "polychromy."

[31.] 48 Columbia Heights, bet. Middagh and Vine Sts. 1865.

[32.] 56 Middagh Street, bet. Hicks and Henry Sts. 1829. Porch added ca. 1845.

Bold, Doric columns give it a great deal of **guts** and style.

[33a.] Middagh Street, bet. Hicks and Willow Sts. ca. 1817.

One of the earliest streets in the Heights, it has most of the remaining wood houses. Aside from the glorious No. **24,** they are now a motley lot: No. **28: 1829,** mutilated beyond recognition; No. **30: 1824,** Greek Revival entrance and pitched roof still recognizable, in spite of the tawdry asphalt shingles; No. **25: 1824,** mutilated; No. **27: 1829,** Italianate brownstone in wood shingles with painted trim; No. **29:** similar to **27;** Nos. **31** and **33: 1847,** mutilated.

[33b.] 24 Middagh Street /formerly **Eugene Boisselet House,** SE cor. Willow St. 1824.

The **Queen** of **Brooklyn Heights** houses (Nos. 2 & 3 Pierrepont Place are the twin-kings). Wood-painted, gambrel-roofed **Federal** house with a garden cottage connected by a garden wall. Special notes are the exquisitely carved Federal doorway and quarter-round attic windows. Throughout, proportion, rhythm, materials, and color are in concert.

[33b.]

[34.] 20–26 Willow Street, SW cor. Middagh St. 1846.

No-nonsense Greek Revival, painted brick and brownstone "terrace." Straightforward, austere, yet elegant. Two-story porches at the rear view the harbor, flanked by visually containing bearing-walls. (No. 22 was the **Henry Ward Beecher** house.)

[35a.] 11 Cranberry Street /formerly **Mott Bedell House.** ca. 1840.

Brownstone and Flemish-bond brick Greek Revival.

[35b.] 13, 15, and 19 Cranberry Street. ca. 1829-1834.

An original matching row (note window lintels and arched entries of 13 and 19), all altered. Above a basement apartment, No. 19 is occupied as a single-family dwelling. Note the handsome modern fence on Willow Street, with a sliding gate.

[36.] Church of the Assumption (Roman Catholic), Cranberry St. bet. Hicks and Henry Sts. 1908. Beatty & Berlenbach.

The facade is cut-rate late Italian Renaissance, in glazed brick and terra cotta. **Alberti** might shudder, but he is indirectly responsible for it.

[37a.] Plymouth Church of the Pilgrims, Orange St. bet. Hicks and Henry Sts. 1849. J. C. Wells. Church house and connecting arcade, 75 Hicks St. 1913. Woodruff Leeming.

Henry Ward Beecher was here from 1847 to 1887. Excepting the porch, it is an austere box of a barn in brick, articulated by relieving arches. The **Tuscan** porch was added long after Beecher left. The Church house is "Eclectic" Classic Revival. Its principal virtue is the enclosure, together with the connecting arcade to the church, of a handsome garden court. Here, **Henry Ward Beecher,** as seen through the eyes and hands of **Gutzon Borglum,** sculptor, holds forth (perhaps holds court). Unfortunately, in this era of vandalism, the churchyard, which could be a pleasant place of repose, is locked.

[37b.] 69 Orange Street, bet. Hicks and Henry Sts. ca. 1829.

[38a.] 47–47A Willow Street. ca. 1860.

When you're greedy, divide your property into its smallest saleable components. Here, the less-than-12-foot internal dimensions are brilliantly arranged in spite of that greed!

[38b.] 57 Willow Street/formerly **Robert White House,** NE cor. Orange St. ca. 1824.

The **Orange Street wall** is a lusty composition of chimneys, pitched roofs, real and blind windows.

[39.] 70 Willow Street/formerly **Adrian van Sinderen House,** bet. Orange and Pineapple Sts. ca. 1839.

A wide **Greek Revival** house, originally free standing, now cheek-by-jowl with **Jehovah's Witnesses** to the north. Former owners filled the southern gap with a stair (ca. 1933).

[37a.]

[40.] Hotel Margaret, 97 Columbia Hts. NE cor. Orange St. 1889. Frank Freeman.

Brooklyn here **foresaw** metal and glass construction of post-World War II. The ornate sheet metal panels have a nautical look with their exposed rivet heads: appropriate for its harbor-watching tenants.

[41.] Jehovah's Witnesses of Brooklyn Heights, 107 Columbia Hts. SE cor. Orange St. 1960. Frederick G. Frost, Jr. & Associates.

Local residence for those who proselytise their faith. Heights citizens fear that too much Heights land and architecture will be gobbled up for the Witnesses' **expansion** as success in gaining adherents breeds need for even greater plant, personnel, and activities.

[42.] 13 Pineapple Street, bet. Columbia Hts. and Willow Sts. ca. 1830.

[43.] Towers Hotel, 25 Clark St. NE cor. Willow St. 1928. Starrett & Van Vleck.

Comfortably affluent materials: brick on random ashlar on granite. The four corner towers are a **Brooklyn landmark,** illuminated after sundown.

[44.] 131–133 Hicks Street bet. Clark and Pierrepont St. ca. 1848.

Tudor-arched brownstones, with cast-iron Gothic stair rails.

Willow Street, Clark to Pierrepont Streets.

[45a.] 102 Willow Street/Dansk Somandskirke.

[45b.] 104 Willow Street. ca. 1829.

[45c.] 109 Willow Street. 1905.

People who embrace archeology frequently miss the point. This **neo**-Federal house is gross, with fat columns, ill-proportioned windows, crudely cut lintels, and thick joints between brickwork.

[45d.] 108–112 Willow Street. ca. 1880.

The "shingle style" in **Brooklyn.** Picturesque massing and profiles produce odd internal spaces and balconies, for our contemporary fun. Terra cotta reliefs, elaborate doorways, bay windows, towers, dormers. The English architect **Richard Norman Shaw** was group leader for these fantasies: in his bailiwick he produced what the English called "Queen Anne."

[40.]

[45f.]

[45e.] 118–122 Willow Street. Remodeled. ca. 1850.

[45f.] 155–159 Willow Street. ca. 1829.

Three charmers (in a league with 24 Middagh) in excellent condition and not far from their original state. A tunnel leads from No. **159** (note flush glass lights set in pavement at 157) to the "stable" at No. **151** (post-Civil War). The skew line of their joint facades dates from an earlier geometry than Willow's present line,

BROOKLYN HTS. CIVIC CENTER

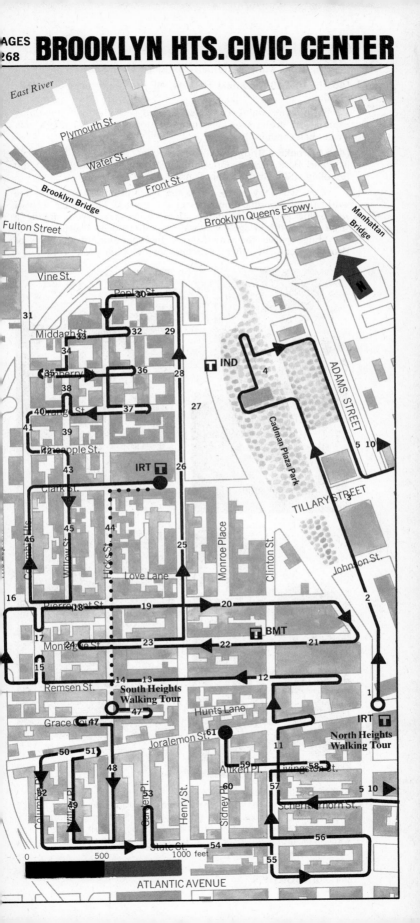

aligning them with the formerly extended **Love Lane.**

[46a.] 210–220 Columbia Heights, NE cor. Pierrepont St. 1852–1860.

Two pairs and two singles, altered, but the best remaining example of group-mansions in brownstone. Note No. **210's** rich Corinthian capitals.

[46b.] Brooklyn Bridge, across East River, bet. Adams St., Brooklyn, and Park Row, Manhattan. 1883. John A. and Washington Roebling. [See Bridges and Tunnels.] ☆

Considered by many to be the most beautiful bridge in the world despite Gothic flourishes in the towers. The spider web of supporting and bracing cables richly enmeshes anyone taking a stroll across the bridge's walkway—recommended. The opening of the bridge paved the way for the incorporation of the City of Brooklyn (and the other boroughs) into Greater New York.

[36.]

[45a.]
[45b.]

End of North Heights tour.

This is a convenient point to break the tour into two segments: if tired, you may regain the subway at the St. George Hotel (IRT Seventh Avenue line), two blocks away along Clark Street; if not, walk back along the Esplanade to Remsen Street, left on Remsen, right on Hicks, to Grace Court.

South Heights Walking Tour: From Grace Court Alley circuitously to Joralemon Street.

[47a.] Grace Court.

Its charm is largely derived from the juxtaposition of Grace Church and the double garden lots of Remsen Street's houses that back up to it. The back of **46** Remsen Street is graced with an imported Romanesque chapel, a rich, multi- and curved-faceted bay window. Check your watch against the bronze sundial above.

[47b.] Grace Court Alley.

A real mews (for Remsen Street mansions). No. 14's arched bearing wall of tooled brownstone ashlar is bold, almost industrial. No. **12** has rock-face granite (man-tooled) base, lintels, sills and spandrel course, in a plain brick face. Nos. **2** and **4**, brick with brownstone quoins.

[52.]

[47c.] Grace Church, SW cor. Grace Court and Hicks St. 1847. Richard Upjohn. Parish House to the west, 1931.

Upjohn, after a radical year completing the **Church of the Pilgrims** (Our Lady of Lebanon) went "straight," back to a more academic brownstone Gothic. A recent bit of urban charm is the entrance court, off Hicks at the south side, leading to the parish house; a backwater for pedestrians, crowned by the umbrella of a glorious elm some 80 feet tall. **Benches** are available.

[48a.] 263 Hicks Street. Altered ca. 1890.

Rock-faced brownstone "Romanesque" stoop and fourth floor gabled roof.

[48b.] 262–270 Hicks Street.

A shingle-style terrace, designed as a group composition. The corbelled brickwork, shingles, and picturesque profiles are romantic, and promised "identity" for the separate occupants. Each is different from its neighbor but part of the overall architectural composition.

[48c.] Engine Co. 224, N.Y.C. Fire Dept., 274 Hicks St. 1903. Adams & Warren.

A house for fire engines, in scale with its house neighbors. A Renaissance Revival building, cum dormers.

[48d.] 276–284 Hicks Street.

Five brick arches once swallowed carriages (two round, three elliptical). Note the sculptured woman's head on the dormer of No. **276.**

[48e.] St. Charles Orthopaedic Clinic, 281 Hicks St. Altered 1921.

A nonindustrial use of the spiral stair: a handsome, elegant cast-iron form that enriches the street.

[49a.] 43–49 Willow Place. ca. 1846.

This now-bedraggled Greek Revival colonnade comes from a day when colonnades denoted "class."

[49b.] 38, 40, 44, 48 Willow Place (three separated buildings, one a double house). 1966. Joseph & Mary Merz.

These three buildings have given new life to **Willow Place** in terms of 1966 needs, materials, and techniques, but with great respect for the nature and scale of the Heights. Garages occupy ground-floor space, and cement block (in a special 8 by 8-inch size), here used sensitively and handsomely, assumes a dignity most thoughtless users miss by a mile.

[49c.] 2–8 Willow Place. ca. 1847.

[50.] 29–75 Joralemon Street, bet. Hicks and Furman Sts. N side. 1844–1848.

Twenty-four houses step down Joralemon's hill. Basically Greek Revival, several have been altered. The stepping of the row gives a pleasant rhythm to the group, each pair roughly 30 inches up (or down) from its paired neighbors.

[49a.]

[51.] 58 Joralemon Street, bet. Hicks and Willow Sts. S side. ca. 1847.

The world's **only** Greek Revival subway ventilator.

[52.] Riverside Houses, 4–30 Columbia Pl. SW cor. Joralemon St. 1890. William Field & Son.

On the river's side they stood, until truncated by the **Brooklyn-Queens Expressway** construction. The original surrounded a central garden, part of which is still contained by the remaining units and the wall of the expressway.

Alfred T. White was a prominent, and paternalistic, Brooklyn citizen, whose motto "philanthropy plus 5%" made these, along with Tower and Home Houses [see WC Brooklyn 4], the original limited-profit housing: enlightened self-interest in the long term.

[53.] Garden Place, bet. Joralemon and State Sts.

A handsome urban space, one block long, contained on four sides. Note the terra cotta, brick, and limestone Queen Anne (No. 26), the Hansel and Gretel carriage house (No. 21), and the intruders from Queens ("tapestry brick" is the real estate man's highest accolade to these: Nos. 17, 19, 19A). No. 54 has been faced with artificial stone (colored stucco) of the **most** obnoxious kind.

[54.] 103-107 State Street, NW cor. Sidney Pl. ca. 1848.

A trio, but only **107** still has the elegant cast-iron balcony that allows French doors to the living room floor with visual security.

[55.] 175 Clinton Street, bet. State St. and Atlantic Ave. E side. ca. 1840. Remodeled.

Revival of Revival, embellished with all sorts of added attractions: a Mansard roof, bowed bay window, Ionic colonnettes, Renaissance Revival cornice. It has the unreal air of a movie set.

Atlantic Avenue

A fashionable shopping street before the Civil War; its character was later maintained by placing the **Brooklyn-Jamaica railroad** in a tunnel for its last mile of trackage to the **"South Ferry."** It clearly marks **Brooklyn Heights'** south border, separating it from **Cobble Hill** and is now the social and shopping center of the local **Near Eastern** (Lebanese and Syrian) community, with exotic shops for both food and "gifts," mostly in the block on the north side between Clinton and Court Streets. [**Alwan** (food), **183**; **George Malko** (food), **185**; **Sahadi** (food), **187**; **Sahadi** (gifts), **199**; **Rashid** (Arabic records), **191**; **Malko Importing** (food), **197**; **Malko Importing** (gifts), **199**;] Baklawah, halvah, dried fruits, nuts, pastries, dates, dried beans, copper and brasswork, goatskin drums, inlaid chests.

  [63.]

[56.] 168–170 State Street, bet. Clinton and Court Sts. ca. 1890.

The huge, leaf-decorated cornices of these elegant tenements loom over the street.

Clinton Street, bet. State and Joralemon Streets.

[57a.] 138–40 Clinton Street. ca. 1855.

Lintels and cornice lush with volutes and garlands, in cast iron. The detail and profiles survived well in comparison to those carved in brownstone.

[57b.] 133–139 Clinton Street. ca. 1851.

Gas lamps, constantly lit, add a "ye olde" air, but with great taste.

[58.] 57 Livingston Street bet. Clinton and Court Sts. N side. ca. 1848.

A lusty **Greek Revival** house in the garden of **Packer Collegiate Institute.**

[59.] St. Charles Borromeo Church (Roman Catholic), Sidney Pl. NE cor. Aitken Pl. 1869.

A simplified brick Gothic revival in maroon-painted brick. The plain interior is decorated with wood "carpenter-Gothic" arches and trim.

[60a.] Sidney Place, bet. State and Joralemon Sts.

A wider, more varied, more "charming" version of **Garden Place.** Its architecture ranges more widely, including all that Garden Place offers, but adds a church, **St. Charles Borromeo,** and such specialties as a seven-story Greek Revival girls' residence. The front gardens on the east side between State and Aitken are unusual [See 155-159 Willow Street.] Nos. **31** through **49** form a variably altered Greek Revival row **(1846–1851).**

[60b.] 18 Sidney Place, opposite Aitken Pl. W side. ca. 1838.

Bold Doric columns and entablature signalled an "important" mansion (originally three stories and basement); three more floors were added for its life as a **girls' residence.** The result is startling at first glance, for it looks no more than a neat, seven-story Greek Revival house.

[61a.] 135 Joralemon Street, opposite Sidney Pl. E side. ca. 1833.

Opposite-hand plan from **24 Middagh.** Their similarities are concealed by the post-Civil War porch with cast ironwork, and the fact that this house is contained between two large buildings.

End of Tour: To reach subways (IRT and BMT), walk east on Joralemon Street to Borough Hall.

MISCELLANY

[62.] Fulton Street, NW cor. Front St. ca. 1890.

Pressed metal (sheet steel) was once a distinguished, inexpensive, and modern material. New industrial processes made it possible, in the mid-19th Century, to construct elaborate but economical cornices, interior ceilings, and parts of building facades. Here, not part, but all the facade is pressed, achieving a warmed-over but delightful **Renaissance** effect with, surprisingly, "Romanesque" windows on the second floor. Tap it—it's hollow!

 [63.] Eagle Warehouse, 28 Fulton St. opposite Front St. S side. 1870. Additions, 1910. Frank Freeman.

The brick arch bears elegant bronze lettering, and is screened by a bronze gate. The machicollations (a word every cocktail party one-upsman should know) are equalled only in a few remaining brick armories.

[64.] Water Street warehouses, Water St. bet. New Dock and Main St. N side. ca. 1890.

Naked brickwork conjures great power. These arched bearing walls are in the functional tradition of Victorian architecture, seeking direct and economical ways of handling quantities of space— here, for warehousing.

FORT GREENE/CLINTON HILL

"To the rear of the boisterous city hall quarter was Brooklyn's other fine residential district, **the Hill.** Located in the center of the city and surrounded by diverse elements, its position was not unlike that of **the Heights;** but its elegant residences were fewer in number and their owners slightly further removed from the traditions of genteel respectability. It abounded in churches and middle class houses, the majority of whose owners worked in **New York,** but took pride in living in **Brooklyn." Harold C. Syrett, The City of Brooklyn, 1865–1898.**

These precincts rank with **Cobble Hill** and **Park Slope** as unsung areas of urban delight. Clustering around **Fort Greene Park** and the **Pratt Institute Campus** are blocks of handsome brownstones, occasional mansions and a surprisingly rich inventory of churches and other institutions. Its edges at Flatbush Avenue and along the old **Navy Yard** are roughened by cheap commercial areas, but the body is solid and handsome in large part. From a vantage point at the foot of the **Martyr's Monument** in **Fort Greene Park,** a prospect of the neighborhood and harbor suggests that perhaps this, rather than **Prospect Park,** should have been so named.

Walking Tour: From Washington Avenue station of Myrtle Avenue Elevated to vicinity of Atlantic Avenue Terminal, L.I.R.R. (BMT and IRT Subways converge here). An unusual and pleasant introduction to these neighborhoods is by the Myrtle Avenue "el". Sailing over the low buildings of Fort Greene, you feel the varying quality of old brownstone street, new housing project, park, and mansion. Alight at Washington Avenue.

[1.] Willoughby Walk Apartments, Hall St. to Emerson Pl., Myrtle Ave. to Willoughby Ave. 1957. S. J. Kessler.

[2.] St. Mary's Episcopal Church, 230 Classon Ave. NW cor. Willoughby Ave. ca. 1920.

Very comfortable English country chapel. It looks peaceful.

[3a.] Pratt Row, 220–234 Willoughby Ave. 171–185 Steuben St., 172–186 Emerson Pl. 1910.

[3b.] Pratt Institute Campus, Willoughby Ave. to DeKalb Ave., Classon Ave. to Hall St. 1887 to the present. Various architects.

Originally five blocks; renewal gave the opportunity to make a single, campus-style superblock. The separate buildings were built to conform to a geometry of streets that no longer exists. The in-between buildings were removed in favor of grass and parking lots, giving a **surrealist** result: street architecture with both streets and most of the adjacent facades removed.

.] [6.]

[3c.] Library/formerly **Pratt Institute Free Library, Pratt Institute,** Hall St. bet. Willoughby and DeKalb Aves., E. side. 1896. William B. Tubby. Alterations, John Mead Howells.

Tubby's stubby: strongly articulated brick piers give a bold face to Hall Street. A free Romanesque Revival, but with a classical plan. Originally Brooklyn's first **Free** Public Library, it was restricted to Pratt Students in 1940.

[3d.] Main Building, Pratt Institute, near Willoughby Ave. on the old bed of Ryerson St. 1887. William Wingren.

Pratt is a professional school of art, graphics, architecture, engineering, home economics, and library science. Old **Charles Pratt** ran it as his personal paternalistic fiefdom until his death in **1891.**

A **gung-ho** Romanesque Revival; its innards have been tortured

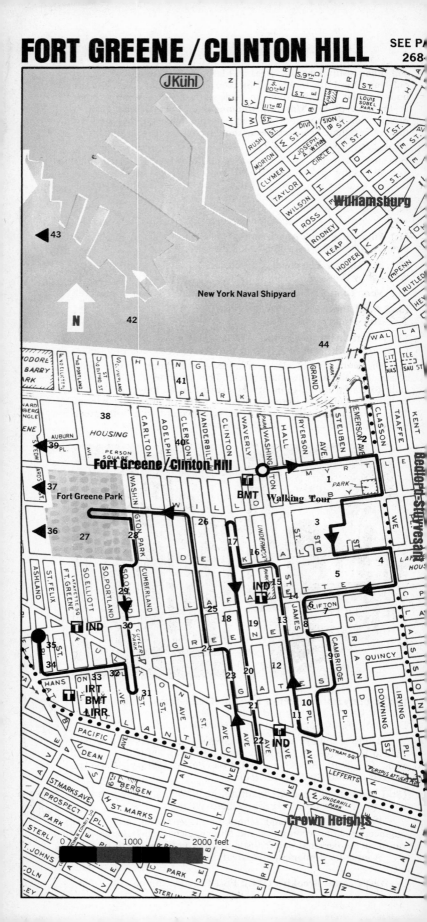

FORT GREENE / CLINTON HILL

JKühl

Williamsburg

S. 9TH ST.
S. 10TH ST.
LOUIS SOBEL PARK
DIVISION ST.
RUSH
MORTON
CLYMER
TAYLOR
WILSON
ROSS
RODNEY
KEAP
HOOPER
JOSEPH A WYM CIRCLE
WAL LA
LITTLE NAS SAU ST.
PENN
RUTLEDGE
HEY

New York Naval Shipyard

▶43

⬆
N
42

44

THEODORE BARRY PARK
EVOLLIOTT PL.
NO PORTLAND
S. OAKLAND ST.
S. PORTLAND
HING PARK
41
GRAND

WARD BERG ANGLE
GREENE S EDW
39
AUBURN PL.
38 HOUSING
PERSON SQUARE
CARLTON
ADELPHI
CLERMONT
40
VANDERBILT
CLINTON
WAVERLY
WASHINGTON
PARK
HALL
RYERSON
STEUBEN AVE
EMERSON AVE
CLASSON
TAAFFE
KENT
2

Bedford-Stuyvesant

Fort Greene / Clinton Hill

🅣
BMT
Walking Tour

1 PARK

3

37 ▶
Fort Greene Park
36 ▶
27
28
26
WASHINGTON PARK
WILL
DE
17
16
UNDERWOOD
15
K ST.
B ST.
T ST.
4
5
LAF HOUS
CP

ASHLAND
ST. FELIX
SO ELLIOTT
LAFAYETTE FT. GREENE
SO PORTLAND
SO OXFORD
29
30
CUMBERLAND
CARLTON
25
18
F
19
PARK AVE
14
JAMES
13
CLIFTON 6
7
G
8
CAMBRIDGE
9
QUINCY
IRVING
DOWNING

🅣 IND

35
34
33
32
31
HANS ON ST.
🅣 IRT BMT LIRR
FT GREENE
24
23
20
12
10 PL.
11
GATES
CRISPUS ATTUCKS PL
PUTNAM SQ
LEFFERTS

PACIFIC
DEAN
STMARKSAVE
PROSPECT PL
PARK
STERLI
ST JOHNS
LCOLN
LEY
BERGEN
ST. MARKS
HG
H ST. GREENE
21
22 🅣 IND
UNDERHILL PARK

Crown Heights

0   1000   2000 feet
A COURT 500
PARK
STERLIN

THESE ARE A FEW OF NEW YORK'S OUTSTANDING BUILDINGS WHICH ARE GLAZED WITH LIBBEY · OWENS · FORD GLASS

LINCOLN CENTER

Philharmonic Hall
Harrison & Abramovitz

New York State Theater
Philip Johnson

Metropolitan Opera House
Harrison & Abramovitz

Vivian Beaumont Theater, Library and Museum
Eero Saarinen; Skidmore, Owings & Merrill

AMERICAN BROADCASTING CO.
Emery Roth & Sons

CHASE MANHATTAN BANK
Skidmore, Owings & Merrill

ALLIED CHEMICAL
Smith, Haines, Lundbergh & Wahler

UNION CARBIDE
Skidmore, Owings & Merrill

TIME-LIFE
Harrison & Abramovitz

COLUMBIA BROADCASTING SYSTEM
Eero Saarinen

BANKERS TRUST
Emery Roth & Sons associated with Henry Dreyfuss

MUSEUM OF MODERN ART
Philip Johnson

MADISON SQUARE OFFICE BLDG.
Charles A. Luckman Assoc.

UNITED NATIONS SECRETARIAT
Harrison & Abramovitz

PEPSI-COLA
Skidmore, Owings & Merrill

140 BROADWAY
Skidmore, Owings & Merrill

WEAVER HALL, NYU
Warner, Burns, Toan & Lundy

SOCONY-MOBIL
Harrison & Abramovitz

LIBBEY · OWENS · FORD GLASS COMPANY
Toledo, Ohio

by necessary surgery, as educational space-needs changed.

[4.] 88th Precinct, N. Y. C. Police Dept., 300 Classon Ave. SW cor. DeKalb Ave. ca. 1890; south half, 1924.

Mini-Romanesque Revival, it packs an arcuated castle into a tight site, with small scale.

[5.] University Terrace, DeKalb Ave., St. James Pl. and Lafayette Ave. 1963, Kelly & Gruzen.

The balconies are **recessed** within the body of the building, rather than appliqué. This containment on three sides solves not only a design problem, but also the possibility of **vertigo.**

[6.] Higgins Hall, Pratt Institute/formerly **Adelphi Academy,** St. James Pl. bet. Clifton Pl. and Lafayette Ave. E side. 1887–1888.

The brickmasons have been loose again with piers, buttresses, round arches, segmental arches, reveals, corbel-tables. The nature of the material is exploited and exaggerated. Henry Ward Beecher laid the cornerstone of the north (**older**) building, and Charles Pratt gave the latter.

[7.] Clifton Place, St. James Pl. to Grand Ave. ca. 1870.

[8.] St. James Place, Lafayette Ave. to Gates Ave. ca. 1870.

[9.] Cambridge Place, Greene Ave. to Gates Ave.

[10.] 202–210 St. James Place, bet. Gates Ave. and Fulton St. W side. ca. 1885.

When bored by the excesses of the uniform row, architects turned to picturesque variety, giving **identity** of detail and silhouette to each tenant.

[11a.] Brown Memorial Baptist Church, 484 Washington Ave. SW cor. Gates Ave. ca. 1895.

A pinch of **Lombardian Romanesque** decorates a square-turreted English Gothic body. The white watertables against red brick are a bit jazzy.

[12.] 460 Washington Avenue, bet. Gates and Greene Aves., W side. ca. 1890.

A **Queen Anne** porch surrounds a brick and cast terra cotta body.

[13a.] 400–404 Washington Avenue, NW cor. Greene Ave. ca. 1885.

Romanesque Revival trio.

[13b.] 396–398 Washington Avenue, bet. Greene and Lafayette Aves. W side. ca. 1890.

Bearded giants in the gables. Orange terra cotta Queen Anne.

[14a.] Emmanuel Baptist Church, 279 Lafayette Ave. NW cor. St. James Pl. 1887, Francis H. Kimball. ☆

Porous **Ohio** sandstone was sculpted into an approximation of French 13th Century Gothic. The interior is a Scotch Presbyterian preaching room that is startling in contrast, with radial seating fanning from the pulpit and baptismal font.

[14b.] Apostolic Faith Mission/formerly **Orthodox Friends Meeting House,** 265 Lafayette Ave. NE cor. Washington Ave. 1868.

A simple **Lombardian Romanesque** box polychromed with with vigor by its new tenants.

[15a.] Underwood Park, Lafayette Ave. bet. Washington and Waverly Aves. N side.

Site of the former **John T. Underwood** mansion, this park was donated to the city on its demolition.

[15b.] Graham Home for Old Ladies, 320 Washington Ave. bet. DeKalb and Lafayette Aves. 1851.

Free Georgian with a touch of Romanesque; great brick piers flank its three bays.

[16.] 285–289 DeKalb Avenue, NW cor. Waverly Ave. ca. 1890.

A trio of slate-roofed, brownstone, and brick Romanesque. Note the cast terra cotta frieze.

[17a.] 271 Clinton Avenue, bet. DeKalb and Willoughby Aves. ca. 1890.

Still beautifully groomed, this mansion sports striped awnings in the summer, a vestige of pre-air conditioning New York that enriched the summer cityscape remarkably.

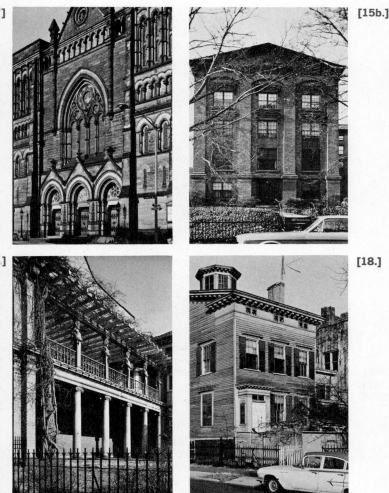

[15b.]

[18.]

[17b.] St. Joseph's College for Women/formerly **George DuPont Pratt Residence,** 245 Clinton Ave. bet. DeKalb and Willoughby Aves. 1901. Babb, Cook and Willard. ☆

Charles Pratt, the elder, refiner of kerosene at **Greenpoint,** joined his oil empire with that of John D. Rockefeller's Standard Oil Company in 1874. At the marriage of each of his sons, he presented the new couple with a house for a wedding present. Three still remain, at **229, 241,** and **245 Clinton Avenue,** opposite their father's at **232.** The last son, Harold I., responsive to the changing fashion and the consolidation of Brooklyn with New York, built *his* nuptial palace on Park Avenue at 68th Street. [See UES Manhattan.]

[17c.] Residence, Bishop of Brooklyn (Roman Catholic)/formerly **Charles Millard Pratt Residence,** 241 Clinton Ave. bet. DeKalb and Willoughby Aves. E side. 1893. William B. Tubby. ☆

"**Richardsonian**" **Romanesque** of bold, strong forms, without the fussy picturesqueness of lesser acolytes than **Tubby.** Note the spherical bronze lamp at the great arched porte-cochère and the semicircular conservatory to the south.

[17d.] Caroline Ladd Pratt House/formerly **Frederick B. Pratt Residence,** 229 Clinton Ave. bet. DeKalb and Willoughby Aves. E side. ca. 1898. Babb, Cook and Willard. ☆

Attached on one side and freestanding on the other, it forms a neat and handsome urban transition. The pergola-ed entry supported by truncated **caryatids** and **atlantides** does the trick. The house proper is grey and white Georgian Revival.

[17e.] St. Joseph's College for Women/formerly **Charles Pratt [Sr.] Residence,** 232 Clinton Ave. bet. DeKalb and Willoughby Aves. W. side. ca. 1875. ☆

The **manor** house and gardens of the Pratt family; Italianate, a freestanding equivalent of the brownstone row mansion.

[17c.]

[18.] Skinner House, 200 Lafayette Ave. SE cor. Vanderbilt Ave. 1812. Altered. ★

Extraordinary relic from the days these precincts were farm country. **Greek Revival** clapboard, weathered and shuttered, it has been inhabited by the **Skinner** family since 1900.

[19.] Clinton Hill Development, Section 2, Clinton Ave. to Waverly Ave., Lafayette Ave. to Greene Ave. 1955. Harrison & Abramovitz, Irwin Clavan.

[20a.] 410 Clinton Avenue, bet. Greene and Gates Aves. W side. ca. 1890.

Monolithic monochromy, modulated with brick, colored mortar and cast terra cotta ornament, spell **Queen Anne,** a style allowing great license to the architect who **yearns to be a virtuoso** in creating original detail.

[20b.] 405 Clinton Avenue, bet. Greene and Gates Aves. ca. 1890.

[21.] 487 Clinton Avenue, bet. Gates Ave. and Fulton St. 1890.

[22.] Church of St. Luke and St. Matthew, 510–524 Clinton Ave. bet. Fulton St. and Atlantic Ave. W side. 1890.

The Episcopalians begat Baptist temples in the 1880's and 90's. Eclecticism gone **beserk:** battered **Egyptian**-like walls, **Romanesque** arches, **Ruskinian Gothic** granite-brownstone polychromy.

[23.] 374–434 Vanderbilt Avenue, bet. Gates and Greene Aves. W side. ca. 1880.

An almost perfectly preserved row; 30 Italianate brownstones stepping down the hill. Note that the balustrades are cast iron, painted to look like Brownstone: **industrialization rears its head.**

[24a.] Church of the Messiah and Incarnation, 80 Greene Ave. SE cor. Clermont Ave. 1865. James H. Giles. Finished, 1892. R. H. Robertson.

A **"beehive"** caps a colonnaded drum on a brick and terra cotta landmark tower reaching **130** feet.

[24b.] Roman Catholic Brothers' Residence, 75 Greene Ave., NE cor. Clermont Ave. ca. 1885.

Dour; Hollywood would cast it as an "orphan asylum" for a **Charlotte Brontë** novel. In fact, the neatly dressed granite blocks and Mansard roof may be **austere,** but complementary landscaping makes a rich package.

[25a.] New York Community College/formerly **Brooklyn Masonic Temple,** 317 Clermont Ave. NE cor. Lafayette Ave. 1909. Lord & Hewlett.

They took the word *"temple"* literally in 1909. Some of the polychromy that archeologists believe was used on **4th Century B.C. Greek temples** is recalled here in fired terra cotta ornament.

[25b.] Church and School of Our Lady Queen of All Saints, 300 Vanderbilt Ave. NW cor. Lafayette Ave. 1913. Gustave Steinbach.

[25a.]

George Mundelein, later Cardinal of Chicago, commissioned this building while pastor of St. John's parish. A **glassy** church (**stained**) and a **glassy** school (**clear**) suggest on the one hand that stained-glass box, the **Sainte Chapelle** of Paris, and on the other, slim-mullioned modern school architecture. The sculpture is impressive in both quality and quantity; **36** saints are "in residence."

[26.] Fort Greene Jewish Center/formerly **Simpson Methodist Church,** Clermont Ave. SE cor. Willoughby Ave. 1870.

[27.] Fort Greene Park, DeKalb Ave. to Myrtle Ave., Washington Park to St. Edwards St. 1860, Frederick Law Olmsted and Calvert Vaux.

From its summit there is a prospect of **Brooklyn** and the harbor that suggests this might have better been the park to be named *"Prospect."*

[27a.] Prison Ship Martyr's Monument, center of Fort Greene Park. 1908. Stanford White; A. A. Weinman, Sculptor.

A memorial to those 11,500 *unlucky* American patriots who died in prison ships anchored in Wallabout Bay (*near the Navy Yard*) during the Revolution. The world's largest **Doric** column bears a brazier of bronze by sculptor **Weinman.** Nearby is the **world's most elegant comfort station**, a square "di-style in antis" Doric temple by the same architect.

[28.] Washington Park, the portion of Cumberland St. facing Fort Greene Park, Myrtle Ave. to DeKalb Ave.

Lined with mansions in a social overflow from **Clinton** and **Washington** Avenues on the "Hill" to the east; now mostly rooming houses. Note the bronze balconies on No. **180** and the porticoed **Queen Anne** brownstone at No. **198.**

[46.]

[3

[29a.] South Oxford and South Portland Streets, DeKalb Ave. to Lafayette Aves.

Two handsome, tree-shaded blocks of brownstones.

[29b.] The Roanoke, 69 S. Oxford St. near Lafayette Ave. E side. ca. 1890.

An early **Brooklyn** apartment house (as opposed to tenement).

[30.] Lafayette Avenue Presbyterian Church, 85 S. Oxford St. SE cor. Lafayette Ave. 1862, J. C. Wells.

Noted architecturally largely for its numerous windows by the **Tiffany** studios (six of eight upper windows; all but one below).

[31.] Church of St. Simon the Cyrenian, 175 S. Oxford St. bet. Hanson Pl. and Atlantic Ave. E side. ca. 1895.

A splendid mansion is now, happily, used as a church. **Black Forest Queen Anne:** ornamented stucco, ornamented terra cotta, ornamented brick.

[32.] Hanson Place Seventh Day Adventist Church/formerly **Hanson Place Baptist Church,** 88 Hanson Place. SE cor. S. Portland St. 1862.

Cream and white Greek Revival reminiscent of the many churches of the **Kremlin.** Victorian milk glass.

[33.] Norwegian Seamen's House and Restaurant, 62 Hanson Pl. SE cor. S. Elliott Pl. 1929.

A pleasant, bright restaurant overlooks a garden; **inexpensive** Norwegian food and beer. Handsome sweaters are available for purchase.

[34a.] Hanson Place Central Methodist Church, 144 St. Felix St. NW cor. Hanson Pl. ca. 1930.

Gothic restyled in modern dress, an exercise in *massing* brick and limestone. The street level contains stores, a surprising but intelligent adjunct to churchly economics.

[34b.] Williamsburgh Savings Bank, 1 Hanson Pl. NE cor. Flatbush Ave. and Ashland Pl. (Times Square). 1929. Halsey, McCormick and Helmer.

Brooklyn's **skyscraper** counts more by its own uniqueness. From Manhattan this strongly marks the center of **commercial action**. For 25 cents the bank offers a complete view of Brooklyn from its observatory.

[35.] Academy of Music, 30 Lafayette Ave. bet. Ashland Pl. and St. Felix St. 1908, Herts and Tallant.

End of tour: One block south is **Times Plaza** where a choice of mass transit facilities are available to get you back.

MISCELLANY

[36.] Founders Hall, Long Island University/formerly **Brooklyn Paramount Theatre,** 385 Flatbush Ave. Extension, NE cor. DeKalb Ave. 1928.

Brooklyn's leading movie palace was converted, in two steps, to university use: the office tower, in **1950**; the 4400-seat auditorium, in **1962**; the 12 intervening years witnessed the **swan song of pop corn** in these marble halls. A new campus is being given form to the north and features a distinguished newcomer:

[36a.] The Maltz Building (Humanities-Social Science Center), L. I. University. 1967. Davis, Brody Assocs; Horowitz and Chun.

The stripped concrete frame of a warehouse is provided with new guts and a new veneer. Service towers at north and south contain elevators, stairs, and mechanical ventilation.

[36b.] The Brooklyn Hospital, DeKalb Ave. to Willoughby St., Ashland Pl. to Ft. Greene Park. 1920. J. M. Hewlett. Alterations/ expansion, 1967. Rogers, Butler & Burgun.

[37.] Kingsview Cooperative Apartments, Willoughby St. to Myrtle Ave., Ashland Pl. to St. Edwards St. 1957. Brown and Guenther.

Neat cooperative housing surveys **Fort Greene Park.**

[38.] Fort Greene Houses, Park Ave. (Brooklyn-Queens Expwy.) to Myrtle Ave., Carlton Ave. to Prince St. 1944. Candela, Fouilhoux, Harrison, Mayer, Dennison, Hohauser, Kahn, Butler, Churchill, Stein, and Kahn.

Thirty-five hundred apartments *(14,000 persons)* on 38 acres. Within its bounds are the **Church of St. Michael and St. Edward, Cumberland Hospital,** and **P.S. 67. New York's** largest public-housing project will be dwarfed by Co-Op City, the middle-income cooperative under construction on the former environs of **Freedomland,** in the **Bronx**: there will be 15,500 units **(60,000 people!).**

[39.] Church of St. Michael and St. Edward, 100 St. Edward Pl. in Ft. Greene Housing Project, W of Myrtle Ave. ca. 1890.

Twin conical-capped towers in the manner of a **Loire Valley 17th Century** chateau. The interior is **pop-art** plaster, painted and gilt, with huge sheets of pictorial stained glass (done by the "Norman Rockwell" of the medium).

[40.] Public School 46, Brooklyn, Edward Blum School, 100 Clermont Ave. bet. Myrtle and Park Aves. 1958. Katz Waisman Blumenkranz Stein Weber, Architects Associated.

An austere white-glazed brick body, embellished with sculptured canopies and chimney, and play-horses in the play-yard by sculptor **Constantino Nivola. Blum** was son-in-law of **Abraham Abraham;** each headed the Abraham & Straus department store.

[41.] U.S. Naval Receiving Station, 136 Flushing Ave. Flushing Ave. to Park Ave., Clermont Ave. to Vanderbilt Ave. 1941.

Rare naval structures, in that they are urban housing in its strictest sense, modern and permanent.

[42.] The New York Naval Shipyard (Brooklyn Navy Yard), East River to Flushing Ave., Hudson and Navy Sts. to Kent Ave. 1801–1966.

Brooklyn's **oldest** industry, the then-shipyard was purchased by the Navy in 1801, abandoned in 1966. **Seventy-one thousand** naval and civilian personnel labored here during World War II.

[43.] Commandant's House, Quarters A, New York Naval Shipyard, near the dead end of Evans and Little Sts. 1805. Attributed to Charles Bulfinch. ★

Only a **glimpse** at its rear is now possible, for **Navy** gates intervene. A photograph must satisfy most below the rank of **Admiral.**

[44.] U.S. Naval Hospital, 263 Flushing Ave. bet. Squibb Pl. and Oman Rd. N side. 1838. Martin E. Thompson. ★

[45.] Bethel Seventh Day Adventist Church, 457 Grand Ave. NE cor. Lefferts Pl. ca. 1885.

The **obtuse** intersection of Lefferts and Grand suggested a stepped form to this architect. The **piered, arched, corbeled,** and **articulated** brickwork has a fresh modern flavor.

[46.] Mechanics Building/formerly **Lincoln (Republican) Club,** 67 Putnam Ave. bet. Irving Pl. and Classon Ave. N side. 1890. R. L. Daus.

Elegant **Republicans** left this florid structure, marking the memory of these streets with remembrances of better times. The bracketed tower is in the **Wagnerian Victorian** idiom popularized by the fantastic Bavarian royal castle, **Neuschwanstein.**

[47.] 418 Classon Avenue, bet. Quincy St. and Gates Ave. W side. ca. 1885.

A **Romanesque** trio arranged as a single composition.

[4.]

PARK SLOPE/PROSPECT PARK

A wonderland of pinnacles, arches, unrestrained ornament; in short a display of **Victoriana.** The district owes its name to the rise in topography that culminates in Prospect Park. Though the terrain begins its ascent in the lowland around the Gowanus Canal, the Park Slope area is normally defined as that lying east of Fourth Avenue and opposite Prospect Park. Despite its proximity to the park, the area was slow to develop. As late as 1884 it was still characterized as **"fields and pastures."** Edwin C. Litchfield's Italinate villa, completed in 1857, alone commanded the view to the harbor from the hill it occupies today off Prospect Park West. The primary stage of the park's construction was already complete in 1871, yet the Slope lay quiet and tranquil, bypassed by thousands of persons on the **Flatbush Avenue horsecars** making their way to the newly created recreation area. By the mid-80's, however, the potential of the Slope became apparent, and mansions began to appear on the newly built grid of streets.

The lavish homes clustered along Plaza Street and Prospect Park West and eventually caused this stretch to be named **"The Gold Coast."** Massive apartments then invaded the area after World War I, feeding upon the large, underutilized plots of land occupied by the first growth. These behemoth apartments, concentrated at Grand Army Plaza, are a contrast to the richly imaginative brick dwellings of Carroll Street and Montgomery Place, the mansions and churches and clubs that still remain, and to the remarkably varied row houses occupying the side streets as they descend toward the skyscrapers of Manhattan to the west.

Walking Tour A: From newsstand on street at Grand Army Plaza Station of the IRT Seventh Avenue Subway south into Park Slope and return. Cross Plaza Street, proceed south and admire:

[5.]

[1.] The Montauk Club, 25 Eighth Ave. NE cor. Lincoln Pl. 1891. Francis H. Kimball. ☆

A Venetian Gothic palazzo whose canal is the narrow lawn separating it from its Indian head-encrusted, cast-iron fence. This exclusive club bears the name of a local tribe, which explains the liberal use of Indians in the frieze, column capitals, and elsewhere in this confectioner's delight. Continue south on Plaza Street and turn right—into Berkeley Place.

[2.] George P. Tangeman Residence, 276 Berkeley Pl. bet. Plaza St. and Eighth Ave. 1890. Lamb & Rich.

[3.] 64–66 Eighth Avenue, bet. Berkeley Pl. and Union St. W side. 1889. Parfitt Bros.

Two very special limestone row houses by popular architects of the period; client: Stephen Underhill. Take a peek to the right down Union Street.

[4.] 889–903, 905–913 Union Street, bet. Eighth and Seventh Aves., N side. ca. 1890–1895.

Nos. 889–903 comprise a widely eclectic design of Baroque pediments, elliptical and half-round arches, bold lintels, oriel windows, and delicately embossed friezes. Continue south on Eighth Avenue to President Street. Turn right.

[5.] Missionary Servants of the Most Holy Trinity Residence, 869 President St. W of Eighth Ave. N side. ca. 1890.

A most unusual town house. The broad expanse of roman brick is interrupted by two metal-covered oriel windows bracketed out from the masonry wall by **Viollet-le-Duc**-inspired struts. Retrace your steps and proceed up President Street toward the Park.

[6.] 940–946 President Street, W of Prospect Park West.

Four quaint brick houses. The easterly pair are unusual in that they share a common court area beginning above the parlor floor. No. 946 was the Tollefsen Studio of Music. It housed a fascinating private **collection of antique musical instruments** and mementos of the musical scene. Turn right on Prospect Park West past Nos. 16 and 17 by Montrose W. Morris (1898) and turn right again into Carroll Street.

[7.] Carroll Street, bet. Prospect Park West and Eighth Ave. 1887–1911.

The north side of this street is as calm, orderly, and disciplined in its row housing as the south side is delightfully chaotic. This block of Carroll Street is visual evidence of a significant change of style:

863,   N side. 1890. Napoleon LeBrun.
878–876, S side. 1911. Chappell & Bosworth.
872–864, S side. 1887. William B. Tubby. Queen Anne shingles
             and brick.
862–856, S side. 1889. George B. Chappell. Arched doorways.
848,   S side. ca. 1905. A narrow bay window on columns is its
             facade.
846–838, S side. 1887. C. P. H. Gilbert. Three 40-foot beauties.

[8.]

[8.] Thomas Adams Jr. Residence, 115–119 Eighth Ave. NE cor. Carroll St. 1888. C.P.H. Gilbert.

A Richardsonian Romanesque brownstone mansion with terra cotta trim. Wonderful old heap now divided into apartments. Exterior well cared-for. Continue west on Carroll Street across Eighth Avenue and turn south into Fiske Place. The 212-foot-high spire you see ahead on Carroll Street is that of the:

[9.] Old First Reformed Church, 126 Seventh Ave NW cor. Carroll St. 1892. George L. Morse.

[10.] 12, 14, 16 Fiske Place, bet. Carroll St. and Garfield Pl. W side. ca. 1890.

A three-unit row whose bay windows are handled like an academic exercise in design: first a square, then a semicircle, last a triangle. Very neat and very successful. As a matter of fact the developer thought so too — the same grouping occurs in the same sequence one block west at 11, 15, 17 Polhemus Place. Turn left onto Garfield and left again onto Eighth Avenue. As you do, take note that James A. Farrell, elected president of the United States Steel Corporation in 1911, lived at 249 Garfield Place during his tenure.

What shall we call it? Naming apartment buildings to give them a personality must have begun with Manhattan's Dakota. At the northwest corner of Garfield Place and Eighth Avenue are four more modest works with names like The Serine, The Lillian, and Belvedere, but the Gallic influence won out on number four: **Ontrinue.**

Turn east onto Montgomery Place.

[11.] Montgomery Place, bet. Eighth Ave. and Prospect Park West. 1887–1892.

One of the finest streets in New York. Though only one block long, it displays a magnificent variety of homes built as a real estate scheme of Harvey Murdock. His wish was to create row houses that broke away from the traditional disciplined and repetitive approach. He commissioned C. P. H. Gilbert, a noted architect of the period, to create the picturesque grouping, and the results speak for themselves. A 1930's vintage amber brick six-story *moderne* apartment closes the vista at Eighth Avenue — a very successful termination in a totally different style. On the north side, Nos. 11, 17, 19, 21, 25 are by C. P. H. Gilbert; No. 47 by R. L. Daus. On the south side, Nos. 14–18, 36–48, 54–60 are all by C. P. H. Gilbert.

[13.]

Turn right at Prospect Park West and proceed south.

[12.] Brooklyn Ethical Culture School/formerly **Henry J. Hulbert Residence,** 49 Prospect Park West bet. 1st and 2nd Sts. W side. 1883. Montrose W. Morris.

When designed, this Indiana limestone-faced **extravaganza** was alone at the top of a slope that reached toward the harbor. As a result, Hulbert, a paper merchant, asked his architect to provide a second-story porch facing west to enjoy the view. Little did he know how useless that porch would become in the next few years of the Slope's growth or, for that matter, to what use his **dream house** would eventually be put. The residence was purchased by the Brooklyn Ethical Culture Society in 1928.

The edifice next door at No. 53 is the meeting house of the group, formerly the **William H. Childs Residence,** William B. Tubby, architect. Continue south along Prospect Park West to 4th Street. On your left in the park you will see:

[13.] Litchfield Mansion/or **Ridgewood**/ *or* **Grace Hill Mansion,** Prospect Park West bet. 4th and 5th Sts. E side. 1857. Alexander Jackson Davis. ★ Annex, 1911–1913, Helmle and Huberty.

The villa was built for Edwin C. Litchfield, a lawyer whose fortune was made in midwestern railroad development. In the 1850's he **acquired about one square mile** of virtually vacant land extending from 1st Street to 9th Street and from the Gowanus Canal to the projected line of Tenth Avenue, just east of his mansion — a **major portion of today's Park Slope.** (One of his enterprises was the improvement of the swampy shore of the Gowanus Canal, a dredge-and-fill operation carried out by the **Brooklyn Improvement Company,** whose handsome two-story Classical Revival main office still stands at the southwest corner of Third Avenue and 3rd Street.)

The mansion is the best surviving example of **Davis's Italianate style,** but more than 80 years as a public office have eroded most of its original richness. Its original exterior finish, stucco simulating cut stone, has been stripped off exposing the common brick beneath.

End of tour. Since you're in Prospect Park, take a leisurely stroll back to Grand Army Plaza.

Michel's Restaurant, 346 Flatbush Ave. bet. Seventh and Eighth Aves. NE 8–4552. Sprawling, table-clothed, family restaurant with a wide variety of food on its menu. It has a bar and Old New York-type waiters. Closed Mondays.

Walking Tour B: From newsstand on street at Grand Army Plaza Station of the IRT Seventh Avenue Subway to Bergen Street Station of same subway. Proceed south on St. Johns Place. The silhouetted church spires you see on this lovely street are those of:

[14a.] Memorial Presbyterian Church, Seventh Ave. SW cor. St. Johns Pl. 1883.

[14b.] Grace M. E. Church (Methodist), Seventh Ave. NE cor. St. Johns Pl. 1883. Parfitt Bros.

Note the brownstone steeple of the former and the ornate Moorish and Romanesque detailing of the latter's stonework along St. Johns Place. Turn right on Seventh Avenue and you will find:

[15.] Lillian Ward Mansion, 21 Seventh Ave. SE cor. Sterling Pl.

The entire east blockfront from St. Johns to Sterling is filled with a group of fine structures beginning with the Grace M. E. Church and its parsonage and anchored by the Ward Mansion. Note the fanciful circular tower hanging out into space at its corner and the polychromed and finialed pitched roof. This Victorian town house and its neighbors at Nos. 23–27 were built as a group. Miss Ward was a noted diva of the early 20th Century.

Plane Crash: In the morning mist of December 16, 1960, two airliners collided in the air over New York. The pilot of one attempted an emergency landing in Prospect Park but made it only to the intersection of Seventh Avenue and Sterling Place. The plane sliced the cornice off a small apartment building west of Seventh Avenue (the light-colored brick marks the spot) and came to rest with its nose at the doorstep of the Ward Mansion. A church on Sterling Place was destroyed by the resulting fire, but miraculously the mansion was untouched.

Retrace your steps on Seventh Avenue south to St. Johns Place. On your right between Sixth and Seventh Avenues are St. John's Episcopal Church at No. 139 and two robust Victorian town houses across the way at Nos. 176 and 178.

[16.] St. John's Episcopal Church, 139 St. Johns Pl. W of Seventh Ave. 1869.

[17a.] Brooklyn Conservatory of Music, 58 Seventh Ave. NW cor. Lincoln Pl. ca. 1888.

[17b.] Lincoln Plaza/formerly **F. L. Babbott Residence,** 153 Lincoln Pl. bet. Sixth and Seventh Aves. N side. ca. 1888.

[17c.] 139 Lincoln Place, bet. Sixth and Seventh Aves. N side ca. 1885.

[18.] Sixth Avenue Baptist Church, Sixth Ave. NE cor. Lincoln Pl. 1880.

In amongst the variety of row house construction are these bits of architectural punctuation, each using brick in a very special way.

[19.] St. Augustine's Roman Catholic Church, 116 Sixth Ave. bet. Sterling and Park Pls. W side. 1888–1892. Parfitt Bros. ☆

Sixth Avenue is one of Park Slope's most beautiful streets, block after block containing rows of amazingly well preserved row housing. St. Augustine's provides an **oasis** along the stately avenue, both spatially and in change of scale. The **crusty tower** with its mottled brownstone contrasts with the smoothness of the row housing. It is one of the most elaborate and architecturally distinguished Roman Catholic churches in Brooklyn (which has **as many Roman Catholics as Rome**).

[20.] Cathedral Club of Brooklyn/originally **The Carlton Club,** 85 Sixth Ave. NW cor. St. Marks Pl. 1890.

Built as an exclusive clubhouse, it changed hands successively to the Monroe Club, the Royal Arcanum Club and in 1907, through the efforts of a young priest, to the Cathedral Club, a Roman Catholic fraternal organization. The priest went on to become Cardinal Mundelein of Chicago.

[18.]

Scandia Foodshop, 244 Flatbush Avenue, east of Sixth Avenue. NE 8-1077. "That's Nokkel-Ost. Here, have a taste!" This is the way cheese is sold at this gourmet's paradise. A wide variety of foodstuffs from all over the world complemented by a friendly atmosphere and mouth-watering displays.

[21.] "Pintchikville," Flatbush Ave. and Bergen St. in every direction.

If **"pop art"** had its origins in New York, certainly this area must have been influential in giving it impetus. Building after building has been raucously decorated in **bright colors** all calling attention to Pintchik's, an emporium for every sort of home decoration material: linoleum, paint, tile, carpeting, lamps. There is an immense scale to the advertising which covers every inch of the old facades on both sides of the streets.

End of tour. The Bergen Street stop of the IRT Seventh Avenue Subway is close by.

MISCELLANY

[22.] Vechte-Cortelyou House, James J. Byrne Memorial Playground, 3rd St. W of Fifth Ave. 1699.

Known as the "Old Stone House at Gowanus," the building was rebuilt by the Park Department in 1935, with the original stones. The most severe fighting in the **Battle of Long Island** took place here, General Stirling's troops fighting a delaying action with Cornwallis' superior numbers permitting Washington a successful retreat.

World's Largest Clock Factory: In 1877 the Ansonia Clock Co. established a factory on the east side of Seventh Avenue between 12th and 13th Streets and employed 1500 workers. It was the world's largest clock factory in its time. The brick Functional Tradition buildings still exist at the site.

22

Grand Army Plaza: Laid out in 1866 by Olmsted & Vaux as monumental approach to their Prospect Park from the City of Brooklyn, which then lay to the north of the park. Most of the features of the plaza today **date from several decades later,** when the plaza and the park itself were embellished with many features of the Classical Revival style, conspicuously **white and formal** in contrast with the **picturesque, naturalistic** architecture of the original park. Of course, Classicism was appropriate in the plaza, always a **formal** concept, but even in the park itself the two distinct waves of construction have turned out to be complementary.

The oval island at the center of it all (not easy to reach on foot; be careful!) is laid out at fitting scale, with a double ring of **formally trimmed sycamores** surrounding a generously laid out **complex of stairs and terraces,** and a **fountain.** Around the **John F. Kennedy Memorial [24a.]** at the north end (1965, Morris Ketchum, Jr. and Assocs. architects; Neil Estern, Sculptor), the scale shrinks noticeably. This little memorial, New York's **only official memorial** to President Kennedy, was originally designed as a marble cube with a flame on top, later abandoned as an unsuitable duplication of the **perpetual flame** in Arlington Cemetery; its present form is a compromise, with a bust applied to its side in an unusual way. **The Bailey Fountain** (1932, Edgerton Swarthout, Architect; Eugene Savage, Sculptor) **[24b.]** at the center of the island, rates high for scale; Neptune and his Tritons at the base are amusing.

The structure that dominates the plaza — the neighborhood, for that matter — is the 80-foot high **Soldiers' and Sailors' Memorial Arch [24c.],** erected in 1892 (21 years after Prospect Park was "substantially completed") from a competition-winning design by John H. Duncan, architect of **Grant's Tomb.** The arch itself was meant as an **elegant armature for sculpture** dedicated to the Union forces of the Civil War. It carries its sculpture well — in fact, the empty pedestals on the north side are its weak points. The first part to be seen is Frederick MacMonnies' **huge quadriga atop the arch,** placed there in 1898. Inside the arch itself is its most subtle work, bas-reliefs of Lincoln (by Thomas Eakins) and Grant (by William O'Donovan), placed in 1895. On the south pedestals are **two bristling**

PARK SLOPE / PROSPECT PARK

N

Park Slope

Crown Heights

IRT

BMT

IRT

Grand Army Plaza

Walking Tour B

Walking Tour A

Walking Tour D

The Zoo

Walking Tour C

PROSPECT PARK

Brooklyn Museum

BOTANIC GARDENS

IRT

BMT

BEEKMAN

JKLM

WESTBURY

BMT

The Lake

IND

PARADE GROUNDS

C BROOKLYN

1000   2000 feet

groups representing the Army and the Navy by MacMonnies, dating from 1901.

While the arch was being embellished, a **necklace of Classical ornaments** was being strung across the park entrances facing it. [**25.**] Four 50-foot Doric columns rising out of some entangling fasces and topped with **harpy-like eagles** (by MacMonnies), railings, bronze urns, and lamp standards, and two ten-sided **"temples"** were all designed by **Stanford White** and completed in 1894. Of the whole ensemble, the temples—with their polished granite **Tuscan columns,** Guastavino vaulting, and bronze finials—probably show White's abilities best (note the lamp standards).

[**26.**] **Main Branch (Ingersoll Memorial), Brooklyn Public Library,** Grand Army Plaza at intersection of Flatbush Ave. and Eastern Pkwy. 1941. Githens & Keally; Paul Jennewein, reliefs; Thomas H. James, screen over entry.

Prospect Park: Once past Stanford White's ring, one sees Olmsted & Vaux's park **much as they conceived it.** They considered it a better work than their first collaboration, **Central Park.** There are several reasons, none of which reflect on Central Park. The main one is that, since the commission did not result from a competition (with its inevitably fixed site and program), Olmstead & Vaux had a **chance to change the problem given,** and they succeeded. (Delay of construction due to the Civil War aided their efforts.) Almost half the land the City set aside for a park in the 1850's lay **to the**

[24c.]

northeast of Flatbush Avenue, the main artery to Flatbush (then an independent town); it centered about the reservoir on Prospect Hill (since filled and used as a playground). Olmsted & Vaux rejected a scheme [**a.**] that **so completely bisected the projected park,** recommending instead that the area be expanded to the south and west. [**b.**] In lopping off the land to the northeast, they lost the hill that gave the park its name, but they also got rid of the reservoir (a rather negative feature of Central Park to this day) and provided a tract on which related institutions (today, the **Library,** the **Brooklyn Museum,** and the **Brooklyn Botanic Garden**) could be located without consuming park space (as the Metropolitan Museum does in Manhattan). Another encumbrance reduced considerably here is road area; with a more compact shape and without transverse roads, Prospect Park **gives up a much smaller portion of its area to cars** (originally carriages).

Walking Tour C (Prospect Park): Grand Army Plaza to Southeast Entrance at Parkside and Ocean Avenues.

Enter between the east (left) pair of Doric columns. Note statue of **James Stranahan** (1891, Frederick MacMonnies, Sculptor), whose personal 24-year crusade is largely responsible for Prospect Park and the Brooklyn parkways. Note also pine grove along walk, which is repeated in opposite corner as the symmetry of the entrance composition blends into the **picturesque layout** of the park. Like all walks entering the park, this one quickly loses visual connection with the point of entrance through **twists** and the **modeling** of terrain.

Turn right at first fork to **Endale Arch [27.]** first structure completed in the park (1867), a dramatic transition into bright sunlight and a half-mile vista down **Long Meadow.** The arch itself is simplest **bucolic Gothic,** with touching "posies" ornamenting the peaks; only vestiges remain of the wood interior, which once had benches in niches.

Once through the arch, note the corresponding (but architecturally distinct) **Meadow Port Arch [28.]** to the right at the west entrance to the meadow. Follow path to left along the edge of the

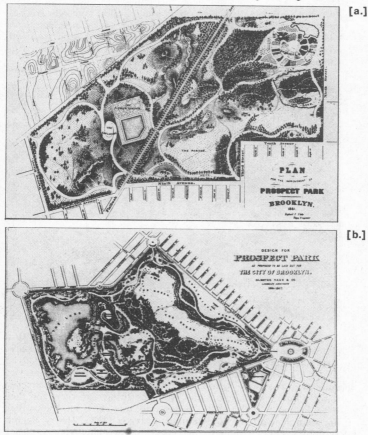

[a.]

[b.]

meadow. Note that active (but not regimented) **recreation on the meadow itself** is deftly separated from (but visible from) the tree-dotted hillsides along the encircling walks.

About 500 feet ahead a set of steps rises to the left; go a bit beyond them for a better view of the meadow, then back, up the steps, and across the road. On the other side, go left along a stretch that was once a rustic arbor (foundations still visible). Go right at next fork down curving walk to the **Rose Garden** (1895, designer unknown) **[29.]** now desolate except for a few rose bushes and the empty concrete basins that once held exotic water lilies. Turning right across the center of the rosebed circle, take the steps leading down to the **Vale of Cashmere,** an unusual melding of Classical architectural elements (1894, possibly McKim, Mead & White) **[30.]** and picturesque landscaping (older Calvert Vaux). Deep in a hollow facing due south, the Vale supports **lush groves of bamboo** and **multitudes of birds**—some uncommon in New York. (There are almost always bird-watchers.) The pools are silted and the **Classical balustrades** have fallen, but the thriving plants and remaining details show what the place must have once been, and may be again.

Follow the brick path along the east side of the Vale (left as you enter) straight out into **a little meadow** from which there are glimpses of Long Meadow across the road. Continue over the **crest of a rise** (part of the **terminal moraine** ridge that cuts across the park from northeast to southwest) and down the wooded slope into **Battle Pass. [31.]** The park road at this point follows roughly the alignment of the original road from Flatbush to Brooklyn, and it was at this pass that Revolutionary **volunteers** put up brief resistance against British troops advancing toward New York in 1776 (see **marker** at left, foot of hill, for details).

The Zoo: An optional detour at this point is to the Prospect Park Zoo, just to the south, which offers public toilets and light refreshments, built in 1935 on the site of a pond. Its neat semicircle of buildings was designed by Aymar Embury II and decorated with reliefs and murals by WPA artists representing scenes from Kipling's *Jungle Books.*

[35.]

At **Battle Pass,** cross the road and climb the stair ahead to a plateau that is the site of a **"dairy,"** an original feature of the park. Turn left at the top of the stairs and follow the brow of the plateau across the **bridle path** (careful!) and past the old **red brick service building,** then turn right and cross high boulder bridge over a return loop of the bridle path. From the bridge, go right and then left up steps, then left at "T" along walk that skirts knoll on which the **John Howard Payne Monument** stands (1873, Henry Baerer, Sculptor). **[33a.]** Climb to the crest for sweeping view of Long Meadow; the red brick picnic house is directly across the meadow, the more elegant Palladian **Tennis House** (1910), Helmle and Huberty) **[33b.]**, to its left. Return to walk below and take first left on walk along edge of slope. At next "T," go right, down steps. Stop where the walk takes a sharp right for view of boulder bridge crossed earlier.

Continue descent into a **deep rocky glen,** through which a brook trickles (usually). Turn left at bottom, crossing small boulder bridge, and follow path along brook. Turn right at the end of this walk and pass through triple **Nethermead Arches** (1868–1870, Calvert Vaux **[34.]** where walk, brook, and bridle path all pass under the Central Drive. Continue along the brook, past some specimen trees, into the **Music Grove.** The "pagoda" here, rebuilt in 1896 (designer unknown), has been the site of summer **Goldman Band** concerts for decades. Cross Music Grove and bear right on the walk that crosses **Lullwater Bridge.** From the bridge there is a fine view of the white terra cotta-faced **Boathouse** (1905, Helmle and Huberty). **[35.]★** From the other side of the bridge, there is a long view down the Lullwater meandering toward the Lake. At the end of the bridge turn left for closer look at the Boathouse (note, in particular, the bronze lamp standards). From the Boathouse take the path south past the **Camperdown elm** (a rare specimen protected by an ugly fence), then turn left through the **Cleft Ridge Span** (1871–1872, Calvert Vaux) **[36a.]** with its polychrome tile inner surface easily visible in this lofty arch.

Through this span is the formal **Garden Terrace,** with oriental-style walls and planters by Calvert Vaux. **[36b.]** Bear right and then left to the **Oriental Pavilion** (1870–1874), **[36c.]** at the top of the terraces, facing the lake. The pavilion has suffered over the years—its interior filled with a refreshment stand and its polychrome slate roof covered with asphalt shingles. But the view down the axis to the lake has suffered even more, for the semicircular **cove** at the foot of the terraces is now filled by the **Kate Wollman Memorial Skating Rink.** Walk down the axis of the garden, past the **statue of Lincoln** (1869, H. K. Brown, Sculptor) and look, with Lincoln, at the high wire fence and exposed refrigeration equipment that stand at what was, until 1961, the edge of the lake. To the left is the **skating shelter** (1960, Hopf & Adler). **[37.]**

After a short detour to the right, to an area where the lake edge is in its original condition, return across the **axis of the garden** and the skating shelter, turning right at the parking lot (which was a **"carriage concourse"** from the very beginning, and undoubtedly influenced the siting of the rink) and continue to the edge of the lake. Passing a **World War I Memorial** (1920, A. D. Pickering, Designer), continue around the edge to the **landing shelter** (probably a reconstruction of the original. ca. 1870, Calvert Vaux), sole survivor of many **rustic shelters** once bordered the lake. From here, follow the path parallel to the lake edge, then bear left across the drive, and continue straight out of the park through the **Classical porticos** with redwood trellises (1904, McKim, Mead & White) to the intersection of Ocean and Parkside Avenues.

End of tour: To the left across Ocean Avenue is the BMT Brighton Line Parkside Avenue station.

For further views of the lake and a look at some of the park's finest Classical structures, instead of leaving the park at this point follow the walk along the south side of the park, between Parkside Avenue and the park drive, to the Croquet Shelter (1906, McKim, Mead & White; Stanford White. Restored, 1966–1967) [38.]☆ and on to Park Circle entrance, a remarkable successful Classical composition (1897, McKim, Mead & White, Architects; Frederick MacMonnies, Sculptor of the two "Horse Tamers" groups). [39.]

Botanic Garden, Brooklyn Museum: The triangle formerly known as Institute Park (contained by Eastern Parkway, Flatbush and Washington Avenues), which **Olmsted & Vaux rejected in their plan** for the park, was reserved for related institutional uses. It now accommodates the Brooklyn Botanic Garden, the Brooklyn Museum, and the main Brooklyn Public Library. The **garden and museum,** both **divisions** of the Brooklyn Institute of Arts and Sciences, are contiguous with one another and offer more than the expected horticultural specimens and works of art. The garden has some interesting examples of **landscape architecture,** and the museum (which is not just an art museum, but an **art school** and an **anthropological museum** as well) houses extensive decorative arts collections, 25 period rooms, **a whole Dutch Colonial house,** and—in a recently opened garden—a collection of exterior decorative elements from **demolished** New York buildings.

Walking Tour D (Botanic Garden to Brooklyn Museum): From the BMT Brighton Line Prospect Park station on Flatbush Avenue near Empire Boulevard (can also be reached from Grand Army Plaza station of IRT Seventh Avenue Subway by B41 bus) to the IRT

Seventh Avenue Subway Eastern Parkway station. Cross the street to the Lefferts Homestead, go back along Empire Boulevard to the Fire Department Bureau of Communications, and then enter the Botanic Gardens.

[40a.] Flatbush Turnpike Tollgate, Empire Blvd. entrance road to Prospect Park. N side. Ca. 1855.

A wooden guardhouse moved from its old position at Flatbush Turnpike (now Flatbush Avenue) is all that remains of the days when roads were **privately built** and **tolls** charged for their use.

[40b.] Lefferts Homestead, Flatbush Ave. N of Empire Blvd. W side. In Prospect Park. 1777–1783. ☆ Hours: call SO 8-2300. Admission free.

[41.] Brooklyn Central Office, Bureau of Fire Communications, N.Y.C. Fire Dept., 35 Empire Blvd. bet. Flatbush and Washington Aves. N side. 1913. Frank J. Helmle. ☆

Its Classical form would never lead you to guess that all fire alarms in Brooklyn are recorded and dispatched within.

Brooklyn Botanic Garden: Enter the garden through the Palladian South Gate. Its 50 acres are **intensively planted** with just about every variety of tree and bush that will survive in this climate; the collection of small flowering plants is not so comprehensive. Undoubtedly, the most popular attraction of the garden, which generates traffic jams at the end of April, is the grove of flowering **Japanese cherry trees,** possibly the finest in America. For a simple tour of the garden, touching the main examples of garden design, follow the east side of the garden (easily done by consistently staying to the right). For **seasonal attractions** (the cherry blossoms, roses, lilacs, azaleas) not on this route, ask the guard (on a **motor scooter**) for directions. On the east edge of the garden a few hundred feet from the south entrance is a reproduction of the **Ryoanji Temple stone garden** in Kyoto. **[42.]** Constructed with

[42.]

painstaking authenticity in 1963, this replica lacks all of the atmosphere that history and natural setting give to the original, but it offers an opportunity unique in this area to contemplate a Zen-inspired, virtually **plantless** landscape composition.

Just north of the Ryoanji are the **greenhouses** (Mondays–Saturdays, 10 AM–4 PM; Sundays and Holidays, 12:15–4 PM. Free) facing a plaza with pools of **specimen water lilies.** The conservatory has a **tropical jungle section** and a **desert section,** but its prize exhibit is the collection of **bonsai** (Japanese miniature trees), unequalled in the U.S. North of the conservatory is another **formal terrace,** planted with **magnolias** (which make a dazzling display in early to mid-April), in front of the garden's **School-Laboratory-Administration Building** (1918, McKim, Mead & White) **[43.],** originally painted white, not the present aquatic green. Farther

north is the **Japanese Garden, [44.]** (1915, Takeo Shiota, Designer), gift of philanthropist Alfred Tredway White. It resembles a **stroll garden of the Momoyama period** but is not copied from any one particular example. Around its small pond are examples of almost every traditional plant and device; this overcrowding fails to achieve the serenity of really good Japanese prototypes. North of the Japanese Garden is the **gate to the Brooklyn Museum** grounds.

[45.] Brooklyn Museum, Eastern Pkwy. SW cor. Washington Ave. 1897–1924. McKim, Mead & White. ★ Mondays–Saturdays, 10 AM–5 PM; Sundays and holidays, 1–5 PM. Free, except for special exhibits.

Wilbour Library of Egyptology (3rd Floor), 1935. Howe & Lescaze.

Frieda Schiff Warburg Sculpture Garden, 1966. Ian White, Designer.

From the south parking field there is a forbidding view of the unfinished, unpainted rear of the museum. The **raw ends** of elaborately decorated side walls and handsome dome revealingly demonstrate the **stage-set concept** of Classical Eclecticism. Across the parking lot is the Sculpture Garden of architectural decoration. It is laid out to accommodate **temporary exhibits and concerts,** as well as its permanent collection, including pieces of McKim, Mead & White's Pennsylvania Station (a column base and capital; a figure that supported one side of a huge clock), Coney Island's **Steeplechase Amusement Park** (a roaring lion's head and a lamp standard), and capitals from the first-floor columns of Louis Sullivan's **Bayard (Condict) Building,** still standing on Bleecker Street, Manhattan. Enter the museum from the Sculpture Garden.

Curios and antiquities: Just inside the south entrance of the museum is the Gallery Shop, the largest museum shop in the U.S., with an extensive stock of hand-crafted toys, jewelry, textiles, ceramics, and so on, from all over the world. And very good buys at that!

The austere architecture of the museum lobby dates from its remodeling in the 1930's, under WPA sponsorship, during which the lobby was moved down one floor and the monumental exterior stairway removed; stark functionalism replacing the Classical impressiveness. The information desk will offer directions to the collections as well as information on concerts, lectures, and movies in the museum. Among the outstanding exhibits in architecture and interior design are the **Jan Martense Schenck House** (originally built in 1675 in the Flatlands section of Brooklyn), dismantled in 1952 and reconstructed inside the museum, and a suite of rooms from the **John D. Rockefeller, Sr., Mansion,** built in 1866 at 4 West

54th Street (Manhattan), redecorated ca. 1884 in Moorish style by Arabella Worsham. A 1967 improvement to the museum is the **Study Storage Gallery** (Brown, Lawford & Forbes), in which over 1000 paintings are made accessible in a limited space by use of sliding panels and revolving pylons.

Leaving the museum by the main entrance (on Eastern Parkway), note the well-detailed parking space and entrance doors (but rather strange vestibule) that were designed to replace the stair up to the portico. Flanking the entrance are two sculptured female figures (1916, Daniel Chester French, Sculptor), representing **Manhattan** and **Brooklyn.** Although they look as if created for this location, they were placed here in 1963 when their places at the Manhattan end of the **Manhattan Bridge** were destroyed in a roadway improvement program.

End of tour: The Eastern Parkway station of the IRT Seventh Avenue Subway is directly in front of the museum.

BEDFORD-STUYVESANT

The name is an amalgam of two communities of the old City of Brooklyn; **Bedford,** its western portion, and **Stuyvesant Heights,** its eastern. Today it is New York's **second Negro ghetto,** overshadowed only by Harlem, and that only because of the latter's location on Manhattan Island. It probably **surpasses Central Harlem** in Negro population, though it differs markedly from its Manhattan counterpart in its large number of home-owners (17 percent of the households) and is therefore more **conservative in its politics.** The southern and western parts consist of masonry row housing of varying quality and of very **fine churches** whose spires create this community's **lacy skyline.** The northeastern reaches have considerable numbers of **wooden tenements** containing what are reputed to

[4.]

be some of the worst **slums** in the country—fire traps and vermin-infested hovels that are a disgrace to the city and an insult to those whose bare-subsistence income forces residence in them.

Where Bedford-Stuyvesant has good housing, however, it is *very* good. Particularly from the outside, where the facades of its brownstones and brickfronts create a **magnificent townscape,** it is as good or better than many fashionable parts of Brooklyn and even competes well with some of Manhattan's neighborhoods. Parts of Chauncey, Bainbridge, Decatur, McDonough, and Macon Streets and the southern end of Stuyvesant Avenue are superb. Hancock Street, between Nostrand and Marcy Avenues, was considered a showplace of its time; it exhibits much of this same quality even today. Alice and Agate Courts, short streets isolated from the macrocosm of the street pattern, are particularly unique spaces in the often anonymous grid.

The area encompasses 500 acres and houses about 400,000 persons, placing it within the 30 largest American cities.

[1.] Lefferts Place Park, Lefferts Pl. bet. Classon and Franklin Aves. N side. 1966. M. Paul Friedberg & Assoc., Landscape Architects; Pratt Planning Dept., Designers.

One of a number of "vest pocket" parks of minimal size intended to fill narrow vacant lots, which otherwise become dumping grounds for rubbish. This one was built with local labor, both as an economy measure and as an attempt to encourage community involvement. Another effort by the same team: Quincy Street Park between Stuyvesant and Reid Avenues.

[2a.] Convent of the Sisters of Mercy, 273 Willoughby Ave. bet. Classon Ave. and Taaffe Pl. N side.

[2b.] St. Patrick's R.C. Church, Kent Ave. NW cor. Willoughby Ave. **Rectory,** 285 Willoughby Ave. **Academy,** 918 Kent Ave.

Rope walks: Not an invention to cross a jungle swamp but a long narrow building used for the spinning of rope. In 1803 one was erected 1200 feet long in the two blocks north of the Convent of the Sisters of Mercy. It was so long that a tunnel was built for it to pass beneath intersecting Park Avenue.

[5e.]

[3.] 361 Classon Avenue and **386–396 Lafayette Avenue.** SE corner.

A group of romantically conceived brick row houses designed as a picturesque grouping in the best Victorian tradition. Compare richness of massing with the monotony of its latter-day brick neighbors across the avenue, a low-rent housing project.

[4.] Malcom Brewery/later Franklin Brewery/later Wallabout Warehouse, 394-412 Flushing Ave. SE cor. Franklin Ave. ca. 1885.

This robust structure towers above adjacent construction in this industrial fringe of Bedford Stuyvesant. Its distinctive silhouette is a landmark to the thousands of motorists who pass it every day on the Brooklyn-Queens Expressway nearby. At the Skillman Street corner are older buildings dating from 1863.

[5a.] 374-376 Franklin Avenue, SW cor. Quincy St. ca. 1865.

A frame double house out of Andrew Jackson Downing's sketchbooks of Victorian country houses. The southerly half still has the original vertical battens as its siding—its partner has been insensitively "modernized" with wide clapboards. A refreshing change of scale and material on otherwise redundant Franklin Avenue, a main southbound artery.

[5b.] 118 Quincy Street, SE cor. Franklin Ave. ca. 1890.

A modest example of the lavish apartments built in the community in the last decade of the 19th Century.

[5c.] Evening Star Baptist Church, 265 Gates Ave. NW cor. Franklin Ave. 1917.

Reminiscent of Frank Lloyd Wright's Unity Temple outside of Chicago, this stuccoed church is unique in the entire city in design.

[5d.] Plaza North Motor Hotel, 218 Gates Ave. bet. Franklin and Classon Aves. S side.

An urbane masonry town house originally, this Mansard-roofed structure has been painted a sterile white throughout its exterior.

[5e.] 212 Gates Avenue, bet. Franklin and Classon Aves. S side.

This romantic Victorian country house predated the establishment of the fire district, which then necessitated the use of masonry walls; it is carpenter-Gothic in the best American tradition.

[6.] Aurora Grata Scottish Rite Cathedral, 1160 Bedford Ave. NW cor. Madison St. 1891.

Bedford Avenue in this vicinity is a nondescript collection of gas stations and other marginal commercial activities. This red and white fantasy is a welcome relief. Its history dates back to 1877 when the Aurora Grata Lodge of Perfection, a Masonic unit, bought the old Dutch Reformed Church and Parsonage which stood at this site. It was rebuilt for Masonic services, a function it still serves today. The belfry is capped by a beautiful Scottish Rite emblem in bronze.

[7.]

[7.] Bergen Tile/formerly **Brooklyn Traffic Court**/formerly **Temple Israel,** 1005 Bedford Ave. NE cor. Lafayette Ave. 1892. Parfitt Bros.

When originally dedicated in 1892 the story took two columns on the front page of the *Brooklyn Daily Eagle*. This was the most **resplendent** Jewish **house of worship** in Brooklyn. Its president was Abraham Abraham (of Abraham & Straus). Speakers at the ceremony included the ministers of the most fashionable churches in New York. The **amber-toned brick exterior,** copper dome, and green, yellow, and gold interior were a striking eclectic expression of **Romanesque** and **Byzantine** forms. Its architects were among the most sought after in Brooklyn.

By the end of World War I, however, the affluent German Jewish congregation who commissioned this work had left the Bedford area. The building became **Traffic Court** for Brooklyn. Quite a letdown. But even this use, which, it might be argued, required a **monumental** space for dispensing **justice** (?) was only temporary. In recent years it has become an **emporium** for the **sale of linoleum,** resilient tile, and other such materials. The monumental arched entry is now emblazoned with a polychromed sign advertising its contemporary wares. A sad tale.

[8.] Engine Co. 209/Ladder Co. 102/34th Battalion, N.Y.C. Fire Department, 850 Bedford Ave. bet. Myrtle and Park Aves. W side. 1965. Pedersen & Tilney.

Certainly the most sophisticated and finest new architectural work in an area void of much recent construction. The brick set into **exposed concrete** and the sensitive modulation of the facade to catch the sun make this **fire station** distinctive yet harmonious with the best parts of its surrounding area. The old fire station this building replaced, dating from 1869, can be seen on the same side of Bedford Avenue between Myrtle and Willoughby.

b.]   [12c.]

[14.]

[9.] Empire State Warehouse Co./formerly **Long Island Storage Warehouse Co.** and **Jenkins Trust Co.,** 390–398 Gates Ave. SW cor. Nostrand Ave. 1906.

A neo-Baroque work noted more for the impact of its cupola upon the skyline than anything else.

[10.] Brownstone row housing, Jefferson Ave. bet. Nostrand and Marcy Aves. ca. 1885–1890.

Merely one of dozens of streets in the area of staid neo-Renaissance brownstones. In 1890, F. W. Woolworth, the variety store merchant, moved from his first home here (365A Quincy St. bet. Marcy and Tompkins Aves.) to No. 209. It is interesting that Woolworth chose to live in this section of the City of Brooklyn when business demands required that his center of operation be New York. (He later left for a magnificent mansion he commissioned on Fifth Avenue overlooking Central Park.) [See UES Manhattan 6b.]

[12d.]  [1?

[11.] Hancock Street, bet. Nostrand and Tompkins Aves. Mostly last decade of 19th Century. Various architects.

This two-block stretch contains some of the finest town houses in all of Brooklyn.

[12a.] Renaissance Apartments, 488 Nostrand Ave. SW cor. Hancock St. ca. 1890. Montrose W. Morris.

[12b.] Alhambra Apartments, 29 Macon St., 86 Halsey St. W side of Nostrand Ave. ca. 1890. Montrose W. Morris.

Two stylish apartment blocks of the **Gay Nineties** along Nostrand Avenue. The Alhambra is the better, except that the ground floor has been altered on Nostrand Avenue to provide for stores on this busy market street. Morris is best known for the Hulbert Mansion (now Brooklyn Ethical Culture School) in Park Slope. [See Park Slope 12.]

[12c.] Bedford-Stuyvesant Youth in Action/formerly **Girls' High School**/originally **Central High School,** 475 Nostrand Ave. bet. Halsey and Macon Sts. E side. 1885, 1891, 1911.

A Gothic Revival fairyland with all the tricks of the trade well employed. The adjacent side streets have many fine row houses of the period. (Look for oriel window on 64 Macon St. and see 68–74 Macon St. just around the corner.)

[12d.] 74 Halsey Street, bet. Nostrand Ave. and Arlington Pl. S side. ca. 1890.

A fine brick residence with the most exuberant iron railings. Imagine bounding up those front steps!

 [13.] John C. Kelley Residence, 247 Hancock St. bet. Marcy and Tompkins Aves. N side. ca. 1895. Montrose W. Morris.

A disciplined neo-Renaissance town house on a 81 by 100 foot site for an Irish immigrant who made good. It was regarded as one of the finest houses in the neighborhood. Legend has it that the brownstone was selected, piece by piece, to guarantee its quality.

Governors: The closest thing to a system for determining street names in Bedford-Stuyvesant is in the blocks between Marcy and Stuyvesant Avenues. Each was named after a Governor of the State of New York: William L. Marcy, Daniel D. Tompkins, Enos T. Throop, Joseph C. Yates, Morgan Lewis, and, of course, Peter Stuyvesant. Yates Avenue became Sumner Avenue when confusion arose between it and Gates Avenue.

[14.] Boys' High School, 823 Marcy Ave. bet. Putnam Ave. and Madison St. W side. 1891. J. W. Naughton.

A splendid Romanesque Revival work complete with elaborately decorated terra cotta trim, a lofty bell tower, arched entrances, and all other hallmarks of this style. It is perhaps one of the great buildings of New York.

[15.] St. George's Episcopal Church, 800 Marcy Ave. SW cor. Monroe St. 1887. Richard W. Upjohn.

One of Upjohn's more modest works.

[16.] Tompkins Avenue Congregational Church/now **First A.M.E. Zion Church** and **Bedford-Stuyvesant Youth in Action,** 480 Tompkins Ave. SW cor. McDonough St. 1889. George B. Chappell.

When you drive south on Tompkins Avenue, the immense campanile of this church is an important landmark in the distance, reminiscent of the tower in Venice's **Piazza San Marco.** The immensity of the church and parish house is evident only when it is reached. While a Congregational church, it was the largest edifice of that denomination in this country and was second in membership. It later merged with the Flatbush Congregational Church. [See C Brooklyn 4.] At one time it was called **Dr. Meredith's Church,** after its well-known minister.

[19a.]

[17.] McDonough Street, particularly bet. Marcy and Stuyvesant Aves. ☆

These five blocks of this street are among those being considered for preservation in a Bedford-Stuyvesant Historic District. It would provide a great cross section of various architectures along its length.

[18.] 13th Regiment Armory–N.Y. State National Guard, 357 Sumner Ave. bet. Jefferson and Putnam Aves. E side. 1894. R. L. Daus.

[19.] Greene Avenue, bet. Sumner and Stuyvesant Aves.

These two blocks of Greene Avenue have three distinctions: they contain an unusual brick church, known today as the Antioch

JKuhl

Williamsburg

Fr. Greene-Clinton Hill

Park Slope

N

Prospect Park

Crown Heights

Brower Pk.

Tompkins Pk.

IND

IRT

BEDFORD-STUYVESANT

Baptist Church; they have a variety of unique town houses slipped in among the repetitive rows of brownstones and brick fronts; and they display the **signs.** What signs? Signs like these, stencilled white on a black surround: "Re-Frain From Bad Language," "Organization Is Power," "Cars Should Be Seen and Not Heard," "Please Keep Your Music Sweet and Low." The signs are reminders that this is a proud community and one which hopes to raise itself by its bootstraps from its present state closer to what it was in the **Mauve Decades.**

The **Antioch Baptist Church** was formerly known as the Greene Avenue Baptist Church, completed in 1892, an outgrowth of a congregation established in 1854. The bowed central portion cantilevering out over the lower story is an unusual detail and helps to make this modest church a vigorous addition to the street. **[19a.]**

McDonald's Dining Room, 327 Stuyvesant Ave. NE cor. Macon St. 773–2774.

A good eating place in a community that sorely lacks them.

[20.] Mount Lebanon Baptist Church, 228–230 Decatur St. SE cor. Lewis Ave. ca. 1890.

[21.] 111–137 Bainbridge Street, bet. Lewis and Stuyvesant Aves. N side. ca. 1890–1900.

A rich assortment of individually styled row houses—quite a departure from the formal restraint of a typical brownstone grouping with a stable cornice line. Here the roof line is constantly changing: false masonry gables, Mansard, conical and octagonal spires on towers, and so on. Note the rest of this block. Also see Decatur Street between Howard and Saratoga Avenues **[21a.].**

[21a.]

[22.] Fulton Park, Chauncey and Fulton Sts. at Stuyvesant Ave.

The rumble of the "A" train below does not affect the serenity of this sliver of green space along squalid Fulton Street. The neighborhood immediately surrounding the park is named after it and because of its high quality is considered an important asset in the work of renewing Bedford-Stuyvesant. North of the park on Chauncey Street are a fine set of small-scale row houses with stoops intact.

City Center: The geographical center of New York City lies within Bedford-Stuyvesant. To be exact, it occurs in the middle of the block between Lafayette and Greene Avenues, 200 feet west of Reid Avenue. It is presently the site of a less-than-distinguished public school.

CROWN HEIGHTS

The name Crown Heights is today applied to the triangle east of Washington Avenue between Atlantic Avenue on the north and Empire Boulevard and East New York Avenue on the south. However, the handsome portion surrounding Grant Square at Bedford Avenue and Bergen Street was originally considered part of the **Bedford community** whose southern boundary is now Atlantic Avenue.

Crown Heights, the 19th Century **Crow Hill,** actually includes a succession of hills south of Eastern Parkway. The old designation derisively recalls a Negro **squatters' colony** in the Utica Avenue section. One of its early thoroughfares was Clove Road, a two-mile, north-south link from the Village of Bedford to Flatbush, dating from 1662. (A bit still remains above Empire Boulevard east of Nostrand Avenue.)

The community is in transition, with large colored and Jewish populations. Many **West Indian** immigrants reside in the area; French and **"very British"** English are commonly heard in the streets.

[1a.] Ulysses S. Grant Statue, Grant Sq. 1896. William Ordway Partridge, Sculptor.

Presented by the Union League Club of Brooklyn.

[1b.] Union League Club of Brooklyn/now **United Lubavitcher Yeshivoth,** Bedford Ave. SE cor. Dean St. 1892. Lauritzen & Voss.

The most resplendent club in Brooklyn was built to serve the social needs of Republican Party stalwarts residing in the Bedford community to the north. In 1915 it became the home of the **Unity Club,** an exclusive Jewish social club. Today it is a Hassidic religious school. [See Williamsburg.] Note the faces of Lincoln and Grant in the stonework and the eagle crest with outstretched wings supporting the immensely scaled bay window.

[1a.]

[1e.]

[1c.] 1345 Bedford Avenue, 1123–1133 Dean Street, NE corner. **1234–1251 Dean Street** N side bet. Bedford and Nostrand Aves. ca. 1890.

Fussy but charming Victorian row houses. Also see 1081–1087 and 1097–1099 Dean Street on the west side of Bedford Avenue.

[1d.] Erskine Funeral Home, 1341 Bedford Ave. bet. Dean and Pacific Sts. E side.

Probably not a funeral establishment originally, but unmistakably one now.

[1e.] Imperial Apartments, 1339 Bedford Ave. SE cor. Pacific St.

ca. 1892. Montrose W. Morris.

Advertising at the time as, "Elegant and well conducted apartment hotel in the fashionable part of the Bedford Section." Its immense apartments ("the largest in Brooklyn") have been subdivided, and the opulence of the building is visible only in the grimy glazed terra cotta arches and column capitals and in the huge, bronze bay windows on the exterior. Morris was responsible for many such buildings.

[1f.] St. Bartholomew's Episcopal Church, 1227 Pacific St. bet. Bedford and Nostrand Aves. N side. ca. 1893. George B. Chappell.

One of the most charming romantic churches in the city. Interior is lovingly designed. [See Park Slope 7. and Bedford-Stuyvesant 16 for other works.]

[1g.] Medical Society of the County of Kings, 1313 Bedford Ave. bet. Atlantic Ave. and Pacific St. E side. 1903. D. Everett Waid & R. M. Cranford.

[1h.] 23rd Regiment Armory, 1322 Bedford Ave. bet. Atlantic Ave. and Pacific St. W side. 1892. Fowler & Hough.

This battlemented fortress for the National Guard, with its handsome round tower and arched gateway, complete with portcullis, lacks only a moat to be right out of King Arthur's realm.

St. Marks Avenue: Row houses, town houses, and mansions.

[2a.] St. Marks Avenue, bet. Franklin and Bedford Aves.

Superbly preserved brownstone and other row housing.

[2b.] 669, 673, 675–677 St. Marks Avenue, bet. Rogers and Nostrand Aves. N side. ca. 1890.

[2c.] 758 St. Marks Avenue, bet. Nostrand and New York Aves. S side. ca. 1890.

[1b.]

[3a.] 800 St. Marks Avenue, bet. New York and Brooklyn Aves. S side. ca. 1890.

The Abraham Abraham Residence. A. A. was at the time he commissioned this house a partner in Wechsler & Abraham, the forerunner of today's Abraham & Straus, Brooklyn's largest department store. Among his philanthropic accomplishments was the founding of nearby Brooklyn Jewish Hospital, built in 1894 as Memorial Hospital for Women and Children. The porch on the house is an addition. Note the stables in the rear on Prospect Place. Also see **834, 836, and 847 Prospect Place,** narrow, Victorian single houses.

[3b.] 814 St. Marks Avenue, bet. New York and Brooklyn Aves. S side. ca. 1905.

The Ludwig Nissen Mansion, a miniature of the Potsdam Palace, was commissioned by a German emigré who became a well-known jeweler.

[3c.] 820 St. Marks Avenue, bet. New York and Brooklyn Aves. S side. ca. 1890.

[3d.] 839 St. Marks Avenue, NE cor. Brooklyn Ave. ca. 1898. Russell Sturgis.

Originally the Dean Sage Residence, now the St. Louis Convent.

Hats, anyone? In 1855 most hats sold in the U.S., and in the provinces of Britain as well, were produced in Brooklyn. (They were mostly beaver hats.) The Knox Hat Company building still stands at the northwest corner of Grand Avenue and Dean Street.

[4a.]

[4.] Brooklyn Children's Museum, Brower Park, Brooklyn Ave. bet. St. Marks Ave. and Park Pl. **North Bldg: L. C. Smith Residence,** ca. 1890. **South Bldg: William Newton Adams Residence,** 1867. **[4a.]**

Both these buildings, regrettably, are in their terminal stages. The Brooklyn Children's Museum, organized in 1899 (the first of its kind in the world), is looking forward to a brand-new facility. The Italianate villa of the Smith Family was a familiar landmark in Brower (formerly Bedford) Park to those motorists who regularly use Brooklyn Avenue. The so-called Spanish Adams House, a curiously designed building, was the home of noted historian James Truslow Adams, as well as his grandfather.

MISCELLANY: The following entries, all to be found in West Central Brooklyn, are not located in the specific neighborhood areas previously covered for this sector of the borough. Each is well worth viewing.

[5.] Union Methodist Church/formerly **New York Avenue Methodist Church,** 121 New York Ave. bet. Bergen and Dean Sts. E side. 1891. Parfitt Bros. (?)

Marvelous, fresh, Romanesque Revival church. Clearly articulated massing of clerestory, tower, and transepts.

[6.] Loehmann's, 1476 Bedford Ave. NW cor. Sterling Pl.

Man's gift to the middle-class matron. An extravagantly decorated bit of orientalia, the work of its founder, Mrs. Frieda Loehmann. Since her death at 88 in 1963 it has been reopened under new management. Noted for its fantastic buys in the realm of one-of-a-kind samples and manufacturers' overstocks of women's chic fashions. On a busy day it's quite a spectacle; no fitting rooms!

[7.] President Street, bet. Brooklyn and New York Aves. 1905–1920.

Both sides of this one-block stretch are lined with lavish masonry mansions of 20th Century vintage. They do not compare with their Victorian predecessors, but lavish setbacks from the street and their large sites create a luxurious sense of space in this otherwise densely built-up area.

WEST CENTRAL BROOKLYN

Cobble Hill: The area south of elegant Brooklyn Heights contains many fine examples of row housing. Overlooked until the late 1950's when an enterprising real estate dealer rediscovered the Revolutionary War name, **Punkiesberg**, a redoubt at today's Atlantic Avenue and Court Street. Translation into English as Cobble Hill transformed the community in both name and desirability.

[1a.] Hoagland Laboratory, Long Island College Hospital, 335 Henry St. SE cor. Pacific St. 1888. John Mumford.

Though a licensed doctor, Cornelius Nevius Hoagland made his fortune as president of the Cleveland Baking Powder Co. The eclectic Dutch-Romanesque Revival building became the first lab in this country founded by private means for bacteriological, histological, and pathological research. Note early Art Nouveau copper signs on both street facades.

[1b.] Nurses Residence, Long Island College Hospital, 349 Henry St. NE cor. Amity St. 1963.

A handsome, contemporary addition to this hospital's urban campus.

[2.] R. L. Cutter Residence/formerly **Aaron De Graw Residence,** 219 Clinton St. SE cor. Amity St. ca. 1844. Altered, 1891, D'Oench & Simon.

The tower added for viewing the harbor became so high that the first residential elevator in Brooklyn was installed from basement.

[3.] Verandah Place, bet. Clinton and Henry Sts. ca. 1850.

A pleasant row of stable buildings, long neglected but now converted into charming residences. Thomas Wolfe lived in one of them. A blandly designed playground and ill-scaled light standards do their best to intrude.

Square Knots: If you're interested in seeing what pastimes are possible using rope and your own ingenuity, stop in at P. C. Herwig's shop at 264 Clinton Street, just off Verandah Place. His specialty is cordcraft, and he has both the materials and the know-how.

[1b.]

[4.] Tower and Home Apartments, Hicks St. bet. Warren and Baltic Sts. E side. 1878–1879. Hicks St. SE cor. Baltic St. 1877. **Warren Place Workingmen's Cottages,** 1878–1879. William Field & Son.

Completion of the **"sun-lighted tenements"** in newly social-conscious Late Victorian London inspired these 226 low-rent apartments and 44 cottages financed by businessman **Alfred Tredway White.** Innovation of outside stairs and access corridors achieved floor-through layouts and good ventilation. Common bathing facilities were provided in the basement. The tiny, 11½-foot-wide **cottages** line a private pedestrian way called **Warren Place.** None

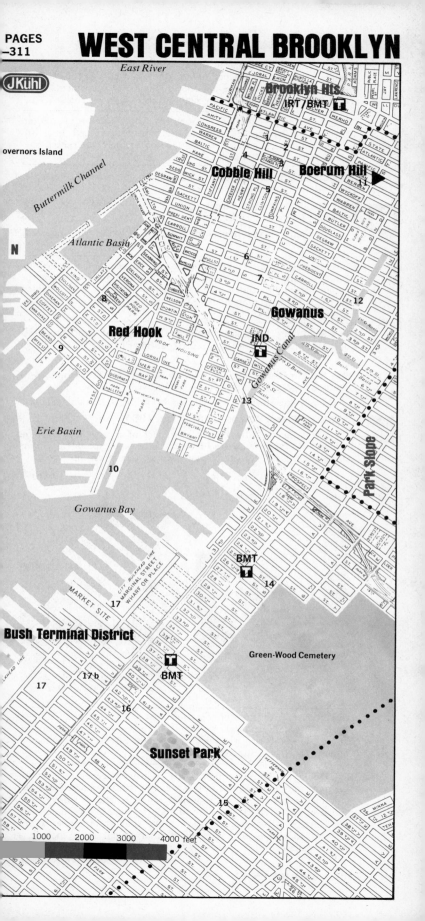

has a back yard, but a rear access space is provided. These six-room dwellings rented for $18 per month (they had cost $1150 each to build, exclusive of land). Four-room, "high-rise" apartments went for $1.93 a week. The **first low-rent "project"** in New York.

Winny's Mom: At 426 Henry Street just below Kane a plaque on an 1848 brownstone indicates that it was the original Leonard Jerome Residence. It was here that Jennie Jerome was raised; she later became Lady Randolph Churchill, mother of Winston.

[5a.] Christ Church Episcopal, 320 Clinton St. SW cor. Kane St. 1842. Richard M. Upjohn.

[5b.] 301–311 Clinton Street, 206–224 Kane Street, and 10–12 Tompkins Place. ca. 1850.

Nine pairs of row houses in an Italianate mode. Very unusual; very lovely.

Cafiero's Restaurant, 97 President St. bet. Hicks and Columbia Sts. 624-9650. Simply but expertly prepared Italian food in an open-kitchen setting. Friendly waiters, fragrant aromas, and presided over by a warm Italian mama. Wine and beer. Closed Mondays. Early dinner to 8 PM only.

[6a.] St. Paul's Protestant Episcopal Church of Brooklyn, 435 Clinton St. NE cor. Carroll St. 1867–1884. Richard M. Upjohn & Son.

[6b.] Rankin Residence/ now **Guido & Sons Funeral Home,** 440 Clinton St. SW cor. Carroll St. ca. 1840.

Handsome, three-story, salmon brick Georgian single house.

[7.] 98 1st Place, SW cor. Court St. ca. 1860.

An Italianate villa that is now part of a row house group. Incidentally, **1st through 4th Places** are interesting spatial variations on the street grid because of their deep setbacks from the street.

[9.

Dennett Place: An atmospheric street that seems more like a stage set for Maxwell Anderson's *Winterset* than a brick and mortar reality. It lies between Court and Smith Streets and connects Luquer with Nelson Streets.

Red Hook: Partly residential, partly industrial, generally squalid. The most impressive things in this area are the docks and the ships. Its immense low-rent housing project of the Thirties is simply that: immense. Though these units are four stories high like Williamsburg and Harlem River Houses, they prove that scale alone is not sufficient to create an environment, that design must include a broader palette.

[8.] Pioneer Street, bet. Van Brunt and Richards Sts. ca. 1840.

Out of nowhere appears this charming row of early houses, by far the best bit of environment in the area.

[9.] Brooklyn Clay Retort and Firebrick Works, Beard to Van Dyke Sts. bet. Van Brunt and Richards Sts. ca. 1860.

Two sturdy **granite warehouses,** on the north sides of both Beard and Van Dyke Streets just west of Richards, and a **manufactory** with original masonry chimney on the south side of Van Dyke are all that remain of this major enterprise. Clay from South Amboy, New Jersey, was barged in to nearby **Erie Basin** and converted to firebrick here.

[9.]

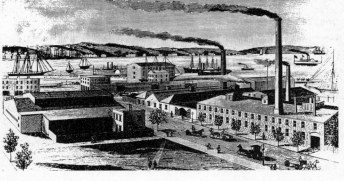

Erie Basin: The scythe-shaped breakwater defining Erie Basin was the idea of enterprising William Beard, a railroad contractor who completed it in 1864. He charged ships seeking to haul American cargoes 50 cents per cubic yard to deposit the rock they had carried as ballast from overseas ports. Incidentally, the longest dead-end street in New York is Columbia Street at Erie Basin. Drive out and see ocean-going vessels parallel parked in the adjacent slips and the dry docks of Todd Shipyard Corporation across the way.

[10.] Port of N. Y. Authority Grain Elevators, Henry St. Basin. (Best seen from Columbia Street.)

Concrete silos dramatically lined up to receive grain shipments from incoming ships.

Boerum Hill: As Cobble Hill before it, Boerum Hill is also a relatively new name for this community trying to revive itself from its **neglected past.** Though the area claimed by the neighborhood association is larger, the most intense concern is for streets such as State, Pacific, Dean, and Bergen east of Court and west of Fourth Avenue. In the mid-19th Century this was a **fashionable district,** as the **fine row housing** will itself indicate. Visitors to the area included Washington Irving, James Fenimore Cooper, and William Cullen Bryant. Sidney Lanier lived briefly at 195 Dean Street.

[11a.] Baptist Temple, 306 Schermerhorn St. SW cor. Third Ave. 1894.

This Romanesque Revival fortress is a continuing center of fundamentalist preaching—the intersection it overlooks is officially Temple Square but has acquired the name, "Brimstone Square." Understandable.

[11b.] Brooklyn Boys Boarding School/later **Public School 15, Brooklyn/**now **Board of Education Certificating Unit,** 475 State St. NE cor. Third Ave. ca. 1840.

Gowanus: A shabby, dull, and monotonous part of Brooklyn. Its most interesting physical features are the **man-made structures** that cross the waterway bearing its name. Before 1911 the fetid Gowanus Canal was known derisively as **Lavender Lake.** At that time the

Butler Street pumping station at its northern terminus began **piping the stale waters** into Buttermilk Channel, inviting fresh water to enter by tidal action. It hasn't helped much.

[12.] Carroll Street Bridge, Carroll St. and Gowanus Canal. 1889.

A unique retractile bridge. The driveway retracts diagonally to shore on special tracks in order to clear the Canal for a passing boat.

[13.] IND Subway High-Level Crossing, Smith and 9th St. Station over Gowanus Canal. 1933.

The ground in these parts proved so poor for tunnel construction that the IND Coney Island Line rises over a hundred feet to meet the Canal's navigational clearances. This leaves the Smith and 9th Street subway station high and dry. Spectacular piece of construction, but regrettably of little visual merit save that of size.

Green-Wood Cemetery

Opened in 1840, this cemetery covers 478 acres and includes the highest point in Brooklyn (216 feet above sea level.) It would be worth visiting merely for its **hills, ponds,** and **plantings,** and its **superb view** of the harbor, but it has much more. Most of the more than one-half million buried there (including Henry Ward Beecher, Currier and Ives, Peter Cooper, Samuel F. B. Morse, "Boss" Tweed, and Lola Montez) are symbolized by **extraordinary mausoleums** and **monuments.** The cemetery is open daily 9 AM–5 PM and can be entered from any of three gates (Prospect Park West at 20th St.,

[14a.]

37th St. near Ft. Hamilton Pkwy.; and **Fifth Ave. at 25th St.**), but the latter **[14a]**☆ is the main gate, with an extraordinary Gothic Revival **gate house** (1861, Richard Upjohn & Son). Alan Burnham has called these gates the "culmination" of the Gothic Revival movement in New York. The gate structure includes offices and a clock tower, all built of **brownstone** with **polychrome slate** roofs on the office wings. The composition has exaggerated verticals and is deliberately squeezed horizontally, the clock face barely fitting within a face of the central steeple.

[14b.] Weir & Co. Greenhouse, Fifth Ave. SW cor. 25th St.

Sunset Park: A neighborhood named after its park, a sloping green oasis with sweeping views of the harbor. The community is heavily Scandinavian in heritage.

[15.] Alku, "Alku" Toinen, Finnish Cooperative Apartments, 816–826 43rd St. bet. Eighth and Ninth Aves. S side. 1916.

No. 816, a not too unusual apartment building, is reputedly the first cooperative dwelling in New York.

[16.] St. Michael's Roman Catholic Church, 4200 Fourth Ave. SW cor. 42nd St. 1905. Raymond F. Almirall.

Brooklyn's own Sacre Coeur, except that the egg-shaped domes are grouped on its 200-foot tower.

Bush Terminal District: Created by Irving T. Bush in 1890, this is an industrial and warehouse city within the city containing loft, freight depot, and pier facilities.

[17a.] Bush Terminal, 28th St. to 50th St. Upper Bay to Second Ave. (irregular) ca. 1911. William Higginson.

Block after block of eight-story, white-painted concrete loft buildings are the visual evidence of the mammoth industrial and warehousing enterprise. Some older red brick buildings still exist in the vicinity of First Avenue and 43rd Street.

[16.]

[17b.] National Metal Co./now **loft space,** 4201–4207 First Ave. SE cor. 42nd St. ca. 1885.

Its ornamental red brick tower is a local landmark—and enigma.

[18.] 2nd Battalion, New York Naval Militia, 5100 First Ave. bet. 51st and 52nd Sts. W side. 1904.

Magnificent arched naval armory; no attempt here to disguise the structural form with a romantic facade of crenellated towers and battlements. Incidentally, a submarine is often moored at the rear.

N

NORTHERN BROOKLYN

Town of Bushwick/Boswijck-Town of the Woods

Established as a town in 1660; Town of Williamsburgh separated from Bushwick in 1840; annexed to City of Brooklyn in 1855.

This area, which includes the three communities of **Bushwick-Ridgewood, Williamsburg,** and **Greenpoint** was often referred to as **The Eastern District** after the merger of 1855, to distinguish it from the remaining and older portion of the City of Brooklyn, **The Western District.** In general this term has fallen into disuse except in connection with the names of a local high school and a freight terminal. Much of this part of Brooklyn is devoted to **working-class** residential areas clustered between industrial concentrations strung along the **East River** and **Newtown Creek.** It is in this precinct that many **fortunes were made** in sugar, oil, rope, lumber, ship building, brewing, and glue.

BUSHWICK-RIDGEWOOD

Malt and hops, barley and barrels, beer and ale. Obermeyer and Liebmann, Ernest Ochs, Claus Lipsius, Danenberg and Coles. The history of the **Bushwick** we see today has been the **history of brewing.** Even now, two major breweries maintain mammoth operations in the area—Rheingold and Schlitz. Beer came to Bushwick in the middle of the 19th Century when a large German population emigrated here after the unsuccessful uprisings in "der Vaterland" in 1848 and 1849.

In its early years the community was noted largely for farming, the produce being sold locally as well as ferried to Manhattan's markets. By the 1840's **Peter Cooper** had moved his **glue factory** here from Manhattan, land values in Murray Hill having so risen that an odoriferous glue manufactory on the old site was no longer practical. Cooper, always a **shrewd businessman,** chose this undeveloped area of Brooklyn near main roads connecting the ferries to New York with the farms of Long Island. The site today is that of Cooper Park Houses, a low-rent housing project. It is named after the adjacent park given to the City of Brooklyn in 1895 by the Cooper family.

[1.] Breweries for Rheingold and Schlitz, off Bushwick Ave. bet. Forrest and Jefferson Sts. W of Evergreen Ave.

On Forrest, George, Noll, and Stanwix Streets stand two mammoth brewery complexes that interlock the original buildings of the 1880's and their 20th Century counterparts. The richness of the 19th Century designs finds no match in the new except where the boldness of the industrial forms overcomes the self-consciousness of the contemporary architecture. The collection of buildings spills over the streets and forces some of them to be closed to traffic either formally, by gates and uniformed guards, or practically, by the trucks waiting their turn to be loaded.

a.] [6.]

[3b.]

[2.] St. Mark's Lutheran Church/formerly St. Mark's Evangelical Lutheran German Church, 626 Bushwick Ave. SE cor. Jefferson St. 1892.

Very prominent as a landmark; its verdigris-covered spire dominates Bushwick Avenue for most of its length.

[3a.] William Ulmer Residence/later Dr. Frederick A. Cook Residence/now Davis Medical Building, 670 Bushwick Ave. SW cor. Willoughby Ave.

A solid, stolid brick fortress as befits a brewer, its builder. Dr. Cook, a later owner, was a well known but not too successful explorer of the Arctic regions in the 1890's.

[3b.] Mrs. Catherine Lipsius Residence/now Franciscan Residence–Pranciskonv Vienuolynas, 680 Bushwick Ave. SE cor. Willoughby Ave. ca. 1885. Theobald Engelhardt.

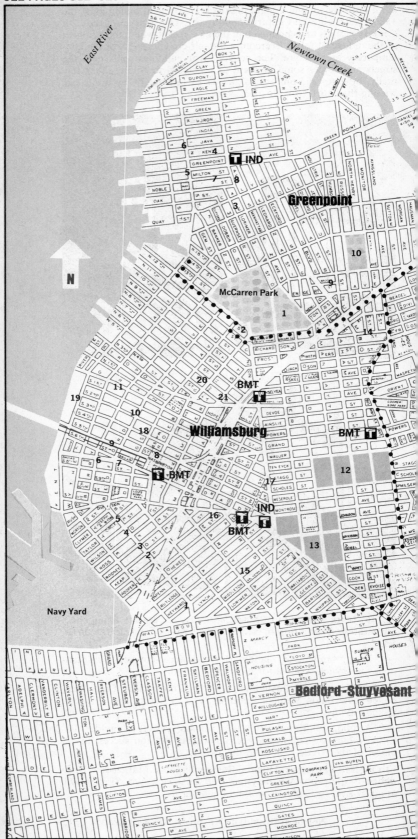

East River

Newtown Creek

Greenpoint

McCarren Park

Williamsburg

BMT

IND

BMT

Navy Yard

Bedford-Stuyvesant

N

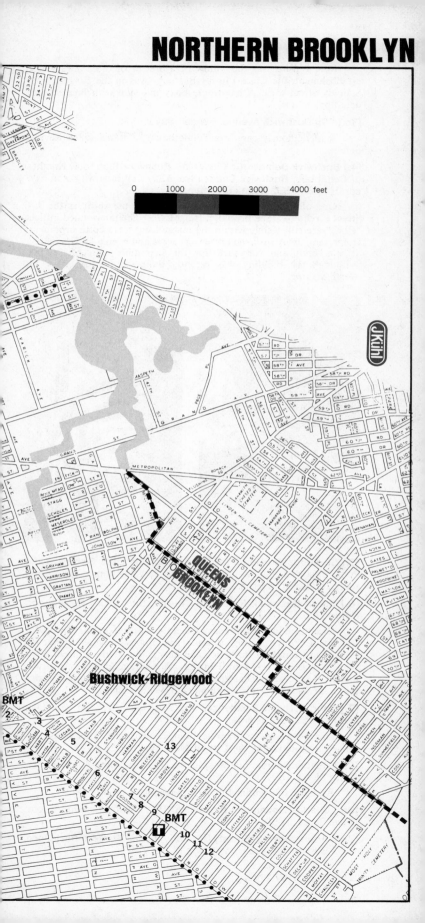

Bushwick-Ridgewood

Mrs. Lipsius was the widow of a brewer of the 1880's whose establishment, the Claus-Lipsius Brewery, was in the Forrest-Noll-Stanwix Street area. A handsome boxy mansion with fine exterior detailing.

[3c.] 696 Bushwick Avenue, SW cor. Suydam St.

A meticulously cared-for frame house of Renaissance Revival detail.

[4.] Bushwick Democratic Club/later **Bushwick Club**/now **Knights of Columbus, Bushwick Council No. 132,** 719 Bushwick Ave. NW cor. Hart St. 1892. Frank Freeman.

One of Freeman's finer works: in the same spirit as the **Jay Street Firehouse.** [See Brooklyn Heights 7a.] The intertwined initials "BDC" are still visible within the magnificent terra cotta ornament. Containing finely furnished meeting rooms and even a bowling alley, it was built and furnished for the incredible sum of $62,000. Although the building was recently damaged by fire, it is still worth visiting.

[4.]  **[4.**

[5.] St. Augustine Home for the Aged of the Little Sisters of the Poor, Bushwick Ave. bet. DeKalb Ave. and Stockholm St. N side. After 1875. Parfitt Bros.

[6.] South Bushwick Reformed Church, Bushwick Ave. NW cor. Himrod St. 1853. ★

Organized in 1851 by farmer members of the original Bushwick Reformed Church, dating back to 1654. First known as the **Second Reformed Church of Bushwick** and now as the **White Church.** First minister was the **Rev. John Himrod,** after whom adjacent street was named. Large-scaled baroque columns and ornate capitals enrich the main facade of this white-painted wood edifice.

[7.] John F. Hylan Residence, 959 Bushwick Ave. bet. Bleecker and Menehan Sts. N side.

One of a row of unpretentious brownstones, this house belonged to a **mayor of the City** of New York (1918–1925).

[8a.] Gustav Doerschuck Residence, 999 Bushwick Ave. NW cor. Grove St. ca. 1890.

Another substantial brewer's mansion in brick.

[8b.] Charles Lindemann Residence, 1001 Bushwick Ave. NE cor. Grove St. ca. 1890.

[8c.] Arion Singing Society/formerly **Louis Bossert Residence,** 1002 Bushwick Ave. SE cor. Grove St. ca. 1890.

This square red brick double house with Mansard roof and attached extensions was originally the home of **Louis Bossert,** a successful millwork manufacturer whose plant was in nearby Williamsburg at Union and Johnson Avenues. The building now is the home of an organization which began as the **Arion Männerchor,** literally the **Arion Men's Choir,** the leading German singing society of the Eastern District. (In 1887 **Arion Hall** was erected for its meetings and concerts. It still stands at **13 Arion Place.**) Bossert went on to become the founder of the **Hotel Bossert** in Brooklyn Heights. [See Brooklyn Heights 14.]

Grove Street: It owes its name to a park called Boulevard Grove at the intersection of that street with Bushwick Avenue. Picnics were being held there as early as 1863.

8a.]  [9a.]

[9a.] 1020 Bushwick Avenue and **37–53 Linden Street,** SW cor. Linden St.

A group of the richly decorated and carefully crafted row houses. As is usual in this period the corner house is treated as a special design problem using the vocabulary of the entire composition. The frieze of terra cotta girding the entire group is superb.

[9b.] George W. Shellas Residence, 1027 Bushwick Ave. NE cor. Linden St.

[10.] Bushwick Avenue Central Methodist Episcopal Church/now **Bushwick Avenue Methodist Church,** 1130 Bushwick Ave. NE cor. Madison St.

[11.] Mrs. J. A. Gramberg Residence, 1150 Bushwick Ave. SE cor. Putnam Ave. ca. 1885.

[12.] Bushwick Avenue Congregational Church/now **Bethesda Baptist Church,** Bushwick Ave. SW cor. Cornelia St. 1896. Parfitt Bros. (?)

A strikingly handsome brick church with a magnificent belfry and a raised clerestory section over the auditorium. Regrettably, it has suffered in recent years from lack of maintenance. It is reminiscent of the Union Methodist Church of Brooklyn in Crown Heights. [See Crown Heights 5.]

Bakery-N. Di Marco, Prop., 291 Central Ave. NW cor. Bleecker St. In the shadow of St. Barbara's across the street this **old Italian bakery** and one-time **coffee house** still exudes the flavor of Italy, both visually and gustatorially. You may not be able to identify which of the pastries are **canoli** and which are **genoice** or **pastichiatta ricotta.** Don't be put off. Let your eyes decide, and your taste buds will be rewarded.

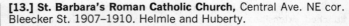

[13.] St. Barbara's Roman Catholic Church, Central Ave. NE cor. Bleecker St. 1907–1910. Helmle and Huberty.

A gleaming white and cream neo-Renaissance pastiche visible from many parts of the adjacent community because of its two tall encrusted towers. Built in a Mediterranean vein for a largely German Catholic parish, today it serves a community with an Italian heritage as well.

[13.]

WILLIAMSBURG

That's right, without the final "h", even though a major institution, the Williamsburgh Savings Bank, spells its name the old way. (The "h" fell when it consolidated with the City of Brooklyn in 1855.)

Though it shares its current spelling with the well-known restoration in Virginia, the resemblance ends there. Our Williamsburg, formerly part of the **Town of Bushwick,** later a village and city in its own right, was named after its surveyor, **Benjamin Franklin's grandnephew,** Col. Jonathan Williams. Richard M. Woodhull started the community when he purchased 13 acres of land at the foot of today's South 2nd Street in 1802. He had Williams survey it, established a ferry to Manhattan, and proceeded to go bankrupt by 1811.

Thomas Morrell and James Hazard picked up where Woodhull had failed. They also established a ferry to the Grand Street Market in Corlears Hook and provided an outlet for the **farmers** of Bushwick to **sell their produce** in Manhattan. The impetus to the growth of the area, however, was the establishment of a **distillery,** in 1819. The distillery is gone (it is site of the Schaefer Brewery), but the district, together with adjacent Bushwick-Ridgewood, still has both active and latent concentrations of alcohol-producing establishments—mostly **breweries** of varying vintages.

The most significant influence upon the community was the opening of the Williamsburg Bridge in 1903. Overnight the community changed from a **fashionable resort** with hotels catering to such sportsmen as Commodore Vanderbilt, Jim Fisk, and William C. Whitney to an **immigrant district** absorbing the overflow from New York's Lower East Side. (*The New York Tribune* of the period characterized the Bridge as "The Jew's Highway.") Its elegant families moved out, and the mansions and fine brownstones of the post-Civil War era fell into disuse and were soon converted to multiple dwellings.

Hassidic Community: Along Bedford Avenue are arrayed such a group of mansions, brownstones, and some ornate apartment houses. The area also contains the most concentrated Hassidic Jewish community. This unique settlement, recalling **Late Medieval Jewish**

life in its dress and customs, is a result of the persecution of the eastern European Jewish community in World War II. In 1940, *Rebbe* Joel Teitelbaum and several of his flock reached these shores and chose Williamsburg—even then a **heavily Orthodox** area—as their home. By the end of the war, the remaining survivors from Hungary migrated to the new settlement and reestablished their lives there. **Beards** and **uncut forelocks** of hair identify the men; shaven but **wigged heads** identify the women. Long **black frock coats** and **skull caps** are in evidence everywhere among its male population, young and old, and in the winter, the **fur-trimmed hat,** the *shtreimel,* is certain to make its appearance. Evidence of its residents' heritage is everywhere apparent, from the proliferation of Yiddish signs on the mansions to the identification of small business establishments catering to the group.

Bedford Avenue: The sequence is northbound with the direction of traffic; the house numbers decrease as we proceed.

[1.] 675–665 Bedford Avenue, bet. Heyward and Rutledge Sts. E side.

An entire blockfront of magnificently encrusted tenements following in the footsteps of the more elegant mansions further north on the avenue.

[2a.] 571 Bedford Avenue, bet. Keap and Rodney Sts. E side.

Rough-hewn stone and an obviously affluent client made this building a showplace.

[2b.] Hawley Mansion/later **Hanover Club**/now **Young Israel of Brooklyn,** 561 Bedford Ave. SE cor. Rodney St. ca. 1875. Conversion, 1891. Lauritzen & Voss.

Built by O. F. Hawley, a successful lumber dealer whose yard was down Rodney Street at Kent Avenue, the building was vacated by him in 1890. Prominent men in the community seized this opportunity to convert the building into a clubhouse, and in 1891, after alterations and enlargement, it was opened as the Hanover Club. William Cullen Bryant became its first president and held office until 1899.

[2c.] Congregation Arugath Habosem, 559 Bedford Ave. NE cor. Rodney St. ca. 1890.

An imposing mansion, now minus the conical, Spanish tile roof over its round corner tower.

[3.] Joseph F. Knapp Residence/later a dancing academy/now **Yeshiva Umesivta Torah V'Yirah D'Satmar,** 554 Bedford Ave. NW cor. Ross St. 1894.

Built by the president of Metropolitan Life Insurance Company.

 [4a.] Frederick Mollenhauer Residence/later **The Congress Club/** now **Yeshiva Yesoda Hatora of K'Hal Adas Yereim,** 505 Bedford Ave. NE cor. Taylor St. 1896. Lauritzen & Voss.

This handsome neo-renaissance limestone mansion occupies a corner site and is still impressive today. Built by one of the sons of John Mollenhauer, who in 1867 founded the Mollenhauer Sugar Refinery, subsequently the National Sugar Refining Company (Jack Frost). The original refinery, no longer there, was at Kent Avenue at Rush Street and later at South 11th Street.

[5a.] Congregation Tiffereth Israel/formerly **First Reformed Dutch Church of Williamsburg,** 491 Bedford Ave. SE cor. Clymer St. 1869.

The Tree that Grows in Brooklyn: Williamsburg, a swampy, low-lying area, became the ideal spot for the culture of the ailanthus tree. First imported from China about 1840, it found great popularity here because of its supposed powers to dispel the disease-producing vapors presumed to come from swampy lands. See Betty Smith's novel of Williamsburg life.

[5b.] Dr. Charles A. Olcott Residence/later **Entre Nous Club,** 489 Bedford Ave. NE cor. Clymer St.

[5c.] "The Rebbe's House," Grand Rabbi Joel Teitelbaum Residence, 500 Bedford Ave. NW cor. Clymer St.

A recently installed bronze grillwork forms the ceremonial entrance at the top of the stoop in this mansarded row house. Home of the Grand Rabbi of Satmar, one of four leaders of Hassidic sects in the Williamsburg community.

[5d.] Clymer Street, bet. Bedford and Lee Aves. N side.

The **march of history** is particularly well documented in a group of buildings that still remain on this side street. No. 169–171 seems to have been the home of Knickerbocker Hall, a **concert hall** that also provided studio space for individuals such as Mr. William A. French, dancing teacher. Duhamel and Singer, **carriage makers** to the carriage trade, later occupied the building. No. 163–165, a splendid brick structure, was a **livery stable** operated by Douglass and Peterkin to service the carriages of the aristocratic families who resided nearby; No. 159 is their old storage building. Subsequently, the Douglass **stables** occupied the entire row and quartered the prize-winning trotters from the Union Race Course there. (Union Course was located on the south side of Jamaica Avenue in the vicinity of 76th Street across the Queens County line.) In 1911 the buildings became the home of Kestler Brothers' **garage**—the motor car had come into existence! At No. 173 an elaborate two-story carriage house which was the home of the first and, for a period, the only **steam fire engine** owned by any Eastern District volunteer company. They called themselves "Victory Engine Company No. 13."

Peter Luger Steak House, 178 Broadway, West of Bedford Avenue, EV 7-7400. Polished oak tables bare of coverings, waiters wearing white aprons down to the floor, and superb but simply prepared food. These are the characteristics of this out-of-the-way, but highly respected, restaurant. It began as Charles Luger's Cafe, Billiards, and Bowling Alley in 1876. It's been pretty much the same as you presently see it since 1887. The side entrance on Bedford Avenue just south of Broadway looks undisturbed since then. Special luncheons include beef stew, pot roast, and prime ribs of beef. The specialty of the house *is* steak, and some authorities consider that it may be the best available in the city. See what you think.

While on Broadway, let's diverge a bit from Bedford Avenue:

[6a.] 97 Broadway, bet. Bedford Ave. and Berry St. N side. 1870.

A cast-iron facade with Mansard roof. Its prime function today is to support an immense sign facing the adjacent Williamsburg Bridge. At one time it was the home of the Kings County Fire Insurance Company.

[6b.] 103 Broadway, bet. Bedford Ave. and Berry St. N side. ca. 1875.

Another cast-iron wonder.

[7a.] Kings County Savings Bank, 135 Broadway NE cor. Bedford Ave. 1868. King & Wilcox, William H. Wilcox. ★

Bands of vermiculated Dorchester stone alternate with smooth ones to enliven the exterior of the banking floor of this splendid Second Empire masterpiece. Victorian at its best, even the interior is carefully preserved, the gas-lit chandeliers all being in evidence (even though wired for electricity). Let's hope the trustees of the Bank will continue to extend its life.

[7b.] 134–136 Broadway, SW cor. Bedford Ave. 1888 (?). Frank J. Helmle. Formerly the Nassau Trust Company.

[7c.] Williamsburgh Savings Bank, 175 Broadway NW cor. Driggs Ave. 1875. George B. Post. ★

An eclectic combination of Florence's *Il Duomo* on a Roman base. One of the landmarks of Williamsburg, particularly to the tens of thousands who pass it daily on the BMT Jamaica Elevated. Later additions in 1906 as in 1925 were by Helmle, Huberty, and Hudswell, and they carry out Post's ideas very well.

[10.]

[8a.] Holy Trinity Cathedral of the Ukrainian Orthodox Church in Exile/formerly **N. Y. C. Magistrate's Court,** 117–185 S. 5th St. NW cor. New St. 1906. Helmle and Huberty. ★

The more common progression from religious to sectarian uses in a building's life is here reversed. Built as a court, this opulent marble monument is now a cathedral. That's how it goes.

[8b.] Washington Plaza, S. 4th St. to Broadway, S. 5th Pl. to Havemeyer St.

Formerly a ganglion for half the **trolley empire** in Brooklyn, the Plaza is now a depot for nondescript green buses belching forth diesel fumes even though resting between runs. Some of the old wooden sheds and a signal tower remain, but the mass of **overhead copper wires** are now only a memory. Furthermore, the space is cut into pieces by the elevated BMT and Brooklyn-Queens Expressway which slice through it with melancholy abandon. In the northwest corner, a **forecourt** for the Ukrainian Cathedral, is a formally executed plaza which is the only part of the whole deserving the title. It contains, among other things, a fine equestrian statue, **George Washington at Valley Forge,** by Henry M. Shrady. Unveiled in 1906.

[9.] Fruitcrest Corporation/formerly **The Bedford Avenue Theater,** 109 S. 6th St. bet. Bedford Ave. and Berry St. 1891. W. W. Cole, Builder.

Opened by an actress named Fannie Rice in a farce, *The Jolly Surprise.* Its history as a theater was short-lived. It was sold in 1908 after a period during which it was known as the Empire Theatre.

[7a.]

[7

[8a.]

[1

And back to Bedford Avenue for one last entry:

[10.] 324 Bedford Avenue, NW cor. S. 2nd St. ca. 1866

Built as the headquarters of the Williamsburg Gas Light Company but vacant now after service as a branch office of the Brooklyn Union Gas Co. Its cast-iron facade is rusted and resembles the best Maori-R or Cor-Ten finish obtainable. The building awaits its fate. It is far too fine a work of architecture to permit demolition, particularly since it marks a famous site in the history of the community. The structure sits adjacent to the former location of the Old City Hall of the City of Williamsburgh and on the site of its park and bell tower.

Grand Street

[11a.] North Side Bank/later **Manufacturer's Trust Co.**/now **J.**

Nikolas Guaranteed Lacquers, 33–35 Grand St. bet. Kent and Wythe Aves. N side. 1889. Theobald Engelhardt.

[11b.] Palace Hall/formerly **Palace Rink,** 89–93 Grand St. bet. Wythe Ave. and Berry St. N side.

These two buildings offer some indication of the importance of Grand Street when it was one of the main streets of Williamsburg and led down to the ferryboat to Manhattan. Though the two divergent street grids are arranged about Grand Street as their central axis (it lies between North 1st and South 1st Streets), it never attained the importance of Broadway.

The Fourteen Buildings: The turn Grand Street takes at Union Avenue marks the beginning of the site of the Fourteen Buildings. The street was laid out between Union and Bushwick Avenues so that it would pass through the property of a group of men who then built for themselves a series of Greek Revival frame dwellings. Each had a dome and a colonnaded porch of fluted wood columns. The houses were arranged one per block on both sides of Grand Street with two extras slipped in. This was in 1836. By 1837 each of the men had suffered the consequences of that year's financial panic and the houses changed hands. In 1850 all still remained, but by 1896 only one was left. Today there is no sign on this busy shopping street of that bygone elegance.

[12.] Williamsburg Houses, Maujer to Scholes Sts., Leonard St. to Bushwick Ave. 1937. Board of Design: Richmond H. Shreve, Chief Architect; with James F. Bly, Matthew W. Del Gaudio, Arthur C. Holden, William Lescaze, Samuel Gardstein, Paul Trapani, G. Harmon Gurney, Harry Leslie Walker, and John W. Ingle, Jr., Associates.

It is amazing that such a large committee could have come up with this early, large, and **very successful solution** to the problem of low-rent subsidized housing. In New York City today, only Harlem River Houses, among low-rent projects of the same period, compare favorably insofar as their impact on the **cityscape.**

[13.] Lindsay Park Houses, Montrose Ave. to Moore St., Union to Manhattan Aves. 1966–1967. Kelly & Gruzen.

A middle-income, Title 1 urban renewal project 29 years younger than Williamsburg Houses.

[14a.] 492–494 Humboldt Street, bet. Richardson and Herbert Sts. E side. **[14b.] 201 Richardson Street,** bet. Humboldt and N. Henry Sts. N side. ca. 1850's.

Three houses of a somewhat larger number (of which the others have been remodeled) that formed one of Brooklyn's four colonnade rows. (Two were in Brooklyn Heights, one still in existence; the other was also in Williamsburg.)

Colonnade Row: Only records remain of the least known of Brooklyn's four colonnade rows. This one was on the east side of Kent Avenue, between South 8th and South 9th Streets in Williamsburg. (The last of the group was removed in the 1920's.) Among the families who shared the extraordinary views across the river were the Walls and the Berrys. Dr. Abraham Berry became the first mayor of the City of Williamsburgh in 1852; William Wall became the second and the last in 1854.

MISCELLANY

[15.] 17th Corps Artillery Armory/formerly **47th Regiment Armory**/formerly **The Union Grounds,** Marcy to Harrison Aves., Heyward to Lynch Sts. 1883. Henry Mundell.

The site of early baseball games in the 1860's between the Cincinnati Red Stockings, the Philadelphia Athletics, the New York Mutuals, and the Brooklyn Eckfords.

[16.] Temple Beth Elohim/now **Talmud Torah Pride of Israel,** 274

Keap St. bet. Marcy and Division Aves. 1876.

The first Hebrew congregation in Brooklyn, dating from 1851. Merged with Union Temple on Eastern Parkway in the 1920's when its founding Reform German Jewish Congregation departed.

[17a.] Deutsch Evangelische St. Petri Kirche/now **Iglesia de Dios Pentecostal Missionera,** 262 Union Ave. NE cor. Scholes St. 1881.

[17b.] N. Y. C. Department of Sanitation District Office/formerly **P. S. 69, Brooklyn,** 270 Union Ave. bet. Scholes and Stagg St. E side.

[17c.] South Third Street Methodist Church, 411 S. 3rd St. bet. Union Ave. and Hewes St. N side. 1855.

Three wonderful brick buildings controlling a peculiar triangular intersection of street grids.

[18.] Industrial School Association, Main Branch/now **Yeshivath Torah Vodaath & Mesivta,** 141 S. 3rd St. bet. Driggs and Bedford Aves. N side.

Originally a school for the reeducation of vagrants, started by the New England Congregational Church (now known as Light of the World Church on S. 9th Street east of Driggs Ave.)

[17a.]
[17c.]

[2

[19.] American Sugar Refining Company (Domino Sugar)/formerly **Havemeyer and Elders Sugar Refining Company,** 292–350 Kent Ave. bet. S. 5th and South 2nd Sts. W side.

Bulky, bold, and brutal masonry behemoths.

[20.] St. Matthew's First Evangelical Lutheran Church, 197–199 N. 5th St. bet. Roebling St. and Driggs Ave. 1864.

Note the battered buttresses trying to look as though they are necessary to support this charming brick church.

[21.] Church of the Annunciation (Roman Catholic), 255 N. 5th St. NE cor. Havemeyer St. ca. 1870.

A crisply detailed and lovingly maintained basilica. Nothing unnecessary to the full impact has been added, nor can any small bit of detail be removed. A gem of a building. Note the two parochial school structures across Havemeyer Street to the west.

Subway kiosks: The famed and late-lamented cast-iron IRT subway kiosks were cast in a successful foundry that once existed in Williamsburg. The Hecla Iron Works flourished on Berry Street in the northern part of the community.

A short course in Fiberglas is a few short blocks away.

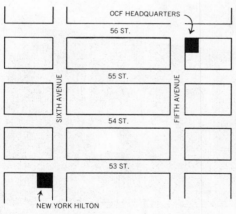

OCF HEADQUARTERS

56 ST.

55 ST.

54 ST.

53 ST.

SIXTH AVENUE

FIFTH AVENUE

NEW YORK HILTON

Come to the Owens-Corning Fiberglas headquarters. We have a special exhibit for architects. It includes many of the new things you can do with Fiberglas* products. Sorry, we don't have the Merchandise Mart to show you all of them. However, as soon as we hear of a new use, we hurry up and get it in the exhibit. We make sure you take home nothing but the freshest ideas. But if you can't find the time to visit our place, don't despair. Just look for our representative in your home town phone book. He's our walking, talking, Fiberglas exhibit.

Industrial & Commercial Const. Mat. Div., 717 Fifth Ave., New York 10022

OWENS-CORNING

FIBERGLAS

T-M REG U S PAT OFF

325

*T-M (Reg. U.S. Pat. Off.) O-CF. Corp.

GREENPOINT

Greenpoint (local pronunciation: **Greenpernt**) is a quiet community whose central area has a charm unknown to most outsiders.

Greenpoint's modern history begins with the surveying of its lands in 1832 by **Dr. Eliphalet Nott,** President of Union College, Schenectady (America's first architecturally planned campus), and **Neziah Bliss.** Within two years all the area was completely laid out in streets and lots. Much of it was then purchased for development by A. C. Kingsland, a mayor of New York, and **Samuel J. Tilden** who went on to fame in politics and is remembered for the establishment of a free public library system in New York City.

The area became a great ship building center soon afterward, and it is here at the **Continental Iron Works,** in a building which stood at West and Calyer Streets, that Thomas F. Rowland built the ironclad **Monitor** from designs by John Ericsson. The **"Yankee cheese box on a raft"** was launched January 30, 1862, and defeated the Confederate **Merrimac** at Hampton Roads, Virginia, two months later. That same year (December 20th) the Monitor foundered off Cape Hatteras and was lost.

By 1860 the so-called **Five Black Arts** (printing, pottery, gas, glass, and iron) were firmly established in Green Point, as it was first known. In 1867 **Charles Pratt** established his oil refinery to meet the need for refined by-products of petroleum. (The first successful tapping of oil in Titusville, Pa., came in 1859.) Pratt's product, a widely-used, high-grade kerosene, later gave rise to the remark, "the holy lamps of Tibet are primed with Astral Oil." The sale of **Astral Oil** provided the wealth which later made possible Pratt Institute, as well as the **Astral Apartments** in Greenpoint.

[1.]

[1.] McCarren Park Swimming Pool, McCarren Park, Lorimer St. bet. Bayard St. and Driggs Ave. E side. ca. 1935.

One of four WPA-built swimming pools erected in Brooklyn during the Depression. The entrance pavilion combines a weightless, four-sided, masonry arch with an open clerestory level just below its roof. Somehow, its form is just right for announcing a dip in the pool.

[2.] Russian Orthodox Church of the Transfiguration, 228 N. 12th St. SW cor. Berry St. 1922. Louis Allmendinger. ☆

The five, luscious, onion-domed cupolas on this church are visible from far and wide. The real treat, however, is inside the cream-colored brick building. The interior is surprisingly small—it seats only about 250. The **central cupola** is supported by four huge columns painted to resemble **richly veined marble.** The three altars are divided from the body of the church by an *iconostasis,* a **hand-**

carved wooden screen on which icons painted by monks in the Orthodox Monastery of the Caves in Kiev are displayed. Around the screen are miniature light bulbs—those around the door flicker off and on as it is opened into the **sanctuary.**

A visit must include the **celebration of the Mass.** The architecture, the aroma of the swinging container of incense, the service sung and **chanted** in Latin, Slavonic, and English when all put together are overwhelming—a deeply moving saturation of the senses.

[2.]

[3.] Green Point Savings Bank, 807 Manhattan Ave. SW cor. Calyer St. 1908. John Pierce. ☆

A granite temple with a finely executed Doric portico.

[4a.] St. Elias Greek Rite Catholic Church/formerly **Greenpoint Reformed Church,** 149 Kent St. bet. Manhattan Ave. and Franklin St. N side. Church, 1870; Chapel, 1880.

This version of a 16th Century German Romanesque church was originally the home of Greenpoint's Dutch Reform Congregation. In 1891 it became a Greek Rite Catholic church. Unfortunately neither tower is complete, each lacking a Mansard roof.

[4b.] Church of the Ascension (Episcopal), 129 Kent St. bet. Manhattan Ave. and Franklin St. N side. 1866.

A random ashlar stone building with a very unusual and quite contemporary roof line.

[5.] Greenpoint Branch of the Corn Exchange Bank/now **Met-maint Electric Company,** 144 Franklin St. NE cor. Greenpoint Ave.

[6.] The Astral Apartments, 184 Franklin St. bet. Java and India Sts. E side. 1886. Lamb & Rich.

Commissioned by Charles Pratt as housing for his refinery workers and others, this collection of six adjacent apartment buildings was patterned after the earlier **Peabody Apartments** in London. **Alfred Tredway White** had already pioneered in similar projects south of Brooklyn Heights. [See WC Brooklyn 4.]

[4a.]

Milton Street: This interesting block stretches up hill between Franklin Street and Manhattan Avenue culminating at the entrance to St. Anthony's Church and sums up the finest values of Greenpoint.

[7a.] 93–103 Milton Street, N side.

Ten brickfront row houses with delicate hoodmolds over windows and doors.

[7b.] 118–120 Milton Street, S side.

Mansard-roofed: very tiny; small in scale. Note entries are along sides of building rather than in front.

[7c.] 119–123, 125–127 Milton Street, N side.

Each pair is handled as one composition—the slight forward projection of the entryways provides a verticality in their boxy facades that puts these two-story dwellings in scale with their taller neighbors. Nos. 125–127 have been insensitively altered.

[7d.] 122–124 Milton Street, S side.

No. 124 is the parsonage of St. John's Lutheran Church across the way. At first glance this pair seems to be meant as a symmetric grouping. Look carefully though—they are not and were not meant to be!

[7e.] 138 Milton Street, S side. **Greenpoint Reformed Church.**

Before 1891 this congregation occupied St. Elias Greek Rite Catholic Church two blocks north on Kent Street. Today they occupy this modest house. Note the similarity in design and approach with Nos. 119–125 across the street.

[7f.] 139–151 Milton Street, N side.

[7g.] 155 Milton Street, N side. **St. John's Lutheran Church,** 1892.

Cut into stone in the finest German antique fashion are the words "Evangelisch Lutherisch St. Johannes Kirche." This was one of the most popular churches of Greenpoint's German population.

[8.] 862 Manhattan Avenue, at end of Milton St., E side. **St. Anthony of Padua Roman Catholic Church,** 1874.

The 190-foot spire of this church, located at the point of a subtle change of direction in Manhattan Avenue, is a center of focus, not only for Milton Street, but for much of central Greenpoint as well.

[9.] St. Stanislaus Kostka Roman Catholic Church, 607 Humboldt St. SW cor. Driggs Ave.

In this eastern part of Greenpoint, the spires of this church dominate the low skyline. (It holds the largest Polish Catholic congregation in Brooklyn.) The church is characterized by a heavy encrustation of stone ornament, in rich contrast to the demure rows of low-rise amber brick apartments that line the nearby streets.

[10.] Monsignor McGoldrick Park, Driggs to Nassau Aves., Russell to Monitor Sts. **Shelter pavilion,** Helmle and Huberty. ☆

CENTRAL BROOKLYN

Town of Flatbush/Vlackebos

Established as a town in 1652; Town of New Lots separated from Flatbush in 1852; annexed to the City of Brooklyn in 1894.

Until the 1880's Flatbush was a rather quiet place with a **distinctively colonial character.** The introduction of the Brooklyn, Flatbush, and Coney Island Rail Road, now the Brighton Line of the BMT, encouraged real estate men in enterprises that by the turn of the 20th Century had transformed the farm land into a **fashionable suburb.** The names of these subdivisions are still used in some cases, dimly remembered in others: **Prospect Park South,** the most affluent of those existing today, **Vandeveer Park** (close perusal of Brooklyn IRT destination signs will show this area listed instead of the Flatbush Avenue terminal of the Nostrand Avenue Line), **Ditmas Park, Fiske and Manhattan Terraces,** and a host of others like Matthews Park, Slocum Park, and Yale Park.

Earlier there were a series of abortive attempts to establish grids of houses on the countryside, such as **Parkville,** the off-axis grid surrounding Parkville Avenue (1852) and **Windsor Terrace,** between Vanderbilt and Greenwood Avenues in the corridor separating Green-Wood Cemetery from Prospect Park (1862). These projects were never so successful as those that hugged the natural interruption of through streets caused by the cut of the railroad to Brighton Beach.

FLATBUSH

[1.] 111 Clarkson Avenue, bet. Bedford and Rogers Aves. N side.

Victoriana at its most outlandish. But why the onion domes?

[2a.] Flatbush Reformed Dutch Church and Parsonage, Flatbush Ave. SW cor. Church Ave. **Church,** 1793–1798. Thomas Fardon; ★

[2b.] Parsonage, Kenmore Terrace NE cor. E. 21st St. 1853.

Third edifice to occupy this site; the earliest, built 1654, was the first church on Long Island. Original building was one of three

churches built according to a **mandate of Gov. Peter Stuyvesant.**
(The others were Flatlands Reformed Dutch and First Reformed.)

[2c.] Erasmus Hall Academy/now part of **Erasmus Hall High
School,** Flatbush Ave. SE cor. Church Ave. 1786. ★

Established as a private academy by the Flatbush Reformed
Dutch Church across the street; built of local materials by parishioners, with those later adversaries, **Hamilton and Burr,** both contributing to the building fund; became first secondary school
chartered by State Board of Regents. In 1896 it was given to the
City of Brooklyn, and Academy changed to High School.

Warning: Rule 9, Erasmus Hall Academy, 1797, states "No student shall be permitted to practise any species of gaming nor to
drink any spiritous liquors nor to go into any tavern in Flat Bush
without obtaining consent of a teacher."

[2d.] Kenmore Terrace, E of E. 21st St. bet. Church Ave. and Albemarle Rd.

[2e.] Albemarle Terrace, S of Kenmore Terrace.

What an unfortunate expression "dead end" is, particularly
when applied to these two short and delightful streets.

[1.]

PROSPECT PARK SOUTH

The streets between Church Avenue and Beverly Road, and between Coney Island Avenue and the open cut for the BMT Brighton
Line contain as unique a community as any in the city. The entrances to most of its streets are guarded by pairs of sturdy brick
piers containing cast-stone plaques with the letters **PPS** formed
into a monogram. This area is **Prospect Park South,** characterized
at the time of its initial development as *"Rus in Urbe,"* an expression not inappropriate even today. Lining its streets are a series of
lavish, turn-of-the-century, single-family **residences** that have somehow withstood the pressures of change.

PPS is a monument to the vision of Dean Alvord. What he
conceived was a rural park within the confines of the grid. He
wanted to abandon the row house concept and build detached
houses under careful restrictions. To this end he installed all his
utilities and paved the streets before selling one plot of land.
Trees were planted, not along the curb, but on the building line,
in order to give the streets a sense of breadth. The species were
carefully chosen. Alternating every 20 feet were Norway maples,
for permanence, and Carolina poplars, for immediate shade. The
poplars, Alvord and his architect, John Petit, reasoned, being short-
lived, would die out as the maples reached maturity.

[3a.] 84 Buckingham Road, SW cor. Church Ave.

Tudoresque.

[3b.] 85 Buckingham Road.

Note the Palladian window over the entrance and the harmonizing curve in the eave.

[3c.] 104 Buckingham Road.

Originally the Russell Benedict Residence. As stately a portico as one could wish.

[3d.] 115 Buckingham Road.

Originally the M. G. Gillette Residence. A volumetric exercise in Late Victorian house design. Witty juxtaposition of mass with void. Note shingle siding and the delicacy of the shadow lines cast.

[3e.] 125 Buckingham Road.

Surprisingly, the carved wooden columns with their florid capitals harmonize quite well with the finely-scaled clapboard siding in the pediment and on the walls.

[3f.] 131 Buckingham Road.

Originally the Dr. F. S. Kolle Residence. Known at the time as "The Japanese House." In contrast to the later exoticism of oriental moderne in other parts of Brooklyn, the restraint of the carefully adapted Japanese temple detailing is a welcome note. The form of the residence is that of a standard, boxy, two-story-plus-attic dwelling. The handling of details—porch, balcony, and eave lines—gives the Japanese effect. Dr. Kolle was a German emigre who later established a practice in radiology in New York.

[3g.] 143 Buckingham Road, NE cor. Albemarle Rd.

A more traditionally romantic house of the period on a large corner plot.

Back yards: Today's four-track BMT Brighton Line, which abuts the rear yards of the houses on the east side of Buckingham Road, was, at the time of the original development, only a two-track operation. In 1907, the Brooklyn Rapid Transit Company, successors to the original railroad and precursors of the BMT, widened the cut, thus narrowing the back yards of these houses to the nominal amount visible today.

  [3f.]

[3h.] 1519 Albemarle Road. NW cor. Buckingham Rd.

A later, masonry dwelling obviously influenced in both form and detail by the work of the Chicago School of architects.

[3i.] 1510 Albemarle Road. SE cor. Marlborough Rd.

A stately mansion, with later additions of a two-story sun porch and greenhouse. Note stable in rear on Marlborough Road and the repeat of the Corinthian colonnade.

[3j.] 1305 Albemarle Road. NE cor. Argyle Rd.

The articulation of the two-story, colonnaded portico with the one-story porches on either side makes a dynamic and robust facade of wood neobaroque design.

Street Furniture: An original Prospect Park South cast-iron street sign still stands at the southeast corner of Beverly and Marlborough Roads.

[3j.]

[11.]

[4.] Flatbush–Tompkins Congregational Church Parish House/ formerly **Flatbush Congregational Church,** 451 E. 18th St. SE cor. Dorchester Rd. Pre–1900.

A boldly curved, dark-shingled parish house with handsome fenestration, now interconnected with later buildings of the church itself (Additions, 1909, Allens & Collens/L. E. Jallade). The present church joined with the former Tompkins Congregational Church. [See Bedford-Stuyvesant 16.]

 [5a.] George W. Van Ness Residence, 1000 Ocean Ave. bet. Ditmas and Newkirk Aves. W side. 1899. McKim, Mead & White.

[5b.] Thomas H. Brush Residence/now **Community Temple Beth Ohr,** 1010 Ocean Ave. NW cor. Newkirk Ave. 1899. McKim, Mead & White.

This pair sets the tone for all the lavish homes that line the west side of Ocean Avenue in this block. No. 1010 was at one point the home of Gilda Gray, "shimmy" star of the Twenties; since 1937, it has housed a synagogue.

[6.] 2693 Bedford Avenue, bet. Foster Ave. and Farragut Rd. E side.

Juxtaposition of circular recesses in an otherwise rectilinear house produces a feeling of cut-out paper dolls. Delightful Victorian showpiece.

[4.]

EAST FLATBUSH/RUGBY

[7.] Downstate Medical Center of the State University of New York. Complex occupies area roughly bounded by Clarkson and New York Aves., Linden Blvd., and E. 37th St.

Basic Sciences Building	1954–1956 Voorhees, Walker, Smith, Smith & Haines
Hospital and Intensive Care Unit	1966 Office of Max O. Urbahn
Dormitories	1966 Office of Max O. Urbahn
Garage	1967 William Lescaze & Assoc.

[8.] Gen. George W. Wingate High School, 600 Kingston Ave. bet. Winthrop St. and Rutland Rd. W side. 1955. Kelly & Gruzen.

[9.] East New York Savings Bank, Kingsboro Branch, Kings Highway and E. 98th St.

WINDSOR TERRACE

[10a.] Engine Company 240, N.Y.C. Fire Department, 1309 Prospect Ave. bet. Greenwood Ave. and Ocean Pkwy. E side. 1896.

Charming Victorian fire station that has regrettably lost its conical turret.

PARKVILLE

[11.] Parkville Congregational Church, 18th Ave. NW cor. E. 5th St. 1895.

This congregation claims one of the handsomest country churches in all of Brooklyn. The stepped-back bracketing of the roof eave adds a marvelous staccato note.

Bocci: Using the sandy roadbed of the dormant railroad tracks as their court (4'–8½" is a perfect width) and portable wooden planks as their backstops, a group of die-hard Italians play their game of Latin bowls under the BMT Culver Shuttle at 37th Street and Church Avenue. You can find them there any weekend, weather permitting.

SOUTHWESTERN BROOKLYN

Town of New Utrecht/Nieuw Utrecht

Established as a town in 1662; annexed to City of Brooklyn in 1854.

The old Town of New Utrecht includes the present-day communities of Bay Ridge, Fort Hamilton, Dyker Heights, Borough Park, Bath Beach, and much of Bensonhurst. At various times in its past, other, barely remembered communities existed here: Blythebourne, Mapleton, Lefferts Park, and Van Pelt Manor; and the area was largely rural until the beginning of the 20th Century.

BAY RIDGE–FORT HAMILTON–DYKER HEIGHTS

Some of the most desirable residential sites in Brooklyn lay along the high ground overlooking the Narrows and Gravesend Bay, and this strip, along Shore Road, was once the site of **magnificent mansions.** The **ornate villa** of E. W. Bliss, of Greenpoint fame; Neils Poulson's **cast-iron fantasy,** by the founder of Williamsburg's Hecla Iron Works; **Fontbonne Hall,** the home of Tom L. Johnson, the "three-cent mayor of Cleveland," and many others lined the bluff overlooking the harbor. In the Chandler White residence the group headed by Cyrus Field and Peter Cooper first gathered to discuss the laying of the **Atlantic Cable.** The Bliss mansion was once the home of Henry C. Murphy where, in 1865, Murphy met with Kingsley and McCue to formulate the original agreement for building the **Brooklyn Bridge.** Except for Fontbonne Hall, now a private school, all the mansions have been supplanted by endless ranks of elevator apartment buildings, forming a palisade of red brick along the edge of Shore Road.

[1.] Flagg Court, 7200 Ridge Blvd. bet. 72nd and 73rd Sts. W side. 1933–1936. Ernest Flagg.

Flagg Court, named after its architect, who was also responsible for the Singer Tower, is a 422-unit housing development contained in six contiguous buildings. In the center is an arcaded courtyard with a swimming pool and an amusing diving board tower in the form of a **Hindu chatri.** Among the project's unique qualities: reversible fans below all windows, a workable early substitute for air conditioning; windowshades on the outside of the windows; the underside of concrete floor slabs serving as the ceilings of the rooms below, and an auditorium of vaulted concrete arch construction.

[2a.] 129 Bay Ridge Parkway, bet. Ridge Blvd. and Colonial Rd. N side. Early 20th. Cent.

[2b.] 131 76th Street, bet. Ridge Blvd. and Colonial Rd. N side. Early 20th Cent.

[2c.] 122 76th Street, bet. Ridge Blvd. and Colonial Rd. S side. Early 20th Cent.

These three houses sit high on an inland embankment that runs parallel to the water's edge; best views are from Colonial Road. At 76th Street the precipice is so steep that a flight of steps replaces the roadway, one of the few times in Brooklyn that the pedestrian is unquestionably king.

[3a.] 8205 11th Avenue, SE cor. 82nd St. (Dyker Heights).

A handsome, clapboarded country villa of Italianate origin. The view from the tower room is a spectacular one of the nearby harbor.

[3b.] 8302 11th Avenue, SW cor. 83rd St. (Dyker Heights).

[3c.] 8310 11th Avenue, bet. 83rd and 84th Sts. W side (Dyker Heights).

[3d.] 1101 84th Street, NE cor. 11th Ave. (Dyker Heights).

[3e.] 8220 Narrows Avenue, NW cor. 83rd St.

Bumpety stone and seemingly thatched roofs make these fairy-tale residences seem like mirages right out of Hansel and Gretel. They look good enough to eat!

[4.] National Shrine Church of St. Bernadette (Roman Catholic), 8201 13th Ave. bet. 82nd and 83rd Sts. E side. 1937.

What a surprise! Parabolic arched plaster bents support the roof, and thick stained glass in the medieval manner throws saturated color over all the surfaces of the interior in this small, but impressive, church from an unpopular architectural period.

[3e.]

[5.]

[5.] James P. Farrell Residence, 119 95th St. bet. Marine Ave. and Shore Rd. N side. ca. 1850.

A splendid Greek Revival wood-frame house inundated, but not drowned, by an adjacent sea of red brick apartment blocks. Painted gray but with no detail changed, this miraculously preserved gem sits next to an unpretentious outbuilding (No. 125) which is askew from the building line of 95th Street. Presumably, the main building was moved to this point and set parallel to the street in the vicinity of its humble neighbor.

[6a.] St. John's Episcopal Church, 9818 Fort Hamilton Pkwy. NW cor. 99th St. 1834.

This stone and wood edifice is known as the "Church of the Generals" because it has attracted numerous military leaders to its services from adjacent Fort Hamilton. Generals Robert E. Lee and "Stonewall" Jackson worshipped here.

[6b.] Fort Hamilton Veteran' Hospital, 800 Poly Place bet. Seventh and Fourteenth Aves. S side. 1950. Skidmore Owings & Merrill.

BOROUGH PARK

Built up largely during the 1920's with numerous one- and two-family houses as well as larger apartment buildings, this section was rural except for scattered villages at the turn of the century. Perhaps the most interesting of these settlements was **Blythebourne,** which lay southwest of the intersection of New Utrecht Avenue and 55th Street along the Brooklyn, Bath Beach & West End Rail Road, today's BMT West End line. It was started in the late 1880's by **Electus B. Litchfield,** the son of Edwin C. Litchfield of Prospect Park fame. A number of houses were quickly built, as well as a series of Queen Anne cottages and two churches, but before the community could take hold, a politician purchased the area north of Blythebourne and east of New Utrecht Avenue and named it Borough Park. A real estate agent at the time warned the Litchfield family to sell its holdings, explaining that the *pogroms* in Eastern Europe would soon cause a **mass migration** to the outskirts of Brooklyn, forcing land values down. Mrs. William B. Litchfield, who controlled the property at the time, decided not to sell. The prediction was partially fulfilled; the **Borough Park** section did become a heavily Jewish community, but the **land values,** instead of falling, **rose tremendously.** As a result, Blythebourne was swallowed up by Borough Park and is remembered today only in the name of the local post office, Blythebourne Station.

[9.]

[

[7.] Franklin Delano Roosevelt High School, 5801 19th Ave. bet. 59th and 55th Sts. 1965. Raymond & Rado.

The precast concrete facade of the four-story central wing of this high school adds an important note of variety and a change of scale to an otherwise monotonous area, visually.

BENSONHURST–BATH BEACH

This present-day, lower-middle-class residential area preserves the family name of Charles Benson whose farm was subdivided into the gridiron we see today. At New Utrecht and 18th Avenues the original Village of New Utrecht was settled back in 1661, on a site now marked by the 1828 New Utrecht Reformed Church.

[8.] Cropsey House, 1740 84th St. SE cor. Bay 16th St.

The name of Cropsey is today most identified with the avenue bearing that name. Behind a woven wire fence stands this Victorian wood house of the Cropsey Family, built by the grandfather of Judge Andrew Cropsey.

[9.] New Utrecht Reformed Church and Parish House, 18th Ave. bet. 83rd and 84th Sts. E side. Church, 1828; Parish House, 1892. ★

Within sight of the crude steel frame of the BMT Elevated structure stands this delicate church, built in **meeting house style,** with the original stones of its predecessor (erected in 1700). The parish house is in the robust Romanesque Revival style. A **Liberty Pole** stands in front of the church; its ancestors dating back to 1783 and replaced six times since.

Liberty Pole: To harass the British garrisons or to signify their defeat, Revolutionary patriots erected flagpoles, called Liberty Poles, on which to raise the flag of independence. Lightning and dry rot have taken their toll of the originals, but in some communities a tradition has developed to replace them.

S

SOUTHERN BROOKLYN

Town of Gravesend/S'Gravensande

Established as a town in 1645; annexed to City of Brooklyn in 1894.

Of the six original towns of Brooklyn, Gravesend is unique in a number of ways. First of all, it was settled by a group of **English** rather than Dutch colonists. Second, its list of patentees was headed

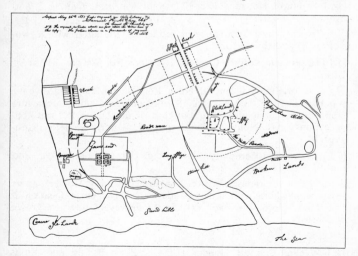

by the name of a woman, a precocious admission of the **equality of the sexes.** Third, Gravesend Village was laid out using a set of sophisticated **town-planning** principles resembling those of both New Haven and Philadelphia. (Remnants of the plan are still visible today, but only in the street layout.)

In 1643 **Lady Deborah Moody** and her flock chose to settle in Gravesend after a bitter sojourn in New England where they found the same religious intolerance they had fled from in their native land. The free enjoyment of *most* opinion in religious matters, which characterized Nieuw Amsterdam, made Gravesend an obvious haven for them.

In the 19th Century the territory of Gravesend became a great resort. No less than three **racetracks** were built within its bounds at various times, one northeast of Ocean and Jerome Avenues in Sheepshead Bay, another southeast of Ocean Parkway and Neptune Avenue in Brighton, and a third southwest of Ocean Parkway and Kings Highway, just north of the original village square. Before the development of Coney Island as a public beach and amusement area, it was the location of a number of fashionable hotels and piers, immense pinnacled wooden structures benefiting from the **imagination and wit** of Victorian decoration. Regrettably, there is little left of its raucous spirit and lively architecture. Coney was revived in the 1920's with the completion of subway connections to Manhattan, but as a recreation area it has lost popularity and been outmoded by more attractive resorts accessible by automobile. Only the dismembered corpus remains—the soul is gone.

GRAVESEND

[1.] Gravesend Village, Village Rd. North to Village Rd. South, Van Sicklen St. to Village Rd. East, at intersection of Gravesend Neck Rd. and McDonald (formerly Gravesend) Ave. ca. 1686.

[1a.] Hicks-Platt House/also called **Lady Moody House,** 27 Neck Road bet. McDonald Ave. and Van Sicklen St. N side. Mid-17th Cent.

First publicized as Lady Moody's own home in the 1890's by William E. Platt, a real estate developer, for purposes of publicity. Confusion seems to stem from the noted lady's ownership of this site as well as that of her own home in the northeast quadrant of the village. The house is far more famous than its present-day condition and recent architectural indiscretions warrant. That it adjoins a public school makes its desecration that much more deplorable.

[1b.] Ryder-Van Cleef House, 38 Village Rd. North bet. McDonald Ave. and Van Sicklen St. S Side.

[1c.] Hubbard House, 2138 McDonald Ave. bet. Avenue S and Avenue T. W side.

Two nearby Dutch Colonial residences, the latter with a two-story wing added in 1925.

[1d.] Gravesend Reform Church, 145 Neck Rd. NW cor. E. 1st St. 1894.

The original building at Neck Road and McDonald Avenue was built in 1655. This Victorian Gothic edifice is quite a departure from the earlier, plain white churches of the Dutch Reform congregations. Art Nouveau lettering and a porte-cochère distinguish it.

[1e.] Gravesend Cemetery, Neck Road bet. McDonald Ave. and Van Sicklen St. S side. 1650.

One of the oldest cemeteries in the city; Lady Moody's grave exists somewhere within its boundaries, but its exact location is lost. Many old markers still exist in the graveyard now overgrown with brush.

SHEEPSHEAD BAY

[2.] Wyckoff-Bennett House, 1669 E. 22nd St. SE cor. Kings Highway. ca. 1766. ★

The most impressive of all early houses in Brooklyn still in private ownership, this one is dated by a number cut into one of the wooden beams. Used as quarters by the Hessians during the Revolutionary War, it contains the following inscriptions scratched into its 4 by 7-inch panes of window glass:

Toepfer Capt of Regt de Ditfurth
MBach Lieutenant v Hessen Hanau Artilerie

[3.] Elias Hubbard Ryder House, 1926 E. 28th St. bet. Avenue S and Avenue T. W side. ca. 1822 or earlier.

[4.]

Gerritsen Beach: A community of 1600 year-round bungalows on tiny plots, narrow streets barely two cars wide, a volunteer fire company building, and lots of community spirit. Off Gerritsen Avenue along undeveloped Marine Park.

[4.] Junior High School 43, Brooklyn, 1401 Emmons Ave. bet. E. 14th and E. 15th Sts. N side. 1965. Pedersen & Tilney.

Cast-in-place concrete. The long, low facades along the side streets, often the downfall of recent public school designs, are here perhaps the most successful parts of an altogether splendid project.

Lundy Bros. Restaurant, Ocean and Emmons Aves. Pointing like an arrow toward Sheepshead Bay, Ocean Avenue terminates at the water's edge and at Lundy's. Big, brash, noisy, crowded but oh, what seafood! Quartered in two stories of a rambling, mission-style, stuccoed building, and serving as many as 5000 meals a day; a visit to Lundy's is a special treat for anyone in New York. Don't mind the brusque waiters—just dig in and enjoy!

CONEY ISLAND

[5.] Coney Island Hospital, Ocean Pkwy. NE cor. Shore Pkwy. 1953–1957. Katz Waisman Blumenkranz Stein Weber, Architects Associated.

Renowned as a landmark to vast numbers of motorists, it announces arrival at Coney Island even though it isn't actually in the district. Light brick masses are fussily articulated, and its southern facade, seasoned with sunshades, a symbol of its period. Handsome in overall appearance but less successful close up.

[6a.] William E. Grady Vocational High School, 25 Brighton 4th Rd. bet. Brighton 4th and Brighton 6th Sts. N side. 1956. Katz Waisman Blumenkranz Stein Weber, Architects Associated.

This is one of the most ebulliently conceived buildings in the entire school system. The curved and pitched forms of the gym and auditorium are played against the simple mass of the classroom wing. On the south facade is a sculpture by Constantino Nivola; on the west, a mosaic mural by Ben Shahn. As in the hospital, this work suffers in its small-scale details.

[7a.] New York Aquarium, Boardwalk NE cor. W. 8th St. Exhibit Building, 1955. Harrison & Abramovitz. **Osborn Laboratories of Marine Sciences,** 1965. Goldstone & Dearborn.

A "must" visit, mainly for the quality of its exhibits. The Exhibit Building falls short trying to reconcile the programmatic re-

[6a.]

quirements of museum and those of a shoreside amusement park. The Lab, however, is more successful. White whales, sea horses, octopi, colorful sea anemones, and other fascinating sea life make the trip abundantly worthwhile. Parking available, or take BMT Brighton Line or IND "D" Train to West 8th Street stop. Hours: Winter, 10 AM–5 PM. Admission charge.

[7b.] Amusement area, bet. W. 8th St. and W. 16th St. and bet. Surf Ave. and the Boardwalk.

As each Memorial Day rolls around, signifying the opening of a new season at Coney Island, the number of amusements decrease. The immense spiderweb of the Wonder Wheel still remains, but Steeplechase is gone. Luna Park is gone. Dreamland is gone. A number of roller-coasters and carousels remain. The Bowery, a circus midway of a street, located between the Boardwalk and Surf Avenue, still provides some life. The automobile has taken the middle class to other resorts.

Nevertheless many rides remain, as do games of skill, corn-on-the-cob, slices of watermelon and cotton candy. The rides and buildings reveal all sorts of architectural styles, many vernacular in origin, the work of local carpenters. It would be pointless to single out any special events since "change" is the battlecry. Look around—there's plenty to see and to enjoy.

Nathan's Famous, Surf Ave. SW cor. Stillwell Ave.

With Steeplechase Park gone, Nathan's Famous remains Coney's greatest institution. Once upon a time it cost a nickel to get to Coney, and a nickel bought a **hot dog** at Nathan's. Those days are gone forever! Open all year for stand-up, delectable treats, such as delicatessen sandwiches, clams on the half-shell, **"shrimp-boats"** (shrimp cocktails in miniature plastic dinghies) and sundry other appetizing morsels. Our mouths are watering!

Shatzkins' Famous Knishes, 1500 Surf Ave. SW cor. W. 15th St.

One block west of Nathan's Famous is this other "**famous**." Here the **knish** is raised to a high art. (Knishes have become, with pizza, a symbol among politicians of their catholicity in the appreciation of ethnic foods.) In most parts of New York, a knish (the "k" *is* sounded resoundingly) is a potato substance about four inches square, an inch-and-a-half thick, and **as heavy as lead**. Here it is a pastry-covered delicacy with a filling of apple, blueberry, cherry, cheese, kashe (groats), or potato, of course. You can see a whole battery of bakers preparing knishes right behind the counter and, as a result, get them fresh from the oven.

[7c.] Steeplechase Pier, Boardwalk bet. W. 16th and W. 19th Sts.

Ravaged by fire numerous times (like most of Coney Island), this pier is no longer so elegant a spot as it was years ago. It is now a favored fishing dock operated by the city. A walk along its thousand feet provides cool breezes and wonderful vantage points for the summer fireworks or for the setting sun. Try your hand at catching fluke, bluefish, flounder, or other of the fish in season.

[8.] 2835–37 W. 37th Street, bet. Neptune and Canal Aves. E side.

Mykonos in Brooklyn, complete to the textured stucco and the whitewashed surfaces. Mediterranean memories must have been vivid among the masons responsible for this vernacular conversion of two adjacent two-family houses of standard design.

Sea Gate: A smug private community at the west end of Coney Island. We couldn't get past the guards. Since we suspect it will be the same for you, we say nothing further!

.]

SOUTHEASTERN BROOKLYN

Town of Flatlands/Nieuw Amersfoort

Established as a town in 1666; annexed to the City of Brooklyn in 1896.

The name **Flatlands** aptly describes this area. It is flat, much of it still marshy. A considerable part of the territory bordering Jamaica Bay is a result of **land-fill** operations. The area includes much of Midwood, a desirable residential area; the inland portion still known as Flatlands, part of which is being developed as an industrial park; and the shorefront areas of Floyd Bennett Field, Bergen Beach, Mill Basin and Canarsie.

[1.] Johannes Van Nuyse House, 1041 E. 22nd St. bet. Avenues I and J. E side. ca. 1800. ☆

Originally at East 22nd Street and Avenue M, this farmhouse was moved about 1916 and turned perpendicular to the street in order to fit the lot. The distinctive Dutch colonial gabled end is therefore the street facade. Woodwork and oval window in hall are Federal, other interior details of the 19th Century. Portico at entrance dates from 1952 restoration.

[2.] Joost Van Nuyse House/also called **Coe House,** 1128 E. 34th St. bet. Flatbush Ave. and Avenue J. W side. 1744, 1793. ☆

FLATLANDS

[3.] Pieter Claessen Wyckoff House, 5902 Clarendon Rd. at intersection of Ralph and Ditmas Aves. SW cor. Pre-1641. ★

Located in an area of Brooklyn in which mapped streets have not as yet been paved, this venerable (and venerable looking) relic is hard to pinpoint easily by location. Some historians consider it the oldest extant building in the state.

[3.]

[4.] Vitagraph Co. Inc.–Warner Bros. Pictures Inc., 791 E. 43rd St. bet. Farragut and Glenwood Rds. E side. ca. 1925.

Atop these storage vaults for highly inflammable motion picture film is a ventilation system that creates a roofscape of startlingly dramatic proportions—an exciting complement to the wide variety of industrial forms found around the city.

[5a.] Flatlands Dutch Reformed Church, 3931 Kings Highway bet. Flatbush Ave. and E. 40th St. 1848. Henry Eldert, Builder. ★

One of three Brooklyn churches established by order of Gov. Peter Stuyvesant (other two are Flatbush Reformed Dutch and First Reformed). Handsomely sited at the end of a tree-lined walk, this starkly simple Gothic Revival church stands where two earlier churches stood, the first, built in 1663, being octagonal in plan. Note names in adjacent cemetery: Lott, Sprong, Voorhees, Kouwenhoven, Wyckoff.

[5b.] Van Pelt–Woolsey House, 4011 Hubbard Pl. bet. 40th St. and Kings Highway.

Located on a demapped portion of Hubbard Place (the other part has numbers of two digits only). Alterations have confused, but not entirely concealed, its Dutch Colonial origins.

[6.] Hendrick I. Lott House, 1940 E. 36th St. bet. Fillmore Ave. and Avenue S. W. side. ☆

This house illustrates a pattern of growth perhaps better than others of its origins. The small wing dates back to 1676 (its small window openings supposedly result from fear of Indian attack). The main part was built by Lott himself in 1800. The projecting roof eaves have square pillars on one side and Ionic on the other, showing the changes in fashion through the years.

[4.]

[8b.]

[7a.] Stoothof–Baxter House, 1640 E. 48th St. bet. Avenue M and Avenue N. W side. Before 1796.

[7b.] Douwe Stoothoff–John Williamson House, 1587 E. 53rd St. bet. Avenue M and Avenue N. E side.

Dutch Colonial farmhouse; poorly altered.

CANARSIE

[8a.] Bay View Houses, Shore Pkwy. NE cor. Rockaway Pkwy. 1955. Katz, Waisman, Blumenkranz, Stein, Weber, Architects Associated.

For its time this was an exceedingly sophisticated middle-income housing development. Each tower building is neatly split by a narrow service core clearly expressed on the exterior. The rear of each core, at the fire exit stairs, is a subtle checkerboard of brick with carefully studied window and door locations. The front facade of each core is a wire mesh screen enclosing sky lobbies— outdoor porches on each floor intended as play areas for children requiring parental supervision. The project suffers from a site plan that pays little attention to the street grid or to any other discipline recognizable to a visitor.

 [8b.] Bankers Federal Savings Bank, 1764 Rockaway Pkwy. SW cor. Avenue L. 1961. La Pierre, Litchfield & Partners.

In an area devoid of sophisticated architecture, despite the large amount of post-Korean War construction, it is refreshing to find a work such as this. Built of rough-textured, precast concrete panels with a pleasant juxtaposition of semiprivate garden courts between the exterior walls and the banking room itself. By not being oppressively saccharine in its materials or details it may have a chance to grow on the community.

[9.] Pepsi Cola Bottling Plant, 9701 Avenue D. NW cor. Rockaway Ave. 1956. Skidmore, Owings & Merrill.

A classic SOM curtain wall overlooks what is today still a primordial *zumpf,* a low-lying marsh on one side and a railroad siding on the other. The curtain wall does not lend itself to turning the corners of the polygonal site; neither do rock-throwing, neighborhood scamps help the glass maintain its integrity.

Look Out for Trains! Canarsie is the site of the only remaining subway grade crossing in the city. The BMT 14th Street–Canarsie Line crosses East 105th Street at Farragut Road, complete with ringing bells, flashing lights, and striped crossing gates.

EASTERN BROOKLYN

Town of New Lots
Separated from the Town of Flatbush in 1852; annexed to the City of Brooklyn in 1886.

[1c.]  [

Three major neighborhoods exist within this sector. **Highland Park,** also called **Cypress Hills,** lies above Atlantic Avenue; **Brownsville** occupies the roughly triangular area between East 98th Street, East New York Avenue and the tracks of the Long Island Railroad; **East New York** makes up the remainder south to Jamaica Bay and east to the Queens boundary or "City Line," as its residents often call it, a relic of the days when Brooklyn was a city unto itself.

HIGHLAND PARK–CYPRESS HILLS

[1a.] 278, 279, and 361 Highland Boulevard, bet. Miller Ave. and Barbey St.

Three distinctive residences of a large number that once occupied this high ground. In recent years many have been displaced by new multiple dwellings, to take advantage of the phenomenal views from this hillside location.

[1b.] 101 Sunnyside Avenue, bet. Hendrix St. and Miller Ave. N side. ca. 1930.

Nestled against a sharp precipice, this brick apartment house has an interesting entry in a *neo*-neo-Romanesque style. The upper part of the building is quite simply handled and looks impressive, towering above the adjacent small-scaled residences at the foot of the hill.

[1c.] 48 Van Siclen Avenue, bet. Arlington Ave. and Fulton St. W side.

An unusual building for this community; monumental in scale for its two-story height and narrow width. Modified Palladian window, rustication of facade, and elaborate cornice treatment overwhelm the shortsighted addition of a tinplate awning stretching across front.

[2a.] 130 Arlington Avenue, 71 Schenck Avenue, SE cor. ca. 1900.

Two similar houses, differing only in response to their sites (one is at the intersection). Eclectic in design, they combine a Baroque portico and Dutch Colonial gambrel roofs sheathed in Spanish tile. Obviously intended for wealthy owners, they look quite lovely on tree-lined and stately Arlington Avenue.

[4a.]

BROWNSVILLE

Brownsville is at exactly the other end of the economic ladder. It is a poor area, largely **non-white,** with old and dilapidated housing predominating and nondescript, subsidized low-rent projects as a questionable change of pace. This **neighborhood** was first subdivided from farmland by **Charles S. Brown** in 1865, and the community owes its name to him. By 1883 only 250 frame houses existed in the village. But in 1887 a group of real estate men purchased land and began to encourage **Jewish immigrants** in the congested Lower East Side to move here. The arrival of the Fulton Street "el" in 1889 encouraged the influx, and the settlement became a great concentration of poor, Eastern European Jews. The community was not free of problems normally associated with deprived areas. Some of **Murder Incorporated's** most notorious leaders grew up on its streets. The completion of the New Lots branch of the IRT in 1920–1922 further improved rapid transit connections to Manhattan, and the area grew mildly prosperous. **Pitkin Avenue** is still a major shopping street which, in the 1920's through 1940's, attracted shoppers from a much larger region. The movie house still functioning at Pitkin and East New York Avenues was one of the great ornate **picture palaces** of New York. Following World War II, the Jewish population began to leave, and the area, never very well

[3.]

[4

[8.]

[8

maintained, settled into a neglected slum of apartments, tenements, and two- and four-family housing. The slum clearance, although well intended, has been the *coup de grace* for the neighborhood, destroying what little character it had in the first place.

[3.] Pitkin Theatre/formerly **Loew's Pitkin Theatre,** Pitkin Ave. NE cor. Saratoga Ave.

Through the years this theater has been a landmark along this brassy shopping street. Its carefully decorated masonry exterior led to one of those outlandish, fairytale auditoriums of the great era of the picture palace, complete with twinkling stars and moving clouds across its ceiling-sky.

[4a.] Belmont Avenue Pushcart Market, Belmont Ave. bet. Thatford and Stone Aves.

346 **BROOKLYN**

One of the few street markets remaining in the city. This one sprung up because the Long Island Railroad siding at nearby Junius Street was the center of a **wholesale fruit and vegetable market.** The tradition evolved of selling the less-apptizing remainders of the early morning bargainings in the vicinity. To provide a vehicle for such sales to the local community, a pushcart market began. Though efforts are constantly being made to displace these activities from the streets, this colorful, **old-world market place** has weathered all storms, but the construction of a low-rent housing project across the street may be its death knell.

[4b.] Belmont Avenue Baths, 15 Belmont Ave. bet. Thatford Ave. and Osborn St. N side.

Just below the sheet metal cornice of this building there is lettered, in the finest tradition of the *Architectural Review,* a sign, **Russian and Turkish Baths;** in front, a massive hanging sign makes the same pitch in grime-encrusted neon tubing; over the sidewalk, the sagging cantilever of a canvas canopy advertises more of the same.

Such dilapidation indicates that the great tradition of the Turkish bath is almost gone. In the heyday of Brownsville the baths were the equivalent of bars in other ethnic communities. They were a place to **steam out one's problems** in both perspiration and conversation.

[5.]Betsy Head Memorial Playground Bathhouse, Strauss St. to Hopkinson Ave., Dumont to Livonia Aves. ca. 1939.

Liberal use of glass block and a parasol roof delicately balanced on parabolic ribs distinguish this bathhouse, one of a series of such projects constructed by the WPA during the Depression.

[9.]

The Shtetl: What Brownsville lacked in physical amenities, it more than made up in the richness of its social life. It was a recall of the life of the *shtetl,* the small Jewish community in Eastern Europe. Pitkin Avenue was the street for the grand promenade, its Yiddish-speaking community being addicted to thrashing out the social and political problems of the hour while **spatziering** down the avenue. At one time, a cafeteria called Hoffman's was the area's glittery but modest version of a Delmonico's of another era and of an entirely different social class. Amboy Street, the home of a youth gang immortalized in Irving Shulman's *The Amboy Dukes,* became, in 1916, the home of the first birth control clinic in America, established by the pioneer in this field, Margaret Sanger.

EAST NEW YORK

[6.] Bradford Street, bet. Sutter and Blake Aves.

This street preserves a sense of the early settlement of East

New York. Gaily painted, the block conveys a charm that must have been attractive to the families who moved here from the more crowded adjacent areas during the period of its peak development. At No. 408 is a converted house, typical of those on the block, with the euphonious name, St. Stephen's Halibethan Cathedral.

[7.] Christian Duryea House, 562 Jerome St. bet. Dumont and Livonia Aves. ca. 1787. ☆

A traditional Dutch Colonial farmhouse. The overhanging roof on the south side, a trademark of this style, has been removed.

[8.] New Lots Reformed Dutch Church and Parish House, 620 New Lots Ave. SE cor. Schenck Ave. 1823. ★

Built by the Dutch farmers of this area who decided that weekly trips to the Flatbush Church were too arduous. Their handiwork, far more vernacular than the other Dutch Reformed churches of the period, is in many ways the freshest of the group today. The cupolas, detailing, and proportions of both buildings are superior.

[9.] Public School 306, Brooklyn, 970 Vermont St. NW cor. Cozine Ave. 1966. Pedersen & Tilney.

At the edge of the built-up section of New Lots is this superb, cast-in-place concrete school. In an area of flat monotony and long eerie vistas down empty streets, the boldly raked stair towers and handsome massing of the long, low volumes of the building add richness and an air of mystery to the otherwise bland skyline.

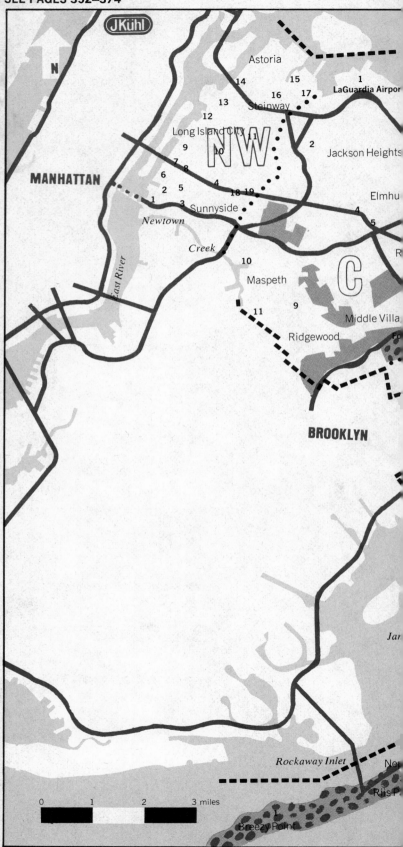

JKühl

N

Astoria

14   15   1
      16   17   LaGuardia Airport
13   Steinway
12
Long Island City   11
9   NW
10   2   Jackson Heights
7 8
6   4   Elmhu
2 5   18 19
MANHATTAN
1   3   Sunnyside   4
Newtown   5
Creek   R
                              C
      10
Maspeth
11   9
                              Middle Villa
Ridgewood   Fo

BROOKLYN

East River

Jar

Rockaway Inlet   Ne

0   1   2   3 miles   Riis P.

Breezy Point

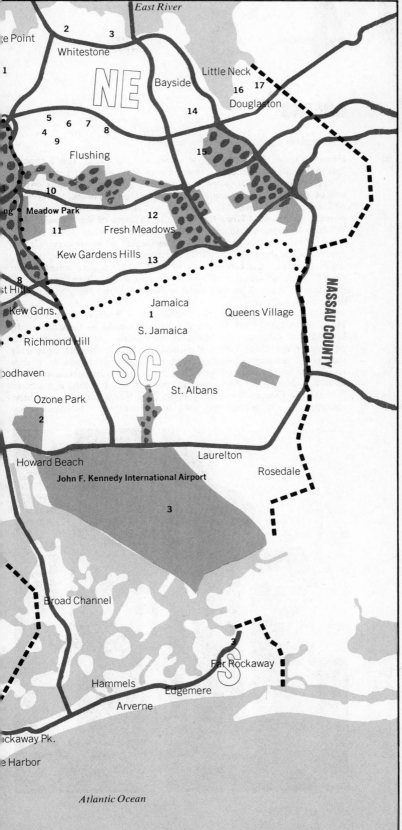

East River

e Point

2   3

Whitestone

1

NE   Bayside

Little Neck

16   17

Douglaston

14

5   6   7

4   8

9

Flushing   15

10

Meadow Park   12

ng

11   Fresh Meadows

Kew Gardens Hills   13

8

st Hills

Kew Gdns.   Jamaica
                    1
                   S. Jamaica   Queens Village

Richmond Hill   NASSAU COUNTY

oodhaven   SC

Ozone Park   St. Albans

2

                                        Laurelton
Howard Beach
                                              Rosedale
          John F. Kennedy International Airport

                              3

          Broad Channel

                                        3
                              Far Rockaway

Hammels   Edgemere
          Arverne

ockaway Pk.

e Harbor

                    Atlantic Ocean

4

QUEENS

Borough of Queens/Queens County

Home of both *local* municipal airports, LaGuardia and Kennedy International; its residents are unable to forget this fact, the **drone of jets, props, and jet-props** ever reminding them as planes **swoop out of the sky** and into these **all-weather aerodromes.** Awareness of modern technology is balanced by contact with nature—with **postage stamp-sized front lawns** or the vastness of the **Jamaica Bay Wildlife Refuge,** not to mention the borough's other parks, 16,397 acres in all. Queens has not only **the largest park acreage** (almost equivalent to the total of that in the remaining four boroughs) but, understandably, **the largest area as well,** 114.7 square miles (126.6 including inland waters), almost a *third* of the city's entire area. In population, it **ranks second only to Brooklyn** and the gap between them is closing fast.

As a borough it is predominantly a bedroom community. However, a good deal of **industry thrives within its boundaries.** In Long Island City and in Maspeth, and along the extensive rights of way of the Long Island Railroad are manufacturers of **a wide variety of products,** ranging from surgical instruments to pianos to biscuits and crackers. The LIRR makes it **a transportation center** as well, aided by the Pennsylvania and by many trucking operations.

Before Queens became a borough, it was **a far larger county,** encompassing its present-day area as well as that of Nassau (a new

county created as a by-product of consolidation into Greater New York in 1898). The name stems from Catherine of Braganza, **Queen** of Charles II.

The vastness of Queens and its relatively late development has encouraged the retention of the old town, village and subdivision names for its various communities. From a **strong sense of pride** and identification with **the outlying suburbs** a resident never refers to himself as a "Queensite" but rather as living in Flushing or St. Albans or Forest Hills. If pressed further, the response to **"Where do you live?"** becomes **"Long Island."**

NORTHWESTERN QUEENS

Long Island City
Separated from the Town of Newtown in 1870.

Between 1870 and 1898, the year of **consolidation** into Greater New York, Long Island City was, in fact, a *city*. It encompassed not only the area we still identify with its name, but the adjacent **communities** of Hunter's Point, Ravenswood, Astoria, Steinway, and Sunnyside.

LONG ISLAND CITY, HUNTER'S POINT AND RAVENSWOOD

The combination of these areas forms THE industrial concentration in New York City, in appearance, if not in fact. Laced by IRT and BMT Elevateds, the passenger yards of the Pennsy, the Long Island Railroad in an open cut, and the IND underground, it is a great **transportation nexus.** From the "els," from a car, or on foot, the factory agglomeration makes itself felt: above, alongside, and even below you as you cross endless trestles over deep scars in the flat landscape.

Hunter's Point in the southwest corner is a mixed **factory and residence district.** Ravenswood, along the East River above the Queensboro Bridge has a number of **high-rise housing** projects in its midst, as well as a major Con Edison power generator whose

candy-striped stacks (and their produce) are landmarks on both sides of the river.

[1a.] Long Island City Station, L.I.R.R., 2nd St. NW cor. Borden Ave.

This old masonry warhorse marks the site of the ferry connection between Long Island and East 34th Street in Manhattan, which all suburban riders on the Long Island Railroad were forced to take to reach New York. In 1910 a direct rail connection into Pennsylvania Station was opened via the East River Tunnels.

[2.] St. Mary's Roman Catholic Church, 10-08 49th Ave., SE cor. Vernon Blvd.

The modest steeple on this humble red brick edifice is still tall enough to dominate the immediate skyline, though no competition for Manhattan's towers at arm's reach across the river.

Steinway Tunnels: The twin tubes of the IRT Flushing Line under the East River were originally begun in 1892 by piano king William Steinway as a trolley car connection to Manhattan. The Panic of 1893 and Steinway's death in 1896 interrupted the project until August Belmont Jr., the IRT financier, revived it in 1902. The tunnel, with reversing loops at each end (the loop under the Grand Central IRT station still exists) became the first connection between Manhattan and Queens in 1907, though it was not put into regular use until converted to subway operation in 1915.

[5a.]

[3.] Russ Toggs Manufacturing and Distribution Center, 27-09 49th Ave. SE cor. 27th St. 1965. Robert E. Levien, Engineer.

A bulky, brutal, brick box which reaches for the top of the nearby, high-level approach of the Long Island Expressway. As a result, its roof becomes the obvious place for an immense neon sign on a delicate latticework of angle iron supports. From the street, the factory reads strongly against its confused industrial background; from the highway the sign is all that can be captured at 50 m.p.h.

[4.] Sunnyside Yards, Pennsylvania R.R., Jackson Ave. and Northern Blvd. to Skillman Ave. 1910.

Seventy-nine tracks having a total length of about 40 miles make it the largest passenger railroad yard in the world. Built to service cross-country trains arriving at Pennsylvania Station. It has magnificent potential for air-rights development.

[5a.] Engine Co. 258, Hook & Ladder Co. 115, N.Y.C. Fire Department, 10-40 47th Ave. bet. Vernon Blvd. and 11th St. S side. 1903. Bradford L. Gilbert.

Robust multistory fire house with stepped Dutch gable (false) at roof.

[5b.] 45th Avenue, bet. 21st and 23rd Sts. ★

A street of virgin row houses complete with original stoops and cornices. Proposed by the Landmarks Preservation Commission as part of an **Historic District.**

[6a.] Kilmoyler Realty Corp., 42-16 Vernon Blvd. bet. Bridge Plaza South and 43rd Ave. W side. 1892.

Romanesque Revival amber brick jewel with Sullivanesque terra cotta trim. It stands with integrity among the artifacts of industrial blight.

[6b.] Queensboro Bridge. [See Bridges and Tunnels.]

This is the ornate cantilevered bridge whose intricate latticework was always the backdrop for swank N.Y. apartments in **Hollywood films** of the Forties. Surprisingly, its completion in 1909 did not cause the migration across the river that the Williamsburg and Manhattan Bridges before it had done. The last **trolley car** to see service in New York shuttled back and forth across the Queensboro, stopping at the **elevator tower** on Welfare Island to take on and discharge passengers. The trolley and the vehicular elevators were discontinued in 1955 when a bridge was completed between the island and Ravenswood.

[7.] Queensbridge Houses, Vernon Blvd. to 21st St., 40th Ave. to Bridge Plaza North. 1939. William F. R. Ballard, Chief Architect; Henry S. Churchill, Frederick G. Frost, Burnett C. Turner, Associates.

Once the largest public housing project in the country (3149 units in 26 six-story buildings occupying six superblocks.) They predate the overuse of red brick—theirs is a handsome light brown with dark red window frames.

[8.] Brewster Building, 27-01 Bridge Plaza North bet. 27th and 28th Sts. 1910. Stephenson & Wheeler.

A bulky masonry structure distinguished by a handsomely sculpted clock tower, of which only the supports are visible today. This is where the Brewster carriage was produced, and later the Rolls-Royce automobiles, shipped knocked-down from England and assembled here.

[9.]

[9.] Barkin-Levin Factory (Lassie Coats)/now **Structural Display Co., Inc.,** 12-12 33rd Rd. SW cor. 13th St. 1958. Ulrich Franzen.

Built for an expatriate clothing manufacturer from the over-crowded garment district of Manhattan. Crisp lines and sophisticated detailing somehow never mixed with the drab surroundings—actually seemed overwhelmed by them.

[10.] Famous-Players Lasky Corp. (Paramount Pictures)/later **Eastern Service Studios**/now **U.S. Army Pictorial Center,** 35th Ave. bet. 34th and 38th Sts. Both sides. 1919.

Ernst Lubitsch, Ben Hecht, and Charles MacArthur produced films here, one of a number of old film studios that can still be found in the city. The monumental porte-cochère at 35-11 35th Avenue is a distinctive note. **[10a.]**

[11.] New York and Queens County Rail Road Co. Station/now **warehouse,** Northern Blvd. SE cor. Woodside Ave. ca. 1885.

Built as main station for a street railway and railroad company later absorbed by L.I.R.R. system. Twin masonry towers and a robust archway (now blocked) joyfully announced the impending trip into Queens.

ASTORIA AND STEINWAY

The original settlement was **Hallet's Cove** along the East River at the foot of 30th Avenue. It was named after **William Hallet,** to whom Gov. Peter Stuyvesant granted a patent for 1500 acres in 1654. As a suburb, its growth coincided with the introduction of a **steam-powered ferry** in 1815. By 1839 the area was incorporated, friends of John Astor winning a bitter factional fight in naming it **Astoria** after him.

The year 1842 saw the completion of the turnpike to Greenpoint, Brooklyn. Soon shipping trade was established in **lumber,** particularly in **exotic foreign woods.** Shipping and lumber magnates built **mansions** just north of the Cove on the mound called Hallet's Point, some of which still exist. The availability of both lumber and cheap land persuaded **William Steinway** to establish a 400-acre company town in the Seventies near the foot of Steinway Street. The **piano factory,** some **row housing,** and his **mansion** remain.

[12.] Sohmer Piano Co., 11-02 31st Ave. SE cor. Vernon Blvd.

Steinway's competitor is also established in this area in a prominent high-rise structure with a distinctive curved Mansard tower.

[13a.] 26-35 4th Street, bet. 26th and 27th Aves. E side. ca. 1835. ☆

One of the lumber dealer's mansions, unfortunately stripped of detail. Until 1966 a far finer one remained at corner. **[13b.]**

[13b.]

[13c.] First Reformed Church of Astoria/formerly **Reformed Dutch Church of Hallet's Cove,** 27-26 12th St. bet. 27th and 28th Aves. 1888.

Built to serve the early community, it still remains a charming country church tucked away on a side street.

[13d.] 25-37, 25-39 14th Street, bet. Hoyt and 26th Aves. E side.

A palatial frame mansion with a Doric portico across its breadth. Set far back from the adjacent building lines, it is easy to miss.

[14a.] Astoria Park, Shore Blvd. to 19th St., Ditmars Blvd. to Hoyt Ave.

[14b.] Triborough Bridge. [See Bridges and Tunnels.]

[14c.] Hell Gate Bridge/officially **New York Connecting Railroad Bridge.** [See Bridges and Tunnels.]

The purpose of this bridge is to provide a route for through trains of the Pennsylvania and the New York, New Haven and Hartford Railroads to get through New York. The trestle taking the trains from the East River Tunnel out of Pennsylvania Station up to the height of the bridge deck dominates much of this part of Queens. The bridge itself is a handsome and boldly masculine structure of the overhead-arch type.

[15.] Steinway Mansion, 18-33 41st St. bet. Berrian Blvd. and 19th Ave. ca. 1875. ☆

Surmounting a knoll overlooking the East River, **piano manufacturer** William Steinway's dark gray granite home was a showplace of its time. Down at the heels today, it still exudes a **glamorous** quality. (The **factory** of Steinway & Sons is at the northwest corner of 19th Avenue and 38th Street. Row housing from the original **company town** can still be seen on the south side of 20th Avenue east of Steinway Street.)

[16.] Lawrence Family Graveyard, 20th Rd. SE cor. 35th St. 1703. ★

[17.] Lent Homestead, 78-03 19th Rd. at 78th St. N side. ca. 1729. ★

One of the best preserved Dutch farmhouses in the city.

SUNNYSIDE

A residential area that sprang up following the completion of the IRT Flushing Line in its vicinity in 1917. Though surrounded by industry and cemeteries, proximity and excellent means of access to Manhattan have assured its stability. Its most significant feature is Sunnyside Gardens.

[11]

[18.] Sunnyside Gardens, 43rd to 51st Sts., 39th Ave. to Queens Blvd. First units, 1924. Henry Wright, Clarence S. Stein, and Frederick Ackerman.

Roughly 70 acres of what had been barren and mosquito-infested land was converted to a community of one-, two-, and three-family homes and apartment buildings by the limited-dividend City Housing Corporation. The scheme, acclaimed for its site planning, holds to the regular street grid and provides green areas in the middle of each block. By today's standards, however, the design is pallid.

[19.] J. Sklar Manufacturing Co., 38-04 Woodside Ave. bet. Barnett and 39th Aves. W side.

A campus of Tudoresque pavilions set on a manicured lawn disguises this manufactory of surgical instruments. For once, a factory becomes a visual amenity to the community.

[15.]

NORTHEASTERN QUEENS

Town of Flushing/Vlissingen
Settled in 1642; chartered in 1645.

The name Flushing is commonly associated with the growth of **religious freedom** in the New World. The town, founded by English settlers, received its patent from Dutch Governor Kieft who stipulated in its text that the **freedom of conscience** of the townspeople was to be **guaranteed.** Kieft's successor, Peter Stuyvesant, attempted to suppress the **Quaker sect,** a number of whose adherents had settled in Flushing. Quaker and non-Quaker residents banded together against Stuyvesant and were successful in having the patent's stipulation recognized and observed. Among these settlers was the **Bowne family** whose house, dating from the 17th Century, can still be seen. The old **Quaker Meeting House** of the same period also remains as a testament to this struggle for religious liberty.

COLLEGE POINT

This community gets its name from an ill-fated Episcopal divinity school begun in 1836 by the **Rev. William A. Muhlenberg,** but never opened. Prior to this time its name was Strattonsport, after **Eliphalet Stratton** who purchased the land from the Lawrence family, early settlers, in 1790. At first, College Point was virtually an island separated from the Village of Flushing by creeks and flooded marshland and connected by a route known to this day as **College Point Causeway.** Land fill and recent development have begun to change this, but the isolation of the area is still visible in the **flats near Flushing Airport,** a private aircraft facility.

INDUSTRIES

Despite the new name, glass is still very much our business. Within recent months, in fact, we have developed a complete line of environmental control glasses with few limitations.

If you are concerned with visual comfort, glare for example, PPG makes tinted glasses with light transmissions ranging from 74 percent to 5 percent.

If your problem is thermal insulation, PPG offers a glass with a remarkable U-Value of 0.30.

If heat gain is a factor, you will want to know more about SOLARBAN TWINDOW, a new PPG product that admits only 40 BTU's/hr/sq.ft.

We call the proper application of these new environmental control products, GLASS CONDITIONING*. A PPG Architectural Representative is available in all major cities to consult with you. Phone him . . . or write to: PPG Industries (Pittsburgh Plate Glass Company), One Gateway Center, Pittsburgh, Pa. 15222.

PPG

makes the glass that makes the difference

*GLASS CONDITIONING is a PPG Service Mark

In its Civil War phase the district became a **lusty industrial community,** only a few vestiges of which remain. It attracted a large German and Swiss population whose **beer gardens** and **picnic groves** were the focus of Sunday outings by German-born Manhattanites. Following the war the **Poppenhausen family** (Adolph was majority stockholder of the Long Island Railroad) purchased large amounts of property and established an adult education institute bearing its name.

[1a.] 23-27 122nd Street, bet. 23rd and 25th Aves. E side. ca. 1870.

A mansarded Victorian country house, a colorful example of a number still to be found in this community.

[1c.]

[1b.] Poppenhausen Institute, 114-04 14th Rd. SE cor. 114th St. 1868.

One of the earliest free adult evening schools in this country, it was established in this handsome masonry structure by Conrad Poppenhausen, to train men for the local industries. It still offers evening courses today.

[1c.] First Reform Church (of College Point) and Parish House. 14th Ave. NW cor. 119th St. 1872.

A lovely, white, country church and its sprightly Carpenter-Gothic parish house. A real find!

WHITESTONE

The original community saw its major growth in the streets radiating from 14th Avenue and 150th Street. Though settled in 1645 it took the establishment of a **tinware factory** to convert it from a rural settlement into a thriving manufacturing center. A bit of industry survives, but the area is best known for its housing resources: the private community of **Malba,** west of the Bronx-Whitestone Bridge, **Beechhurst,** and the relatively recent Levitt House development now known as **Le Havre,** in the shadow of the Throgs Neck Bridge.

[2.] Dr. George W. Fish Residence and Carriage Houses, 150-10 Powell's Cove Blvd. at 150th St. S side, ca. 1860. ☆

To get a peek at these it is necessary to take a circuitous route: 149th Street north from 3rd Avenue; continue bearing right in a broad arc to the cul-de-sac at its end. Note the lovely views of the Bronx-Whitestone Bridge from this area.

[3a.] Le Havre Houses/formerly **The Levitt House Development,** vicinity of 12th Ave. and 162nd St. 1957–1958. Alfred Levitt.

Neat, boxy, well-scaled apartment development using painted concrete block for its exterior walls. The jazzy pastel colors, different for each building, are a false note.

[3b.] Cryder House, 166-25 Powell's Cove Blvd. at 166th St. N side. 1963. Hausman & Rosenberg.

A single handsome apartment tower standing out dramatically from the smaller scaled construction in the vicinity. Great views of Long Island Sound and the Throgs Neck Bridge.

FLUSHING

Until the end of World War II Flushing was a charming **Victorian community** laced with some six-story Tudor apartment construction from the late Twenties and early Thirties. Many of its streeets were lined with **rambling white clapboard houses** dating from the last quarter of the 19th Century. On its outskirts were vast reaches of undeveloped rolling land.

The construction of the Bronx-Whitestone Bridge together with its connecting highways for the **1939 New York World's Fair** set the stage for a change that was nipped in the bud by the war emergency. After the end of the conflict the **rush to build** was on.

[4a.] St. George's Episcopal Church, Main St. bet. 38th and 39th Aves. W side. 1854. Wills & Dudley. ☆

Miraculously, this stately Gothic Revival church has withstood the revolutionary changes population increase has wrought on Main Street. Francis Lewis, a signer of the Declaration of Independence, was a church warder here in the original building, completed in 1761.

Prince's Nursery: North of Northern Boulevard, from the site of today's RKO Keith's theater west to Flushing Creek, was a tree nursery, the first in the country, established by William Prince in 1737. The eight acres had, by 1750, become the Linnaean Botanic Garden. All traces of the site are erased, but not its produce. To this day Flushing displays 140 genera consisting of 2000 species of trees.

[5a.] Quaker Meeting House, 137-16 Northern Blvd. bet. Main and Union Sts. S side. 1694–1717. ☆

Austere and brooding, this medieval relic timidly looks out upon the never-ending stream of cars on Northern Boulevard. On its rear facade, facing the quiet graveyard, are two doors, originally separate entrances to the meeting house for men and women. The wood-shingled, hip-roofed meeting house has been continuously used since the 17th Century for religious activities by the Society of Friends, except for a hiatus as a British hospital, prison, and stable during the Revolution.

[5b.] Flushing Municipal Courthouse, 137-15 Northern Blvd. NE cor. Linden Pl. 1862. ☆

A well-preserved Romanesque edifice of the Civil War era. Its masonry is painted cream with dark brown trim.

[6a.] Bowne House, 37-01 Bowne St. bet. 37th and 38th Aves. E side. 1661. ★

Built by John Bowne, a Quaker, this house was the first indoor meeting place of the forbidden Society of Friends; earlier they had met clandestinely in the nearby woods. Bowne was a central figure in the dispute with Gov. Peter Stuyvesant over religious freedom. The interiors are carefully maintained and contain a wide variety of colonial furnishings.

Hours: Tuesdays, Saturdays, and Sundays. 2:30–4:30 PM Free.

[6b.] First Congregational Church of Flushing, Parish House, and Parsonage, Bowne St. bet. 38th and Roosevelt Ave. W side.

A dignified trio of 19th Century wood structures on a broad green carpet of grass.

[5b.]

[6c.] Reformed Church of Flushing, Roosevelt Ave. NE cor. Bowne St. ca. 1895.

[6d.] The Weeping Beech Tree, 37th Ave. W of Parsons Blvd. 1847. ★

An immense canopy of drooping branches hangs down about its broad trunk and makes almost a natural shelter. The street on which it stands has been turned into a cul-de-sac, providing a virtually traffic-free setting.

[7.] North Shore Oldsmobile, 149-04 Northern Blvd. SE cor. 149th St. 1963. Rigoni & Reich.

A contemporary and quite sophisticated temple for the sale of cars. But is a temple the appropriate form?

[8.] William K. Murray House/Kingsland Homestead, 40-25 155th St. SE cor. Roosevelt Ave. 1775. ★

Once the home of the family for which Manhattan's Murray Hill is named. There are plans to move the building to a more appropriate setting near the Weeping Beech Tree. [See NE Queens 6d.]

[9.] St. Thomas Hall/later **St. Joseph's Academy,** Kissena Blvd. NE cor. Sanford Ave. 1838–1839.

[10.] Booth Memorial Hospital, 56-33 Main St. NE cor. Booth Memorial Drive. 1957. William Francis Schorn. **Williams Memorial Residence for the Aging,** 1965, Kelly & Gruzen.

[11.] Public School 219, Queens, 144-39 Gravett Rd. E of Main St. 1966. Caudill, Rowlett & Scott.

The russet colored (and awkward) domed roof of the experimental kindergarten wing is the most apparent feature of this school. Large panes of tinted glass and the lush interior make the space seem less designed for play than for *dis*play.

[12.] Fresh Meadows Housing Development, 186th to 197th Sts., Long Island Expwy. to 73rd Ave. (irregular). 1949. Voorhees, Walker, Foley & Smith; 20-story addition, 1962, Voorhees, Walker, Smith, Smith & Haines.

This 166-acre development on the site of the old Fresh Meadows Country Club was a post-World War II project of the New York Life Insurance Co. The project benefits from a good site plan and includes a mix of row housing, low- and high-rise apartments, as well as a regional shopping area, a theater, schools, and other appropriate amenities. Of planning rather than architectural distinction.

[13.] Triborough Hospital, Parsons Blvd. SE cor. Goethals Ave. 1940. Voorhees, Walker, Foley & Smith.

BAYSIDE, DOUGLASTON, LITTLE NECK

Bayside is an outlying portion of Flushing with an attractive **suburban character** maintained by an abundance of detached houses and low-rise apartments. It was originally settled by William Lawrence in 1664 and **remained largely rural** until linked to Manhattan by the L.I.R.R.'s East River Tunnels in 1910.

[6b.]

Douglaston and Little Neck lie east of Cross Island (Belt) Parkway, New York's **circumferential highway,** and, as a result, many assume they are part of adjacent Nassau County. The part above Northern Boulevard certainly lends credence to this assumption since the community physically resembles the **prosperous commuter towns** on the adjacent North Shore. Originally the entity was known as Little Neck (for the peninsula jutting out into the Sound), but in 1876 the western part was renamed Douglaston after **William B. Douglas** who had donated the L.I.R.R. Station there. The area is hilly and supports a wide variety of **exotic trees.** Peculiar to Douglaston are the Chinese maidenhair tree and the Chinese weeping cypress.

[14.] Bell Homestead, 38-08 Bell Blvd. bet. 38th and 39th Aves. W side. ca. 1845. ☆

[15.] Queensboro Community College, 56th Ave., Kenilworth Rd. to Cloverdale Blvd. 1967. Frederick Wiedersum & Assocs./Holden, Egan Wilson & Corser.

A handsome unified collection of campus buildings to supplant temporary and undistinguished earlier facilities.

[16a.] Cornelius Van Wyck House, 37-04 Douglaston Pkwy. (126 West Drive) SW cor. Alston Pl. 1735. ★

[16b.] Douglaston Club/formerly **George Douglas Residence/** originally **Wynant Van Zandt Residence,** Douglaston Pkwy. (West Drive) SE cor. 32nd Ave. (Beverly Rd.) Before 1835. Numerous additions.

[16c.] 205 32nd Avenue, (Beverly Rd.) NE cor. 237th St. 1964. Sachs & Tinnerello.

Neat new residence respectful of this stately community of older homes.

[17.] Morrell-Morgan House, 39-30 Little Neck Pkwy. bet. L.I.R.R. and 40th Ave. W side. West wing, 17th Cent. Main wing, 18th Cent. ☆

CENTRAL QUEENS

Town of Newtown/Middleburg

Settled in 1652; chartered by the Doughty Patent of 1640.

The old Town of Newtown encompasses the present-day communities of Jackson Heights, Corona, Elmhurst, Rego Park, Forest Hills, Maspeth, Ridgewood, and Glendale. The western part is relatively inactive, with many **old frame buildings** remaining; the eastern and northern parts are **dense apartment districts,** Jackson Heights having developed before World War II; the stretch along Queens Boulevard in Forest Hills and Rego Park afterward. Forest Hills is named after **Forest Hills Gardens,** the successful town-planning and real estate scheme of the **Russell Sage Foundation;** Rego Park abbreviates the phrase, "really good."

The center of **"New Towne" (1665),** the outgrowth of Middleburg, an **English Puritant settlement** under Dutch auspices, occupied the winding stretch of Broadway, north of Queens Boulevard. Vestiges of the community remained well into the 20th Century although only a **few church buildings remain** today.

After consolidation in 1898 the name, Newtown, quickly fell into disuse, the immediate community becoming known as Elmhurst, a name of **Germanic origin,** the ethnic heritage of many residents of this and the adjacent districts of Glendale and Ridgewood. The **"Newtown Pippins,"** grown in the apple orchards of the area, were prized by the English to whom they were extensively exported for the manufacture of cider.

[1.] LaGuardia Airport, Grand Central Pkwy. at 94th St. Jackson Heights, 1939. Delano & Aldrich. Central terminal and control tower, 1965. Harrison & Abramovitz.

Built as New York's **second municipal airport** (after Floyd Bennett Field in Brooklyn).

The **central terminal** is a sweeping arc of a building echoing the elliptical form of an extraordinarily **successful traffic interchange;** less successful is the shape of the control tower, which resembles the hyperbolic cooling towers of English steam generating plants. Flanking the terminal building, with a **"flying wing"** pergola at its roof, are the old individual hangars dating from 1939 and the **Marine Terminal,** lurking on the western edge of the field and originally built to serve the **seaplane transports** of the Thirties; today it is a facility for private aircraft.

[2.] Lexington School for the Deaf, 30th Ave. bet. 73rd and 75th Sts. N side. Jackson Heights. 1967. Pomerance & Breines.

A large school facility replacing an outmoded one in Manhattan. Handsome design expressing the structural frame within.

Flushing Meadow Park: Straddling the Flushing River, one-time navigational facility into the village of Flushing and the boundary between the towns of **Flushing** and **Newtown,** is present-day Flushing Meadow Park. Originally **a swamp,** it became known as the "**Corona dump**" after land fill operations had begun there. Its transformation into a park was due to its being chosen as the site of the **New York World's Fair of 1939–1940,** the site serving the same purpose for the 1964–1965 Fair.

Remnants of both fairs remain: The New York City Building and the Amphitheater **from 1939;** the U.S. and New York State pavilions, the theme structure and other works **from 1964.** In addition, a zoo and botanic garden are now established in the park, the Museum of Science and Technology built for the '64 Fair is slated for expansion, and Shea Stadium occupies much of the parking field of the '39 **Fair.**

[3a.] Shea Stadium, Grand Central Pkwy. to 126th St., Northern Blvd. to Roosevelt Ave. 1964. Praeger-Kavanagh-Waterbury, Engineers-Architects.

The basically simple form and sheer size of this new home for the **N.Y. Mets Baseball Club** impressively dominate the flat terrain for miles. The exterior gives the impression of scraps of colored paper caught on a giant wire basket after a wind storm—the result of an arbitrary applique of pastel-colored screens. Unique feature is the rotating tiers of infield seating which permit conversion to a football stadium.

[3b.] Museum of Science and Technology, Flushing Meadow Park at 111th St. and 48th Ave. 1964. Harrison and Abramovitz. Expansion, 1968, Office of Max O. Urbahn.

The original building, an **undulating tapestry of stained glass** set into precast concrete panels, exhibits a variety of fascinating displays on space travel and atomic energy. The adjacent "**space park,**" where full-size rockets and other space hardware reach into the sky, makes a successful and far less self-conscious pitch for your attention. The addition will be a **powerful reinforced concrete pavilion** whose scale and mass should be appropriate to the scale of its exhibits.

[3b.]   [3d.]

[3c.] United States Pavilion, New York Worlds Fair, 1964–1965, Flushing Meadow Park. 1964. Charles Luckman Assocs.

An immense square donut with stained-glass walls built on four stilts around a pyramidal podium and topped by a thin cornice. Is this America?

[3d.] New York State Pavilion, New York Worlds Fair, 1964–1965, Flushing Meadow Park. 1964. Philip Johnson and Richard Foster, Architects; Lev Zetlin & Assocs., Structural Engineers.

One of the few pavilions in the 1964–1965 Fair that attempted to utilize fresh technological developments as generators of form. In this case the **tubular perimeter columns** (as well as those supporting the observation decks) were **slip-formed** of concrete in a continuous casting operation; the **translucent roof** is a double diaphragm of radial cables separated by vertical pencil rods to dampen flutter, a common problem in cable suspension roofs. Altogether, a thoroughly successful **fair pavilion.**

[4a.] Reformed Dutch Church of Newtown, and Fellowship Hall, 85-15 Broadway, SE cor. Corona Ave., Elmhurst. **Church,** 1831. **Hall,** ca. 1860.

[4b.] St. James Episcopal Church, 84-07 Broadway, NE cor. Corona Ave. Elmhurst. 1849.

This church is an outgrowth of one built in 1734. [See 4c.]

[4c.] St. James Episcopal Church/now St. James Fellowship Hall, Broadway, SW cor. 51st Ave. Elmhurst. 1734.

The original St. James built on land granted by the town. The steeple on the west end of this somber Colonial relic was removed at the turn of the century.

[4d.] Queens Boulevard Medical Group, Health Insurance Plan of Greater New York, 86-15 Queens Blvd. bet. Broadway and 55th Ave. N side. Elmhurst. 1957. Abraham W. Geller & Assocs.

This medical office building sits atop the IND subway tunnel and thus requires its basement utility area to be on the roof. The resulting form, mastaba-like in quality, plus the articulate detailing and choice of color and materials make it a gem. Unfortunately, it suffers from some gross signs added during its short life.

[4d.]

[5a.] Macy's Queens, 87-11 Queens Blvd. bet. 55th and 56th Aves. N side. Elmhurst. 1965. Skidmore, Owings & Merrill.

Take a difficult site, consider that a department store requires exterior walls only as *enclosure,* calculate the parking problem, add the SOM touch and you get Macy's Queens, a circular department store girded by a concentric parking garage. What could be more logical? Luckily, a recalcitrant property owner refused to part with the southwest parcel, forcing a notch to be cut into the squat cylinder of precast concrete panels; a welcome punctuation.

[5b.] First National City Bank, Queens Boulevard-55 Branch, 87-11 Queens Blvd. (next to Macy's Queens). 1966. Skidmore, Owings & Merrill.

A small, bronze-colored aluminum and glass cylinder complements the larger crystalline concrete cylinder of Macy's.

[5c.] Lefrak City, Junction Blvd. to 99th St., 57th Ave. to Long Island Expwy. Elmhurst. 1962–1967. Jack Brown.

Hardly a city!

[5d.] Alexander's Rego Park, Queens Blvd. NW cor. 63rd Rd., Rego Park. 1960. Morris Ketchum Jr. and Assocs.

The first of the branch department stores to be built in this part of Queens.

[6a.] Walden Terrace, 98th to 99th Sts., 63rd Dr. to 64th Rd. Rego Park. 1948. Leo Stillman.

Their buff brick facades and unusual detail make this two-block group of apartments distinctive in an area suffering from an over-abundance of stripped-down red brick blocks. They have a mysterious and intriguing continental look about them.

[6b.] Parkside Memorial Chapels Inc., 98-60 Queens Blvd. SW cor. 66th Ave., Rego Park. 1961. Henry Sandig.

A funeral chapel conceived in Mesopotamian forms (at least on the outside) and 20th Century materials (textured concrete block).

[7.] Forest Hills Gardens, 71st (Continental) Ave. to Union Turnpike, Long Island R.R. right-of-way to uneven line south of Greenway South. 1913–present. Grosvenor Atterbury, Architect, and Frederick Law Olmsted, Jr., Landscape Architect, original team.

"Apart from its convenient location, within a quarter of an hour of the center of Manhattan Island, the Forest Hills Gardens enterprise differentiates itself ... from other suburban development schemes most notably in that its size permits a unique layout of winding streets, open spaces and building lots and thus permits the development of an ideally attractive neighborhood, while its financial backing is such that the realization of the well studied plans is assured in advance beyond peradventure." Alfred Tredway White in a promotional booklet of 1911.

[7.]

White, who had pioneered in housing for the working class [See WC Brooklyn 4] would not have been disappointed. This project, originally meant as a **working-class community** and sponsored by the Russell Sage Foundation, has become one of Queens' most **exclusive** residential enclaves. It is also a splendid combination of good planning and of romantic, picturesque architecture.

[8.] "Pretzel Intersection," Grand Central Pkwy., Union Turnpike, and Van Wyck Expwy. 1939–1964.

A highway engineer's fantasy come true. Best view is from an upper floor window of Queens Borough Hall at 120-55 Queens Boulevard (near Union Turnpike) or from an airplane slowly circling the city.

[9.] United States Cremation Co. Ltd./Fresh Pond Crematory/ formerly **United States Colombaria Co.,** 61-40 Mt. Olivet Crescent, NW cor. 62nd Ave. Maspeth. ca. 1905.

A pompous Classical Revival crematory in an otherwise uninteresting area of Queens. Note the adjacent country church whose cornerstone reads 1837.

[8.]

[1a.]

[10.] United Parcel Service Distribution Center, 56th Rd. bet. 46th and 58th Sts. N side. Maspeth. 1967. Francisco & Jacobus.

The physical requirements of an efficient conveyor-belt distribution system forced the erection of long, narrow, and very high fingers of construction out to the truck bays. To give the buildings visual amenity, an unusual Mansard roof in crisp corrugated metal siding was used, creating a clever, truck-scaled complex which somehow works.

Niederstein's Restaurant, 69-16 Metropolitan Ave. at 69th St. 1854. Judged by its appearance, this must have begun as a roadside tavern and inn on the road from Greenpoint, Brooklyn to Jamaica. The stables are still visible on the west side of this old wooden structure. Also known as a good place to eat. DA 6-0717.

[11.] Adrian Onderdonck House/now **American-Moninger Green-house Manufacturing Co. Inc.,** 1820 Flushing Ave. bet. Cypress and Onderdonk Aves. S side. Maspeth. 1731.

The only remaining example of the group of Dutch Colonial farmhouses that had withstood the onslaught of heavy industry onto their farmlands in the first half of the 20th Century. Regrettably, the owners of this one have appended a brick taxpayer, which occupies its front yard.

SOUTH CENTRAL QUEENS

Town of Jamaica/Rustdorp
Settled in 1656; chartered in 1660.

The communities lying within the boundaries of the old Town of Jamaica contain as a group the **widest contrasts** of any in Queens. Some, like Ozone Park, Richmond Hill, and Woodhaven, are quiet residential communities; Jamaica itself, on the other hand, is a bustling market place with department stores, specialty shops and theaters. **Affluence** is markedly visible in the Jamaica Estates area along Grand Central Parkway; **poverty** and **squalor** mark the Negro slum of South Jamaica; in the St. Albans area, though, is a lovely, tree-lined, Negro middle-income community. Parts of Jamaica date from the 17th and 18th Centuries; Kew Gardens, Richmond Hill, Queens Village, from the 19th; the eastern and southern areas like Howard Beach and Cambria Heights seeing their most **intensive growth** in the last decades.

[1a.] King Mansion, King Park, Jamaica Ave. bet 150th and 153rd Sts. N side. North section, 1730; west section, 1755; east section, 1806. ★

[1b.] Grace Episcopal Church and Graveyard, 155-03 Jamaica Ave. bet. 153rd St. and Parsons Blvd. 1862. Dudley Field. Additions, 1901–1902. Cady, Berg & See. Graveyard, ca. 1734. ★

[1c.] Prospect Cemetery, 159th St. SW cor. Beaver Rd. 1662.

The first public burial ground in Jamaica. In the early days of this community the wealthy were mostly buried in church—laymen under their pews, clergymen in the chapel or beneath the pulpit. Less affluent parishioners were interred in the churchyard. Anyone else was buried in Prospect Cemetery.

[2.] Aqueduct Race Track, Linden Blvd. to Southern Pkwy., IND Rockaway Line right-of-way to 114th St. 1894. Reconstruction, 1959. Arthur Froehlich & Assocs.

"The Big A," as it is currently known, is the last race track entirely within city boundaries. As land values increase, these enormous operations sell to developers (like Jamaica Race Track, now Rochdale Village). The name relates to the Ridgewood Aqueduct, Brooklyn and Queens' first large-scale water system, which still follows Conduit Avenue, the service road of Southern Parkway, in from its reservoirs on Long Island.

Frappes and sundaes: Frank Jahn's is a real 1890's ice cream parlor at 117-03 Hillside Avenue (near 117th St. and Jamaica Ave.). Complete with marble countertops, leaded-glass Coca Cola chandeliers, and wild, just wild, ice cream concoctions. Very crowded on date nights.

[3.] John F. Kennedy International Airport, Van Wyck Expressway and Southern Pkwy. 1942 to present.

Rescued from the swampy waters of adjacent Jamaica Bay, Kennedy Airport's **4900 acres** are roughly equivalent in area to Manhattan Island south of 34th Street. It is so large that it is quite possible to run up a dollar's tariff on your taxi's meter just covering the distance between the terminal and Kennedy's outer edge—Manhattan lies about 15 miles farther west. The dollar will be well spent, however, for the trip will take you past every architectural cliché of the past decade, some very handsome works, and some less distinguished hangovers from earlier periods as well.

Kennedy is best known for its **Terminal City,** housing the various passenger terminals, a control center, a central heating and cooling plant, three chapels, and a multitude of parking stalls. In addition, the airport has a cargo complex and service and storage facilities for the airline companies, as well as a hotel, a Federal office building, and other service structures.

[3a.] International Hotel. 1958, 1961. William B. Tabler.

For all intents and purposes, the gateway building to this aircraft empire.

[3b.] Federal Office Bldg. 1949. Reinhard, Hofmeister & Walquist.

[3c.] First National City Bank, JFK Branch. 1959. Skidmore, Owings & Merrill.

The stilts holding this exquisite glass box above its roadside site express just the right amount of diffidence about becoming associated with the rest of Terminal City.

[3m.]

[3h

[3f.]

[3d.] Eastern Airlines/Mohawk Airlines. 1959. Chester L. Churchill.

[3e.] Northwest Airlines, Northeast Airlines, Braniff International. 1962. White & Mariani.

A simple box with a sea of mushroom columns at the porte-cochere. The bold numbers at each gate are a welcome bit of identi-fication in what is so often an anonymous collection of redundancies.

[3f.] Pan American Airways. 1961. Tippetts-Abbett-McCarthy-Stratton, Architects and Engineers; Ives, Turano & Gardner, Assoc. Architects. Zodiac figures: Milton Hebald, Sculptor.

A genuine architectural attempt to answer the problem of all-weather connections to the planes. The suspended 4-acre elliptical roof canopy soars 110 feet beyond the terminal's enclosure on 32 radial, prestressed girders. Unfortunately the concept is compro-mised by an overabundance of distracting detail.

[3g.] International Arrivals Building. 1957. Skidmore, Owings & Merrill. Lobby sculpture, Alexander Calder.

This 2000-foot-long building is perhaps the most noticeable in Terminal City, because of both its arched, central pavilion and its central control tower, the highest element in the complex. The most successful parts of the building are its provision for watching the customs check of incoming passengers from the upper level and the string of airline reception areas that populate its two lateral wings. (It is possible to bar hop for almost half-a-mile in sumptuous surroundings if you are discreet.) The two 1,000-foot corridors con-necting the gates, however, are fatally monotonous and strangely surrealistic.

[3g.]

[3h.] Trans World Airlines. 1962. Eero Saarinen & Assocs.

Romantic, dramatic, voluptuous, eerie, disconcerting, loving, swooping, soaring—controversial. Well worth a visit to judge for yourself. Don't forget a trip through the "umbilical cord" to the entrance gates to the planes.

[3i.] Domestic Arrivals Building. 1969 (?). I. M. Pei & Partners.

Design established as a result of closed competition. Comple-tion date uncertain.

[3j.] Chapels. 1966. **Our Lady of the Skies (Roman Catholic),** George J. Sole. **Protestant,** Edgar Tafel & Assocs. **Jewish,** Bloch & Hesse.

[3k.] Central Heating and Refrigeration Building. 1957. Skidmore, Owings & Merrill.

On axis with their International Arrivals Building, across the fountain-studded mega-mall, this glass display case for condensers, compressors, pumps, and pipe is a multicolored fantasy and thoroughly wonderful.

[3l.] American Airlines. 1960. Kahn & Jacobs. Stained glass, Robert Sowers.

One of this world's most frustrating experiences is to enter this terminal, with the expectation of seeing its immense (largest in the world) stained glass facade illuminated by sunlight streaming through its colorful panes, only to find it hidden from view.

[3m.] United Airlines, Delta Airlines. 1961. Skidmore, Owings & Merrill.

A fastidiously detailed, subtly curving terminal building, with elaborate attention paid to every element.

[3n.] Gulf Oil Gasoline Station. 1959. Edward D. Stone.

A miniature New Delhi Embassy far too pretentious for automobile servicing.

Statistics: Kennedy's Terminal City can handle 6000 cars in its central parking area, using 10 miles of roadways. In its center is a 220-acre park with a trapezoidal reflecting pool and fountain. It has increased in passenger traffic at a rate far exceeding anyone's expectations. In 1953 a forecast was made of 5.4 million passengers by 1965. Late the same year the date was moved up to 1960. In 1958, 5.9 million had used the facility; in 1960, 9.0 million did. In 1965 Kennedy served 16.2 million passengers, and the curve still seems to be rising.

[3l.]

SOUTHERN QUEENS

Portion of Town of Hempstead/Hemstede

Settled and chartered in 1664.

This narrow spit of land, a **breakwater for Jamaica Bay,** was so inaccessible prior to the coming of railroads in 1868–1878 that it was an exclusive **resort** second only to **Saratoga Springs.** The accessibility afforded by rail connections by 1900 drove **society**

leaders out to more remote parts of Long Island's south shore at the Hamptons. Neponsit, Belle Harbor, and portions of Far Rockaway retain **traces of this former splendor.** (The IND Subway has replaced the L.I.R.R. as the operator of the trestle connection across Jamaica Bay—a lovely summer ride.)

After the **departure of high society** the area became a resort for the middle class. But in parts of the peninsula, this too has changed in recent years. The Hammels and Arverne, both east of the terminus of the **Cross Bay Bridge,** have seen the wood frame cottages and tenements become **squalid slums.** Various public housing projects and privately sponsored but publicly assisted **middle-income projects** dot the area; more are planned. Unfortunately they are grim in appearance and amazingly unresponsive to the beach-front sites they occupy. The potential development of a great recreational area at **Breezy Point,** thanks to the successful fight waged by a number of civic-minded citizens, holds out the greatest hope for the area.

[1.] Breezy Point, Tip of Rockaway Peninsula west of Beach 193rd St.

Appropriately named, these windswept dunes are the site of a private shorefront community with ferry access to Sheepshead Bay, Brooklyn. Its most conspicuous landmarks are a few abandoned concrete frames for a high-rise apartment development. In 1963, owing to pressure from a group of public-spirited citizens, municipal authorities courageously acquired title to the site for future beachfront development. It is planned to include Fort Tilden to the east, creating an uninterrupted public beach and park stretching 3½ miles from Riis Park to the western tip of the peninsula.

[2.] Jacob Riis Park, Beach 149th to Beach 169th Sts. 1937.

A mile of sandy beachfront graced by simple and handsome WPA-era buildings. In addition to swimming, there are other recreational possibilities, such as handball, paddle tennis, and shuffleboard, as well as a boardwalk for strolling. In the winter this is a haven for Polar Bear Club enthusiasts, and the 13,000-car parking field becomes an aerodrome for radio-controlled model aircraft flights. Refreshments available year 'round, as are lockers during the swimming season (at a nominal charge).

Amusement Park: Rockaway Playland is the one-square-block amusement section in the Rockaways, a neat and confined package of rides and games. Located between Beach 97th and Beach 98th Streets along Shore Front Parkway.

[3.] Congregation Knesseth Israel, 728 Empire Ave. SE cor. Reads Lane, Far Rockaway. 1964. Kelly & Gruzen.

An elaborate building complex containing an octagonal sanctuary, enclosed on three sides by a religious school and social activities center. Successfully occupies prominent site on main route of this comfortable quasi-suburban section of Far Rockaway.

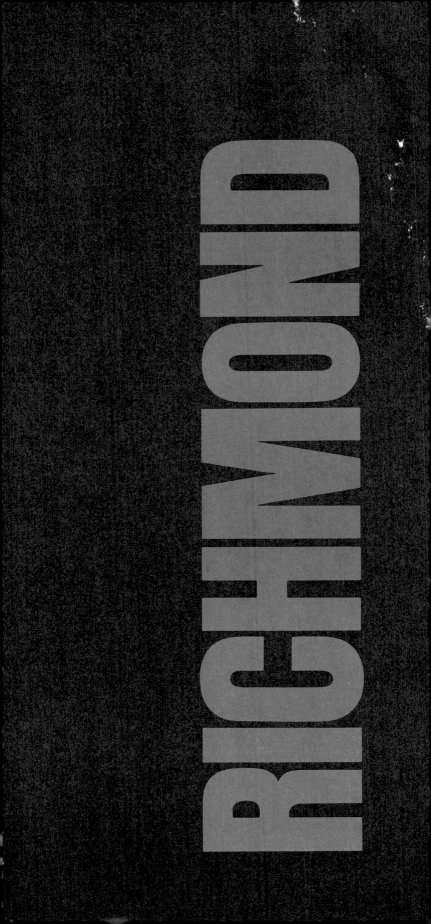

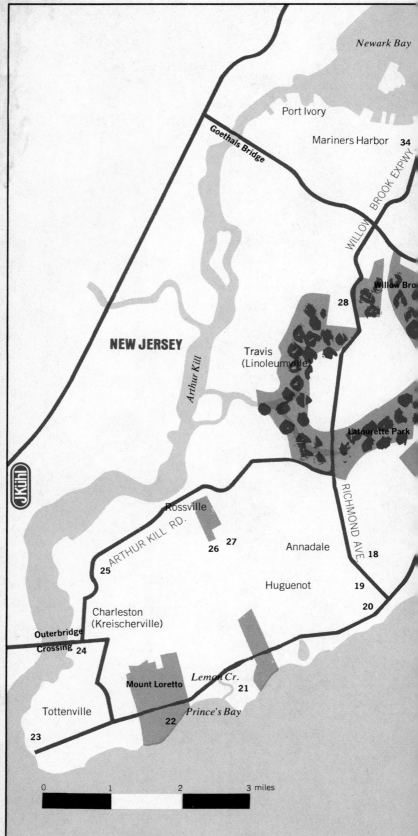

Newark Bay

Port Ivory

Mariners Harbor 34

Goethals Bridge

WILLOW BROOK EXPWY

Willow Bro

28

NEW JERSEY

Arthur Kill

Travis
(Linoleumville)

Latourette Park

RICHMOND AVE.

Rossville

ARTHUR KILL RD.

26 27

Annadale 18

25

Huguenot 19

20

Charleston
(Kreischerville)

Outerbridge
Crossing 24

Mount Loretto   Lemon Cr.

21

Prince's Bay

Tottenville

22

23

JKfihl

0   1   2   3 miles

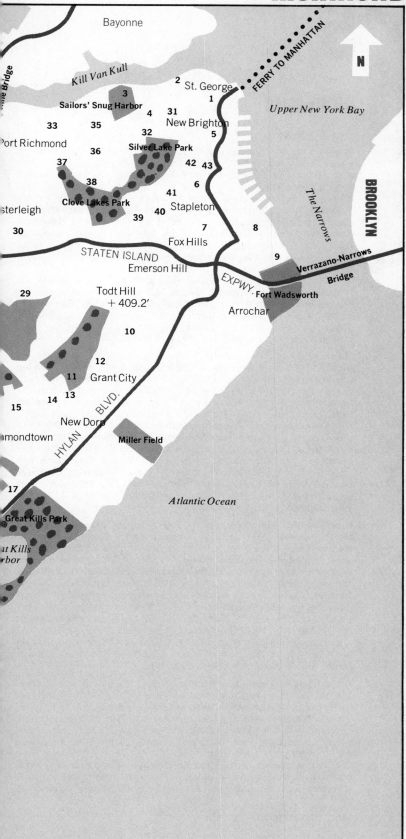

RICHMOND

Bayonne

Kill Van Kull

ine Bridge

2 St. George

1

FERRY TO MANHATTAN

N

3

Sailors' Snug Harbor

4

31

New Brighton

5

Upper New York Bay

33   35

Port Richmond

32

36

Silver Lake Park

42   43

37

38

6

Clove Lakes Park

41

sterleigh

40

Stapleton

39

30

7

8

The Narrows

BROOKLYN

STATEN ISLAND

Fox Hills

Emerson Hill

9

Verrazano-Narrows

EXPWY

Bridge

Fort Wadsworth

29

Todt Hill

+ 409.2'

Arrochar

10

12

11

Grant City

BLVD.

13

14

15

New Dorp

HYLAN

mondtown

Miller Field

17

Atlantic Ocean

Great Kills Park

t Kills

rbor

RICHMOND

Staten Island

For most tourists, Staten Island is nothing more than the terminus of a **spectacular ferry ride.** Few venture ashore to explore. If one does step ashore, first glimpses are very discouraging; drab brick houses, huge gasoline stations, and gaudy pizza parlors predominate. Persevere. Behind the listless dingy facade are **hills as steep as San Francisco's,** with breathtaking **views of the New York harbor;** mammoth, crumbling mansions surrounded by **mimosa and rhododendron,** rutted dirt roads, four-foot blacksnakes and fat, **wild pheasant,** ridges where archeologists still find Indian artifacts, Dutch farmhouses, **Greek temples,** Victorian mansions beyond Charles Addams' wildest **fantasies.**

The triangular island is 13.9 miles long and 7.3 miles wide. It is two and one-half times the size of Manhattan and ranks **third in area** among the city's boroughs. **Population** is equal to Manhattan's in 1840—about 270,000, a mere eight persons per acre. This **low density** can be expected to change rapidly as a result of the completion of the Verrazano Bridge, to top 500,000 by 1985.

Hills and Dales: One always is aware of being on an island. A slight, salty **dampness** in the air, a **brackish** smell, a buoy **braying forlornly** in the distance, a feeling of isolation, proclaim the fact.

Down the backbone of the island, from St. George to Richmondtown, runs a range of hills formed by an outcropping of **serpentine rock.** These hills—Fort, Ward, Grymes, Emerson, Todt, and Lighthouse—are dotted with elegant mansions of the 19th and 20th Centuries, many of them taken over by **private schools** and charitable **institutions.** Others remain palatial residences protected from the hoi polloi by high fences and private roads. (Private associations pay for street lamps, telephone poles, and upkeep.) **Todt Hill,** often proclaimed the **highest point** on the Atlantic coast, is a dinky 409.2 feet compared with Mt. Desert Island's Cadillac Mountain at 1532. The view, however, is justly famous.

Links to the Mainland: Staten Island is an **Othmar Ammann lover's paradise.** All four bridges connecting the island to the mainland were constructed under his design supervision. In the north, the steel arch of the **Bayonne Bridge,** opened in 1931, connects Port Richmond and Bayonne. In the northwest, the **Goethals Bridge,** a cantilever structure built in 1928, joins Elizabeth and Holland Hook. In the southwest is the **Outerbridge Crossing**—named not for its remoteness from Manhattan but for Eugenius Outerbridge, first chairman of the Port of N.Y. Authority. It also opened in 1928 and spans the Arthur Kill between Pleasant Plains and Perth Amboy. The **Verrazano Bridge,** completed in 1964, provides a crossing to Brooklyn. For several years city planners have been discussing a masstransit link to Manhattan, with no results.

Once Upon a Time: The island is rich in historical associations. Indians and Dutch colonialists seem absurdly distant and irrelevant in Manhattan. The crush of **towering skyscrapers** inhibits the play of the imagination on which a sense of history thrives. On Staten Island, however, a **Dutch Colonial farm** is still set out in fields surrounded by old apple trees. Here it is still possible to envision the life of our forebears.

History books notwithstanding, Staten Island was first "discovered" by the Algonquin Indians. It was first *seen* by a European, **Giovanni da Verrazano,** in 1524, and named **Staaten Eylandt** 85 years later by Henry Hudson while on a voyage for the **Dutch East India Company.** Following a number of unsuccessful attempts, the first permanent settlement by 19 French and Dutch colonists was established in 1661 near the present **South Beach.** The island was renamed **Richmond** (after King Charles II's illegitimate son, the Duke of Richmond) following the English capture of New Amsterdam in 1664.

Until the Revolution, inhabitants went quietly about their business, farming, fishing, oystering, shipbuilding. The revolution brought 30,000 hungry, lusty **redcoats** and **Hessian mercenaries** who occupied the island from 1776 to 1783. Initially Loyalist in sentiment, islanders greeted **Admiral Howe** with boisterous celebrations. But the 3000 islanders were hard put to provide food, fuel, hay for the occupying army and rapidly lost some of their fondness for the British. The island was the scene of several **skirmishes** between patriots, encamped on the Jersey shore, and the King's troops.

In the 1830's, the island began to develop into a **summer retreat** for wealthy, if not particularly prominent, families from New York and the South, who moved into the New Brighton area. A small literary colony sprang up around the eminent eye specialist, **Dr. Samuel MacKenzie Elliott.** [See 33a.] James Russell Lowell, Henry Wadsworth Longfellow, Francis Parkman came to Elliott for treatment and stayed on the island to recuperate. Here Italy's patriot, **Giuseppe Garibaldi,** lived in exile for three years, and **Frederick Law Olmsted** opened a wheat farm. But Staten Island's connection with famous people has always been rather tenuous; more typical were **gentleman farmers, shipbuilders** and **oyster captains.**

[3b.]

Sailors' Snug Harbor

The **Civil War** may have benefited oyster captains, but other islanders suffered the dislocation of a new army. The island became the **assembly point for Union regiments** in the process of organization. Fields and orchards were turned into **camps** and **training fields.** This exacerbated an already touchy situation. Confederate sympathies were strong on the island—many Southerners had sent their wives and children up from Virginia and Maryland to the comparative safety of Staten Island's hotels. [See 5.] Lootings, burnings, riots of the **anti-draft citizenry** plagued the island, and **abolitionists** had a hard time protecting their homes from the **angry mobs.**

After the war the island continued to develop, albeit slowly. The industrial revolution brought to the island's shores **brick and linoleum factories,** breweries, dye and chemical plants, **wagon and carriage makers.** Farming continued to be a leading occupation. Growth was so sluggish, however, that in 1871 the Legislature appointed a committee to study the problem. This, the first of endless analyses of

Staten Island's **lack of growth** or (as is more popular today) **excessive growth,** pointed to the **prevalence of malaria** (mosquitos prospered in the island's marshes) and **poor ferry service.** Indeed, the preceding decades had seen one ferry's hull crushed by ice, another blown up as the result of a boiler explosion. Prospective passengers were understandably alarmed.

The rural nature of the island, however, did attract the sporting set from across the bay. Here the **first lawn tennis court in America** was built in 1880, and the **first American canoe club** founded. Lacrosse, cricket, rowing, fox hunting, fishing, bathing, and cycling engaged **weekend enthusiasts.** But by the beginning of the 20th Century, the island's popularity had begun to wane. Fantastic schemes worthy of **Barnum and Bailey** were developed in a last-ditch attempt to lure the tourist trade. One promoter imported **Buffalo Bill's Wild West Show,** complete with **sharpshooting Annie Oakley,** "Fall of Rome "spectacles, and herds of girls and elephants.

[9b.]

Today and Tomorrow: During the last half-century the dangers threatening the island's natural advantages of space, air, grass, and trees have increased. Park areas are being **menaced by expressways.** On humid, stagnant days, lawns shrivel up and die from chemical fallout, and citizens hastily retreat to the safety of air conditioned homes. Meadows have been **scraped clean of trees,** natural streams buried, **hills leveled** in preparation for jerry-built housing developments. Wild salt marshes are now city garbage dumps. The outlook is grim—particularly to a person who remembers what rural Staten Island was once like. But to a person who knows how rare **a blade of grass** is in Manhattan or Queens, the island, by contrast, is positively pastoral. With its waterfront areas as yet unspoiled by shorefront drives, its wooded hills as yet **unscarred by bulldozers,** the island still has a marvelous potential for recreational and residential development. Whether this potential is realized or recklessly squandered will be determined within the next decade.

Staten Island Ferry Ride

"We were very tired, we were very merry—
We had gone back and forth all night on the ferry."

Edna St. Vincent Millay

Drawbridges and rusty chains clank, engines shudder and grunt, the throaty whistle blasts, and the ferry churns out into the oily waters of New York harbor. Petulant gulls hover aloft, commuters, inured to the spectacular, settle behind newspapers while tourists crowd to the rail. Children and even some adults become very merry.

Ferries leave every 10 or 15 minutes on weekdays, every 20 minutes on Saturdays and Sundays. Fare: a ridiculous **five cents.** Enter through the aquamarine tile building, singularly lacking the grace of the **old terminal** next door designed by Walker & Morris around 1900. Upon boarding, move to the far end of the second deck. From this position, Brooklyn lies to the left, and Governors Island is immediately ahead; Ellis Island, the old immigration station, and the **Statue of Liberty,** bound to produce **a lump in the throat** for even the most callous, appear in succession on the right.

The **first glimpse** of Staten Island is attractive. Steep, wooded hills rise behind the civic center of St. George; **Greek Revival porticos** appear along the waterfront, and **Gothic spires** and **Italianate towers** of schools and churches top hills on the right. On a misty or, more likely, smoggy day, the aspect is momentarily reminiscent of **a small Italian town.** Romance is quickly dispelled by the brutally efficient red brick ferry terminal, with its pea green tile interior—more suggestive of an athletic shower room than of a **gateway.**

Advice for Touring: A map is absolutely necessary. A newspaper stand inside terminal may have one. A better bet, however, is an inexpensive Chamber of Commerce map sold at Toder's Newspaper Store, 32 Bay Street (open mornings only, on Saturdays and Sundays). A car is not a necessity but offers distinct advantages.

Carless tour: See St. George, then take Bus 114 to Richmondtown, look around restoration project, proceed to Tottenville on Bus 113 to see Conference House. Return by Staten Island Railroad to St. George.

Driving tours: Don't try to do the whole island in one day. Distances are deceptively long, roads poorly marked, buildings hard to find. Specific driving instructions are given to save time. If you must be independent, go ahead but with fair warning.

Restaurants: They are few and far between. For lunch, soda fountains or coffee shops are the best bet. For supper, Carmen's is highly recommended. Note: By New York standards, decor in all restaurants is atrocious.

Carmen's, 750 Barclay Ave., southern section of the island near Hylan Blvd. and Woods of Arden Rd. Open 4–12 PM every day except Tuesday. Spanish and Mexican food. Indigenous and excellent. Dinner only. Closed Tuesdays. 984-9786.

Jones' Steak House, 945 Manor Rd., near Todt Hill. bet. Croak and Liberty Aves. Open 11:45 AM–10 PM. Good steaks at reasonable prices. Lunch and dinner. Closed Mondays. 442-9628.

The Shoal's, 2 Shell Rd. off Nelson Ave. Great Kills Harbor. The service leaves something to be desired, but food—mostly seafood—doesn't. Call for hours, YU 4-6316.

Ann's Sugarbowl, 1113 Victory Blvd. near Clove Rd. Luncheonette-dinner with ordinary, but good, food. Open 2–11 PM every day except Mondays. 442-9553.

Trimarche's Restaurant, 1650 Hyland Blvd. near Dongan Hills. bet. Altar and Cromwell. Open during the week, Noon–3 PM, 5–10 PM; Saturdays, 5–10 PM; Sundays, Noon–10 PM. Dull decor but food is fine. Italian cooking or American steaks and chops. Occasionally has excellent wines. EL 1-7755.

Eggers Confectionery, 1400 Forest Ave. near Burnside Ave. Serves excellent homemade ice cream. Highly recommended. Open 2–10 PM daily except Tuesdays. 442-9529.

ST. GEORGE-NEW BRIGHTON

[1a.] Original Chief Physician's House, U.S. Coast Guard Base, 1 Bay St., adjacent to ferry. 1815. (Visiting by appointment.) ☆

Gambrel roof of handsome, Federal-style building can be seen from Richmond Terrace, picturesquely peeking over base's high brick wall. Fussy bay windows capped by scalloped roof added to facade later.

[1b.] Borough Hall, Richmond Terrace opposite ferry terminal. 1906. Carrère & Hastings.

This elegant brick structure in the style of a French town hall welcomes the passenger emerging from the ferry building. Has light, graceful quality similar to that found in the same architects' design for the New York Public Library in Manhattan.

 [1c.] County Court House, Richmond Terrace next to Borough Hall. 1919. Carrère & Hastings.

Slightly pretentious Italian Renaissance structure with Greek Revival portico. Designed in totally different style from its neighbor. Purists may object, but effect is pleasing.

[1d.] Family Court House, 100 Richmond Terrace bet. Wall St. and Hamilton Ave. S side. 1930. Sibley & Fetherston.

Has finely detailed Doric columns and simple unornamented facade. Looks pleasantly remote from the heavy problems that are pondered by judges and juries inside.

If driving, continue west along Richmond Terrace, once fashionable for Sunday outings in horse and carriage, now blighted by oil refineries in New Jersey, factories and railroad further down. If walking, go back towards Borough Hall to see Brighton Heights Reformed Church, then proceed to Richmondtown. [See 16.]

[1e.] Staten Island Institute of Arts and Sciences, 75 Stuyvesant Pl. NW cor. Wall St. Hours: Tuesdays–Saturdays, 10 AM–5 PM; Sunday, 2–5 PM.

Dioramas of Staten Island's flora and fauna. Uninteresting unless you're keen on Indians (has locally found artifacts) or cicadas (large, privately owned collection, seen by appointment only).

[1f.] Brighton Heights Reformed Church, St. Mark's Pl. SW cor. Fort Pl. on hill behind Borough Hall. 1866. ★

 [2a.] Columbia Hall, 404 Richmond Terrace bet. St. Peter's Pl. and Westervelt Ave. 1835. ☆

Columbia Hall and Brooks House (next door) are last two remaining examples of **Temple Row,** the name given to ten Greek Revival mansions built by wealthy New Yorkers and Southern planters along the Terrace. House has fine Doric columns and carefully sculpted laurel wreaths in the frieze. Operated as a public bar with red peppermint decor and a restaurant catering to private banquets only.

[2b.] Brooks House, 414–418 Richmond Terrace SE cor. Westervelt Ave. 1835. ☆

[3a.] Neville House, 806 Richmond Terrace bet. Clinton Ave. and Tysen St. ca. 1770. ★

Built by a retired officer, later turned into a saloon called the "Old Stone Jug." Current occupants have attempted to suburbanize the house with pastel paint job, ceramic flamingos, and picket fence but have failed to destroy handsome proportions.

[3b.] Sailors' Snug Harbor, Richmond Terrace bet. Tysen St. and Kissell Ave. S side. 1831–1833. Martin E. Thompson. ☆

An impressive and dignified row of Greek Revival buildings looking like administrative offices for a college or a civic center, scarcely like dormitories for retired seamen. The Harbor was founded in 1801 by Captain R. R. Randall, the son of a privateer. Income from his 21-acre estate in Greenwich Village supports the 100-acre home and provides about 800 mariners with food, tobacco, and movies. Greek grandeur of the buildings is tarnished by wooden "doghouse" entrances stuck on facades to protect residents from cold drafts.

[3c.] Chapel, Sailors' Snug Harbor, Richmond Terrace. ca. 1854. ☆

Turn around, go back along Richmond Terrace towards St. George, turning south on Franklin Avenue to see Pendleton House.

[4.] W. S. Pendleton House, 22 Pendleton Pl. bet. Franklin and Prospect Aves. W side. 1855. ☆

A thoroughly delightful shingle-style house with orange slate roof, tiny Gothic windows, a silly tower pierced by dormers facing four points of the compass. Ideal home for Snow White and the Seven Dwarfs. Competes with Horrmann Castle [See 41] as most fantastic home on the island.

Take Franklin Avenue back to Richmond Terrace; proceed towards St. George. Turn right directly after Borough Hall, go up Hyatt Street to Brighton Reformed Church [See 1f]. Go down St. Mark's Place to Bay Street. Go south on Bay Street, keep eyes peeled for the Planter's Hotel.

Free port: Between Tompkinsville and Stapleton there are blocks of deserted deep-water piers. These, built between 1921 and 1923 by Mayor John Hylan, were the first of several attempts to boost Staten Island's maritime life. The docks were never used, became known as "Hylan's Folly." In 1937, the island was designated a free port. This does not mean you can buy a Leica or Drambuie at bargain prices. It means that German cuckoo clocks or Colombian pepper can be landed duty-free for storing, repacking, and re-exporting. Strangely this special privilege also failed to activate the dormant port. A huge, 135-acre project for containerized cargo handling is being considered for the area.

[2a.]

[5.] Planter's Hotel, 360 Bay St. NW cor. Grant St. ☆

Easy to miss. Years of neglect, ungainly fire escape, and drain pipes tacked on facade have defaced the once-fashionable hotel patronized by wealthy Southerners during the 19th Century.

[6.] U.S. Marine Hospital, Seamen's Fund and Retreat Building, Bay St. NW cor. Vanderbilt Ave. ca. 1837. ☆

Imposing stone and granite facade with two-story pierced gallery. Doesn't have grimly efficient appearance of modern hospitals; is unscientifically gracious. Perhaps this is why it's due for demolition.

If interested in Italian history, make a right on Chestnut Street to visit Garibaldi Memorial, otherwise continue south on Bay.

[7.] Garibaldi Memorial, 420 Tompkins Ave. SW cor. Chestnut St. 1840. ★

An unlikely refuge for fiery Italian patriot Giuseppe Garibaldi, who lived here with his friend **Antonio Meucci** between 1851 and 1853. Restlessly awaiting an opportunity to return to Italy, Garibaldi made candles in a nearby factory, killed time fishing and "shooting thrushes" (the only game available). **Museum,** housed in altered Federal farmhouse, has letters, photographs describing Garibaldi's life and documenting Meucci's claim to **invention of telephone** prior to Alexander Graham Bell. Hours: Tuesdays–Fridays, 11 AM–5 PM; weekends, 1 PM–5 PM.

Fig Trees: Italians on the island love ripe figs. Consequently, many backyards are decorated with weird trees bundled up like mummies in winter, laden with clusters of ripe figs in summer. Presence of this tree is foolproof clue to nationality of its owner. Garibaldi memorial is no exception—an Italian caretaker lives on the second floor.

Go back to Bay Street. Turn south.

[8a.] St. Mary's Roman Catholic Church and Rectory, 1101 Bay St. bet. St. Mary's and Virginia Aves. E side. 1858. ☆

Turn left on Hylan Boulevard for Austen Cottage and old New York Yacht Club. Don't miss.

[8b.] Austen Cottage, 2 Hylan Boulevard, overlooking the water. ca. 1700. ☆

Original stone cottage built by a Dutch merchant is in back. Low clapboard front was remodeled in 1843, possibly by James Renwick, architect for Manhattan's St. Patrick's Cathedral. During the Revolutionary War, the commander of the Hessian mercenaries was stationed here. A breathtaking site overlooking the Narrows and the Verrazano Bridge.

[8c.] F. Bredt House/formerly **N.Y. Yacht Club,** 30 Hylan Boulevard ca. 1859. ☆

Behind the Austen house, set back from road. Another incredible view, enhanced here by meadows and horse paddock. Its tenure as a club ended in 1880; now an apartment house. Rambling plan with spacious bay windows framed by Egyptoid forms.

[8d.]  [8e.

[8d.] St. John's Protestant Episcopal Church, 1331 Bay St. SE cor. New Lane. 1869. Arthur Gilman. ☆ **Rectory,** 1862. ☆ **Parish House,** 1865. ☆

More likely to be found at Yale University than on Staten Island. A fine example of Victorian Gothic style built of rose-colored granite with handsome stained-glass windows. Unfortunately, original steeple has been altered. The first child baptized in original frame building of this parish was Cornelius Vanderbilt, born in nearby Stapleton in 1794.

Backdoor to America: An important strategy conference brought Winston Churchill to the island's shores during World War II. The Prime Minister secretly debarked from British cruiser anchored off Stapleton and took the B&O Railroad directly to Washington to confer with President Roosevelt. Thus you might say the island is the backdoor to America.

Turn right on Belair Road for Nathaniel Marsh Home.

[8e.] Nathaniel Marsh Home, 30 Belair Rd. bet. Bay St. and Wingham Home Ave. S side ca. 1860. ☆

Sits elegantly atop hill, surrounded by beautiful trees. Pink brick festooned with wisteria vines, stylish Italianate bays on two sides.

[9a.] Von Briesen Park, S end of Bay St. at Ft. Wadsworth.

One of the island's prettiest parks. Nicely landscaped to retain hilly terrain—pleasing contrast to the flat parks of Manhattan. Unusual trees. Spectacular view of Verrazano Bridge and Fort Weed.

[9b.] Fort Weed, Fort Wadsworth Reservation, S end of Bay St. ca. 1840. ★

Gate and guards look ominous, but actually visitors are welcome. Drive in to point overlooking Fort Weed. Romantic legend depicts Algonquin Indians standing here spellbound by the sight of Hudson's ship, the *Half Moon* entering the Narrows in 1609. Since those sylvan times, Dutch, British, and Americans in times of war have stood watch here, scanning the horizon for enemy ships.

Park Land: Of all the boroughs, Staten Island has the smallest percentage of park land. The island has 4943 acres of Parks Department property or 12.7 percent of the total land, compared with 17 percent in New York City, 22 in the Bronx.

We suggest you now take Verrazano Bridge home and come back another day via the bridge to see Richmondtown and southern sections of the island. When you do, take Richmond Road exit off the bridge. Go south. This boulevard once known as Kings Highway was one of main stagecoach routes from New York to Philadelphia.

[10.] Billiou-Stillwell-Perine House, 1476 Richmond Rd. bet. Norden St. and Forest Rd. 1662–1830. ☆ Opposite Carroll's Florist. Hours: Saturdays, and Sundays, 2–5 PM.

Like the house the Pecks built, this one has additions sprawling in every direction. Looking at the building from the front and reading from left to right, you see rooms added on in 1790, 1680, 1662, 1830. The original one-room fieldstone farmhouse with steep pitched roof built in 1662 is best seen from the back. Walk around house; take a look outside and in particular at the magnificent open-hearth fireplace.

Half a mile south on Richmond Road on the west side is a fascinating church complex containing samples of Dutch Colonial, Greek Revival, Roman Revival, and Victorian architecture, all within a stone's throw of each other.

[11a.] New Dorp Moravian Church, 1256 Todt Hill Rd. N of Richmond Rd. W side. 1844. ☆ **Parsonage,** ca. 1870. ☆ **Parish House,** 1913. ☆

This "new" church is older than many of New York's "old" ones. The pretentious, gray stucco parish house in Classical Revival style was the gift of William H. Vanderbilt, son of Cornelius.

[11b.] Old New Dorp Moravian Church, in the Moravian Cemetery. 1763. ☆

A good example of Dutch Colonial style. Has sweeping roof extending over eaves to form porch. Building originally served as church and parsonage; now catering to the very young as well as the very old, it is both church school and cemetery office.

[11c.] Vanderbilt Mausoleum, rear of Moravian Cemetery. 1886. Richard Morris Hunt. Entire cemetery—☆

Carved out of the "living rock" with ornate entrance added at the face of the stone outcropping. A trip through the rest of the cemetery provides beautiful, if morbid, walks and drives.

Drive up Todt Hill Road, make a right on Flagg Place to see Flagg Residence and Richmond Country Club.

[12a.] Ernest Flagg Residence, Gatehouse and Gate, 209 Flagg Pl. N side. ca. 1900. Ernest Flagg. ★

For many years the palatial residence of architect Ernest Flagg, responsible for Singer Tower and United States Naval Academy at Annapolis. Marvelous use of serpentine rock, quarried locally, contrasted with white clapboard on upper stories. The lavish estate with enormous swimming pool, barn, row upon row of fruit trees now quarters 23 seminarians.

[12b.] Richmond County Country Club, 135 Flagg Pl. N side. ca. 1845. ☆

Go back to Richmond Road and continue south.

[13.] Lakeman House, 2286 Richmond Rd. bet. Bryant and Otis Aves. W side. ca. 1674. ☆

For Dutch Colonial addicts only. Look for Moravian Florist shop on left side of street. Completely hidden behind greenhouses is a fieldstone house with gambrel roof. Next to the Billop House, this is the earliest example on the island of two-story construction—rare in the 17th Century. Paneling on fireplace and walls, visible through window *inside* the greenhouse added to the building's front, is now a backdrop for gladiolas and flowerpots. Buy a flower to placate owner.

Penguins: The Bronx zoo has on display several penquins caught on Staten Island. Incredulous? You should be. These aquatic birds thrive on the cold, rugged shore of the other Staten Island, located off the eastern tip of South America, between the Straits of Magellan and Cape Horn.

[14.] Mayer House/formerly **J. M. Davis House,** 2475 Richmond Rd. bet. Altamont Ave. and Odin St. W side. ca. 1854. ☆

[15a.] Moore-McMillen House/formerly **Rectory of the Church of St. Andrew,** 3531 Richmond Rd. opposite Kensico St. W side. 1818. ★

A very good example of Federal style. Extremely handsome doorway and neatly articulated cornice. Behind house is good view of lighthouse.

If pressed for time, hurry on to Richmondtown. Otherwise turn right on Lighthouse Avenue to see pre-fab Wright House, lighthouse, and Tibetan museum.

[15c.]

[1

[15b.] Cass House, 48 Manor Court W of Lighthouse Ave. 1959. Frank Lloyd Wright.

Best seen driving up Lighthouse Avenue toward the lighthouse. Long, low, pre-fab building clings precariously to cliff edge taking full advantage of the view. Cream colored masonite building with tacky metal roof, totally lacking dignity or style. Only Wright-designed residence within city-limits.

[15c.] Staten Island Lighthouse, Edinboro Rd. 1909. ★

Can be seen from Lighthouse Avenue. This lighthouse, strangely distant from rocks and pounding waves, stands calmly amid lawns and homes. The octagonal structure of yellow brick with fanciful Gothic carpentry supporting walkway is a pleasant change from pure white cylindrical lighthouses familiar to yachtsmen. The beacon provides range lights to guide ships into Ambrose Channel off Sandy Hook.

[15d.] Jacques Marchais Center of Tibetan Art, 340 Lighthouse Ave. near Windsor Ave. S side. Hours: Tuesdays and Thursdays, 3–5 PM; 2nd and 4th Sundays of each month, 2–5 PM. Open June 1st to October 31st only. Admission 50¢.

The largest privately owned collection of Tibetan art outside of Tibet. A rare treat—if you enjoy Tibetan sculpture, scrolls, paintings.

Continue east on Lighthouse Avenue; make a left on Ascot, a right on Meisner.

[15e.] Nathaniel J. Wyeth House, 190 Meisner Ave. bet. Rockland Ave. and London Rd. W side. ca. 1850. ☆

A lovely, ivy-covered, deserted mansion hidden behind lush rhododendron bushes and pine trees. Planting and siting offer the privacy that newer homes have sacrificed to wide, showy lawns. Has elaborate ten-sided cupola, surrounded by captain's walk.

Go back to Richmond Road. Proceed to Richmondtown.

Richmondtown: The site of an ambitious project involving the **restoration** and **reconstruction** of approximately 31 buildings under the direction of the Staten Island Historical Society, and the Department of Parks. It is proposed as an Historic District by the Landmarks Preservation Commission.

At its founding in 1685 Richmondtown was humbly known as **"Cocclestown"** or more commonly "cuckoldstown"—presumably after oyster and clam shells found in streams nearby. Here, in 1695, the Dutch erected the Voorlezer House, their **first meeting house,** used for both church services and teaching school. Subsequently a **town hall** and **gaol** were built. By 1730 the town was thriving. It had a new court house, one tavern, about a dozen homes, and the Church of St. Andrew. This tiny town was now the largest and most important town on the island. As such, the name Cocclestown was considered inappropriate and changed to the more staid Richmondtown. By the time of the **American Revolution,** when British occupied it, Richmond had a blacksmith shop, a general store, a poorhouse, a tanner's shop, a Dutch Reformed Church, a grist mill, and several more private homes.

[16a.] Staten Island Historical Museum, Court and Center Sts. 1848. ☆ Open daily except Monday, 2–5 PM; Sundays, 2–6 PM.

To get your bearings, study model of Richmondtown restoration project. On display are odd bits of Americana of varying interest—china, lithographs, furniture, toys, a marvelous collection of tools. Note photos around gallery (second floor) to see beautiful buildings you've missed—most have met wrecking ball fate.

[16b.] Third Court House, end of Center St. 1837. ☆ Opposite Historical Museum.

[16c.] Stephens House and General Store, Court St. cor. Center St. 1837. ☆

Fascinating reconstruction of 19th Century store—everything from ginger beer to quinine pills. Musty smell of soap and candles delights modern-day shopper used to antiseptic, cellophane-wrapped goods in supermarkets. Storefront is perfectly plain—no neon signs, no billboards.

[16d.] St. Patrick's Roman Catholic Church, 53 St. Patrick's Pl. ca. 1866. ★

[16e.] Lake-Tysen House, Richmond Rd. near Center St. W side.

ca. 1740. ☆

One of the best examples of the Dutch Colonial style remaining in the metropolitan area and luckily saved at the last minute from destruction when it was moved in 1962 from original site in New Dorp. Low-pitched gambrel roof has lovely sensuous line accented by dormers and chimneys; porch is supported by trim pillars. Roofing is particularly handsome—in sharp contrast to some modern roofing seen on old homes on the island. Interior includes original paneling and woodwork. Alone merits the trip from Manhattan.

 [16f.] Voorlezer House, Arthur Kill Rd. at end of Court St. 1696. ☆

Archetypical little red schoolhouse, called Voorlezer because in communities unable to obtain a minister, a layman named a voorlezer was chosen by the Dutch congregation to teach school and conduct church services. This house not only served these purposes but also was a residence for the voorlezer. About 20 such houses were built in the Hudson Valley, but this is the only one now remaining. It is the oldest known elementary school building in the United States. The interior features hand-hewn beams, wide floorboards, tasteful replica of colonial classroom.

[16g.] St. Andrew's Protestant Episcopal Church, Old Mill Rd. SE cor. Arthur Kill Rd. 1872. William H. Mersereau. ★

Pelts, anyone? Staten Island muskrats used to end up in Hudson Seal coats. A peak year would bring 40,000 pelts. As late as the 1940's, over 20,000 of these furry rodents were being trapped annually on the island.

 [16h.] Latourette House/now **Latourette Park Clubhouse,** Latourette Park and Richmond Hill. 1839. ☆

Go back towards Richmond, make a right on Arthur Kill Road, left on Giffords Avenue. If you've had enough sightseeing for the day, take Nelson Avenue to Hylan Boulevard. Turn north; take Hylan Boulevard back to bridge, perhaps visiting Great Kills Park, or driving down to Roosevelt Boardwalk, or South Beach. Such a detour would not be to see beautiful beaches (they aren't) but to see vast waterfront potential as yet unused. This route will take you past Trimarche's Restaurant and the Shoals. On way back note Holmes Cole House.

If continuing the tour, make a right on Amboy Road to old Amboy Road to see a Richard Upjohn church, then make a left on Arden Road, another left on Koch Boulevard to see a contemporary school and playground.

[17.] Holmes Cole House, 3425 Hylan Boulevard at SW cor. Justin Ave. ca. 1730. ☆

A fine site overlooking Great Kills Park. House sits on a little rise with dormers drinking in the vista. Landscaping sharply contrasts with modern bulldozer approach.

[18.] St. Alban's Protestant Episcopal Church and Rectory, 76 Old Amboy Rd. bet. Pacific and Richmond Aves. S side. ca. 1855. Richard Upjohn. ☆

A gem. Board-and-batten Carpenter Gothic style with vertical boards and steeply pitched roof. Entrance is not opposite apse area but from one side—an interesting variation.

[19.] Public School 55, Richmond, and Playground, Koch Blvd. NE cor. Woods of Arden Rd. School, 1965; Playground, 1967, Richard J. Stein.

Refreshing departure from usual brick-box schools. Has exposed masonry on exterior and interior, four sculptures by Nivola, and tasteful graphics by Chermayeff and Geismar. Playground promises to be equally exciting. Instead of bulldozing the hillside site into a large asphalt plateau, the architect is creating an imaginative multi-level playground with lawns and trees on upper level; ramps and amphitheater leading to lower level of paved game areas.

Cut down to Hylan Boulevard. Go south.

Land boom: Note large tracts of wooded, undeveloped land, occasionally marked by cement gate posts and rusty fire hydrants. These "improvements" were put in during a speculative land boom of the Twenties that subsequently fizzled. Much of this land is City-owned.

[20.] Poillon House, 4515 Hylan Blvd. near Woods of Arden Rd. ca. 1720. ☆

Hard to find—set back from road. Extensively remodeled in the 19th Century. Before he became a park designer, Frederick Law Olmsted lived here, running a wheat farm, planting trees, experimenting with landscaping. Later, when Olmsted began work on Prospect Park, he moved up to Clifton, commuting daily to Brooklyn via the nearby ferry.

Turn left on Seguine Avenue to reach Prince's Bay. Visit Carmen's Restaurant, if it's right time of day.

Prince's Bay: Once a prosperous fishing and oystering village. Oysters from here were so famous that fashionable restaurants in New York and London carried "Prince's Bays" on their menus. Now an area of run-down shacks with tar paper flapping, paint peeling.

[21a.] Seguine House, 440 Seguine Ave. bet. Wilbur St. and Purdy Pl. W side. ca. 1840. ★

Grand, but ugly; two-story pillars are fat and chunky, fanlight in middle of pediment, awkward. Still, building's Southern-style grandeur in this run down setting is appealing. Splendid site—look back at the house from marina area.

[21b.] Purdy Hotel, 509 Seguine Ave. NE cor. Purdy Pl. ca. 1690. ☆

Two-story addition made in 1800 (on left) and enclosed porches are nicely integrated with original structure. Once upon a time guests had a lovely view of clipper ships and schooners sailing into the Narrows; now, an unlovely vista of smokestacks.

Take Seguine Avenue back to Amboy Road; make a left.

Historic District: From Seguine Avenue to Page Avenue, Amboy Road has been proposed as an historical district. This 2-mile stretch of road is the Georgetown of Staten Island. A drive miraculously free of gasoline stations, run-down bars, dreary rooming houses. Result is a delightful stretch of old buildings dating from 1820 to 1860 with newer houses tastefully related to older structures.

At Sharrott Avenue take detour back down to Hylan Boulevard to see Prince's Bay Lighthouse.

[22.] Prince's Bay Lighthouse and Keeper's House/now **Residence of the Mission of the Immaculate Virgin,** Mount Loretto. ca. 1868. ☆

From Hylan Boulevard there is a good view of rusticated brownstone lighthouse up on hill, with beacon now replaced by statue of the Virgin Mary. An enviable residence and dining hall for priests who care for nearly a thousand children from broken homes. Grounds include 600 acres of sweeping meadows and glorious views.

Proceed to Billopp/Conference House, either on Hylan Boulevard or Amboy Road.

[23a.] Billopp House/Conference House, foot of Hylan Blvd. ca. 1680. ☆

[23a.]

The house was built by British **naval captain,** Billopp, the gentleman responsible for Staten Island's inclusion in New York City. He **sailed around the island** in 23 hours, thereby winning the island for New York. Billopp's, descendants remained in **British Loyalist** tradition. During the Revolutionary War, Colonel Thomas Billopp was **thick as thieves** with Lord Howe. On several occasions, patriots in Perth Amboy, rowed across the **Arthur Kill** and kidnapped the Tory officer.

Go left on Saterlee Street for Biddle House.

[23b.] Captain Biddle House, 70 Saterlee St. at NW cor. Shore Rd. 1840. ☆

Take Craig and Bentley Roads to Arthur Kill Road; head north.

Arthur Kill Road, a fascinating drive, runs past Charleston, a marine graveyard, Rossville, Fresh Kills reclamation project, desolate salt marshes—the real backwoods of Staten Island. Charleston, formerly known as Kreischerville, after Balthazar Kreischer who started a brick factory in 1854, is an area rich in clay. Old clay pits can still be visited; several brick-making firms operated here during the 19th Century. Rossville, now an eastern ghost town, was the site of the old Blazing Star Ferry to New Jersey, in service from 1757 to 1836. Stage coaches going between New York City and Philadelphia took the ferry, propelled by sail or oars, here or in Tottenville.

[24a.] Blomeley House/Captain Abraham Cole House, 4927 Arthur Kill Rd. bet. Botany Pl. and South Bridge St. W side. ca. 1830. ☆

Classically simple house—oddly unpretentious for Staten Island. Crisply detailed doorway has flanking Ionic columns capped by a plain architrave.

[24b.] Kreischer House, 4500 Arthur Kill Rd. bet. Allentown Lane and Englewod Ave. E side. ca. 1885. ★

Queen Anne style *par excellence*. Its fanciful Gothic embellishments, lacy balustrade, delicate turret with open-air balcony might be made of sugar, covered with white icing.

Industrial graveyards: Stucker's automobile graveyard and Witte Marine Equipment are off Arthur Kill Road between Chemical Lane and Rossville Ave. N Side. Surrealistic outdoor museums. Largest automobile graveyard on the East Coast; rusting navy destroyers, barges.

[25.] J. Winant House/formerly **Blazing Star Tavern,** 2390 Arthur Kill Rd. bet. Engert and St. Lukes Aves. S side. ca. 1750. ☆

A comfortable stopping place for stagecoach travelers weary of bouncing over rutted roads.

At Rossville, note picturesque Sleight Family Graveyard (1750–1850) at foot of Rossville Avenue, then go south on Rossville Avenue, left on Woodrow Road. ★

[26.] Woodrow Methodist Church and Hall, 1109 Woodrow Rd. bet. Rossville Ave. and Vernon Ave. N side. ca. 1847. ★

This lovely example of Greek Revival style is almost, but not quite, spoiled by ungainly arcaded bell tower added in late 19th Century. Spacing and proportions of Ionic columns in portico is especially fine.

[27.] Captain Cole House, 1065 Woodrow Rd. next to Woodrow Methodist Church ca. 1836. ☆

This house and church next door nicely complement each other; let us hope they will continue to do so.

Take Woodrow Road back to Arthur Kill Road, turning north on Richmond Avenue. Road traverses Latourette Park. If a bird lover, take a left at Travis Avenue to visit William T. Davis Wildlife Refuge, if Dutch Colonial lover, take a right on Richmond Hill Road to see Decker Farm, otherwise, continue to Victory Boulevard and Staten Island Expressway. Houseman House en route. Make a detour to Jones' Steak House, if it's lunch time. Note church, truck farm, Christopher House, en route.

[28a.] Sylvanus Decker Farm, 435 Richmond Hill Rd. bet. Kelly Blvd. and Forest Hill Rd. ca. 1800. ★

A cozy clapboard farmhouse, owned by the Staten Island Historical Society. It will be restored as a farm of the 1830's, with barns, carriage shed, orchard of cherry, pear, and apple trees.

[28b.] Asbury Methodist Episcopal Church, Richmond Ave. bet. Signs Rd. and Rockland Ave. W side. 1845. ★

Fine brickwork accented by white clapboard. Directly opposite is one of the few remaining truck farms on the island. Drop in for fresh lettuce, romaine, cauliflower, dandelion and watercress.

[29.] Christopher House, 819 Willowbrook Rd. bet. South Cannon Ave. and Forest Hill Rd. N side. ca. 1767. ★

South side of Staten Island Expressway; turn onto South Cannon Avenue and from there to Willowbrook Road. Set **way back**

from road, protected by shaky bridge and snarling dog, house is hard to find and always was. Thus, during the Revolution, it was an ideal meeting place for **Patriot Committee of Safety.** Members of the Committee spied on British encamped on the island and reported their activities to New Jersey patriots whenever it was possible to **elude sentries** located along the Arthur Kill. An important historical monument now sadly neglected by **motorists whizzing by** on nearby expressway.

Farms: In 1886, there were 300 farms on the island. By 1948, the number had dwindled to 35; by 1967, to a handful, including one farm specializing in organically grown crops. Problems of rising taxes, industrial zoning, air pollution, have made it difficult for most farmers to resist selling their land to real estate developers. Some farmers, unwilling to waste green thumbs, have turned to green-house flower-growing operations.

[30.] Houseman House, 308 St. John's Ave. NE cor. Watchogue Rd. ca. 1750. ☆

One-story frame and fieldstone section of house with steeply pitched roof is typical Dutch farmhouse. An addition with dormers was made in 1770. During the Revolution, Loyalist Garrett House-man lived here. He refused to reveal his hiding place for silver and money to New Jersey patriots; suffered cruel punishment at their hands.

Tour of northern section of the island focuses on mansions built during the 19th Century—some modest, some grandiose. From St. George, drive down Richmond Terrace to Franklin, then left on Buchanan.

[18.]

[31.] Pritchard House, 66 Harvard Ave. NW cor. Park Pl. 1845. ★

Hidden behind box hedge, birch trees, festooned with wisteria, a charming yellow stucco home with blue trim. Greek Revival style with Italian-palazzo flavor provided by quoin work and arched windows visible from Park Place.

[32.] Nicholas Muller House, 200 Clinton Ave. NW cor. Prospect Ave. 1855. ☆

Continue west on Richmond Terrace, turning left on Bard Avenue to see Elliott House.

[33a.] Dr. Samuel MacKenzie Elliott House, 69 Delafield Pl. bet. Davis and Bard Aves. N side. 1850. ★

Frilly serpentine verge board decorates an otherwise straight-forward stone exterior. Trim is painted aquamarine, a favorite color for Staten Islanders. Focal point of small literary colony, appro-

Building or remodeling?

Move up to Stainless Steel—we've got the cost down!

Here's the first truly cost-competitive stainless steel fenestration system—USS ULTIMET Stainless Steel Wall Framing. There has never been a stainless steel system like it.

All USS ULTIMET components are roll-formed—for precise part-to-part uniformity and fit, greater strength, lower cost fabrication, and faster, lower cost erection.

USS ULTIMET framing is first-quality nickel-chrome stainless steel—in a new softline architectural finish. Includes narrow-stile doors and horizontally-pivoted sash. Meets NAAMM test requirements.

USS ULTIMET flush-glazed components can be erected more simply and quickly than ever before possible with stainless steel fenestration. Most members just lock into place. No on-site cutting. No welding, no exposed fasteners.

And USS ULTIMET components give the architect a completely integrated series of structurally efficient and easily fabricated and erected stainless steel shapes that lend themselves to a great variety of architectural expressions and applications.

If you want to use stainless steel fenestration in building or remodeling, don't let cost worry you any longer. USS ULTIMET Stainless Steel Wall Framing is available now, at a price you can afford.

For a copy of "USS ULTIMET Stainless Steel Wall Framing," write United States Steel, Room 4375, 525 William Penn Place, Pittsburgh, Pa. 15230. Or contact a USS Architectural Products Representative through your nearest USS Construction Marketing or Sales Office. USS and ULTIMET are trademarks.

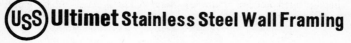

(USS) **Ultimet Stainless Steel Wall Framing**

priately since Dr. Elliott was eye doctor to the literati.

Swing back to Richmond Terrace to see Pelton House, Reformed Church of Staten Island, Mariners' Harbor.

[33b.] Kreuzer-Pelton House, 1262 Richmond Terrace. Foot of Pelton Ave. 1722–1840. ★

Stone cottage on the right dates from 1722; central frame section was added in 1770; two-story Georgian tile roofing and flaking paint make it hard to imagine Revolutionary days when house was used as headquarters for British General Courtlandt Skinner, commander of forces occupying Staten Island. Here Skinner entertained Prince William Henry, later King William IV.

[34.] Reformed Church of Staten Island, 54 Richmond Ave. Opposite Church St. ca. 1854; **Chapel,** 1898. ☆

Site of the first religious congregation on Staten Island, organized in 1663. A reproduction of the original church, which was built in traditional Dutch Colonial style—six sides surmounted by a belfry —will be reconstructed at Richmondtown. Present church is a chunky version of Greek Revival style.

Mariners Harbor: A prosperous community during the heydey of oystering. Now few remain of the imposing mansions built along the shore by oyster captains. In the 1840's, 40 or 50 sloops would be moored in the Kill opposite these houses, known as Captain's Row.

Go back along Richmond Terrace to Bard Avenue, turn right to see Curtis House, Garner Mansion.

[35.] George W. Curtis House, 234 Bard Ave. NW cor. Bard and Henderson Ave. 1850. ☆

Curtis, a dedicated abolitionist and supporter of Lincoln, was a delegate to Republican National Convention that nominated Lincoln. In this house he hid both Wendell Phillips and Horace Greeley from mobs of angry Staten Islanders, who generally supported the Southern cause. Note hipped roof penetrated by four bracketed gables.

[36a.] W. T. Garner Mansion/now **St. Vincent's Hospital Convent,** NE cor. Castleton and Bard Aves. 1887. ☆

Huge Victorian mansion proclaims by size, if not by beauty, the prodigious wealth garnered by businessmen in the late 19th Century. General Grant considered retiring here, but his wife, visiting the house on a damp day, was plagued by mosquitoes that thrived in Staten Island's marshes and swamps.

[36b.] St. Mary's Protestant Episcopal Church, NE cor. Castleton and Davis Aves. 1853. **Rectory,** 1924; **Parish Hall,** 1914. ☆

Modeled after English Village Gothic prototype. Later additions are tastefully in keeping with original structure.

Take Clove Road to Delafield Avenue; turn right.

[37.] Scott-Edwards House, 752 Delafield Ave. bet. Clove Rd. and Raymond Pl. S side. ca. 1730. Remodeled ca. 1849. ★

Prohibition Park, a wooded tract of 25 acres, was set up in 1898 for teetotalers. Lots were sold to prohibitionists throughout the country. Streets were named for dry states—Maine, Ohio, Virginia—and Prohibition Party presidential candidates—Bidwell, Wooley, Fiske. A huge auditorium was built for lectures and sermons on religion and science. The area, just south of Port Richmond, is known today as Westerleigh, but the original street names still remain to admonish unwary residents of the evils of alcoholic spirits.

[38a.] Clarence T. Barrett Park and Zoo, 614 Broadway bet. Raleigh Ave. and Glenwood Pl. Parking facilities on Glenwood Pl. Open daily 10 AM–5 PM.

Small, nice zoo specializing in snakes. Only zoo in America exhibiting all 32 species of rattlesnakes. Snake-lovers are reassured by hand-printed notice: "None of these snakes is fixed—all have full possession of fangs."

Continue down Clove Road to Tyler Street, go left.

[38b.] Gardiner-Tyler House, 27 Tyler St. bet. Broadway and North Burgher. N side. ca. 1835. ★

Opposite St. Peter's Cemetery. Once-elegant mansion now surrounded on three sides by phalanx of modern bungalows. President John Tyler's widow resided here during the Civil War. Being a woman of Southern sympathies, Mrs. Tyler displayed a Confederate flag in upstairs room until outraged Unionists invaded the house and forcibly removed the unpatriotic emblem.

Continue on Clove Road (noting Vanderbilt house in passing) to Howard Avenue, make a left. Drop in at Ann's Sugarbowl for refreshments.

[39.] Vanderbilt House, 1197 Clove Rd. bet. Waldron Ave. and Victory Blvd. N side. 1830. ☆

Exquisite detailing on windows. Discreet Vermont-style house.

[40a.] Cunard Hall, Wagner College, 631 Howard Ave. bet. Campus Rd. and Hillside Ave. E side. ca. 1851. ☆

Administration building of Wagner, a four-year liberal arts Lutheran college. Named Bellevue, but mansion's glorious view is now obstructed by modern brick dorms.

The "back lot": Fox Hills just east of Grymes Hill was the area where Civil War battle scenes for *Birth of a Nation* were filmed by D. W. Griffith.

[40b.] Oneata, Wagner College, 631 Howard Ave. next to Wagner Athletic Field. ca. 1865. ☆

Named Oneata, Seminole for "kissed by the dawn" because of gorgeous view. French windows opening on spacious porch, slate Mansard roof, corner windows capped by towers may soon be kissed by the wrecker's ball. The college has expansion plans.

[62.]

[40c.] August Horrmann Library, Wagner College, 631 Howard Ave. bet. Campus Rd. and Hillside Ave. E side. 1961. Perkins and Will.

Nice combination of brick and glass well-integrated with site.

[41.] Horrmann Castle, 189 Howard Ave. Opposite Greta Pl. E side. ca. 1915. ☆

A fantastic monstrosity worthy of King Ludwig of Bavaria combines Rhineland castle, Renaissance mansion, Flemish stepped gables, Spanish tiled roof, Queen Anne chimneys. This grotesque and delightful creation is topped by a crow's nest with onion-shaped cupola.

Drive around Grymes Hill area. The posh place to live. Take Victory Boulevard to Cebra Avenue and turn right.

[42.] Ward-Nixon House, 141 Nixon Ave. ca. 1835. ☆

One of the finest Greek Revival mansions left, now an apartment house. Imposing Ionic portico, finely detailed cornice, applied pilasters, and chintz curtains at windows. Brick bungalows are creeping up on all sides, ready to ambush their Greek rival.

[43.] St. Paul's Protestant Episcopal Church and Rectory, 225 St. Paul's Ave. bet. Clinton St. and Tartar Pl. E side. 1870. Edmund Potter. ☆

English Village style—rough, dark stone, handsome rose window, steep-pitched roof.

End of Tour.

MISCELLANY

[44.] New Brighton Village Hall, 66 Lafayette Ave. 1871. ★

[45.] Christ Church, 76 Franklin Ave. 1905. ☆

[46.] Hamilton Park Cottage, 105 Franklin Ave. ca. 1855. ☆

[47.] Jonathan Goodhue House/"Woodbrook," 304 Prospect Ave. ca. 1855. ☆

[48.] Decker House, 2091 Forest Ave. ca. 1770. ☆

[49.] Crocheron House, 47 Travis Ave. ca. 1824. ☆

[50.] School District #3, 4108 Victory Blvd. Rebuilt, 1896. ☆

[51.] T. Robjohn House/formerly **YMCA Building,** 651 Broadway. ca. 1845. ☆

[52.] Sunny Brae House, 27 Colonial Court. ca. 1875. ☆

[53.] New Dorp Light Station, Altamont Ave., New Dorp Heights. ca. 1854. ★

[54.] Staten Island Savings Bank, 81 Water St. ca. 1909. ☆

[55.] Edgewater Village Hall, Tappan Park and Canal St. ca. 1889. ☆

[56.] Mariners' Family Home, 119 Tompkins Ave. ca. 1855. ☆

[57.] King House, 29 McClean Ave. ca. 1870. ☆

[58.] Fountain Family Graveyard/formerly **First Baptist Church of Staten Island Graveyard,** Richmond and Clove Rds. 1800–1840. ☆

[59.] Kornbau House, 2585 Amboy Rd. New Dorp. ca. 1850. ☆

[60.] Old Administration Building, U.S. Coast Guard Base, 1 Bay St. ca. 1867. ☆

[61.] The Institute for Basic Research in Mental Retardation, Willowbrook State School, off Victory Boulevard. 1967. Fordyce & Hamby.

[62.] Monsignor Farrell High School, Amboy Rd. bet. Tysen Rd. and Arc Pl. 1962. Charles Luckman & Assocs.

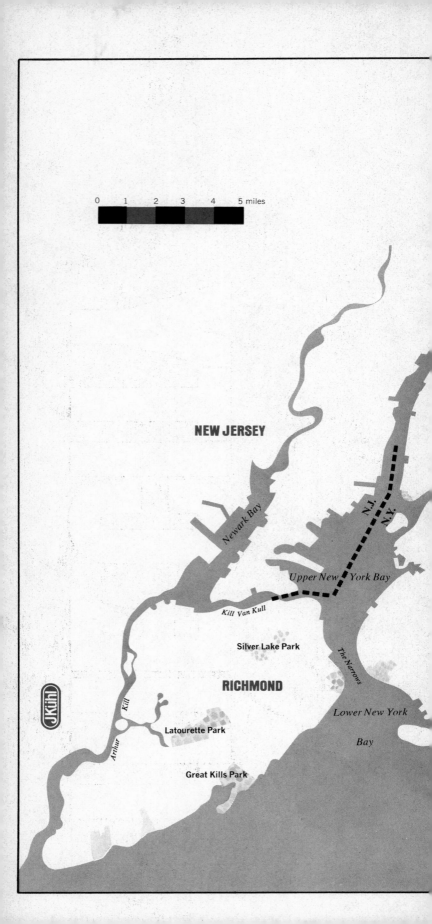

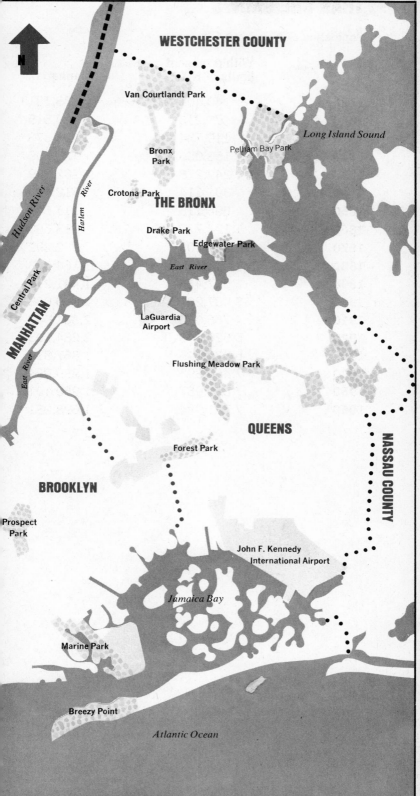

NEW YORK CITY

WESTCHESTER COUNTY

N

Van Courtlandt Park

Long Island Sound

Hudson River

Harlem River

Bronx Park

Pelham Bay Park

Crotona Park

THE BRONX

Drake Park

Edgewater Park

East River

Central Park

LaGuardia Airport

MANHATTAN

East River

Flushing Meadow Park

QUEENS

Forest Park

NASSAU COUNTY

BROOKLYN

Prospect Park

John F. Kennedy International Airport

Jamaica Bay

Marine Park

Breezy Point

Atlantic Ocean

THAR SHE GROWS

Population of New York City

	Within present limits of N.Y.C.	Manhattan
1790	49,401	33,131
1800	79,216	60,515
1810	119,734	96,373
1820	152,056	123,706
1830	242,278	202,589
1840	391,114	312,710
1850	696,115	515,547
1860	1,174,779	813,660
1870	1,478,103	942,292
1880	1,911,698	1,164,673
1890	2,507,414	1,441,216
1900	3,437,202	1,850,093
1910	4,766,883	2,331,542
1920	5,620,048	2,284,103
1930	6,930,446	1,867,312
1940	7,454,995	1,889,924
1950	7,891,957	1,960,101
1960	7,781,984	1,698,281

The Bronx	Brooklyn	Queens	Richmond
1,781	4,495	6,159	3,835
1,755	5,740	6,642	4,564
2,267	8,303	7,444	5,347
2,782	11,187	8,246	6,135
3,023	20,535	9,049	7,082
5,346	47,613	14,480	10,965
8,032	138,882	18,593	15,061
23,593	279,122	32,903	25,492
37,393	419,921	45,468	33,029
51,980	599,495	56,559	38,991
88,908	838,547	87,050	51,693
200,507	1,166,582	152,999	67,021
430,980	1,634,351	284,041	85,969
732,016	2,018,356	469,042	116,531
1,265,258	2,560,401	1,079,029	158,346
1,394,711	2,698,285	1,297,634	174,441
1,451,277	2,738,175	1,550,849	191,555
1,424,815	2,627,319	1,809,578	221,991

City of New York in 1960 had a population greater than the combined total of 13 states:

Alaska	226,167
Delaware	446,292
Hawaii	632,772
Idaho	667,191
Maine	969,265
Montana	674,767
Nevada	285,278
New Hampshire	606,921
North Dakota	632,446
Rhode Island	859,488
Utah	890,627
Vermont	389,881
Wyoming	330,066
	7,611,161

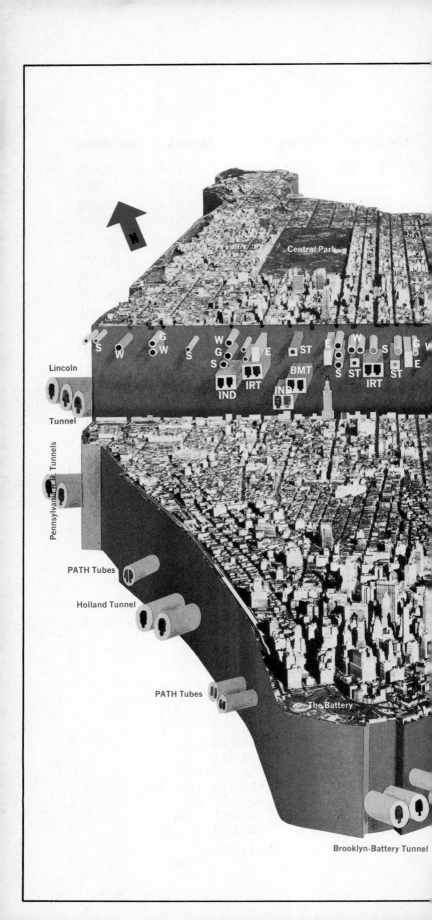

NEW YORK UNDERGROUND

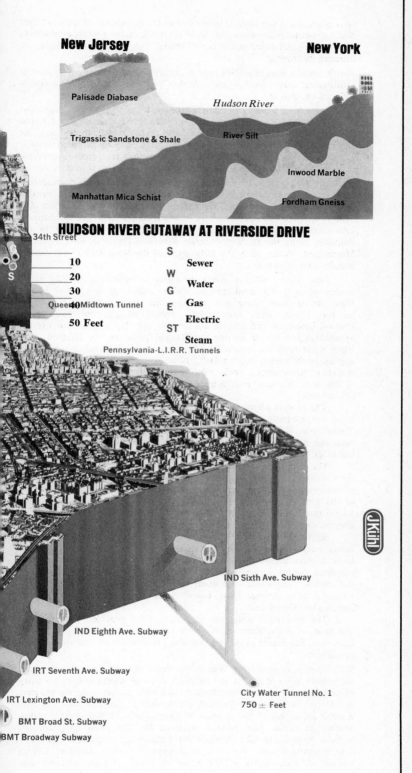

New Jersey

New York

Palisade Diabase

Hudson River

Trigassic Sandstone & Shale

River Silt

Inwood Marble

Manhattan Mica Schist

Fordham Gneiss

HUDSON RIVER CUTAWAY AT RIVERSIDE DRIVE

34th Street

10	S — Sewer
20	W — Water
30	G — Gas
Queens Midtown Tunnel 40	E — Electric
50 Feet	ST — Steam

Pennsylvania-L.I.R.R. Tunnels

IND Sixth Ave. Subway

IND Eighth Ave. Subway

IRT Seventh Ave. Subway

IRT Lexington Ave. Subway

BMT Broad St. Subway

BMT Broadway Subway

City Water Tunnel No. 1
750 ± Feet

JKühl

GEOGRAPHY OF THE CITY

New York is a water city: It is situated at the confluence of a major river and the ocean, waterways that have played a major role in establishing the fundamental form of the city. Through the years they have also influenced its growth.

New York is a port city: Not only is there an abundance of shoreline but also natural deep channels and a harbor well protected from the vicissitudes of an open sea.

New York is an island city: Appropriately, all of New York's boroughs except one, The Bronx are located on islands: Manhattan, Long Island (shared with two suburban counties), and Staten Island. In addition, the city is encrusted with other bits of land that poke up from its waters: Governors, Welfare, and Rikers Islands, to name a few, and the extensive and convoluted collection in Jamaica Bay which forms a wildlife preserve.

Geology: Throughout the city the signposts of its geological development are everywhere apparent. The very location of its skyscrapers, divided into two distinct areas on Manhattan Island, Financial District and Midtown, reflects the places where bedrock comes closest to the surface. Less abstract indications of the city's geology can be found in the Palisades along the Hudson opposite Riverside Drive, in Fort Tryon or Morningside Parks, or in the hilly areas of the West Bronx and central Brooklyn and Queens.

New York's relative youth *as a city* is in strong contrast to its *geological* age. Fordham gneiss, which makes up the ridge of the West Bronx and along whose spine the Grand Concourse winds its way, dates from the earliest period of all, the Archeozoic. Inwood limestone and marble are next in age. (In a boat tour around Manhattan just before leaving the Harlem River for the Hudson, their white substances are clearly visible in the stone cliffs of a community appropriately named Marble Hill.) Next in age is the Manhattan schist, a mass of metamorphic rock covering the deeper limestone strata, which is the firm bedrock providing the superb foundations for the city's skyscrapers.

The general physical form of the city and its immediate region, the form we recognize today, dates from a much later period, that of the Triassic Age. The Palisades, the lowlands, the gorge of the Hudson, and even the brownstone, still so frequently found on New York's older buildings, are a product of this period.

The coming of the Ice Age 20,000 to 25,000 years ago provided the finishing touches to the pattern of the city. The glacier pushed ahead of it a mound of gravel, rock, and other debris. This mound is still visible as the terminal moraine which runs from the southern tip of Staten Island (and forms its backbone) to the Narrows, where it is interrupted, only to rise again to form Long Island's spine as well.

South of these hills, particularly in Brooklyn and Queens, is the sandy outwash deposited by the melted glacier, to this day giving rise to such place names as Flatlands. This melting of the glacier converted the once deeper gorge of the Hudson River into an estuary and filled the shallow depressions with water to form the East and Harlem Rivers (actually tidal straits), Long Island Sound, and the shallow bays of Jamaica and Gravesend.

The geological accidents of history have provided the city with 578 miles of waterfront, innumerable beaches and overlooks, and, perhaps most important of all, a substratum to support its upward-reaching skyscrapers.

New York Underground: Within the geological strata and below the city's 6000 miles of streets and its many miles of waterways are a variety of underground channels which even most New Yorkers take for granted. A trip on the subway or through a vehicular or railroad tunnel is only a small indication of the vastness and complexity of New York's underground networks. The subways account for 134 miles of below-the-surface routes; the other tunnels for perhaps an additional ten miles. The magnitudes for other such underground systems, however, are of entirely different order: 62,000 miles of electrical wires and services;

7800 miles in gas mains; 20 *million* miles of wire (in cables) for telephones; over 50 miles of steam mains that heat fully one-seventh of Manhattan's buildings; not to mention water mains, sewers, coaxial cable for television, and the now-unused pneumatic tubes that once sped mail between post office branches at 30 MPH *below* the streets (rather than 8 MPH *on* them.

If one were to calculate the amount of space invested in the subsurface facilities necessary to make the metropolis function, carved through its primeval rock and muck, enough area to support a small city would result. And within New York there are such underground "cities" even now, in Rockefeller Center, at Grand Central Terminal and its passages below grade to adjacent buildings, and in the proposals for the World Trade Center.

Though it is there, though it functions amazingly well, it remains an enigma, even for those who regularly patrol and repair the subworld mazes; perhaps the diagram will give some indication of their phenomenal complexity.

NEW YORK MILESTONES

1524   Giovanni da Verrazano, an Italian, explores New York Bay and coastline of North America for Francis I of France.

1525   Esteban Gomez, a Portuguese, discovers what may have been Hudson River for Charles V of Spain.

1609   Henry Hudson explores harbor and Hudson River from Sandy Hook to Albany for Dutch East India Company.

1613   Adriaen Block and crew reside on Manhattan Island at site of 41 Broadway and construct new ship after fire destroys original.

1614   Block sails completed ship into Long Island Sound and draws "First Figurative Map" of New Netherland showing Manhattan as an island.

1624   First colonists, consisting of 30 Dutch and Walloon families, reach New Netherland; some establish residence on Manhattan and Governors Island as first settlement of Dutch West India Company.

1626   Island of Manhattan purchased from Manhates tribe by Director General Peter Minuit for 60 guilders (or the familiar $24.)

1633   First church built at what is now 39 Pearl Street.

1636   Jacques Bentyand Adrianse Bennett moves to Brooklyn, buying land at Gowanus from the Mohawk tribe. Jacobus Van Corlaer acquires what is later to become Corlaer's Hook.

1638   Ferry established from Dover and Pearl Sts. in Manhattan to Fulton St., Brooklyn. Oldest deed to land on Manhattan granted to Andries Hudd in Harlem, for an area between 109th and 124th Sts. later to be known as Montagne's Flat after Jean De la Montagne, an early settler.

1639   Staten Island first settled under David de Vries; settlement later wiped out by local Indians. Jonas Bronck purchases land from Indians in what was to become The Bronx.

1641   Board of Twelve Men formed in New Amsterdam, the beginning of representative government. It is soon dissolved.

1643   Theological disputes in neighboring New England encourage English migration to Nieuw Amsterdam. Anabaptist John Throgmorton of Salem settles what is now Throgs Neck; Lady Deborah Moody, another Anabaptist settles Gravesend; Anne Hutchison establishes settlement north of Throgmorton in East Bronx.

1645   Vlisingen (Flushing) founded by 18 patentees.

1646   Breuckelen (Brooklyn) established as a town. Yonkers originates as farm in the West Bronx settled by Adriaen Van der Donck and called "der Jonkheer's Landt."

1648   First pier in colony built on the East River at Schreyer's Hook. First housing law in N. Y. deals with fire prevention. This law followed by others dealing with sanitation, zoning of land use, arrangement of street pattern and lots.

1651   Director General Peter Stuyvesant, appointed in 1647, establishes farm or "bouwerie" at today's Bowery.

1653   First municipal government established in any area later to become part of U.S. City limits set at Collect Pond (Foley Square). Wood palisades with six bastions are erected from river to river which give Wall Street its name. Prison and poor house appear.

1654   First Jewish settlement: Jacob Barsimon from Holland, Asser Levy and 22 others from Brazil.

1655   Dutch Reformed Church built in Flatbush, the first church on Long Island.

1656   Rustdorp, now Jamaica, receives a charter. Corner of Whitehall and Pearl Sts. becomes site of first public market place.

1658   Village of Harlem founded.

1659   First Latin School opens at 26 Broad St. First hospital building started on Bridge St.

1660   First post office in Nieuw Amsterdam opens.

1661   Bowne house built in Flushing. First permanent settlement in Staten Island at Oude Dorp near South Beach.

1664   British capture Nieuw Amsterdam for Duke of York and rename it New York in his honor.

1670   Merchants Exchange established at Broad St. and Exchange Pl. at site of old "curb market." Staten Island purchased from Indians for sixth and last time.

1673   New York to Boston mail service started. Dutch recapture New York, rename it New Orange, lose it the following year to British through Treaty of Westminster.

1676   Broad St. canal filled in; the Great Dock, along Water Street between Whitehall and Coenties Slips to remain until 1750 as only place of dockage.

1682   Jews establish cemetery which still exists near Chatham Square.

1683   Staten Island becomes Richmond County.

1693   Kings Bridge, first crossing of the Harlem River, built by Frederick Philipse.

1697   Street lights erected on every seventh house.

1704   New City Hall finished at Wall and Nassau Sts., present site of old Sub-Treasury Building.

1713   Ferry service between the Battery and St. George, Staten Island, implemented.

1725   New York Gazette, city's first newspaper established.

1729   First Jewish synagogue building, Sheareth Israel, opened on Beaver Street.

1731   City divided into seven wards by Montgomerie Charter, granted by governor to city officials expanding their administrative powers. It will remain in force 100 years.

1732   First theater opens. Site of Bowling Green Park leased to citizens for playing bowls.

1733   The New York Weekly Journal established by John Peter Zenger who, two years later in his acquittal on a charge of libel, establishes principle of freedom of the press.

1740   Ferry from Bay Ridge, Brooklyn to Staten Island established.

1757   First History of New York published in London by William Smith of New York.

1762   Samuel Fraunces, a Negro, purchases house of Etienne de Lancey at Pearl and Broad Sts. and converts it into a tavern.

1763   Ferry service to Paulus Hook, now Jersey City, established.

1766   Roger Morris House, now known as Jumel Mansion erected. St. Paul's Chapel, oldest existing church building on Manhattan, dedicated.

1776   First water works begun. Proclamation of Declaration of Independence sets off Revolutionary War. Numerous battles will occur in New York and Long Island.

1783 Revolutionary War ends.

1784 New York City becomes capital of State.

1785 First *daily* newspaper in city, *The Daily Advertiser,* established— the city's third.

1786 Bowling Green first laid out as a park.

1787 Erasmus Hall Academy established in Brooklyn.

1788 New City Hall of 1704 remodelled by Maj. Charles P. L'Enfant to serve as Federal Hall till 1790.

1789 Federal Constitution becomes effective; first Congress meets in Federal Hall until 1790 when capital shifts to Philadelphia.

1790 Captain Robert Richard Randall purchases 21 acres of farm land in what is now Greenwich Village; later left to Sailors Snug Harbor.

1791 Yellow Fever epidemic spurs settlement of outlying districts, Greenwich Village.

1794 Bellevue, Lindley Murray estate on the East River becomes site of hospital for contagious diseases bearing estate's name. Madison Square purchased as a potter's field.

1796 Collect Pond (Foley Square) becomes site of James Fitch's experiment with a steamboat using screw propeller.

1797 Albany becomes capital of State superseding New York. Washington Square purchased as municipal potter's field replacing Madison Square.

1798 Another yellow fever epidemic causes 2086 deaths.

1799 Manhattan Company founded by Aaron Burr as water company —clause in charter permits banking operations as well. St. Mark's in the Bouwerie opens; replaces earlier chapel at same site. Archibald Gracie builds his mansion on site of Old Revolutionary War fort—now Mayor's official residence.

1800 Alexander Hamilton's home, The Grange, is built; later moved to its present temporary site. Suburbs around Union Square being developed; beginning of row house expansion.

1801 Brooklyn Navy Yard established. Sailors' Snug Harbor founded in Manhattan; present holdings in Staten Island purchased 30 years later with proceeds from Manhattan land rentals.

1803 Cornerstone for present City Hall laid. Yet another yellow fever epidemic.

1805 Free School Society organized, but first building not erected until 1809. It will supervise city's public schools until 1853.

1806 Madison Square becomes site of Federal Arsenal superseding its use as potter's field.

1810 Steamboat, first demonstrated on Hudson by Robert Fulton in 1807, now placed in service between New York and New Jersey.

1811 John Randel Jr. produces grid-iron plan for Manhattan known as Randel Survey or Commissioner's Map under Commissioners Gouverneur Morris, Simeon De Witt, and John Rutherford.

1812 Present City Hall opens as does first Tammany Hall, center of Democratic Party politics.

1815 Union Square Park laid out; enlarged in 1832.

1816 Village of Brooklyn incorporated, encompassing the downtown area and its environs.

1819 First steamship to cross Atlantic leaves N.Y., heralding new shipping era for port. *Another* yellow fever epidemic strikes. Advertisements for Brooklyn Heights, a suburban development, appear.

1820 New York becomes the nation's most populous city.

1823 Bryant Park purchased as a potter's field. A. T. Stewart Co., retailers, founded.

1825 Erie Canal opens giving city supremacy in trade to middle west. Freight rates drop from $100 to $6 per ton by 1830's.

1826   Lord & Taylor, retail merchants, founded.

1828   Old potter's field converted to Washington Square Park.

1829   First large reservoir (holding 233,000 gallons) completed at 14th St. and the Bowery (now Fourth Ave.)

1830   Broadway stage line between Bowling Green and Bleecker Street inaugurated. Notorious "Five Points" district, the intersection of Cross, Anthony, Little Water, Orange, and Mulberry Sts. (now Park, Worth, Baxter, and Mulberry Streets) is condemned as "focus of social and housing problems and source of cholera."

1831   Gramery Park established by Samuel Ruggles as private park. University of the City of New York, later to become NYU, incorporated—use of stone cut at Sing Sing Prison for new buildings precipitates city's first labor demonstrations as stone cutters riot.

1832   New York and Harlem Railroad, incorporated 1831, opens on today's Bowery and Fourth Avenue from Prince to 14th Sts. as first railroad in city. Uses horse drawn vehicles.

1833   Sailors' Snug Harbor opens in Staten Island.

1834   Village of Brooklyn incorporated as City of Brooklyn. New York and Harlem R.R. extended north along Fourth Ave. (Park Ave. South) and Park Avenue, first to 84th St. and then to Harlem.

1835   "Great Fire" destroys 674 buildings in vicinity of Hanover and Pearl Sts. Panic of 1837 causes 98 business failures in N.Y.C. *alone* totaling $60 million.

1837   New York and Harlem R.R. extended to Harlem. One-sixth of Manhattan covered with buildings and paved streets—rest remains farms and gardens.

1839   First steam locomotives on New York and Harlem R.R.

1840   Edgar Allan Poe moves into cottage now located in Poe Park, Bronx.

1841   St. John's College founded in the Bronx. Becomes Fordham University in 1904.

1842   Croton Aqueduct opens, bringing water to reservoir in what is now Bryant Park. Astor Library founded by John Jacob Astor. Present Sub-Treasury Building at Wall and Nassau Sts. erected as Customs House. Charles Dickens visits NYC.

1843   Potter's field established at Randall's Island.

1844   First storm sewers installed—not connected to houses.

1845   Second "Great Fire" destroys more than 300 buildings.

1847   Old potter's field opened as Madison Square Park.

1848   Immigration from Germany increases as a result of Revolution there.

1849   Free Academy, authorized by Legislature in 1847, opens at southeast corner of 23rd St. and Lexington Ave. In 1866 its name becomes College of the City of New York.

1850   Castle Gardens at the Battery, formerly Fort Clinton, welcomes Jenny Lind under auspices of P. T. Barnum. Giuseppe Garibaldi arrives in Staten Island to work as candlemaker prior to returning to Italy and victory. Fifty years of large-scale tenement construction begins.

1851   Hudson River R.R. completed from New York to Albany.

1852   William Marcy "Boss" Tweed begins political career when elected alderman of Seventh Ward (Manhattan).

1853   Act of Legislature authorizes Central Park through efforts of William Cullen Bryant and others. World's Fair held in iron and glass Crystal Palace at west end of Bryant Park. Assay Office established and Clearing House formed by city's banks.

1854   Academy of Music at northeast corner of 14th St. and Irving Pl. opens.

1855   Castle Garden converted into immigration station. First "model tenement" built by the Association for Improving the Condition of the Poor. Located on a lot running through from Elizabeth to

Mott Sts., its tenancy was restricted to "colored persons." Upper floors contained rooms for concerts, lectures, and meetings.

1856 Site of Central Park purchased.

1857 Financial panic.

1858 Competition for design of Central Park draws 33 entries and proclaims Olmsted, Vaux & Co. winners; work begins the same year. Crystal Palace destroyed by spectacular fire. R. H. Macy's Department Store founded.

1859 Cooper Union for the Advancement of Science and Art opens first building at Astor Pl. and Fourth Ave. Legislature authorizes acquisition of Prospect Park in Brooklyn.

1860 City ends 20-year period of expansion establishing it as great metropolis of the western world. Staten Island Steam Railway opens from Edgewater to Tompkinsville.

1862 John Ericsson's Monitor, the Northern ironclad, launched in Greenpoint, Brooklyn. Hansom cabs first appear in the city.

1863 Draft riots against mass conscription, exempting those who could raise $300 fee. Civic leaders forced to recognize wretched conditions of housing from which the mobs poured. Eventually spurred establishment of powerful Board of Health.

1865 Volunteer fire fighting system, ridden by inefficiency, finally replaced by professional Metropolitan Fire District.

1867 N.Y. Chapter American Institute of Architects is founded. West Side Development Plan providing for establishment of Riverside Park is adopted. Prospect Park, built from design by Olmsted, Vaux & Co., first opens to the public. First tenement house law establishes minimum standards for size of rooms, ventilation, and sanitation.

1868 Plan for consolidation into five boroughs proposed by Andrew H. Green of Brooklyn, later to be called "Father of Greater New York." Killed in 1903 by insane boy. Elevated railroad using cable and stationary steam engines opens on Greenwich St. between Battery and Cortlandt St.

1869 First definitive apartment building built by Rutherford Stuyvesant at 142 E. 18th St., Richard Morris Hunt, architect. (Demolished 1956.) Potter's field moved to Harts Island. Black Friday as Jay Gould and Jim Fisk corner gold market.

1870 Work begins on John A. and Washington A. Roebling's New York and Brooklyn Bridge. Equitable Life Assurance Society Building opens at 120 Broadway, first office building to utilize passenger elevators. Destroyed by fire in 1912. Experimental pneumatic subway running 312 feet under Broadway from Warren to Murray Sts. opens. 20 passengers pay 20¢ each for the ride. Plans for improving Madison Square, Washington Square, and Union Square Parks adopted. Cable elevated extended along Ninth Ave to 30th St. with substitution of rolling steam locomotives.

1871 Steam trains appear on Greenwich Street elevated. Grand Central Depot, nation's largest, opens.

1873 Financial panic.

1874 P. T. Barnum opens Hippodrome at corner of 27th St. and Madison Ave. All of the Bronx west of Bronx River annexed to NYC, formerly only Manhattan.

1877 First tenements erected around central court sponsored by Alfred Treadway White in his Tower and Home Apartments at Hicks and Baltic Sts., Brooklyn. President Rutherford B. Hayes opens original building of Museum of Natural History at its present site.

1878 Sixth Avenue elevated opens from Rector Street to Central Park. By 1880 service reaches 155th St. Apartments spring up rapidly along the route.

1879 The newspaper, *Sanitary Engineer,* holds competition for a tenement plan to fit on a typical 25' x 100' lot. Prize-winning "dumbbell plan" by James F. Ware, architect, is one of 209 entries. Plan widely condemned.

1880	Metropolitan Museum of Art opened by President Hayes. Broadway first illuminated by Brush electric arc lamps.
1882	Commercial lighting by electricity becomes available as Thomas Edison's first generating plant opens at 257 Pearl Street.
1883	Dakota Apartments open at 72nd St. and Central Park West. The New York and Brooklyn Bridge opens, first bridge over East River, longest suspension bridge of its time. Metropolitan Opera House opens on west side of Broadway between 39th and 40th Sts. and incurs a first season deficit! (Demolished, 1967.)
1884	Report made to Legislature recommending acquisition of various park and parkway lands in the Bronx.
1885	"Main Line," first Brooklyn "air-borne" elevated opens.
1886	Statue of Liberty unveiled on Bedloe's (now Liberty) Island. Elevated railway first links the Bronx with Manhattan.
1888	The year of "Great Blizzard" also sees first steel skeleton building erected, Tower Building, at 50 Broadway. Elevated lines begin use of electric propulsion. Fulton Street elevated opens in Brooklyn.
1890	Second Madison Square Garden opens on block between 26th and 27th Sts., Madison and Lexington Aves. from designs by Stanford White. (First one on site opened in 1879.)
1891	Carnegie Hall and New York Botanical Garden open.
1892	Ellis Island replaces Castle Garden as immigration station. Grand Boulevard and Concourse in the Bronx proposed by Louis J. Heintz; Act of Legislature passes in 1895.
1894	People vote to merge counties into a Greater New York and to extend rapid transit to link them.
1895	Harlem Ship Canal opens along the old route of the Harlem River and a specially constructed channel at Spuyten Duyvil. Area of the Bronx east of Bronx River annexed to New York City.
1896	Aquarium opens in old Castle Garden.
1897	Trolley service begins across Brooklyn Bridge.
1898	Greater New York established under new charter uniting five counties with population of 3,400,000 persons. Harlem River Speedway (now Drive) opens as only N.Y. street with *no speed restrictions.*
1899	New York Zoological Park (Bronx Zoo) established. Children's Museum, first in world intended primarily for children, founded in Brooklyn. Demolition of reservoir in Bryant Park.
1900	Construction begins on first permanent subway. Negroes begin to replace Italians and Jews in Harlem. 82,652 tenements house 70% of New York City's population.
1901	Tenement House Law passed marking end of the dumbbell plan and the beginning of the so-called New Law tenement.
1902	Fuller (Flatiron) Building opens at Fifth Ave. and 23rd St.
1903	Williamsburg Bridge opens. New York Stock Exchange Building opens at Broad and Wall Sts.
1904	Subway service opens from City Hall to W. 145th St. Pneumatic tube mail tunnel opened between old main post office, Manhattan, (City Hall Park) and main post office, Brooklyn.
1905	Municipal ferry service to Staten Island begun, inaugurating 5¢ fare.
1906	Harry K. Thaw, Pittsburgh millionaire, kills architect Stanford White on Madison Square Garden roof. Jerome Park Reservoir opened from New Croton Aqueduct.
1908	East River (subway) Tunnel between Bowling Green, Manhattan and Joralemon St., Brooklyn opens. McAdoo Tunnel, first of Hudson Tubes, opens from Manhattan to Hoboken. High pressure water system for fire fighting established north to 23rd St. Broadway Line of IRT extended to Kingsbridge in the Bronx.
1909	Queensboro and Manhattan bridges open. Metropolitan Life Insurance Co. Building opens at NE corner of Madison Avenue and 23rd St.

1910   Forest Hills Gardens, planned as working class community, financed by Russell Sage Foundation. Pennsylvania Station opens. Gimbel Brothers Department Store, started in Vincennes, Indiana in 1842, opens a New York store.

1911   New York Public Library opens at east end of Bryant Park. Triangle Shirtwaist Co. fire at Washington Pl. and Greene St. (still in existence as one of N.Y.U.'s buildings) kills 145. Brooklyn Botanic Garden opens.

1913   Grand Central Terminal opens. Municipal Building opens. The Armory Show at 69th Regiment Armory proves to be sensation as first US showing of "modern" art.

1916   First zoning resolution in U.S. takes effect in NYC. Black Tom explosion of munitions ships at Jersey City piers causes $40 million in damage.

1917   Catskill water system opens delivering 250 million gallons of water to city daily.

1918   Malbone Street (now Empire Blvd.) Tunnel subway wreck (BMT) in Brooklyn kills 97.

1920   After Gov. Alfred E. Smith's warning of severe housing shortage in state, Legislature passes law permitting cities to abate real estate taxes until 1932. One billion dollars worth of housing stimulated by this abatement in NYC alone.

1921   Port of New York Authority established.

1922   First Regional Plan begun by Regional Plan Association, financed by Russell Sage Foundation.

1923   The "setback law" limiting height and configuration of new buildings adopted.

1924   Sunnyside Gardens, in Queens, admits first residents.

1925   Columbia University and Presbyterian Hospital join forces to create the Medical Center at Broadway and 168th St. Madison Square Garden at Madison Square demolished.

1926   Limited Dividend Housing Companies Law passed by Legislature permits condemnation of housing sites, local tax abatement; requires limits on rents and profits, sets income limitations for tenants.

1927   Holland Tunnel opens linking Canal Street with Jersey City.

1928   New York Medical Center opens. Goethals Bridge and Outerbridge Crossing open connecting Staten Island with New Jersey.

1929   Stock market falls sharply portending Great Depression. First Regional Plan completed. The NY State Multiple Dwelling Law supersedes 1901 Tenement House Act.

1931   Empire State Building and George Washington Bridge open. Floyd Bennett Field, first city-owned airport, opens. Bayonne Bridge opens between Staten Island and New Jersey.

1933   Franklin D. Roosevelt assumes office as president, Fiorello LaGuardia elected Mayor as head of Fusion reform administration, following resignation of Mayor James J. Walker the previous year. Independent Subway to Queens opens.

1934   NYC Housing Authority formally established through the Municipal Housing Authorities Act.

1935   Work begins on East River Drive. First public sponsored housing project in country opens its first apartments.

1936   Triborough Bridge opens. First Houses at Avenue A and E. 3rd St. completed.

1937   U.S. Housing Act passes, providing for a pattern of loans and grants to local housing authorities.

1938   City Charter of 1936 becomes effective.

1939   New York World's Fair of 1939–40 opens in Flushing Meadow Park, Queens. World War II begins; Germany invades Poland.

1940   Queens-Midtown Tunnel opens, linking Manhattan with Queens. Construction starts on Brooklyn Battery Tunnel; to be interrupted by war. Parkchester, first Metropolitan Life Insurance Co. "village" opens in the Bronx. 12,000 units are provided with only 400 having more than 2 bedrooms. 62 families per acre.

1941 U.S. enters war. Redevelopment Corporations Law passes Legislature.

1942 Redevelopment Companies Law passes Legislature; applies terms of 1941 law specifically to insurance companies, presaging Stuyvesant Town.

1945 U.S. Army Bomber crashes into Empire State Building between 78th and 79th floors. World War II ends; "Atomic Age" begins.

1946 Army plane crashes into Bank of Manhattan Co.'s building at its 58th floor. The United Nations selects New York as its permanent headquarters. Its interim meetings are held at Hunter College, the New York City Building of the 1939–40 World's Fair at Flushing Meadow Park, and at old Sperry Gyroscope Plant in Lake Success, Long Island.

1947 Rockefeller family gives $8,500,000 tract at First Ave. north of 42nd St. to the United Nations. Stuyvesant Town built by Metropolian Life Insurance Co., under Redevelopment Companies Law. Houses 25,000 persons at 25% coverage at density of 100 families per acre.

1948 Work begins on permanent United Nations Headquarters. Subway fare rises to 10¢, Fifth Ave. bus fare to 10¢, New York International Airport at Idlewild, Queens opens.

1949 Title I National Housing Act of 1949 encourages municipalities to acquire and resell substandard areas below cost for private redevelopment.

1950 Brooklyn Battery Tunnel opens following war's interruption.

1951 Fresh Meadows, NY Life Insurance Co. housing development in Queens, opens. Density 17 families per acre; 11,000 residents.

1952 Lever House opens on Park Avenue; catalyst for its metamorphosis. Legislature establishes Transit Authority.

1953 Subway fare rises to 15¢.

1954 National Housing Act of 1954.

1955 Lincoln Center project proposed; approved by City. Mitchell-Lama (Limited Profit Housing Companies) Law passed by Legislature to aid private middle-income housing.

1956 Ebbetts Field sold as site for housing; Brooklyn Dodgers leave New York.

1957 NYC passes Fair Housing Practices Law, outlawing discrimination, nation's first. Manhattantown scandal explodes; sponsors in Title I project fail to develop site while profiting from its tenants for 5 years.

1958 Seagram Building completed on Park Avenue.

1959 Ground broken for first Lincoln Center unit, Philharmonic Hall.

1960 Proposal for World Trade Center along East River, to cost $250 million, made by Downtown-Lower Manhattan Assoc.

1961 NYC Charter revision approved in public referendum. New Zoning Law passed. Port of NY Authority backs World Trade Center in Hudson Terminal area; to cost $355 million.

1963 Protests fail to stop demolition of Pennsylvania Station. City approves Breezy Point recreation project after citizen pressure.

1964 Port Authority proposes twin 1350-foot towers for World Trade Center, tallest buildings in world. NY World's Fair of 1964–65 opens.

1965 World Trade Center estimates rise to $525 million. CBS Building opens.

1966 Federal Departments of Housing and Urban Development (HUD) and Transportation established by Congress. Lower Manhattan Plan, commissioned by City Planning Commission, issued.

1967 Centennial of NY Chapter, American Institute of Architects.

STREET SPECTACLES

January/ February	Lunar New Year Celebration (Chinese)	Two days of Lunar New Year	Chinatown
	Feast of St. Francis de Sales (Italian)	January— No fixed date	E. 12th St. bet. 2nd & 3rd Aves.
	Feast of St. Agatha	February 5th	Little Italy bet. Baxter & Canal Sts.
March/ April	St. Patrick's Day Parade	March 17th	Fifth Avenue
	Easter Egg Rolling Contest	Saturday before Easter	Central Park
	Easter Parade	Easter Sunday	Fifth Avenue
	Cherry Blossoms	April into May	Brooklyn Botanic Garden
May/June	May Day Parade	May 1	Union Square
	Loyalty Day Parade	Nearest Saturday to May 1	Fifth Avenue
	Hungarian Independence Day Parade	May 15	E. 82nd St. to Riverside Dr. and W. 98th St.
	Norwegian Independence Day Parade (Brooklyn)	May 17	Eighth Ave. & 50th St. Bklyn to McKinley Park (Bay Ridge)
	Armed Forces Day Parade	Third Saturday in May	Fifth Avenue
	I Am an American Day Ceremonies	Third Sunday in May	Central Park Mall
	National Maritime Day Parade	May 22	Sixth Ave. from W. 44th St. to Rockefeller Center
	Washington Square Out-Door Art Show	Late May thru June	Around Washington Sq. Park
	Memorial Day Parade	May 30th	Riverside Dr., 72nd St. to 95th St. Manhattan.
	St. Joseph's Day Festival	May—No fixed date	Brooklyn
	Puerto Rican Parade	First Sunday in June	Fifth Avenue
	Madonna delle Grazie Festival (Italian)	June—No fixed date	Cherry St.
	Feast of San Antonio (Italian)	Week of June 13th	Sullivan St. below Houston St.
	Blessing of the Fleet	Fourth Sunday in June	Sheepshead Bay
	Fireworks	Tuesdays 9 P.M. June, July, August	Coney Island
	San Juan's Day (Puerto Rican)	Last weekend in June	Downing Stadium Randall's Island
	Irish Feis (pronounced fesh)	June—No fixed date	No fixed place
July/ August	Feast of Our Lady of Mount Carmel (Italian)	Week of July 16th	First Ave. and 115th St.
	Feast of O-bon (Japanese)	Saturday night in July closest to full moon	Riverside Park at W. 103rd St.

CONTINUED ON P. 416

BRIDGES & TUNNELS

BRIDGES

No.	Name	Water-crossing	Between	Type (2)
1.	George Washington	Hudson River	Manhattan-N. J.	Susp.
2.	Throgs Neck	East River	Bronx-Queens	Susp.
3.	Bronx-Whitestone	East River	Bronx-Queens	Susp.
4.	Rikers Island	East River	Queens-Rikers Is.	Fixed
5.	Triborough	East River	Queens-Wards Is.	Susp.
		Harlem River	Man.-Randalls Is.	Lift.
		Bronx Kills	Bx.-Randalls Is.	Fixed
6.	Hell Gate	East River	Queens-Wards Is.	Arch
7.	Wards Is. (Ped.)	East River	Man.-Wards Is.	Lift.
8.	Welfare Island	East R./ E. Chan.	Qns.-Welfare Is.	Lift.
9.	Queensboro	East River	Man.-Queens	Cant.
10.	Williamsburg	East River	Man.-Brooklyn	Susp.
11.	Manhattan	East River	Man.-Brooklyn	Susp.
12.	Brooklyn	East River	Man.-Brooklyn	Susp.
13.	Verrazano-Narrows	The Narrows	Bklyn.-Richmond	Susp.
14.	Henry Hudson	Harlem River	Man.-Bronx	Arch
15.	Broadway	Harlem River	Manhattan	Lift.
16.	University Heights	Harlem River	Man.-Bronx	Swing
17.	Washington	Harlem River	Man.-Bronx	Arch
18.	Alexander Hamilton	Harlem River	Man.-Bronx	Arch
19.	High Bridge	Harlem River	Man.-Bronx	Arch
20.	McCombs Dam	Harlem River	Man.-Bronx	Swing
21.	145th Street	Harlem River	Man.-Bronx	Swing
22.	Madison Avenue	Harlem River	Man.-Bronx	Swing
23.	Third Avenue	Harlem River	Man.-Bronx	Swing
24.	Willis Avenue	Harlem River	Man.-Bronx	Swing
25.	174th Street	Bronx River	Bronx	Truss
26.	Westchester Avenue	Bronx River	Bronx	Bascule
27.	Eastern Boulevard	Bronx River	Bronx	Bascule
28.	Unionport	Westchester Creek	Bronx	Bascule
29.	Eastchester	Eastchester Creek	Bronx	Bascule
30.	Hutchinson R.P. Ext.	Eastchester Creek	Bronx	Bascule
31.	Pelham	Eastchester Bay	Bronx	Bascule
32.	City Island	Pelham Bay Narrows	Bronx	Swing
33.	Whitestone Expwy.	Flushing River	Queens	Bascule
34.	Flushing	Flushing River	Queens	Bascule
35.	Roosevelt Avenue	Flushing River	Queens	Bascule
36.	Little Neck	Alley Creek	Queens	Fixed
37.	Hunter's Point Ave.	Dutch Kills	Queens	Bascule
38.	Midtown Highway	Dutch Kills	Queens	Fixed
39.	Borden Avenue	Dutch Kills	Queens	Retract.
40.	Hawtree Basin (Ped.)	Hawtree Basin	Queens	Fixed
41.	Nolins Avenue	Shell Bank Basin	Queens	Bascule
42.	North Channel	North Channel	Queens	Bascule
43.	Cross Bay	Jamaica Bay	Queens	Bascule
44.	Hook Creek	Hook Creek	Queens-Nassau	Fixed
45.	Pulaski	Newtown Creek	Queens-Bklyn.	Bascule
46.	Greenpoint Ave.	Newtown Creek	Queens-Bklyn.	Bascule
47.	Kosciusko	Newtown Creek	Queens-Bklyn.	Fixed
48.	Grand Street	Newtown Creek	Queens-Bklyn.	Swing
49.	Metropolitan Ave.	English Kills	Brooklyn	Bascule
50.	Union Street	Gowanus Canal	Brooklyn	Bascule
51.	Carrol Street	Gowanus Canal	Brooklyn	Retract.
52.	Third Street	Gowanus Canal	Brooklyn	Bascule
53.	Third Avenue	Gowanus Canal	Brooklyn	Fixed
54.	Ninth Street	Gowanus Canal	Brooklyn	Bascule
55.	Hamilton Avenue	Gowanus Canal	Brooklyn	Bascule
56.	Mill Basin	Mill Basin	Brooklyn	Bascule
57.	Cropsey Avenue	Coney Island Cr.	Brooklyn	Bascule
58.	Stillwell Avenue	Coney Island Cr.	Brooklyn	Swing
59.	Ocean Avenue	Sheepshead Bay	Brooklyn	Fixed
60.	Marine Parkway	Rockaway Inlet	Bklyn.-Queens	Lift.
61.	Bayonne	Kill Van Kull	Richmond-N. J.	Arch
62.	Goethals	Arthur Kill	Richmond-N. J.	Truss
63.	Outerbridge Cross'g	Arthur Kill	Richmond-N. J.	Truss
64.	Lemon Creek	Lemon Creek	Richmond	Retract.
65.	Fresh Kills	Richmond Creek	Richmond	Bascule

TUNNELS

No.	Name	Water-crossing	Between
1.	Lincoln	Hudson River	Manhattan-N. J.
2.	Holland	Hudson River	Manhattan-N. J.
3.	Brooklyn-Battery	Upper N. Y. Bay	Manhattan-Brooklyn
4.	Queens-Midtown	East River	Manhattan-Queens

Yr. Compl.	Max. Span. Length (Feet)	Maximum Clearance above M.H.W. (3) (Feet)	Credits (1)	Operator (4)	No.
1931	3,500.	212.	O.H. Ammann, Cass Gilbert.	PA	1.
1961	1,800.	142.	O.H. Ammann	TBTA	2.
1939	2,300.	150.	O.H. Ammann, Aymar Embury II.	TBTA	3.
1966		52.		DPW	4.
1936	1,380.	143.	O.H. Ammann, Aymar Embury II.	TBTA	5.
1936				TBTA	
1936	383.	55/135		TBTA	
1917	1,087.	135.	Gustav Lindenthal.	NYCR	6.
1951	312.2	55/135		DPW	7.
1955	418.	40/103		DPW	8.
1909	1,182.	135.	Palmer & Hornbostel	DPW	9.
1903	1,600.	135.	L. L. Buck.	DPW	10.
1909	1,470.	135.	G. Lindenthal, Carrère & Hastings.	DPW	11.
1883	1,595.5	133.	J.A. & W.A. Roebling.	DPW	12.
1964	4,260.	228.	O.H. Ammann.	TBTA	13.
1936	800.	142.5	E.H. Praeger, C.F. Loyd.	TBTA	14.
1962	304.	24.3/135		DPW	15.
1908	264.5			DPW	16.
1888	508.8	133.5		DPW	17.
1963	1,526.0	103.0		DPW	18.
1848	322.0±	102.		DP	19.
1895	408.5	29.2		DPW	20.
1905	300.	25.2		DPW	21.
1910	300.	25.		DPW	22.
1898	300.	25.8		DPW	23.
1901	304.	25.1		DPW	24.
1928	190.	30.5		DPW	25.
1938	83.	17.2		DPW	26.
1953	118.7	26.6		DPW	27.
1953	75.	17.5		DPW	28.
1922	127.7	12.5		DPW	29.
1941	160.5	35.		DPW	30.
1908	80.	17.5		DPW	31.
1901	164.8	12.3		DPW	32.
1939	174.	35.		DPW	33.
1939	107.	25.		DPW	34.
1925	212.	25.6		DPW	35.
1931	44.5	7.3		DPW	36.
1910	71.5	88.		DPW	37.
1940	126.5	90.		DPW	38.
1908	82.	4.		DPW	39.
1963	72.	18.		DPW	40.
1925	43.	10.		DPW	41.
1925	123.	26.3		DPW	42.
1939	131.	17.5		TBTA	43.
1931	34.17	4.1		DPW	44.
1954	176.6	55/135		DPW	45.
1929	180.	27.4		DPW	46.
1939	300.	125.		DPW	47.
1903	227.	9.		DPW	48.
1933	111.	10.72		DPW	49.
1905	56.	8.3		DPW	50.
1889	45.2	4.7		DPW	51.
1905	56.	7.3		DPW	52.
1889	40.3	13.		DPW	53.
1905	56.	7.3		DPW	54.
1942	66.3	19.		DPW	55.
1940	165.	35.		DPW	56.
1931	155.	11.25		DPW	57.
1929	250.	5.7		DPW	58.
1917	46.2	7.8		DPW	59.
1937	40.	55/150		TBTA	60.
1931	1,675.	150.	O.H. Ammann, Cass Gilbert.	PA	61.
1928	672.	135.	O.H. Ammann.	PA	62.
1928	750.	135.	O.H. Ammann.	PA	63.
1958	34.	4.		DPW	64.
1931	81.	11.74		DPW	65.

NOTES:

1. Credits for bridges list engineer or chief engineer, followed by architect. To conserve space, name of firm or design agency not included.
2. Abbreviations: Susp. — Suspension, Cant. — Cantilever, Retract. — Retractile.
3. M.H.W.—Mean High Water.
4. Abbreviations: PA—Port of New York Authority; DPW—N.Y.C. Department of Public Works; NYCRR—N. Y. Conecting Railroad. DP—Department of Parks.
5. Tube refers to location of tube in question (i.e. N means northernmost tube).

Yr. (5) Compl./Tube	Length/Tube (5)	Credits	Operator	No.
1945 N	7,482. N		PA	1.
1937 C	8,216. C			
1957 S	8,006. S			
1927	8,558. N	C.F. Holland, Ole Singstad.	PA	2.
	8,371. S			
1950	9,117.	Ole Singstad.	TBTA	3.
1940	6,414. N	Ole Singstad.	TBTA	4.
	6,272. S			

STREET SPECTACLES CONTINUED

	St. Stephen's Day Picnic and Parade (Hungarian)	Sunday nearest August 20	
	Washington Square Outdoor Art Show	Late August thru mid September	Around Washington Square Park
September/ October	Labor Day Parade	Odd numbered years	Fifth Avenue
	Feast of San Gennaro (Italian)	Week of September 19	Mulberry St. Little Italy
	Steuben Day Parade (German)	Last Saturday in September	Fifth Avenue
	Pulaski Day Parade (Polish)	October 5th or nearest Sunday	Fifth Avenue 26th to 52nd Sts.
	Columbus Day Parade	October 12th	Fifth Avenue 44th to 83rd Sts.
November/ December	Veteran's Day Parade	November 11th	Fifth Avenue
	Macy's Thanksgiving Day Parade	Thanksgiving Day morning	Central Park West to Herald Square via Broadway
	Rockefeller Center Tree Lighting Ceremony	Second Thursday in December at dusk	Rockefeller Plaza

PHOTO & LITERARY CREDITS

Location of photos are noted in the following manner: Where all photographs on one page are credited to the same source, only the page number is listed. Where photographs on a page are from multiple sources, the position on the page has been abbreviated: T, top; B, bottom; L, left; R, right.

Introduction: Ewing Galloway—4,5. **Manhattan:** John Albok—152 R. Gil Amiaga—201. Peter Blake—37. CBS Photo—134 R. Louis Checkman—156 R. John Clarke—143 BL. Columbia University, Columbiana Collection—200. George Cserna—67 L,117 R,128 R,176,184 L,196 R. Richard Dattner—205, 206,207,208,211 TR,213. Dept. of Parks—144 R. John Dixon—83 L,85,86,87, 88,89 L,109,115 R,121,123 BR,124,125 L,136 L,139 L. Ann Douglass—42,47, 48,49,50,52,53,55,57 TL,57 B,58 R,59,61,62 L,63,64,67 R,68,70,104 L,105, 108,111,113,126,127 TL,127 TR,127 BL,136 R,137. Empire State Building Corp.—102 R. Roger Feinstein—143 TL,143 TR,144 L,148,187,193,195,197. Samuel H. Gottscho—128 L. Douglas Haskell—112. David Hirsch—141. Peter Hujar—77 TR. John Kraif—167. J. Alex Langley—120 L. Eric Locker—23. Long Island Historical Society—29. Macy's Inc.—102 L. David McAdams—194. Norman McGrath—162 R. Merkle Press,Inc.—89 R. Joseph Molitor—162 L. Museum of the City of New York—142,143 BR; (J. Clarence Davies Collection) 204 B. N.Y.C. Housing Authority (Louis Marinoff)—196 L. New York University—65. Erick Pollitzer—123 BL. Port of New York Authority—27 L, 209,210. Louis Reens—204 T. Riverside Church—189. Rockefeller Center,Inc. —133. Ben Schnall—115 L. St. Luke's Hospital—198. Ezra Stoller—24,110, 120 R,139 R,140,158 R,175,184 R. United Nations—123 T. Roberta Warne— 150,152 L. Norval White—10,11,14,15,16,17,18 L,19,20,21,22,27 R,28,30,32, 33,35,36,39,72,75,77 TL,77 BL,77 BR,92,93,95,97,98 L,99,156 L,158 L,159, 161 L,165 TR,165 B,168,170,171,172,178,179,180,181,182,183,185. Elliot Willensky—100,153. Dan Wynn—134 L. Yeshiva University—211 TL,211 B. **Bronx:** Louis Checkman—238. Roger Feinstein—219,220,221,222,224,226, 230,232,234,236,237,240. Museum of the American Indian—239. Museum of the City of New York—229. Ben Schnall—231. John Veltri—235. **Brooklyn:** Brooklyn Botanic Garden—292,293. Brooklyn Children's Museum—305. George Cserna—343 B. Dept. of Parks—288,290. John Dixon—279 R,280 L. Long Island Historical Society—250,257,258 L,259,261,281,285,286 B,289, 294,306,309,310,328. N.Y.C. Housing Authority (Louis Marinoff)—322 BR. Louis Reens—336 R. Ben Schnall—339,347. Ezra Stoller—340. Norval White —251,253,254,255,258 R,260,262,264,265,266,267,269,273,274,275,276,327. Elliot Willensky—278,279 L,280 R,284,286 T,295,296,297,298,299,302,303, 304,308,311,313,316,317,318,319,322 TL,322 TR,322 R,324,326,330,331, 332,333,335,336 L,341,342,343 T,344,345,346. **Queens:** Jay Hoops Studio— 365 L. Ezra Stoller—335,365 R,370 TL,370 TR,371. Triborough Bridge & Tunnel Authority—368 T. Norval White—367. Elliot Willensky—352,353,354,356, 357,358,360,362,363,368 B. **Richmond:** Mina Hamilton—380,383,384,386 R,389,390,392. Elliot Willensky—386 L.

Literary Credits: P. 186: Hughes, Langston, *The Sweet Flypaper of Life.* Simon and Schuster. New York. 1955. P. 208: Jeanneret-Gris, Edouard, (Le Corbusier), *When the Cathedrals Were White.* (trans. Francis E. Hyslop, Jr.) Reynal & Hitchcock. New York. 1947. Harcourt, Brace & World. P. 268: Syrett, Harold C. *The City of Brooklyn, 1865–1898.* Columbia University Press. New York. 1944. P. 380: Millay, Edna St. Vincent, From "Recuerdo," *Collected Poems.* Harper & Row. New York. Copyright 1922, 1950 by Edna St. Vincent Millay. By permission of Norma Millay Ellis.

ARCHITECTURAL STYLE GUIDE

CLASSICAL REVIVAL

COLONIAL

GEORGIAN/FEDERAL

GOTHIC REVIVAL

GREEK REVIVAL

ITALIANATE

MODERN

INDEX

Beaux Arts Apartment Hotel, 122
Beck Memorial Presbyterian
   Church, 224
Bedford Park, 230
   on map, 216
Bedford-Stuyvesant, 294
   on map, 244, 300–301
Bedford-Stuyvesant Historic District
   (proposed), 299
Bedford-Stuyvesant Youth in
   Action, 298, 299
Bedloes Island: see Liberty Island
Beecher, Henry Ward, 251, 260, 261,
   272, 310
Beekman family, 120
Beekman Place, 123
Beekman Tower Apartments, 123
BEER, FREDERICK
   Washington Irving (1885), 92
BELFATTO AND PAVARINI
   Church of the Epiphany (1967), 93
   Our Lady of Grace Church
      (1967), 242
   St. Brendan's Church (1966), 233
BELGIOJOSO, PERESSUTTI & ROGERS
   Olivetti-Underwood Corp.
      Showroom (1954), 126
BELL, MIFFLIN E.
   Brooklyn Central Post Office
      (1885-1891), 251
BELLUSCHI, PIETRO
   Juilliard School of Music
      (1968), 140
   Pan Am Building (1963), 116
Belmont, August Jr., 354
Belmont (on map), 216
Belmont Avenue Pushcart Market, 346
Belnord Apartments, 144
BENDER, RICHARD
   Colombian Center (1966), 162
Bensonhurst, 336
   on map, 244
BERG, CHARLES I.
   15 East 70th Street (1907), 173
BERGER, R.
   480 Broome Street (1885), 38
   37-43 Greene Street (1884), 37
Berry, Abraham, 323
Bertine Block, 219
Best & Company, 104
Berwind, Edward, 159
Betsy Head Memorial Playground
   Bathhouse (1939), 347
BIEN, SYLVAN
   Vladeck Houses (1940), 41
BIEN & PRINCE
   Hotel Carlyle (1929), 175
Billiou-Stillwell-Perine House, 385
Billopp, Christopher, 390
Billopp House/Conference House, 390
Bishop Manning Memorial Wing,
   Trinity Church, 20
BISSELL, GEORGE
   Chester A. Arthur (1898), 95
   Abraham De Peyster (1896), 14
BITTER, KARL
   Abundance, 156
   Peace (N.Y. State Supreme
      Court), 96
   Carl Schurtz (1913), 199
   Franz Sigel (1907), 148
Blackwell's Island: see Welfare Island
Blazing Star Ferry (site), 391
BLESCH AND EIDLITZ
   St. George's Church (restored
      1897), 90
   see also Eidlitz, Cyrus L. W.
BLOCH & HESSE
   Jewish Chapel at Kennedy Airport
      (1966), 371
Block Beautiful (19th St. at Irving
   Pl.), 93
Bloomingdale, 144
   on map, 149
Bloomingdale Insane Asylum

   (site), 198
BLUM, GEORGE & EDWARD
   11 East 74th Street (1919), 174
   9 East 74th Street (1919), 174
Blythebourne (form. town,
   Brooklyn), 336
Board of Estimate, 3, 30
Boerum Hill, 309
   on map, 307
BOGARDUS, JAMES
   Cast-Iron Building (1848), 27
   85 Leonard Street (1862), 35
   Watchtower (1857), 190
BOLTON, CHARLES W.
   Abyssinian Baptist Church
      (1923), 195
BOLTON, WILLIAM JAY
   windows, Church of the Holy
      Apostles, 87
Bonnier's, 161
Booksellers' Row, 79
Booth, Edwin, 94
BORGLUM, GUTZON
   Henry Ward Beecher, 261
   Daniel Butterfield, 202
BORING, W. A., JR.
   Heights Casino (1905), 258
BORING AND TILTON
   United States Immigration Station
      (1898), 213
Borough Hall-form. Brooklyn City
   Hall, 250
Borough Hall, Old (Bronx), 227
Borough Park, 336
   on map, 244
Boswijck: see Bushwick-Ridgewood
BOSWORTH, WILLIAM WELLES
   American Telephone and Telegraph
      Building (1917), 21
   Cartier, Inc.-form. Morton F. Plant
      Residence (remodeling—
      1917), 128
   12 East 69th Street (1914), 172
Botanic Garden (Bklyn.), 291, 292
Botanical Garden (Bronx), 224
BOTTOMLEY, WAGNER & WHITE
   River House (1931), 124
Bowery, The (Bouwerie), 78, 405
Bowery Savings Bank, 120
Bowling Green, 11, 406
Bowne House, 362
BOWYER, GORDON AND URSULA
   Vidal Sassoon/Charles of the Ritz
      (1965), 160
Boys' High School, 299
Bradford, William, 17
Brady, Diamond Jim, 111
Bredt F. House, 384
Breezy Point, 374
Brentano's, 127
BREUER, MARCEL
   New York U.: Julius Silver
      Residence Center (1964);
      Hunter College Library and
      Classroom Buildings (1959);
      Technology Building and
      Begrisch Lecture Hall
      (1964), 231, 232
   Whitney Museum (1966), 174
Breukelen: see Brooklyn
Brevoort family, 43, 59, 61
Brewster Building, 355

BRIDGES
   Brooklyn Bridge, 3, 29, 264, 334,
      409, 410, 414
   George Washington Bridge, 208,
      209, 414
   Manhattan Bridge, 33, 414
   Queensboro Bridge, 355, 414
   Verrazano-Narrows Bridge, 414
   Williamsburg Bridge, 41, 318, 414
   see also Bridges and Tunnels,
      pp. 414–415 for complete table
      of Greater New York bridges

POST, GEORGE B. & SONS
Statler-Hilton-form. Hotel
Pennsylvania, 101
Potter Building, 30
POTTER, E. C.
lions, New York Public Library, 109
POTTER, EDMUND
St. Paul's Protestant Episcopal
Church (1870), 396
POTTER, W. A.
Church of St. Paul & St. Andrew
(1895), 144
Church of the Divine Paternity
(1898), 142
St. Martin's Church (1888), 192
Trinity School, 145
POTTER'S FIELDS (site)
Bryant Park, 108, 407
Madison Square, 95, 408
Randall's Island, 408
Washington Square Park, 65, 408
Powell, Adam Clayton, 195
PRAEGER, E. H.
Henry Hudson Bridge (1936), 415
PRAEGER-KAVANAGH-WATERBURY
Shea Stadium (1964), 365
Pratt, Charles, 269, 273, 326, 328
residence, 274
Pratt Institute, 269, 272, 326
PRATT PLANNING DEPT.
Lefferts Place Park-design
(1966), 295
Premier, The, 185
PRICE, BRUCE
100 Broadway, Bank of Tokyo-
form.-American Surety Company
(1895), 20
Richard Morris Hunt Memorial
(1898), 172
12 West 10th Street, 59
21 East 21st Street (1878), 95
PRICE, H. BROOKS
Hispanic Society of America North
Building (1910–1926), 206
PRICE, MARTIN
Central University Library-Yeshiva
U., associate (1967), 211
Science Center, Belfer Graduate
School, Yeshiva U., associate
(1968), 211
PRICE, THOMAS D.
Conservatory Garden (1936), 153
PRINCE, HARRY M.
Concourse Village (1968), 228
James Weldon Johnson Houses
(1947), 197
see also Bien & Prince
Prince's Bay, 389; on map, 376
Prince's Nursery (site), 361
Prohibition Park: see Westerleigh
Prison Ship Martyr's Monument, 275
Prospect Park, 278, 288
maps, 244, 287, 300
Prospect Park South, 329, 330
Prospect Park Walking Tour, 288;
map, 287
Public Baths of New York City, 99
Public housing: see Housing
Developments, Public housing
Public School 36, 201
Public School 43, 339
Public School 46, 277
Public School 55, 388
Public School 57, 197
Public School 107, 196
Public School 199, 141
Public School 219, 362
Public School 306, 348
Puck Building, 40
Punkiesberg: see Cobble Hill
Purdy Hotel, 390

Q

Quaker Meeting House, 361
Quaker sect, 202, 253, 358, 361, 362
Queens, 352–374

map, 350
Queens Boulevard Medical Group,
H.I.P., 366
Queens County: see Queens
Queens-Midtown Tunnel, 403, 414
Queens Village, 369
on map, 351
Queensboro Bridge, 355, 414
on map, 155
Queensboro Community College, 363
Queensbridge Houses, 355
QUINN, EDMOND T.
Edwin Booth (1916), 94

R

Racquet and Tennis Club, 118
Railroad flats, 40
RAILROAD STATIONS
Grand Central, 114, 115
Long Island City, 354
Pennsylvania Station, 101
RAMSEY & SLEEPER
25 East 83rd Street (1938), 176
Randall, Robert Richard, 43, 382, 407
Randall's Island, 214, 408
on map, 9
Randel, John, Jr., 43, 407
Ravenswood: see Long Island City
RAYMOND & RADO
Franklin Delano Roosevelt High
School (1965), 336
Japan Airlines Ticket Office
(1956), 133
KLM-Royal Dutch Airlines Ticket
Office (1959), 127
RAYMOND LOEWY-WILLIAM SNAITH, INC.
1025 Fifth Avenue (1955), 176
RCA Building, 132
Recreation: see Amusements and
Sports; Parks; Stadiums
Red Hook, 308
on map, 307
REED, C. A.
Grand Central Terminal
(1903–1913), 115
Rego Park, 364
on map, 350
REILLY, PAUL C.
Church of Our Savior (1959), 106
REILLY, ROBERT J.
James Weldon Johnson Houses
(1947), 197
REINHARD & HOFMEISTER
Rockefeller Center (1931–1940), 132
REINHARD, HOFMEISTER & WALQUIST
Federal Office Bldg. (1949), 370
Reliance Films (site), 89
Renaissance Revival architecture:
see ARCHITECTURAL STYLE GUIDE
RENWICK, JAMES, JR.
Calvary Church (1846), 94
Grace Church (1846), 76
Greystone-form. Cleveland E.
Dodge Residence (1863), 236
Rhinelander Gardens (site), 60
Riverdale Presbyterian Church
(1863), 235
St. Ann's Church (1869), 253
St. Patrick's Cathedral
(1858–1879), 128
St. Stephen's Church (1854), 97
RENWICK, W. W.
All Saints School (1904), 194
St. Aloysius' Church (1904),
192, 194
RENWICK & CO.
71 Franklin Street, 35
RENWICK & SANDS
Cathedral High School (1865), 47
Graymore Friars-form. St. Joseph's
Church School (1869), 47
RENWICK, ASPINWALL & RUSSELL
All Saints' Church (1889–1894), 194
All Saints Rectory (1886–1889), 194
806 Broadway (1888), 76
RENWICK, ASPINWALL & SANDS

National Lutheran Council
(1896), 96
Renwick Triangle, 76
RESTAURANTS
Al & Dick's Steak House, 114
Algonquin, The, 110
Ann's Sugarbowl, 381
Au Canari d'Or, 164
Barclay Hotel, 125
Bemelmans Bar, 175
Blarney Stone, 122
Brasserie, 118
Caesar's Pastry Shop, 48
Café de la Paix, 138
Café Français, 132
Café Nicholson, 162
Caffé Reggio, 70
Cafiero's Restaurant, 308
Caliban's (bar), 97
Carmen's, 381
Casey's, 54
Castilla's Restaurant, 32
Cavanaugh's Restaurant, 83
Charles French Restaurant, 60
Charley Brown's, 116
Cheetah, 114
Chez Vous, 48
Chez Yvonne L'Escargot, 24
Chumley's, 50
Colony Restaurant, The, 161
Copacabana, 157
Copenhagen, 138
Delmonico's Restaurant (Oscar's
Delmonico), 18, 24
Dominick's Oyster & Chop
House, 227
Dominick's Restaurant, 238
Eggers Confectionery, 381
El Parador, 98
El Radiante, 221
English Grill, 132
Faicco's Sausages, 48
Fountain Café, 151
The Four Seasons, 118
Frank Jahn's, 369
Fraunces Tavern, 16, 24
Gage & Tollner's, 252
Gino's, 164
Grand Central Oyster Bar, 716
Grand Ticino, 70
Ground Floor, The, 135
Hanover Square Restaurant, 26
Harouto Restaurant, 66
Hong Fat Restaurant, 34
Hye Oriental Food Shop, 98
Il Bambino Restaurant, 62
Il Faro Restaurant, 79
Joe King's Rathskeller, 93
Joe's, 164
Joe's Restaurant, 71
Jones' Steak House, 381
Joy Luck Coffee Shop, 34
Kabuki, 26
Kass & Goldstein Soda
Fountain, 112
Keen's English Chop House, 101
King Wu Restaurant, 34
La Crêpe, 58
La Fonda del Sol, 133
L'Étoile Restaurant, 157
Le Bijou Restaurant, 46
Le Pavillon, 120
Le Provençal, 158
Le Veau d'Or, 163
Le Voisin, 160
Lindy's, 114
Lion's Head, The, 46
Louis Restaurant, 241
Lüchow's, 90
Lundy Bros. Restaurant, 339
Marchi, 98
Martell's, 183
Mary's Restaurant, 48
McSorley's Old Ale House, 79
Meenan's, 122
Michel's Restaurant, 282

Minetta Tavern, 70
Mme Romaine de Lyon, 161
Nash Pastry Shop, 212
Nathan's Famous, 340
Niederstein's Restaurant, 368
Norwegian Seamen's House &
Restaurant, 276
Nu Deli Gallery, 50
O'Henry's Steak House, 68
Old Homestead Restaurant, 57
Old Seidelberg, 122
Oscar's Salt of the Sea, 166
Oviedo Restaurant, 64
Paddy's Clam House, 101
Paolucci's Restaurant, 39
Paul & Jimmy's Place, 93
The Peacock Cafe, 68
The Penthouse Restaurant, 199
Peter Luger Steak House, 320
Pete's Tavern, 93
Piemonte Restaurant, 63
P. J. Moriarty's, 101
P. J.'s, 119
The Playboy Club, 157
Rainbow Room, 132
Ratner's Restaurant, 79
Rockefeller Center, 132
Roseland, 114
Rumpelmayers, 138
Sardi's, 113
Sayat Nova, 54
Schlitz Inn, 220
Schrafft's, 111
Serendipity, 164
Shatzkins Famous Knishes, 340
Shine's, 101
Shoals, The, 381
Sign of the Dove, 166
Sixty-Eight Restaurant, 62
Solowey's, 101
St. Regis-Sheraton Hotel, 130
Stage Delicatessen, 114
Stanhope Hotel Outdoor Cafe, 176
Steinberg's Dairy Restaurant, 144
Suerken's Restaurant, 36
Sutter's French Café, 58
Sweet's Restaurant, 24
Tavern on the Green, 138
Teddy's Restaurant, 35
Trattoria, 116
Trimarche's Restaurant, 381
21 Club, 120
Whyte's Downtown, 24, 31
Wo Ping, 34
Yellow Fingers, 163
Ye Olde Chop House, 26
Ye Waverly Inn, 55
Zum Zum, 26, 116

Rheingold Brewery, 312
RHIND, J. MASSEY
left entrance, bronze doors, Trinity
Church, 20
Rhinelander Gardens (site), 60
Rhinelander Mansions (site), 66
Rice Stadium, 240
Richmond: see Staten Island
Richmond County: see Staten Island
Richmond Hill, 43, 71, 369
on map, 351
Richmondtown, 387
on map, 377
RIDDLE, THEODATE POPE
Theodore Roosevelt Association-
form. Theodore Roosevelt House
(remodeling 1923), 94
Ridgewood (Bklyn.): see Bushwick-
Ridgewood
Ridgewood (Queens), 364
on map, 350
Ridgewood: see Litchfield Mansion
Riis (Jacob) Park, 374
on map, 350
Riis Plaza, 79
Riker's Island (on map), 216
RISSE, LOUIS
Grand Concourse (1892), 227

see also Vaux & Withers
Wolfe, Thomas, 306
Women's House of Detention, 58
Wood/wood-frame house, 50, 260
Woodhaven, 369
   on map, 351
Woodrow Methodist Church and
   Hall, 391
Woolworth Building, 29
Woolworth family, 158, 298
World of Darkness (Bronx Zoo), 224
World Trade Center (proposed-1975),
   14, 27, 412
   on map, 12
Worth, William J., 96
WRIGHT, C.
   32-34 Greene Street (1873), 37
WRIGHT, FRANK LLOYD
   Cass House (1959), 386
   Guggenheim, The (1959), 177
   Mercedes-Benz Showroom
     (1955), 119
WRIGHT, HENRY
   Sunnyside Gardens (1924), 357
Wyckoff-Bennett House, 338

X

XIMENES, ETTORE
   Verrazano Monument (1909), 10

Y

YAMASAKI, MINORU
   World Trade Center (proposed-
     1975), 27
Yankee Stadium, 228
YELLIN, SAMUEL
   wrought-iron work, Central Savings
     Bank, 142
Yellow fever epidemics, 407
Yeshiva University, 210–211
Yonkers, 405
YORK & SAWYER
   Bowery Savings Bank (1923), 121
   Brick Presbyterian Church
     (1938), 179
   Central Savings Bank (1928), 142
   Federal Reserve Bank of New York
     (1924), 23

Flower & Fifth Avenue Hospital/
   New York Medical College
   (1921), 181
14 East 71st Street (1913), 173
Greenwich Savings Bank
   (1924), 101
Manufacturer's Hanover Trust
   Company-form. Brooklyn Trust
   Company (1915), 257
New York Academy of Medicine
   (1926), 181
New York Historical Society,
   central portion (1908), 142
660 Park Avenue (1927), 168
27 East 69th Street (1922), 172
YOSHIMURA, JUNZO
   Japan Airlines Ticket Office
     (1956), 133
YOUNG & CABLE
   U.S. Office Building (1886), 15
Young Men's Hebrew
   Association, 183

Z

Zenger, Peter, 229, 242, 406
ZETLIN, LEV & ASSOCS.
   New York State Pavilion, World's
     Fair (1964–1965), 366
ZION & BREEN
   Samuel Paley Plaza, landscape
     (1967), 128
Zoning laws and resolutions
   1916: 21, 27, 89, 111, 125, 411
   1961: 21, 412
ZOOLOGICAL PARKS
   Bronx Zoo, 223
   Central Park, 152
   Clarence T. Barrett Park and
     Zoo, 394
   Flushing Meadow Park, 365
   Prospect Park Zoo, 290
ZORACH, WILLIAM
   bas reliefs, Civil and Municipal
     Court (1960), 31
   John Howard Melish, 258
ZUCKER, A.
   132–140 Greene Street (1885), 38
Zukor, Adolph, 89

NOTES

NOTES

NOTES

GEORGIAN FEDERAL MODERN CLASSICAL REVIVAL ROMANESQUE REVIVAL

GOTHIC REVIVAL ITALIANATE GREEK REVIVAL COLONIAL RENAISSANCE REVIVAL